HOMEOWNERSHIP
BUILT TO LAST

HOMEOWNERSHIP BUILT TO LAST

Balancing Access, Affordability, and Risk after the Housing Crisis

ERIC S. BELSKY
CHRISTOPHER E. HERBERT
JENNIFER H. MOLINSKY

Editors

JOINT CENTER FOR HOUSING STUDIES
HARVARD UNIVERSITY
Cambridge, Massachusetts

BROOKINGS INSTITUTION PRESS
Washington, D.C.

Library of Congress Cataloging-in-Publication data

Homeownership built to last : balancing access, affordability, and risk after the housing crisis / Eric S. Belsky, Christopher E. Herbert, and Jennifer H. Molinsky, Editors, Joint Center for Housing Studies, Harvard University, Cambridge, Massachusetts.
     pages   cm
Includes bibliographical references and index.
     ISBN 978-0-8157-2564-0 (pbk. : alk. paper) 1. Home ownership—United States.
2. Mortgage loans—United States. 3. Housing—United States—Finance. I. Belsky, Eric S., editor of compilation.
     HD7287.82.U6H664 2014
     333.33'80973—dc23   2014015497

9 8 7 6 5 4 3 2 1

Typeset in Adobe Garamond

Composition by Cynthia Stock
Silver Spring, Maryland

Contents

Acknowledgments

A book exploring so important and complex a topic as the sustainability of homeownership in the wake of the housing crisis requires the insights and talents of many. We count ourselves fortunate to have worked with such dedicated and adept authors, funders, advisers, and staff in the process of producing *Homeownership Built to Last*.

The papers in this volume were originally written for and presented at a symposium convened by the Joint Center for Housing Studies in April 2013. The symposium brought together researchers, policymakers, and industry leaders to reflect on the lessons of the housing crisis for sustaining homeownership for low-income and minority families. We are deeply grateful to the event's funders, the Ford Foundation, NeighborWorks America, and Bank of America Charitable Foundation, for providing the support that enabled us to assemble such an exceptional group of authors and participants. We are especially appreciative of George McCarthy, Jerry Maldonado, and Lisa Davis of Ford for their continued encouragement of Joint Center symposia and their deep commitment to improving understanding of the housing markets and policy in order to improve housing opportunities for low-income people.

We want to offer special thanks to the advisory committee that helped us shape the symposium's content and research questions: Janis Bowdler, Eileen Fitzgerald, Edward Golding, Jerry Maldonado, George McCarthy, Andrew Plepler, Janneke Ratcliffe, and Gordon Whitman. The breadth of their expertise and depth of insights were instrumental in shaping the research agenda. Special thanks go to the contributing authors for their exceptional efforts to draw lessons from the housing and foreclosure crisis. Their chapters offer a fuller understanding of both the value and the pitfalls of homeownership, thoughtfully reconsider the role of government in supporting homeownership, and point the way forward to a better system of assessing and balancing risks and sustaining homeownership for those who have the potential to gain so much from it. We also deeply appreciate the moderators, discussants, speakers, and attendees of the symposium for a very thoughtful and energizing debate about how we move on in the wake of the housing crisis.

We owe a great debt of gratitude to our colleagues and friends at the Joint Center for Housing Studies who supported the symposium, this book, and us with their professionalism, expertise, and good humor. Many thanks go to Pamela Baldwin, Kerry Donahue, Mary Lancaster, Angela Flynn, and Jackie Hernandez for their meticulous work on *Homeownership Built to Last,* and to all staff who assisted with the symposium and provided research support to papers included in this volume: Elizabeth La Jeunesse, Irene Lew, Ellen Marya, Dan McCue, Rocio Sanchez-Moyano, and Abbe Will. And special thanks go to Nicolas Retsinas, director emeritus of the Joint Center, for his wise counsel and support of the event.

Finally, we offer our deepest gratitude to our spouses, Cynthia, Tracey, and Andy, for their encouragement and support.

INTRODUCTION

Balancing Access, Affordability, and Risk after the Housing Crisis

JENNIFER H. MOLINSKY, ERIC S. BELSKY,
AND CHRISTOPHER E. HERBERT

The ups and downs in U.S. homeownership over the last two decades are without precedent. Though the first few years of the millennium brought the highest homeownership rate the nation had ever seen, they were followed by a half decade of devastating foreclosures in which millions saw their hopes of building wealth through homeownership dashed. The costs—financial, psychological, and social—have been enormous. Yet even in the aftermath of these dramatic events and despite headlines proclaiming the death of homeownership in the United States, Americans overwhelmingly still aspire to own. And though the downturn took a particularly hard toll on homeowners of color and those with low incomes, many advocates still view access to homeownership as an important part of a strategy to build wealth among historically disadvantaged households.

In spring 2013 the Harvard Joint Center for Housing Studies, with support from the Ford Foundation, NeighborWorks America, and the Bank of America Charitable Foundation, convened a symposium to reexamine the goals of homeownership and its risks and rewards, particularly for low-income and minority households. The event explored the lessons to be learned from the housing crisis and Great Recession and considered how homeownership can be made more sustainable over time to increase the likelihood that its benefits will be realized. The symposium was structured around thought-provoking original research commissioned from leading academics that forms the chapters of this book. It was further enriched by the participation of nearly 100 policymakers, industry leaders, housing advocates, and scholars.

Here we introduce the motivation for the symposium and this book: the housing crisis, the questions that have arisen in its aftermath about the role of low-income homeownership in the housing boom and bust, and the ongoing debate about how the nation moves forward in its homeownership policy. We then draw lessons from the chapters that follow, examining how to achieve the appropriate balance among breadth of access to homeownership, affordability, and limitation of the risks assumed by homeowners, investors, and taxpayers.

The Housing Boom and Bust and Its Aftermath

The past two decades have seen remarkable changes in U.S. homeownership rates. After two decades of stagnation from the 1960s to early 1990s, the national homeownership rate rose to an all-time high of 69.3 percent in 2005, an increase of 5 percentage points since 1994. Rates for minorities climbed more steeply: the homeownership rate for African Americans climbed from 42.8 percent in 1994 to 49.7 percent in 2005; for Hispanics, from 41.6 percent to 49.3 percent; and for Asians, from 51.7 to 60.0 percent. Homeownership expanded among lower-income households as well: from 1994 to 2002, the rate for those with annual incomes of $25,000 or less rose over 5 percentage points from 44.0 percent to 49.7 percent.[1]

Yet these gains were nearly all erased in the wake of the housing crisis and Great Recession. By 2013 the national homeownership rate was down to 64.9 percent and had yet to stop falling. While Hispanic and Asian householders had maintained some of their gains, the homeownership rate for African Americans and those making under $25,000 a year had dropped back to levels not seen since the mid-1990s.

As is evident in figure 1, minority homeownership rates have historically lagged those of whites. While numerous factors have contributed to racial and ethnic differences in homeownership, disparities in access to mortgage financing have certainly played a role. The mid-twentieth-century expansion of homeownership was built on a system of Federal Housing Administration (FHA) preferences, intended to stimulate home building for new suburban homes, as well as outright discrimination against communities of color and older urban neighborhoods through FHA redlining, in which strict appraisals, construction standards, escrow of tax and insurance, and an encouragement of racially "homogeneous" neighborhoods effectively excluded lower-income people and people of color from the program's opportunities.[2] The legacy of these policies

1. Joint Center for Housing Studies tabulations of U.S. Census Bureau's *Current Population Survey*, various years. Income categories are inflation-adjusted to 2012 dollars using the Consumer Price Index All Urban Consumers for All Items.

2. Carliner (1998).

Figure 1. *Homeownership Rates, 1994–2013*[a]

Percent

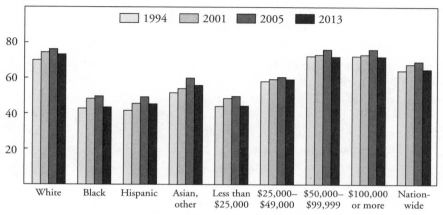

Source: Joint Center for Housing Studies tabulations of data from U.S. Census Bureau, *Current Population Survey,* various years.

a. Income categories are inflation-adjusted to 2012 dollars using the Consumer Price Index All Urban Consumers for All Items.

has been long lasting. Oliver and Shapiro note that because of historical discrimination and ongoing bias, "black families have been denied the benefits of housing inflation and the subsequent vast increase in home equity assets," reinforcing racial disparities in wealth over time.[3] Even after equal opportunity in mortgage lending was made law in the mid-1960s, discriminatory practices in lending and housing markets (as well as in labor markets) have persisted and diminished access to homeownership.[4]

Because erratic incomes, shortage of funds for down payments, and poor or absent credit all decrease access to financing, homeownership rates for lower-income people, many of whom are minorities, have also fallen far short of rates for higher-income families. Lower-income people are also less likely to sustain ownership over time as their households are more prone to extended periods of unemployment and have less savings to fall back on to weather unexpected expenses.

Given these historic gaps, the homeownership gains made from 1994 to 2004 were particularly promising. But the substantial losses suffered in the years following by people of all incomes, races, and geography—but disproportionately by lower-income and minority households—inevitably led to questions about

3. Oliver and Shapiro (2006, p. 22).
4. Yinger (1997); Ross and Yinger (2002); Turner and others (2013).

the role of the expansion of homeownership in producing the housing crisis and about the true value of homeownership for these groups. Below we discuss the causes of the rise and fall of homeownership rates during the last two decades and their relationship with the housing boom and bust.

The Expansion of Low-Income and Minority Homeownership

Policy changes and regulatory shifts, technological advances in the mortgage industry, a booming economy, and shifting demographics all played a role in the expansion of overall and lower-income and minority homeownership rates beginning in the mid-1990s.

The genesis of policymakers' focus on increasing homeownership can be traced in large part to the concept of "asset building," which entered the community development lexicon in the early 1990s. Homeownership was seen as an important vehicle for asset building, especially for low-income people.[5] This concept helped drive the Clinton administration to adopt the goal of increasing homeownership rates among lower-income and minority households to close the gap with higher-income and white households.[6] However, the adoption of this goal was not accompanied by any landmark new programs. Instead, the president's bully pulpit was used to focus the attention of all levels of government, nonprofit organizations, and the housing industry on this homeownership goal, and to foster public-private partnerships in support of it.[7] One concrete step taken was an expansion of education and counseling to better prepare potential owners. Another was a modest increase in direct assistance to lower-income homebuyers through down payment and other forms of financial assistance offered by the HOME Investment Partnerships Program, the Affordable Housing Program of the Federal Home Loan Banks, and NeighborWorks America. A series of reforms at the Federal Housing Administration also aimed at increasing access to mortgage financing.[8]

The George W. Bush administration continued this emphasis on increasing homeownership among historically disadvantaged groups. Its main programmatic contribution was the introduction of the American Dream Downpayment

---

5. Sherraden (1991); Belsky and Calder (2005); von Hoffman (2012).

6. The Clinton administration's National Homeownership Strategy asserted that homeownership could help build assets, which could provide the capital needed to start a small business, finance college tuition, and generate financial security for retirement; give control over living space; strengthen and stabilize communities; and help generate jobs and economic growth. U.S. Department of Housing and Urban Development (1995).

7. Haurin and others (2005), Herbert and Belsky (2006).

8. Changes to FHA programs included higher loan limits (after 1998), faster processing, more flexibility in using gifts for down payments, simpler methods for calculating down payments, reforms to the appraisal process, and automated underwriting. See Eggers (2001).

Initiative in 2003, a carve-out from the HOME program to provide funding for down payment and closing cost assistance for low-income first-time homebuyers.

More significantly, the emphasis on expanding homeownership opportunities also coincided with a series of regulatory shifts to encourage greater lending to previously underserved groups. The Federal Housing Enterprise Safety and Soundness Act of 1992 established affordable housing goals for the government-sponsored enterprises (GSEs), Fannie Mae and Freddie Mac, specifying target shares for the loans they backed made to low-income borrowers and to borrowers in underserved areas and low-income communities. The combination of new underwriting technology (described below) and increased pressure on Fannie Mae and Freddie Mac to provide a secondary market outlet for loans to underserved borrowers allowed lenders to reach out to these markets and also helped reduce the share of lower-income borrowers relying on FHA financing beginning in the mid-1990s.[9] But as discussed below, there remains a difference of opinion as to how much this pressure led Fannie Mae and Freddie Mac to take excessive risks. An equally if not more compelling reason for their expanded risk taking was the pressure to regain significant market share lost to nonprime lenders.

New changes to the Home Mortgage Disclosure Act and the Community Reinvestment Act (CRA), originally adopted in the 1970s, also increased pressure on lenders to serve minority and low-income households and communities in the 1990s. Beginning in 1989, the Home Mortgage Disclosure Act's reporting requirements were expanded to include data on applications made to lending institutions, lenders' decisions, and applicants' race and income. Lawsuits and a widely cited study by the Federal Reserve Bank of Boston that found discrimination in lending led to greater pressure on lenders to comply with antidiscrimination laws.[10] CRA standards were tightened while concurrent changes in banking regulation and trends in bank mergers and acquisitions made CRA ratings more important to financial institutions.

In efforts to comply with the CRA, lenders reaching out to underserved borrowers found that many would-be borrowers met their risk standards, which allowed them to expand their market without taking on excessive risk.[11] Thus, while regulations and public disclosures of lending patterns may have pressured banks and thrifts to take action, these institutions profited from this business and took it to scale.

At the same time, technological innovations in mortgage finance, particularly data-driven mortgage scoring systems, led to the recognition that low-income homeownership could be a profitable business. Statistical models produced

9. An and others (2007); An and Bostic (2009).
10. Munnell and others (1996).
11. Laderman and Reid (2009).

consumer credit scores, valued assets, and assessed the risk of mortgage default, allowing lenders to identify first-time and low-income borrowers who represented tolerable risks but who would otherwise have been denied loans. The systems allowed for one underwriting risk to offset another, and these so-called compensating factors helped decrease rejection rates.[12] (At least one carefully done study suggests that such offsetting was done without adding much to risk and with the costs typically spread across a broader pool of loans.)[13] Indeed, at least through the 1990s—a period when half of the 1994–2004 surge in homeownership rates occurred—neither the CRA nor the GSE goals appear to have led to any dramatic increases in the risk profiles of banks, thrifts, Fannie Mae, or Freddie Mac.[14] Instead, these regulations resulted in extension of credit to creditworthy borrowers previously denied loans.[15]

The rise of the nonprime lending market also expanded credit availability through both subprime and manufactured home lending. While a large majority of subprime loans during the 1990s were used to refinance existing homes and so did not support moves into homeownership, subprime loans nonetheless contributed a nontrivial share of the increase in conventional home purchase loans for low-income and minority homebuyers. Between 1993 and 1998, subprime lending accounted for 30.5 percent of this increase among black homebuyers, 22.3 percent among Hispanics, and 26.1 percent among borrows in lower-income census tracts, with the remainder of the increase from prime and manufactured housing loans. In 1998, 15.6 percent of loans to African American borrowers and 10.4 percent to Hispanic borrowers were subprime, compared to 4.6 percent to white borrowers, while 12.0 percent of loans in lower-income census tracts were subprime compared to 5.0 percent in the highest-income tracts. Meanwhile, loans for manufactured homes made up nearly as large a share of the overall increase, accounting for 27 percent among blacks, 19 percent among Hispanics, and 22 percent among lower-income homebuyers.[16] Another study examining lending to low-income borrowers in low-income neighborhoods over the 1993–2001 period also documented the importance of subprime and manufactured home lending, which together accounted for 28 percent of the growth in home purchase loans to this market segment. But this study also highlights the important role played by FHA, which accounted for 32 percent of home purchase lending growth by low-income borrowers in low-income neighborhoods.[17]

---

12. Belsky and Richardson (2010).

13. Gates, Perry, and Zorn (2002).

14. Ding and others (2011); Reid and Laderman (2011); Hernández-Murillo, Ghent, and Owyang (2012).

15. Ambrose and Thibodeau (2004); Bhutta (2011, 2012).

16. Canner, Passmore, and Laderman (1999, p. 712–13).

17. Apgar and Calder (2005, p. 109).

Indeed, subprime originations were particularly plentiful in lower-income and minority areas underserved by conventional credit. The percent of home purchase mortgages originated by subprime specialists grew from 2.4 percent in 1993 to 13.4 percent in 2001 in low-income minority neighborhoods and rose even more steeply for refinances.[18] Predatory lending practices associated with some subprime loans also began to put borrowers at risk.[19]

Finally, but significantly, the country was experiencing the longest peacetime economic expansion in its history, with rising incomes and mortgage interest rates that were much lower than a decade earlier, which helped more people afford homeownership.[20] Demographics also played a role as the large baby boomer population advanced into older age brackets characterized by higher homeownership rates, helping to drive overall increases in the national home-ownership rate.[21] As result of all these changes—the attention to homeownership brought by two presidential administrations, regulatory changes, technological shifts in the mortgage market, and the economic boom and demographic shifts that favored homeownership—overall homeownership rates expanded through the late 1990s and into the early 2000s to historic highs. Gains among minorities and low-income groups helped to narrow gaps with white and middle- and upper-income groups (figure 1).

Even as the overall homeownership rate crested, however, the housing and mortgage markets continued to expand (figure 2). While the scale and variety of nonprime credit grew during the 1990s and the start of the 2000s, beginning in 2004 an explosion of alternative forms of credit spurred the housing market to greater heights. Subprime, Alt-A, piggyback, and home equity lending boomed as Wall Street sought to capture more consumers in a saturated market.[22] With rating

18. Joint Center for Housing Studies (2001), cited in Belsky and Richardson (2010, p. 23).

19. Goldstein (1999, p. 7) notes that not all subprime loans are predatory. Rather, "loans become predatory when they target a particular population, take advantage of the borrower's inexperience and lack of information, manipulate a borrower into a loan the borrower cannot afford to pay, or defraud the borrower or investor."

20. Historical mortgage interest rate tables at www.freddiemac.com/pmms/pmms30.htm.

21. Indeed, Gabriel and Rosenthal (2005) find most of the increase in homeownership in the 1990s to be attributable to demographic factors, which also help explain the persistent gaps between white and minority homeownership.

22. Subprime loans are typically made to borrowers who would not qualify for a prime loan due to poor credit histories, most typically defined as a credit score below 620. Alt-A loans are made to borrowers with near prime credit scores but who fail to meet traditional guidelines for prime credit for other reasons, such as limited or no documentation of income or assets, higher debt-to-income ratios, and nonowner occupancy. Piggyback loans refer to multiple loans obtained from one or more lenders to finance property purchase, allowing the first mortgage to not exceed 80 percent of the home value, thus obviating the need for mortgage insurance. See Fligstein and Goldstein (2011) on the home equity lending boom.

Figure 2. *Homeownership Rates versus Share of Nontraditional Loan Originations, 1990–2008*[a]

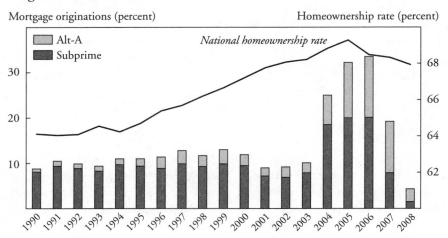

Sources: Inside Mortgage Finance (2009); U.S. Census Bureau, *Current Population Survey*, various years.
a. Subprime and Alt-A shares are of the dollar volume of all originations.

agencies bestowing "AAA" ratings on large portions of securities backed by these risky nonprime loans, global investor demand for these instruments was strong, further spurring lenders to aggressively market new lending products.[23]

Subprime lending alone expanded from nearly 10 percent of the mortgage origination market in 1994 to 20 percent of a much larger market in 2005. The expansion of lending contributed to the inflation of a housing price bubble because buyers had easier access to mortgage credit than ever before. Certainly other factors contributed to the bubble, including initially low inventories of homes for sale and low interest rates. The expectation of further sharp home price increases in turn contributed to rising demand for homes, as homebuyers sought to benefit from the rapid escalation of home prices—and avoid being locked out if they hesitated. Demand for housing also came increasingly from investors who, perhaps for the first time in history, could easily get loans to buy homes with high leverage. This helps explain why the homeownership rate actually began to dip by 2005 even as the single-family market continued to boom. As a bubble mentality took hold, lenders and borrowers, as well as regulators and investors, allowed or took great risks. Lenders were willing to lend to borrowers based on stated—but undocumented—incomes and assets or to borrowers with excessive debt-to-income ratios or at high combined loan-to-value

23. Zandi (2009).

ratios. Meanwhile, cash-out refinancings and other home equity lending further increased borrowers' leverage.

Subprime lending increased default risk due to a number of factors, often layered together. To begin with, borrowers in this segment had poor credit histories, reflecting unstable incomes and limited savings that among other factors made default more likely from the start. But these loans also came with higher interest rates, requiring higher shares of income, and often had adjustable interest rates with low initial teaser rates that caused a further payment shock when loans adjusted to their fully indexed rate, usually after two years. Consumers often had limited understanding of how often and how much loan payments might change, or that they would have to pay property taxes and insurances that were not escrowed into the mortgage. Despite being targeted to borrowers with better credit histories, Alt-A loans also had higher default risk, reflecting the prevalence of nontraditional mortgage terms (such as interest only or payment options that allowed for negative amortization); higher cumulative loan-to-value ratios, including associated piggyback loans; higher housing payment burdens that were hidden by the lack of income documentation; and lower purchaser motivation to maintain ownership in the case of investor loans. With the boom in nonprime lending, many who would not otherwise be able to access credit to purchase a home were able to do so, but default risk increased substantially.[24]

In 2007, as house price growth stalled and interest rates began to climb, subprime delinquency rates jumped (figure 3). The rise in delinquencies was driven in part by borrowers who had high loan-to-value loans originated under loose underwriting standards and little equity to draw upon to refinance when faced with rising payments on adjustable loans. In earlier years these borrowers had been able to refinance into a new loan to address their financial difficulties, but as house price growth stalled and lenders pulled back, the option to refinance dried up and defaults spiked. Another contributing factor was a rise in early payment defaults (those occurring in the first three months of the loan) as buyers walked away as home prices softened. Presumably many of these buyers were speculators who could walk away from loans at the first sign of trouble without losing their primary residences. Agreements with investors required originating lenders to repurchase these early defaulting loans. At a time when they could not raise the capital to do so, this led to high-profile lender bankruptcies that undermined confidence in Alt-A and subprime lending and to a pullback in credit. By the end of 2008, nonprime loans in private asset-backed securities (ABS) accounted for 15 percent of outstanding mortgage debt but fully half of serious delinquencies.[25]

---

24. Gramlich (2007).
25. Belsky and Richardson (2010, p. 80).

Figure 3. *Average Annual Rate of Foreclosure Starts by Loan Type,
1998–2012*

Share of all loans (percent)

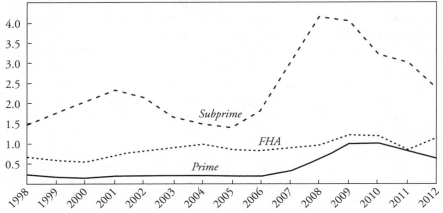

Source: Joint Center for Housing Studies tabulations of the Mortgage Bankers Association *National
Delinquency Survey,* various years.

Defaults quickly spread to the prime markets as the financial crisis deepened
and spawned the Great Recession, with job losses and drops in home prices
becoming the primary causes of default.[26] The overall foreclosure start rate
jumped, tripling from 2006 to 2008 (from 0.6 percent to 1.8 percent), though it
was much higher in some of the nation's hardest hit counties.[27] Mortgage applications and loan originations dropped off dramatically after 2006, both falling
overall about 25 percent from 2006 to 2007, more so for Hispanic and black
households than for whites.[28] The lengthy periods of unemployment that characterized the recession made it particularly difficult for borrowers to cover mortgage payments and increased the likelihood of default.[29] As of November 2013,
CoreLogic estimated that the total number of foreclosures completed since the
foreclosure crisis began in earnest in late 2008 was a bleak 4.7 million. Black
and Hispanic owners have been disproportionately affected, as have minority
communities.[30] Indeed, the most distressed communities in 2010 were those in

26. Been and others (2011); U.S. Department of Housing and Urban Development (2010).
27. Kochhar, Gonzalez-Barrera, and Dockterman (2009, p. ii).
28. Kochhar, Gonzalez-Barrera, and Dockterman (2009, p.14).
29. Been and others (2011).
30. Bocian, Li, and Ernst (2010).

which the highest-risk loans were made during the boom. As Apgar notes, in 2010 borrowers in the most intensely distressed neighborhoods were 2.5 times more likely to have high-cost loans and nearly twice as likely to have piggy-back loans as those in low-distress neighborhoods.[31] The costs to individuals from foreclosures and collapsing home prices have been enormous, with some $8.2 trillion in housing wealth lost between 2006 and 2011.[32] But entire neighborhoods have suffered as well, with concentrated foreclosures further depressing housing values, increasing municipal costs, and producing a precipitous drop in home purchase lending.[33] Additionally, in the wake of the housing crisis, many existing homeowners became renters, driving the homeownership rate down from its peak.

Narratives of Homeownership's Role in the Housing Crisis and Direction for the Future

The facts of the housing crisis and recession are clear: millions of homes lost to foreclosure, millions more homeowners underwater on their loans, trillions in lost housing equity, and the loss of homeownership gains among historically disadvantaged populations in part because the housing finance system and housing markets went so seriously awry. There is broad consensus that responses to the foreclosure crisis were not sufficient to meet the scale of the problem and caused additional suffering on the part of distressed homeowners. In the aftermath ABS investors exited the market, others tightened underwriting, and the share of the market accounted for by loans backed by Fannie Mae, Freddie Mac, and FHA surged.

Yet there is still considerable debate about the role played in the housing boom and subsequent bust by the extension of homeownership to millions of lower-income Americans, including those with lower credit scores and whose loans had low down payments or high debt-to-income ratios. Most agree that there was a substantial loosening of credit and that this was a key factor in the inflation of an unsustainable housing bubble in the early to mid-2000s. There is disagreement, however, about why credit became less constrained, particularly about how much this loosening was driven by regulatory pressures to serve low-income borrowers.

One view is that a combination of factors worked together to expand credit and reduce borrowing constraints, including deregulation of mortgage markets, which facilitated the development of a wider range of products; global

31. Apgar (2012, p. 22).
32. Joint Center for Housing Studies (2012).
33. Mallach (2009); Bocian, Li, and Ernst (2010, p. 3); Apgar (2012, p. 22) citing Avery and others (2011, pp. 47–49).

liquidity that led to low interest rates and to investors seeking higher returns by taking greater risks; innovative financial securities that seemed to offer protection against risk but in reality often did not; and failure of regulation to prevent excessive risk taking in the market. The bubble mentality also drew people into the market in pursuit of gains from house price appreciation, including many who had no intention of occupying properties but were instead looking to flip them. Even among owner-occupants, the bubble mentality fed the assumption that it would be possible to take equity out of a house because rising house prices would more than repay it if a home had to be sold to cover it.

In this view, to which we subscribe, specific efforts to support increased low-income and minority homeownership did not play a prominent role in the housing crisis. The market was expanding the availability of credit in the nonprime space, but largely in pursuit of profits rather than to fulfill government-imposed affordable housing goals and conform to CRA rules. The riskiest lending occurred in the subprime sector, which had been an area of concern for some time among homeownership advocates worried about the high cost and risky terms offered to many lower-income and minority buyers. As these advocates feared, the expansion of subprime lending reflected a failure of regulation to adequately protect consumers. In contrast, efforts to expand lending in response to regulatory pressures from GSE housing goals or CRA inducements were expanding credit through fairly safe means, without the high default risk or high costs characterizing nonprime loans.

In this narrative there is a fairly bright line between nonprime (subprime and Alt-A) lending and that done to meet GSE goals or CRA inducements. Although the GSEs did purchase AAA-rated subprime tranches and purchased and securitized Alt-A loans, their most disproportionate share of losses came from Alt-A loans that were not typically targeted to low- and moderate-income borrowers.[34]

The fault instead lies in part in a long list of lapses of regulation that permitted the private market to go off the rails, including a lack of transparency in credit default swap and collateralized debt obligation markets, inattention to overly optimistic ratings of large tranches of subprime mortgage-backed securities, allowance of off-balance-sheet short-term bank funding of longer-term risky mortgages, failure to use existing authorities to regulate forcefully when problems were detected, and failure to pass new regulations to address the problems until after the crisis. These regulatory lapses also included preemption by federal regulators of state laws that regulated loan interest rates and loan terms and prohibited alternative mortgages (only a handful of states retained the right to regulate certain loan products and terms); the lifting of restrictions

---

34. Park (2010); Weicher (2010). See Freddie Mac (2009); this analysis indicates that Alt-A loans accounted for a majority of realized losses on 2008 lending.

on different kinds of financial service providers being part of a broader holding company structure (for example, banking, investment, and insurance companies), which shifted the center of activity in many bank holding companies to trading; the lifting of leverage caps on investment banks and permission for them to apply to have much higher caps; failure to use existing authorities like the 1994 Home Ownership and Equity Protection Act to clamp down on emerging predatory lending practices; weak regulation and supervision of the ABS channel and capital adequacy of creators of credit default swaps; weak regulation of ratings agencies; and inadequacy of the capital requirements for Fannie Mae and Freddie Mac. In all, these factors helped foster a race to the bottom, where lenders, investors, and guarantors each contributed to relaxation of underwriting standards, lending processes, and risk assessment of securities, all in pursuit of expanded market share and profits.[35]

A counternarrative lays more of the blame for the relaxation of underwriting and the inflation of the housing bubble on government efforts to expand lending. In this view the GSEs made a significant contribution to the expansion of subprime and Alt-A lending after they became subject to affordable housing goals, starting in the early 1990s.[36] According to proponents of this view, subsequent increases in those goals by the Clinton and Bush administrations put even more pressure on Fannie Mae and Freddie Mac, and this in turn gave incentives to lenders to downgrade their underwriting standards to push "affordable" loans through. In this narrative Wall Street followed the GSEs rather than led them.

Yet the affordable housing goals were raised by both the Clinton and Bush administrations because the GSE shares of the low-income market were in fact lagging the market level, and the GSEs' significant push into the Alt-A market in 2004, in particular, was more profit driven than goals driven as this coincided with a sharp drop in their market share to nonprime lenders, again following the market.[37] Indeed, at first the GSE goals were modest. While they were raised in 1995 and then again sharply in 2001, it was not until 2005, when a more onerous home purchase subgoal was imposed on them, that Fannie Mae and Freddie Mac really had to struggle to avoid taking heavy risks to meet the goals. Prior to that change, Fannie Mae and Freddie Mac were able to meet goals primarily through multifamily rental loans that carried little risk. Even after 2005, however, failure to meet the affordable housing goals did not result in material hardship for the GSEs and so may not have been the reason they took on riskier loans. Indeed, in years in which the GSEs failed to meet their goals, this failure reflected unusual market circumstances, and regulators found the goals for those

35. Belsky and Richardson (2010).
36. Wallison (2011).
37. Weicher (2010); Jaffee (2010).

years to have been infeasible.[38] Finally, research suggests that the GSEs did not have a significant effect on low-income homeownership rates.[39] While the GSEs *did* have a bigger presence in the Alt-A market than in the subprime market, most of these loans were not even goals-eligible since income was either not documented, above low-income cutoffs, or inflated.

While GSE involvement in direct subprime lending, defined at least as the industry mostly did, was limited, their involvement in the purchase of AAA-rated tranches of subprime securities was significant.[40] While some have argued that Fannie Mae and Freddie Mac made the market for these securities, their willingness to buy only the highest-rated tranches was unlikely to have been consequential since the demand for AAA securities of all types is broad and deep. Instead, the buyers of the junior tranches were arguably the ones who made the market by absorbing these riskier investments for which demand was more limited. Furthermore, low spreads on these AAA securities were indicative of broad market demand for them. Indeed, as risks mounted, spreads even on the underlying subprime mortgages narrowed. Finally, another sign that demand for subprime securities was extremely strong is the fact that a synthetic securities market was developed that amounted to many multiples of the face amount of actual subprime loans originated.

The narrative blaming government regulations for the deterioration of credit also faults the CRA for incentivizing lenders to make lower-quality loans. Yet there is very little evidence that CRA loans were either a significant part of the market or that they performed poorly.[41] Canner and Bhutta found that only 6 percent of subprime loans were made to CRA-qualified borrowers or in low- to moderate-income neighborhoods by CRA-covered lenders, while other studies found that loans originated by institutions with CRA obligations were not more risky than those of other lenders.[42] And despite the severity of the downturn—which rendered the size of initial down payments somewhat less important at the margins because price drops exceeded 5 or 10 percent in so many markets—tailored loan programs that served low-wealth and even lower–credit score borrowers in many cases performed relatively well. For example, Ding and his colleagues found that loans in the Community Advantage Program—if anything somewhat more aggressive than typical CRA lending because the program was

---

38. Federal Housing Finance Agency (2010).

39. Bostic and Gabriel (2006).

40. An alternative view holds that the GSEs did have exposure to subprime loans by using higher credit score (FICO) cutoffs and low loan-to-value loans, including loans with second mortgages. See Pinto (2011).

41. Bhutta and Canner (2009); Reid and others (2013).

42. Canner and Bhutta (2008), cited in Jaffee (2010, p. 19); Apgar and Duda (2003); Reid and others (2013).

designed to demonstrate the feasibility of new standards, with the Ford
tion standing in the first loss position—performed much better than s
loans, with default rates that were generally fully 70 percent lower. They note
that unlike subprime mortgages but very typical of loans originated by banks
for CRA credit, Community Advantage Program loans were typically fixed-rate,
thirty-year, fully amortizing loans with no prepayment penalties.[43] FHA loans
too have had more success: figure 3 shows the FHA foreclosure start rate well
below that of subprime loans.

Moving Forward

Though the debate continues about the causes of the housing crisis and Great
Recession, nearly all would acknowledge that a clear lesson from the housing
boom and bust is that a substantial loosening of restrictions on the availability of
credit, indiscriminately and with little regard for a borrower's ability or willingness to repay, can have catastrophic results for borrowers, communities, and the
financial system as a whole. But less clear is the degree to which lending standards can be relaxed without exposing individuals or society to excessive risks.
The salient aim now is the correct balance among access to mortgage credit,
affordability of financing, and risk—for individuals, institutions, and taxpayers.

Nearly all understand that there are trade-offs between reducing risk and
providing access to mortgage credit for the lower and middle parts of the market, and that achieving perfect performance is impossible when the causes of
so many defaults are idiosyncratic (such as illness, divorce, or job loss).[44] The
central question is what level of failure is acceptable, which must be assessed
both for the housing finance system as a whole as well as at the community
and individual levels. The near meltdown of the financial system in 2008 has
highlighted the very real need to be concerned with the degree of systemic risk
arising from mortgage lending. But even if systemic risk is managed, there also
remains a question of how much risk an individual borrower should be allowed
to bear. Is 10 percent risk of losing a home to foreclosure too high for an individual (or the surrounding community) to bear—or acceptable given the potential individual and societal benefits of sustained homeownership? If those that
take higher levels of expected risk are geographically concentrated, should that
alter the level of acceptable risk due to negative neighborhood externalities? In
a society whose wealth distribution has been so shaped by people's opportunities to take a chance on homeownership (chances that have, over long stretches,
paid off handsomely in terms of wealth accumulation relative to renting), many

43. Ding and others (2011).
44. Couch (2013); Cutts and Merrill (2008). See also chapter 13 in this volume.

would like to allow broad access to home loans but in a context of better educated, protected consumers and in which lenders do not take excessive risks. But even if we agree about the degree of risk that is acceptable, how confident are we that we can adequately assess that risk?

Most would agree that there is clearly a greater need for attention to borrowers' ability to pay—both to protect them and to protect against systemic risk. Better safeguards are needed to align the incentives of originators and investors, with mechanisms potentially including greater transparency in transactions and requiring "skin in the game" by originators or earn-outs based on loan performance. Better access to wholesale mainstream capital is needed in the market to avoid perpetuating dual markets in which some groups are served only by specialized niche lenders and so are subject to different, and generally more disadvantageous, treatment in both the origination and loan servicing markets. A more unified market would also have the advantage of some degree of risk pooling in setting prime loan prices.[45] Better servicing with aligned incentives is also needed at scale. And there is a clear value for consumers to be better educated about the risks, costs, and financial responsibilities of homeownership. Finally, there is growing recognition that not enough attention was paid to these matters previously, by either consumers or investors, given the degree to which consumers were unprotected from mortgage fraud and in too many cases poorly treated in both the loan origination process and subsequently in the servicing process during the foreclosure crisis.

The chapters that follow mine the lessons of the housing boom and bust to address these critical questions regarding the value of homeownership, the rationale for public support, government's role in ensuring access and mitigating risk, and the best means to help homeowners sustain ownership over time.

The Value of Homeownership

Americans have long found the idea of owning one's home deeply appealing, associating homeownership with increased privacy, independence from landlords and rent increases, control over one's living space, greater wealth, better outcomes for children, and opportunities such as higher-quality schools and safer communities that, for a multitude of reasons, often accompany living in areas dominated by single-family owner-occupied housing.[46] Various rationales have been used for public policy's support of homeownership through the decades, including that homeownership makes better citizens and stronger communities and that it is a route to greater opportunity and financial security for those of modest means.

---

45. Ranieri and others (2013).
46. Drew and Herbert (2013).

Yet ownership has not been without its risks, as the recent foreclosure crisis unambiguously demonstrated. Questions now center on whether homeownership still has the same wealth-building potential that benefited homeowners in the past, whether it is a preferred path to stronger communities and better social outcomes, and how we can lend more safely to avoid systemic problems and also help low-income and minority borrowers enjoy the benefits of ownership.

Three chapters explore homeownership's potential benefits to individuals and society. Amid recent concerns about the rising racial wealth gap, john a. powell and Kaloma Cardwell argue that racial discrimination has been socially constructed and reinforced through housing and credit policy throughout the past century. The legacy of discrimination, segregation, and systematic denial of homeownership opportunities has left minorities with less access to wealth-building opportunities and fewer assets, an impediment to accessing homeownership today.

Christopher Herbert, Daniel McCue, and Rocio Sanchez-Moyano find that, indeed, homeownership remains a path to wealth for the majority of people who are able to choose it, a finding that held even through 1999–2009, and even for minorities and lower-income households, who experienced positive wealth gains, though lower than those of higher-income nonminorities. The authors also found that even after controlling for income, initial wealth, and the recent major collapse in house prices, homeowners have more wealth than renters. This suggests that homeownership is still the best available path to wealth building. However, Herbert, McCue, and Sanchez-Moyano acknowledge that homeownership entails considerable risks for which not all buyers are prepared and that the timing of the purchase is critical to outcomes.

Homeownership is associated with nonfinancial benefits as well. In their chapter William Rohe and Mark Lindblad explore the social benefits of owning, providing an updated review of literature on the topic as well as a consideration of how the housing crisis may have changed perceptions of the value of homeownership and the actual social benefits that have previously been associated with it. While they find that previous positive associations between homeownership and personal satisfaction, political and social participation, and some child outcomes still hold, they also find that negative experiences with homeownership are demonstrably associated with increased stress, anxiety, and depression and note that one's experience during the crisis is likely to shape perceptions about the value of homeownership going forward.

These three chapters contribute to the debate on why low-income and minority homeownership warrants public intervention, considering its role in creating opportunities for building wealth and reducing wealth disparities in society, providing entrée to other opportunities, and creating stability for households and communities. Aside from the fact that homeownership has both private and social benefits, the *desire* to own persists, rebounding even after the recent unprecedented foreclosure crisis. The implication is that policy interventions are needed to make sure that people can pursue this desire in a fair, safe, and informed way with their eyes open about the risks as well as potential benefits of homeownership.

Consumer Choices and Homebuyer Programs

Despite Americans' persistent desire to own, decisions about tenure and specific home purchases are complex, and potential homeowners may not always make choices that are in their best interests. In her chapter Carolina Reid finds that decisions to own among lower-income households were driven not by economic cost-benefit analysis but by aspirations related to belonging, achievement, higher-quality housing, more control, and escape from violence. She identified a strong optimism bias in those seeking to buy, which discounted past employment disruptions and other forms of volatility that are likely to make maintaining homeownership challenging. Reid also finds that borrowers use simple rules of thumb about affordability that may be misleading, and that they rely on experts in the home-buying process, such as real estate agents and mortgage lenders, who may inflate their expectations about what is affordable.

In his chapter J. Michael Collins provides a framework for policymakers to use when designing and evaluating programs to subsidize low-income homeownership. The framework focuses on scalability, the extent to which a program converts renters to buyers, its target population, efficiency of administration, extent of subsidy recapture, extent of positive neighborhood externalities (such as making a particular community more attractive to investment), the impact of the policy on default risk, and the extent to which the policy allows or prevents mobility on the part of the homebuyer. Collins examines the most significant existing subsidy mechanisms, finding that all fail to satisfy some key criteria, most commonly either failing to provide a meaningful level of assistance to a well-targeted population or suffering from a lack of scale.

Finally, Jeffrey Lubell urges a new way to think about ownership. The "own or rent" decision is usually thought of as binary, but Lubell suggests considering options that fall on the continuum between. Shared equity approaches can limit downside risk and, though they limit upside potential as well, allow some to own who otherwise could not and help keep housing affordable through successive owners. He stresses the value of shared equity approaches as a way to economize on subsidies by retaining a portion of them for the benefit of future generations of homebuyers and—in the case of community land trusts—for the stewarded model of lasting, affordable ownership housing stock it establishes. A fundamental challenge, however, is bringing these models to scale given the need for funding, a lack of standardization in approaches, and the need for ongoing management of what may be relatively small numbers of homes at the jurisdiction level. Shared equity arrangements also must overcome consumer confusion about the nature of these arrangements as well as political opposition to the limits placed on equity accumulation for lower-income owners targeted by these programs.

Assessing and Mitigating Risk

The conditions under which households borrowed and how their loans were serviced mattered enormously through the financial economic crisis of 2007–11. These conditions included timing of purchase, the amount of debt borrowers carried relative to their home's value at the time of loan origination, the type of loan product they had, the underwriting standards applied to their loan, and the industry channel through which they received their loan. The financial crisis represented a tragic but vast natural experiment on the impact of these conditions on default risk, treatment of nonperforming loans by servicers, and loss severity.

In the aftermath of this disastrous experience, the credit box has greatly tightened. Vast groups of potential owners will have a hard time obtaining credit in this environment but might nonetheless represent acceptable risks. Three chapters examine what we can learn from the last decade about the circumstances under which credit can be extended to borrowers who appear to present a higher risk of default, focusing on ongoing efforts to develop better and alternative credit scoring methods and the role and availability of low-down-payment loans as well as long-term fixed-rate loans.

Marsha Courchane, Leonard Kiefer, and Peter Zorn analyze the performance of mortgages originated over the past decade to assess how well traditional automated underwriting scorecards could be used to extend credit to borrowers with low down payments (loan-to-value ratios of 90 percent or higher), weak credit histories (credit scores less than 720), and living in low-income census tracts. A critical step in applying these scorecards is to determine the level of default risk that is acceptable, which they note is not a scientific question but one that must balance policy, regulatory, and business considerations. They find that sizable shares of these higher-risk borrowers could be approved for mortgages through automated systems employing default standards deemed reasonable based on the experience of the previous decade. In contrast, they note that few borrowers in this group would qualify for loans under current qualified mortgage or the initially proposed qualified residential mortgage standards with high-down-payment requirements. Their findings drive home the point that use of automated underwriting systems that allow one or more underwriting standards to compensate for others affords greater access to creditworthy borrowers and is a more holistic way to evaluate default risk than relying on static criteria. But they also caution that traditional automated underwriting systems are unlikely to be a panacea for providing access to credit to the targeted population. While they see these systems as preferable to static regulatory regimes, they acknowledge the potential of prepurchase counseling and high-touch origination and servicing to help reduce risks. They also point out the value of considering nontraditional sources of data, such as rental payment history, when assessing borrower risk, even though they may not be easy to incorporate into these models. In short, automated underwriting is likely to remain only one of the effective tools used to responsibly extend credit to targeted populations.

In their chapter Stephanie Moulton and Roberto Quercia examine the role of state housing finance agencies (HFAs), many of which have been branching into new financing strategies. The authors focus on the techniques HFAs use to create access and limit risk that might be put to use outside of specialized lending. HFAs provide a prominent example of successful specialized lending that utilizes a combination of counseling, careful underwriting and diligent servicing to achieve greater success, as measured by loan performance among borrowers who did not fit conventional underwriting standards. Still, there are a variety of questions about whether this approach can be scaled up. One concern is that these specialized programs might not be as good models as they may first appear because of self-selection of borrowers into them. There is also the question of whether it is possible to make "high touch" features "low touch" by automating them to reduce costs and achieve scale. But while evidence suggests that under the right conditions, low-down-payment lending can produce relatively low levels of default, not enough attention has been given to exploring what makes smaller specialized low-down-payment programs successful.

Finally, Andrew Davidson, Alex Levin, and Susan Wachter ask in their chapter whether we can return to mortgage lending and relative house price stability such as the nation saw from 1980 to 2000. This period stands in contrast to the 2000–07 period, which was characterized by massive inflows of nontraditional mortgage credit that increased price volatility and concurrently both credit and systemic risk. The authors note that this expansion of credit did not result in increased homeownership rates after 2004 but did allow real estate investors to play a large role in the housing boom, pushing the bubble to greater heights. The authors find that while it is clear that systemic risk is increased by the procyclical erosion of lending standards, there is no consensus on how to avoid this. But they also note that while no system is perfect, fixed-rate long-term mortgages with robust, standardized securitization have historically been associated with financial stability, while also promoting liquidity and suitability.

Government's Role

In debates about the future of the housing finance system, a central area of disagreement is over the appropriate role of government as mortgage guarantor—or if it should play this role at all. One view is that government presence distorts the market and inevitably leads to excessive risk taking. While the question of market distortion is one matter, it is worth pointing out that the government has had a significant presence in the mortgage market since the Great Depression. A systemic crisis did not erupt until the mid-2000s when the most excessive risk taking occurred first, and importantly, not in the markets implicitly or explicitly backstopped by the federal government but rather in the purely private ABS market. The counterview is that a government guarantee is needed to create stability in the housing sector—a sector too prone to systemic risk and too important for the economy and households for the government not to step in to rescue during times of national crisis. In many respects the debate about the government role is not primarily an issue of availability of credit for low-income or minority households but of the strength of the broader mortgage market. But absent a broad-based guarantee, mortgage costs would likely be higher and thus would restrict access for households with lower income and wealth.

The question of government's role as guarantor has been widely examined and so is not covered here; however, three chapters take on the issue of government regulation of lending activity, with an eye on three specific questions. First is the critical question of whether there ought to be a "duty to serve" provision to ensure that the benefits derived from government action accrue to a broad set of households. Adam Levitin and Janneke Ratcliffe reexamine the rationale for a duties-to-serve mandate in their chapter, focusing on the experience to date with the CRA and GSE housing goals and how this might inform decisions about whether and how to impose such a duty in a reconstituted mortgage market. The authors argue that banks' special-purpose charters and role in a government-constituted market entail social responsibilities, including provision of access to financial services in all communities within the constraints of safety and soundness. They make suggestions for improving duties-to-serve requirements, including expanding them to all mortgage lenders, imposing additional duties on the nation's largest banks, and improving tools to ensure compliance.

Second is the issue of whether a dual market is inevitable or necessary, or whether a unitary market that can serve all homebuyers, with some degree of average cost pricing, is preferable. Low-income and minority borrowers have historically been served through different channels than middle- and upper-income borrowers: through the FHA in the 1970s and continuing through the 1990s; through subprime specialists and brokers to some degree in the mid-1990s and to a significant degree in the mid-2000s; and through the FHA again in the late 2000s and early 2010s.

The expansion of credit to underserved sectors of the market in many respects naturally creates a segmented market, as the industry attempts to offset the higher risks of these borrowers with higher interest charges. In addition, there may be a need for different underwriting processes to vet borrowers with more complex risk profiles. Yet many of the concerns that arose from the rise of subprime lending related to issues of market segmentation, as borrowers who fell into the subprime segment faced not only much higher costs but also lighter regulatory oversight, riskier loan terms, and fewer loss mitigation options. Instances of fraud, deceptive lending practices, and other forms of predatory lending all appeared to be higher in the subprime channel.[47]

Raphael Bostic's chapter takes on the question of dual markets directly, examining their history and arguing that ultimately different lending channels are needed in order to expand access to homeownership. But, he argues, policy's role is to limit the risks to which homebuyers may be exposed as a result of a dual market. Bostic explores the government's role in preventing abuses in a dual market and encouraging innovation that is sustainable and responsible. He points to the Dodd-Frank Act and the creation of the Consumer Financial Protection Bureau as positive steps in the safe expansion of credit, and calls for a government role in realigning the incentives of mortgage brokers, increasing mortgage counseling and financial literacy to prepare people for homeownership, and promoting responsible innovation, potentially by funding the testing of new products.

A third critical question is whether government should impose restraints on household and financial sector leverage and, if so, how severe these restraints ought to be. In his chapter Mark Calabria argues that the housing crisis resulted in large measure from high leverage on the part of both homeowners and lenders. Thus in his view the government's role should be to establish higher capital requirements for lenders and higher loan-to-value ratios for borrowers to reduce risk, given that this risk can impose such significant costs.

Sustaining Ownership

The last theme of the book, and a key concern in the aftermath of the housing crisis, is how to help low-income and minority families sustain homeownership over time, which sharply increases the odds that its benefits will be realized. Patricia McCoy and Mark Cole explore lessons learned from servicing and counseling efforts in the past half decade.

Cole's chapter is based on insights gleaned from the work of the counseling organization CredAbility in engaging and counseling distressed homeowners. Data gathered from millions of counseling sessions reveal historically high levels of families in distress in the wake of the Great Recession. Record numbers have been driven to delinquency and default but by many different events and circumstances, including income losses from job loss or illness, falling home prices, interest rate shocks, and unexpected repair costs. While there is wide variation in the demographics of distressed owners, they are older than in the past,

---

47. Engel and McCoy (2011); Immergluck (2009); Gramlich (2007); Goldstein (1999).

portending bleak retirement prospects for those who were at or near peak earning years and had hoped to rely on their home as a nest egg or at least a hedge against rent inflation in their retirement. In reaching out to distressed owners, Cole points out the importance of a neutral third party endorsed by a lender, and how often a single answered call from the right neutral party could make a difference in putting owners on a path toward resolution. But he also notes that traditional servicing does not engage well with owners reluctant to take the first steps toward resolution on their own, who instead turn inward and wait. In results from a post-loan modification support program, Cole also stresses the importance of regular, ongoing contact; that one-time financial transactions do not change habits; and that sustainability in loan modifications requires a comprehensive view of a family's finances and of the events that affect them.

McCoy takes a broader view of the servicing industry in her paper. Among the serious failings of the system brought into relief by the foreclosure crisis were misaligned incentives and capacity problems, which inhibited servicers from quickly pursuing loss mitigation strategies; moral hazard concerns that limited the use of principal reduction strategies that held promise for loss mitigation for lenders and owners alike; funding and implementation constraints of federal programs that slowed and narrowed the government's response; and the voluntary nature of participation in federal loan modification and refinance programs. She notes the importance of keeping homes occupied whenever possible to avoid vacancies that can drag down the value of surrounding homes. She also discusses how families became delinquent for different reasons, which warrant different approaches. Like Cole, McCoy emphasizes the need for early intervention, and she also stresses the need to tackle barriers to foreclosure prevention, such as misaligned incentives for servicers and reliance on outdated technology.

Together, Cole and McCoy make the case for active, early engagement with distressed owners and for solutions that address their entire financial picture and that make sense given their unique circumstances (whether they have suffered a shock to their income or they are underwater). They argue that better servicer incentives are needed and that the intervention of a trusted third party that knows the system is a particularly effective form of loss mitigation.

Conclusions

The chapters in this volume point the way forward. While the authors are not in total agreement on every point, all understand that despite the risks homeownership poses to consumers, communities, and the financial system, it has historically played a special role in household wealth building in the United States and in fostering a range of social benefits. Taken together, the essays in this collection suggest at least four broad approaches to reducing the risks of homeownership while preserving its benefits. First, lenders should draw more extensively on what we know about how to select loan applicants likely to sustain homeownership and about how to pair them with products that increase their chances of doing so, even through a decline in home prices. Second, government should play a role in ensuring that borrowers with different risk profiles and who are served through different market channels do not face substantially different risks. Third, markets benefiting from critical government supports ought to be charged with ensuring that these benefits are widely available. Finally, much has been learned about effective methods for helping borrowers in trouble, and servicers should be given incentives to employ these methods so as to mitigate losses to investors and borrowers alike.

Policymakers and businesses will continue to debate what constitutes an acceptable level of risk and what pricing of that risk will best protect the financial system and the taxpayer. However, supporting broad access to homeownership—by well-informed and financially prepared consumers—will rightfully remain a bedrock goal of the financial system and should be a central concern of housing policy moving forward.

References

Ambrose, Brent W., and Thomas G. Thibodeau. 2004. "Have the GSE Affordable Housing Goals Increased the Supply of Mortgage Credit?" *Regional Science and Urban Economics* 34, no. 3: 263–73.

An, Xudong, and Raphael W. Bostic. 2009. "Policy Incentives and the Extension of Mortgage Credit: Increasing Market Discipline for Subprime Lending." *Journal of Policy Analysis and Management* 28, no. 3: 340–65.

An, Xudong, and others. 2007. "GSE Loan Purchases, the FHA, and Housing Outcomes in Targeted, Low-Income Neighborhoods [with Comments]." *Brookings-Wharton Papers on Urban Affairs:* 205–56.

Apgar, William. 2012. *Getting on the Right Track: Improving Low-Income and Minority Access to Mortgage Credit after the Housing Bust.* Harvard University, Joint Center for Housing Studies.

Apgar, William, and Allegra Calder. 2005. "The Dual Mortgage Market: The Persistence of Discrimination in Mortgage Lending." In *The Geography of Opportunity: Race and Housing Choice in Metropolitan America,* edited by Xavier N. De Souza Briggs, pp. 101–23. Brookings.

Apgar, William, and Mark Duda. 2003. "The Twenty-Fifth Anniversary of the Community Reinvestment Act: Past Accomplishments and Future Regulatory Challenges." *Federal Reserve Bank of New York Economic Policy Review* 9, no. 2: 169–91.

Avery, Robert B., and others. 2011. "The Mortgage Market in 2010: Highlights from the Data Reported under the Home Mortgage Disclosure Act." *Federal Reserve Bulletin* 97, no. 6: 1–60.

Been, Vicki, and others. 2011. "Decoding the Foreclosure Crisis: Causes, Responses, and Consequences." *Journal of Policy Analysis and Management* 30, no. 2: 388–96.

Belsky, Eric S., and Allegra Calder. 2005. "Credit Matters: Building Assets in a Dual Financial Services Market." In *Building Assets, Building Credit: Creating Wealth in Low-Income Communities,* edited by Nicolas P. Retsinas and Eric S. Belsky, pp. 10–41. Brookings.

Belsky, Eric S., and Nela Richardson. 2010. "Understanding the Boom and Bust in Nonprime Mortgage Lending." Working Paper. Harvard University, Joint Center for Housing Studies.

Bhutta, N. 2011. "The Community Reinvestment Act and Mortgage Lending to Lower Income Borrowers and Neighborhoods." *Journal of Law and Economics* 54, no. 4: 953–83.

————. 2012. "GSE Activity and Mortgage Supply in Lower-Income and Minority Neighborhoods: The Effect of the Affordable Housing Goals." *Journal of Real Estate Finance and Economics* 45, no. 1: 238–61.

Bhutta, Neil, and Glenn B. Canner. 2009. "'Did the CRA Cause the Mortgage Market Meltdown?" *Community Dividend* (Federal Reserve Bank of Minneapolis) (www.minneapolisfed.org/publications_papers/pub_display.cfm?id=4136).

Bocian, Debbie Gruenstein, Wei Li, and Keith S. Ernst. 2010. *Foreclosures by Race and Ethnicity: The Demographics of a Crisis.* Durham, N.C.: Center for Responsible Lending.

Bostic, Raphael W., and Stuart A. Gabriel. 2006. "Do the GSEs Matter to Low-Income Housing Markets? An Assessment of the Effects of the GSE Loan Purchase Goals on California Housing Outcomes." *Journal of Urban Economics* 59, no. 3: 458–75.

Canner, Glenn B., and Neil Bhutta. 2008. "Staff Analysis of the Relationship between the CRA and the Subprime Crisis." Board of Governors of the Federal Reserve System, Division of Research and Statistics (http://www.federalreserve.gov/newsevents/speech/20081203_analysis.pdf).

Canner, Glenn B., Wayne Passmore, and Elizabeth Laderman. 1999. "Role of Specialized Lenders in Extending Mortgages to Lower-Income and Minority Homebuyers." *Federal Reserve Bulletin* 85, no. 11: 709–23.

Carliner, Michael S. 1998. "Development of Federal Homeownership 'Policy.'" *Housing Policy Debate* 9, no. 2: 299–321.

Couch, Robert M. 2013. *The Great Recession's Most Unfortunate Victim: Homeownership.* Bradley Arant Boult Cummings LLP (www.jchs.harvard.edu/sites/jchs.harvard.edu/files/misc13-1_couch.pdf).

Cutts, Amy Crews, and William Merrill. 2008. "Interventions in Mortgage Default: Policies and Practices to Prevent Home Loss and Lower Costs." In *Borrowing to Live: Consumer and Mortgage Credit Revisited,* edited by Nicolas P. Retsinas and Eric S. Belsky, pp. 203–54. Harvard University, Joint Center for Housing Studies and Brookings.

Ding, Lei, and others. 2011. "Risky Borrowers or Risky Mortgages? Disaggregating Effects Using Propensity Score Models." *Journal of Real Estate Research* 33, no. 2: 245–77.

Drew, Rachel Bogardus, and Christopher Herbert. 2013. "Post-Recession Drivers of Preferences for Homeownership." *Housing Policy Debate* 23, no. 4: 666–87.

Eggers, Frederick J. 2001. "Homeownership: A Housing Success Story." *Cityscape* 5, no. 2: 43–56.

Engel, Kathleen C., and Patricia A. McCoy. 2011. *The Subprime Virus: Reckless Credit, Regulatory Failure, and Next Steps.* Oxford University Press.

Federal Housing Finance Agency. 2010. "The Housing Goals of Fannie Mae and Freddie Mac in the Context of the Mortgage Market: 1996–2009." Mortgage Market Note 10-02 (February 1).

Fligstein, Neil, and Adam Goldstein. 2011. "Catalyst of Disaster: Subprime Mortgage Securitization and the Roots of the Great Recession." Working Paper. University of California-Berkeley, Institute for Research on Labor and Employment.

Freddie Mac. 2009. "Cost of Freddie Mac's Affordable Housing Mission." June 4 (http://fcic-static.law.stanford.edu/cdn_media/fcic-docs/2009-06-04%20Freddie%20Mac-%20Cost%20of%20Affordable%20Housing%20Mission.pdf).

Gabriel, Stuart A., and Stuart S. Rosenthal. 2005. "Homeownership in the 1980s and 1990s: Aggregate Trends and Racial Gaps." *Journal of Urban Economics* 57, no. 1: 101–27.

Gates, Susan Wharton, Vanessa Gail Perry, and Peter M. Zorn. 2002. "Automated Underwriting in Mortgage Lending: Good News for the Underserved?" *Housing Policy Debate* 13, no. 2: 369–91.

Goldstein, D. 1999. *Understanding Predatory Lending: Moving toward a Common Definition and Workable Solutions.* Harvard University, Joint Center for Housing Studies and Neighborhood Reinvestment Corporation.

Gramlich, Edward M. 2007. *Subprime Mortgages: America's Latest Boom and Bust.* Washington: Urban Institute.

Haurin, Donald R., and others. 2005. *Homeownership Gaps among Low-Income and Minority Borrowers and Neighborhoods.* U.S. Department of Housing and Urban Development.

Herbert, Christopher E., and Eric S. Belsky. 2006. *The Homeownership Experience of Low-Income and Minority Families: A Review and Synthesis of the Literature.* U.S. Department of Housing and Urban Development.

Hernández-Murillo, R., A. Ghent, and M. Owyang. 2012. "Did Affordable Housing Legislation Contribute to the Subprime Securities Boom?" Working Paper 2012-005B. Federal Reserve Bank of St. Louis (http://research.stlouisfed.org/wp/2012/2012-005.pdf).

Immergluck, Daniel. 2009. *Foreclosed: High-Risk Lending, Deregulation, and the Undermining of America's Mortgage Market.* Cornell University Press.

Inside Mortgage Finance. 2009. *2009 Mortgage Market Statistical Annual.* Bethesda, Md.

Jaffee, Dwight M. 2010. "The Role of the GSEs and Housing Policy in the Financial Crisis." Paper presented to the Financial Crisis Inquiry Commission. Washington, February 27.

Joint Center for Housing Studies. 2001. *The State of the Nation's Housing 2001.* Harvard University.

————. 2012. *The State of the Nation's Housing 2012*. Harvard University.

Kochhar, Rakesh, Ana Gonzalez-Barrera, and Daniel Dockterman. 2009. *Through Boom and Bust: Minorities, Immigrants and Homeownership*. Washington: Pew Hispanic Center.

Laderman, Elizabeth, and Carolina Reid. 2009. "CRA Lending during the Subprime Meltdown." In *Revisiting the CRA: Perspectives on the Future of the Community Reinvestment Act*, edited by Prabal Chakrabarty and others, pp. 115–33. Federal Reserve Banks of Boston and San Francisco.

Mallach, Alan. 2009. *A Decent Home: Planning, Building, and Preserving Affordable Housing*. Chicago: American Planning Association.

Munnell, Alicia H., and others. 1996. "Mortgage Lending in Boston: Interpreting HMDA Data." *American Economic Review* 86, no. 1: 25–33.

Oliver, Melvin L., and Thomas M. Shapiro. 2006. *Black Wealth/White Wealth: A New Perspective on Racial Inequality*. New York: Routledge.

Park, Kevin. 2010. "Fannie, Freddie, and the Foreclosure Crisis." University of North Carolina, Center for Community Capital.

Pinto, Edward J. 2011. "Government Housing Policies in the Lead-up to the Financial Crisis: A Forensic Study." American Enterprise Institute (http://www.aei.org/files/2011/02/05/Pinto-Government-Housing-Policies-in-the-Lead-up-to-the-Financial-Crisis-Word-2003-2.5.11.pdf).

Ranieri, Lewis S., and others. 2013. "The Future of Home Finance: Who Will Qualify?" Berkeley, Calif.: Rosen Consulting Group (www.ranieripartners.com/Literature Retrieve.aspx?ID=192075).

Reid, C., and E. Laderman. 2011. "Constructive Credit: Revisiting the Performance of Community Reinvestment Act Lending during the Subprime Crisis." In *The American Mortgage System: Crisis and Reform*, edited by Marvin Smith and Susan Wachter, pp. 159–86. University of Pennsylvania Press.

Reid, Carolina, and others. 2013. *Debunking the CRA Myth—Again*. University of North Carolina, Center for Community Capital.

Ross, S. L., and J. Yinger. 2002. *The Color of Credit: Mortgage Discrimination, Research Methodology, and Fair-Lending Enforcement Lending*. MIT Press.

Sherraden, Michael. 1991. *Assets and the Poor: A New American Welfare Policy*. Armonk, N.Y.: M.E. Sharpe.

Turner, M. A., and others. 2013. *Housing Discrimination against Racial and Ethnic Minorities 2012: Full Report*. U.S. Department of Housing and Urban Development.

U.S. Department of Housing and Urban Development. 1995. *Homeownership and Its Benefits*. Urban Policy Brief 2 (www.huduser.org/publications/txt/hdbrf2.txt).

————. 2010. *Report to Congress on the Root Causes of the Foreclosure Crisis*.

von Hoffman, Alexander. 2012. "The Past, Present, and Future of Community Development in the United States." Working Paper W12-6. Harvard University, Joint Center for Housing Studies.

Wallison, Peter J. 2011. "Financial Crisis Inquiry Commission Dissenting Statement." In *The Financial Crisis Inquiry Report*, Official Government Edition, pp. 441–49. U.S. Government Printing Office.

Weicher, John C. 2010. "The Affordable Housing Goals, Homeownership and Risk: Some Lessons from Past Efforts to Regulate the GSEs." Paper presented at the conference "Past, Present, and Future of the Government-Sponsored Enterprises," Federal Reserve Bank of St. Louis. November 17 (http://research.stlouisfed.org/conferences/gse/Weicher.pdf).

Yinger, John. 1997. *Closed Doors, Opportunities Lost: The Continuing Costs of Housing Discrimination.* New York: Russell Sage Foundation.

Zandi, Mark. 2009. *Financial Shock: A 360° Look at the Subprime Mortgage Implosion, and How to Avoid the Next Financial Crisis.* Upper Saddle River, N.J.: FT Press.

PART I

Making the Case for Homeownership as a Policy Goal:

Has the Experience of the Housing Bust Changed the Calculus?

1

Homeownership, Wealth, and the Production of Racialized Space

john a. powell AND KALOMA CARDWELL

One of the hard-won insights of the twentieth century is that race—and the stratification experienced with it—is a social construct. Although this concept is still contested, it has gained currency even among conservatives, including members of the Supreme Court. What is less explored is *how* race is constructed and what might be done to reconstruct it. We fail to understand how race not only shapes the identity of the racial other but also how it shapes the identity of the dominant racial group. It is not the constructed nature of race that is the problem but how it is constructed and the way that construct is applied.

It is important then to understand what work race and other types of "othering" processes are doing, and how we construct and maintain these processes.[1] In the United States, racial identity and stratifications are the manifestations of othering that give shape and meaning to the dominant norm of whiteness and the ideology of radically separate individualism. This chapter explores the role of housing as one—if not the primary—mediating institution for the propagation of racial meaning and racial distribution in modern America.

Housing is key to the construct of race in contemporary American society. Patterns of residential living not only shape and define the meanings of race, but they are the primary explanatory variable in producing racial inequality. We live in institutions and structures that shape who we are and our life chances. These

---

1. "Othering" is the (conscious or unconscious) process of differentiating oneself from other people.

frameworks are sometimes referred to as opportunity structures. Housing is at
the hub of these opportunity structures since it is instrumental to the life chances
of individuals, families, and communities. For example, housing defines educational opportunities through tax policies that rely heavily on local property taxes
to fund schools. In turn, jurisdictional boundaries, which define tax policy, shape
housing patterns in dynamic relation. This is not a natural role of housing. It has
not always played that role in the United States and often does not play that role
in other societies.

More deeply, housing is central to conceptions of who belongs in our imag-
ined community. It defines, next to marriage and sex, the most intimate conceptions of our self and our community. In the American context, these spaces
acquire racialized meanings. Think of racial profiling: it is most extreme when
nonwhites are in a white space. There is an implicit understanding that nonwhites either do not belong or are strangers in white space, which may be imag-
ined as a neighborhood, a town, or even the entire country. When Arizona and
other states allow police to stop nonwhites for looking "un-American," such
policies create or maintain racialized and regulated spaces. While these laws are
clearly directed at Latinos, housing segregation has a similar effect on blacks and
others who might be American but still do not belong. This helps to explain how
a school district targeted and investigated a young black mother in Ohio who
sought to enroll her children in a school district in which she did not reside, or
how a young black teenager taking a shortcut returning from a convenience store
for candy and a soda would arouse suspicion near a gated community.

Growing patterns of both racial and socioeconomic segregation—normalized
as natural preferences of individuals or the operations of market forces—are central to the broader trends of increasing inequality in American society. Today,
more than ever, housing patterns are linked to regional, national, and even global
forces. Whereas technological developments—such as the automobile and industrialization—changed living patterns in the past, today's access to credit markets,
bifurcated labor markets, public policy, and global financial trends shape patterns
of residential living as much as individual choice.

U.S. Policy and Housing

A review of the history of housing policy in the United States illustrates the ways
in which federal, state, and local governments have directly shaped and influenced historical and contemporary housing patterns.

Historical Housing Policies

Despite the widespread segregation of public life in so many ways, before 1900
housing segregation was not the norm. Other mechanisms for othering existed,

not the least of which were explicit laws that regulated social status and belonging for people in physical proximity. Most Americans did not reside in the cities, and rural black and white families lived near one another. The great migration and the waves of black migrants to the North, as well as the industrialization of the South, changed those patterns. But as more and more Americans moved to cities, in areas where explicit laws were more relaxed, new practices for defining race and belonging emerged.

Between 1870 and 1970, U.S. homeownership developed alongside waves of black and immigrant migrations, technological advancements (for example, automobiles) that opened up new housing markets (for instance, suburbs), and shifting labor markets that were linked to global events (such as World War I). There was also a shift in the function of laws and the workplace. As blacks moved north and west, the South shifted to other practices for race making, and a developing housing market would be employed for this purpose. As a consequence barriers to black homeownership evolved. Before 1900 deed restrictions, which only covered single parcels and did not keep blacks from migrating into white communities, were not uncommon. After 1910 and until 1948—years in which migration reached record levels—"improvement associations" used restrictive covenants that contractually forbade blacks from owning, occupying, or leasing residents' property.[2] Moreover, real estate agents used different screening and rent requirements for blacks.

The Home Owners' Loan Corporation (HOLC) helped homeowners refinance urban mortgages but excluded blacks through HOLC's neighborhood quality ratings system and "redlining." Redlining used the color red on maps to indicate which neighborhoods were the poorest quality. Neighborhoods in red rarely received HOLC loans, which effectively and systematically undervalued racially or ethnically mixed neighborhoods. Black areas were always redlined.[3] Private banks adopted the HOLC loan system, including its process for generating maps and ratings.

The Federal Housing Administration (FHA), created in 1937, and the Veterans Administration, created in 1944, extended the HOLC's practices. The FHA loan program guaranteed the value of collateral for loans made by private banks, making low down payments (such as 10 percent) the new norm. Moreover, the FHA loan program established low monthly payments: repayment periods were extended to twenty-five or thirty years, and fully amortized loans were encouraged.[4]

These homeownership benefits, however, did not apply equally to blacks. The 1939 FHA loan program's *Underwriting Manual* explained: "If a neighborhood

2. De Graaf (1970, pp. 336–37); Drake and Cayton (1945, pp. 182–90); Kusmer (1976, pp. 46, 167).
3. Jackson (1985, pp. 199–201).
4. Jackson (1985, p. 204).

is to retain stability, it is necessary that properties shall continue to be occupied by the same social and racial classes."[5] Ultimately, it would not be until the 1950s that the FHA stopped encouraging the use of racially restricted covenants. Thus white middle-class areas received the majority of FHA and Veterans Administration mortgages. St. Louis County, a suburb surrounding St. Louis, received five times as many FHA loan program mortgages and nearly six times the loan money as did St. Louis between 1934 and 1960. Similar patterns were found in New York, where per capita FHA loan program lending in suburban Long Island was eleven times that in Brooklyn and sixty times that in the Bronx. In addition, some cities, such as Paterson and Camden, New Jersey, had zero FHA mortgages in some years. These practices not only directed government and private resources along racial lines, they helped create modern racial dynamics, generating racial meaning and identity. The new, emerging middle class came to be known in a way that did not exist prior to these practices: it specifically meant being white—not ethnic, not black, and not other. While this lending process was and still is deeply racialized, it had implications for othering beyond race.[6]

Historically, real estate agents have been active facilitators of housing discrimination. They used flat refusal, deception, and different screening, deposit, and rent requirements for black applicants. Helper's surveys in the 1950s provide insight into these practices.[7] In one study agents believed "few or very few banks were willing to make loans to Blacks, and half of the agents confirmed that banks would not make loans to areas that were Black, turning Black, or threatened with the possibility of Black entry."[8] Another study of real estate practices found that in Chicago 80 percent of agents refused to sell blacks properties in white neighborhoods, and 68 percent refused to rent to blacks in such neighborhoods. Half of those who would sell or rent to blacks likely applied restrictive conditions.[9]

The Highway Act of 1956 generated tremendous development that not only broke up black neighborhoods but led to further disinvestment in these areas by indirectly subsidizing the development of white suburbs. For the whites who could not leave the central cities—later to be renamed the inner cities—urban renewal functioned as urban removal and further marginalized and destroyed strong black communities to create roads and safe buffers for white elites still bound in cities. The destruction of these neighborhoods also created a housing boom for large public housing projects, also known as vertical ghettoes.

5. Unless otherwise indicated, most of the content in this paragraph is from Jackson (1985, pp. 203, 208, 211, and 213).

6. Consider bans on group homes for people with disabilities or "nontraditional" families.

7. Helper (1969, p. 322).

8. Helper (1969, p. 337).

9. Helper (1969, pp. 201 and 317).

Thus government and private markets were not just directing resources to the emerging white middle class; these actors also denied and destroyed resources in existing black communities. Again, these processes created a new form of both blackness and whiteness, deepening and reinstitutionalizing the othering. The dynamic would be acknowledged—but not changed—years later in the Kerner Commission Report.[10]

In the sales and rental markets, whites were systematically advantaged through the marketing of nonadvertised units and disparate types of credit assistance.[11] In 1989 the *Atlanta Journal-Constitution* conducted one of the largest studies on racial housing discrimination, examining 10 million applications to savings and loan associations between 1983 and 1989. The newspaper discovered that the overall rejection rate was 11 percent for whites and 24 percent for blacks. In three of the five years evaluated, high-income blacks were rejected more often than low-income whites across thirty-five metropolitan areas.[12]

Other studies confirmed widespread discrimination. In 1977 the U.S. Department of Housing and Urban Development (HUD) conducted an extensive assessment of housing discrimination in forty metropolitan areas with central cities containing at least an 11 percent black population.[13] Nationwide, whites were favored on 48 percent of transactions in the sales market and on 39 percent of those in the rental market. Blacks had a 60 percent chance of experiencing unfavorable treatment in rental markets in Detroit, Indianapolis, and Los Angeles, and in sales markets in Cincinnati, Columbus, and Detroit. Another study estimated that in the 1980s blacks averaged a 20 percent chance of experiencing discrimination in the sales market and a 50 percent chance in the rental market.[14]

In 1988 the Housing Discrimination Study repeated HUD's 1977 survey and found that widespread discrimination was similar to that in 1977.[15] The study indicated that whites were advantaged in 45 percent of the transactions in the rental market and 34 percent of those in the sales market. Additionally, more bias was documented in the marketing of nonadvertised units (for example, 60 percent and 90 percent of rental and sales units, respectively, made available to whites were not brought to the attention of blacks). And whites received more

10. U.S. National Advisory Commission on Civil Disorders (1968).

11. Galster (1990); Mikelsons and Turner (1991); Turner, Edwards, and Mikelsons (1991); Yinger (1991a, 1991b).

12. See Bill Dedman, "Blacks Denied S&L Loans Twice as Often as Whites," *Atlanta Journal-Constitution,* January 22, 1989.

13. Wienk and others (1979).

14. Galster (1990).

15. The findings of the 1988 Housing and Discrimination Survey are summarized in the following reports: Mikelsons and Turner (1991); Turner, Edwards, and Mikelsons (1991); Yinger (1991b).

favorable credit assistance in 46 percent of sales encounters and were offered more favorable terms in 17 percent of rental transactions.[16]

The Housing Acts of 1949 and 1954, which ushered in public housing, did not reverse these trends. These acts provided "federal funds to local authorities to acquire slum properties, assemble them into large parcels, clear them of existing structures, and prepare them for redevelopment."[17] Federal funding was tied to stipulations that required replacement housing to be made available to displaced families. Multistory, high-density public housing projects were built almost always in or adjacent to black neighborhoods. Such "urban renewal" continued for two decades. It halted in the 1970s, when white communities and political forces adamantly resisted mandates to build projects in white neighborhoods.

Housing and Wealth

U.S. housing policy affects more than just housing: since housing is a hub of opportunity, housing policy is about the creation and distribution of opportunity. Segregation, then, is not just about the distribution of people but the distribution of opportunity. Housing policy has both enabled and constrained the generational life chances of millions of Americans. For whites it created the middle class. For blacks it created significant gaps in, and distance from, opportunity and well-being. A brief exploration of the federal government's response to the Great Depression is illustrative.

In the aftermath of the Great Depression, widespread foreclosures and inaccessible credit led to another shift in the housing market and new barriers to black homeownership. Established in 1933, the HOLC became "the first government-sponsored program to use, on a mass scale, long-term, self-amortizing mortgages with uniform payments."[18] In other words, opportunity was created and distributed. The percentage of families living in owner-occupied dwellings increased from 44 percent to 63 percent between 1934 and 1969, with the purchase price of new suburban homes being cheaper than rental prices for comparable dwellings in the city.[19]

Legislative acts continued to distribute opportunity and improved life chances for many, in particular for white men born in the 1920s. Katznelson, among many others, asserts that the Servicemen's Readjustment Act of 1944, more commonly known as the GI Bill of Rights, is probably the single most important legislation in the creation of middle-class America. Of the men born in the

16. Yinger (1991b).
17. Massey and Denton (1995, p. 55).
18. Jackson (1985, p. 208).
19. Jackson (1985, p. 204).

1920s, 80 percent were eligible for benefits under the GI Bill.[20] Between 1944 and 1971, $95 billion flowed to former soldiers, as "millions bought homes, attended college, started business ventures, and found jobs commensurate with their skills."[21] Similar to New Deal housing legislation, racial compromises were structured into the GI Bill, and black veterans' life chances were shaped much differently than white veterans' life chances.

Before the GI Bill's passage, southern congressmen negotiated racialized provisions that would constrain the life chances and wealth of blacks for generations. The final GI Bill authorized states, not the federal government, to determine eligibility for the bill's educational benefits. Furthermore, the "South's desire to preserve Jim Crow and maintain white supremacy in the states of the former confederacy" was not limited to southern efforts that altered who received a GI Bill–assisted education.[22] The negotiated final bill also authorized the Veterans Administration to adopt the same housing standards and policies as the FHA. Thus black veterans' ability to accumulate wealth was handicapped significantly. As Oliver and Shapiro note, the value of the average housing unit tripled from 1970 to 1980.[23] The housing boom in the 1970s, typically described in purely economic terms, was a racialized and uneven source of opportunity.

Interventions and Deregulation

There are a number of challenges and difficulties in addressing our entrenched racialized structures and practices. One is that we often fail to acknowledge that racial practices are constantly changing, without necessarily improving across every indicator and certainly without any final resolution. We name the problem in one era not as a problem of race but as a specific or salient problem of that era. People have been proclaiming the end of the issue of race since the abolition of slavery and the end of the Civil War. If we address slavery, Jim Crow, mass incarceration, individual prejudice, and elect a black president, then we believe the problem has been solved. Our analysis, narratives, and rush to "move on" perpetuate a dysfunctional blindness to the complicated dynamics of race.

In addition, we also fail to understand just how deeply issues of race have affected the American national identity—who we are, our institutions, and our values.[24] We have not acknowledged or addressed our deep ambivalence toward race. It is not just that we do not understand race; we often have conflicting

---

20. Katznelson (2005).
21. Katznelson (2005).
22. Oliver and Shapiro (2006, p. 108).
23. Oliver and Shapiro (2006).
24. powell (2012).

approaches to race both within the country and ourselves.[25] When we look at important legislation and rules designed to deal with race, this ambivalence is often present but seldom noticed. Moreover, these efforts and missed opportunities have resulted in partial successes and disturbing racial arrangements and outcomes. Again, the federal government's response warrants our attention.

Following a series of episodes of mass civil disobedience in the mid- and late 1960s, often triggered by incidents involving police brutality, President Lyndon Johnson formed the Kerner Commission to identify the causes of racial unrest. The commission concluded that the United States "was moving toward two societies, one black, one white—separate and unequal."[26] In particular, the commission identified residential segregation as a significant cause of racial inequality.

Conflicting approaches to race, both within the country and ourselves, are apparent in the evolution and enforcement of the Civil Rights Act of 1968. In 1968 Congress passed Title VIII of the Civil Rights Act of 1968 (Fair Housing Act), which prohibited persons from refusing to rent or sell a home to any person because of race and authorized HUD to enforce these provisions. The Fair Housing Act, once one of the most filibustered bills in history, passed in the aftermath of institution- and country-defining events—the Detroit riots of 1967 and the assassination of Martin Luther King Jr. The Fair Housing Act, however, was not the watershed moment it could have been. From its inception the Fair Housing Act lacked critical enforcement mechanisms. The Supreme Court recognized this reality in 1972: "HUD has no power of enforcement."[27] Initially, the Fair Housing Act was primarily an antidiscrimination act that was limited to "aggrieved persons" who initiated private suits on their own. Other limiting provisions (for example, those that placed the burden of costs and attorneys' fees on plaintiffs) further weakened an act whose individualistic nature made it inherently inadequate and ill-suited to remedy systemic and institutional harms.

Other limitations went beyond the Fair Housing Act's design. President Richard Nixon appointed George Romney, Mitt Romney's father and an opponent of housing segregation, as his first secretary of HUD. In an effort to preempt and respond to Romney's efforts to enforce the act, southerners saw fit to refer to Nixon as "Mister Integrator" and "Anti-South." Nixon responded, in part, by putting and keeping Romney on a tight leash.[28] At first, and with Nixon's position on housing in mind, Romney attempted to discreetly push for fair housing enforcement without making formal policy announcements. Such efforts did not

25. This conflict is increasingly being exposed to those who follow the research in the cognitive sciences. See Kang (2011).

26. U.S. National Advisory Commission on Civil Disorders (1968).

27. *Trafficante* v. *Metropolitan Life Insurance*, 409 U.S. 205, 210 (1972).

28. Unless otherwise indicated, most of the material discussed in this and the following four paragraphs is taken from Hannah-Jones (2012).

last long. Nixon eventually "froze Romney out" and "ordered HUD to stop all efforts to pressure cities and states to foster integrated housing." George Romney resigned in 1972. Undoubtedly, *the problem* is not merely a specific problem of that era. For most of its history, indifference and opposition have undermined the Fair Housing Act. A senior HUD official under President Bill Clinton spoke to this legacy: "People say integration has failed. It hasn't failed because it's never been tried."[29] Similarly, experts estimated that between 1968 and 1995, about 2 million housing discrimination incidents occurred every year; by contrast, only 400 fair housing cases were decided during that time period.

Other apparent conflicts are observable in the structures of the agencies responsible for the act's enforcement. Commenting on HUD's structural conflicts and its racialized identity, a former assistant secretary of HUD under the Clinton administration stated: "HUD is . . . the most disfavored of all agencies and FHEO [Fair Housing and Equal Opportunity Office] is the most despised of all."[30] In 2012 the Fair Housing and Equal Opportunity Office, HUD's civil rights arm, employed blacks and whites at a ratio of almost two to one—57 percent and 27 percent, respectively. Moreover, employees in the fair housing office reportedly make less than comparably experienced employees in HUD. (The division responsible for disbursing funds to communities, the Community Development division, is 51 percent white and 32 percent black.)

Such conflicts, though structural and deeply rooted in historical forces, reflect choices. Between 1974 and 1983, HUD did not withhold any block grants—money cities and states would apply for in order to build roads—from any communities that violated the Fair Housing Act. Using 1988 as a starting point, some researchers could only identify two instances in which HUD chose to withhold block grants from communities. On the other hand, Montgomery County, Maryland, traditionally one of the nation's wealthiest and whitest suburbs, chose to take a more proactive approach. In the 1970s, Montgomery County officials enacted "inclusionary zoning" ordinances that mandated affordable units in each large development. ("Exclusionary zoning" refers to zoning tools that block or slow housing growth in a community, make housing more expensive, or that limit construction of rental units.) In essence a structural solution was implemented for a structural problem. In a span of three decades, this suburb's black population more than tripled to 18 percent, and its segregation levels are below the national average.

Yet such efforts and outcomes are not typical. In fact, HUD exacerbated segregation by subsidizing segregated housing. For years much of HUD's staff and budget prioritized building new units, regardless of whether the communities

29. Quoted in Hannah-Jones (2012).
30. Quoted in Hannah-Jones (2012).

who were receiving millions were complying with fair housing regulations. A 2009 internal HUD study noted that many communities applied for block grants without completing the required paperwork, including an "analysis of impediments" to fair housing, which was "apparently not performed at all." Also telling, the study found that one-third of the grant materials needed to be updated, with one out of ten receiving no updates since the 1990s.

Inclusionary zoning ordinances similar to those implemented in Montgomery County not only provide a mechanism for institutional and systemic harms to be addressed, they also illuminate why success has been limited. Simply put, when disconnected from structural solutions, antidiscrimination requirements are insufficient. Congress eventually recognized this dynamic and realized further action was needed.

In 1983 Congress amended the Fair Housing Act to require HUD to "affirmatively further fair housing." More importantly, Congress took a significant step in affirming that fair housing is still the critical strategy to address structural and systematic inequality.[31] Recent progress in enforcement has been documented, and HUD has shown signs that it is willing to enforce this critical requirement. The Obama administration has reportedly doubled the funding for private fair housing enforcement agencies to over $40 million dollars, threatened to cut off block grants worth millions of dollars, and rejected requests from states that were asking for billions. These efforts suggest the Obama administration recognizes that private or individual responses and solutions are insufficient. Nevertheless, the Fair Housing Act has had mixed results, a track record also associated with other related legislative acts.

In the 1970s two pieces of legislation were enacted to address discriminatory credit practices in the housing market. The first was the Home Mortgage Disclosure Act of 1975, which mandated lending institutions to report public loan data to the federal government, including the applicant's race, gender, and income; the amount, type, and approval or denial of loan; and the census tract of the home.[32] The second was the Community Reinvestment Act of 1977 (CRA), which required institutions chartered by the Federal Deposit Insurance Company to officially end redlining practices in communities of color and other lower-income communities. Though few believe redlining really ended, and despite strong evidence that race continues to play a critical role in the credit market, there is a push by bankers and others to weaken the CRA.

Bankers, who by no means were the only ones, rushed to move on without accounting for housing's racialized history. As a result they incorporated

31. All content in this paragraph from powell (2012).
32. Squires, Hyra, and Renner (2009).

dysfunctional blind spots into securitized processes, and opportunities once again were missed. One of the most important missed opportunities was the recent work concerning private securitization. Securitization created an explosion in the amount of capital and liquidity in the mortgage market.[33] Since black and Latino markets were undercapitalized—in part due to decades of redlining—this was an opportunity to address this lack, and to some extent securitization did. Capital poured into these communities, and for a short time the homeownership gap, if not the segregation gap, began to close. What was not noticed by most—until it was too late—were the terms and unsustainability of these practices.

As shown below, these practices were deeply racialized but not necessarily based on racial animus; in some cases they were well-intentioned efforts to make more resources available to previously excluded communities. But not enough attention was paid to the existing structures of segregation and disinvestment that these new approaches were built upon.[34] It is also worth noting that the big push for addressing the issue of a dual credit market is not necessarily coming from white homeowners, who might be reluctant to live with nonwhites. Instead, there is a big and organized push from a banking and mortgage industry that does not want to see its prerogatives limited. While this tension is often present, it seldom is in such plain view.[35]

These shifts in credit tell a story that is not just about the private credit market and missed opportunities but also government complicity and neglect. Beginning in the early 1980s, there was a restructuring of the financial industry and credit markets. First, important legislation was passed, including the Depository Institutions Deregulation and Monetary Control Act of 1980 and the Garn-St. Germain Depository Institutions Act of 1982, which permitted lending institutions to charge any rate of interest they chose and to provide adjustable-rate mortgage loans. The former established the "groundwork for risk-based pricing in mortgage lending."[36]

Second, the Riegle-Neal Interstate Banking and Branching Efficiency Act of 1994, which allowed for multiple branch banking, expanded the purview of federally chartered banks. This legislation arguably produced a more competitive banking environment on a local level, increasing the potential provision of financial services to black and other minority and low-income borrowers in compliance with the Community Reinvestment Act of 1977.

---

33. "Securitization" is defined here as the "process of pooling assets, such as mortgage loans, and then reselling them to investors." Peterson (2006, p. 3).

34. This insight could be important as we examine racialization further into the twenty-first century. But this requires a different understanding of race and racialization than the dominant discourse.

35. powell and Menendian (2011).

36. Squires, Hyra, and Renner (2009).

Third, and most important, the Gramm-Leach-Bliley Act, also known as the Financial Services Modernization Act of 1999, repealed the Glass-Steagall Act.[37] A provision within the act enabled commercial banks and investment banks to exist within the same top-tier holding company, known as a financial holding company. Creation of the financial holding company charter facilitated the use of the "originate to distribute model," whereby banks originate loans and resell them within structured products, rather than holding the loans on their balance sheets until maturity. The incentive to make good loans was thus dramatically reduced.

Last, the Commodity Futures Modernization Act of 2000 deregulated these new products, including credit default swaps on them, by excluding them from regulation by the Securities and Exchange Commission and the Commodity Futures Trading Commission.

With the invention of securitization in the 1970s, government-sponsored enterprises (GSEs) entered the business of securitization.[38] GSEs "guaranteed the principal and interest income of their securities even when mortgagors defaulted" and enabled "larger capital markets to directly invest in American homeownership at a lower cost than the older depository lending model of business."[39] As the biggest players in the secondary mortgage market, Fannie Mae and Freddie Mac set many of the standards for the entire mortgage market. They were government chartered but became private corporations in 1968 and 1970, respectively, and were subsequently traded on the New York Stock Exchange. Private institutions, including investment banks, financial holding companies, and thrift holding companies, followed in the practice of securitization with the passage of the Secondary Mortgage Market Enhancement Act of 1984 and entered the business of subprime mortgages. The private securitization of mortgages and other forms of credit became increasingly important.

These developments also created new ratings and different forms of securities. As their market share grew, the GSEs were pushed into mimicking the private market, including the subprime loan market. In the mid-2000s, the GSEs lowered their standards. As a result a new market opened up, consisting of agency mortgage-backed securities that were considered subprime but with a federal guarantee. Following massive losses due to "risky but not subprime mortgages," inadequate capital to cover declining property values, and fears of instability in the housing market, the federal government put Fannie Mae and Freddie Mac under conservatorship in 2008. The Treasury Department gave both companies

---

37. The Glass-Steagall Act refers to four provisions within the Banking Act of 1933 that limited activities and affiliations between investment and commercial banks.

38. These GSEs included Fannie Mae and Freddie Mac.

39. Peterson (2006, p. 14).

an infusion of capital.[40] The story following the large loss was to shift much of the blame onto black and Latino communities and even the CRA.

With the creation of securitized mortgages, clients and communities that had historically been discriminated against became sought after in the housing market. Traditionally, the volume of mortgages was in proportion to the amount of deposits with the bank; in contrast, with the securitization of mortgages, the volume of mortgages was limited by "the number of potential borrowers and [investors willing] to purchase mortgage-backed securities."[41] New demand was generated for banks to increase their pool of borrowers in this new system, thereby expanding credit to black and other historically marginalized communities while also securing a new market for profit generation.[42]

The history of racialized residential segregation of blacks created the geography for "reverse redlining," where "high-cost loan products" are disproportionately directed toward black and other communities of color.[43] The spatial effects of historical segregation coupled with the historical inability of blacks and other communities of color to access mortgage credit as a result of discrimination in the credit markets were important factors in generating the foreclosure crisis. They created conditions that enabled subprime lending in communities of color. These communities were targeted for "differentially marketed risky subprime loans" that were securitized and sold in secondary markets.[44] Even though financial holding companies and stand-alone investment banks were often not directly making these loans, they were enabling their origination by purchasing them to resell as structured products. In short, the market for structured products incentivized banks and other lenders to extend credit to those who would become subprime borrowers through what can be called "predatory structured finance."[45] Thus institutions engaging in sponsoring and administering the securitization of mortgages were also participating in predatory lending practices.[46]

Moreover, during this period of time, the government incentivized rather than discouraged excessive risk taking.[47] First, Federal Reserve Chairman Alan Greenspan encouraged homeowners to take out variable-rate mortgages, rather than fixed-rate mortgages.[48] This placed homeowners at risk if interest rates went

40. Thomas and Van Order (2011).
41. Rugh and Massey (2010, p. 631).
42. Rugh and Massey (2010, p. 631).
43. Squires, Hyra, and Renner (2009).
44. Rugh and Massey (2010, p. 629).
45. Peterson (2006, p. 4).
46. Predatory lending is the practice of "imposing unfair and abusive loan terms on borrowers." See Federal Deposit Insurance Corporation (2006, p. 1).
47. Stiglitz (2010).
48. Greenspan (2004).

up.[49] Second, in 2003 Greenspan brought interest rates down to an unprecedented low of 1 percent, thereby increasing demand for mortgages.[50] Inevitably, short-term interest rates rose (rising to 5.25 percent in 2006), creating a crisis for those who had taken out the largest mortgages they were told they could afford or that their banks would give them. For many their only option was default.[51]

The mortgage crisis consequently had disproportionate effects on black borrowers and homeowners, as well as Latinos, the elderly, people with disabilities, and those with poor credit.[52] It has been estimated that "subprime lending accounted for 43 percent of the increase in black home ownership during the 1990s."[53] Furthermore, subprime lending disproportionately affected black middle- and upper-income borrowers for whom creditworthiness was not an issue. For example, across Ohio upper-income blacks received subprime loans 47.51 percent of the time, whereas lower-income whites received them 28.50 percent of the time.[54] These high rates of subprime lending in black communities were not related to lending under the CRA. As Bhutta and Canner's findings demonstrate, only 6 percent of subprime loans were made to low-income borrowers or individuals in neighborhoods subject to CRA oversight.[55]

Thus, as occurs with uneven geographic development, the effects of foreclosures were disproportionately felt in black neighborhoods. As Rugh and Massey argue, the higher the degree of black-white segregation in a metropolitan area, the greater the number and higher the frequency of foreclosures.[56] For example, in the city of Atlanta, middle-income black borrowers were "35 percent more likely to go into foreclosure" than middle-income white borrowers.[57] Yet because consumer protection laws were outpaced by the financial technology of securitization, victims of subprime lending had little legal recourse because it was almost impossible to hold any one institution accountable for the predatory practices.[58]

As a consequence of the financial crisis, Congress passed the Dodd-Frank Wall Street Reform and Consumer Protection Act in 2010. In terms of the mortgage crisis, the act first seeks to address subprime lending by making all mortgage originators, including institutions that are not banks or thrift holding companies,

49. Stiglitz (2010).
50. "Greenspan Goes for Broke," *The Economist,* June 26, 2003 (www.economist.com/node/1875594).
51. Stiglitz (2010).
52. Peterson (2006).
53. Williams, Nesiba, and McConnell (2005, p. 193, table 1).
54. Dillman, Pleasants, and Brown (2006).
55. Bhutta and Canner (2009, table 2).
56. Rugh and Massey (2010, p. 635).
57. Anacker, Carr, and Pradhan (2012).
58. Peterson (2006).

subject to consumer protection laws and standards for the origination of all mortgages. It therefore attempts to align the incentives of borrowers, banks, and investors in structured products. Second, it prohibits discrimination against "consumers of equal credit worthiness but of different race, ethnicity, gender, or age."[59] Nevertheless, the act does not address critical problems in the secondary market; it fails to incentivize "an inclusive market" that provides access to adequately financed housing loans through the secondary market, leaving a "credit vacuum" in communities already devastated by the foreclosure crisis.[60] In the end the act was a compromise that largely gave in to the demands of the banking community.

Few attempts were made to address the underlying racialized housing and credit market. In the midst of the crisis, the government reached out to help save the banks but refused to do anything but offer the weakest response to the needs of borrowers and homeowners. The Home Affordable Modification Program and Home Affordable Refinance Program have been notable, high-profile failures.[61] Though there is evidence that the former has had some positive effects, the program fell well short of its goal of facilitating 3 to 4 million modifications. Ultimately, these programs did not change the behavior of the biggest banks.[62]

By all accounts what has been adopted and is being considered is likely to deepen the dual housing and credit market. Some call for an explicit dual market, where loans are given to borrowers who could put down 20 percent, which banks could then sell. If borrowers put down less, banks would be required to hold on to the loan. The idea is to incentivize banks to check the viability of the loan. Such a plan would lock a large number of blacks and Latinos and some poor whites out of the housing market. The response by the head of HUD is that perhaps some people should not be homeowners. This is the position being advanced by an African American president and a Democratic secretary of HUD. The Republicans have been even more insistent that banks be left to do what they do without government intervention. The problem of a deeply racialized market has been reconstructed, recast as the fault not of the banks or lack of oversight but of low-income borrowers—and particularly borrowers of color. This approach risks deepening the racial divide into future generations.

Rather than exacerbating the status quo, banking institutions must play a critical role as vehicles for extending and fairly distributing credit. The question remains: in the shadow of redlining and subprime lending, how can the United States incentivize the extension of credit to all borrowers in a racially just and ethical way to ensure wealth creation in black and other communities of color?

59. Haberle (2011).
60. Haberle (2011).
61. Pierce and Kiel (2011).
62. Kiel (2012).

Ending Residential Segregation and Creating Sustainable Structures and Relationships

This chapter has described a number of tools and practices that have been used both to perpetuate a segregated housing market and construct race in a particular way. There are many more that could be included. Some of these will be important to address and understand if this country is to have a truly integrated housing market. But before considering how we might get there, there are two important things to address.

The first is that housing is just a tool. It is conceivable that we could have an integrated housing market and find some other mediating practice and norms to reproduce racial meaning and stratification. There is no single force producing racial meaning. Too often we have assumed that there was only one issue and that if we addressed that issue, everything would change. When we fall prey to that illusion, we focus all our efforts on a singular strategy and fail to address the shifts and accommodation that systems can and do make to limit change.

We cannot be in a rush to move on from a process that is not a complete move forward. For example, the shift from slavery to Jim Crow and sharecropping was a move, but it was not a move to full belonging and an end of racial stratification. The end of formal slavery did not ensure freedom. Similarly, the transition from Jim Crow to what some call "colorblind" racism has been a move but not one leading to an end to racial meaning and racial stratification. Consider "stop and frisk" practices in New York, mass incarceration of people of color throughout the country, and the disenfranchisement of millions of blacks who are nonetheless counted for white congressional districts.[63] There are ways to reproduce racial stratification that we have not even thought of. The point is not to detract from the importance of addressing de facto housing segregation but rather to continue to be aware of emerging innovative racial practices.

The second point is similar to the first. We have to be willing to state our goal and work toward it. The goal is not to end intentional discrimination or to repeal a particular racist law. The goal is to have a truly just set of arrangements and outcomes for housing, schools, and other institutions in our society that support fully belonging. It is not enough to have a just process, although there is value in that. As stated in the opening of this chapter, we are calling for a society where all groups are full members and fully belong. This requires more than just new structures; it also calls for a new culture and a new way of being. When Wechsler claimed that the call for integration in *Brown* v. *Board of Education* was not rooted in neutral principles and in some important ways impinged on the

---

63. Sommerstein (2010).

rights of whites, he was not entirely wrong.[64] True integration cannot occur or survive in a society committed to racial exclusion and stratification, whether de jure or de facto. As a society we have not agreed on that goal—and without that agreement whatever processes we implement will lose their force.

References

Anacker, Katrin, James Carr, and Archana Pradhan. 2012. "Analyzing Determinants of Foreclosure of Middle-Income Borrowers of Color in the Atlanta, GA Metropolitan Area." Research Paper 2013-01. George Mason University, School of Public Policy. July 14 (http://ssrn.com/abstract=2106055).

Bhutta, Neil, and Glenn B. Canner. 2009. "Did the CRA Cause the Mortgage Market Meltdown?" *Community Dividend,* March 1 (www.minneapolisfed.org/publications_papers/pub_display.cfm?id=4136).

De Graaf, Lawrence B. 1970. "The City of Black Angels: Emergence of the Los Angeles Ghetto, 1890–1930." *Pacific Historical Review* 39, no. 3: 323–52.

Dillman, Jeffrey, Carrie Bender Pleasants, and David M. Brown. 2006. "The State of Fair Housing in Northeast Ohio." Cleveland: Housing Research and Advocacy Center (www.nhlink.net/housing/OHIO_Lending_Disparities2006.pdf).

Drake, St. Clair, and Horace R. Cayton. 1945. *Black Metropolis: A Study of Negro Life in a Northern City.* New York: Harcourt, Brace.

Federal Deposit Insurance Corporation, Office of Inspector General. 2006. "Challenges and FDIC Efforts Related to Predatory Lending." Report 06-011 (www.fdicoig.gov/reports06/06-011.pdf).

Galster, George C. 1990. "Racial Steering by Real Estate Agents: Mechanisms and Motives." *Review of Black Political Economy* 19, no. 1: 39–63.

Greenspan, Alan. 2004. "Understanding Household Debt Obligations." Remarks at the Credit Union National Association 2004 Governmental Affairs Conference. Washington. February 23 (www.federalreserve.gov/boarddocs/speeches/2004/20040223/).

Haberle, Megan. 2011. "Finishing What Dodd-Frank Started: Why Housing Finance Reform Still Matters" (www.alternet.org/speakeasy/2011/06/30/finishing-what-dodd-frank-started-why-housing-finance-reform-still-matters?page=entire%2C0).

Hannah-Jones, Nikole. 2012. "Living Apart: How the Government Betrayed a Landmark Civil Rights Law." *ProPublica,* October 28 (www.propublica.org/article/living-apart-how-the-government-betrayed-a-landmark-civil-rights-law).

Helper, Rose. 1969. *Racial Policies and Practices of Real Estate Brokers.* University of Minnesota Press.

Jackson, Kenneth T. 1985. *Crabgrass Frontier: The Suburbanization of the United States.* Oxford University Press.

Kang, Jerry. 2011. "Getting Up to Speed on Implicit Bias." March 13 (http://jerrykang.net/2011/03/13/getting-up-to-speed-on-implicit-bias/).

64. *Brown* v. *Board of Education,* 347 U.S. 483 (1954); Wechsler (1959, p. 1).

Katznelson, Ira. 2005. *When Affirmative Action Was White: An Untold History of Racial Inequality in Twentieth-Century America.* New York: Norton.

Kiel, Paul. 2012. "Foreclosure Fail: Study Pins Blame on Big Banks." September 11 (www.propublica.org/article/foreclosure-fail-study-pins-blame-on-big-banks).

Kusmer, Kenneth L. 1976. *A Ghetto Takes Shape: Black Cleveland, 1870–1930.* University of Illinois Press.

Massey, Douglas S., and Nancy A. Denton. 1995. *American Apartheid: Segregation and the Making of the Underclass.* Harvard University Press.

Mikelsons, Maris, and Margery A. Turner. 1991. *Housing Discrimination Study: Mapping Patterns of Steering for Five Metropolitan Areas.* U.S. Department of Housing and Urban Development, Office of Policy Development and Research.

Oliver, Melvin L., and Thomas M. Shapiro. 2006. *Black Wealth/White Wealth: A New Perspective on Racial Inequality.* New York: Routledge.

Pendall, Rolf. 2000. "Local Land Use Regulation and the Chain of Exclusion." *Journal of the American Planning Association* 66, no. 2: 125–42.

Peterson, Christopher. 2006. "Predatory Structured Finance." Working Paper 1709. *bepress Legal Series.* September 7 (http://law.bepress.com/expresso/eps/1709).

Pierce, Olga, and Paul Kiel. 2011. "By the Numbers: A Revealing Look at the Mortgage Mod Meltdown." *ProPublica.* March 8 (www.propublica.org/article/by-the-numbers-a-revealing-look-at-the-mortgage-mod-meltdown).

powell, john a. 2012. *Racing to Justice: Transforming Our Conceptions of Self and Other to Build an Inclusive Society.* Indiana University Press.

powell, john a., and Stephen Menendian. 2011. "Beyond Public/Private: Understanding Excessive Corporate Prerogative." *Kentucky Law Journal* 100: 83–164.

Rugh, Jacob, and Douglas Massey. 2010. "Racial Segregation and the American Foreclosure Crisis." *American Sociological Review* 75, no. 5: 629–51.

Sommerstein, David. 2010. "Urban, Rural Areas Battle for Census Prison Populace." *All Things Considered,* NPR. February 15 (www.npr.org/templates/story/story.php?storyId=123663462).

Squires, Gregory D., Derek S. Hyra, and Robert N. Renner. 2009. "Segregation and the Subprime Lending Crisis." Paper presented at the Federal Reserve System Community Affairs Research Conference. Washington, April 16 (www.kansascityfed.org/publicat/events/community/2009carc/Hyra.pdf).

Stiglitz, Joseph E. 2010. *Freefall: America, Free Markets, and the Sinking of the World Economy.* New York: Norton.

Thomas, Jason, and Robert Van Order. 2011. "A Closer Look at Fannie Mae and Freddie Mac: What We Know, What We Think We Know and What We Don't Know." Working Paper. George Washington University (March) (http://business.gwu.edu/creua/research-papers/files/fannie-freddie.pdf).

Turner, Margery A., John G. Edwards, and Maris Mikelsons. 1991. *Housing Discrimination Study: Analyzing Racial and Ethnic Steering.* U.S. Department of Housing and Urban Development, Office of Policy Development and Research.

U.S. National Advisory Commission on Civil Disorders. 1968. *The Kerner Report.* Repr., New York: Pantheon, 1988.

Wechsler, Herbert. 1959. "Toward Neutral Principles of Constitutional Law." *Harvard Law Review* 73, no. 1: 1–35.

Wienk, Ronald, and others. 1979. *Measuring Racial Discrimination in American Housing Markets: The Housing Market Practices Survey.* U.S. Department of Housing and Urban Development.

Williams, Richard, Reynold Nesiba, and Eileen Diaz McConnell. 2005. "The Changing Face of Inequality in Home Mortgage Lending." *Social Problems* 52, no. 2: 181–208.

Yinger, John. 1991a. *Housing Discrimination Study: Incidence and Severity of Unfavorable Treatment.* U.S. Department of Housing and Urban Development, Office of Policy Development and Research.

———. 1991b. *Housing Discrimination Study: Incidence of Discrimination and Variations in Discriminatory Behavior.* U.S. Department of Housing and Urban Development, Office of Policy Development and Research.

2

Is Homeownership Still an Effective Means of Building Wealth for Low-Income and Minority Households?

CHRISTOPHER E. HERBERT, DANIEL T. McCUE, AND ROCIO SANCHEZ-MOYANO

In many respects the notion that owning a home is an effective means of accumulating wealth among low-income and minority households has been the keystone underlying efforts to support homeownership in recent decades. The renewed emphasis in the early 1990s on boosting homeownership rates as a policy goal can be traced in no small part to the seminal work by Oliver and Shapiro and by Sherraden, which highlighted the importance of assets as a fundamental determinant of the long-run well-being of families and individuals.[1] The efforts of these scholars led to a heightened awareness of the importance of assets in determining life's opportunities, enabling investments in education and businesses, providing economic security in times of lost jobs or poor health, and passing on advantages to children. Assessments of differences in asset ownership placed particular emphasis on the tremendous gaps in homeownership rates according to race-ethnicity and income and the importance of these gaps in explaining differences in wealth. In announcing their own initiatives to close these homeownership gaps, both President Clinton and President Bush gave prominence to the foundational role that homeownership plays in providing financial security.[2]

The authors thank Eric Belsky, Jennifer Molinsky, Carolina Reid, and conference participants for helpful comments and suggestions.
1. Oliver and Shapiro (1990); Sherraden (1991).
2. Herbert and Belsky (2006).

But while faith in homeownership's financial benefits is widespread, there have long been challenges to the view that owning a home is necessarily an effective means of producing wealth for lower-income and minority households. In 2001 the Joint Center for Housing Studies (JCHS) hosted a symposium with the goal of "examining the unexamined goal" of boosting low-income homeownership.[3] The general conclusion that emerged from this collection of papers was that lower-income households do benefit from owning homes, although this conclusion was subject to a variety of "caveats and codicils."[4] A few of these caveats related to whether financial benefits were likely to materialize, with research finding that all too commonly homebuyers sold their homes for real losses while alternative investments offered higher returns.[5] In perhaps the most comprehensive critique of the policy of fostering low-income homeownership, Shlay's review of existing scholarly evidence cast doubt on the likelihood that either the financial or social benefits of owning would be realized.[6]

These criticisms have only grown louder in the aftermath of the housing bust, as trillions of dollars in wealth evaporated, leaving more than 10 million homeowners owing more than their homes are worth and causing more than 4 million owners to lose their homes to foreclosure.[7] Many of the criticisms concerning the financial risks of homeownership are not new, but the experience of the last five years has certainly given new impetus to these arguments. However, there are also concerns that changes in the mortgage market and in consumer behavior may have exacerbated these risks, increasing the odds that owners will, at best, be less likely to realize any financial gains from owning and, at worst, face a heightened likelihood of foreclosure.

The goal of this chapter is to reassess, in the light of recent experience, whether homeownership is likely to be an effective means of wealth creation for low-income and minority households. Has the experience of the last decade proven the arguments of earlier critics of homeownership? Have changes in the market affected whether these benefits are liable to be realized? The chapter takes three approaches to addressing these questions. We begin by presenting a conceptualization of the risks and rewards of homeownership as a financial choice, with a particular eye toward whether the odds of a beneficial outcome are less for lower-income and minority owners. This review also assesses whether recent experience has altered this calculus—as opposed to just raising awareness

3. Retsinas and Belsky (2002b).
4. Retsinas and Belsky (2002a, p. 11).
5. Belsky and Duda (2002); Goetzmann and Speigel (2002).
6. Shlay (2006).
7. Joint Center for Housing Studies (JCHS;2012); Kiviat (2010); Li and Yang (2010); Davis (2012).

of the proper weighting of the likelihood of realizing the benefits while sidestepping the risks. Our second approach is a review the existing literature examining the financial benefits of owning a home, including both studies simulating the returns to owning and renting as well as studies using panel surveys to track actual wealth accumulation among owners and renters. Finally, we examine data from the Panel Study of Income Dynamics covering the last decade to assess how owning a home has been associated with changes in household financial balance sheets over this period.

To preview our conclusions, we find that while there is no doubt that homeownership entails real financial risks, there continues to be strong support for the association between owning a home and accumulating wealth. This relationship held even during the tumultuous period from 1999 to 2009, under less than ideal conditions. Importantly, while homeownership is associated with somewhat lower gains in wealth among minorities and lower-income households, these gains are on average still positive and substantial. In contrast, renters generally do not see any gains in wealth. Those who buy homes but do not sustain this ownership also do not experience any gains in wealth but typically are left no worse off in wealth terms than they were prior to buying a home—although of course there may still be substantial costs from these failed attempts at owning, in terms of physical and mental health as well as future costs of credit.

We conclude that homeownership continues to represent an important opportunity for individuals and families of limited means to accumulate wealth. As such, policies to support homeownership can be justified as a means of alleviating wealth disparities by extending this opportunity to those who are in a position to succeed as owners under the right conditions. The key, of course, is to identify the conditions under which lower-income and minority households are most likely to succeed as owners and so realize this potential while avoiding the significant costs of failure.

Assessing the Financial Risks and Rewards of Homeownership

Before turning to evidence about actual financial returns to homeownership, it is helpful to start by framing the arguments about why homeownership is thought to be an effective means of generating wealth as well as the counterarguments about why these benefits may not materialize, particularly for lower-income and minority homeowners. We then consider how changes in mortgage markets and consumer behavior may have altered the likelihood that owning will lead to financial gains. This framing helps provide a basis for interpreting the findings from the following two sections of the chapter that examine evidence about the association between homeowning and wealth accumulation.

The Potential Financial Benefits of Owning

The belief that homeownership can be an important means of creating wealth has its roots in five factors. First, the widespread use of amortizing mortgages to finance the acquisition of a home results in forced savings as a portion of the financing cost each month goes toward principal reduction. While modest in the early years of repayment, the share of the payment going toward principal increases over time. For example, assuming a thirty-year loan with a 5 percent interest rate, a homeowner will have paid off about 8 percent of the mortgage after five years, 19 percent after ten years, and nearly a third after fifteen years. Assuming that individuals purchase a home while in their early thirties and persist in paying off their mortgages over a thirty-year period, these forced savings will represent a sizable nest egg when they reach retirement age. In addition, an often overlooked aspect of the forced savings associated with homeownership is the accumulation of the down payment, which often entails a committed effort to accumulate savings over a short period to buy a home.

Second, homes are generally assumed to experience some degree of real appreciation over time, reflecting increased overall demand for housing due to growth in both population and incomes against a backdrop of a fixed supply of land located near centers of economic activity. Shiller has been the most notable critic of this point of view, arguing that over the very long run, real house prices have only barely exceeded inflation.[8] Lawler, however, has argued that Shiller's house price estimates and measures of inflation result in an underestimate of real house price growth.[9] Analysis of trends in real house prices across a range of market areas supports the conclusion that these trends reflect a complex interaction of supply and demand factors in local markets that defy simple categorization.[10] At a national level, the Federal Housing Finance Agency house price index indicates that between 1975 and 2012, the compound annual growth rate in house prices has exceeded inflation by 0.8 percentage points. Even at a modest rate of increase, the compounding of these returns over a longer period of time can produce a substantial increase in real home values. Assuming just a 0.8 percent annual real increase in house values over thirty years, an owner will experience a real gain of about 26 percent in the overall house value.

A third factor contributing to wealth gains through homeowning is the use of financing to leverage gains in home values since a homebuyer with a modest down payment gets the benefit of increases in the overall asset value despite his

8. Shiller (2005).
9. Lawler (2012).
10. Capozza and others (2002); Gallin (2006).

or her small equity stake. Through this leverage, the rate of return on an investment in a home can be substantial even when the increase in house values is modest. Consider the case in which a buyer puts down 5 percent and the house appreciates at 4 percent annually. After five years the home will have increased in value by nearly 22 percent—or more than four times the initial 5 percent down payment. Even allowing for selling costs of 6 percent, this would represent an annualized return of 31 percent on the owner's initial investment. Even nominal increases in home values that do not exceed inflation can result in real returns. In the above example, if inflation matched the 4 percent growth in home prices, the owner would still have earned a substantial real return on the initial investment.

Federal income tax benefits from owning a home can also be substantial. The ability to deduct mortgage interest and property taxes is the most apparent of these benefits. Taxpayers who are able to make full use of these deductions receive a discount on these portions of ongoing housing costs at the taxpayer's marginal tax rate, ranging from 15 percent for moderate-income households up to 39 percent for the highest tax bracket. In addition, capital gains on the sale of a principal residence up to $250,000 for single persons and $500,000 for married couples are also excluded from capital gains taxation, which is currently 15 percent for most households and 20 percent for the highest income bracket.[11]

Finally, owning a home provides a hedge against inflation in rents over time. Sinai and Souleles find that homeownership rates and housing values are both higher in markets where rents are more volatile, indicating the value placed on being able to protect against rent fluctuations.[12] Under most circumstances mortgage payments also decline in real terms over time, reducing housing costs as a share of income. For long-term owners this can result in fairly substantial savings in the out-of-pocket costs for housing. Assuming a fixed-rate mortgage, inflation of 3 percent, 1 percent growth in both real house prices and the costs of property taxes, and insurance and maintenance expenses, real monthly housing costs would decline by about 10 percent after five years, 15 percent after ten years, and 30 percent by the last year of the mortgage. Once the mortgage is paid off, the out-of-pocket costs of owning in real terms are less than half the payments made at the time of purchase. Housing costs for renters, in contrast, would be expected to keep pace with inflation in housing prices.

---

11. An additional tax benefit that is often overlooked is the fact that while owner occupants benefit from the use of their home as a residence, they do not have to pay any tax on these benefits, referred to as the implicit rental income from the property (that is, the rent one would have to pay to occupy the home) (Ozanne 2012). The loss of revenue to the U.S. Treasury from this exclusion is substantial, outweighing the costs of the mortgage interest deduction.

12. Sinai and Souleles (2005).

The Potential Financial Risks of Owning

Combined, the financial benefits outlined above can fuel significant wealth accumulation. But as the last few years have made painfully clear, the financial benefits associated with owning a home are not without risk. To begin with, house prices can be volatile. That was certainly the case in the wake of the housing bust, as nominal prices fell nationally by some 25 percent or more (depending upon the specific price index used), with the hardest hit markets experiencing declines of more than 40 percent. Almost no area of the country was spared from some degree of decline. According to the Federal Housing Finance Agency index, nominal prices fell in every state with the exception of North Dakota.[13] But while recent experience is notable for the breadth and depth of price declines, there are other examples of fairly significant price declines over the last few decades, including declines of between 10 and 20 percent in some "oil patch" states in the 1980s and in New England, California, and Hawaii in the early 1990s.

There are also a number of markets where house price trends have historically been more stable, but in these areas long-run real price increases have either not kept pace with inflation or have been modest. House price growth has been particularly weak in a number of markets in the Midwest and South. Based on long-run state level indexes from the Federal Housing Finance Agency, between 1975 and 2012 there were ten states in these regions where the compound annual growth in house prices did not exceed general price inflation.[14] In nine other states house price growth did beat inflation, but by less than 0.25 percent on an annual basis. Thus in about two-fifths of states real house price growth was either nonexistent or trivial. At the other extreme, there were seventeen states, mostly along the Pacific coast and in the Northeast, that experienced real house price growth of more than 1 percent a year over the same period, including five states that exceeded 2 percent.

There are also peculiar aspects of owning a home that further exacerbate the financial risks of these investments. Homeowners make a significant investment in a specific location and cannot diversify the risk of home price declines by spreading this investment across assets or across markets. Home values are also high relative to incomes and so account for a large share of household wealth. Wolff reports that in 2010 the value of the principal residence accounted for two-thirds of total wealth among households in the middle three quintiles of the

13. Federal Housing Finance Agency, "All Transactions Home Price Index" (www.fhfa.gov/Default.aspx?Page=87).

14. Federal Housing Finance Agency, "All Transactions Home Price Index" (www.fhfa.gov/Default.aspx?Page=87).

wealth distribution.[15] With so much wealth tied up in one asset, homeowners are particularly vulnerable to changes in home values. The use of debt financing for a large share of the purchase further magnifies these risks, with even small drops in prices wiping out substantial shares of homeowner equity. Indeed, at the height of the housing bust, the number of households underwater on their mortgages was estimated by CoreLogic to have exceeded 12 million, while Zillow placed the number closer to 15 million.[16]

When assessed purely on the basis of real growth in values over time, housing also compares poorly to the returns offered by investments in diversified portfolios of stock or bonds. Goetzmann and Speigel compare the change in home prices in twelve market areas between 1980 and 1999 to a range of alternative investments and find that housing as an investment asset was consistently outperformed by all of the financial alternatives considered, leading them to conclude that it is "surprising that housing continues to represent a significant portion of American household portfolios."[17] However, Flavin and Yamashita take a more expansive view of the returns on housing investments by including the value derived from occupying the unit, the use of financial leverage, and the ability to claim income tax deductions.[18] This fuller treatment of housing's returns finds that the average rate of return was slightly below returns for investments in stocks, but the variance of these returns was also lower and so somewhat less risky. Still, even if the returns to housing are deemed to be competitive with alternative investments, the concern remains that it accounts for an excessive share of low-wealth households' portfolios.

Housing investments are also handicapped by high transaction costs associated with buying and selling these assets. Homebuyers face fees for mortgage origination, title search and insurance, state and local taxes, home inspections, and legal fees, all of which can add up to several percentage points of the home value. Real estate broker commissions typically also command 6 percent of the sales price. These high transaction costs can absorb a significant share of home price appreciation from the first few years of occupancy. Given these high costs, homeowners who are forced by circumstances to move within a few years of buying will face the risk of losing at least some share of their initial investment even if home values have risen modestly.

The need to maintain the home also imposes financial risks on owners. While routine maintenance can keep both the physical structure and the home's major systems in good working order, major investments are periodically needed, such

15. Wolff (2012).
16. CoreLogic (2013) and Zillow (2012).
17. Goetzmann and Speigel (2002, p. 260).
18. Flavin and Yamashita (2002).

as painting the exterior or replacing the roof or heating system. While owners may have the opportunity to plan for these investments over time, in some cases a system will fail with little warning and produce an unexpected cost that the owner cannot afford, creating a financial strain that in the most extreme cases can jeopardize the ability to maintain ownership.

Finally, the financial costs of failing to sustain homeownership are high—in addition to the traumatic impacts that foreclosures can have on the health and psychological well-being of the owner.[19] Owners who default on their mortgage will not only lose whatever equity stake they had in the home, they are also likely to deplete their savings in a bid to maintain ownership and suffer significant damage to their credit history, making it difficult and costly to obtain credit for several years to come.

Factors Contributing to Wealth Accumulation through Homeownership

Whether and to what extent a homebuyer will realize the potential benefits of owning while avoiding succumbing to the risks depends on a complex set of factors. Herbert and Belsky present a detailed conceptual model of the factors that contribute to whether homeownership produces wealth over the life course, which is briefly summarized here.[20] The most obvious factor is the timing of purchase relative to housing price cycles. The recent boom and bust in house prices presents a prime example. Homebuyers who bought in the early 2000s were poised to benefit from the massive run-up in prices that occurred in many markets, while those that bought in the mid-2000s entered just in time for the historic freefall in prices that followed. While other price cycles in recent decades may not have been as dramatic, the consequences for wealth accumulation of buying near troughs or peaks would have been similar. Belsky and Duda examined data on repeat sales in four market areas between 1982 and 1999 and found that roughly half of the owners who bought and sold their homes within this time period failed to realize gains that beat inflation, assuming a 6 percent sales cost (although most did earn a return in nominal terms).[21] Whether owners realized a positive return depended strongly on where in the housing price cycle they bought and sold their homes. Belsky and Duda conclude that "although the golden rule of real estate is often cited as location, location, location, an equally golden rule is timing, timing, timing."[22] Their conclusion points to another critical factor in how likely a home is to appreciate in value: in what market and in which specific neighborhood the home is located. As noted above, there have

19. Carr and Anacker (2012).
20. Herbert and Belsky (2006).
21. Belsky and Duda (2002).
22. Belsky and Duda (2002, p. 223).

been sizable differences across market areas in long-term house price trends, with areas along the coasts experiencing real gains of 1 percent a year or more over the last several decades while areas in the Midwest and South have had little or no gains. But there are also substantial variations in price trends across neighborhoods within a single market.[23] Whether a household bought a home in Boston or Cleveland is an important factor in the returns realized, but so is whether the home was in a desirable area or a declining neighborhood.

The terms of financing used to buy the home also matter. Higher interest rates lower the share of payments that are devoted to principal reduction in the early years of repayment, slowing wealth accumulation. Higher monthly interest payments also erode the ability of the household to meet other expenses and to save on an ongoing basis. Indeed, even modestly higher interest rates can add up to substantial amounts over the life of the mortgage. For example, over a thirty-year term, a loan for $150,000 at 7 percent interest will require $69,000 more in interest payments than a 5 percent loan. Higher origination fees also sap savings, reducing the quality and size of home that is affordable and lowering the rate of return on housing investments.

Choices about refinancing over time can also exert a strong influence on wealth accumulation. Taking advantage of declines in mortgage interest rates to reduce financing costs can save owners hundreds of dollars each month, and tens of thousands over the life of a mortgage—although continually resetting the term of the mortgage will reduce opportunities for forced savings. On the other hand, refinancing to take cash out of the property can erode wealth accumulation, particularly if the extracted funds are used to finance consumption rather than investments in the home, education, business, or financial opportunities. Wealth accumulation will be further undermined if the new loan comes with high fees and higher interest rates. Of course, the ability to tap housing wealth as a buffer against income shocks is one of the virtues of developing this cushion, but using home equity to finance an unaffordable lifestyle is an unsustainable path.

A host of other factors come into play in determining how much housing wealth is realized over the span of a lifetime. For example, buying higher valued homes—if successful—can produce more wealth both through forced savings and by earning returns on a higher valued asset. By the same means, those who trade up to more expensive homes over time may also accrue greater housing wealth. The age at which a first home is purchased can also be significant, giving the household a longer period to accumulate wealth. Of course, the quality of the home purchased and the owner's ability to maintain it will also affect both ongoing maintenance costs and how much the home appreciates over time.

23. For reviews of this literature, see Herbert and Belsky (2006); Dietz and Haurin (2003); McCarthy, Van Zandt, and Rohe (2001).

But arguably the most fundamental factor—the true golden rule of how to accumulate wealth through homeownership—is whether ownership is sustained over the long term. Housing booms aside, many of the financial benefits are slow to accumulate, including the gradual buildup of forced savings, the compounding of values at low appreciation rates, and the decline in monthly housing costs in real terms over time. The expression "time heals all wounds" may also be applicable to many of homeownership's most critical risks. The losses associated with buying near the peak of a price cycle will diminish over time as owners benefit from the next upswing in prices. And even in areas where real growth in house prices does not occur or is limited, over the long term, owners will still amass some degree of wealth through paying off the mortgage and as a result of savings from lower housing costs. On the flip side, a failure to sustain homeownership—particularly when the end result is a foreclosure—will wipe out any accrued wealth and bring additional costs in the form of a damaged credit history that will make borrowing more difficult and costly in the future.

To some degree whether or not ownership is sustained will depend on choices that owners make over time, including whether the home they buy is affordable, whether they make prudent choices about refinancing, and whether they maintain the home to avoid larger home repair bills. But sustainable ownership also depends on whether the household can ride out any number of significant events that can fundamentally alter its financial circumstances, such as loss of a job, a serious health problem, or change in the family composition due to the birth of a child, death, divorce, or the need to care for a parent or relative. Over the course of a lifetime, these events are likely to befall almost everyone. Whether homeownership can be sustained in the wake of these events depends on the ability of the household to adjust to changed circumstances and whether it has enough available savings to cushion the blow.

Impediments to Wealth Creation among Lower-Income and Minority Homeowners

Up to this point, this discussion has considered homeownership's financial risks and rewards in a general sense. But this chapter's specific focus is the potential for homeownership to serve as an effective means of wealth accumulation for lower-income and minority households. How are the odds of generating wealth as a homeowner likely to differ for these households?[24]

In keeping with the fundamental importance of sustained homeownership for accumulating wealth, the chief concern is that these groups of homebuyers

---

24. Galster and Santiago (2008) provide a useful framing of this issue and a comprehensive review of the relevant literature.

face more difficulties in maintaining ownership. Studies analyzing panel data to document homeownership spells among first-time buyers consistently find that low-income and minority owners have a lower probability of maintaining homeownership for at least five years. In an analysis of the National Longitudinal Survey of Youth from 1979 through 2000, Haurin and Rosenthal find that ownership is less likely to be sustained among both these groups.[25] Specifically, only 57 percent of low-income buyers were found to still own their first home five years later, compared to 70 percent of high-income owners (with income categories defined by income quartiles at age twenty-five). First homeownership spells were also found to be much shorter for minorities, averaging 4.4 years for blacks and 5.4 years for Hispanics compared to 6.5 years among whites. In an analysis of the Panel Study of Income Dynamics covering the period from 1976 through 1993, Reid had similar results, with only 47 percent of low-income owners still owning their first homes five years later compared to 77 percent of high-income owners (with incomes here defined according to average income in the years prior to homeownership compared to area median incomes).[26] Reid further found that minorities had a harder time staying in their first home, with 42 percent of low-income nonwhites still owning after five years compared to 54 percent of low-income whites.

While these results raise clear concerns about the high risk of failed homeownership among these groups, the focus on a single homeownership spell may overstate the extent to which homeowning is not sustained in the long run. Haurin and Rosenthal also examine subsequent tenure experience in their panel and find that the share of households that return to owning a second time is very high for both whites and minorities.[27] Over the twenty-one-year period in their panel, 86 percent of whites who ever bought a home either never returned to renting or resumed owning after a subsequent spell as a renter, with only slightly lower rates for blacks (81 percent) and Hispanics (84 percent). However, they do find that minorities have longer intervening spells as renters, which reduces the overall amount of time they can accumulate benefits from owning.

Another critical difference in the financial returns to owning for low-income households is that they often derive little benefit from the ability to deduct mortgage interest and property taxes from federal taxable income. In order to benefit from these tax provisions, the amount of available deductions must exceed the standard deduction, which stood at $5,950 for individuals and $11,900 for married couples in 2012. For taxpayers with lower valued homes, particularly married couples, the costs of mortgage interest and property taxes, even when

25. Haurin and Rosenthal (2004).
26. Reid (2004).
27. Haurin and Rosenthal (2004).

added to other deductions for state taxes and charitable contributions, may not greatly exceed the standard deduction. In addition, the value of these deductions depends on the taxpayer's marginal tax rate, which is lower for low- and moderate-income households. In fact, the share of the total value of the mortgage interest deduction going to moderate-income households is fairly small. According to estimates from the Joint Committee on Taxation, only 3 percent of the total deductions went to filers with incomes under $50,000, 9 percent to those with incomes between $50,000 and $75,000, and 11 percent to those with income between $75,000 and $100,000, leaving 77 percent of the benefit going to those earning above $100,000.[28] To the extent that these tax benefits swing the financial scales in favor homeownership, this tilting is not very evident for low- and moderate-income tax filers.

There are also systematic differences in mortgage terms and characteristics by income and race-ethnicity that can also affect the financial returns to owning. The development of the nonprime lending industry that began in the 1990s and came to full blossom during the housing boom produced much greater variation in mortgage terms and pricing than had previously been evident. A fairly extensive literature has documented the greater prevalence of subprime lending among minorities and, to a lesser extent, low-income borrowers and communities.[29] As described above, higher costs of financing can significantly reduce the financial benefits of owning. While the expansion of financing options beyond a "one size fits all who qualify" approach to lending has the potential to extend homeownership opportunities to a greater range of households, there is significant evidence that the cost of credit was often higher than risk alone would warrant. Bocian, Ernst, and Li present perhaps the most compelling evidence through an analysis of a large data set on nonprime loans that documents a wide range of risk measures, including credit scores as well as income and race-ethnicity.[30] They find that even after controlling for observable differences in credit quality, both blacks and Hispanics were significantly more likely to obtain high-priced mortgages for home purchase, while blacks were also more likely to obtain higher-priced refinance loans. These higher costs of borrowing not only limit the wealth-producing capacity of homeownership, they also increase the risk of failing to sustain homeownership. In fact, Haurin and Rosenthal find that a 1-percentage-point increase in the mortgage interest rate increases the rate of homeownership termination by 30 percent.[31]

28. U.S. Congress (2013).

29. See, for example, Bradford (2002); Calem, Gillen, and Wachter (2004); Apgar and Calder (2005); Avery, Brevoort, and Canner (2007); Belsky and Richardson (2010).

30. Bocian, Ernst, and Li (2008).

31. Haurin and Rosenthal (2004).

Low-income and minority borrowers are also less likely to refinance when interest rates decline. In an analysis of loans guaranteed by Freddie Mac during the 1990s, Van Order and Zorn find that low-income and minority borrowers were less likely to refinance as interest rates fell.[32] Their analysis also found that once borrower risk measures and loan characteristics were taken into account, there were no remaining differences in refinance rates by income—although this just indicates that refinancing may be constrained by credit factors. Minorities, on the other hand, still had lower rates of refinancing even after controlling for these factors, suggesting that there were impediments to refinancing by these borrowers that were in addition to measurable credit factors. Nothaft and Chang analyze data from the American Housing Survey from the late 1980s through 2001 and also find that minority and low-income owners were less likely to refinance when interest rates declined.[33] These authors use their results to estimate the forgone savings from missed refinance opportunities, which are more than $20 billion each for black and low-income homeowners.

To the extent that low-income and minority homebuyers may be more likely to purchase homes in poor condition, they are also exposed to greater risks of high costs of maintenance and repair. Herbert and Belsky find that compared to whites, black and Hispanic first-time homebuyers were more likely to buy homes that were moderately or severely inadequate as characterized by the American Housing Survey—6.5 percent for blacks and 8.8 percent for Hispanics compared to 4.3 percent among whites.[34] A similar gap was also evident between low- and high-income households. While there has been little study of the incidence of unexpected home repair needs, a study by Rohe and his colleagues of participants in homeownership counseling programs found a fairly significant incidence of the need for unexpected repairs.[35] Roughly half of 343 recent homebuyers reported that they had experienced a major unexpected cost in the first few years after buying their home, with the most common problem being a repair to one of the home's major systems.

Finally, there are also concerns that lower-income households and minorities may be more likely to purchase homes in neighborhoods with less potential for house price appreciation. This is a particularly salient issue for minorities given the high degree of residential segregation by race and ethnicity that continues to be evident in the United States. However, Herbert and Belsky present a detailed review of this literature and conclude that "taken as a whole the literature indicates that there is no reason to believe that low-value segments of the housing

32. Van Order and Zorn (2002).
33. Nothaft and Chang (2005).
34. Herbert and Belsky (2006).
35. Rohe and others (2003).

market will necessarily experience less appreciation than higher-valued homes. In fact, at different points in time and in different market areas, low-valued homes and neighborhoods have experienced greater appreciation rates. Although the opposite is also true."[36] The evidence about differences in appreciation rates by neighborhood racial composition is less definitive. Here Herbert and Belsky conclude that "it does appear that homes in mostly black areas may be less likely to experience appreciation, but this conclusion is tempered by the small number of studies and the fact that they mostly analyzed trends from the 1970s and 1980s, which may no longer be relevant."[37]

Findings by Boehm and Schlottmann regarding differences in wealth gains from homeownership by race and income are instructive in this regard.[38] They find that over the period from 1984 to 1992, there was little difference in appreciation rates in the specific neighborhoods where minorities and low-income households lived. Instead, they found that differences in housing equity accumulation were tied to the lower valued homes and the shorter duration of ownership for lower-income and minority households. Thus differences in appreciation rates may be less of a factor than other considerations in whether housing leads to wealth accumulation.

Reassessing the Calculus of Wealth Accumulation through Homeownership

As the above review has shown, there were significant concerns about the risks of homeownership as an investment well before the housing bubble burst. For critics of homeownership as a wealth-building tool, the experience of the housing bust was in many respects a confirmation of their fears. Still, there were several market developments during the boom years that magnified these preexisting risks. Most notably there was a marked increase in the prevalence of riskier mortgages, including those calling for little or no documentation of income, adjustable rate loans that exposed borrowers to payment shocks from the expiration of initial teaser rates or reduced payment options, allowances for higher debt-to-income ratios, and greater availability of loans for borrowers with very low credit scores. Down payment requirements also eased as loan-to-value (LTV) ratios of 95 percent or more became more common, and borrowers also used "piggyback" second mortgages to finance much of the difference between a home's value and a conforming first mortgage at an 80 percent LTV ratio.

Not unrelated to the greater availability of mortgage credit, house prices also exhibited much greater volatility than in the past, with a dramatic increase in prices that greatly outpaced trends in both incomes and rents and belied an

36. Herbert and Belsky (2006, p. 76).
37. Herbert and Belsky (2006, p. 77).
38. Boehm and Schlottmann (2004).

unsustainable bubble. The greater availability of credit also increased the opportunity for lower-income households to mistime the market. Belsky and Duda found that during the 1980s and 1990s, purchases of lower valued homes were less likely to be transacted around market peaks, so buyers of these homes were less likely to buy high and sell low.[39] They speculated that this was due to the natural affordability constraints that took hold as markets peaked. But during the boom of the 2000s, lower valued homes experienced greater volatility in prices, arguably reflecting much greater credit availability at the peak than was true in past cycles.[40]

However, there are good reasons to believe—or certainly to hope—that the conditions that gave rise to this excessive risk taking and associated housing bubble will not be repeated any time soon. The Dodd-Frank Act includes a number of provisions to reduce the degree of risk for both borrowers and investors in the mortgage market. The qualified mortgage (QM) is aimed at ensuring that borrowers have the ability to repay mortgages by requiring full documentation of income and assets, setting tighter debt-to-income standards, and excluding a variety of mortgage terms that expose borrowers to payment shocks. The qualified residential mortgage (QRM) is aimed at ensuring greater protections for investors in mortgage-backed securities by requiring the creators of these securities to retain an interest in these investments if the loans included in the loan pool do not conform to certain risk standards that essentially mirror those of the qualified mortgage. Dodd-Frank also established the Consumer Financial Protection Bureau to fill a gap in the regulatory structure by creating an agency charged with looking out for consumers' interests in financial transactions. Beyond these regulatory changes, there is also a heightened awareness of the risks of mortgage investments on the part of private sector actors who have suffered significant financial losses with the bursting of the housing bubble. Regulatory changes aside, these private actors are unlikely to embrace riskier lending any time soon. The Federal Reserve and other federal regulators are certainly more attuned to the possibility of a bubble in housing prices and so are more likely to act in the event that signs of a bubble reemerge.

But even in the absence of the excessive risks of the last decade, homeownership will remain a risky proposition. Thus, at best, there may be a return to the market conditions that existed prior to the boom and to the real risks that these conditions posed for investments in owner-occupied housing. In that regard an assessment of experience in wealth creation through homeownership prior to the boom is relevant for what one might expect in the future.

On the other hand, it does seem likely—and arguably even desirable given how tight credit has become—that some greater degree of risk taking will emerge

39. Belsky and Duda (2002).
40. JCHS (2011).

to make credit available to the many lower-income and lower-wealth households that would like to own a home. In fact, the QM standard of a total debt-to-income ratio of up to 43 percent does curtail the higher levels that became evident during the boom, but this cutoff still represents a liberalization of standards for conventional mortgages that prevailed in the 1990s. There also may have been a shift in consumer attitudes toward mortgage debt, with fewer households seeking to pay off mortgages over time and thus expose themselves for longer periods to the risks associated with these leveraged investments. Over time, as conditions return to normal and the market adjusts to new regulatory structures, mortgages originated outside of the QM and QRM boxes are likely to appear. In that regard an assessment of the experience of homeowners through the boom and bust is instructive as a stress test of how likely homeownership is to build wealth under more extreme market conditions.

The next two sections of the chapter attempt to assess homeownership's potential for wealth building from these two perspectives—first, by presenting a review of the literature assessing homeownership's association with wealth building prior to the 2000s, and then by analyzing data from the last decade to examine how homeownership was associated with changes in wealth through the turbulent conditions of the 2000s.

Review of Previous Studies Assessing the Financial Returns to Homeownership

As the discussion up to this point has intended to illustrate, whether owning a home will lead to the accumulation of wealth is the result of a complex set of factors related to the choices that households make in buying their home and how these choices interact with market conditions, both at the time of purchase and over time. This complexity makes it quite difficult to assess whether in practice owning is likely to be an effective means of increasing a household's wealth. A further complicating factor is that there is a substantial selection bias in who becomes a homeowner, as there is reason to believe that those who are most secure in their financial condition and most inclined to save are more likely to become owners. For this reason comparisons of the wealth profiles of owners and renters may not be able to attribute any observed differences solely to the influence of homeownership on the ability to accrue wealth.

There are two broad classes of studies that have attempted to assess the financial benefits of homeownership in light of these challenges. One group relies on simulations that compare the theoretical costs and benefits of owning and renting under a variety of assumptions about market conditions and household choices. A key appeal of these studies is that they essentially remove concerns about selection bias by assuming otherwise identical households operate under a consistent set of decision rules. They can also isolate the influence of specific factors on financial outcomes to shed light on the paths that are most likely to make owning or renting more beneficial. But while these studies highlight the potential financial returns to owning and renting, they do not capture how households are likely to actually behave in these situations, and so they leave open the question of whether the *potential* returns of these tenure choices are likely to be realized in practice.

Another class of research relies on panel studies that track households over time to examine how choices about owning and renting are correlated with changes in wealth. The findings from this type of analysis provide evidence of whether in *practice* owners are more likely to accrue wealth than renters and how this experience differs by income and race-ethnicity. Where the theoretical comparisons of owning and renting also generally focus on a single spell of home-ownership—that is, the financial outcome associated with the period between buying and selling a single home—panel studies can track households through multiple transitions in and out of owning to assess outcomes from a series of tenure choices over time. The main drawback of these studies is the lingering concern that owners may be inherently different from renters in ways that observable household characteristics cannot capture. Some of these studies employ statistical methods to try to control for this selection bias, although it is doubtful that these controls can fully account for these differences.

Both classes of studies provide important insights into the opportunities and drawbacks of homeownership as a means of increasing household wealth. When viewed as a whole, the findings from both streams of research help paint a clearer picture of whether and how homeownership may help foster wealth creation. The sections that follow highlight key findings from each of these literature strands.

Simulations of the Financial Returns to Owning and Renting

Beginning with Mills, there have been a number of studies that have simulated the financial returns to owning and renting under a variety of assumptions to identify whether and under what circumstances owning or renting is likely to be more financially beneficial.[41] While the studies differ in important respects, the general approach is to compare the "all-in" costs of owning (including mortgage interest, property taxes, insurance, maintenance, and transaction costs along with offsetting gains in property value) to the costs of renting a comparable housing unit. Either implicit or explicit in these comparisons is that renters save and invest both the initial investment that owners make in buying their homes as well as any annual savings in housing costs.

---

41. Mills (1990); Capone (1995); Belsky, Retsinas, and Duda (2007); Rappaport (2010); Beracha and Johnson (2012).

There are a host of assumptions that underlie these calculations, but among the most influential factors are the estimate of market rents as a share of house values, the length of time the home is owned, the basis for simulating trends in house prices and rents over time, the treatment of income tax benefits, and the financial return earned on alternative investments. The studies differ in fundamental ways related to the range of assumptions tested and the method for comparing returns to owning and renting. Not surprisingly, given such differences these studies reach somewhat different conclusions about which tenure choice is likely to be preferred. But collectively the studies lead to some general conclusions about the relative financial merits of owning and renting.

Perhaps the most fundamental conclusion drawn from these studies runs counter to the prevailing sense that homeownership is a powerful source of wealth, finding that under a variety of conditions renting is often more likely to be a better financial choice than owning. Belsky, Retsinas, and Duda compare owning and renting in four different market areas chosen to represent different degrees of price appreciation and volatility over the period studied from 1983 through 2001.[42] They focus on holding periods of three, five, and seven years during their window of study and report the share of different holding periods where owning results in higher financial returns than renting. Overall they find that in only 53 percent of the three-year holding periods would owning be preferred to renting. Even when they increase the holding period to seven years—which allows for more time to work off the high transaction costs of buying and selling a home—the proportion only increases to 63 percent. Rappaport reaches a similar conclusion based on an analysis of national trends in market conditions between 1970 and 1999 and an assumed ten-year period of owning a home.[43] He finds that owning a home unambiguously built more wealth in about half of the possible ten-year periods, whereas renting was clearly better in another quarter and likely, but not unambiguously, preferred in the remaining periods. Finally, Beracha and Johnson come to a similar conclusion in an analysis of all possible eight-year holding periods given actual market conditions at both the national and regional level between 1978 and 2009.[44] They find that in 65 to 75 percent of cases, renting offered greater opportunities for accruing wealth than owning, depending on whether renters employ a more conservative or aggressive investment approach.

In parsing the findings of these studies, we found several factors that are the critical drivers of the results. Perhaps the most obvious is the importance of the timing of home purchase relative to market cycles in prices and interest rates.

42. Belsky, Retsinas, and Duda (2007).
43. Rappaport (2010).
44. Beracha and Johnson (2012).

Depending on the future course of prices, rents, and interest rates, one or the other tenure would be strongly preferred at different points in time. The importance of timing may be most clearly demonstrated by Belsky, Retsinas, and Duda when they consider different holding periods among owners.[45] In general, it would be expected that longer holding periods should favor owning as more time is allowed to overcome high transaction costs, pay down additional principal, and ride out price cycles. Instead, they find that in most markets the likelihood of owning being preferred to renting was little changed by the holding period as short holding periods offered the possibility of catching only the upswing in prices, while longer holds made it more likely that owners would share in some portion of a downturn. Only in Chicago, which did not experience dramatic swings in prices, were longer holding periods found to be much more likely to benefit owning.

Still, the issue of a holding period is an important consideration. Recognizing that a longer holding period would always favor homeownership, studies by both Mills and Capone solved for the holding period that was needed for owning to yield a higher return than renting. In his base case scenario, Mills found a holding period of slightly longer than seven years was needed for owning to be preferred.[46] The more recent studies that have shown the importance of market timing either assumed a single fixed holding period of eight to ten years (as in Beracha and Johnson and in Rappaport) or a range of relatively short holding periods (as in Belsky, Retsinas, and Duda). If owning does become more favorable over a longer period of time—for example, slightly longer than eight to ten years—these assessments would not capture this. In fact, many households move in and out of homeownership over time, so a more complete assessment of the financial implications of tenure choice would take into account multiple homeownership spells. While one spell of owning may yield low returns, if homeowning is sustained or resumed, then the household may yet benefit from the next upswing.

Another important factor driving the findings consists of assumptions made about rents as a share of house value. How much renters have to pay to rent a comparable home is obviously a key driver of financial outcomes as it determines how much they can save annually by renting, thereby adding to their wealth. However, this ratio is difficult to estimate, both because of systematic differences in the nature of the owner- and renter-occupied stock and because market values and rents are hard to observe simultaneously.

Mills found that among the variables used in his simulation, his results were most sensitive to the ratio of rents to house values since a single percentage-point-change

45. Belsky, Retsinas, and Duda (2007).
46. Mills (1990).

up or down led to fluctuations in the required holding period from three to twenty-three years.[47] Capone built on Mills's study to examine the rent-versus-buy decision specifically for lower-income households.[48] He makes note of the importance of the rent-to-price ratio assumption and argues that Mills's assumption of 7 percent was well below the ratios observed in low-cost segments of the market, where ratios of 10 to 12 percent were more reasonable. Under Capone's assumption that renters faced much higher rents relative to values, he found that owners only needed to hold onto their homes for about three years for owning to be preferred.

In contrast, Belsky, Retsinas, and Duda rely on rent-to-price ratios in the range of 5 to 7 percent, while the series used by Beracha and Johnson—derived by Davis, Lehnert, and Martin—appears to average about 5 percent.[49] In both cases these assumptions are more favorable to renting than the assumptions used by either Mills or Capone. In recognition of the importance of this assumption, Rappaport structures his analysis to estimate the rent-to-price ratio that is the break-even point between owning and renting. He then compares this estimate to what he feels is a plausible range for this ratio of between 5 and 10 percent based on analysis of different market areas over time. At the higher end of this range, owning would almost always be preferred, while his findings for the lower end of the range lead to him to conclude that owning is clearly preferred to renting in only about half of the holding periods considered. In short, high or low values of this ratio can swamp other considerations; yet, as Rappaport demonstrates, pinning down actual values for this ratio is not an easy task.[50]

Several of the studies have examined how important tax benefits are to whether owning makes more financial sense than renting. Mills assumes that owners can take full advantage of tax benefits at a 28 percent marginal rate. When he reduces the marginal rate to 15 percent, he finds that owning is never preferred. Capone, though, demonstrates that this knife edge does not hold if a higher rent-to-price ratio is assumed. In his base case analysis, owners are only assumed to benefit from tax benefits if they exceed the standard deduction. Since he assumes a much more modest house, in keeping with his focus on lower-income households, the tax benefits are essentially nonexistent. As a result, reducing the tax benefits in his analysis does not change his conclusion that owning is a better financial choice even after only a few years. Belsky, Retsinas, and Duda also examine the importance of tax benefits for lower-income owners. Like Capone they adjust the value of tax deductions to account for the size of the home purchased and the amount

47. Mills (1990).
48. Capone (1995).
49. Beracha and Johnson (2012); Davis, Lehnert, and Martin (2008).
50. Rappaport (2010).

of the standard deduction. They also find that tax benefits by themselves generally do not change the calculus of whether owning beats renting financially. So while tax benefits are an important factor among higher-income households, as Mills found, they have little effect on the calculus for lower-income households. Capone and Belsky, Retsinas, and Duda find that despite the limited benefits from tax breaks under a variety of circumstances, lower-income households can fare better financially by owning.[51]

Belsky, Retsinas, and Duda also make a unique contribution by examining how the returns to homeownership are affected by higher mortgage costs.[52] They examine two scenarios: one where owners face interest rates that are 2 percentage points higher than prime rates and another where they are 5 percentage points higher. Under the first scenario, the likelihood that owning would be preferred to renting is decreased by moderate amounts (between 6 and 17 percentage points), whereas under the latter scenario, owning is rarely a better financial choice than renting. In short, they find that higher interest rates do reduce the financial appeal of homeownership, although the impact is most pronounced at extremely high levels.

Lastly, and in some ways most critically, the finding that renting offers the potential for higher returns than owning depends in large part on renters taking steps to invest the annual savings in housing costs compared to renting. Building on the study by Beracha and Johnson, Beracha, Skiba, and Johnson examine how variations in key assumptions regarding trends in prices, rents, interest rates, down payment shares, and the returns available from alternative investments affect the buy-versus-rent financial calculus.[53] They find that modifying most factors in isolation has only a moderate effect on whether renting is favored over owning. However, when they drop the assumption that renters actually invest any annual savings in housing costs on top of the initial down payment, they find that renting rarely results in higher wealth than owning. Thus they find that the forced savings aspect of homeownership is of fundamental importance in determining whether owning will lead to greater wealth.

This finding is echoed in the results of Boehm and Schlottmann, who employ a unique approach to simulating the impact of homeownership on wealth accumulation.[54] This study uses the Panel Study of Income Dynamics (PSID) to model the probability of moving in and out of homeownership on an annual basis over the period from 1984 through 1992. These same data are also used to estimate the house value that a household would opt for if a home

51. See Mills (1990); Capone (1995); Belsky, Retsinas, and Duda (2007).
52. Belsky, Retsinas, and Duda (2007).
53. Beracha and Johnson (2012); Beracha, Skiba, and Johnson (2012).
54. Boehm and Schlottmann (2004).

were purchased in a given year. The estimated house value is then inflated based on house price trends in the census tract where the household resided to yield each household's expected gain in wealth from homeownership. This analysis finds that while minorities and low-income households do accrue wealth from homeownership, the amounts are much less than for higher-income whites, both because the former own for fewer years and because they buy lower valued homes. But significantly, while the expected wealth accumulation among these households is less than that earned by higher-income whites, it is still positive. The authors also use the PSID to document that these same low-income and minority households essentially had no growth in nonhousing wealth over the same period. So in that regard the estimates of potential wealth created through homeownership were all the more important.

Evidence from Panel Surveys about Wealth Accumulation through Homeownership

As the findings from Beracha and Johnson and from Boehm and Schlottmann suggest, the theoretical advantages of renting may not be realized if in practice renters do not take advantage of the opportunities afforded to them for saving derived from the lower cost of renting.[55] In contrast, studies making use of panel surveys that track households over time provide insights into the wealth accumulation associated with actual choices about renting and owning. These studies universally find that owning a home is associated with higher levels of wealth accumulation even after controlling for a range of household characteristics. While the gains are also consistently smaller in magnitude for lower-income and minority households, these studies also find that in contrast to owners, renters with similar characteristics experience little or no gains in wealth. These findings hold even when steps are taken to account for selection bias in who becomes a homeowner. Although these methods may not fully account for the differences between owners and renters, there remains a strong case that homeowning does make a positive contribution to household balance sheets regardless of income or race-ethnicity.

Haurin, Hendershott, and Wachter were among the first to use panel survey data to track wealth trajectories associated with homeownership.[56] The primary focus of their study was on the accumulation of wealth in anticipation of becoming an owner rather than on how owning a home over time contributes to wealth accumulation, but their findings provide important insights into one way in which homeownership adds to wealth. They use the National Longitudinal Survey of Youth to track young renters age twenty to twenty-eight from

---

55. Beracha and Johnson (2012); Boehm and Schlottmann (2004).
56. Haurin, Hendershott, and Wachter (1996).

1985 through 1990 and observe both their annual wealth levels and the timing of any transitions into homeownership. They find that household wealth goes up markedly during the transition to homeownership, increasing by 33 percent on average in the year prior to buying a home and then more than doubling in the year they first own. When they examine factors that contribute to this jump in wealth, they find that marrying makes a significant contribution along with an increase in hours worked and a slightly higher incidence of inheritance and gifts. Their results suggest that an important mechanism by which homeownership adds to wealth is through the incentive to save in anticipation of buying a home. Even before any returns are realized on the investment in the home itself, the drive to become an owner results in substantially higher wealth than among those who remain renters. Adding to this effect, Haurin and his colleagues also find that wealth increases more rapidly in the years after becoming a homeowner—by 17 percent annually on average among their sample.

Reid uses panel data from the PSID for the period 1976 through 1994 to examine the financial outcomes of homeownership among low-income households who bought their first home at some point during this period (with low-income households defined as those with incomes consistently below 80 percent of area median income before first buying a home).[57] She takes two approaches to examining the returns to homeownership for this group. First, she estimates the change in home values for both low-income and minority homeowners compared to higher-income and white owners. She finds that the rate of increase in home values for these groups was fairly modest, failing to beat the returns that would have been earned on an investment in Treasury bills over the same time. Reid then examines wealth holdings of households by tenure status at the end of her period of observation. She finds that while low-income and minority owners generally built much less wealth than higher-income and white households, the amount of their housing wealth was nontrivial and was many times larger than their other forms of wealth. Like Boehm and Schlottmann, she also finds that those who were renters at the end of the period essentially held no wealth of any kind. Reid, however, does not undertake a multivariate analysis to control for other factors that may account for the differences between owners and renters. Nor does she factor in the impact of failed efforts at homeownership on wealth. But the fact that home equity accounts for such a large share of wealth among low-income and minority households points to the important role that owning a home played in fostering wealth accumulation.

The study by Di, Belsky, and Liu was the first to directly assess the relationship between homeownership and wealth accumulation over time while attempting to account for household characteristics and to include some measure of

57. Reid (2004).

potential selection bias in who becomes an owner.[58] The study uses the PSID to track households who were renters in 1989 through 2001 to observe transitions into and out of homeownership. The change in household wealth over time is then modeled as a function of starting wealth, a range of household character-istics thought to influence wealth, and, their principal measure of interest, the amount of time spent as an owner. To take into account a household's propen-sity to save, the study uses the PSID from 1984 through 1989 to estimate the share of income that was saved as an indication of savings behavior prior to the period when tenure transitions are observed. The measure of prior savings is then included to account for this tendency in assessing differences in savings behav-ior after buying a home. Their principal finding is a positive and statistically significant association between additional years of homeownership and changes in wealth. The authors include a square term for the number of years owned to take into account anticipated impacts of the timing of moves into homeowner-ship over the period, as there was an initial decline in house values during the first years of their panel followed by more robust increases in later years. This square term is negative and significant, indicating those who bought earlier in the period had lower cumulative gains in wealth. The largest estimated gains in wealth of $13,000 per year of ownership occurred among those who owned for eight years. But for those who owned for the maximum possible period of twelve years, the gains were only $3,333 per year. Prior savings tendency was positively associated with increases in wealth as expected but was not statistically significant and so did not appear to capture any important difference in household behavior that was not already accounted for by other explanatory variables.

Turner and Luea undertake a very similar analysis using the PSID sample for the period from 1987 to 2001.[59] In contrast to Di, Belsky, and Liu, who only include initial renters, their study sample includes all households in the sample as of 2001 that were age sixty-five or younger, regardless of whether they were renters at the start of the period. The study pools observations for the sample on household wealth from three points in time: 1994, 1999, and 2001. For each observation they include a count of the number of years the household has owned a home since 1988 as their explanatory variable of interest. The approach used in this study attempts to control for selection bias into homeownership by estimating a random effects model that includes a household-specific con-stant term. Turner and Luea also separate the sample into two income classes to see whether the association between homeownership and wealth growth differs by income. Low- and moderate-income (LMI) households were those who had incomes below 120 percent of area median income in all three periods when

58. Di, Belsky, and Liu (2007).
59. Turner and Luea (2009).

wealth was observed. The results indicate that each year of homeownership is associated with nearly $14,000 in additional wealth, perhaps not surprisingly quite similar to the amount found by Di, Belsky, and Liu using the same survey over a nearly identical period (although with a somewhat different sample). When controls are included for LMI status, Turner and Luea find that these households have somewhat lower wealth accumulation of between $6,000 and $10,000 a year. But they note that since the average wealth holding of LMI households in 2001 was about $89,000, this annual rate of increase accounts for a fairly sizable share of total wealth.

In an unpublished dissertation, Mamgain extends the work of Turner and Luea by employing a two-stage model to add stronger controls for selection into homeownership.[60] Like most of the other studies, Mamgain's analysis also uses the PSID, but his period of observation is from 1999 through 2007. Despite the different time period examined, when he replicates Turner and Luea, his analysis yields similar results regarding the magnitude of the association between homeownership and wealth (although by ending the study period in 2007, it does not include the sharp loss of both housing and financial wealth that subsequently followed). When Mamgain adds additional controls to his model to capture the intention to move, the respondent's health status, ownership of other real estate, and an estimate of the current LTV ratio, he finds a somewhat lower impact for additional years of owning, but the estimate is still significant and positive. Importantly, when he employs his two-stage approach to include both a selection term and an instrumental measure of current tenure, his estimate of the impact of each additional year on owning does not change. He also estimates separate models by income level and finds that there is no difference in the impact of owning across income classes—all are positive and significant. In short, like other researchers, Mamgain finds no significant impact of selection bias in his findings, and he also deduces that low-income owners are likely to benefit from owning homes.[61]

None of the studies estimating statistical models to assess the contribution of homeownership to wealth accumulation analyzed whether there were differences in this experience by race and ethnicity. As discussed above, there are significant racial and ethnic differences in residential location, size of home, and characteristics of financing used, all of which could contribute to differences in wealth

---

60. Mamgain (2011).

61. He does differ from previous studies in how he estimates the contribution of owning to wealth gains, by focusing on impacts at much lower household wealth levels. He finds that assuming wealth of about $2,500 for the lowest income group (at or below 150 percent of the poverty level), owning a home only adds a few hundred dollars a year to the household's bottom line. But with total wealth set a level well below the median among owners in this income class, this result seems implausible. Mamgain (2011).

outcomes. Shapiro, Meschede, and Osoro use the PSID from 1984 through 2009 to examine specifically the factors associated with more rapid growth in wealth among whites compared to blacks over this period.[62] Tracking the same set of households over this time frame, they find that gains in median wealth among whites exceeded those among blacks by $152,000. Based on the results of a multivariate analysis, they find that the single largest driver of this divergence in wealth was the additional time whites spend as homeowners, which they estimate accounted for 27 percent of the additional gains among whites. The next most significant factors were differences in income (20 percent), unemployment spells (9 percent), lower shares with a college education (5 percent), and differences in inheritance and financial support from family (5 percent). They also find that years of homeownership exerted a stronger influence on gains in wealth for blacks than it did for whites. While the authors do not attempt to control for any selection bias for who becomes a homeowner, none of the previous studies that have taken these steps have found that such controls changed their findings.

Conclusions Drawn from the Previous Literature

Studies presenting simulations of the financial returns to renting and owning make a convincing case that in many markets over many periods of time and under a variety of assumptions renting ought to support greater wealth accumulation than owning. However, as virtually all of the panel studies document, in practice owning has consistently been associated with greater increases in wealth, even after controlling for differences in household income, education, marital status, starting wealth, inheritances, and other factors. Importantly, these same studies also consistently find that owning has a positive effect on wealth accumulation among both lower-income households and minorities, although the gains are smaller than for higher-income households and whites generally. Housing wealth among lower-income and minority households also often accounts for a substantial share of total wealth for these groups. On the other hand, renters in these same demographic groups are consistently found to accrue little to no wealth over time.

How can we reconcile the findings from simulation studies that renting should often be more financially advantageous than owning with the findings from the analysis of panel surveys that unambiguously find owning to be more favorable? One explanation may be that behavioral issues play a key role. Efforts to save for a down payment lead to a large jump in wealth that is then further supported by at least modest appreciation and some paydown of principal over time. Renters may have the opportunity to accrue savings and invest them in higher yielding opportunities but lack strong incentives and effective mechanisms for carrying

62. Shapiro, Meschede, and Osoro (2013).

through on this opportunity. There is also likely some degree of selection bias at work in who becomes a homeowner. While studies do control for income, education, marital status, and other factors that would contribute to differences in the ability to save, there are likely differences in motivation and personal attributes that are related to both savings practices and whether someone becomes an owner. While controls included in studies to capture this effect have not diluted the association between homeownership and increases in wealth, this may simply reflect the challenge of measuring these elusive factors.

Studies using panel surveys may also make the benefits of homeownership appear more assured than they actually are by not fully capturing the impact of failed attempts at owning on changes in wealth. Studies to date have focused on measuring homeownership as the number of years spent as a homeowner, which does not distinguish short sustained spells of owning from similar periods of owning that end in foreclosure or other financial distress. So while homeownership *on average* may increase wealth, it is undoubtedly the case that for some share of households owning a home had a negative impact on their balance sheet.

Finally, the studies reviewed here may also not fully reflect changes that have occurred over time in both market conditions and household behavior. Most of the studies cited reflect experiences of owners during the 1980s and 1990s and so do not capture the market dynamics that began in the late 1990s and came to full bloom during the boom years of the 2000s, including the much greater availability of and appetite for high LTV loans, higher-cost loans, sharp swings in house prices, and much higher risks of default even before the national foreclosure crisis began. The next section turns to an analysis of data from the 2000s to examine whether findings about homeownership's positive association with wealth accumulation held over this period, particularly for low-income and minority households who were most likely to have used high-cost mortgage products.

Experience with Homeownership and Wealth Accumulation through the Boom and Bust

Given the substantial changes in the availability, cost, and terms of mortgage financing that began in the 1990s and accelerated through the mid-2000s and the accompanying boom and bust in home prices, there is good reason to believe that the experience of homeowners in accumulating wealth over the last decade may have been substantially different from what is documented in much of the existing literature for earlier periods. In this section we present information from the PSID on changes in household wealth through the housing market boom and bust of the 2000s. Whereas previous studies have focused solely on how each additional year of homeownership contributes to household wealth, we are also interested in assessing how failed attempts at homeownership affect wealth to assess the downside risks of owning as well.

Specifically, we examine changes in net household wealth from 1999 to 2009, the latest year for which complete PSID survey data were available. Of course, since the period of observation is only through 2009, we do not capture the full extent of the housing market downturn. In fact, much of the decline in nominal home prices had occurred by then, with the CoreLogic home price index hitting a low in March 2009, some 30 percent below the 2006 peak. Prices fluctuated over the next two years, reaching a new low in March 2011 that was 5 percent below the 2009 level. But while much of the loss in home values had occurred by 2009, a large share of foreclosures had yet to occur. Still, the period studied does capture the elevated levels of default and foreclosures among subprime mortgages during the years leading up to the broader housing market meltdown and the first national wave of foreclosures from 2007 into 2009. Thus the results provide some indication of the sustainability of homeownership through the years when more subprime and exotic mortgage products became widespread as well as during the initial stage of the national housing crisis.

Previewing our conclusions, we find that, on average, homeownership's contribution to household wealth over this period was remarkably similar to that found in earlier periods. The results also confirm previous findings that while lower-income households and minorities realized lower wealth gains from owning, on average these gains were positive and significant. The results also show that a failure to sustain homeownership is associated with a substantial loss of wealth for established owners, although those who made a failed transition from renting to owning are no worse off financially than those who remained renters over the whole period. Thus, despite the many ways in which market conditions over this period might have been expected to undermine homeownership's wealth-building potential, our analysis of the PSID finds that owning maintained a strong association with improvements in wealth over the decade from 1999 to 2009.

The sample is constructed by starting with all household heads in 1999. The starting year was selected because it was the first year the survey included detailed questions on household wealth after more Hispanic households were added to the survey panel in 1997 to account for the surge in immigration that occurred since the original PSID panel was constructed in the 1960s. Our sample includes all household heads in 1999 that were still heads or spouses in 2009, although we drop households that were missing from more than two intervening surveys.[63]

---

63. Respondents who drop out of the survey are more likely to be lower-income and minorities, and so we opted to keep some respondents with missing survey years in order to not exclude a disproportionate share of these households.

We include both owners and renters at the start of our period of observation to observe how changes in wealth varied with different tenure trajectories over the period. The sample is limited to those under age fifty-five in 1999 to avoid including households entering into retirement years when wealth is less likely to accumulate and more likely to be tapped for living expenses.

Table 2-1 presents summary statistics for the PSID sample included in the analysis. There were a total of 4,143 households in the sample. The sample includes a fairly large number of African Americans but a smaller number of Hispanics. Household income in each survey year is adjusted to constant 2011 dollars and then averaged across all surveys in order to categorize households by longer-term income. Four income categories are defined that roughly correspond to income quartiles for the entire sample, with cutoffs selected at the nearest $10,000 increment. The exclusion of older households from the sample reduced the share of lowest quartile households more than other income categories.

For much of our analysis we focus on estimates of total net wealth, which is the value of all assets (including savings, pensions, financial investments, businesses, farms, and real estate including the primary residence) less all outstanding debt.[64] While in some respects our main concern could be with home equity, we focus more broadly on total net wealth, both because home equity can be tapped for other investments and because owning a home may contribute to decreases or increases in other wealth if, for example, differences in monthly housing costs affect savings rates. Of note, home values are self-reported by respondents, who have been found in other surveys to overestimate values by between 3 and 6 percent.[65] This tendency to overstate home values should be kept in mind in evaluating our findings since it will contribute to some inflation in homeowner net wealth. However, given that housing equity is only a portion of total net wealth, a modest overstatement of home values is unlikely to explain much of the total differences in wealth observed.

Table 2-2 presents levels and changes in net wealth over the decade for key demographic groups. Overall, compared to African Americans and Hispanics, median wealth among whites was nearly ten and five times higher, respectively, in 1999. The lowest-income-quartile households also had very little wealth, amounting to only a fraction of that held by higher-income households. Virtually all groups experienced an increase in real net wealth over the decade, in part reflecting the fact that we are tracking a consistent set of households and so

---

64. For convenience, net wealth is sometimes referred to in the text as "wealth." In this chapter we do not focus at all on wealth measures, which is the value of all assets without regard to debt levels.

65. Bucks and Pence (2006).

Table 2-1. *Sample Characteristics*[a]

Units as indicated

	Unweighted	Weighted	Weighted share (percent)
Race/ethnicity			
White	2,366	62,918	73
African-American	1,343	11,676	14
Hispanic	296	7,706	9
Other	114	2,908	3
Missing	24	425	0
Total	4,143	85,633	100
Age			
Under 25	416	6,966	8
25–34	1,143	23,652	28
35–44	1,470	27,993	33
45–54	1,112	26,984	32
Missing	2	38	0
Total	4,143	85,633	100
Average income 1999–2009 (2011 dollars)			
< $40,000	1,021	17,438	20
$40–69,999	1,071	21,914	26
$70–109,999	1,065	22,754	27
$110,000 and up	986	23,527	27
Missing	0	0	0
Total	4,143	85,633	100
Education			
Less than high school	743	12,754	15
High school	1,254	23,338	27
Some college	987	21,018	25
College or more	964	25,086	29
Missing	195	3,437	4
Total	4,143	85,633	100
Region			
Northeast	586	15,703	18
Midwest	1,037	22,883	27
South	1,702	26,345	31
West	799	20,194	24
Foreign country	17	489	1
Missing	2	18	0
Total	4,143	85,633	100
Beginning tenure			
Own	2,295	49,454	58
Rent	1,848	36,179	42
Total	4,143	85,633	100

Source: JCHS calculations based on 1999-2009 PSID.

a. Characteristics are as of 1999 with the exception of race/ethnicity and income. Race/ethnicity is based on 2009 survey response to take advantage of higher response rate to this survey question. Income is average of household income over the entire period in 2011 dollars. Hispanics may be of any race. Whites, African-Americans exclude Hispanics. Rent includes those reported to pay no cash rent or live in 'other' tenure situation.

Table 2-2. *Net Wealth by Demographic Characteristics, 1999 versus 2009*
2011 dollars

	Median net wealth		Mean net wealth	
	1999	2009	1999	2009
Race/ethnicity				
White	66,200	144,500	245,800	571,400
African American	6,800	17,400	47,900	130,900
Hispanic	14,900	30,900	64,900	139,900
Total	43,200	101,700	201,900	467,400
Age				
Under 25	3,800	23,400	16,300	87,000
25–34	15,100	60,600	71,600	300,500
35–44	54,700	103,800	207,000	380,000
45–54	134,300	182,400	357,900	798,900
Total	43,200	101,700	201,700	466,200
Average income 1999–2009				
< $40,000	3,000	3,700	26,800	57,300
$40–69,999	19,200	41,900	63,000	428,100
$70–109,999	59,400	130,000	176,200	313,100
$110,000 and up	200,000	418,300	484,700	952,200
Total	43,200	101,700	201,600	466,000

Source: JCHS calculations based on 1999–2009 PSID using sample weights.

capturing the tendency for wealth to accumulate with age.[66] Gains in wealth are much larger for whites and high-income households, while the lowest-quartile households are the only group to show essentially no gains in wealth. As a result, differences in wealth by race-ethnicity and income grew wider over the decade. Table 2-2 also shows changes in mean wealth. Given the skewed distribution of wealth, mean values are much higher than medians and show larger gains, but the relative experience across demographic groups in mean wealth gains over the decade is similar.

66. For example, among all households included in our analysis, median net wealth increased from $43,200 to $101,700 over the decade. But if all households surveyed in 1999 and 2009 are considered, net wealth actually declined from $79,000 to $65,200. In general, trends in wealth from the overall PSID sample are consistent with findings from other surveys.

Tenure Transitions

A key focus of our analysis is to document the frequency of movements into and out of homeownership, both to assess how well households sustained homeownership over this turbulent period and how these changes in tenure were associated with changes in net household wealth. We begin by dividing the sample into those that were owners and renters in 1999. We then categorize households by their tenure at the end of the period, taking into account whether there were any intervening changes in tenure.[67] The following six categories of tenure transitions emerged:

—*always own,* which includes those reported to own a home in all periods;

—*own with interruption,* which includes those who owned in both 1999 and 2009 but had one or more spells as a renter in the middle of the study period;

—*owner to renter,* which includes those who started as an owner but ended the period as a renter;

—*rent to own sustained,* which includes those who began as renters but ended as owners;

—*rent to own not sustained,* which includes those who began as renters, transitioned to owning at some point, but ended the period renters; and

—*always rent,* which includes those reported to rent a home in all periods.

Table 2-3 presents the distribution of households by the tenure transitions over the observation period. One striking aspect of the distribution is that a fairly significant share of households—roughly two-thirds—did not change tenure over the ten-year period of observation. Also there are no sharp differences by race-ethnicity or income in these shares, with the second income quartile being somewhat less likely to not change tenure (57 percent) and the highest-income quartile being the least likely to change (76 percent).

Another interesting aspect of the tenure transitions is that despite the upheavals in the housing market over this period, a large majority of households (91 percent) that started out as owners were still owners at the end of the period. It is true that the homeownership survival rates were somewhat lower among African Americans (83 percent) and the lowest-income quartile (77 percent), but even among these groups a large majority of 1999 owners also owned a home in 2009.

A lower share of renters that transitioned to owning over the period still owned at the end of the period, but even this share was quite high at 81 percent. Again, the rates were somewhat lower for African Americans (70 percent) and the

---

67. During the period covered by our study, the PSID was conducted every two years in odd-numbered years. We observe tenure in the year of the survey, for a total of six times from 1999 through 2009. Since we do not observe tenure in even-numbered years, we may miss some brief switches in tenure, but we assume that periods of owning of less than two years are few in number and so unlikely to substantially bias our estimates.

Table 2-3. *Distribution of Tenure Transitions, 1999–2009*[a]

Percent

Tenure change 1999 to 2009	Total	Race/ethnicity			Average income 1999–2009			
		White	African American	Hispanic	Under $40,000	$40,000–69,999	$70,000–109,999	$110,000 and up
Start as owner	58	64	35	48	27	49	66	81
Always own	49	55	26	40	17	37	57	74
Own with interruption	4	4	3	5	3	4	5	4
Owner to renter	5	5	6	3	6	7	4	3
Start as renter	42	36	65	52	73	51	34	19
Rent to own sustained	21	21	19	22	16	25	26	15
Rent to own not sustained	5	4	8	6	7	7	4	2
Always rent	17	12	38	24	50	19	5	2
Total	100	100	100	100	100	100	100	100
Key subtotals								
Share with stable tenure	65	66	64	64	67	57	62	76
Share owned at some point, but rent in 2009	10	9	14	9	14	15	8	4
Share of starting owners still owning in 2009	91	92	83	93	77	85	93	97
Share of "rent to own" groups that own in 2009	81	83	70	79	69	77	88	91

Source: JCHS calculations based on 1999-2009 PSID using sample weights.

a. Categories based on starting and ending tenure. Categories may include multiple transitions. For example, "rent to own sustained" includes households that transitioned in owning more than once over the observation period.

lowest-income quartile (69 percent), but even for these groups a large majority of those moving into owning were still owners in 2009. Of note, these rates appear to be higher than those reported in previous studies, such as those by Reid and by Haurin and Rosenthal, where only about half of lower-income and minority homeowners were found to still be owners five years after purchasing a home.[68] One difference is that these other studies only considered first-time homebuyers, while we do not screen our sample for tenure prior to 1999. Another important difference is that we allow for transitions back into owning for those who have an intervening period as renters. Finally, renters who first bought a home in 2005 or later were observed for fewer than five years in our sample, so the mingling of different periods of observation may elevate our estimates. Still, of those that bought in 2001 and 2003, a substantial 77 and 82 percent, respectively, owned a home in 2009.[69]

Overall, 10 percent of all households that owned at some point over the study period were renters in 2009, with the share slightly higher at 14 percent among African Americans and households in the bottom half of the income distribution. We do not investigate the factors contributing to these returns to renting and so do not know what share of these transitions were due to financial hardship rather than other reasons for a return to renting. But even absent the costs of a default or foreclosure, the high transaction costs of buying and selling homes mean that these owners are less likely to realize financial benefits from owning. However, the number of households experiencing a transition out of homeownership as of 2009 was a fairly small share of the overall sample.

Tenure Transitions and Changes in Net Wealth

These different tenure trajectories were associated with large differences in wealth across households, including both differences in starting wealth and how much was gained over the decade (table 2-4). The starting wealth levels in 1999 were strongly indicative of households' future tenure. The wealthiest households in 1999 were those most likely to consistently own over the period, while those who rented the entire time had the lowest wealth. Among owners, those who no longer owned by 2009 had the least wealth in 1999. Renters in 1999 overall had much lower wealth than owners, but those who later became owners and sustained it through 2009 had the highest starting wealth, roughly twice that of those who bought but did not sustain ownership.

The largest gains in wealth were experienced by both those who owned the whole period and those that transitioned into owning and sustained it, for whom the median change in wealth was $74,700 and $73,300, respectively. In keeping

68. Reid (2004); Haurin and Rosenthal (2004).
69. Authors' calculations based on PSID study sample.

Table 2-4. *Net Wealth by Tenure Transition Categories, 1999 versus 2009*
2011 dollars

	Median net wealth			Mean net wealth		
	1999	2009	Median change[a]	1999	2009	Mean change
Start as owner						
Always own	139,700	238,000	74,700	353,000	755,600	402,600
Own with interruption	81,000	145,900	41,700	190,000	468,100	278,100
Owner to renter	52,700	9,200	−28,500	159,800	142,000	−17,800
Start as renter						
Rent to own sustained	8,100	94,400	73,300	38,200	298,100	259,900
Rent to own not sustained	3,800	4,200	−1,800	18,300	50,800	32,500
Always rent	1,500	1,100	0	32,500	50,500	18,000
Total	43,200	101,700	28,700	201,600	466,000	264,400
	Median home equity			Mean home equity		
Start as owner						
Always own	64,800	108,000	41,400	97,700	170,200	72,500
Own with interruption	37,800	62,900	15,400	59,300	106,200	46,900
Owner to renter	33,800	0	−33,800	71,800	0	−71,800
Start as renter						
Rent to own sustained	0	50,300	49,300	0	89,500	89,500
Rent to own not sustained	0	0	0	0	0	0
Always rent	0	0	0	0	0	0
Total	10,800	47,200	12,400	53,800	105,600	51,800
	Median non-housing wealth			Mean non-housing wealth		
Start as owner						
Always own	55,400	97,500	19,700	255,300	585,400	330,100
Own with interruption	26,300	45,600	12,700	130,700	361,900	231,200
Owner to renter	16,200	9,200	500	88,000	142,000	54,000
Start as renter						
Rent to own sustained	8,100	26,600	13,600	38,200	208,600	170,400
Rent to own not sustained	3,800	4,200	−1,800	18,300	50,800	32,500
Always rent	1,500	1,100	0	32,500	50,500	18,000
Total	18,900	31,500	7,000	147,800	360,500	212,700

Source: JCHS calculations based on 1999–2009 PSID using sample weights.

a. The median change is the change in wealth for the median household in the category shown, which differs from the change in the median for the two time periods shown.

with the expectation that movements out of homeownership would reduce the financial gains from owning, owners who experienced a period as renters in the middle of the study period had lower median gains in wealth, although at $41,700 the amount was still substantial. Meanwhile, those who started out as owners in 1999 but were renters by 2009 experienced a substantial decline in wealth, with a median loss of $28,500. While not all of these losses may be attributable to the movement out of homeownership, this result is certainly consistent with the substantial costs associated with a failed homeownership experience.[70]

Those who made the transition from renting to owning but did not sustain it saw modest changes in wealth, as the median household in this group lost $1,800. Those who rented the entire period experienced little change in wealth, with the median household experiencing no change. Considering that renters that sustain ownership experienced substantial increases in wealth, while both those that failed to sustain owning and those who remained renters on net experienced no change in wealth, from a financial perspective the movement into homeownership could be characterized as "nothing ventured, nothing gained." Of course, this only considers changes in wealth and does not consider the consequences of losing a home to foreclosure for the psychological and physical well-being of these individuals or the ongoing financial costs of a damaged credit history.[71]

When we look specifically at wealth in home equity, we find that it represents a substantial share of median wealth gains for households in all groups who owned in 2009. For those who owned for the entire observation period, the median gain in home equity was $41,400 against the median gain in non-housing wealth of $19,700. Home equity gains were even more important for those who transitioned from renting to owning and sustained it. The median increase in home equity for this group was $49,300 compared to median gains

70. The 2009 PSID asks a retrospective question about whether any members of the household experienced a foreclosure on a previously owned home during the 2001–08 period. There were ninety-nine respondents in our panel that reported a foreclosure during this period, about half of whom were owners in 1999 and half renters. Among this group median net wealth fell from $14,900 to $1,300 over the period. The moderate starting wealth reflects the mix of owners and renters at the start of the period. The very low ending wealth suggests that foreclosures may lead to more significant declines in wealth than the figures for all those who return to renting suggest.

71. The reported changes also represent the median change and do not take into account the experience of those who fared worse. Among those who started as renters, bought a home, and failed to sustain ownership over the period, those at the bottom 10th percentile of wealth change lost $55,300 over the period. Even among those who moved from renting to owning and still owned in 2009, the bottom 10th percentile saw a fall in net wealth of $43,100. In short, while the "typical" renter who failed to sustain owning ended the period where he or she began, some clearly suffered substantial losses. And even among those that sustained ownership, not all experienced gains over the period.

in nonhousing wealth of $13,600. Those who owned at both the beginning and end of the period but experienced some period as a renter in the middle also had a majority of their wealth gains in home equity, with a median gain of $15,400 compared to a median gain of $12,700 in nonhousing wealth. The reverse is true for owners who became renters by the end of the period, with losses in home equity accounting for a large share of the declines in net wealth among this group. The median loss of home equity was $33,800 while the median change in other wealth was positive though modest, at $500.

Timing of Home Purchase and Changes in Wealth

Given the dramatic rise and fall in home prices in many markets between 1999 and 2009, it would be expected that the timing of entry into homeownership would have a substantial impact of changes in net wealth. Table 2-5 presents estimates of net household wealth from each wave of the PSID over the study period for households that were first observed to have made the transition into homeownership in each survey year. For example, the top row of the table shows the median net wealth among households in each survey year for those who first bought a home in 2001, while the next row shows the same information for those who first bought in 2003, and so on. The year the household was first observed to own is shown in bold in table 2-5. Similar to the findings of Haurin, Hendershott, and Wachter, we find that wealth increases substantially in the first year of observed homeownership.[72] Much of this initial gain likely reflects efforts to accumulate a down payment to support the move into owning but also includes some gains in home values in the initial year or two of ownership. Wealth gains are also generally found to be larger in the years following home purchase than in the years preceding it.

In fact, the boost from rapidly rising home prices after purchase during the boom is evident in the wealth trends shown. Those who bought in 2003 and 2005 experienced much bigger gains in wealth immediately following home purchase than those who bought in earlier or later years. The median jump in wealth in the first year of owning for these two groups was $57,700 and $68,100, respectively. In comparison, those who bought in 2001 and 2007 had wealth gains in the first year of owning of $33,700 and $37,900, respectively. Those who were first observed to own in 2009 would have bought since the last survey in 2007 and so would have been most likely to experience a substantial decline in home values immediately after buying. In fact, these buyers did experience a much smaller increase in net wealth, but they still gained $17,600. The more modest gains no doubt include actual losses in wealth from the decline in home values, but not enough to overcome whatever increased savings occurred as part

---

72. Haurin, Hendershott, and Wachter (1996).

Table 2-5. *Trends in Median Wealth among Renters Transitioning to Owning*[a]
Units as indicated

First year reporting owning a home	Wealth by year (2011 dollars)						Share sustaining owning (percent)
	1999	2001	2003	2005	2007	2009	
2001	10,800	**44,500**	53,800	83,500	93,300	73,400	77
2003	9,500	9,500	**67,200**	88,700	108,700	81,800	82
2005	3,800	7,100	17,100	**85,200**	113,400	82,400	77
2007	4,100	4,100	3,700	6,600	**44,500**	30,400	86
2009	2,800	5,100	2,900	4,400	8,700	**26,300**	100
All	7,000	15,900	32,300	62,700	87,500	67,600	81
Households that sustain owning							
2001	13,500	**52,100**	67,200	107,700	139,900	128,900	
2003	9,500	9,500	**61,700**	97,900	135,600	100,700	
2005	5,700	7,100	15,900	**93,300**	130,200	120,600	
2007	5,400	4,400	2,200	7,500	**46,900**	40,900	
2009	2,800	5,100	2,900	4,400	8,700	**26,300**	
All	8,100	16,500	37,900	70,300	106,300	94,400	
Households that fail to sustain owning							
2001	4,600	**23,800**	15,100	20,400	7,300	4,200	
2003	7,400	8,600	**67,200**	53,000	20,800	7,900	
2005	2,000	6,500	18,300	**55,300**	58,000	1,000	
2007	2,200	0	12,200	3,100	**21,800**	11,500	
All	3,800	11,400	21,600	27,400	19,600	4,200	

Source: JCHS calculations based on 1999-2009 PSID using sample weights.
a. Figures shown in bold represent year of transition into homeowning.

of the move into owning. While much smaller than the wealth gains observed for homebuyers in any other period, the gain for the 2009 group was still substantially larger than the wealth gains observed for renters between any two periods.

Aside from those who first owned as of 2009, all other cohorts did experience a substantial drop in median net wealth between 2007 and 2009, with larger percentage declines the later in the period the household purchased a home. Among those who bought in 2001, median net wealth dropped by 21 percent whereas among those who bought in 2007, median net wealth declined by 32 percent. Since the top panel of table 2-5 includes both households that continued to own for the remainder of the period as well as those who moved back into renting, these trends include declines not just in home values but also from the impact of defaults and foreclosures. In fact, between 77 and 86 percent of each cohort still owned a home as of 2009, with other households transitioning back to renting.

As shown in the middle panel of table 2-5, those who sustained owning through 2009 generally had higher wealth levels at the end of the period and suffered lower losses of wealth. The bottom panel shows those who failed to sustain owning. The same pattern of a big jump in median wealth in the year of first owning is observed, but over the next few years all of these gains are lost as households transition back to renting. By 2009 the medians for all of the cohorts were roughly back to the same wealth levels as in 1999. The lone exception to this pattern is among buyers in 2007 for whom 2009 wealth was several times higher than in 1999, but this may simply be due to the very small number of households (22) in this group. Thus the move to homeownership provided a temporary boost to wealth, although the move back to renting did not result in losses in wealth beyond the starting point—at least for the typical household.

Regression Analysis of Changes in Wealth

The tabulations of changes in wealth provide some indication of how different tenure histories contributed to changes in net household wealth, but since a variety of factors contribute to these changes and may also be correlated with homeownership, the tabulations do not isolate the association of homeownership and wealth. A regression analysis of changes in wealth is useful to estimate this association while controlling for these other factors; it also provides an opportunity to examine if these associations differ by race-ethnicity or income.

We estimate a regression model to predict wealth in 2009 as a function of starting wealth, a range of demographic characteristics, geographic location, and the respondents' experiences as homeowners over the observation period. Given the highly skewed distribution of wealth, it is necessary to transform wealth into a more linear measure to reduce the influence of extreme values on the estimated coefficients. Past studies of homeownership and wealth using the PSID have used a logarithmic transformation of wealth, but this approach presents challenges in that wealth that is negative or zero is not defined as a logarithm. Di, Belsky, and Liu address this by setting all negative and zero values of wealth to 1, which truncates the independent variable and removes the possibility that failed homeownership could lead to negative wealth positions.[73] Turner and Luea exclude these observations from their model but include a selection measure for those with positive wealth to account for this bias.[74] Following Pence, we estimate a

---

73. Di, Belsky, and Liu (2007).
74. Turner and Luea (2009).

median regression model that employs an inverse hyperbolic sine transformation of wealth that allows for both negative and zero values and reduces the influence of extreme values of wealth on the results.[75]

Of note, unlike previous studies, we do not attempt to account for selection bias in who becomes an owner. In contrast, Di, Belsky, and Liu employ a measure for previous savings behavior to capture some intrinsic differences between renters and those who became owners, Turner and Luea employ a random effects model, and Mamgain uses an instrumental variable approach.[76] However, none of these studies found a significant impact from these controls on their findings. Given the difficulty of finding an effective control for these selection issues, our approach is to simply assess the association between owning and changes in wealth while recognizing that the association does not prove a causal link. But our analysis will still help identify whether owning is associated with gains in wealth even in the midst of significant volatility in housing prices and the proliferation of high-risk lending.

In the base model (model 1), wealth in 2009 is assumed to be a function of starting wealth, average income over the period, race-ethnicity, age, changes in marital status, whether children are in the household, education level, and geographic region in 1999. We also include an indicator for whether the household received inheritance or financial gifts at any time during the study period. Our main variable of interest is the number of years spent as a homeowner during the period from 1999 to 2009. Since we only observe tenure every other year, we assume that every survey response is equal to two years of owning. This will overstate the years of owning in the first year owning is observed since it is unlikely that the purchase always take place immediately following the previous survey, but this assumption is conservative by assuming the maximum number of years a respondent could have owned. To assess whether the association between homeownership and wealth changes differs by race-ethnicity and income, we then estimate models that first include variables interacting the measure of years owned with dummy variables for African Americans and Hispanics (model 2), and then add interaction variables for each of the income quartiles (with the $70,000–109,999 income band in the left out category for comparison) (model 3). A final model then interacts the years owned with dummy variables indicating whether the respondent fell into the own to rent, rent to own sustained, rent to own not sustained, or own with interruption categories to see what effect these different trajectories have on wealth accumulation.

---

75. Pence (2006). We do drop the ten highest and ten lowest values of wealth from the sample to remove the influence of these outliers on the results. The sample in the regression model also excludes twenty-two cases for which race-ethnicity was not known.

76. Di, Belsky, and Liu (2007); Turner and Luea (2009); Mamgain (2011).

In general the models fit the data well, and results are consistent with expectations. In the base model, ending wealth has a positive and statistically significant relationship with wealth in 1999, being in the highest-income quartile, living in regions other than the Midwest (the left out category), receiving gifts or inheritance, and getting married during the observation period (table 2-6). Negative and statistically significant relationships are found with being in the two lower income quartiles, being African American or of "other" race, having less than a college degree or higher in education (the left out category), being younger than twenty-five or thirty-five to forty-four years old in 1999 (relative to the left out category of being forty-five to fifty-four years old), and getting divorced or having children. There is also a significant and positive association between changes in wealth and each additional year spent as a homeowner. When evaluated at the sample median wealth of $69,200, each year of owning is found to increase wealth by $9,500. This result is very close to the findings of Di, Belsky, and Liu and of Turner and Luea reviewed above.[77]

When interaction terms are added for years owned and the race-ethnicity variables (model 2), most of the remaining estimated coefficients are similar to the base model, although neither the African American variable nor the two youngest age categories are still statistically significant. The results do find that homeownership is associated with lower wealth gains for African Americans and Asians, but owning is still found to be associated with a fairly large increase in net wealth for both of these groups. Specifically, combining the base tenure variable with the interaction term, African American homeowners are estimated to see increases of wealth of $8,400 compared with $10,500 for white homeowners. The coefficient on the variable interacting Hispanics with years owned is not statistically significant but is close to zero in any event.

Model 3 then adds interaction terms for income quartiles. Including these variables reduces the significance of the remaining age variables, but other coefficients remain similar. This model finds that the two lowest-income quartiles actually had modestly higher increases in wealth from each year of homeownership while the highest income quartile had much lower returns. This result may be an indication that households owning higher valued homes had more to lose in the downturn. When the interaction terms with income are added, the interaction term for African Americans shows somewhat lower gains for owners. Each additional year of owing for an African American is now estimated to add $6,900 to wealth, compared to $10,000 for whites.

Finally, model 4 adds interaction terms for the different categories of tenure transitions over the period. Consistent with the findings from the tabulations, households that fail to sustain homeownership do not realize any financial

77. Di, Belsky, and Liu (2007); Turner and Luea (2009).

Table 2-6. *Median Regression Model Results, Marginal Effects of Independent Variables*[a]

Variable	Model 1	Model 2	Model 3	Model 4
Constant	**91,600**	**79,300**	**84,000**	**82,100**
Wealth 1999	**2.3**	**2.3**	**2.4**	**2.5**
Income quartile 1	**–43,900**	**–44,800**	**–57,300**	**–58,100**
Income quartile 2	**–23,500**	**–22,900**	**–38,100**	**–33,700**
Income quartile 4	**38,300**	**38,800**	**91,100**	**79,900**
African American	–20,800	–6,000	1,300	–700
Hispanic	–5,600	–2,100	–1,500	4,000
Asian	15,200	**73,800**	35,600	6,200
Other race	**–27,900**	**–38,600**	–26,100	–25,200
Northeast	**14,600**	**16,700**	**15,300**	**12,300**
South	**10,400**	**11,000**	**10,000**	**10,300**
West	**17,000**	**18,100**	**19,000**	**17,300**
Other region	**50,100**	**59,000**	**42,900**	**49,300**
Less than high school	**–29,800**	**–28,500**	**–27,400**	**–21,900**
High school	**–23,800**	**–21,900**	**–21,200**	**–18,200**
Some college	**–20,900**	**–20,700**	**–21,200**	**–18,900**
Missing education	–9,900	–10,400	–7,800	–4,800
Age under 25	**–11,700**	–6,600	–4,400	–7,700
Age 25–34	–7,000	–6,700	–6,200	–4,800
Age 35–44	**–7,700**	**–6,800**	–4,400	–3,100
Always married	–5,700	–5,600	–3,800	–6,600
Got married	**14,600**	**14,700**	**13,500**	3,900
Got divorced	**–27,800**	**–28,700**	**–28,000**	**–13,000**
Has children	**–10,800**	**–11,500**	**–12,500**	**–10,800**
Receive inheritance or gift	**7,500**	5,700	6,400	7,800
Years owned	**9,500**	**10,500**	**10,000**	**9,300**
Years owned * African American		–2,100	–3,100	–2,900
Years owned * Hispanic		–100	–500	–1,500
Years owned * Asian		**–5,500**	–2,300	–500
Years owned * other race		2,500	1,400	700
Years owned * income quartile 1			1,900	**2,900**
Years owned * income quartile 2			1,700	1,500
Years owned * income quartile 4			**–4,800**	–3,700
Years owned * own with interruption				1,400
Years owned * own to rent				**–13,700**
Years owned * rent to own sustained				3,600
Years owned * rent to own not sustained				**–10,500**
Number of observations	4,101	4,101	4,101	4,101
Pseudo R^2	0.407	0.408	0.410	0.431

Source: JCHS calculations based on 1999–2009 PSID.

a. Values statistically significant at 5 percent level shown in bold. The transformation of wealth was based on a value of θ of 0.0001 based on maximum likelihood estimation. Marginal effects evaluated at sample median wealth in 2009 of $69,200. To be consistent with the transformation of 2009 wealth, an inverse hyperbolic sine transformation was also applied to the 1999 wealth variable so that the marginal effects of this coefficient are not comparable to that shown for other variables.

benefits from owning. Those who start as renters and return to renting by 2009 are found to lose about $1,200 for each year of owning. Those who start as owners but end as renters are found to lose $4,400 per year of owning. Renters who make a successful transition to owning are actually found to gain even more from owning—$12,900 for each year compared to $9,300 for those who owned for the whole period. Surprisingly, owners who experienced a period of renting also gained more from each year of owning than the average owner ($10,700).

The coefficients on the other interaction terms for race-ethnicity and income are similar in this model. African Americans are still found to benefit from each year of homeownership, but at a lower rate than whites ($6,400). The coefficient on Hispanic owners also suggests that the gains to Hispanics are less than for whites and slightly higher than for African Americans, but these differences are not statistically significant. Households in the lowest-income quartile are found to have slightly higher gains ($12,200) while those in the highest-income quartile have lower gains ($5,600).

In general, the results of the regression models are highly consistent with the findings from the previous literature examining the association between homeownership and wealth gains—despite the differences in market conditions that prevailed during the 2000s. Overall, owning a home is consistently found to be associated with increases of roughly $9,000–$10,000 in net wealth for each year a home is owned. Also consistent with earlier studies, African Americans are found to benefit less from owning a home, but each year of owning is still associated with gains in net wealth of between $6,000 and $8,000, which is substantial considering the generally low levels of wealth among African Americans. In contrast to earlier studies, however, we find that lower-income households actually had slightly higher gains from owning compared to households in the third income quartile, while the highest-income households had much lower gains. This difference may well reflect the fact that higher-income households owned higher valued homes and so suffered greater absolute losses in wealth when house prices dropped.

Conclusions

Even after the tremendous decline in housing prices and the rising wave of foreclosures that began in 2007, homeownership continues to be a significant source of household wealth and remains particularly important for lower-income and minority households. As has become painfully clear, owning a home is not without risk. But even during a time of excessive risk taking in the mortgage market and extreme volatility in house prices, large shares of owners successfully sustained homeownership and created substantial wealth in the process (at least through 2009). While African American and lower-income households were somewhat less likely to sustain homeownership, these groups also experienced sizable gains in net wealth on average that were associated with owning, while renters saw few gains. Owners who failed to sustain homeownership did suffer substantial losses in wealth, but much of the wealth was associated with the move into homeownership, so these households essentially fell back to their initial wealth levels. At least in terms of household wealth, failed attempts at owning do not appear to leave the typical household worse off than when it started.

Our analysis highlights two primary mechanisms by which owning appears to generate wealth over a decade-long period. Most obviously, owners can accrue substantial wealth through appreciation in home prices, as evidenced by the outsized gains realized among those who first became owners during the 2003 and 2005 PSID waves as home prices took off. But fluctuations in home prices are a two-edged sword, and a significant share of these gains was subsequently lost when the bottom fell out of the market. The other mechanism by which owning is associated with increases in wealth is through the large increase in savings that occurs when households make the move to owning. This is evidenced among those first buying between 2007 and 2009, who, despite the troubled housing market, had gains in net worth of $18,000, more than tripling the amount they held before buying a home. Over a longer period of time, the paydown of principal will further add to these gains, although the period studied was too short to capture this effect. But this forced savings aspect is arguably an important way that owning leads to wealth creation over the long run since it is at work under all market conditions. While studies simulating the financial returns to owning and renting find that renting is often more likely to be beneficial, in practice renters rarely accumulate any wealth. In no small part this seems traceable to the difficulties households face in trying to save absent either a clear goal or an automatic savings mechanism.

Of course, our examination of the PSID does not attempt to account for selection bias in who becomes a homeowner. Therefore our results cannot attribute a causal link between owning a home and wealth increases, just that there is an association. Our analysis does control for a range of household attributes that are associated with the ability to save, including starting wealth, age, educational status, income, and marital status. Still, there may yet be differences between owners and renters in personality and motivation that are unmeasured by available data and that make important contributions to the differences between these groups. But if homeownership itself were a drain on finances—or even neutral—we would not expect to find such a strong association between owning and wealth gains while controlling for other household characteristics. While it may still be the case, as suggested by the simulation studies, that under the right conditions, renters would come out ahead of owners, in practice we do not observe these outcomes. And while owners could potentially fare better financially if they were to rent, there is still strong evidence that owning is financially beneficial given the strong positive association with wealth gains.

It is also important to bear in mind that the desire to own a home is not solely—or even primarily—motivated by financial goals. Homeownership's appeal lies in its strong associations with having control over one's living situation, the desire to put down roots in a community, and the sense of efficacy and success that is associated with owning.[78] If the only reason to support homeownership were to foster wealth, then other means for encouraging savings in a more safe and secure way would be best. But the fact that homeowning is strongly preferred for a host of other reasons by most individuals as they age provides further support for policies to promote homeownership out of equity concerns to help individuals and families achieve this important goal. The social benefits of homeownership lend further credence to the value of supports for homeownership.[79] But policies to support homeownership need to take into account the very real risks involved and ensure that when households take the plunge to buy a home, they must be able to sustain homeownership and thus realize the financial benefits offered.

Still, it is inevitable that some owners will not succeed. A key challenge for policymakers is to assess what degree of failure risk is appropriate. From a wealth perspective, the opportunity to realize fairly substantial gains if owning is maintained against the risk of essentially falling back to starting wealth levels if it is not suggests that there is reason to err on the side of fostering attempts at owning. But the calculation also needs to factor in the nonfinancial costs of failure for these families and individuals as well as impacts on the surrounding community. To avoid tilting the playing field too sharply toward homeownership and enticing those with low odds of success toward this goal, it is important that housing policies are more tenure neutral, providing supports for renters and owners alike to find affordable, good quality housing. The fact that homeownership will not be appropriate or desirable for all low-income households also argues for a broader range of policies to promote savings and wealth accumulation among those of limited means.

References

Apgar, William, and Allegra Calder. 2005. "The Dual Mortgage Market: The Persistence of Discrimination in Mortgage Lending." In *The Geography of Opportunity: Race and Housing Choice in Metropolitan America,* edited by Xavier N. De Souza Briggs, pp. 101–23. Brookings.

Avery, Robert B., Kenneth P. Brevoort, and Glenn B. Canner. 2007. "The 2006 HMDA Data." *Federal Reserve Bulletin* 93: A73–A109.

78. Reid (2013); Drew and Herbert (2013).
79. Rohe and Lindblad (2013).

Belsky, Eric S., and Mark Duda. 2002. "Asset Appreciation, Time of Purchase and Sale, and the Return to Low-Income Homeowners." In *Low-Income Homeownership: Examining the Unexamined Goal,* edited by Nicolas Retsinas and Eric Belsky, pp. 208–38. Brookings.

Belsky, Eric S., Nicolas Retsinas, and Mark Duda. 2007. "The Financial Returns to Low-Income Homeownership." In *Chasing the American Dream,* edited by William M. Rohe and Harry L. Watson, p. 191–212. Cornell University Press.

Belsky, Eric S., and Nela Richardson. 2010. "Understanding the Boom and Bust in Nonprime Mortgage Lending." Working Paper. Harvard University, Joint Center for Housing Studies.

Beracha, Eli, and Ken H. Johnson. 2012. "Lessons from over 30 Years of Buy versus Rent Decisions: Is the American Dream Always Wise?" *Real Estate Economics* 40, no. 2: 217–47.

Beracha, Eli, Alexandre Skiba, and Ken H. Johnson. 2012. "A Revision of the American Dream of Homeownership?" Unpublished manuscript, November 28.

Bocian, Debbie Gruenstein, Keith S. Ernst, and Wei Li. 2008. "Race, Ethnicity and Subprime Home Loan Pricing." *Journal of Economics and Business* 60, no. 1: 110–24.

Boehm, Thomas P., and Alan Schlottmann. 2004. *Wealth Accumulation and Home Ownership: Evidence for Low-Income Households.* U.S. Department of Housing and Urban Development, Office of Policy Development and Research.

Bradford, Calvin. 2002. *Risk or Race? Racial Disparities and the Subprime Refinance Market.* Washington: Center for Community Change.

Bucks, Brian K., and Karen Pence. 2006. "Do Homeowners Know Their House Values and Mortgage Terms?" Finance and Economics Discussion Working Paper 2006-03. Washington: Federal Reserve Board of Governors.

Calem, Paul S., Kevin Gillen, and Susan Wachter. 2004. "The Neighborhood Distribution of Subprime Mortgage Lending." *Journal of Real Estate Finance and Economics* 29, no. 4: 393–410.

Capone, Charles A., Jr. 1995. "Taxation and Housing Tenure Choice: The Case for Moderate-Income Homeownership." *Journal of Housing Economics* 4: 328–49.

Capozza, Dennis R., and others. 2002. "Determinants of Real House Price Dynamics." Working Paper 9262. Cambridge, Mass.: National Bureau of Economic Research.

Carr, James H., and Katrin B. Anacker. 2012. "Long-Term Social Impacts and Financial Costs of Foreclosures on Families and Communities of Color: A Review of the Literature." Washington: National Community Reinvestment Coalition (October).

CoreLogic. 2013. *CoreLogic Equity Report Third Quarter 2013* (www.corelogic.com/research/negative-equity/corelogic-q3-2013-equity-report.pdf).

Davis, Morris A. 2012. "Questioning Homeownership as a Public Policy Goal." Policy Analysis Paper 696. Washington: Cato Institute (May 15).

Davis, Morris A., Andreas Lehnert, and Robert F. Martin. 2008. "The Rent-Price Ratio for the Aggregate Stock of Owner-Occupied Housing." *Review of Income and Wealth* 54, no. 2: 279–84.

Di, Zhu Xiao, Eric Belsky, and Xiaodong Liu. 2007. "Do Homeowners Achieve More Household Wealth in the Long Run?" *Journal of Housing Economics* 16, no. 3: 274–90.

Dietz, Robert D., and Donald R. Haurin. 2003. "The Social and Private Micro-Level Consequences of Homeownership." *Journal of Urban Economics* 54, no. 3: 401–50.

Drew, Rachel Bogardus, and Christopher Herbert. 2013. "Post-Recession Drivers of Preferences for Homeownership." *Housing Policy Debate* 23, no. 4: 666–87.

Flavin, Marjorie, and Takashi Yamashita. 2002. "Owner-Occupied Housing and the Composition of the Household Portfolio." *American Economic Review* 92, no. 1: 345–62.

Gallin, Joshua. 2006. "The Long-Run Relationship between House Prices and Income: Evidence from Local Housing Markets." *Real Estate Economics* 34, no. 3: 417–38.

Galster, George C., and Anna M. Santiago. 2008. "Low-Income Homeownership as an Asset-Building Tool: What Can We Tell Policymakers?" In *Urban and Regional Policy and Its Effects*, vol. 1, edited by Harold Wolman, Howard Wial, and Margery Austin Turner, pp. 60–108. Brookings.

Goetzmann, William N., and Matthew Speigel. 2002. "The Policy Implications of Portfolio Choice in Underserved Mortgage Markets." In *Low-Income Homeownership: Examining the Unexamined Goal*, edited by Nicolas Retsinas and Eric Belsky, pp. 257–74. Brookings.

Haurin, Donald R., Patric H. Hendershott, and Susan M. Wachter. 1996. "Borrowing Constraints and the Tenure Choice of Young Households." Working Paper 5630. Cambridge, Mass.: National Bureau of Economic Research.

Haurin, Donald R., and Stuart S. Rosenthal. 2004. *The Sustainability of Homeownership: Factors Affecting the Duration of Homeownership and Rental Spells*. U.S. Department of Housing and Urban Development, Office of Policy Development and Research (December).

Herbert, Christopher E., and Eric S. Belsky. 2006. *The Homeownership Experience of Low-Income and Minority Households: A Review and Synthesis of the Literature*. U.S. Department of Housing Development, Office of Policy Development and Research.

JCHS (Joint Center for Housing Studies). 2011. *The State of the Nation's Housing 2011*. Harvard University.

————. 2012. *The State of the Nation's Housing 2012*. Harvard University.

Kiviat, Barbara. 2010. "The Case against Homeownership." *Time Magazine,* September 11 (www.time.com/time/magazine/article/0,9171,2013850,00.html).

Lawler, Thomas. 2012. "On the Upward Trend in Real House Prices." *Calculated Risk Finance and Economics* (www.calculatedriskblog.com/2012/12/lawler-on-upward-trend-in-real-house.html).

Li, Wenli, and Fang Yang. 2010. "American Dream or American Obsession? The Economic Benefits and Costs of Homeownership." *Business Review* Q3: 20–30.

Mamgain, Abhishek. 2011. "Do Low-Income Households Benefit from Homeownership?" Ph.D. dissertation. University of Southern California.

McCarthy, George, S. Van Zandt, and William M. Rohe. 2001. "The Economic Costs and Benefits of Homeownership: A Critical Assessment of the Research." Working Paper 01-02. Arlington, Va.: Research Institute for Housing America (May).

Mills, Edwin S. 1990. "Housing Tenure Choice." *Journal of Real Estate Finance and Economics* 3, no. 4: 323–31.

Nothaft, Frank E., and Yan Chang. 2005. "Refinance and the Accumulation of Home Equity Wealth." In *Building Assets, Building Credit: Creating Wealth in Low-Income Communities,* edited by Nicolas Retsinas and Eric Belsky, pp. 71–102. Brookings.

Oliver, Melvin L., and Thomas M. Shapiro. 1990. "Wealth of a Nation." *American Journal of Economics and Sociology* 49, no. 2: 129–51.

Ozanne, Larry. 2012. "Taxation of Owner-Occupied and Rental Housing." Working Paper 2012-14. Congressional Budget Office (November).

Pence, Karen M. 2006. "The Role of Wealth Transformations: An Application to Estimating the Effect of Tax Incentives on Saving." *Contributions in Economic Analysis and Policy* 5, no. 1: 1–24.

Rappaport, Jordan. 2010. "The Effectiveness of Homeownership in Building Household Wealth." *Economic Review* (Federal Reserve Bank of Kansas City) 95, no. 4: 35–65.

Reid, Carolina Katz. 2004. "Achieving the American Dream? A Longitudinal Analysis of the Homeownership Experiences of Low-Income Households." Working Paper 04-04. University of Washington, Center for Studies in Demography and Ecology.

———. 2013. "To Buy or Not to Buy? Understanding Tenure Preferences and the Decision-Making Processes of Lower-Income Households." Harvard University, Joint Center for Housing Studies.

Retsinas, Nicolas P., and Eric S. Belsky, eds. 2002a. "Examining the Unexamined Goal." In *Low-Income Homeownership: Examining the Unexamined Goal,* edited by Nicolas Retsinas and Eric Belsky, pp. 1–14. Brookings.

———. 2002b. *Low-Income Homeownership: Examining the Unexamined Goal.* Brookings.

Rohe, William M., and Mark Lindblad. 2013. "Reexamining the Social Benefits of Homeownership after the Housing Crisis." Harvard University, Joint Center for Housing Studies.

Rohe, William M., and others. 2003. "Individual and Neighborhood Impacts of Neighborhood Reinvestment's Homeownership Pilot Program." Washington: Neighborhood Reinvestment Corporation.

Shapiro, Thomas, Tatjana Meschede, and Sam Osoro. 2013. "The Roots of the Widening Racial Wealth Gap: Explaining the Black-White Economic Divide." Waltham, Mass.: Institute on Assets and Social Policy.

Sherraden, Michael. 1991. *Assets and the Poor: A New American Welfare Policy.* Armonk, N.Y.: M. E. Sharpe.

Shiller, Robert J. 2005. *Irrational Exuberance.* New York: Crown Publishing.

Shlay, Anne B. 2006. "Low-Income Homeownership: American Dream or Delusion?" *Urban Studies* 43, no. 3: 511–31.

Sinai, Todd, and Nicholas S. Souleles. 2005. "Owner-Occupied Housing as a Hedge against Rent Risk." *Quarterly Journal of Economics* 120, no. 2: 763–89.

Turner, Tracy M., and Heather Luea. 2009. "Homeownership, Wealth Accumulation and Income Status." *Journal of Housing Economics* 18, no. 2: 104–14.

Wolff, Edward N. 2012. "The Asset Price Meltdown and the Wealth of the Middle Class." Working Paper 18559. Cambridge, Mass.: National Bureau of Economic Research.

U.S. Congress, Joint Committee on Taxation. 2013. *Present Law, Data, and Analysis Relating to Tax Incentives for Residential Real Estate.* Congressional Report JCX-10-13. 113 Cong. 1 sess. (April 22).

Van Order, Robert, and Peter Zorn. 2002. "Performance of Low-Income and Minority Mortgages." In *Low-Income Homeownership: Examining the Unexamined Goal,* edited by Nicolas Retsinas and Eric Belsky, pp. 322–47. Brookings.

Zillow. 2012. *Zillow Negative Equity Report.* June (http://zillow.mediaroom.com/file.php/1478/Zillow+Neg+Equity+Report_Q2+UPDATED.pdf).

3

Reexamining the Social Benefits of Homeownership after the Foreclosure Crisis

WILLIAM M. ROHE AND MARK R. LINDBLAD

The recent foreclosure crisis and ensuing economic recession have been unprecedented in modern times. The loss of wealth due to the decline in value of real estate has been dramatic. Between 2006 and 2011 house prices fell more than 30 percent nationally, wiping out over $8 trillion in home equity.[1] At the height of the foreclosure crisis, one of every four homeowners with mortgages owed more on their mortgages than their homes were worth.[2] Moreover, many people have been put out of their homes and had their credit ratings severely damaged. Mortgage foreclosures increased from the 1980–2006 average foreclosure rate of 0.32 percent to over 4.9 percent in 2010.[3] Between 2008 and 2011, more than 4 million homeowners lost their homes to foreclosure, and there are many more homeowners who were forced to sell, often at prices that were less than they owed on their mortgages. Recent data also indicate that there are an additional 2 million homeowners who are at least 90 days delinquent on their mortgage payments, suggesting that the high foreclosure rate will continue for some time to come.[4]

Given these recent events, it is reasonable to ask, first, if the bloom is off the rose of homeownership. One of the attractions of homeownership is that it has

1. Joint Center (2012).
2. Belsky (2013).
3. Mortgage Bankers Association (2012).
4. Joint Center (2013).

been seen as a good financial investment. The sharp decrease in housing values may have seriously undermined that view of homeownership. As one writer recently put it, "The national psyche has absorbed the tribulations of the millions of people who have been living in homes worth less than their mortgages, struggling to make payments and yet unable to sell."[5] Another attraction of homeownership is that it is perceived to provide more stability and control over one's living environment. Homeowners were thought to be more secure than renters since they were not subject to landlords raising the rent or not renewing the lease. Again, the recent spike in foreclosures and forced sales may have seriously undermined this belief among both existing and prospective homeowners. Not only have many people been directly affected by the foreclosure crisis, a much larger number have been indirectly affected by knowing someone who has or by exposure to the extensive press coverage on the crisis.

A second and related question is whether the social benefits of homeownership found in past research, such as greater political participation and positive educational outcomes for children, still apply. That research was conducted at a time when a very small proportion of homeowners were experiencing heightened economic and psychological stress due to difficulty in making mortgage payments, mortgage delinquency and foreclosure, and dramatic declines in home equity. Might the recent, noticeable increases in these problems affect the attitudes, behavior, and health of homeowners? Research, for example, has tended to support a positive relationship between homeownership and residential satisfaction. But will this relationship be as strong or hold at all given the large number of vacant homes in many neighborhoods? Other research has tended to support a positive relationship between homeownership and both psychological and physical health. Will this relationship continue given the large number of homeowners that have been under considerable stress in trying to make their mortgage payments? The answers to these questions have important policy implications as the federal commitment to and subsidy of homeownership has been justified by claims that it provides a variety of social benefits both to individuals and society.

This chapter has several purposes. First, it presents a conceptual model of how the foreclosure crisis and related recession might affect both interest in and the social impacts of homeownership. A second purpose is to review the limited empirical evidence on how, if at all, the recession and foreclosure crisis have altered interest in homeownership or its actual impacts. A third purpose is to provide an updated review of the research on the social impacts of homeownership, most of which was conducted before the recession. Fourth, we draw some preliminary conclusions about how the recession and foreclosure crisis may have altered these social impacts and what additional research is needed on

5. Shiller (2013).

this important topic. The discussion focuses on five social impacts: psychological health, physical health, parenting and children's academic achievement and behavior, social and political participation, and neighborhood-social capital.

A Conceptual Model of the Impacts of the Foreclosure Crisis on the Social Benefits of Homeownership

Both the perceived and the actual social benefits of homeownership found in previous research may have been substantially altered by the spikes in home depreciation, mortgage stress, and foreclosure in recent years. The purpose of the conceptual model presented in figure 3-1 is to explore how direct and indirect experience with homeownership during the foreclosure crisis might be expected to affect the perceived benefits of homeownership among both prospective buyers and current homeowners. For the sake of completeness, the model also suggests how the recent homeownership experience may affect the capacity to own as well as the desire to own.

Starting with the "tenure" box in the center of the model and moving to the left, the model suggests that the tenure decision—to buy or to continue renting—is a function of both the desire to own and the capacity to own. The desire to own, in turn, is influenced by the perceived benefits of owning, which include economic aspects, such as wealth creation, and social-psychological aspects, such as greater control over the living environment. Continuing to the left, the model suggests that those perceived benefits are influenced by cultural attitudes toward owning and the active promotion of homeownership by the leaders, real estate agents, builders, and others involved in the housing industry. Homeownership is an important goal of a very large percentage of Americans and has become a cultural symbol of social and economic success.[6] At the same time, the desire to own has also been reinforced by government programs and by advertising campaigns sponsored by housing industry players.[7]

We argue, however, that the perceived benefits of homeownership are also influenced by both direct and indirect experience with homeownership. This is shown in the model as a feedback loop between homeownership experience and the perceived benefits of homeownership. As mentioned above, this influence may be direct—individuals may have had a good or bad homeownership experience—or indirect—they know someone who has had a good or bad homeownership experience.

The key elements of the homeownership experience can be organized into three categories: economic, physical, and social. The economic aspects include

6. Rohe and Watson (2007).
7. Vale (2007).

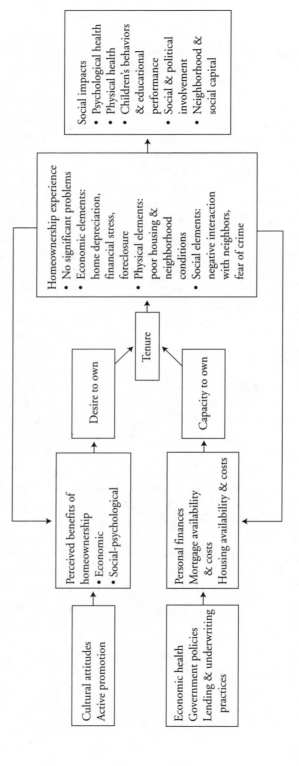

Figure 3-1. *A Conceptual Model of the Effects of the Recession on Attitudes toward and Impacts of Homeownership*

the value of the home, the mortgage as a portion of the budget, and the ability to meet mortgage payments. In most places and times, prerecession home prices increased over time, but from 2007 to 2012, a very large proportion of the housing stock depreciated. Moreover, due to the spike in unemployment and the reliance on predatory and "creative" mortgage products, many homeowners have been under great stress trying to keep up with their mortgage payments, and many of those either have been forced to move or have lost their homes through foreclosure. Physical elements of the homeownership experience include the quality of the house and the neighborhood in which the house is located. The recession may have reduced the financial abilities of homeowners to maintain their homes, and the increase in foreclosure rates may have led to neighborhood deterioration. Finally, the social elements of the homeownership experience include owners' sense of security and control over their homes. The sharp increase in foreclosures and forced sales may have decreased the sense of residential security among homeowners. It is reasonable to believe that these substantial increases in negative homeownership experiences and their coverage in the media may have altered the perceived benefits of homeownership among prospective homebuyers; hence the bifurcated feedback loop in the model. It is also reasonable to believe that the actual benefits of homeownership, as described in earlier research, may no longer be operative.

To understand how the social impacts of homeownership may have changed, it is helpful to consider the proposed theories as to what aspects of homeownership are responsible for its social impacts. Table 3-1 summarizes five major theories on how ownership may lead to specific positive outcomes and three theories on how it may lead to specific negative outcomes; it also suggests the ways that the recession may have influenced each outcome. The first theory of positive impacts is that homeownership leads to wealth creation, which in turn leads to enhanced life satisfaction, to being able to afford better quality health care, and to higher rates of civic engagement.[8]

During the recent recession, home values fell dramatically in many communities, resulting in massive decreases in household wealth. Homeowner equity plummeted by over $6 trillion.[9] This suggests that the wealth-related benefits of homeownership should be substantially reduced, particularly among those with "underwater" mortgages (that is, they owe more than the house is currently worth).

A second theory of positive impacts is that homeownership leads to greater residential stability, which, in turn, leads to better school performance among children and higher levels of civic engagement and social capital among adults.[10]

---

8. Grinstein-Weiss and others (2010); Harkness and Newman (2002).

9. Federal Reserve Bank of San Francisco (2013).

10. Bramley and Karley (2007); Haurin, Parcel, and Haurin (2002).

Table 3-1. *Theories on the Positive and Negative Social Impacts of Homeownership*

Impacts	Expected benefits or liabilities	Possible influence of the recession
Positive		
Anticipation of and actual wealth creation	Improved health, enhanced life satisfaction, civic engagement	Falling home prices reduce or turn negative both anticipated and actual wealth creation
Greater residential stability and security	Higher levels of high school and postsecondary education completion, social capital, civic engagement	Difficulty in paying mortgages and foreclosures decrease residential stability and security
Better dwelling quality	Better school performance and youth behaviors, greater residential satisfaction, greater self-esteem	Difficulty in paying for home improvements reduces the quality of dwellings
Better quality neighborhood, physically and socially	Better schools lead to better educational outcomes; higher homeownership rates lead to enhanced social capital and less crime	Foreclosures result in an increase in vacant homes and rental units in many neighborhoods, thus reducing overall neighborhood quality
Heightened sense of control, social status, accomplishment	Higher levels of life satisfaction and psychological health	Foreclosures and difficulty paying mortgages lead to lower levels of life satisfaction and psychological health
Negative		
Mobility restrictions	Homeowners have more difficulty moving to better homes and neighborhoods	The large number of underwater mortgages limit mobility
Mortgage payment stress and foreclosure	Some homeowners experience considerable stress and other psychological problems	The increase in unemployment will expand the number of homeowners who experience mortgage stress or foreclosure
Home maintenance and repair stress or impacts	Some homeowners cannot afford to maintain their homes, which may lead to health problems	Increased unemployment and underwater mortgages may lead to more unmet home repairs and maintenance

Traditionally, homeowners have remained in their homes considerably longer than renters have in rented housing.[11] Yet the recession has forced many homeowners to move because they were no longer able to pay their mortgages; thus this positive aspect of homeownership may be diminished.

A third theory of positive impacts is that homeowners enjoy better quality housing. Compared to renters, homeowners tend to live in single-family units, often with yards, and they provide more stimulating home environments for their children.[12] Recession-induced reductions in home equity and incomes, then, may have resulted in cutbacks in home maintenance and reduced the quality of the home environment, thereby muting these positive effects of ownership.

A fourth theory of positive impacts is that homeownership allows access to neighborhoods with better schools and amenities, and better physical and social conditions.[13] This theory actually concerns the neighborhood rather than the home itself. Neighborhoods with a higher percentage of single-family homes tend to be maintained at a higher quality and have lower crime rates.[14] The spike in the foreclosure rate, however, has generated an increase in vacant units in areas with high percentages of homeowners, thereby eroding overall neighborhood quality.[15]

A final theory of positive impacts is that homeowners enjoy more control over their homes and therefore experience a heightened sense of personal accomplishment and social status. This, in turn, leads to greater life satisfaction and psychological health. Here again, the heightened number of foreclosures and greater difficulty in making mortgage payments could lower life satisfaction and psychological health among homeowners.

Turning to theories of negative impacts, some have argued that homeownership can trap households, particularly minority and lower-income ones, in areas that they would rather leave.[16] Compared to renters, homeowners face higher transaction costs if they want to relocate, and their homes may be worth less than they owe on their mortgages. The recession only exacerbated this problem as falling real estate values resulted in almost a quarter of all homeowners being "underwater." The second and third negative theories suggest that some homeowners experience considerable psychological stress due to difficulty in either making mortgage payments or maintaining their homes. The recession-induced increase in unemployment and loss of home equity could certainly have increased the prevalence of these negative impacts.

11. Rohe and Stewart (1996).
12. Galster (1987); Haurin, Parcel, and Haurin (2002).
13. Bramley and Karley (2007); Holupka and Newman (2012).
14. Galster (1987).
15. Immergluck (2009).
16. South and Crowder (1997, 1998); Van Zandt and Rohe (2006).

The conceptual model presented in figure 3-1 also highlights the importance of the capacity to own, along with the desire to own, in achieving homeownership. That capacity is affected by individual personal finances (for example, income, savings, and debt), mortgage availability and cost, and the availability and cost of housing. Those factors, in turn, are affected by the status of the local and national economy, government policies, and lending practices. A more detailed discussion of this pathway is beyond the scope of this chapter.

The next section reviews the preliminary evidence on the extent to which the foreclosure crisis has, in fact, affected both the perceived as well as actual benefits of homeownership.

Impact of the Foreclosure Crisis on the Homeownership Model: Preliminary Evidence

Several recent studies address the effects of the foreclosure crisis on attitudes toward homeownership (the upper feedback pathway in the model). That research has focused on three conceptually distinct attitudes:

—the perceived benefits of homeownership as assessed by survey questions on the financial benefits of owning,

—the general desire to own as assessed by questions on homeownership as a personal desire or goal, and

—personal expectations about buying a home at some time in the future as assessed by questions asking respondents whether, were they to move, they would be more likely to buy or to rent, or if they expected to buy a home at some point in the future.

Perceived Benefits of Homeownership

Studies that address the impact of the foreclosure crisis on the perceived benefits of homeownership have been limited to assessing whether owners and renters see homeownership as a good or safe investment. This narrow focus on financial criteria is disappointing given that a recent study that asked respondents the reasons they wanted to own a home found that the three most frequently cited reasons were social considerations: providing a good place to raise children, living in a safe place, and having control over living space.[17]

A Pew Charitable Trusts survey conducted in March 2011 found that a very high percentage of people still consider financial gain as a perceived benefit of homeownership. When a national sample of respondents was asked whether buying a home was the best long-term investment a person can make, 81 percent

---

17. Drew and Herbert (2013).

either strongly or somewhat agreed that it was.[18] A 2013 MacArthur Foundation survey, however, found that only 25 percent of the respondents thought that families today were more or much more likely to build equity and wealth through homeownership than they were twenty or thirty years ago.[19] The reference to the earlier time period may help explain the differences between these two surveys.

The only longitudinal analysis on perceptions of homeownership as a good or safe investment relies on data from Fannie Mae's National Housing Survey. In comparing the responses to a survey question asked in both 2003 and 2012 on whether homeownership is a safe investment, Belsky reports that the share of mortgage holders who thought that homeownership was a good investment declined between 2003 and 2012.[20] Moreover, from 2010 to 2012, the share that viewed housing as a safe investment fell from 82 to 72 percent. Notwithstanding this drop, in 2012 almost three quarters of the respondents still believed housing was a good investment.

Drew and Herbert disaggregate perceptions of the financial benefits of homeownership using Fannie Mae National Housing Survey data collected from June 2010 to October 2011.[21] Overall, they report that 87 percent of the respondents felt that owning a home made more financial sense than renting. Compared to current owners, renters were considerably less likely to view homeownership as financially better than renting, as were younger and lower-income respondents. In none of the subgroups, however, did the percentage favoring ownership drop below 73 percent.

Drew and Herbert also assessed the relationship between the belief that owning is the best financial choice and respondents' personal experiences with housing problems, such as being underwater on their mortgages or knowing of defaults in their neighborhoods.[22] Somewhat surprisingly, their analysis found no statistically significant relationship between personal experience with housing problems and views of owning as a better financial choice among both the renters and current mortgage holders. Two other recent studies, by Collins and Choi and by Bracha and Jamison, also report no statistically significant relationship between both local housing price changes and foreclosure rates, and respondents' views on the financial sense of owning versus renting.[23]

In sum the available evidence suggests that people's perceptions of homeownership as a good investment were not dramatically affected by the foreclosure

18. Pew Research Center (2011).
19. MacArthur Foundation (2013).
20. Belsky (2013).
21. Drew and Herbert (2013).
22. Drew and Herbert (2013).
23. Collins and Choi (2010); Bracha and Jamison (2011).

crisis. The percentage of people holding those views certainly dropped during the early stages of the foreclosure crisis, but that proportion seems to have rebounded relatively quickly. There is also a surprising lack of association between personal experience with housing problems and attitudes toward the financial benefits of homeownership. Unfortunately, we could find little research that has addressed the impact of the foreclosure crisis on other perceived benefits of homeownership, such as whether it provides a greater sense of control.

General Desire to Own

Three recent surveys have assessed the desire to own a home, but due to lack of longitudinal data, it is not clear how the foreclosure crisis has influenced this sentiment. A *New York Times*–CBS poll conducted in June 2011 asked all respondents, "If you were going to move and could afford either, would you prefer to rent or buy?" Seventy-three percent of the respondents said they would prefer to buy. The renters in the sample were asked, "Regardless of whether you think you can afford it, would you like to own someday or would you prefer to continue renting?" A full 85 percent of the respondents said they would like to own someday. Another question asked, "How important a part of the American Dream is owning a home?" A full 89 percent of the respondents thought it was either "very" or "somewhat" important.[24] Similarly, a 2012 survey asked renters, "Is one of your goals to eventually own a home?" A somewhat lower but still substantial 68 percent of respondents said that it was.[25] Finally, in a recent poll sponsored by the MacArthur Foundation, 72 percent of renters said that homeownership was something that they aspired to, and 49 percent reported some degree of worry about not being able to someday own a home.[26] Given these relatively high percentages, it seems safe to conclude that if the foreclosure crisis did influence the desire to own, the effect was neither dramatic nor long term.

Expectations about Buying

Other research has addressed the conceptually distinct indicator of whether respondents expect, rather than desire, to buy a home at some point in the future. One longitudinal study found that the intentions of lower-income renters to eventually purchase a home decreased with the downturn in the housing market between 2004 and 2007.[27] Using more recent Fannie Mae National Housing Survey data, Drew and Herbert construct a measure that distinguishes between those who expect to buy at some point in the future, including current

24. *New York Times* (2011).
25. National Association of Home Builders (2012).
26. MacArthur Foundation (2013).
27. Cohen and others (2009).

homeowners, and those who expect to always rent.[28] Their findings show that 89 percent of all respondents expect to buy a home or another home at some point in the future. However, when only current renters are considered, the percent who expect to buy falls to 74 percent. They also report that black and Hispanic renters are more likely than white renters to expect to own, while both older renters and owners with mortgages are less likely than those under thirty-five years of age to expect to buy in the future. Again, Drew and Herbert report a surprising lack of association between personal exposure to housing market distress and the expectation of buying, although underwater homeowners were significantly less likely to say they expected to buy in the future.[29] Similarly, Martin reports that even among people who lost their homes to foreclosure, most want to buy homes again.[30] Yet those who experience foreclosure reframe homeownership by saying that homes purchased with mortgages are owned by the bank rather than the homebuyer.

Other research has analyzed responses to a question asking whether respondents think it is a good time to buy a home. Engelhardt, for example, suggests that believing it is a good time to buy is an indicator of "positive home-buying sentiment."[31] Using data from the University of Michigan's Survey of Consumer Attitudes from 1993 through the first quarter of 2011, he reports significant declines in the percentage of persons who thought it was a good time to buy in the mid-2000s. By the first quarter of 2011, 80 percent of homeowners thought it was a good time to buy, which was close to the survey's long-term average, while only 63 percent of renters thought it was a good time to buy, which was well below the long-term average.

In sum, recent research on home-buying expectations supports the conclusion that very large percentages of Americans still expect to buy a home at some time in the future. The foreclosure crisis had a negative impact on those expectations, but they have rebounded quite rapidly, particularly among current homeowners. Moreover, the finding that younger renters and owners are more likely than their older counterparts to expect to own bodes well for the future of the homeownership market.

The Social Benefits of Homeownership

This section updates the research literature on the impacts of homeownership on five social constructs: psychological health, physical health, parenting and

28. Drew and Herbert (2013).
29. Drew and Herbert (2013).
30. Martin (2012).
31. Engelhardt (2011).

children's behavior, social and political involvement, and social capital and neighborhood perceptions. The last comprehensive review of the social benefits of homeownership was done by Herbert and Belsky in 2006.[32] Since then much new research has been conducted, often utilizing stronger study design.

Most of the research conducted before 2000 was limited in several ways. First, it failed to control for many covariates of homeownership such as income, wealth, time in residence, and neighborhood characteristics. Thus the associations between homeownership and the outcome variables of interest may have been a result of these uncontrolled covariates and not of homeownership itself. Second, very few studies addressed the potential for self-selection to bias the relationships reported. They did not account for the possibility that certain types of people, say, those who plan on staying in a place a long time or those who value citizen involvement, are more likely to buy homes. Thus the findings may be due to the characteristics of those who buy homes rather than the experience of owning a home. More sophisticated research addresses this potential for self-selection bias by using two-stage models that first predict the decision to own or rent. Examples include propensity score analysis and instrumental variables.[33] Finally, many of the earlier studies analyzed cross-sectional data sets that are limited in their ability to draw causal inferences. They cannot, for example, determine whether homeownership promotes good health or whether healthier people are more likely to be homeowners.

The reviews of the research literature on each of the five social constructs mentioned above begin with a discussion of the importance of the construct, the theory as to how homeownership affects the construct, a summary of the research findings with emphasis on more recent research, and a discussion of the aspects of homeownership that appear to be responsible for any associations found.

Homeownership and Psychological Health

The central tenet underlying the psychological impacts of housing is that dwellings can influence what people think and how they feel. If this is true, then housing can play an important role not only in promoting psychological well-being but also in reducing the incidence and severity of stress that can lead to psychopathologies and mental illnesses. One important characteristic of housing is whether it is owned or rented. Homeownership is associated with other housing characteristics, such as single-family versus multifamily designs, but beyond that association, many believe that compared to renting, ownership itself has positive

---

32. Herbert and Belsky (2006). For earlier reviews, see Dietz and Haurin (2003); Rohe, Van Zandt, and McCarthy (2002).

33. For propensity score analysis, see Guo and Fraser (2009). For instrumental variables, see Murnane and Willett (2011).

psychological impacts. Others suggest that homeownership in certain situations and for certain people can have decidedly negative effects.

THE THEORY

Prior research identifies three ways that homeownership may influence psychological health: self-esteem, perceived control, and financial security. Rohe and Stegman suggest that becoming a homeowner may be seen by both oneself and others as a sign of success.[34] As discussed above, despite the financial and foreclosure crises, owning a home remains an important desire for many Americans. Becoming a homeowner, then, may lead to higher levels of life satisfaction and psychological health, such as greater self-esteem and less depression. Of course, for those who lose their homes, the reverse could be true as it may be experienced as a significant life failure.

Perceived control is a second way that homeownership might influence psychological health. Renters are limited in the customization of their dwelling and have less control over their time in residence. Landlords can decide to not renew the lease or to substantially increase rent. In contrast, homeowners can customize their dwellings in ways that are not possible for renters. Homeowners who stay current on their mortgages can also make their own decision whether to stay in their house or move. Thus homeowners may have a heightened sense of control over their living environment, which may lead to greater residential and life satisfaction and to less depression.

The wealth-building potential of owning a home may also influence psychological health. Fixed-rate mortgages decrease housing costs over time relative to inflation. Repaying principal may combine with house price appreciation to generate gains in home equity. Together these factors may help build wealth among homeowners. Increased wealth, in turn, may translate into higher life satisfaction and self-esteem. If financial interests explain the link between homeownership and psychological outcomes, an important corollary is that homeowners who experience decreases in home equity from depreciating house values, predatory mortgages, or home foreclosure should experience negative effects on psychological health.

RESEARCH ON POSITIVE PSYCHOLOGICAL HEALTH

Early research on how psychological health might be influenced by homeownership emphasized its impacts on psychological orientation. That research found, for example, positive associations between homeownership and overall life satisfaction.[35] This also held true for narrower measures of residential and housing

---

34. Rohe and Stegman (1994a).
35. Rohe and Basolo (1997); Rohe and Stegman (1994a); Rossi and Weber (1996).

satisfaction.[36] However, the research findings on other positive psychological constructs, including perceived control and self-esteem, were mixed. Rossi and Weber reported a positive association between ownership and self-esteem in a cross-sectional study with limited controls, whereas neither Rohe and Stegman nor Rohe and Basolo find any association when using longitudinal data and controlling for housing condition.[37] In general, the earlier research on the impacts of homeownership on psychological health suffered from the limitations discussed above.

A second generation of research addresses some of the shortcomings of prior work. Three rigorous studies have linked homeownership to positive psychological impacts. Diaz-Serrano studied a panel sample of Europeans from 1994–2001.[38] A portion of the sample purchased the homes that they were renting, changing ownership without changing units or neighborhoods. This feature allowed a rare natural experiment given that the housing unit and neighborhood conditions did not change as tenure type changed. The results indicate that homeownership was positively associated with residential satisfaction.

Manturuk studied the connection between homeownership, sense of control, and mental health.[39] Data came from the Community Advantage Panel Survey (CAPS), which consists of a sample of homeowners who received affordable mortgages and a comparison group of low-income renters. The study used established measures shown to be reliable by other researchers. The findings demonstrate an expected link between homeownership and mental health, but the homeownership effect is entirely mediated by a higher sense of control among homeowners. Furthermore, the sense of control is partially mediated by housing experiences: those homeowners who experienced a mortgage delinquency had a lower sense of control than homeowners who had never been delinquent. This study accounts for selection bias while demonstrating how sense of control and financial hardship are causal mechanisms that link homeownership to mental health.

In a separate study, Manturuk, Riley, and Ratcliffe studied how the financial crisis affected the financial satisfaction of CAPS homeowners versus renters.[40] In this study the authors adjusted for selection into homeownership and controlled for household income, net worth, and other socioeconomic variables. Their findings indicate that during the financial crisis, renters and owners experienced similar levels of financial hardship, yet homeowners reported feeling more satisfied with their financial situation.

36. Danes and Morris (1986); Kinsey and Lane (1983); Lam (1985); Morris, Crull, and Winter (1976); Rohe and Basolo (1997); Rohe and Stegman (1994a); Varady (1983).

37. Rossi and Weber (1996); Rohe and Stegman (1994a); Rohe and Basolo (1997).

38. Diaz-Serrano (2009).

39. Manturuk (2012).

40. Manturuk, Riley, and Ratcliffe (2012).

RESEARCH ON NEGATIVE PSYCHOLOGICAL HEALTH

An important contribution of recent research on the impacts of homeownership has been the documentation of negative psychological consequences of mortgage delinquency and foreclosure. The preponderance of research on the psychological impacts of homeownership has been conducted during times of appreciating housing markets and low mortgage delinquency and foreclosure rates. With the recent foreclosure crisis, however, a growing number of researchers have turned their attention to assessing whether negative experiences with homeownership influence psychological stress and mental illness.

In work that predates the foreclosure crisis, Cairney and Boyle linked homeownership and mortgage delinquency to depression, loneliness, and restlessness.[41] They use data from the 1991 General Social Survey and find that homeowners have lower levels of psychological distress than renters. The authors also find that homeowners without mortgages reported lower levels of distress than homeowners with mortgages. Their analysis, however, does not adjust for selection bias or other potentially confounding variables such as dwelling quality.

Through a series of focus groups held in five U.S. cities, Fields, Libman, and Saegert investigated the psychological impacts of mortgage delinquency and foreclosure.[42] Those behind on their mortgage payments reported a variety of negative psychological emotions including anxiety, stress, fear, hopelessness, and depression. Other feelings associated with mortgage delinquency included confusion, victimization, and a sense of betrayal. The authors identify an "emotionality of delinquency" that encompasses respondents' holistic negative psychological responses to mortgage delinquency and foreclosure.

Another qualitative study of mortgage foreclosure was undertaken by Bowdler, Quercia, and Smith.[43] They conducted interviews with twenty-five Latino families who had recently experienced foreclosure. Their findings suggest elevated stress, interpersonal strain, and mental illness during foreclosure proceedings and a sense of loss and disillusionment after the foreclosure was completed.

Pollack and Lynch studied how depression among people receiving foreclosure counseling in Philadelphia compared to a random sample.[44] The authors identify a higher incidence of depression among the group in foreclosure counseling. However, depression, as well as most covariates, was measured in different ways across the two groups. Furthermore, the two samples differed greatly, with the

41. Cairney and Boyle (2004).

42. Fields and others (2007); Fields, Libman, and Saegert, (2010); Saegert, Fields, and Libman (2011); Libman, Fields, and Saegert (2012).

43. Bowdler, Quercia, and Smith (2010).

44. Pollack and Lynch (2009).

comparison group representing the general population rather than homeowners experiencing overall financial distress.

Osypuk and others examined depression among African American mothers in Detroit who had recently given birth.[45] Depression was measured with a validated twenty-item scale. Eight percent of the sample reported a mortgage foreclosure within the past two years. The findings suggest higher levels of severe depression among those who reported a home foreclosure. This cross-sectional study, however, did not control for the time since foreclosure, prior history of depression, and other potentially confounding variables.

Burgard, Seefeldt, and Zelner studied the health effects of housing instability, defined as late rent or mortgage payments, foreclosure, displacement, or homelessness.[46] Housing instability was found to be associated with validated measures of anxiety and depression, but the analysis was cross-sectional.

Two longitudinal studies used stronger research designs that controlled for psychiatric history and financial stressors. McLaughlin and others assessed mental health using validated measures of psychiatric symptomatology.[47] Loss of the home through foreclosure was associated with elevated levels of general anxiety disorder and major depression, but only twenty-five respondents reported home repossession between surveys. Alley and others studied mortgage delinquency in the Health and Retirement Study. They found that older U.S. adults who reported a mortgage delinquency had more depressive symptoms.[48]

Foreclosure *rates* in geographic areas also have been associated with mental illness. Two studies link foreclosures aggregated at the zip code level to medical diagnoses identified through hospital discharge data. Menzel, Moonie, and Thompson-Robinson track diagnostic changes between 2005 and 2008 for twenty-five stress-related measures.[49] They identify a spike in bipolar and depressive disorders in 2007 that coincides with local foreclosures. Currie and Tekin study high foreclosure areas and measure nonelective hospitalizations and emergency room visits.[50] They find positive associations between foreclosure rates and elevated rates of suicide attempts, heart attacks, and strokes. These associations are stronger among minorities, especially Hispanics. Houle and Light analyze state level data and link suicide rates to home foreclosures between 2005 and 2010. When compared to foreclosure starts, foreclosure sales that became real estate owned had the stronger association to suicide rates.[51] The findings of these

45. Osypuk and others (2012).
46. Burgard, Seefeldt, and Zelner (2012).
47. McLaughlin and others (2012).
48. Alley and others (2011).
49. Menzel, Moonie, and Thompson-Robinson (2012).
50. Currie and Tekin (2011).
51. Houle and Light (2014).

three studies are suggestive but far from definitive. The aggregated data do not enable linking of individual foreclosed homeowners to the observed stress disorders and cannot identify whether the home foreclosure itself is the causal factor in psychological stress.

In sum, although the research evidence supports an association between homeownership and both residential and financial satisfaction, evidence of its independent impact on self-esteem, sense of control, and other dimensions of positive psychological health is still limited. The research on the negative impacts on psychological health is also constrained by relatively weak research designs, but it is consistent in finding higher levels of psychological stress, anxiety, and depression among homeowners who are delinquent on their mortgages or who have experience with home foreclosure.

WHAT ASPECTS OF OWNERSHIP SEEM TO BE RESPONSIBLE FOR THE IMPACTS FOUND?

All of the empirical studies above suggest mechanisms by which homeownership could influence mental health. Manturuk shows that sense of control and financial hardship entirely mediate the homeownership effect.[52] In explaining why homeowners have greater financial satisfaction, Manturuk, Riley, and Ratcliffe suggest that owning a home gives people a sense of stability which reduces stress and helps them manage financial hardship.[53] Diaz-Serrano controls for residential mobility and finds that it is not responsible for the positive associations found between homeownership and residential satisfaction.[54] This leads the author to conclude that there is something about ownership itself that is qualitatively different than renting.

Turning to explanations for the negative influence of mortgage delinquency and foreclosure on psychological health, several authors suggest that home foreclosure likely interacts with other stressful events in a homeowner's life.[55] Adverse events such as job loss or divorce may put people at greater risk for psychological stress when home foreclosure starts. The finding by Osypuk and others that housing stressors amplified severe depressive symptoms among new mothers is consistent with this explanation.[56] The drawn-out nature of the foreclosure process may also play an important role. Foreclosure proceedings take months or sometimes years. Thus the prospect of being displaced from one's

---

52. Manturuk (2012).

53. Manturuk, Riley, and Ratcliffe (2012).

54. Diaz-Serrano (2009).

55. Bennett, Scharoun-Lee, and Tucker-Seeley (2009); Fields and others (2007); Libman, Fields, and Saegert (2012).

56. Osypuk and others (2012).

home is a chronic stressor.[57] Finally, Saegert, Fields, and Libman suggest that foreclosure adversely affects mental and physical health by extracting human, social, and financial assets from homeowners and that this may be magnified for first-generation homeowners and for African American households.[58]

Missing from the research on the psychological impacts of foreclosure is clarity about the various stages of home foreclosure and how each might affect mental health. Most foreclosure studies conflate the start of foreclosure proceedings with that of household displacement and actual sale of the home through foreclosure. The mental health impacts may differ for each stage of the foreclosure process. None of the authors clarified how the timing of mental health assessments related to post-foreclosure outcomes such as household displacement, home sale, or mortgage modification. Another unexplored question is at what point people recover psychologically from home foreclosure. Clearly more research is needed to evaluate mental health outcomes at all stages and outcomes of home foreclosure proceedings.

Homeownership and Physical Health

The impact of housing quality and crowding on physical health has been the subject of many research studies. That research has documented strong positive associations between living in poor quality housing and a range of health problems including respiratory conditions, such as asthma; exposure to toxic substances, such as lead; and injuries, such as burns and falls.[59] Research has also focused on the role of overcrowding in the onset of health problems.[60] There is, however, a surprising lack of research on the independent role of housing tenure on health.

THE THEORY

The most obvious connection between homeownership and physical health outcomes is through its relationship to housing conditions. The argument is that owner occupants, compared to landlords, have more incentives for maintaining their homes at a higher level. Housing conditions affect owner occupants on a day-to-day basis; thus they are more likely to act to correct problems as they arise. The condition of owner-occupied homes is also more likely to be taken as a reflection of the occupants' own values or behaviors; they cannot blame poor housing conditions on recalcitrant landlords. In fact, research has shown that the

---

57. Bennett, Scharoun-Lee, and Tucker-Seeley (2009).
58. Saegert, Fields, and Libman (2011).
59. Krieger and Higgins (2002); Rohe and Han (2012); Wilkinson (1999).
60. Cohen (2011); Evans and others (1998); U.K. Office of the Deputy Minister (2004).

homes of owners are generally in better condition than those of renters.[61] Better housing conditions among owners, then, may result in improved health outcomes, particularly if those conditions are directly linked to the genesis of health problems such as dampness, toxic substances, and the presence of allergens.[62]

As discussed above, homeownership is also associated with residential stability, which may result in a greater knowledge of local health care resources, more extensive social support networks, and lower levels of stress. On the other hand, physical health outcomes may be negative for homeowners who would like to move due to difficulties in maintaining their properties, paying their mortgage, or undesirable neighborhood conditions but cannot because their property is worth less than they owe on their mortgages.[63]

Another possible link between homeownership and physical health is that homeowners may tap into home equity they may have accrued to pay for better medical care.[64] However, a counterargument is that assuming the costs of ownership are greater than the cost of renting, homeowners, at least in the early years, may actually have less money to spend on health care. This suggests that the impacts of homeownership on health outcomes may depend on both the relative costs of renting versus owning and the amount of home equity that an owner has at a particular point in time.

RESEARCH ON PHYSICAL HEALTH OUTCOMES

Much of the research on the relationship between tenure and health outcomes has been conducted in the United Kingdom, where homeownership is often used as a proxy for socioeconomic status because the national census does not collect information on income or wealth.[65] Those studies have consistently found positive associations between ownership and a variety of self-reported health indicators.[66] Rahkonen, Arber, and Lahelma, for example, report that homeownership is strongly associated with the health of young adults in Britain.[67] Given the lack of controls for income and wealth, however, this and other studies based on British census data cannot isolate the independent impacts of ownership.

Several British studies address the relationship between homeownership and health using survey data that do contain measures of income. Ellaway and Macintyre, for example, analyze survey data from two neighborhoods in Glasgow

---

61. Galster (1987); Rohe and Stewart (1996).
62. Ellaway and Macintyre (1998); Macintyre and others (1998); Macintyre and others (2003).
63. Smith and others (2003).
64. Rasmussen and Megbolugbe (1997).
65. Macintyre and others (2003).
66. Filakti and Fox (1995); Gould and Jones (1996).
67. Rahkonen, Arber, and Lahelma (1995).

and find that owner occupancy is related to several health indicators even after controlling for income and other socioeconomic characteristics.[68] They also find that homeowners were less likely to report a range of health-related housing problems such as hazards, dampness, and noise. When those housing problems were controlled, however, the impact of tenure on health was no longer statistically significant. In a larger sample of residents in western Scotland, Macintyre and others find similar results.[69] The magnitude of the associations between homeownership and a range of physical and mental health indicators are substantially reduced after housing and neighborhood conditions are controlled. The conclusions drawn from these cross-sectional studies are limited, however, by the small number of control variables included in the analysis and the failure to account for selection bias.

Several U.S. studies have also addressed the association between homeownership and physical health. Robert and House assess the associations between homeownership and health and find that after controlling for education, income, and liquid assets, homeownership was positively related to self-reported health but not to chronic conditions among many of the age categories considered.[70] When Rossi and Weber analyzed data from the National Study of Family Health, they found that self-reported health among homeowners was higher than that among renters.[71] The control variables, however, were limited to age and socioeconomic status. These authors also analyzed data from the General Social Survey and found no statistically significant relationship between ownership and self-reported health.

Several studies have also assessed whether mortgage stress, mortgage default, or foreclosure affects physical health. Nettleton and Burrows analyzed data from the British Household Panel Survey to assess the impacts of mortgage arrears on the subjective well-being and number of doctor visits of homeowners.[72] They find that being in mortgage arrears is associated with lower scores on a general well-being scale for both men and women, and it increased the likelihood that men visited the doctor. The control variables, however, were limited to income, employment, and age. Alley and others, in analyzing a representative sample of U.S. adults over fifty, report that those delinquent on mortgage payments had poorer physical health.[73] Pollack and others used a case-controlled research design to assess rates of hypertension and renal disease and the number of visits to the

---

68. Ellaway and Macintyre (1998).
69. Macintyre and others (2003).
70. Robert and House (1996).
71. Rossi and Weber (1996).
72. Nettleton and Burrows (1998).
73. Alley and others (2011).

hospital over a two-year period prior to foreclosure.[74] Those who experienced foreclosure were found to have higher rates of hypertension and renal disease and were more likely to visit the emergency room, even after controlling for several sociodemographic characteristics. Finally, Cannuscio and others, using the results of an Internet survey conducted in the four U.S. states with the highest foreclosure rates, compare self-reported indicators of health among those who reported no financial strain, moderate financial strain, being in the process of default or foreclosure, and renters.[75] They find that owners who reported no strain had the best health, followed by owners reporting moderate strain and renters. Homeowners who reported being in default reported the poorest health. None of these studies, however, speak to the causal direction between foreclosure and health.

In sum, although many studies have documented an association between homeownership and physical health, there is no convincing evidence that homeownership *causes* better health. Even with the introduction of a limited set of control variables, the simple associations found tend to become nonsignificant, and none of the studies reviewed addressed the issue of selection bias. The research on the impacts of mortgage delinquency and foreclosure on physical health is consistent in finding negative health impacts, but again, the circumstances that led to subjects' inability to pay their mortgages were not controlled in those studies. Clearly much additional research is needed on this topic.

What Aspects of Ownership Seem to Be Responsible for the Impacts Found?

The limited research on the impacts of homeownership on physical health supports the theory that the impact, if there is one, is through its association with higher quality housing and neighborhood conditions. Overall, homeowners have been found to live in better quality houses and neighborhoods, and thus they have better health outcomes. In several studies, when those factors are controlled, ownership does not have an independent impact on physical health. The findings of Robert and House provide some support for the theory that the impact of homeownership on health is through its association with wealth creation, as they find that assets are important in predicting health outcomes.[76] Thus, to the extent that homeownership leads to additional assets, it should enhance health.

The literature on ownership and physical health also suggests that this relationship may vary depending on the homeowner's ability to keep current with mortgage payments. Rather than enhancing physical health, mortgage payment

---

74. Pollack and others (2011)
75. Cannuscio and others (2012).
76. Robert and House (1996).

stress may result in health problems. Moreover, those whose health is in decline may find that homeownership adds to their health problems.[77]

Homeownership, Parenting, and Children's Behavior

Beyond the potential impacts on adults, homeownership also may exert an important influence on the cognitive abilities, school performance, and behaviors of children.

THE THEORY

Through what mechanisms might living in a home that is owned, rather than rented, impart benefits? A variety of answers to this question have been suggested in the literature. One compelling argument is that children benefit from the residential stability associated with homeownership. Research consistently finds that the average time of residence among homeowners is substantially longer than that of renters.[78] The children of homeowners, then, may benefit from this stability in several ways. First, they do not change schools as often. Children who change schools often have been found to do considerably worse in school.[79] Second, residential stability may increase parent participation in local civic organizations, thereby building social networks that are supportive of positive child behaviors. Haurin, Parcel, and Haurin argue that residential stability may "create neighborhood networks that may promote positive child outcomes."[80] Third, some have suggested that homeownership results in access to better quality neighborhoods and schools.[81] Housing that is for sale tends to be located in higher-income, better quality neighborhoods and is often served by better quality schools than areas dominated by rental housing. Fourth, homeownership may require parents to learn home repair and financial, and interpersonal skills that they then pass along to their children.[82] Fifth, homeowners may create a more stimulating home environment for their children.[83] Sixth, improved self-esteem and reduced financial stress among homeowning parents may affect children's behaviors. The improved self-esteem associated with homeownership may translate into more positive interactions with their children. "Greater emotional support should lead to better cognitive outcomes and fewer behavioral problems."[84] Reductions in

77. Smith and others (2003).
78. Rohe and Stewart (1996).
79. Mohanty and Raut (2009).
80. Haurin, Parcel, and Haurin (2002, p. 647).
81. Bramley and Karley (2007); Holupka and Newman (2012).
82. Green and White (1997).
83. Haurin, Parcel, and Haurin (2002).
84. Haurin, Parcel, and Haurin (2002, p. 642).

financial stress due to the accumulation of home equity may have similar positive impacts on parent-child interactions.[85]

Research on Child Outcomes and Parenting

There is a particularly large amount of recent research on the impacts of homeownership on children's cognitive ability and behavioral outcomes. Unfortunately, many of the studies utilize different measures of childhood outcomes—including school performance, cognitive ability, educational attainment, and teenage childbirth—so the number of studies on any one outcome measure is limited. Research has been conducted on the relationship between housing tenure and parenting behaviors, including time spent reading to children, time children spend watching "screens," school involvement, and parental supervision.

Homeownership and Cognitive Ability

The impact of homeownership on child cognitive ability is the most often studied outcome. Although there is some support for the conclusion that homeownership has a positive impact on cognitive ability, most of the better-designed research indicates that once other variables are controlled, the impact of homeownership is not statistically significant.

Based on an analysis of longitudinal data from the National Longitudinal Survey of Youth, Haurin, Parcel, and Haurin found that after controlling for individual and household characteristics—including income, wealth, the gender of the child, and county-level socioeconomic characteristics—the children of homeowning parents had math achievement test scores 9 percent higher and reading achievement scores 7 percent higher than the children of renters.[86] These differences were statistically significant at the 0.1 level. They suggested that these findings resulted from homeowners providing more stimulating home environments for their children.

Four other studies, however, found no statistically significant relationship between homeownership and children's cognitive abilities. Holupka and Newman, in analyzing data from the Panel Study of Income Dynamics (PSID and its Child Development Supplement), did not find a statistically significant relationship between homeownership and measures of either verbal or math ability.[87] Similarly, Barker and Miller, in analyzing both the PSID and the National Longitudinal Survey of Youth data, report that after controlling for mobility, wealth, dwelling types, and vehicle ownership, homeownership had no significant impact

85. Grinstein-Weiss and others (2010); Harkness and Newman (2003).
86. Haurin, Parcel, and Haurin (2002).
87. Holupka and Newman (2012).

on math and reading test scores.[88] Finally, Mohanty and Raut, in analyzing four
different national data sets, report that after controlling for home environment,
neighborhood quality, and residential stability, homeownership had no independent impact on the cognitive abilities of children in any of the four data sets.[89]

Other studies have looked at the impacts of homeownership on high school
and college completion rates. The majority of those studies find that homeownership does positively impact completion rates. Green and White, in analyzing PSID and Public Use Microdata Sample data, report that the children of
homeowners were significantly less likely to drop out of school, yet key variables
including parental wealth, neighborhood attributes, and mobility were not controlled.[90] Aaronson replicated Green and White's analysis and included mobility
as a control variable.[91] He found that the impact of homeownership was reduced,
but it remained statistically significant.

In analyzing a low-income subsample from the PSID, Harkness and Newman
report a positive relationship between homeownership and both high school and
postsecondary education, but they were unable to control for important family
characteristics.[92] Galster and others, in analyzing PSID and U.S. Census data,
report a positive relationship between homeownership and the attainment of
both high school and college degrees, although those relationships fall below
statistical significance when residential stability is controlled.[93] Finally, Green,
Painter, and White tested to see if the amount of the down payments made on
homes influences the degree to which the children of homeowners drop out of
high school by age seventeen.[94] Analyzing PSID data, they find that the children
of homeowners are generally less likely to drop out of school than those of renters, but that this did not apply for homeowners who made no down payment.
This benefit was also found to decrease as time in residence increased. Stable
long-term renters showed results similar to those of homeowners.

Children's Behaviors

Several studies have addressed the impacts of homeownership on child and
teen behaviors. One set of studies assesses the impacts of homeownership on
indexes of either behavioral problems, such as acting out or withdrawal, or positive behaviors, such as getting along with others or thinking before acting. That
research finds either that homeownership does not have a statistically significant

88. Barker and Miller (2009).
89. Mohanty and Raut (2009).
90. Green and White (1997).
91. Aaronson (2000).
92. Harkness and Newman (2003).
93. Galster and others (2007).
94. Green, Painter, and White (2012).

impact on those indexes or that the impacts are confined to specific population subgroups. After controlling for socioeconomic variables, Haurin, Parcel, and Haurin report that homeownership had a small, nonsignificant impact on their behavioral problems index.[95] Similarly, Holupka and Newman, in their study of a lower-income minority sample, find no statistically significant associations between homeownership and behavioral problems in any of their subsamples.[96] In the CAPS sample, Grinstein-Weiss and others found no statistically significant associations between homeownership and a positive behavior index.[97] Such a relationship was found, however, among a subsample of respondents who lived in higher-density areas. This study is limited, however, by its nonrandom sample and lack of controls for length of ownership and residential mobility.

Several other studies have assessed the impact of homeownership on teen childbirth. Green and White reported that the teenage daughters of homeowners were less likely to have a child by the age 18, although as mentioned above, controls for parental wealth, neighborhood attributes, and mobility were not included in the analysis.[98] In a more recent follow-up study, Green, Painter, and White report that their earlier findings hold for homeowners who made a down payment but not for those who failed to make a down payment.[99] They also report that the positive impacts of homeownership attenuated as length of tenure increased. Studies by Galster and others and by Harkness and Newman, however, found no statistically significant relationships between homeownership and teenage daughters having a child.[100]

ENGAGED PARENTING

The impacts of homeownership on parenting have also been addressed in several studies. Grinstein-Weiss and others analyzed CAPS data and found that once they controlled for covariates, the homeowners exhibited no greater levels of parental supervision, expectations that their children will go to college, or volunteering at their children's schools.[101] In another analysis using the CAPS data, Grinstein-Weiss and others did find that homeowners were more likely to limit the amount of screen time allowed their children and to involve children in organized activities.[102] Yet they were no more likely to be involved in their children's school and were less likely to read to their children. Given the small sample in these analyses, it is premature to draw firm conclusions from them.

95. Haurin, Parcel, and Haurin (2002).
96. Holupka and Newman (2012).
97. Grinstein-Weiss and others (2012).
98. Green and White (1997).
99. Green, Painter, and White (2012).
100. Galster and others (2007); Harkness and Newman (2003).
101. Grinstein-Weiss and others (2011).
102. Grinstein-Weiss and others (2010).

In sum, the weight of the evidence does not support the proposition that homeownership has a positive impact on the cognitive abilities of children or that it is related to measures of either positive or negative behaviors, while research on it effect on teen births and parenting behaviors has elicited mixed results. However, the research does support an association between homeownership and the completion of high school and postsecondary education.

WHAT ASPECTS OF HOMEOWNERSHIP SEEM TO BE RESPONSIBLE FOR THE IMPACTS FOUND?

Most of the studies reviewed attempt to shed light on the aspects of homeownership that are responsible for the positive associations found between homeownership and child outcomes. Several studies suggest that the key aspect of homeownership is its relation to residential stability. In several instances studies find positive and statistically significant relationships between homeownership and child outcomes only to see those relationships disappear once length of residence is added as a control variable.[103] In other instances the positive and statistically significant relationships diminish but remain significant.[104] Thus there is considerable evidence suggesting that residential stability is responsible for some of the benefits that have been attributed to homeownership.

Another aspect of homeownership that has been studied is its relationship to the quality of home environments. Both Haurin, Parcel, and Haurin and Mohanty and Raut conducted analyses that support the idea that homeowners, due to greater financial incentives to invest in their homes, provide healthier and more stimulating home environments, which in turn, result in positive child outcomes.[105] Haurin, Parcel, and Haurin trace the influence of homeownership through its impacts on the quality of the home environment, while Mohanty and Raut find that once the quality of the home environment is controlled, the effect of homeownership becomes nonsignificant.[106] Consequently they argue that "subsidized ownership can lead to better child outcomes to the extent that it places a child in a better home environment, in a more stable residence and in a better neighborhood."[107] Clearly more research needs to be done to isolate the aspects of homeownership that are responsible for any positive associations between homeownership and child outcomes.

103. Barker and Miller (2009); Galster and others (2007); Mohanty and Raut (2009).
104. Aaronson (2000).
105. Haurin, Parcel, and Haurin (2002); Mohanty and Raut (2009).
106. Haurin, Parcel, and Haurin (2002); Mohanty and Raut (2009).
107. Mohanty and Raut (2009, p. 465).

Homeownership and Social and Political Participation

Citizen participation in political and social activities, such as voting and involvement in neighborhood and community groups, is an important aspect of American culture. Our democratic form of government is predicated on the assumption that citizens will actively participate in the governing process. A primary form of political participation is voting in national, state, and local elections, but other forms include supporting candidates and calling or writing elected officials. At the same time, there is a long tradition of citizen involvement in voluntary organizations that seek to supplement or expand the issues addressed by government. Citizens join neighborhood organizations, for example, to pick up litter, improve the local schools, or address affordable housing issues. Such volunteer activities are important to the quality of life in American communities.

THE THEORY

Previous research and writing on the link between homeownership and political and social participation has suggested two explanations for the higher rates of participation among homeowners: protecting economic interests and protecting social-psychological interests. The economic argument suggests that, compared to renters, homeowners have greater economic investment in their homes, and thus it is reasonable to expect that they will be more likely to participate in both political and social activities to protect and enhance that investment.[108] Moreover, homeowners have significantly higher transaction costs associated with moving. Owners have to pay a real estate agent, mortgage, and assorted fees when they sell an existing home and buy a new one. While renters also have costs associated with moving, they are typically a small fraction of those borne by owners.

The social argument for greater participation among homeowners is that, compared to renters, homeowners become more emotionally attached to their homes and neighborhoods.[109] Homeowners may participate at higher levels because they want to protect the consumption or use values of their homes. They are more socially ensconced in their neighborhoods and are motivated to protect those relationships. Owned homes may provide their residents with an observable indication of their success in society. Thus perceived threats to home and neighborhood may be experienced as threats to one's sense of social status or self-esteem. Given that homeowners tend to stay in their homes for longer periods of time, there is some question as to whether these social and psychological attachments are solely a function of time in residence rather than ownership.

108. Cox (1982).
109. Logan and Molotch (1987).

Research on Voting and Involvement in Political Activities

Early research on political involvement was consistent in finding that, compared to renters, homeowners are more likely to vote and to engage in other political activities, even after a range of demographic and social factors were taken into account. This was the case for both general population samples and samples of low- and moderate- income households.[110] Gilderbloom and Markham found higher voting rates for upper-income members of the sample but not for the lower-income ones.[111] This first-generation research suffered to a lesser or greater extent from both failure to account for potentially confounding variables and selection bias. In addition, the samples used in this research tended to be geographically limited, raising questions about the generalizability of the results.

The second-generation research has attempted to address one or more of those limitations. Overall, it tends to show that even when selection bias and additional factors are controlled, homeowners are still more likely to vote. DiPasquale and Glaeser, in analyzing data from the General Social Survey, addressed selection bias by using an instrumental variable approach and also controlled for time in residence.[112] They report that compared to the renters in the sample, homeowners were 16 percent more likely to vote in local elections. Manturuk, Lindblad, and Quercia, in comparing voting among a matched sample of lower-income homebuyers and renters, found that homeowners were more likely to have voted in recent local elections.[113] Selection bias was addressed in this study by the use of two-stage modeling. Manturuk, Lindblad, and Quercia also report that homeowners in disadvantaged neighborhoods were more likely to vote than owners in other areas.[114] McCabe, in analyzing data from several years of the Current Population Survey, found that after controlling for residential stability and many other variables, homeowners remained more likely to participate in local elections.[115]

There is one recent study, however, that found no relationship between homeownership and voting. Engelhardt and others, in analyzing data from a random assignment experiment on the impacts of an individual development account program in a single city, report that those who bought homes were no more likely to vote in local elections or to engage in other political activities, including writing a letter or supporting a candidate with their time or money.[116] The

110. Ahlbrandt and Cunningham (1979); Cox (1982); Kingston and Fries (1994); Lyons and Lowery (1989); Rossi and Weber (1996).

111. Gilderbloom and Markham (1995).

112. DiPasquale and Glaeser (1999).

113. Manturuk, Lindblad, and Quercia (2009).

114. Manturuk, Lindblad, and Quercia (2009).

115. McCabe (2013).

116. Engelhardt and others (2010).

relatively small, socially and geographically confined sample, however, limits the generalizability of these findings.

RESEARCH ON PARTICIPATION IN NEIGHBORHOOD AND COMMUNITY ORGANIZATIONS

The early research on homeownership and involvement in neighborhood and community organizations supports the proposition that homeowners are more likely to participate in at least certain types of community groups.[117] Based on the analysis of panel data on a group of low-income homebuyers and a comparison group of continuing renters in Baltimore, Rohe and Stegman and Rohe and Basolo report that homebuyers' participation in neighborhood and block organizations increased significantly after purchasing their homes.[118] Homebuyers were no more likely than the continuing renters, however, to participate in other types of community organizations such as PTA groups. The study by Kingston and Fries, which used data from the General Social Survey, is one of the few to find no relationship between homeownership and participation in voluntary organizations.[119]

More recent research on homeownership and social involvement tends to support the earlier positive findings. DiPasquale and Glaeser, in analyzing data from the General Social Survey, report that homeownership had a strong correlation with the number of nonprofessional organizations to which respondents belonged and with involvement in activities designed to solve local problems.[120] Manturuk, Lindblad, and Quercia, using a matched sample of CAPS owners and renters followed over a four-year period, report that renters who became homeowners during the study period significantly increased their participation in neighborhood organizations.[121] When compared to similar renters, homeowners were more likely to demonstrate instrumental civic engagement, such as participating in neighborhood organizations, but not expressive engagement, such as socializing with neighbors.[122] Similarly, McCabe reports that after controlling for residential stability, homeowners were still more likely to participate in civic and neighborhood associations than were renters.[123]

---

117. Ahlbrandt and Cunningham (1979); Baum and Kingston (1984); Cox (1982); Guest and Oropesa (1986); Pratt (1986); Rossi and Weber (1996).
118. Rohe and Stegman (1994b); Rohe and Basolo (1997).
119. Kingston and Fries (1994).
120. DiPasquale and Glaeser (1999).
121. Manturuk, Lindblad, and Quercia (2012).
122. Manturuk, Lindblad, and Quercia (2012).
123. McCabe (2013).

What Aspects of Ownership Seem to Be Responsible for the Impacts Found?

Many of the studies reviewed above have tried to identify the aspects of homeownership responsible for its associations with both political and social participation. Cox, for example, compared homeowners who reported that making a profit was an important reason for buying to those who said it was less important and found no difference in their levels of engagement in political and social activities.[124] Similar results have been reported by Rohe and Stegman and by DiPasquale and Glaeser.[125]

The more recent research on this issue has made some progress in identifying the underlying factors, but this question is still far from resolved. McCabe found that residential stability was an important predictor of participating in local elections, civic groups, and neighborhood associations.[126] Yet, after controlling for residential stability, homeownership was still a significant predictor of all three measures of participation. Similarly, Manturuk, Lindblad, and Quercia suggest that homeowners engage in a different type of social interaction that is more utilitarian and focused on protecting their own financial and social interests within the neighborhood.[127] A study by Rotolo, Wilson, and Hughes measured the economic interest of homeownership using self-reported home equity levels, which they defined as high, low, or none (for renters).[128] Their findings did not support the hypothesis that home equity relates to volunteering, which implies that noneconomic factors may explain the homeownership effect. Much work is still needed to tease out what it is about homeownership that motivates owners to participate at higher rates.

Neighborhood Perceptions and Social Capital

The proposition that homeownership might influence neighborhood perceptions and social capital has implications for housing policy. If positive homeownership experiences build trust in neighbors, then it may influence the way that residents think and feel about their communities. The reverse may also be true: household displacement and asset loss through foreclosure sale may undermine trust in neighbors. Policies that foster positive homeownership experiences and minimize negative experiences therefore have potential to affect not only individual households but also social capital within communities.

124. Cox (1982).
125. Rohe and Stegman (1994b); DiPasquale and Glaeser (1999).
126. McCabe (2013).
127. Manturuk, Lindblad, and Quercia (2012).
128. Rotolo, Wilson, and Hughes (2010).

Is there any evidence to suggest that perceptions of neighbors matter? Sampson, Raudenbush, and Earls convincingly demonstrate that positive perceptions of neighbors reduce violent crimes within neighborhoods.[129] They analyze crime perceptions and victimization, including homicides. Through multilevel and latent variable models, the authors assess neighborhood effects in Chicago. Their study also links homeownership to crime outcomes, but indirectly, through the intervening measures of how residents view their neighbors. Similarly, other studies connect perception of neighborhoods to safety, walkability, physical exercise, drug and alcohol use, and the mental and physical health of residents.[130]

The Theory

Prior research suggests several mechanisms by which homeownership could influence the perceptions of neighbors and neighborhoods. One possible mechanism is through fostering more informal social interaction in the neighborhood. Manturuk, Lindblad, and Quercia argue that "homeownership produces cohesion and stability, at least in part, by promoting social interaction."[131] In a later study, Manturuk, Lindblad, and Quercia suggest that the type of social interaction matters.[132] Homeowners build cohesion and social capital because they are more utilitarian in protecting their interests within the neighborhood.

A second possible mechanism is that homeowners are more vigilant than renters. Dietz and Haurin suggest that reduced crime victimization among homeowners may reflect greater use of home security systems or participation in neighborhood watch groups.[133]

A third possible mechanism by which homeownership may influence perception of neighbors is that people rationalize past decisions as an ego defense mechanism. Decades of experimental social psychology studies have confirmed processes of cognitive dissonance in which satisfaction increases with costs.[134] Homeownership being the largest purchase most people ever make may lead people to report higher levels of neighborhood satisfaction. The act of choosing a neighborhood may combine with reduced mobility to lead homeowners to see their neighbors and neighborhoods more positively.

A final possible mechanism is that, compared to renters, homeowners pay much more attention to the characteristics of the neighborhoods in which they

129. Sampson, Raudenbush, and Earls (1997).
130. Lin and others (2012); Ross (2000); Ross and Mirowsky (2001); Ross, Mirowsky, and Pribesh (2001).
131. Manturuk, Lindblad, and Quercia (2010, p. 473).
132. Manturuk, Lindblad, and Quercia (2012).
133. Dietz and Haurin (2003).
134. Festinger (1957).

live. Homes are purchased, after all, in particular geographic spaces. This choice of neighborhood is perhaps even more important than the dwelling itself. While researchers increasingly attend to selection bias, such adjustments should be expanded beyond the decision to own or rent. Attention to the potential for neighborhood selection bias seems justified going forward, particularly for the neighborhood-level constructs that we review here.[135]

RESEARCH ON PERCEPTIONS OF NEIGHBORS AND NEIGHBORHOODS

Prior research generally associates homeownership with higher levels of neighborhood satisfaction, friendship formation, attachment, cohesion, trust, and social capital. However, measurement error and level of analysis are particular concerns in studies that link homeownership to neighborhood perceptions because the survey questions no longer focus on the individual respondent. Instead, study participants must shift their attention to their neighbors and neighborhood. Studies that adjust for measurement error and analyze data with multilevel modeling are preferable.

One study used multilevel modeling while predicting neighborhood satisfaction and adjusted for a respondent's decision to own or rent a home. Grinstein-Weiss and others asked lower-income CAPS households to rate their neighborhood as a place to raise children.[136] When neighborhood stability and disadvantage are controlled for, these homeowners express higher levels of neighborhood satisfaction.

Oh included homeownership in models of neighborhood satisfaction, friendship, and cohesion-trust.[137] The study did not address selection bias, but it did include controls for time in residence, neighborhood disorder, and a series of interaction terms. The author reports that homeownership is positively associated with social cohesion but does not predict friendship, neighborhood satisfaction, or sentiment.

The relationship between homeownership and trust of neighbors was investigated by McCabe using the 2006 Social Capital Community Survey.[138] Trust was measured in two ways: general trust of neighbors and a hypothetical scenario gauging the likelihood that neighbors would return lost money. After a series of robustness checks, McCabe concludes that when compared to renters, homeowners are more trusting of their neighbors.

In a study by Lindblad, Manturuk, and Quercia using the CAPS database, neighborhood cohesion, informal social control, and collective efficacy were

135. Galster (2012).
136. Grinstein-Weiss and others (2011).
137. Oh (2004).
138. McCabe (2013).

positively associated with homeownership.[139] The study addressed selection bias and included controls for potential confounding variables such as the respondent's time in residence and neighborhood stability. The findings show that collective efficacy mediates the impact of homeownership on perceptions of neighborhood crime and disorder.

Finally, Manturuk, Lindblad, and Quercia measured social capital in a way that differs from most other housing studies to date.[140] These authors administered what is called a resource generator to capture overall and neighborhood-specific social capital. They addressed selection bias through a two-stage model. The authors found higher neighborhood social capital among homeowners that persists while controlling for overall social capital.

In sum, the reviewed studies largely uphold the link between homeownership and social capital as measured by positive perceptions of neighbors that include greater neighborhood satisfaction, trust, cohesion, connections, and beliefs that neighbors will act in the common good. These perceptions also mediate homeownership's influence on more distal outcomes such as crime and safety in neighborhoods.

What Aspects of Ownership Seem to Be Responsible for the Impacts Found?

The reviewed studies provide rationales for why homeownership might influence perceptions of neighborhoods but make little progress in empirically testing these mechanisms. An exception is the study by Manturuk, Lindblad, and Quercia.[141] These authors suggest that informal social interaction is a causal mechanism that results from the cohesion and stability that come from owning a home. Their results support this idea because the influence of homeownership on social capital was partially mediated by participation in neighborhood groups. Other possible mechanisms such as neighborhood watch groups and home security systems were not analyzed in the studies of crime and safety. No studies explored empirically whether homeowners' higher satisfaction with their neighborhood is simply a rationalization made to justify their large financial purchase. More work is needed to understand why homeownership is associated with higher social capital and positive views of neighbors. Future research on neighborhood outcomes should also empirically adjust for the bias that would arise if homeowners choose their neighborhoods in a selective way that influences neighborhood outcomes.

---

139. Lindblad, Manturuk, and Quercia (2013).
140. Manturuk, Lindblad, and Quercia (2010).
141. Manturuk, Lindblad, and Quercia (2010).

Conclusion

There are many reasons to believe that the foreclosure crisis may have altered attitudes toward home buying and the social impacts that have been associated with
homeownership. This chapter presents a conceptual model as to how that crisis
might have affected both attitudes toward owning as well as the social impacts of
owning. The model focuses on the role that the homeowning experience—such
as mortgage payment stress, having negative equity, and foreclosure—plays in
these outcomes.

The limited information on the impact of the foreclosure crisis on attitudes
toward owning suggests that the impact seems to have been short lived, even
among those who have either direct or indirect experience with mortgage foreclosure. Attitudes toward buying a home have rebounded at a remarkably fast
pace. An apt analogy might be investor interest in the stock market during and
after a crash. In the short run, many people swear off investing in the market.
But as the market recovers, they return to the market relatively quickly. Even
after the dramatic loss of equity and the high foreclosure rates, the early evidence suggests that people seem to believe that, over the long run, owning is
still preferable to renting, at least when it comes to the financial benefits of
homeownership. The long-term cultural preference for owning seems to have
weathered the recent foreclosure crisis. That said, additional carefully designed
research is needed to track the perceptions of homeownership before and after
the foreclosure crisis. There is little in the literature that addresses how the foreclosure crisis has affected the perceived nonfinancial benefits of homeownership, such as whether it is still seen as providing greater residential stability than
rental housing.

Research is also needed on how the foreclosure crisis has influenced the actual
social impacts of homeownership. The literature reviewed in this chapter is, with
a few exceptions, based on data collected before the foreclosure crisis. Thus the
findings that homeownership is related to social involvement, residential satisfaction, and children's completion of high school and postsecondary education may
not hold postcrisis, particularly for those who are under considerable financial
stress due to mortgage payments or who owe more than their homes are worth.

Future research must meet as many of the following criteria as possible if it is
to make important contributions to our understanding of the social benefits of
homeownership. First, it must account for selection bias in who chooses to buy
and where buyers choose to live. Homebuyers may be different from continuing renters in ways that have not been captured in control variables. Moreover,
homebuyers choose to live in particular locations, and those choices threaten
the validity of the causal links that have been drawn between homeownership
and social outcomes such as civic engagement, political participation, and trust

of neighbors. Without addressing selection bias, there is no way to determine whether any associations found are due to homeownership or an artifact of the characteristics of those who seek to own homes.

Second, future research should assess and account for homeowning experiences. As suggested above, experiences such as having to leave one's home due to the inability to make payments, owing more on the mortgage than a house is worth, or even not getting along with neighbors may result in very different social outcomes. Future research should address the question: Under what circumstances does homeownership lead to specific social outcomes?

Third, future research needs to isolate the aspects of homeownership that are associated with particular social outcomes. It needs to be designed to test the importance of length of residence; housing type, size, and condition; and neighborhood conditions. It also should consider home equity, debt leveraging, and how different types of mortgage products may affect stress, health, and other social outcomes. An interesting question is, once these correlates of homeownership are controlled, is there any residual impact that is purely the result of ownership? If one were to rent a home that was similar in type, size, condition, and neighborhood to an owned unit and live in it the same length of time, would there be any difference in the social outcomes? Is there anything that is truly different about owning, or is it just a proxy for other factors that could conceivably be addressed through other public policies or programs? If the positive impacts of homeownership, for example, are largely the result of longer residential stability, policies that improved lease terms among renters would have the same impacts.

Fourth, research needs to consider the effects of homeownership on a wide range of social groups. The research reviewed above varies in the group characteristics of the samples analyzed. Some of the research relies on general population samples while other research relies on population subgroups such as lower-income people. There are reasons to believe that the impacts of homeownership may differ among subgroups since their housing experiences may vary considerably.[142]

Finally, future research needs to use measures of social outcomes that have known validity and reliability. Too often the social constructs are measured with single questions, which lack the comprehensiveness that can be obtained with a multiquestion battery. Thus, whenever possible, validated measures of the social outcomes—such as self-esteem, depression, sense of control, health, and other constructs—should be used. This will both ensure greater accuracy of measurement and allow for valid comparisons among research studies. Although difficult to come by, the use of measures that do not rely on self-reporting will eliminate the social desirability bias that may be influencing respondents' answers.

142. Harkness and Newman (2003); Rohe, Van Zandt, and McCarthy (2002).

Turning to the policy implications, federal homeownership promotion efforts have been at least partially justified by claims that homeownership creates better citizens, results in healthier neighborhoods, and provides a range of other social benefits. Thus it is important to assess the validity of those claims. This is not to say that other good reasons for supporting homeownership do not exist, only that if homeownership is not generating the claimed social benefits, such benefits should not be used as a justification.

The updated literature review presented in this chapter does provide support for several social benefits of homeownership. Even after self-selection and other confounding factors are taken into account, there is considerable evidence that positive homeownership experiences result in greater participation in social and political activities, improved psychological health, positive assessments of neighborhoods, and increased rates of high school and postsecondary school completion. The jury is still out, however, on several other claims including better physical health and improved cognitive abilities and positive behaviors among children.

Our review of early research on the impacts of the foreclosure crisis on attitudes toward homeownership suggests that no extraordinary efforts will be needed to attract American households back into the housing market. Recent research indicates that attitudes toward homeownership as a financial investment have been steadily improving since the height of the foreclosure crisis, although the attitudes of renters have been slower to rebound. Whether this rebound is related to the financial reforms and consumer safeguards or whether it is simply the reassertion of the American belief in the benefits of homeownership is impossible to say.

References

Aaronson, Daniel. 2000. "A Note on the Benefits of Homeownership." *Journal of Urban Economics* 47, no. 3: 356–69.

Ahlbrandt, Roger S., and James V. Cunningham. 1979. *A New Public Policy for Neighborhood Preservation.* New York: Praeger.

Alley, Dawn E., and others. 2011. "Mortgage Delinquency and Changes in Access to Health Resources and Depressive Symptoms in a Nationally Representative Cohort of Americans Older than 50 Years." *American Journal of Public Health* 101, no. 12: 2293–8.

Barker, David, and Eric Miller. 2009. "Homeownership and Child Welfare." *Real Estate Economics* 37, no. 2: 279–303.

Baum T., and P. Kingston. 1984. "Homeownership and Social Activism." *Sociological Perspectives* 27, no. 2: 159–80.

Belsky, Eric S. 2013. "The Dream Lives On: The Future of Homeownership in America." Working Paper W13-1. Harvard University, Joint Center for Housing Studies. January.

Bennett, Gary G., Melissa Scharoun-Lee, and Reginald Tucker-Seeley. 2009. "Will the Public's Health Fall Victim to the Home Foreclosure Epidemic?" *PLoS Medicine* 6, no. 6: 1–5.

Bowdler, Janice, Roberto G. Quercia, and David Andrew Smith. 2010. "The Crisis and Latino Families." *Communities and Banking* 21 (Fall): 3–5.

Bracha, A., and Julian C. Jamison. 2011. "Shifting Confidence in Homeownership: The Great Recession." Public Policy Discussion Paper 12-4. Federal Reserve Bank of Boston.

Bramley, Glen, and Noah Kofi Karley. 2007. "Homeownership, Poverty and Educational Achievement: School Effects as Neighborhood Effects." *Housing Studies* 22, no. 5: 693–721.

Brounen, Dirk, Ruben Cox, and Peter Neuteboom. 2012. "Safe and Satisfied? External Effects of Homeownership in Rotterdam." *Urban Studies* (Edinburgh) 49, no. 12: 2669–91.

Burgard, Sarah A., Kristin S. Seefeldt, and Sarah W. Zelner. 2012. "Housing Instability and Health: Findings from the Michigan Recession and Recovery Study." *Social Science and Medicine* 75, no. 12: 2215–24.

Cairney, John, and Michael H. Boyle. 2004. "Home Ownership, Mortgages and Psychological Distress." *Housing Studies* 19, no. 2: 161–74.

Cannuscio, Carolyn C., and others. 2012. "Housing Strain, Mortgage Foreclosure, and Health." *Nursing Outlook* 60, no. 3: 134–42.

Cohen, Andrew. 2011. "The Supreme Court Declares California's Prisons Overcrowded." *Atlantic,* May 23.

Cohen, Taya R, and others. 2009. "Renting to Owning: An Exploration of the Theory of Planned Behavior in the Homeownership Domain." *Basic and Applied Social Psychology* 31, no. 4: 376–89.

Collins, J. Michael, and Laura Choi. 2010. "The Effects of the Real Estate Bust on Renter Perceptions of Homeownership." Federal Reserve Bank of San Francisco (http://ssrn.com/abstract=1569009).

Cox, K. 1982. "Housing Tenure and Neighborhood Activism." *Urban Affairs Quarterly* 18, no. 1: 107–29.

Currie, Janet, and Erdal Tekin. 2011. "Is There a Link between Foreclosure and Health?" Working Paper 17310. Cambridge, Mass.: National Bureau of Economic Research.

Danes, Sharon, and Earl Morris. 1986. "Housing Status, Housing Expenditures and Satisfaction." *Housing and Society* 13, no. 1: 32–43.

Diaz-Serrano, Luis. 2009. "Disentangling the Housing Satisfaction Puzzle: Does Homeownership Really Matter?" *Journal of Economic Psychology* 30, no. 5: 745–55.

Dietz, Robert D., and Donald R. Haurin. 2003. "The Social and Private Micro-Level Consequences of Homeownership." *Journal of Urban Economics* 54, no. 3: 401–50.

DiPasquale, Denise, and Edward L. Glaeser. 1999. "Incentives and Social Capital: Are Homeowners Better Citizens?" *Journal of Urban Economics* 45, no. 2: 354–84.

Drew, Rachel Bogardus, and Christopher Herbert. 2013. "Postrecession Drivers of Preferences for Homeownership." *Housing Policy Debate* 23, no. 4: 666–87.

Ellaway, A., and S. Macintyre. 1998. "Does Housing Tenure Predict Health in the UK Because It Exposes People to Different Levels of Housing-Related Hazards in the Home or Its Surroundings?" *Health and Place* 4, no. 2: 141–50.

Engelhardt, G. V. 2011. "The Great Recession and Attitudes toward Home-Buying." Special report. Washington: Research Institute for Housing America. December.

Engelhardt, G. V., and others. 2010. "What Are the Social Benefits of Homeownership? Experimental Evidence for Low-Income Households." *Journal of Urban Economics* 67, no. 3: 249–58.

Evans, G. W., and others. 1998. "Chronic Residential Crowding and Children's Well-Being: An Ecological Perspective." *Child Development* 69, no. 6: 1514–23.

Federal Reserve Bank of San Francisco. 2013. "Crisis and Response" (www.frbsf.org/econanswers/crisis.htm).

Festinger, Leon. 1957. *A Theory of Cognitive Dissonance.* Evanston, Ill.: Row, Peterson.

Fields, D., K. Libman, and S. Saegert. 2010. "Turning Everywhere, Getting Nowhere: Experiences of Seeking Help for Mortgage Delinquency and Their Implications for Foreclosure Prevention." *Housing Policy Debate* 20, no.4: 647–86.

Fields, Desiree, and others. 2007. "Understanding Responses to the Threat of Foreclosure among Low Income Homeowners." Graduate Center of the City University of New York, Center for Human Environments (http://web.gc.cuny.edu/che/Final Report7122007.pdf).

Filakti, H., and J. Fox. 1995. "Differences in Mortality by Housing Tenure and by Car Access." *Population Trends* 81 (Autumn).: 27–30.

Galster, George C. 1987. *Homeowners and Neighborhood Reinvestment.* Duke University Press.

———. 2012. "The Mechanism(s) of Neighborhood Effects: Theory, Evidence, and Policy Implications." In *Neighborhood Effects Research: New Perspectives,* edited by M. van Ham and others, pp. 23–56. Dordrecht, Netherlands: Springer.

Galster, George, and others. 2007. "The Impact of Parental Homeownership on Children's Outcomes during Early Adulthood." *Housing Policy Debate* 18, no. 4: 785–827.

Gilderbloom, J. I., and J. P. Markham. 1995. "The Impact of Homeownership on Political Beliefs." *Social Forces* 73, no. 4: 1589–1607.

Gould, M., and K. Jones. 1996. "Analyzing Perceived Limiting Long-Term Illness Using UK Census Microdata." *Social Science and Medicine* 42, no. 6: 857–69.

Green, Richard, Gary Painter, and Michelle White. 2012. "Measuring the Benefits of Homeowning: Effects on Children Redux." Special report. Washington: Research Institute for Housing America.

Green, Richard, and Michelle White. 1997. "Measuring the Benefits of Homeowning: Effects on Children." *Journal of Urban Economics* 41, no. 3: 441–61.

Grinstein-Weiss, Michal, and others. 2010. "Homeownership and Parenting Practices: Evidence from the Community Advantage Panel." *Children and Youth Services Review* 32, no. 5: 774–82.

———. 2011. "Homeownership and Neighborhood Satisfaction among Low- and Moderate-Income Households." *Journal of Urban Affairs* 33, no. 3: 247–65.

———. 2012. "Homeownership, Neighbourhood Characteristics and Children's Positive Behaviours among Low- and Moderate-Income Households." *Urban Studies* 49, no. 16: 3545–63.

Guest, A. W., and R. S. Oropesa. 1986. "Informal Social Ties and Political Activity in the Metropolis." *Urban Affairs Quarterly* 21, no. 4: 550–74.

Guo, S., and M. Fraser. 2009. *Propensity Score Analysis.* Thousand Oaks, Calif.: Sage Publications.

Harkness, Joseph, and Sandra J. Newman. 2002. "Homeownership for the Poor in Distressed Neighborhoods: Does This Make Sense?" *Housing Policy Debate* 13, no. 3: 597–630.

———. 2003. "Differential Effects of Homeownership on Children from Higher- and Lower-Income Families." *Journal of Housing Research* 14, no. 1: 1–19.

Haurin, Donald R., Toby L. Parcel, and R. Jean Haurin. 2002. "Does Homeownership Affect Child Outcomes?" *Real Estate Economics* 30, no. 4: 635–66.

Herbert, Christopher Edward, and Eric S. Belsky. 2006. *The Homeownership Experience of Low-Income and Minority Families: A Review and Synthesis of the Literature.* U.S. Department of Housing and Urban Development.

Holupka, Scott, and Sandra J. Newman. 2012. "The Effects of Homeownership on Children's Outcomes: Real Effects or Self-Selection?" *Real Estate Economics* 40, no. 3: 566–602.

Houle, Jason, and Michael T. Light. 2014 (forthcoming). "The Home Foreclosure Crisis and Rising Suicide Rates, 2005–2010." *American Journal of Public Health* (www. jnhoule.org/storage/AJPH_SuicideForeclosure_final.pdf).

Immergluck, Dan. 2009. *Foreclosed: High-Risk Lending, Deregulation, and the Undermining of America's Mortgage Market.* Cornell University Press.

Joint Center for Housing Studies. 2012. *The State of the Nation's Housing 2011.* Harvard University.

———. 2013. *The State of the Nation's Housing 2012.* Harvard University.

Kingston, Paul W., and John C. Fries. 1994. "Having a Stake in the System: The Sociopolitical Ramifications of Business and Home Ownership." *Social Science Quarterly* 75, no. 3: 679–86.

Kinsey, Jean, and Sylvia Lane. 1983. "Race, Housing Attributes, and Satisfaction with Housing." *Housing and Society* 10, no. 3: 98–116.

Krieger, J., and D. L. Higgins. 2002. "Housing and Health: Time Again for Public Health Action." *American Journal of Public Health* 92, no. 5: 758–68.

Lam, J. 1985. "Type of Structure, Satisfaction and Propensity to Move." *Housing and Society* 12, no. 1: 32–44.

Libman, Kimberly, Desiree Fields, and Susan Saegert. 2012. "Housing and Health: A Social Ecological Perspective on the U.S. Foreclosure Crisis." *Housing, Theory and Society* 29, no. 1: 1–24.

Lin, E.-Y., and others. 2012. "Neighborhood Matters: Perceptions of Neighborhood Cohesiveness and Associations with Alcohol, Cannabis and Tobacco Use." *Drug and Alcohol Review* 31, no. 4: 402–12.

Lindblad, Mark R., Kim R. Manturuk, and Roberto G. Quercia. 2013. "Sense of Community and Informal Social Control among Lower-Income Households: The Role of Homeownership and Collective Efficacy in Reducing Subjective Neighborhood Crime and Disorder." *American Journal of Community Psychology* 51, no. 1-2: 123–39.

Logan, J., and H. Molotch. 1987. *Urban Fortunes: The Political Economy of Place.* University of California Press.

Lyons, W. E., and David Lowery. 1989. "Governmental Fragmentation versus Consolidation: Five Public-Choice Myths about How to Create Informed, Involved, and Happy Citizens." *Public Administration Review* 49, no. 6: 533–43.

MacArthur Foundation. 2013. "How Housing Matters: Americans' Attitudes Transformed by the Housing Crisis and Changing Lifestyles" (www.macfound.org/media/files/HHM_Hart_report_2013.pdf).

Macintyre, S., and others. 1998. "Do Housing Tenure and Car Access Predict Health Because They Are Simply Markers of Income or Self-Esteem? A Scottish Study." *Journal of Epidemiology and Community Health* 52, no. 1: 657–64.

———. 2003. "What Features of the Home and the Area Might Help to Explain Observed Relationships between Housing Tenure and Health? Evidence from the West of Scotland." *Health Place* 9, no. 3: 207–18.

Manturuk, Kim. 2012. "Urban Homeownership and Mental Health: Mediating Effect of Perceived Sense of Control." *City and Community* 11, no. 4: 409–30.

Manturuk, Kim, Mark Lindblad, and Roberto G. Quercia. 2009. "Homeownership and Local Voting in Disadvantaged Urban Neighborhoods." *Cityscape: A Journal of Policy Development and Research* 11, no. 3: 213–30.

———. 2010. "Friends and Neighbors: Homeownership and Social Capital among Low- to Moderate-Income Families." *Journal of Urban Affairs* 32, no. 4: 471–88.

———. 2012. "Homeownership and Civic Engagement in Low-Income Urban Neighborhoods: A Longitudinal Analysis." *Urban Affairs Review* 48, no. 5: 731–60.

Manturuk, Kim, Sarah Riley, and Janneke Ratcliffe. 2012. "Perception vs. Reality: The Relationship between Low-Income Homeownership, Perceived Financial Stress, and Financial Hardship." *Social Science Research* 41, no. 2: 276–86.

Martin, Anne J. 2012. "After Foreclosure: The Social and Spatial Reconstruction of Everyday Lives in the San Francisco Bay Area." Dissertation, City and Regional Planning. University of California, Berkeley.

McCabe, Brian J. 2013. "Are Homeowners Better Citizens? Homeownership and Community Participation in the United States." *Social Forces* 91, no. 3: 929–54.

McLaughlin, Katie A., and others. 2012. "Home Foreclosure and Risk of Psychiatric Morbidity during the Recent Financial Crisis." *Psychological Medicine* 42, no. 7: 1441–8.

Menzel, Nancy, Sheniz Moonie, and Melva Thompson-Robinson. 2012. "Health Effects Associated with Foreclosure: A Secondary Analysis of Hospital Discharge Data." *ISRN Public Health* (http://digitalscholarship.unlv.edu/nursing_fac_articles/129/).

Mohanty, Lisa L., and Lakshmi K. Raut. 2009. "Home Ownership and School Outcomes of Children: Evidence from the PSID Child Development Supplement." *American Journal of Economics and Sociology* 68, no. 2: 465–89.

Morris, E., S. Crull, and M. Winter. 1976. "Housing Norms, Housing Satisfaction and the Propensity to Move." *Journal of Marriage and the Family* 38 (May): 309–20.

Mortgage Bankers Association. 2012. "National Delinquency Survey" (www.mbaa.org/researchandforecasts/productsandsurveys/nationaldelinquencysurvey.htm).

Murnane, Richard, and John Willett. 2011. *Methods Matter: Improving Causal Inference in Educational and Social Science Research.* Oxford University Press.

National Association of Home Builders. 2012. "NAHB National Survey." January 2–5. Washington (www.nahb.org/fileUpload_details.aspx?contentID=173605&from GSA=1).

Nettleton, S., and R. Burrows. 1998. "Mortgage Debt, Insecure Homeownership and Health: An Exploratory Analysis." *Sociology of Health and Illness* 20, no. 5: 731–53.

New York Times. 2011. "The Full Results from the New York Times and CBS News Poll, June 24–28." (www.nytimes.com/interactive/2011/06/30/business/20110630poll-full-results.html?ref=business).

Oh, Joong-Hwan. 2004. "Race/Ethnicity, Homeownership, and Neighborhood Attachment." *Race and Society* 7, no. 2: 63–77.

Osypuk, Theresa L., and others. 2012. "The Consequences of Foreclosure for Depressive Symptomatology." *Annals of Epidemiology* 22, no. 6: 379–87.

Pew Research Center. 2011. "Five Years after the Bubble Burst: Home Sweet Home. Still." Washington (www.pewsocialtrends.org/files/2011/04/Housing-Economy.pdf).

Pollack, Craig, and Julia Lynch. 2009. "Health Status of People Undergoing Foreclosure in the Philadelphia Region." *American Journal of Public Health* 99, no. 10: 1833–9.

Pollack, Craig Evan, and others. 2011. "A Case-Control Study of Home Foreclosure, Health Conditions, and Health Care Utilization." *Journal of Urban Health* 88, no. 3: 469–78.

Pratt, G. 1986. "Housing Tenure and Social Cleavages in Urban Canada." *Annals of the Association of American Geographers* 76, no. 3: 366–80.

Rahkonen, Ossi, Sara Arber, and Eero Lahelma. 1995. "Health Inequalities in Early Adulthood: A Comparison of Young Men and Women in Britain and Finland." *Social Science and Medicine* 41, no. 2: 163–71.

Rasmussen, D. W., and Isaac Megbolugbe. 1997. "The Reverse Mortgage as an Asset Management Tool." *Housing Policy Debate* 8, no. 3: 173–94.

Robert, Stephanie, and James S. House. 1996. "SES Differentials in Health by Age and Alternative Indicators of SES." *Journal of Aging and Health* 8, no. 3: 359–88.

Rohe, William M., and Victoria Basolo. 1997. "Long-Term Effects of Homeownership on the Self-Perceptions and Social Interaction of Low-Income Persons." *Environment and Behavior* 29, no. 6: 793–819.

Rohe, William M., and Hye-Sung Han. 2012. "Housing and Health: Time for Renewed Collaboration." *North Carolina Medical Journal* 73, no. 5: 374–80.

Rohe, William M., and Michael A. Stegman. 1994a. "The Impacts of Home Ownership on the Self-Esteem, Perceived Control and Life Satisfaction of Low-Income People." *Journal of the American Planning Association* 60, no. 1: 173–84.

———. 1994b. "The Impacts of Home Ownership on the Social and Political Involvement of Low-Income People." *Urban Affairs Quarterly* 30, no. 3: 152–72.

Rohe, William M., and Leslie S. Stewart. 1996. "Home Ownership and Neighborhood Stability." *Housing Policy Debate* 7, no. 1: 37–81.

Rohe, William, Shannon Van Zandt, and George McCarthy. 2002. "Social Benefits and Costs of Homeownership." In *Low-Income Homeownership: Examining the Unexamined Goal,* edited by Nicholas Retsinas and Eric Belsky, pp. 381–406. Brookings.

Rohe, William, and Harry Watson, eds. 2007. *Chasing the American Dream: New Perspectives on Affordable Homeownership.* Cornell University Press.

Ross, Catherine E. 2000. "Neighborhood Disadvantage and Adult Depression." *Journal of Health and Social Behavior* 41 (June): 177–87.

Ross, Catherine E., and John Mirowsky. 2001. "Neighborhood Disadvantage, Disorder, and Health." *Journal of Health and Social Behavior* 42 (September): 258–76.

Ross, Catherine E., John Mirowsky, and Shana Pribesh. 2001. "Powerlessness and the Amplification of Threat: Neighborhood Disadvantage, Disorder, and Mistrust." *American Sociological Review* 66, no. 4: 568–91.

Rossi, Peter H., and Eleanor Weber. 1996. "The Social Benefits of Homeownership: Empirical Evidence from National Surveys." *Housing Policy Debate* 7, no. 1: 1–35.

Rotolo, T., J. Wilson, and M. E. Hughes. 2010. "Homeownership and Volunteering: An Alternative Approach to Studying Social Inequality and Civic Engagement." *Sociological Forum* 25, no. 3: 570–87.

Saegert, Susan, Desiree Fields, and Kimberly Libman. 2011. "Mortgage Foreclosure and Health Disparities: Serial Displacement as Asset Extraction in African American Populations." *Journal of Urban Health* 88, no. 3: 390–402.

Sampson, Robert J., Stephen W. Raudenbush, and Felton Earls. 1997. "Neighborhoods and Violent Crime: A Multilevel Study of Collective Efficacy." *Science* 277, no. 5328: 918–24.

Shiller, Robert. 2013. "Today's Dream House May Not Be Tomorrow's." *New York Times,* April 27.

Smith, Susan J., and others. 2003. "Housing as Health Capital: How Health Trajectories and Housing Paths Are Linked." *Journal of Social Issues* 59, no. 3: 501–25.

South, S. J., and Kyle D. Crowder. 1997. "Escaping Distressed Neighborhoods: Individual, Community and Metropolitan Influences." *American Journal of Sociology* 122, no. 4: 1040–84.

———. 1998. "Avenues and Barriers to Residential Mobility among Single Mothers." *Journal of Marriage and the Family* 60, no. 4: 866–77.

U.K. Office of the Deputy Prime Minister. 2004. *The Impact of Overcrowding on Health and Education: A Review of Evidence and Literature.* Wetherby, England (webarchive. nationalarchives.gov.uk/20120919132719/http://www.communities.gov.uk/documents/housing/pdf/138631.pdf).

Vale, Laurence. 2007. "The Ideological Origins of Affordable Homeownership Efforts." In *Chasing the American Dream: New Perspectives on Affordable Homeownership,* edited by William Rohe and Harry Watson, pp. 15–40. Cornell University Press.

Van Zandt, Shannon, and William M. Rohe. 2006. "Do First-Time Homeowners Improve Their Neighborhood Quality?" *Journal of Urban Affairs* 28, no. 5: 491–510.

Varady, David P. 1983. "Determinants of Residential Mobility Decisions: The Role of Government Services in Relation to Other Factors." *Journal of the American Planning Association* 49, no. 2: 184–99.

Wilkinson, D. 1999. "Poor Housing and Ill Health: A Summary of Research Evidence." The Scottish Office, Central Research Unit (www.scotland.gov.uk/Resource/Doc/156479/0042008.pdf).

PART II

Supporting the Home-Buying Process:

Understanding Consumer Preferences and Designing Homebuyer Programs

4

To Buy or Not to Buy? Understanding Tenure Preferences and the Decisionmaking Processes of Lower-Income Households

CAROLINA REID

I am sitting on the lawn of a modest single-family home in Albuquerque, helping a toddler put together her Mega Bloks® as I talk with her mother, a twenty-four-year-old Latina who has lived in the United States her entire life. We are taking advantage of an unusually warm February day, and the interview is going better now that we are at her home rather than sitting in the nearby public library. Earlier in the conversation, I felt as if she were giving me carefully considered answers to my questions about her home search process ("We did a budget to see what we could afford"), but now she is allowing more emotion to come through in her responses. She points to a row of rooftops just visible over her neighbor's backyard—a recently built subdivision that is filled with two-story houses, their newness standing in stark contrast to the older houses in the neighborhood where we are now sitting. "If we could only afford to live there," she says. "That's what I want for my daughter. A house that shows we're providing for her in the right way. That we've made it. So she's not a second-class citizen." She then goes on to explain how she is willing to forgo her careful budget—in addition to increasing the number of hours she works to save a bit more—in order to buy one of those houses.

This one interview encapsulates the challenges of understanding consumer decisions in the homeownership market. It is never simply about an economic utility function. Certainly, buying a home is a financial decision, and every single person I interviewed recognized (and valued) the investment potential of owning a home. The recent housing boom and bust, coupled with the foreclosure crisis, was at the forefront of everyone's mind, and most of the families were watching the real estate reports with keen interest. Were prices going up? Were interest rates going to stay low? Was this the right time to buy? But the interviews also revealed much more complicated motivations for buying a home, highlighting the extent to which a whole host of other nonquantifiable factors—including optimism, identity, and culture—influence consumer decisionmaking processes. These nonquantifiable factors are not negligible, and they have material effects, not only on the financial well-being and vulnerability of the households themselves but also on which neighborhoods benefit from owner-occupied investment.

In this chapter I report on the findings from four focus groups and twenty individual interviews designed to examine how households make decisions about buying a home. The focus groups and interviews were conducted in Oakland, California, and Albuquerque, New Mexico, between December 2012 and February 2013. All of the respondents—forty-three in total—were members of lower-income households (earning less than the median for their respective metropolitan statistical areas), with children, of working age, and who were in the process of buying a house or had bought a home within the last six months. For all of them, this was their first home-buying experience, and all but three were going to be the first generation in their families to own property in the United States. As a result, the data provide rich insights into the processes that influence the home-ownership decisions of lower-income, first-time homebuyers. This chapter summarizes the findings related to three key aspects of the decisionmaking process:

—the factors that motivate the shift from renting to owning,

—the heuristics borrowers use to make financial decisions about their housing choices, and

—the prevalence of "optimism bias" in household decisions about buying a home, and how that optimism stands in stark contrast to lower-income homeowners' vulnerability in the labor market.

The chapter begins with a brief overview of the literature that forms the background for this study, including studies on tenure choice, residential location, consumer decisionmaking, and behavioral economics. It then provides background on the qualitative data as well as some brief statistics that highlight the different contexts of the Oakland and Albuquerque housing markets. The third section presents the findings from the qualitative data, focusing on the three key aspects described above. The final section discusses the potential implications of this study for public policy and suggests directions for future research.

Literature Review

Interestingly, despite the volumes of literature on homeownership, housing tenure choice, and consumer behavior, it was remarkably difficult to find studies that use in-depth qualitative methods to understand the decisionmaking processes of first-time homebuyers, and even more difficult to find studies that focus specifically on lower-income households. Instead, I turned to many different literatures to assemble a framework for thinking about what factors influence the decisionmaking process and what heuristics or biases might be present when households filter information and make choices. The following review focuses on those studies that most inform this research.

First, I draw on the rich literature on tenure choice and residential mobility. Since the early 1980s, there has been valuable research into the factors that influence a household's decision and ability to buy a house, including the relative cost of owning over renting; income, wealth, and credit constraints; and household characteristics, including age and life course stage, education, and race.[1] Related to this research are studies that examine location choice in residential mobility and tenure decisions; many of these studies focus on job accessibility.[2] However, more recent studies have explored the other factors that influence neighborhood preferences, including housing type and open space, personal income and house prices, racial differences, and proximity to retailers and services.[3] Researchers working in these areas have emphasized the importance of situating the transition to ownership within a life course perspective, recognizing that a family with young children may make different residential housing choices than either childless young adults or the elderly. Researchers have also studied how gender roles and intrahousehold dynamics and negotiations influence decisions about residential mobility, particularly among dual-earner families.[4]

These studies all point to the contextual nature of the housing tenure decision and the interdependence of decisions concerning residential mobility, location, and the welfare benefits of multiple people within the household. Nevertheless, these analyses tend to focus on quantifiable attributes that determine housing tenure outcomes as opposed to revealing the processes and heuristics by which consumers make decisions about their housing choices. In addition, as Munro notes, they "typically preserve the central neoclassical assumption of a

---

1. See for example Linneman (1985); Brueckner (1986); Ioannides (1987); Long and Caudill (1992); Wachter and Megbolugbe (1992); Bourassa (1996); Clark and Dieleman (1996); Gyourko and Linneman (1997); Haurin, Hendershott, and Wachter (1997); Hendershott and White (2000); Painter, Gabriel, and Myers (2001); Barakova and others (2003).

2. Waddell (1993); Van Ommeren, Rietveld, and Nijkamp (1997); Horner (2004).

3. Davis (1993); Taylor and Ong (1995); Cameron and Muellbauer (1998); South and Crowder (1998); Gottlieb and Lentnek (2001); So, Orazem, and Otto (2001); Parkes, Kearns, and Atkinson (2002).

4. Bruegel (1996); Jarvis (1999); Cooke (2001); Bailey, Blake, and Cooke (2004); Withers and Clark (2006).

utility maximizing individual."[5] This suggests that there is a value in developing a greater understanding of the heuristics, biases, and other noneconomic motives that might drive consumer choice in the housing market. What forms people's views of what neighborhoods are initially acceptable or unacceptable? How might those preferences differ between different demographic or socioeconomic groups, and how might they change over time? What rules of thumb do households use to determine how much to spend on a house, and are these mutable?

To guide my inquiry in these areas, I reviewed the relevant literature on consumer decisionmaking and behavioral economics.[6] This body of work is helpful in that it challenges the notion of "unbounded" rationality that underlies most models on tenure choice and housing outcomes. Cognitive faculties are not limitless, and consumers often adopt heuristics—rules of thumb—as a way to sort through the vast amounts of information that shape decisions.[7] Heuristics help consumers reduce the amount of work needed to collect and process the array of information related to making a decision (such as a home purchase). Cognitive psychologists have identified a wide range of heuristics people use in decisionmaking (often concurrently), including the representative, availability, and anchoring-and-adjustment heuristics.[8]

All of these biases and rules of thumb are likely to exist to some degree in the homeownership decision, given the fact that buying a home is probably one of the most involved and important decisions a household makes.[9] As Campbell

5. Munro (1995), p. 1610.

6. The literature on behavioral economics and applications to consumer finance is too vast to review here. For excellent reviews, see Mullainathan and Thaler (2001); Thaler and Sunstein (2008); Tufano (2009).

7. Kahneman and Tversky (1974); Shah and Oppenheimer (2008); Gigerenzer and Gaissmaier (2011).

8. The representative heuristic suggests that individuals estimate the likelihood of an event by comparing it to an existing "stereotype" in their minds. See Tversky and Kahneman (1973). So, for example, consumers may use this heuristic in evaluating neighborhood conditions: if they believe that a higher proportion of rental units brings house prices down, they may assume that neighborhoods with more rental units are less desirable, even if that neighborhood actually has higher real estate values.

The availability heuristic relies on immediate examples that come to mind in assessing the probability of a situation. See Tversky and Kahneman (1973); McKelvie (2000). Research has shown that people are preoccupied with highly desirable outcomes, such as winning the sweepstakes, or with highly undesirable outcomes, such as an airplane crash. Consequently, availability provides a mechanism by which occurrences of extreme utility (for example, house price gains or a raise) may appear more likely than they actually are.

The anchoring-and-adjustment heuristic describes cases in which one uses a number or a value as a starting point, known as an anchor, and adjusts information until an acceptable value is reached. See Epley and Gilovich (2006).

9. Gibler and Nelson (2003).

argues, the housing decision is particularly complex from a consumer finance perspective, given the interactions between present and future income, borrowing constraints, and the need to take into account the intricacies of the tax code in financial calculations.[10] However, very little of the recent advances in consumer finance research focuses on the homeownership decision per se, although Fannie Mae has begun to undertake more systematic surveys to understand how borrowers make housing decisions. Since the study here is more qualitative and exploratory in nature, it cannot measure the prevalence of these biases in the larger population. This suggests that there is a significant research opportunity to apply new advances in behavioral economic and psychological methods to housing tenure decisions.

The studies I was able to find on consumer behavior in the home purchase decision did, however, provide an important foundation for my research. First, these studies helped me to frame the steps in the house search process. For example, Talarchek and Cahill both found that movers use a two-stage sequence of information gathering, starting with research to decide which neighborhood to live in and then gathering information on individual housing units within selected neighborhoods.[11] Dibb similarly found that homebuyers use a sequential decision strategy: first they apply a set of "absolute" rules to eliminate properties (for example, those that do not meet minimum requirements for size or location), and then they use "relative" rules to evaluate properties across a range of secondary criteria.[12] Research also suggests that consumers differ in how much data they collect when making housing decisions. A few studies have found that there may be an inverted U-shape relationship between consumer knowledge and the quantity or quality of the search for information.[13] Those who are the least experienced (first-time homebuyers) and those who are the most experienced (have purchased multiple homes) both search less than those with a middle level of experience. Other studies have found that consumers who are more educated usually search more, while inexperienced buyers are more susceptible to external influences such as real estate agents or advertisements and promotions.[14] These research findings are salient for understanding the experience of lower-income first-time homebuyers, who may search less and be more easily swayed by external factors.

10. Campbell (2006). Relevant considerations include the taxation of nominal rather than real interest, the availability of tax-favored retirement accounts, the tax deductibility of mortgage interest, the taxation of capital gains only when these gains are realized through asset sales, and the adjustment of the capital gains tax basis at death.

11. Talarchek (1982); Cahill (1994).

12. Dibb (1994).

13. Bettman and Park (1980); Moorthy, Ratchford, and Talukdar (1997).

14. Bettman and Sujan (1987).

Second, a few studies based on surveys helped me to develop questions related to consumers' expectations of the housing market. During the housing boom in the 1980s, Case and Shiller conducted a survey to understand how consumers think about trends in housing markets and the sources of information that they use to decide how much to pay for a house.[15] While consumers' responses were influenced by whether or not they lived in a "boom" market, the researchers found that many consumers relied on clichés to explain their decisions and opinions rather than on empirical facts. Case and Shiller also found that the majority of homebuyers did not perceive real estate investments to involve a great deal of risk. Their study also provides evidence for the social basis of housing decisions since they found that there was significant discussion among friends and associates about the real estate market.

Third, I drew on a number of studies, conducted largely in Europe, Australia, and New Zealand, that use qualitative methods to examine the role of influences, emotions, and social status considerations in the home buying process. Levy, Murphy, and Lee use in-depth interviews with real estate agents and homebuyers to study how families search for homes, interpret information, and internally negotiate decisions.[16] They find that emotions, feelings, and social collectivities strongly influence the decisionmaking process and that women and men in the household take on different roles in the search process, depending on the family structure.[17] However, their research does not focus on lower-income families and the unique constraints they face in making decisions about housing tenure. Gram-Hanssen and Bech-Danielsen conduct thirteen in-depth interviews to illuminate what priorities determine the choice of a house and what home "signifies" to its residents.[18] The interviews demonstrated how residential neighborhoods are associated with different symbolic values and how these values influence the choice of home. While these authors do explore class differences, their interviews were limited to middle- and upper-income families in Denmark. This chapter fills a gap in the literature by explicitly focusing on the decisionmaking processes of lower-income households in the United States.

Data and Methods

To collect data for this study, I conducted focus groups and interviews at two sites: Oakland, California, and Albuquerque, New Mexico. While the majority

15. Case and Shiller (1988).

16. Levy, Murphy, and Lee (2008).

17. Hempel (1974) similarly finds that husbands and wives take on different roles in the house-buying process.

18. Gram-Hanssen and Bech-Danielsen (2004).

Figure 4-1. *Federal Housing Finance Agency Home Price Index,*
Oakland and Albuquerque, 2000–12

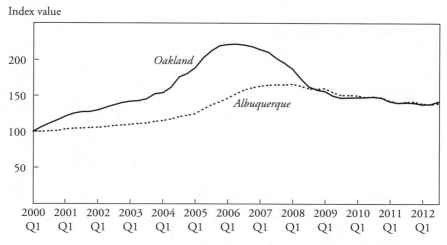

Source: Federal Housing Finance Agency, "House Price Index, Purchase-Only, Not Seasonally Adjusted, through 3rd Quarter 2012."

of data was collected in California, I felt it was important to have a second site as part of the study to see whether California's high house prices influence the nature of lower-income households' decisionmaking processes. I selected Albuquerque because of its greater housing affordability and the fact that New Mexico was relatively insulated from the subprime crisis and subsequent foreclosures (especially compared to other southwestern states such as Arizona and Nevada).

To provide context for the interview sites, figure 4-1 presents the Federal Housing Finance Agency house price index for Oakland and Albuquerque from 2000 to the middle of 2012. Oakland's house values more than doubled between 2000 and 2006 and then dropped significantly afterwards (eroding all the gains during the bubble). In contrast, Albuquerque's housing prices were less volatile during the boom and bust, and the declines after 2007 were not as drastic as in Oakland. Although not reflected in these data, both Oakland and Albuquerque saw significant gains in the first half of 2013, which meant that my interviews occurred during a period of renewed house price appreciation.

In addition to being a less volatile real estate market, Albuquerque remains considerably more affordable than Oakland, particularly when compared against household incomes. Figure 4-2 shows the distribution of owner-occupied home values in Oakland and Albuquerque in 2011. Approximately 55 percent of the homes in Albuquerque were valued at less than $200,000, compared with just

Figure 4-2. *Distribution of House Values in Oakland and Albuquerque, 2011*

Percent owner-occupied stock

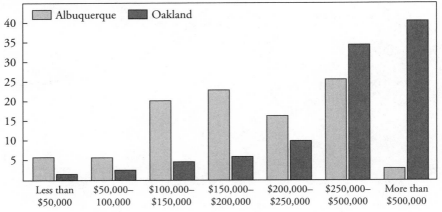

Source: U.S. Census Bureau (2011), table B25075–"Value."

15 percent of the homes in Oakland.[19] While incomes were somewhat lower on average in Albuquerque, the differences were not as large as the differences in house values. Nearly 50 percent of households in Oakland had incomes of under $50,000, compared to 56 percent of households in Albuquerque.[20] As a result, a significantly larger share of residents in Albuquerque lived in owner-occupied units, especially among households headed by individuals under age thirty-five. Only 18 percent of such households in Oakland owned their home compared to 48 percent in Albuquerque.[21]

In Oakland I conducted four focus groups (ranging in size from five to eight participants) and eleven in-depth interviews. In Albuquerque I conducted nine in-depth interviews, although one of these interviews occurred over the phone. (All of the other interviews were conducted in person.) In total the perspectives of forty-three respondents are included in the data. To participate in the study, respondents needed to be working-age adults with children, with a household income of less than $61,000 in Albuquerque and less than $92,300 in Oakland (the area median income for the two respective metropolitan statistical areas). The decision to focus on households with children was deliberate. By narrow-

19. U.S. Census Bureau (2011, table B25075–"Value").
20. U.S. Census Bureau (2011, table S1901–"Income in the Past 12 Months [in 2011 Inflation-Adjusted Dollars]").
21. U.S. Census Bureau (2011, table B25007–"Tenure by Age of Householder").

ing the focus groups and interviews to a specific stage of the life course, I hoped to eliminate some of the life course reasons why households shift tenures and explore the financial aspects of choosing homeownership more explicitly.

Although I initially intended only to conduct focus groups for this study, midway through the data collection process in Oakland, I shifted from a focus group to in-depth interview format. The focus groups' responses were extremely varied, and I wanted to have more time to follow up on individual experiences. While focus groups provide a way to build consensus or identify key cleavages in the opinions, attitudes, and experiences of participants, in this case it seemed like there was more to be gained by talking to respondents one-on-one.[22] The interviews also were helpful because in several cases the respondents offered to show me their current housing situation or the neighborhoods and properties they were considering buying. This provided a stronger qualitative understanding of the local real estate market and how supply and cost constraints were shaping household choices.

To recruit respondents, I relied on a modified "snowballing" strategy, identifying lower-income households through personal contacts and asking them to help me recruit potential respondents (for example, by posting flyers at their congregation or asking workplace friends who were looking for a house if they would be interested in talking to me). I also visited community centers, libraries, and open houses (affordable to lower-income families) and introduced myself and my project to potential respondents, giving them my card and asking them to contact me if they were interested in participating in the study. I also advertised on Craigslist, although I was only able to identify one respondent in this manner. Respondents received a $40 honorarium at the start of the interview or focus group to ensure that none of them felt coerced by the financial incentive to stay for the full time or disclose more information than they felt comfortable discussing. For the focus groups, I provided an additional $50 to the hostess to cover the costs of refreshments.

In both the focus groups and the individual interviews, I used two devices to help elicit information about the respondents and their decisionmaking processes. First, every respondent filled out a brief survey about their financial circumstances (for example, income brackets, job title, current rent, house price search range), housing preferences (for example, did they care more about location or housing quality), and the neighborhoods in which they were concentrating their search. Second, in the one-on-one interviews, I worked with respondents to complete a "life event" chart, where they were asked to identify key aspects of their lives over the past five years and then project what life events they were expecting going forward. The focus groups varied in length from nearly three hours for the first to approximately ninety minutes for the subsequent three. Interviews were

22. Asbury (1995); Morgan (1997).

approximately one hour to ninety minutes long. Both were conducted in an informal, free-flowing format as opposed to following a rigid script.

A few aspects of the respondent sample are worth noting. First, the sample is racially and ethnically diverse. Overall, it is weighted toward first-generation immigrants, especially Latino households, due at least in part to the demographic composition of lower-income households in Oakland and Albuquerque. Out of the forty-three respondents, twenty were of Latino origin, five were from East Africa, and four were Filipino. I see this as one of the strengths of this study: the majority of household and homeownership growth in the United States in coming decades will be among Latino and other immigrant families, so understanding their decisionmaking processes seems to be especially important. Second, the majority of respondents worked in lower skilled, lower paid jobs, meaning that they were unlikely to see significant positive change between their current and future income. Among households in the sample, the median income of households in Albuquerque was $46,000, while in Oakland it was approximately $85,000, well below the respective area median income in each city. Third, I explicitly sought respondents who had not participated in a homeownership counseling program or who were not seeking help from housing nonprofits or local affordable homeownership programs. Research has shown that participation in a prepurchase counseling program changes a respondent's level of knowledge and influences their decisionmaking processes, whereas my goal was to better understand the experiences of families who fall outside of these support systems. None of the respondents in my sample had gone through or were going through official homeownership counseling, although three of the respondents in Oakland and one in Albuquerque had looked into affordable homeownership programs and were considering applying for the subsidy. They knew these programs required financial counseling in order to be eligible.

Despite these efforts to narrow the sample, respondents' answers and experiences were incredibly heterogeneous. While I believe that these focus groups and interviews provide valuable initial insights, significantly more research is needed to develop a clearer understanding of the tenure decisionmaking processes of lower-income households. In addition, it is important to note that all these respondents had already decided to buy a house and therefore do not reflect the experiences of others who may have been more influenced by the recent crisis to stay out of the homeownership market.

Research Findings

This section presents the findings from the focus groups and in-depth interviews related to three key aspects of the homeownership decisionmaking process. First, I examine the reasons and motivations first-time homebuyers give for making the transition from renting to owning. Second, I look at how households determine the house price they can afford. Finally, I show that among my respondents, "optimism bias" plays a significant role in determining the shift to homeownership as well as the amount of resources first-time homebuyers set aside for unanticipated risks.

The Decision to Own

One of the strongest findings—in fact the only finding that was universal among every single respondent in both the focus groups and the individual interviews—was the persistence of the idea that owning a home is part of the "American Dream." Homeownership is not just a housing tenure decision; among respondents it is clear that homeownership embodies the ideals of upward mobility and achievement and that renting is seen as an inferior housing choice. Common statements that captured these ideals included, "Why would you rent if you could own?," "I want to move up the housing ladder," "We're really doing well now; it seems like it's time to stop renting and move up into owning our own place." In other words, while the decision to own is in part a financial decision, it also encompasses important cultural and ideological meanings.

I thought that the foreclosure crisis might have weakened this link, especially since there has been increasing coverage in the news about people rejecting the ideology of homeownership. In the focus groups and interviews, I would challenge the clichéd notion of an American Dream. I would prompt with questions such as, "Don't you think that the foreclosure crisis changed that?" or "But you have much more freedom and flexibility with renting, isn't that valuable to you?" Bearing in mind that these respondents had made the decision to buy—creating a likely selection bias—respondents universally pushed back on these prompts, noting that "homeownership is still the best way to build wealth," "I want to live in my own house, it's better to own," and "Do you own? [Author: Yes.] So why don't you rent if it's so great?" There was some recognition that they were "lucky" not to have bought during the peak of the housing bubble, but the majority of respondents said that they had always wanted to own and that this was the first time that they felt like they could manage it financially.

One of the respondents in Oakland, an African American man in his early thirties who works on social justice issues for a small nonprofit, provided his own assessment of this supposed turn away from homeownership as a preferred tenure. He noted that many of his white friends were choosing to rent "for now" but that this sentiment was less prevalent among his African American friends:

> *The new millennials are supposedly rejecting homeownership. It's critiqued as a capitalist notion—we're supposed to be beyond individual ownership models. Or you hear that homes don't build wealth like they used to. But I think the*

only people who are rejecting homeownership are those who know that they could be homeowners—their parents were, they're of a class that owns, and they're white. It means something different if you've been on the outside. . . . Homeownership matters to us [the African American community] on a whole different level. It's not just about the value of the house; it's about being an owner. Owning land.

His quote exemplifies the fact that homeownership is much more than an economic decision or the fulfillment of a housing "need." Homeownership is also a social practice that positions people within complex hierarchies of power and meaning.[23] Indeed, respondents placed significant weight on "ownership" as signifying a sense of belonging. For African Americans, this idea of belonging tended to be expressed more as the ability to achieve something that had been denied their parents or grandparents as a result of discrimination. For example, another African American respondent told me "For me, the key is becoming a homeowner. I don't care where, I don't care what the house looks like. But I think of my grandfather and how proud he'd be to see I made it." In contrast, among first-generation immigrants, homeownership was more closely associated with notions of citizenship and the "right" to be in this country:

It signifies roots. We're here to stay, and we have the right to be here.

***

I just became a citizen. There's a moment when the official moderating the citizenship ceremony announces that we don't have to carry our green card anymore, because no one can question our right to be here. That's what home-ownership means to me. I'm a citizen and I own land that I can pass down to my kids, who are citizens.

While the linkages between homeownership and identity do not often find their way into economic analyses of tenure choice, they have significant material effects. In my interviews, I found that the aspirational nature of homeownership greatly influenced people's decisionmaking about what kind of house they wanted to buy, and that these aspirations could quickly nullify preconceived notions of how much they could afford or what aspects of the housing bundle they most valued.

Interestingly, while the aspirational nature of homeownership was raised by every single respondent, the aspirations themselves were extremely varied. So while everyone wanted to "move up," what they were moving up "from" and where they wanted to go "to" differed. I identified five intersecting and overlapping motivations for transitioning from renting to owning:

23. Wiese (2004).

—as a signal of achieved economic mobility and the ability to have access to higher-quality and larger housing (greater use value);

—as a signal of belonging, for instance, related to citizenship (for immigrant households) or a right to ownership (African American households);

—as a shift in the locus of control and the idea of having more power over one's own life and housing situation;

—as an investment and an opportunity to build wealth; and

—as a way of providing a better life for their children, sometimes related to educational opportunity but also often articulated as an escape from violence.

These articulated motivations for buying a house led to very different home-ownership choices for the households I interviewed. Based on my own experiences, both as a child and now as an adult parent, I had assumed that neighborhood—and particularly school quality—would be a primary determinant in the initial decisionmaking process. As is reflected in previous literature, I thought households would choose the "best" neighborhoods they could afford and then find the best house within those neighborhood parameters. But through the interviews, I realized that these criteria were not universal. I, and my parents before me, already had achieved many of the aspirational goals that some respondents associated with homeownership: we belonged (while immigrants, we blended in thanks to our whiteness and lack of accent), we already had demonstrated class status (we did not share rooms, even when renting), we were safe (we did not rent in neighborhoods where violence was a part of everyday life), and we felt in control of our lives (we were not at risk of being deported and were not subject to the whims of slum landlords). As a result, for us the decision to buy a house was primarily about its investment potential, both as a tangible asset and as an investment in human capital through the quality of the schools.

In contrast to my personal experience, neighborhoods and school quality—while clearly a factor—were often not the most important decisionmaking criteria for many of these families. I had expected to find significant biases in what people thought constituted a "better" neighborhood—be it nicer homes and fewer renters (for example, a suburban or "white picket fence" vision), the racial-ethnic composition of the neighborhood, and the presence the amenities (such as parks, open space, or retail options). While I certainly found strongly held beliefs about neighborhoods and "what they were like" among respondents, these beliefs did not conform to a homogeneous view of what constitutes a good neighborhood or access to opportunity. For example, I found that there was relatively strong attachment to respondents' current neighborhoods and not as much interest in moving to suburban locales, despite better schools. The decision to stay in place was frequently articulated as a desire to stay connected to existing community ties; many of them worked nearby or relied on the connections they had already established in these neighborhoods to obtain contract work or other employment. In Oakland the distance between respondents' current residences and more affordable suburban locales prevented many families from searching outside their rental neighborhoods; a few respondents noted that they did not want to go "way out there" to find housing.

In the face of economic constraints that shaped where households could afford to buy, many families focused on the other benefits of homeownership instead. The desire for improved housing quality, both in terms of comfort and as an outward symbol of economic mobility, was extremely prevalent across respondents. In Albuquerque in particular, where it is possible for low- and moderate-income families to buy larger houses, six out of the nine respondents were more focused on how the home would improve their housing quality and reflect their rising social status than they were on neighborhood or school quality. Having more space was critical, especially given that many of these households served as anchors for other family members who were still finding their economic footing. One respondent stated:

We really want more than two bedrooms. The houses we're looking at, they have two floors, and three and sometimes even four bedrooms. The kids could have rooms of their own, and my brother wouldn't have to sleep on the couch while he's looking for work.

Another also noted the desire for additional space to accommodate extended family:

Right now, seven of us are living in this tiny two-bedroom rental. I think we're hoping to be able to afford a four-bedroom house, even if the rooms are small. The kids could have one room, my parents the other.

For many, moving to a bigger, new house also symbolized a shift in class status and a move away from "renters," who didn't take care of their properties.

I'm tired of living near neighbors with furniture in their front yards and five broken down cars in the driveway. Some of these new developments, they have really clear rules about what you're allowed to do on your property. I like that.

***

We feel like we're making it and want to see that in our day-to-day life. Not live like renters, but have some space, a nice home.

In Oakland there was less emphasis on house size, with the exception of the focus group that was conducted among East African immigrants. In that focus group, there was a strong consensus that it would be better to move to more distant neighborhoods (for example, in Antioch or Pittsburg–Bay Point, which are characterized by new suburban tract developments that popped up during the subprime and building boom of the early 2000s) to be able to buy a "new" house with more space. As one focus group respondent noted, "If I can't get better than this [current rental], then what's the point? I want something nicer, bigger." The emphasis on and importance of new construction seemed to be particularly strong in this focus group. In contrast, among respondents who were looking primarily in Oakland neighborhoods, size was often less important than quality improvements (perhaps in part because in general houses are smaller and older in Oakland's lower-income neighborhoods). However, the link between house choice and the desire to achieve housing improvements was just as strong. A Filipino respondent was eager to stay in her neighborhood but at the same time wanted something better. She told me, "The house next door, which is just like this one [current rental], came up for sale, but we weren't interested. Why own something that you can rent?"

Motivations related to ownership also corresponded closely with the theme of control. The idea that as homeowners they could "do what they want" to the home was prevalent among the majority of respondents. But I also heard lots of stories about the insecurity of renting and the frustrations of being subject to the whims of the landlord. These ranged from unlawful evictions (usually related to the sale of the building or foreclosure) to unannounced "rehabilitation" projects that required the family to live for months in an apartment or house undergoing construction. Some comments from focus group 2 illustrate these concerns:

If we have to move again, I'll just scream. It sounds so luxurious, just to be in one place.

***

Can you imagine? No one telling you the rent's going up, you can't hang your laundry there, they can't fix the toilet until next week.

***

And no one saying that so-and-so can't stay with you?

There was also significant dissatisfaction with the quality of rental options, which tied the theme of control closely to the goals of improving one's housing use value. Among the rental properties I visited, approximately half showed signs of deferred maintenance, with peeling paint, stained carpets, and sometimes visible mold.

Not surprisingly, wealth building also emerged as an important motive for choosing homeownership. Perhaps the most common quote in my field notes is "I'm tired of paying rent to someone else." Although I explore the financial aspects of the housing decision in more detail below, the more qualitative aspect of this mind-set was the idea of an asset to pass on to their children. With only a couple of exceptions, respondents saw these homes as long-term places to live, not as an investment that they intended to sell in a couple of years. Respondents were thoughtful about the idea that this was the "right" time to buy (especially in Oakland, where newspapers were increasingly touting the return of the real estate market), but unlike interviews I did about mortgage choices during the subprime boom, there was not the same expectation of a large financial windfall associated with buying a house.[24] Some respondents included resale value as one of their top decisionmaking criteria, but this was only true for a minority among those I interviewed.

Finally, although I tried to limit discussion about homeownership being "for the kids," it was clearly central in everyone's mind, be it in terms of an asset to pass on, a yard to play in, or separate rooms for the boys and girls.

Heuristics and the Financial Decisions Related to Homeownership

In addition to understanding the tenure decision, a second goal of the research study was to understand how households make the financial decisions related to buying a house. How do households decide how much to spend? What determines their mortgage choices? How did they relate homeownership to future asset building or other household financial circumstances?

Among the forty-three respondents, I would identify fifteen as very financially astute, with backgrounds in business or accounting. Several of these respondents currently ran their own small businesses—including a grocery store, a cab company, and a hair salon—and were knowledgeable about the tax system and the ways in which the value of homeownership as an investment is related to prevailing interest rates, inflation, and tax benefits. These respondents, while perhaps also motivated by the emotional factors described previously, situated their homeownership decision within a much broader rubric of household finances and analytics related to the state of the housing market. They had thought carefully about the financial costs and benefits of various loan terms and features (including weighing the costs and benefits of an FHA loan, which would allow them to reserve more of their savings for other investments as a result of the lower down payment requirements), the potential returns to homeownership, and the need to consider maintenance and property taxes as part of the overall costs of buying a home.

Among the rest of the respondents, however, there seemed to be many more rules of thumb, misperceptions, and trust in "expert" sources shaping their financial decisionmaking processes. One theme that resonated among many respondents was the "overwhelming" nature of buying a house, and the need to take "a

24. See Reid (2010).

leap of faith" in making the decision to sign on the dotted line. The transcript from focus group 4 is revealing:

> *You know, it's such a big purchase. It's almost too big. At some point you just have to close your eyes and go with your gut.*

***

> *Oh, my God, yes. I think I spent more time shopping for a couch than I did my house.*

***

> *Me too! Once you're talking about that many zeros, and if you really think about what you're signing and what you don't know, it's too much. I think if I had thought about it anymore, I would have gotten cold feet.*

The enormity of the financial decision led many respondents to greatly narrow their focus and exclude information that actually should influence their financial decisions. First, almost everyone anchored their "maximum house price" decision on how their housing costs as a homeowner would relate to their current monthly rent payment. There was a strong consensus that if they could purchase a house and "pay the same as I'm now paying in rent," homeownership was the better decision, and they could afford to make the shift.

> [Respondent] *I used some online calculators to figure out how much I could afford. I tried three or four and kept adjusting the figures so that it worked out so my monthly payment would be the same as my current rent. That gave me a range of around $280,000 to $350,000, depending on the assumptions in the calculator.*
>
> [Author] *Did you look at what the calculators included in the assumptions?*
>
> [Respondent] *A little, but it got confusing between different debt-to-income levels and how much property taxes would be. I figure that I'll be okay as long as I'm in that range.*

***

> *I used some online sites. It was good—it made me realize I need to think about property taxes and my other payments, like my car. But then I noticed that a lot of them are based on different assumptions, so I used several and decided the range I could look in was $185,000 to $265,000. My main goal was to get a house so my monthly payments would be about the same as they are now.*

***

When I realized I could buy a place and pay about the same I am paying in rent, that was what triggered it for me.

This monthly payment figure thus became an important anchor for respondents, and they used this to then subsequently rank and evaluate individual homes. For example, one respondent noted, "If I could get an extra bedroom, I would be willing to pay about $250 more a month." However, because the focus was on monthly payments, many respondents were willing to add on "a little" to get what they wanted but then didn't necessarily recognize that this pushed them into a much more expensive house when the costs were calculated over the long term. Among families who had been looking for a house for a longer period of time, I also found evidence of "anchoring and adjustment," especially in Oakland where a few respondents had bid on houses but had lost out to other buyers.

We started out with a maximum price of $250,000. We figured out that would be around $1,590 in monthly payments, a little less than our current rent of $1,700. But now we've bumped it up to $320,000. Everything under $300,000 we were finding was a foreclosure and in really bad shape.

***

[My husband] wants to keep it under $300,000. But I think we can stretch it a bit further—I'll get a few more clients each month. And I think if we get something a little nicer, it will hold its value better.

***

We started out wanting to pay less. But now we're paying about half our income for the house we bought. It doesn't leave us much, but we got a much nicer house. And we decided it would be better to be happy and save in other areas.

Although respondents anchored their decision on how much to spend based on their rent, I found little evidence that they compared or made any predictions regarding future changes in rents and home prices when thinking about the decision to buy. When I asked, "Do you ever think it might be better to rent than buy?" the first answer was often a variation on, "No, unless you plan on moving again in a few years."[25] When I prompted further with the question, "What if you just looked at it from a financial perspective?" the answer was still generally no. Some respondents noted that during a housing market crash, like the one

---

25. Most respondents had a rule of thumb related to how long one planned to stay in one place before it would make sense to own, and this ranged between three and five years. However, almost all respondents saw this home purchase as "permanent," which greatly conflicts with their previous mobility and life experiences. I also found little evidence that these families were seeing these as "starter" homes.

Oakland had just gone through, it would be better to rent until house prices "hit bottom." But no one suggested that if rents were particularly low, if interest rates were high, or if inflation were low, there might be a reason to do more analysis on the financial trade-offs between renting and owning. Even with further prompting, the links between rental housing market conditions, interest rates, and inflation did not seem to be a part of respondents' decisionmaking process. Inflation was particularly problematic as a financial concept—the majority of respondents thought that inflation was universally "bad," regardless of whether they were owners or renters.

In addition, while most of the respondents had thought about property taxes (in part because these are a standard item in the online cost calculators), the mortgage interest tax deduction did not feature prominently in their decision-making, although a few of them said that their mortgage broker or real estate agent had pointed out that they could possibly afford a bit more since "I would get some money back in taxes."[26] Furthermore, very few of those who were still searching were incorporating homeowner's insurance or earthquake insurance in their calculations of monthly payments. In Albuquerque, where homeowners' association dues are slightly more common, these were on respondents' minds since they were often included in the property brochure. But almost nobody had prepared a detailed budget to calculate not only the expenses related to the mortgage but also other costs, such as water and utilities or potential maintenance issues. Here is a sample discussion about these issues from focus group 2:

[Author] *What about maintenance costs? Are you budgeting for things like a new roof or water heater?*

[Respondent] *Most of the houses we're seeing need a lot of work. But we figure can do that later.*

[Respondent] *We're planning on buying a house and working on it in stages. When we get a little more money, we'll fix up the kitchen or bathroom.*

[Respondent] *Do you know how much a new roof costs? [Lots of discussion, with estimates ranging from $5,000 to $25,000.]*

[Respondent to author] *Do you think we should be budgeting for that? I'm not sure where that money would come from. How often does a house need a new roof?*

In interviewing respondents who had already bought a house, I asked them whether or not their costs after buying a house were lower, higher, or about the

26. A few of the respondents who ran their own businesses were much more focused on the benefits of the mortgage tax deduction.

same as what they had expected or planned for. Universally, the answer was that the costs were significantly higher.

We totally misjudged the costs. There were all sorts of other expenses that weren't at the forefront of our minds.

***

The three months after we bought the house, we tripled our credit card debt. We were so focused on affording the house, we didn't think about the moving costs. And things like buying trash cans for the bathroom or curtains. I think I must have gone to Target every day and walked out with $300 worth of stuff.

While respondents universally underestimated the costs of homeownership, they also seemed to overestimate the financial benefits. Although the recent financial crisis muted respondents' expectations about how much wealth they would build, respondents in Oakland in particular were very attuned to the fact that they were buying in a "down" market and that they expected prices to go up.

It's probably not going to go up as fast as before the crash, but I think it's a good time. Property values here have to go up.

***

I don't think we'll get rich quick. But I think the value will go up, yeah.

In Albuquerque, in contrast, there was significantly less focus on property value appreciation, although in general respondents were optimistic that prices were going to go up in the future. However, at both locations respondents were keenly focused on the equity component of homeownership through forced savings, although that is not how they phrased it. Critically, many respondents were counting on these assets—captured in their home—for their future financial needs, including paying for their retirement or their children's college education. Very few of the respondents reported having significant additional savings other than what they had been putting aside for their down payment, and only six of the respondents in the entire sample had a retirement savings account. Instead, their house was their anticipated savings.

We decided that putting all our savings into a down payment was better than just keeping it in an account. It's a better investment, plus we're no longer paying rent.

***

We see this house as our retirement fund. We don't have any retirement savings now, but this is a good step.

***

We're hoping that we'll build enough equity that this can help us to pay for [our daughter's] college education.

However, even when they did not anticipate significant appreciation in the housing market, respondents greatly overestimated how quickly their assets would grow. With the exception of the more financially sophisticated respondents, I found significant misunderstandings about how mortgage amortization works. The idea that "you're paying rent to yourself" kept coming up as a frame of reference for thinking about the financial benefits of homeownership, with much less attention paid to the interest costs, especially in the first few years of owning a home. My first inkling of this came during the third focus group interview when I thought to ask how much equity one recent homebuyer thought she was building.

[Respondent] *Well, let's see. I pay about $1,200 a month. So over two years, that means I've built up about $28,000.*

[Author] *What about interest?*

[Respondent] *Oh, yes, but I got a really low interest rate—4.2 percent—so that's not very much. So maybe I've built up around $24,000.*

While this respondent was unique in the degree to which she misunderstood amortization, I found that the majority of respondents overestimated the amount of equity they would build and underestimated their interest payments by more than 20 percent.

I also found that "experts"—real estate agents, mortgage brokers, and lenders—contributed to perceptions that homeownership had more benefits than drawbacks. The vast majority of my respondents had turned to others to help them gather and sort through the information related to the home-buying process. While in some cases these were relatives or friends, more than half had hired expert help.[27] All of the respondents were working with real estate agents, and nearly half had a mortgage broker whom they trusted to help them with the finances of the purchase. Throughout the interviews and focus groups, respondents would note that "the real estate agent said . . ." or "our broker suggested. . . ." These pieces of advice were highly valued and clearly given significant weight. In addition, although the sample is small, the analysis suggests that the advice tended toward encouraging the respondents to buy a house sooner rather than later ("She said this is a buyer's market." "Our real estate agent pointed out

27. Consistent with other studies, social networks played a strong role in identifying and selecting experts.

that this is a great time to buy—we may not have the same opportunity later."); expanding the search area and properties that would be considered "acceptable" ("We were only looking in Fruitvale, but she suggested we also look in West Oakland because there's more in our price range."); and suggesting that they "stretch" to buy something more expensive because it would hold its value better (an argument that also emphasized the potential financial benefits of homeownership over time—fixed housing payments and the mortgage interest tax deduction). I found no evidence that any of the advice was directed at more "conservative" decisions—for example, buying a smaller house to start, spending less, or taking into account potential future risks.

Optimism Bias and Future Risks

Perhaps the most important bias that my research detected among respondents was that of overoptimism and a failure to consider the potential downsides of homeownership. Many, if not most, of the respondents have had complicated and tumultuous lives, including forced international relocation due to the Eritrean-Ethiopian war, coming to the United States as children of undocumented immigrants, and personal experiences of violence, layoffs and involuntary job losses, and divorce. During the one-on-one interviews, I had respondents fill out life event charts, noting major changes in either their household or employment circumstances. The amount of volatility and change was remarkable. Out of twenty interviewees, seventeen had experienced significant changes in household composition in the last five years, including divorce, the loss of an income earner in the household (for example, a parent or a sibling moving or passing away), and the birth of additional children. Twelve had experienced job losses and unemployment spells of between four and eight months.

Of interest in these life event charts was how many respondents were deciding to buy during a period of relative prosperity in their lives. New jobs (especially the addition of a second job), a promotion, or a consolidation of households that increased the number of earners all seemed to be important triggers that led families to decide to buy a house. This decision also prompted greater work effort—again, out of twenty interviews, eleven respondents took on a second job (or their partners took on additional work, or both) in order to save for the down payment and increase the value of the house they could afford.[28] Importantly, at the point at which they were deciding to buy a house and how much to spend, respondents likely had higher incomes than is typical for their earning

28. This leads to an important caveat about my interview sample. Although I screened potential respondents according to income, I think many of them provided their "formal" income from their primary job but did not necessarily include "informal" or additional income. This suggests that some of the families I interviewed likely had more income than the area median.

trajectories. However, when I asked what they anticipated happening over the next few years, all of the answers were positive and forward looking:

I think with the experience I'm getting now, I'll be able to start my own business in a couple of years.

***

We're thinking we'd like to have another kid, especially as [my husband] keeps getting raises and earns more.

***

Now that the economy is rebounding, it's good for us. There will be more opportunities for union work and overtime.

No respondents talked about the economy going into a second recession, what they would do if they lost their job, the costs (for example, child care) associated with having additional children, or the potential for house prices to go down again. None of them brought up the possibility that maybe they would get sick or that there would be any conflict in their relationships. As mentioned above, very few had savings or other sources of liquid funds in the case of a sudden negative event.

Moreover, it seemed like respondents strongly discounted their own risks for foreclosure or default, despite the recent crisis.

Those families bought more than they could afford. We're being more careful.

***

We have some friends who went through foreclosure. But they were pretty irresponsible—they bought a new car at the same time they bought their house. . . . I'm not worried that it will happen to us.

Indeed, confidence in the future emerged as one of the key reasons these respondents had gone from seeing themselves as renters to potential owners. The interviews thus point to an important consideration as we think about homeownership for lower-income households. Lower-income homeowners are often very resilient and have developed multiple strategies—including high levels of cohabitation and support across family and friend networks—to build economic stability and make buying a house possible. Indeed, many of the respondents—who tended to be more financially stable than those around them—served as important anchors for their extended families and the community at large. However, there is evidence that income volatility is growing, and housing and labor market downturns may have a more pronounced effect on these families' ability to pay their mortgages, especially when they do not have a savings buffer or other sources of support. In the next section, I explore the policy implications arising from these findings.

Policy Implications

The goal of this research was to provide a qualitative, detailed look at the decisionmaking processes of lower-income households, with a specific focus on those seeking to buy their first home. The small sample size common to in-depth qualitative research can often make it challenging to know how representative the findings are for the broader population. However, I think the results presented here point at least to some important questions that housing policymakers should consider.

First, in the context of poor, urban communities, I think the interviews force us to reconsider the links between housing, tenure choice, and the geography of opportunity. For a wide variety of reasons, it really does appear that people are often deeply connected to "place" and the neighborhoods in which they live.[29] A fair number of the families in this study expressed interest in buying homes in what a policymaker might designate an "undesirable" lower-income community. In some cases this is because they already have roots in that community; in other cases the choice was driven more by cultural familiarity and a feeling of acceptance. Even when given the hypothetical option of living elsewhere (removing the income-price constraint), some respondents said they would still choose to live in the more ethnically diverse, lower-income parts of the city. This suggests that low-income homeownership programs may in fact be an effective way of promoting community development and neighborhood stabilization, and that there is the opportunity to build on that linkage for the benefit of not only the families who become homeowners but also neighboring renters. However, it also suggests that affordable homeownership programs need to be complemented by other policies that focus on improving the quality of urban schools, reducing violence, and building on community assets in order to ensure that lower-income homeowners do not become trapped in disinvested neighborhoods.

Second, the interviews also reveal a deep dissatisfaction with existing rental options—both in terms of size (for example, not enough nice, larger properties available for rent) and instability of tenure (for example, unresponsive landlords and insecure leases). As Immergluck has pointed out, the private rental market in the United States is largely unregulated relative to other industrialized countries, which has contributed to the dichotomy between renting and owning.[30] In part, reducing vulnerability of low-income households in the homeownership market should also entail a focus on improving rental affordability and stability so that families can build savings before buying a home and not be subject to involuntary moves that can disrupt schooling or employment. I was also struck by the

29. Sharkey (2012).
30. Immergluck (2011).

finding that respondents wanted to build assets, but that in this current moment, it was less about house price appreciation than it was about not "paying rent" to someone else. This could be interpreted that people like having something akin to a forced savings or asset-building mechanism, and that rental programs could be attractive if they provided a similar feature—especially if people understand that interest is a significant portion of a monthly payment. It was noteworthy that people thought they were "throwing away" money by paying rent but did not see interest payments in the same light. I think there is significant promise in developing new rental models that address underlying motivations associated with the desire to build savings but that do so without the same level of financial risk as homeownership.

That said, this chapter also reveals that a huge part of the desire to own a home has little to do with financial considerations, and that the heuristics and biases that are present in the homeowning decisionmaking process may not always lead to optimal financial decisions (especially in a volatile labor or real estate market). This suggests that there is still significant room to develop prepurchase interventions that can serve as a counterweight to these biases. There remains a need for prepurchase counseling programs and policies that can help to ensure that these programs are effective as well as reach a greater percentage of first-time homebuyers. The early evidence from these interviews also suggests that we may need to rethink the role of "experts" and recognize that their incentives (even when well regulated) do not necessarily lead them to counsel borrowers to be more cautious or deliberate about their financial decisions. Are there ways to encourage experts—be it real estate agents, brokers, or lenders—to counteract optimism bias and help families make more informed decisions?

Policymakers also need to place greater emphasis on postpurchase interventions and supports. There is increasing evidence that income volatility and risk among lower-income households is growing substantially, suggesting that even prudent financial decisions will not protect these families from the vagaries of the current market-based economy.[31] As Mallach has pointed out, to be a lower-income homeowner is to be at risk.[32] Lower-income homeowners have a smaller financial cushion with which to withstand the impact of negative life events, such as unemployment or serious illness, or to meet unanticipated repair costs, and by virtue of their limited housing choices, they are more likely to buy houses in need of repair. One finding that I think is particularly interesting is the extent to which families are willing and able to save to meet down payment requirements but then do not necessarily extend this behavior and logic to building additional savings. Rather than requiring larger down payments—which tie up

31. Hacker (2008).
32. Mallach (2011).

more of a household's savings in an illiquid form, especially in a down market—maybe it would be better to focus on smaller down payments but either require or encourage a secondary savings account that could be easily tapped into in case of a temporary shortfall in income or unexpected expense? Alternatively, is it possible to develop a "postpurchase" individual development account that would set money aside for home improvements or shortfalls in mortgage payments, funded in part by a share of the monthly loan payments?

Finally, on the research side, there is clearly much more that could be done to understand decisionmaking processes around the choice of tenure and neighborhood. In particular, better experimental and larger-scale studies are needed to document the prevalence and importance of these decisionmaking biases. Emerging methods in behavioral economics or consumer decisionmaking could pinpoint the degree to which these biases are pervasive in a broader population and how important they are for families' long-term financial well-being. That said, the results of this study also caution against commissioning a large number of behavioral economic studies that are conducted on college students in a lab. The motivations and decisionmaking frames of lower-income individuals, as well as those of immigrants and people of color, may be very different from a typical college student who volunteers for a research study. During the interviews I was constantly confronted by the fact that I hold significant biases—about which neighborhoods are "good" or what constitutes "responsible" decisionmaking—that are not universal and are deeply influenced by my own position and experiences. In addition, there were significant differences in responses between the interviews I did in Albuquerque and Oakland, suggesting that context and the extent of supply constraints in the housing market can influence people's thought processes. Critically, we need to see first-time homebuyers as a complex, differentiated group and recognize that class, race, locational, and cultural differences are powerful forces in shaping people's decisions about their housing tenure, finances, and neighborhood preferences. Developing a better understanding of these differences could help us identify what policies are most needed if our goal is to expand access to sustainable homeownership for lower-income and lower-wealth populations.

References

Asbury, J. E. 1995. "Overview of Focus Group Research." *Qualitative Health Research* 5, no. 4: pp. 414–20.

Bailey, A. J., M. K. Blake, and T. J. Cooke. 2004. "Migration, Care, and the Linked Lives of Dual-Earner Households." *Environment and Planning A* 36, no. 9: 1617–32.

Barakova, I., and others. 2003. "Does Credit Quality Matter for Homeownership?" *Journal of Housing Economics* 12, no. 2: 318–36.

Bettman, J. R., and C. W. Park. 1980. "Effects of Prior Knowledge and Experience and Phase of the Choice Process on Consumer Decision Processes." *Journal of Consumer Research* 7, no. 3: 243–8.

Bettman, J. R., and M. Sujan. 1987. "Effects of Framing on Evaluation of Comparable and Noncomparable Alternatives by Expert and Novice Consumers." *Journal of Consumer Research* 14, no. 2: 141–54.

Bourassa, S. C. 1996. "Measuring the Affordability of Home-Ownership." *Urban Studies* 33, no. 10: 1867–77.

Brueckner, J. K. 1986. "The Down Payment Constraint and Housing Tenure Choice." *Regional Science and Urban Economics* 16, no. 4: 519–25.

Bruegel, I. 1996. "The Trailing Wife: A Declining Breed? Careers, Geographical Mobility and Household Conflict in Britain, 1970–89." In *Changing Forms of Employment: Organizations, Skills and Gender,* edited by R. Crompton, D. Gallie, and K. Purcell, pp. 235–58. London: Routledge.

Cahill, D. J. 1994. "A Two-Stage Model of the Search Process for Single-Family Houses." *Environment and Behavior* 26, no. 1: 38–48.

Cameron, G., and J. Muellbauer. 1998. "The Housing Market and Regional Commuting and Migration Choices." *Scottish Journal of Political Economy* 45, no. 4: 420–46.

Campbell, J. Y. 2006. "Household Finance." *Journal of Finance* 61, no. 4: 1553–1604.

Case, K. E., and R. J. Shiller. 1988. "The Behavior of Home Buyers in Boom and Post-Boom Markets." *New England Economic Review,* November-December: 29–46.

Clark, W. V., and F. M. Dieleman. 1996. *Households and Housing: Choice and Outcomes in the Housing Market.* New Brunswick, N.J.: Center for Urban Policy Research.

Cooke, T. J. 2001. "'Trailing Wife' or 'Trailing Mother'? The Effect of Parental Status on the Relationship between Family Migration and the Labor-Market Participation of Married Women." *Environment and Planning A* 33, no. 3: 419–30.

Davis, J. 1993. "The Commuting of Exurban Home Buyers." *Urban Geography* 14, no. 1: 7–29.

Dibb, S. 1994. "Modeling in New Housing Choice: An Application." *Omega: International Journal of Management Science* 22, no. 6: 589–600.

Epley, N., and T. Gilovich. 2006. "The Anchoring-and-Adjustment Heuristic." *Psychological Science* 17, no. 4: 311–18.

Gibler, K., and S. Nelson. 2003. "Consumer Behavior Applications to Real Estate Education." *Journal of Real Estate Practice and Education* 6, no. 1: 63–83.

Gigerenzer, G., and W. Gaissmaier. 2011. "Heuristic Decision Making." *Annual Review of Psychology* 62: 451–82.

Gottlieb, P., and B. Lentnek. 2001. "Spatial Mismatch Is Not Always a Central-City Problem: An Analysis of Commuting Behavior in Cleveland, Ohio, and Its Suburbs." *Urban Studies* 38, no. 7: 1161–86.

Gram-Hanssen, K., and C. Bech-Danielsen. 2004. "House, Home and Identity from a Consumption Perspective." *Housing, Theory and Society* 21, no. 1: 17–26.

Gyourko, J., and P. Linneman. 1997. "The Changing Influences of Education, Income, Family Structure, and Race on Homeownership by Age over Time." *Journal of Housing Research* 8, no. 1: 1–25.

Hacker, J. 2008. *The Great Risk Shift: The New Economic Security and the Decline of the American Dream*. Oxford University Press.

Haurin, D. R., P. H. Hendershott, and S. Wachter. 1997. "Borrowing Constraints and the Tenure Choice of Young Households." *Journal of Housing Research* 8, no. 2: 137–54.

Hempel, D. J. 1974. "Family Buying Decisions: A Cross-Cultural Perspective." *Journal of Marketing Research* 11, no. 3: 295–302.

Hendershott, P. H., and M. White. 2000. "Taxing and Subsidizing House Investment: The Rise and Fall of Housing's Favored Status." Working Paper 7928. Cambridge, Mass.: National Bureau of Economic Research.

Horner, M. W. 2004. "Spatial Dimensions of Urban Commuting: A Review of Major Issues and Their Implications for Future Geographic Research." *Professional Geographer* 56, no. 2: 160–73.

Immergluck, D. 2011. "Critical Commentary: Subprime Crisis, Policy Response and Housing Market Restructuring," *Urban Studies* 48, no. 16: 3371–83.

Ioannides, Y. M. 1987. "Residential Mobility and Housing Tenure Choice." *Regional Science and Urban Economics* 17, no. 2: 265–87.

Jarvis, H. 1999. "Identifying the Relative Mobility Prospects of a Variety of Household Employment Structures, 1981–1991." *Environment and Planning A* 31, no. 6: 1031–46.

Kahneman D., and A. Tversky. 1974. "Judgment under Uncertainty: Heuristics and Biases." *Science* (New Series) 185, no. 4157: 1124–31.

Levy, D., L. Murphy, and C. Lee. 2008. "Influences and Emotions: Exploring Family Decisionmaking Processes When Buying a House." *Housing Studies* 23, no. 2: 271–89.

Linneman, P. 1985. "An Economic Analysis of the Homeownership Decision." *Journal of Urban Economics* 17, no. 2: 230–46.

Long, J. E., and S. B. Caudill. 1992. "Racial Differences in Homeownership and Housing Wealth, 1970–1986." *Economic Inquiry* 30, no. 1: 83–100.

Mallach, A. 2011. "Building Sustainable Ownership: Rethinking Public Policy toward Lower-Income Homeownership." Community Development Discussion Paper. Federal Reserve Bank of Philadelphia.

McKelvie, S. J. 2000. "Quantifying the Availability Heuristic with Famous Names." *North American Journal of Psychology* 2, no. 2: 347–57.

Moorthy, S., B. Ratchford, and D. Talukdar. 1997. "Consumer Information Search Revisited." *Journal of Consumer Research* 23, no. 4: 263–77.

Morgan, D. 1997. *Focus Groups as Qualitative Research*. London: Sage Publications.

Mullainathan, S., and R. H. Thaler. 2001. "Behavioral Economics." In *International Encyclopedia of the Social and Behavioral Sciences,* edited by N. Smelser and P. Baltes, pp. 1094–1100. Oxford: Elsevier.

Munro, M. 1995. "Homo-Economicus in the City: Towards an Urban Socio-Economic Research Agenda." *Urban Studies* 32, no. 10: 1609–21.

Painter, G., S. A. Gabriel, and D. Myers. 2001. "Race, Immigrant Status, and Housing Tenure Choice." *Journal of Urban Economics* 49, no. 1: 150–67.

Parkes, A., A. Kearns, and P. Atkinson. 2002. "What Makes People Dissatisfied with Their Neighborhoods?" *Urban Studies* 39, no. 13: 2413–38.

Reid, C. 2010. "Sought or Sold? Social Embeddedness and Consumer Decisions in the Mortgage Market." Community Development Working Paper 2010-09. Federal Reserve Bank of San Francisco. December.

Shah, A. K., and D. M. Oppenheimer. 2008. "Heuristics Made Easy: An Effort-Reduction Framework." *Psychological Bulletin* 134, no. 2: 207–22.

Sharkey, P. 2012. *Stuck in Place: Urban Neighborhoods and the End of Progress toward Racial Equality*. University of Chicago Press.

So, K., P. Orazem, and D. Otto. 2001. "The Effects of Housing Prices, Wages, and Commuting Time on Joint Residential and Job Location Choices." *American Journal of Agricultural Economics* 83, no. 4: 1036–48.

South, S., and K. Crowder. 1998. "Housing Discrimination and Residential Mobility: Impacts for Blacks and Whites." *Population Research and Policy Review* 17, no. 4: 369–87.

Talarchek, G. M. 1982. "Sequential Aspects of Residential Search and Selection." *Urban Geography* 3, no. 1: 34–57.

Taylor, B., and J. Ong. 1995. "Spatial Mismatch or Automobile Mismatch? An Examination of Race, Residence and Commuting in U.S. Metropolitan Areas." *Urban Studies* 32, no. 9: 1453–73.

Thaler, R. H., and C. R. Sunstein. 2008. *Nudge: Improving Decisions about Health, Wealth, and Happiness*. Yale University Press.

Tufano, P. 2009. "Consumer Finance." *Annual Review of Financial Economics* 1 (August): 227–47.

Tversky, A., and D. Kahneman. 1973. "Availability: A Heuristic for Judging Frequency and Probability." *Cognitive Psychology* 5, no. 1: 207–33.

U. S. Census Bureau. 2011. "2011 One-Year Estimates." In *American Community Survey*.

Van Ommeren, J., P. Rietveld, and P. Nijkamp. 1997. "Commuting in Search of Jobs and Residences." *Journal of Urban Economics* 42, no. 3: 402–21.

Wachter, S. M., and I. F. Megbolugbe. 1992. "Impacts of Housing and Mortgage Market Discrimination: Racial and Ethnic Disparities in Homeownership." *Housing Policy Debate* 3, no. 2: 332–70.

Waddell, P. 1993. "Exogenous Workplace Choice in Residential Location Models—Is the Assumption Valid?" *Geographical Analysis* 25, no. 1: 65–82.

Wiese, A. 2004. *Places of Their Own: African American Suburbanization in the Twentieth Century*. University of Chicago Press.

Withers, S. D., and W. Clark. 2006. "Housing Costs and the Geography of Family Migration Outcomes." *Population, Space and Place* 12, no. 4: 273–89.

5

Developing Effective Subsidy Mechanisms for Low-Income Homeownership

J. MICHAEL COLLINS

Homeownership has captured the attention of policymakers across the world in recent years, and this attention has often been negative. Bank failures based on failed home mortgages and a nearly global housing recession have raised difficult questions about the viability of pro-ownership public subsidies. In the United States, high foreclosure rates have provoked a debate over using limited federal resources to promote home purchases.[1] Yet demand for buying a home remains strong, even among households most exposed to the negative outcomes of failed homeownership.[2] The lure of owning a home remains part of the social and economic fabric of families and communities.[3] In the United States there is a vigorous debate about the optimal role of the public sector in subsidizing home-buying. Policy discussions often include the role of home-buying in stimulating the economy or the role of mortgages in the financial sector. But a common theme throughout is the concern about how to best aid low-income first-time homebuyers.

To be sure, there are widely discussed rationales for public sector support for homeownership. Economists argue that public sector interventions are justified when the private market fails to achieve an efficient outcome. Inefficiencies may arise in the home-buying market in several ways. If homeownership produced

1. Beracha and Johnson (2012); M. Davis (2012); Shlay (2006).
2. Drew and Herbert (2012).
3. Hui, Yu, and Ho (2009).

positive externalities for surrounding communities, then too few renters would become homeowners than would be optimal for society in the absence of incentives from the public sector. Essentially the marginal social benefits of higher homeownership rates are greater than the marginal private benefits of an individual buying a home. Tax deductions and credits, grants, and other subsidies reduce the "price" of ownership (the private marginal cost), which moves the quantity of owners closer to the socially optimal level. More owners may lead to improved overall social welfare.

Yet the evidence of these positive externalities is mixed. Recent studies have shown that positive social benefits of owner-occupied homes are more likely due to who buys a home and when rather than to the tenure of ownership itself.[4] On the other hand, owning a property does generate incentives to invest in one's home and neighborhood. Research seems to support the idea that homeowners work to preserve the value of their property through various mechanisms, including increased civic engagement.[5] Overall, evidence of the positive externalities of greater homeownership is weakly optimistic. Assuming that at least modest positive externalities do exist, making modest supports for home-buying and owning available to all households, regardless of income, may be justified.

Subsidizing homeownership specifically for lower-income buyers stems from additional rationales. The policy argument in favor of subsidizing homeownership for these buyers is rooted in the discrepancies in homeownership rates across households by race and income. Much of the gap in ownership rates can be explained by age and other demographic factors besides income and race. Nonetheless, even controlling for other factors, whites still seem to have better chances of owning a home than blacks or Hispanics, and these differences are concentrated among low-income households.[6] In fact, the racial gap in ownership rates is much lower at higher-income levels. Long-term statistical trends aside, the notion that all families should have a chance to own a home if they want to is a commonly held ideal.[7] Historical failures in real estate and financial markets may have prevented targeted groups from participating in the private benefits of homeownership in the past, and their effects still persist across generations today.[8] To the extent that owned housing may be more likely to be located in places with quality school districts and other services that provide positive environments for families and children, supporting low-income homeownership may enhance intergenerational social and economic attainment.

---

4. Engelhardt and others (2010); Holupka and Newman (2012).
5. Glaeser (2011).
6. Boehm and Schlottmann (2009); Andrews and Sanchez (2011).
7. Bostic and Lee (2009); Cramer (2009).
8. Boehm and Schlottmann (2009).

Going beyond perceptions of social inequality, ownership may also facilitate access to private wealth for lower-income households, wealth that they likely do not accrue in other ways. Historically, home equity is the primary store of nonpension wealth for low-income families.[9] Home equity accrues over decades of ownership due to the paydown of principal, a form of forced savings, and from any house price appreciation. Price appreciation is, of course, volatile, but over time homeowners often realize some gains in value in real terms (adjusting for inflation).[10] However, buying a home is not a sure path to building wealth since the length of ownership, loan terms, and risks of default or foreclosure can all turn an investment with a positive expected net value into a negative proposition.[11] For owners who make it to retirement and pay off their mortgage, an owned home can provide security in old age, an asset that at least produces shelter. Equity in the home might be tapped for consumption via a home equity mortgage or reverse mortgage, or simply from deferred maintenance and depreciation.[12] To the extent that public subsidies succeed in expanding low-income homeownership, financially vulnerable families stand to gain from the wealth-enhancing benefits of ownership, again subject to the caveats concerning length of ownership, loan terms, and default risk.

Despite the arguments supporting public subsidies to facilitate homeownership among the general population—and low-income households more specifically—it is crucial to remember that homeownership can also entail costs to society. Ownership in the United States is closely tied to low-density, energy-intensive, single-family housing, which may be less efficient than denser designs.[13] Moreover, there are a number of costs related to people who buy homes and then fail to maintain them physically or financially. Lenders face unique information failures when underwriting mortgage loans, especially for low-income first-time buyers who have little prior home-buying experience and minimal track records in financial markets. The mortgage lender cannot observe the borrower's true commitment to the home and ability to make timely mortgage payments. In extreme scenarios homeowners default on their home mortgage loans and impose significant costs on neighborhoods and government.[14] Ownership also limits mobility such that households in owned homes may not be able to pursue higher-income jobs in other areas or relocate when local labor markets soften.[15] When evaluating the merit of subsidies, these and other potential downsides

9. Temkin, Theodos, and Price (2010).
10. Kennickell (2012).
11. Galster and Santiago (2008).
12. Herbert and Belsky (2008).
13. Glaeser (2011).
14. Haughwout, Peach, and Tracy (2010).
15. Andrews and Sanchez (2011).

must be taken into account when balancing the marginal social benefits against the costs of ownership.

Although evidence on the benefits of buying a home is mixed and the real downsides to homeownership were made apparent by the recent housing crisis, political support for producing, financing, selling, and maintaining owner-occupied homes is strong.[16] To the extent that the aspirational dream of buying a home remains a symbol of social mobility and economic achievement, the general public also continues to support homeownership.[17] Pragmatically, existing homeowners, entities in the real estate industry, and a host of other constituencies are reluctant to let go of existing public subsidies.

Nevertheless, the political discourse is often dominated by calls for reducing government spending and reforming income tax laws. The deductibility of mortgage interest has been at the center of discussions in recent years, with calls to change or eliminate this long-standing public policy. In this context the rationale, form, and functions of subsidies for home-buying and homeowning need to be critically considered. Policymakers face the task of developing programs and policies that best use public resources based on the overarching public goals involved. This chapter attempts to outline a set of potential criteria to evaluate policy options to promote low-income homeownership, taking into account the inherent trade-offs involved.[18]

Using Subsidies to Lower the Costs of Buying a Home

Policy options for promoting homeownership can be sorted into three broad categories: subsidies, credit enhancements, and regulatory actions.[19] This chapter focuses on the first: explicit subsidies. Subsidies are one of the primary mechanisms that government uses to incentivize first-time homebuyers. The second category, credit enhancement, has been a heated issue in the aftermath of the housing crisis of the late 2000s. Credit enhancements, which involve additional guarantees, insurance, or collateral, increase access to capital used to finance a

16. Basolo (2007); Lerman, Steuerle, and Zhang (2012).

17. Bratt (2008); Drew and Herbert (2012).

18. The definition of "low income" varies. The annual low-income threshold for a family of three including one minor child in fiscal year 2010 was $18,310 as defined by the U.S. Department of Health and Human Services and $14,787 as defined by the U.S. Census Bureau's poverty threshold. The U.S. Department of Housing and Urban Development uses a different formula and allows the definition to vary according to local housing costs. The "50 percent of area median income" threshold means that the criterion for low income varies significantly by geography. For example, in Abilene, Texas, low income for a family of three was defined as less than $23,300 whereas in Marin County, California, that threshold was $48,400.

19. Collins (2007).

home. In some cases enhancements lower the costs of borrowing and might be viewed as a subsidy to buyers. The rise and fall of the government-sponsored enterprises Fannie Mae and Freddie Mac offer a cautionary tale about how credit protections can distort lender and financial institution practices in ways that may not be ideal from a public resources perspective. Nevertheless, the incremental effect of credit enhancements for prospective buyers tends to be small, particularly in equilibrium.[20] The third category, regulations related to credit access, housing standards, zoning, and limits on construction, plays a key role in making mortgages available and determining where and if homes suitable for purchase are developed. Mortgage market regulations are administered by a collection of independent federal agencies and historically do not involve explicit tax expenditures or appropriations. Zoning and building rules are administered at a local level, and the effects vary significantly depending on local housing market conditions.[21] This third category of policies involves far more than ownership preferences and includes land use, environmental stewardship, and community planning. Although both credit enhancements and regulations affect homeownership generally, they are not the focus of this chapter.

Subsidies essentially can be aimed at one of three targets: lowering monthly payments, lowering the initial purchase price, or providing down payment assistance. Monthly payments for a home include paying the mortgage principal, interest, property taxes, and maintenance costs. The primary avenue for subsidizing monthly payments is an interest rate subsidy, which reduces the cost of borrowing. This can be achieved directly through subsidized loans or more broadly through the tax code. That is, the government can either subsidize a lower interest rate on a borrower's mortgage directly or allow borrowers to deduct mortgage interest from their income taxes, lowering their tax burden and indirectly subsidizing mortgage payments. Payments are usually measured relative to income, with a ratio of monthly mortgage payment to monthly gross income commonly used (gross income is income before taxes and withholding for benefits; net or "take home" income is generally 25–30 percent lower). This payment-to-income ratio is one measure, with levels around 0.30 and above considered less affordable and increasing the risk of foreclosure. As a higher percentage of income goes toward housing payments, unexpected nonhousing expenses or temporary drops in income reduce the borrower's ability to make mortgage payments, potentially leading to default. Some countries subsidize monthly housing payments for targeted homeowners more directly, rather than through interest rates or the tax

---

20. Jaffee and Quigley (2009).
21. Glaeser (2011).

code.[22] The closest U.S. example to a direct payment subsidy is the use of rental vouchers for homeownership, but this program operates on a very small scale.[23]

Subsidies for the purchase price of a home are applied at or before the time a new buyer purchases a home. The subsidy may reduce the purchase price below market rates or subsidize construction costs that could not be recouped from the sales price. This form of subsidy can reduce the down payment and mortgage required, thereby lowering monthly payments. This approach raises the possibility that the buyer will resell the home, capture any below-market subsidy, and retain the surplus for him- or herself. In addition, purchase subsidies generally represent large one-time lump sum transfers, which policymakers perceive as costly on a per homebuyer basis (of course, the present value of a thirty-year payment subsidy also may be large but typically is not perceived as being of the same scale). Purchase subsidies are relatively rare and rationed to either specific categories of buyers or specific geographic areas. This distinction—targeting specific borrowers or regions—illustrates the two very different goals associated with purchase subsidies.

One goal of purchase subsidies applied to a specific buyer is to provide financial resources related to the public or private benefits of that household owning a home. The second goal is less focused on the household and more on the neighborhood, with the home purchase viewed as a signal to real estate markets that a particular area is worthy of further investments.

Geographically targeted subsidies also may be designed to stimulate the local economy by employing building tradesmen and suppliers to develop a property into a salable home. However, below-market-rate subsidies for purchasing a home must be a scarce resource since widely available subsidies will simply be absorbed into transaction prices. The homebuyer tax credit of 2008–10 in the United States demonstrates this dynamic. To the extent that a real estate market can anticipate buyers entering the market using purchase subsidies, housing prices will be bid upwards until the last dollar of subsidy is absorbed by an additional dollar of asking price. Some 400,000 first-time buyers in the 2008–10 period claimed an average tax credit of $7,250.[24] The credit was primarily designed to stimulate the housing market and the economy more generally.[25] It was widely available and led to a temporary increase in sales prices rather than a net tangible benefit for first-time buyers, regardless of income level.[26]

22. Atterhog and Song (2009).
23. Olsen (2007).
24. Government Accountability Office (2010).
25. Kocieniewski (2010).
26. Goodwin and Zumpano (2011); Brogaard and Roshak (2011).

The last category of subsidy for home-buying is down payment support, which relates to both payment and price assistance but might be more accurately described as financing assistance. Down payments perform multiple functions in real estate financing. First, the behaviors that potential borrowers must develop to save a 10 or 20 percent down payment are consistent with the skills and behaviors related to managing home mortgage payments, such as budgeting and managing cash flow. Second, lenders can face significant information asymmetries related to a prospective borrower's likelihood of default. Formalized down payment savings plans potentially provide lenders with several years of observable data on a household's financial management habits, which both reduces uncertainty and facilitates efficient loan underwriting.[27] The amassing of savings for a down payment is a signal to a lender that the borrower is likely to be able to manage mortgage debt service obligations. Finally, down payments are most critical in the case of a downturn in property values. The late 2000s illustrated that the combination of little homeowner equity combined with a decline in home values can leave large numbers of homeowners "underwater"—owing a mortgage that exceeds the value of the home. While being underwater does not automatically trigger defaults, the risks of foreclosure are elevated when a borrower has an income decrease or other shock and has negative equity. A 20 percent down payment provides a cushion in the case of a drop in prices and can reduce the probability of default. Thus one potential benefit of down payment subsidies is a reduction in payment defaults due to the added equity the borrower has in the home.[28]

The U.S. Census Bureau has periodically used the Survey of Income and Program Participation to estimate the potential of income and down payment subsidies to increase the share of renters who could afford to buy a home. The last report, using 2004 survey data, shows that only 2 percent of renters were hampered from buying a home *only* by a lack of income, while a lack of savings for a down payment was the *only* barrier for 26 percent. A $5,000 down payment subsidy (in 2004) would have raised renters' ability to buy a home by 10 percentage points.[29] While resting on a number of assumptions and outdated data, these estimates are consistent with other analyses showing that first-time buyers' primary barrier to the purchase of a home is a lack of liquid savings for a down payment and closing costs.[30]

Down payment subsidies can be structured in a number of different ways, including grants and loans. Loans ideally result in the repayment of capital that

27. Atterhog and Song (2009); Ergungor (2010).
28. Ergungor (2010).
29. Savage (2009).
30. See, for example, Listokin and others (2001).

is then reused as a down payment loan for another borrower. These loans can be amortizing, but most often they are designed as "silent" junior liens due at resale or refinance. Because these loans tend to be small, must be monitored over many years, and lose value with inflation, the costs of administering these loans is high relative to the loan amount. Additionally, subsidies in the form of junior liens can constrain owners from taking out additional loans. Instead of loans some assistance programs use down payment grants, which are administratively efficient but strictly one-time in nature. Without monitoring, grants may also encourage borrowers to take out home equity loans or lines of credit after the home purchase in order to tap that equity, eroding the value of down payment subsidies in terms of reduced default risk.

Recent developments will likely result in changes to existing subsidy policies. Under the 2010 Dodd-Frank financial reforms (Wall Street Reform and Consumer Protection Act), the ratio of total monthly debt (including the mortgage payment) to gross income became a key indicator of the quality of mortgage loans. Under Dodd-Frank, a qualified mortgage (QM) is less likely to face regulatory scrutiny and less likely to be challenged in court. The total debt-to-income ratio (DTI) is only binding for borrowers with large mortgage payments relative to income and for borrowers with large amounts of other debt, such as student, car, or consumer loans. Under regulations issued by the Consumer Financial Protection Bureau (CFPB), potential homebuyers with DTIs greater than 0.43 have few options for financing in the traditional mortgage market. This may create an added dimension of public subsidies not just for reducing monthly mortgage debt obligations through payment subsidies but perhaps subsidies for paying down nonhousing debts to enable potential owners to qualify for a mortgage. These rules add further complexity to the use of public subsidies for homeownership going forward.[31]

Whether used for payment support, purchase price, or down payments, subsidies for homeownership can be further divided into two subcategories: those directly appropriated and those provided through the tax code. Appropriated subsidies from the federal government are direct grants, must go through the process of annual budget submissions by the White House, and must then be approved in budget bills in the House and Senate. Tax subsidies are classified as either tax deductions or tax credits. Tax deductions are claimed by taxpayers on their tax returns to reduce taxable income and therefore reduce total tax liabilities. Because of the nation's progressive tax rate structure, reducing $1 of

---

31. Although discussions are ongoing at the time of this writing, a stricter qualified residential mortgage rule promulgated jointly by six federal financial regulators defines the standard for loans allowed to be sold in the secondary market without risk retention. Current qualified residential mortgage standards include a 20 percent down payment and a 36 percent or less DTI.

taxable income in a 33 percent marginal tax bracket is worth $0.33, while a $1 deduction of income in a 15 percent marginal bracket is worth only $0.15. As a result taxpayers with more income in the highest brackets benefit more from tax deductions relative to taxpayers in lower-income tax brackets. Tax credits actually offset the amount of total tax due rather than just reducing the amount of income subject to tax. Since tax credits are of little value to taxpayers with low tax bills, credits are sometimes sold to corporations or individuals with larger tax liabilities. In some cases credits are refundable, meaning that a taxpayer with small or no taxes due can receive a tax refund based on the credit.

Strategies for Subsidizing Low-Income Homeownership

Turning from the general approaches to specific subsidies, the next decision for policymakers is how to implement programs targeted to lower-income first-time buyers. The intent of a subsidy is to change behavior: to incentivize low-income renters to buy their first home and then ideally to sustain ownership over a long enough period to engender the potential positive externalities of homeownership. Barriers to ownership among low-income first-time buyers tend to relate to having both a low income and low levels of net worth (savings less debts). Income subsidies are obviously one general mechanism to aid low-income people to buy homes, as well as to increase consumption of all other goods, but are not aimed at helping renters in general purchase homes. In the United States, there are currently four examples of purported supports for low-income homeownership, each of which is examined briefly below.

Mortgage Interest Deduction

The mortgage interest deduction is a subsidy for homeownership delivered through the tax code. It is by far the largest support for owning a home in the United States and applies to all homeowners, not just those with low incomes. Mortgage borrowers may deduct mortgage interest from taxable income when calculating federal (and usually state) income tax. By reducing tax liabilities for homebuyers, this deduction increases income available for monthly housing payments. The mortgage interest deduction is the second largest tax expenditure for individuals in the federal budget, after the exemption for contributions to pension funds. However, the deduction is primarily an incentive to borrow using more mortgage debt rather than an incentive for lower-income renters to become owners. Most lower-income taxpayers take the standard deduction on their federal income taxes and do not claim the mortgage interest deduction. Only 10 percent of tax filers with incomes under the median income itemize.[32]

32. M. Davis (2012); Government Accountability Office (2010).

The progressive nature of federal income tax rates results in lower-income owners receiving a smaller deduction as a percentage of income than more affluent buyers, even if they itemize their deductions. Recent studies suggest that the mortgage interest deduction is largely capitalized into house prices (depending on the elasticity of local housing markets) and in reality is less of a support of homeownership than many policymakers assume.[33]

Mortgage Payment Subsidies

One of the most well-known mechanisms to reduce borrowing costs for first-time lower-income home buyers is the single-family housing bond, known as a mortgage revenue bond (MRB). MRBs are sold to investors in order to finance below-market interest rate mortgages. Investors are willing to purchase these bonds at below-market interest rates because the income from MRBs is tax free. State housing finance agencies are allocated a per-capita amount of tax-exempt housing bond authority each year. By law MRB-backed loans are limited to first-time homebuyers who earn no more than the median income in their area. If a borrower's income rises above eligible levels, up to half of any profit from the sale of the financed home may be recaptured for up to nine years (although in practice this rarely occurs). MRBs are administered by designated state agencies that issue the bonds and monitor loans. Because of the mechanics of issuing the bonds and the relative value of tax-exempt interest, the value of MRBs to first-time buyers fluctuates over time. In general the resulting payment subsidy is relatively low, typically less than 1 percentage point below prevailing market rates.[34] The housing market recession and historically low current interest rates across the market interest rate yield curve mean that MRB loans may offer no subsidy but simply streamlined access to mortgages for low-income homebuyers with little payment support.[35] MRB loans, for example, are exempt from the CFPB's qualified mortgage regulation restricting debt-to-income ratios. Assuming a return to a more historically average yield curve, MRBs at least have the potential to also offer payment subsidies. The net present value of a 1-percentage-point reduction in interest rate, discounted at inflation (consumer price index) for a $160,000 mortgage is approximately $7,000 over ten years. A similar though smaller-scale financing mechanism is the U.S. Department of Agriculture (USDA) Section 502 direct loan program. Instead of relying on tax-advantaged borrowing, 502 loans are made and held by public agencies with the goal of helping very low income homebuyers in rural areas. The interest rates on these loans can be as low as 1 percent, depending on income.

33. Glaeser (2011); M. Davis (2012); Bourassa and others (2012).
34. Ergungor (2010); Durning (1987).
35. Moulton (2010); see also chapter 8 in this volume.

Down Payment Grants

The Community Development Block Grant (CDBG), HOME Investment Part-nerships Program (HOME), and Federal Home Loan Banks' Affordable Housing Program are all sources of funds used by local governments or nonprofits to make direct grants to first-time homebuyers for down payments. Down payment funds may not be issued as grants but can be provided as an interest-free loan due at the sale of the home. These revolving loan funds allow more households to receive assistance as down payment loans are repaid. Down payment grants and loans are frequently used methods of helping specific populations become first-time homebuyers. Unfortunately, each grant or loan could require $16,000 or more (assuming a $160,000 home price and 10 percent down payment), resulting in far more buyers who qualify than can receive support given the scarcity of grants dollars. In effect this assistance becomes a lottery serving a small share of eligible borrowers. Of course down payment savings subsidies can be smaller and still be effective—even assistance in the range of $1,000 can be enough to help a renter qualify to buy a home in some markets.[36] For example, the American Dream Down Payment Initiative, a demonstration project using HOME funds for down payments from 2004 to 2008, provided an average of $5,000 per homebuyer.[37]

Sales Price-Development Subsidies

Building a home or converting a structure used for another purpose into a dwell-ing suitable for homeownership entails significant costs. Acquiring land for development or an existing unit for renovation is often the most significant cost, but the fixed costs of permits, approvals, and other code requirements are also often high. In some locations the cost of building or renovating affordable homes exceeds prevailing market values. Both the HOME and CDBG programs are used by local governments and nonprofits to subsidize creation of a small number of targeted housing units suitable for affordable homeownership for low-income families. Ideally these subsidies are focused on neighborhoods where the costs of development exceed market values and no private construction would occur in the absence of the subsidies. Although units are typically sold to low-income buyers, the primary intent of these subsidies is to spur real estate markets, with the support of first-time homebuyers as a secondary consideration.

Impacts on Affordability

Table 5-1 illustrates how monthly payment, down payment, and price subsi-dies each can be employed for a buyer of a $160,000 home with an income of

36. Herbert and Tsen (2007).
37. U.S. Department of Housing and Urban Development (2012).

Table 5-1. *Payment, Down Payment, Purchase Price Subsidy Examples*[a]
Dollars unless otherwise indicated

Item	(A) MRB	(B) DPA
House sale price	160,000	160,000
Income	45,000	45,000
Other debt per month	938	938
Loan-to-value ratio	0.9	0.8
Cash required	19,200	35,200
Down payment	16,000	32,000
Closing costs	3,200	3,200
Borrower portion	19,200	19,200
Years to save[b]	7.5	12[c]
Mortgage	144,000	128,000
Market payment (4.5 percent)	730	649
DTI (ratio)	0.44	0.42
Subsidized payment (3.5 percent)	647	575
DTI (ratio)	0.42	0.40
Notes	100 basis points saving from MRB; 10 percent down payment	20 percent down payment

Source: Author's calculations.
a. Based on a $160,000 home and a borrower with an income of $45,000 and $11,500 in consumer debt. See text for definition of acronyms.
b. 5 percent of income saved per year; 5 percent annual return on savings.
c. Without subsidy.

$45,000 and, as the base case in column A, a 10 percent down payment and thirty-year fixed-rate mortgage. The buyer has $11,500 in annual nonmortgage debt obligations, or $938 a month. This is relatively typical for a highly leveraged household that has, for example, student loans, an automobile loan, and credit card debt.[38] Given the CFPB's DTI qualified mortgage regulation, nonmortgage debt levels are important to include in such illustrations. In column A, using a 4.5 percent mortgage interest rate, the DTI is 0.44 and would not meet the QM standard. Using an MRB loan with an interest rate of 3.5 percent reduces the monthly payment by $83, about an 11 percent decrease over the base case. This reduces the DTI to 0.42, which would meet the QM standard. Although not a deep subsidy, in this case the MRB may open up ownership to a renter without first requiring the renter to pay down other debts.

38. Dynan (2012).

Column B shows the same buyer but now with a down payment of 20 percent overall, including down payment assistance (DPA). The additional 10-percentage-point down payment lowers the principal balance and reduces the monthly payment by $81, pushing the DTI to 0.42. In this case the DPA subsidy achieved a similar effect on affordability as the MRB payment subsidy. Combining the DPA with an MRB loan, which is common, reduces the monthly payment by $155 and pushes the DTI down to 0.40. Monthly mortgage payment burdens in this situation are lowered by one-fifth from the base case. Note, however, that saving up the down payment and closing costs is a substantial endeavor for the borrower. A 10 percent down payment and 2 percent closing cost requirement translate to $19,200 in savings required for either case (in column B the borrower would receive $16,000 in down payment subsidy). For a household earning $45,000 per year, saving 5 percent of gross income (not take-home income), invested at a 5 percent annual rate of return, would require four and a half years to accumulate. Coming up with the 20 percent down payment without the down payment subsidy would delay home purchase by an additional four and a half years.[39]

A Framework for Evaluation

If a policy goal is to expand ownership among low-income households, a well-designed subsidy policy focused on low-income first-time buyers specifically might include a number of characteristics. Table 5-2 outlines eight factors that policymakers ought to consider when designing or evaluating new policies to subsidize low-income homeownership.

The first factor is scalability. A number of existing federal programs have small appropriations, have limited administrative capacity, and suffer from a lack of awareness. Programs that promote homeownership need to be large enough to benefit low-income renters so they incorporate the subsidy into their expectations related to the costs of buying a home. An arbitrary benchmark might be serving at least 10 percent of the target market. For example, in a year with 120,000 first-time buyers with incomes at or below the HUD 50 percent of the area median income cutoff, the program ought to serve at least 12,000 first-time buyers. Market share values less than 10 percent might still influence renters to consider buying a home, but at some level programs are likely to become too small and unknown to effectively influence behavior.

The second factor listed in table 5-2, marginal effect, refers to the policy's effectiveness in encouraging renters who would not typically purchase a home in the absence of the program to buy a home. Ideally, a program converts a renter

---

39. Estimates based on real terms; over time income and home values will inflate in nominal terms.

Table 5-2. *Factors for Evaluating Low-Income Homeownership Policies*

Factor	Key indicator	Policy ideal
Scalable	What portion of low-income potential first-time buyers are supported annually?	Larger scale (for example, 10 percent of target market)
Marginal effect	Does the policy primarily induce people who otherwise would not buy a home to buy a home rather than pushing existing buyers to buy larger homes or borrow larger mortgages (intensive margin)?	Extensive marginal buyer
Targeted	Does the policy primarily induce first-time buyers under a certain income level or matching another strategically defined demographic?	Highly targeted
Administrative costs	What portion of the subsidy is required to administer applications, fund transfers, and cover oversight-monitoring (and for how long)?	Low marginal administrative costs
Recapture	Does the program have provisions to "recycle" subsidies for additional buyers or revoke subsidies from buyers who fail to meet targeting criteria or both?	High level of reuse of funds across 3–4 buyers (net of administrative costs)
Neighborhood revitalization	Does the program provide added incentives for the physical improvement of the housing stock in otherwise distressed areas?	Neutral to or promoting acquisition-rehab
Default risk	Does the program develop information useful for underwriting homebuyer risks or reduce-mitigate risks postpurchase or both?	Reveal prepurchase behaviors and create incentives not to default (and to cure in case of delinquency)
Mobility limits	Does the program limit homebuyers from selling or moving if labor market or family contexts change?	Maximum labor market fluidity

who would never buy a home into a homeowner, but the program might also encourage people who would have bought a home within a few years regardless (perhaps when their income is higher) simply to purchase a home now.[40] Potential negative outcomes include incentivizing consumers to purchase bigger homes than they would otherwise consider or encouraging them to take out larger mortgages. These marginal effects—not related to ownership but rather to the intensity of ownership among owners—are not as directly related to expanding the number of owners from targeted income groups. It should be noted that policies focusing on saving for down payments and closing costs may offer the greatest potential for converting the marginal renter into a homeowner, although at significant cost. Because it can take years to accumulate savings, such policies may accelerate owning in the life cycle of some households while for other households homeownership may never have been an alternative without the policy.

The third factor is targeting. The program needs to be designed, tested, marketed, and operated with an explicit restriction to borrowers who fall below particular income thresholds relative to area median incomes. Programs might also serve a wider demographic but offer stronger incentives for lower-income buyers. Without targeting it is difficult to justify new homeownership policies as being directed to support low-income homeownership.

A fourth, and critical, factor is the efficiency of administration. Too often subsidy programs trigger reams of regulatory restrictions that limit access and absorb a significant portion of resources for overhead that should be applied to activities with a direct impact on communities. Administration includes outreach, intake and application processing, disbursement of funds, and monitoring. Since homebuyers may remain in a subsidized home for a decade or more, the present value of ongoing administrative costs can be significant.

A fifth factor is subjecting the subsidy to some form of recapture. Recapture can take two general forms. One is a penalty on buyers who violate the restrictions or terms of the subsidy, such as renting out a purchased home or earning income that exceeds the levels directed in the policy. The other form is some mechanism to boost the scale and sustainability of programs by making their resources recyclable to the extent possible so that a single subsidy can be reused for subsequent first-time homebuyers. For example, a buyer might pay back a down payment subsidy, or the purchase subsidy may be retained to lower the sales price for the next owner of a unit. Both of these approaches can be administratively costly if they entail active monitoring and enforcement, so recapture needs to be balanced against administrative efficiency.

---

40. Generally a first-time buyer is defined as someone who has not owned a home in the last three years.

A sixth factor to consider is a subsidy program's neighborhood externalities. A subsidy focused on a specific geographic area might generate attention for an undervalued part of the housing market. Attractive design and amenities might encourage further private investment that begins to revitalize troubled neighborhoods. However, to the extent that homeownership programs channel low-income homebuyers into disinvested areas that offer fewer amenities or access to opportunities, the neighborhood benefits of owning a home maybe undermined.

The seventh factor is the subsidy's impact on loan default risk. At one extreme, a subsidy could reduce information asymmetry for lender underwriting, lower exposure to negative house price changes, and provide buyers with a more secure position in case of a negative financial shock. At the other extreme, a subsidy could reduce buyers' financial stakes in their homes and leave them with fewer incentives to maintain their properties or keep up with mortgage payments. The ideal program would reduce the probability of default, all else being equal.

The eighth and last factor is that the policy should not impair the ability of the homebuyer to sell or move in response to employment opportunities or household disruptions. Owning a home ties a household to a specific labor market. This can become a significant disadvantage, especially for workers with lower incomes and less human capital, as households try to respond to changes in the local labor market.

Not included in the eight criteria are a number of additional issues policymakers considering approaches to promoting low-income homeownership may also want to consider. One issue is whether "wealth creation" is an explicit goal. One of the benefits of owning over renting is the accumulation of home equity as principal is repaid (and perhaps home values increase). Policies might deliberately enhance or reduce the potential for buyers to build wealth in the form of equity in the property. Another issue is whether the subsidy should be neutral related to preferences for a particular structure type. In some regions detached single-family homes are the predominant structure type, but other areas have a more diverse housing stock including high-density multifamily buildings. Low-density detached homes can contribute to sprawl, traffic congestion, and energy use, all of which may not be socially optimal. In this context programs might award incentives for the purchase of certain structure types. Finally, offering transfers of wealth or income to reward ownership leaves comparable renters who prefer not to own relatively poorer. The implicit trade-off of homebuyer subsidies is that some households for whom renting was optimal are in fact pushed into owning a home.

Together these factors provide a useful tool for assessing policies designed to promote low-income homeownership. With these criteria current policies along with potential policy alternatives for low-income homeownership can be evaluated.

Applying the Framework

Table 5-3 illustrates how the eight criteria can be applied to the four existing policies surveyed in the prior section. The first row describes the mortgage interest deduction (MID), and each column corresponds to a factor outlined in table 5-2. The MID is clearly scalable. In 2010, based on Internal Revenue Service data, more than 37 million taxpayers claimed the deduction.[41] The MID generally has not been found to encourage new homeownership but rather to expand the intensive margin of owning bigger homes and taking out larger mortgages.[42] The MID is also not well targeted. IRS data show that most of the benefits of the MID go to higher-income households. The administrative costs of the MID are low since the deduction is simply entered into the tax form (though income tax filing entails significant administrative costs, the costs of adding the MID to that process are relatively small). There is no recapture mechanism for the MID, nor are there any enforcement regulations. The MID has little bearing on the risks of default for low-income buyers and presents no restrictions on moving or resale that might impair household mobility. Overall, the only advantages of the MID as a public policy are that it has a large scale and is administratively efficient. The MID does little to encourage homeownership among lower-income households and would not be worthy of support in this context.

The next row in table 5-3 covers the mortgage revenue bond program. About 59,127 first-time homebuyers were aided by MRB mortgages in 2010, based on $2.4 million in bond sales.[43] This is a reasonably large scale given that about 5 million homes were sold in 2012, of which about 1.9 million (37 percent) were first-time buyers. Among first-time buyers a little more than one-quarter had low incomes, leaving an estimated 550,000 first-time low-income homebuyers.[44] Based on this estimate, MRBs support about one in ten households within the targeted demographic. The MRB subsidy is shallow, however, and it seems unlikely that the monthly payment reduction of about 1 percentage point (100 basis points) is enough to move renters into owning, relative to borrowing more or buying more housing. Nonetheless, no rigorous studies have evaluated the causal effects of MRBs on owning a home (studies of FHA lending programs, which are similar by some measures, are mixed but generally positive). The MRB program is reasonably well targeted. MRB regulations restrict access to borrowers with incomes under the area median income who are buying homes priced at less than 90 percent of the area mean home sale price. In a strong economy with high

41. Internal Revenue Service (2012).
42. Bourassa and others (2012).
43. National Council of State Housing Agencies, *Fact Book.* press release, May 9, 2013.
44. National Association of Realtors, *2013 Profile of Home Buyers and Sellers,* E186-45-13, press release, November 4, 2013.

Table 5-3. *Illustration of Low-Income Homeownership Policy Criteria: Alternative Policies*[a]

Policy	Scalable	Marginal effect	Targeted	Administrative costs	Recapture	Neighborhood revitalization	Default risk	Mobility barrier
MID	Yes	Intensive	No	Minimal	None	None	No effect	No
MRB	Yes	Intensive?	Yes	Moderate	Yes	Minimal	Mixed	Yes
DPA	No	Extensive	Yes	High	Sometimes	Minimal	Lower	No
Price subsidy	No	Extensive	Yes	Very high	Sometimes	Yes	Lower	Yes
Saving programs	Not currently	Extensive	Yes	Moderate	No	No	Lower	No
CLT	Not currently	Extensive	Yes	High	Yes	Mixed (if new, yes)	Lower	Limited

Source: Author.

a. See text for definition of acronyms.

demand for tax-advantaged bonds, the MRB program can serve a larger number of borrowers with lower overhead costs. At weaker points of the economic cycle, low demand erodes the return on bonds and results in higher administrative costs. This program enforces recapture of a portion of the subsidy for homes that are sold within nine years of the original purchase date in the form of a tax imposed on net sales proceeds, but income levels are not monitored after the loan is made. The subsidy is typically not recycled, as the loan payments are used to fund the bonds—the bonds have lower interest rates than market rates because investors were willing to bid up bond prices to acquire tax advantages. MRBs may target lower-priced units and be used for combined purchase–home rehabilitation loans. In this sense MRBs might support neighborhood improvements, but the use of MRBs for these purposes is limited.

The role of MRBs in default risk is likely mixed. Unlike the MID, the subsidy is not simply capitalized into house prices, so homebuyers may experience a real reduction in housing costs. The mortgage interest rate reduction remains relatively small, however, such that payment ratios are not reduced dramatically. Finally, because of the recapture provisions, which decrease over time, MRBs may actually present at least perceived barriers to mobility for low-income households. In practice borrowers can usually avoid recapture.[45] Overall, the eight-point framework suggests that the MRB has many advantages, especially in terms of scalability and targeting. Nonetheless, it is a small subsidy, and the extent to which MRBs result in higher homeownership rates among low-income households who otherwise would not have owned a home is unclear. The USDA Section 502 direct loan program shares many of the features of the MRBs, with two exceptions: 502 loan distribution is small in scale, with fewer than 2,000 loans generated in 2010, and the subsidy can be adjusted by income level to provide lower interest rates.

The next category of subsidy in table 5-3 is down payment assistance. About 15,000–20,000 homeowners a year are aided across federal down payment assistance programs (HOME, CDBG, Federal Home Loan Banks, and USDA), almost all of whom are first-time low-income buyers. Estimates vary because in practice DPA is often combined with other programs, including MRB loans. Down payment assistance usually does not eliminate all borrower contributions (in addition to closing costs), but it can be used to write down the mortgage balance to both qualify the borrower for lower interest rate loans based on the loan-to-value ratio as well as reduce the monthly payment. The size of DPA

---

45. To owe any recapture, the home must be sold within nine years of purchase, the borrower must earn significantly more income than when he or she bought the home (the equivalent of a 5 percent increase annually), and the borrower must sell the home for more than he or she paid for the property initially.

subsidies limits the policy's scale given existing appropriations levels. Even with more resources, the requisite screening and oversight limit the potential number of borrowers who can be helped annually. Studies suggest that the lack of funds for a down payment is the primary barrier to buying a home for the lion's share of low-income renters. DPA can be substantial enough to make ownership possible for households that are otherwise unable to buy a home; in its absence the difficulty that low-income renters have in saving enough for a down payment would delay homeownership—potentially indefinitely—for this population. DPA is also well targeted through the application process to exclusively channel subsidies to means-tested households.

The oversight structure required for these programs also results in elevated administrative costs. These costs are higher still if the DPA is structured as a silent junior lien loan that has to be monitored and recaptured at resale. Of course, the benefit of those added costs is that the DPA subsidy can be returned to a pool for use with future buyers.[46] Like MRBs, DPA might be used as part of community revitalization strategies, but it is not always implemented in such a manner. One of the most valuable aspects of the DPA subsidy is the potential to lower default risks.[47] As the amount of equity in a home increases, the risk of being underwater on a mortgage decreases. DPA does present some barriers to resale, which could restrict mobility, especially if the home has dropped in value and the silent junior lien for the DPA cannot be repaid. It should also be noted that the source of the down payment may matter in terms of loan performance. During the housing boom, seller contributions to a down payment represented a way to inflate home sales prices in order to rebate cash to sellers to use for the closing. The act of saving for a down payment—including practicing behaviors such as planning, budgeting, and managing funds—may convey skills that support improved loan performance. Savings programs, such as individual development accounts (IDAs), that support savings over time, as well as sweat equity requirements, may also develop complementary skills in borrowers that enhance their ability to maintain their homes and mortgage loans.

The next subsidy covered in table 5-3 affects the sale price, either as a direct discount or an embedded discount in the home construction or development process. As with DPA, subsidizing properties to below-market values can be costly on a per homebuyer basis. This high cost results in a small-scale program, although there are few estimates of the number of new owner-occupied units with final sales prices subsidized by programs such as HOME and CDBG. The

46. Currently, most DPA programs are administered by local nonprofits or state-local government agencies. Servicing these loans could be more efficient with higher-scale centralized processing systems.

47. Ergungor (2010).

marginal effect of sales price subsidies may be significant, however, and has the potential to support renters who otherwise would not have bought a home or would have delayed this purchase for a long time (longer than the three-year window considered in the definition for first-time buyers). Price subsidies are usually targeted to low-income first-time buyers, although local strategies may use such subsidies to encourage moderate-income families or non-first-time buyers to buy homes in particular areas. The administrative costs of providing and monitoring construction subsidies are substantial; the cost of managing the allocation of scarce home price discounts also entails nontrivial costs. The ability to recapture subsidies varies but may be accomplished with a lien on the home or restrictions on resale. (A related version of recapture is a shared equity model, discussed in the next section.)

Neighborhood revitalization is often the primary goal of price subsidies rather than supporting low-income homeownership. The effects of investing in one property in an area may have the potential to generate positive local market effects.[48] The effects of price subsidies on default are unclear, but if the sales price and mortgage are below market prices, the probability decreases that a borrower will owe more than the home is worth in the market. Project-based subsidies also can serve inclusionary purposes to enable selected lower-income households to have access to higher-income neighborhoods, quality schools, or transportation hubs. Finally, price subsidies may require minimum periods of ownership and impose penalties upon owners for resale of the home, factors that may constrain household mobility. Overall, price support subsidies seem to echo the pattern of DPA subsidies: high cost, small scale, and well targeted. Nonetheless, subsidies for purchase price often have an explicit community development aim that may trump any low-income ownership goal.[49]

Alternative Approaches

Overall, the results of this brief survey of existing mechanisms are not encouraging. The largest of the existing subsidy mechanisms, the mortgage interest deduction, does little to promote low-income homeownership. Proposals to reform the MID range from the draconian (complete elimination) to the idealistic (refundable credits available to owners and renters) to the pragmatic (gradually phased-in reductions in total deduction value). While the MID has a wide impact, there is a danger that debate over its value can distract from

---

48. Edmiston (2012); Wyly and others (2001).

49. In fact, encouraging low-income people to buy in areas targeted for revitalization may be counterproductive; moderate-income residents may be required to produce a mixed income distribution.

evidence-based analysis of other programs and approaches. This begs the question: what other alternatives exist?

Savings Programs

Policies that subsidize renters to save for a down payment to buy a home offer an alternative to down payment assistance. Internationally, savings schemes have been part of the homeownership policy strategies used in countries such as the United Kingdom, France, Canada, Singapore, and Australia at various points in time.[50] The program designs vary, but in general they support savings over some period prior to the home-buying process. The subsidy may be in the form of a direct payment, tax incentives for the savings, or earnings in the down payment account, and may also include the use of tax-advantaged retirement or pension accounts for the purposes of a down payment. Subsidizing down payment saving has other advantages. A structured savings program can help renters overcome behavioral problems such as "myopia," procrastination, or lack of self-control. Precommitment to saving could help renters adhere better to a plan to save for a down payment.[51] The arrangement also can be linked to mortgage underwriting. In France, for example, the Plan Epargne Logement is a program administered by private banks that requires potential owners to save for at least eighteen months. The account has minimal interest earnings, but the federal government provides a lump sum subsidy when the borrower takes out a mortgage. The bank has the advantage of observing at least eighteen months of savings behavior, which partially overcomes the information asymmetry lenders face in underwriting first-time buyers.[52]

In the United States, the most widespread mechanisms that might be cast as a down payment savings program are individual development accounts. IDAs are special matched savings accounts restricted for uses such as education, starting a business, and buying a home. In practice, down payments are one of the most common uses of IDAs.[53] A Department of Health and Human Services program called Assets for Independence often matches IDA funds. Match rates vary by program but can be generous, including one-to-one matches or more in some cases. Most programs are operated by community-based organizations on a relatively limited scale. Despite the small scale, these programs may provide opportunities for education, advice, and support for positive financial behaviors that can lead to more sustainable homeownership.[54]

50. Munro (2007); Atterhog and Song (2009); Bourassa, Greig, and Troy (1995).
51. Andrews and Sanchez (2011).
52. Atterhog and Song (2009).
53. Mills and others (2008).
54. McKernan and others (2011).

A very different approach to subsidizing savings is the application of the Low-Income Housing Tax Credit—used to finance rental housing—to structure a lease purchase for current renters. The program requires renters to remain in a qualified unit, building up "equity credits" each month that can be used to buy the unit when the tax credit period expires.[55] Though these credits are not liquid and can only be used to save for a home purchase, they do represent a form of forced savings. The model only works, however, when a nonprofit developer is willing to build the costs of these incentives into the rental structure.

The previously described mechanisms are a heterogeneous set of policy alternatives, but all work with renters to build up savings over a period of a year or more. Turning to table 5-3, the merits of these savings approaches can be analyzed based on the eight policy criteria. Scalability seems possible, although currently both IDAs and lease-purchase arrangements are relatively small scale in the United States. A plan administered by banks, such as the Plan Epargne Logement in France, can certainly operate at a larger scale. Regarding the marginal effect, it seems likely that savings programs benefit renters who need a structure to accumulate the savings required for mortgage underwriting. These programs are also easily targeted by income level. The administrative costs of these programs are all related to enrollment and monitoring during the savings period; once the home is purchased and the funds are dispersed, the administrative burden is largely terminated. The oversight of IDA savings does require an infrastructure. Currently, community-based agencies provide this infrastructure, and administrative costs per dollar of subsidy can be high.[56] Savings programs have no way of guarding against homeowners selling the home to pocket the subsidy or of recapturing the subsidy for future use. There is also no revitalization component to savings strategies. It does seem likely that programs that facilitate the accumulation of savings will lower mortgage default risks. Having more equity and lower loan-to-value ratios help in this regard, and participation in a structured savings plan that is transparent for underwriting the loan may also contribute to lower default rates. Finally, because savings programs concentrate on the prepurchase period, there are no subsequent restrictions on selling a property or moving to seek other opportunities. Overall, savings policies appear to function much like other down payment subsidies, the difference being the longer-term structured savings contributions from the potential homebuyer. This reduces the amount of subsidy required and provides information for lenders that might help screen borrowers and reduce defaults. The period of savings acts a proving ground for potential borrowers where they can gain skills and knowledge as well as practice behaviors that are useful in managing a mortgage and home expenses.

55. Immergluck and Schaeffing (2010).
56. Mills and others (2004).

Limited or Shared Equity Models

There are a variety of partial or shared equity forms of housing, including land trusts, cooperatives, and programs where residents trade off some portion of their equity in property for affordability or security of tenure.[57] Community land trusts (CLTs), for example, are a very different form of homeownership than the alternatives presented in this chapter thus far. Private households purchase homes and then have ground lease contracts that establish a conditional property right for the structure located on the CLT's land. Because it controls the terms of the ground lease, the CLT can restrict the purchase of homes to only low-income buyers and determine the sales price of the structure. The home is sold at a below-market price, creating a subsidy. When the homeowner resells the house, he or she sells it to the CLT for a predetermined price based on a formula that accounts for the buyer's paid-in equity (down payment, principal, improvements) and a portion of any appreciation in the value of the underlying land. In the United States, there are 258 CLTs with about 9,000 total homes.[58] While small in scale, the performance of mortgages on CLT properties has been positive.[59] The structure of CLTs, their targeted income level, and the resale formulas vary, but all are generally designed to help low-income families buy a home and then retain any subsidy so that subsequent borrowers can also benefit from an affordable purchase price. The trade-off is that buyers may not benefit as much from strong home price appreciation, which raises an important issue of whether homeowning should be encouraged as a speculative investment.[60]

An application of the table 5-2 framework reveals several unique advantages of the CLT model. Although the CLT system in the United States is small, the basic model could be administered much like asset management firms govern rental housing. Barriers to scaling up include legal limitations and ambiguities related to the structure of the ground lease and financing. Often CLTs are developed based on new construction or large-scale improvements of multiple existing structures located in a finite geographic area. This requires significant organizational capacity and often public subsidies for administrative costs, as well as subsidies for acquisition and construction costs.[61] All of these factors limit the expansion of CLTs in the United States. The extent of the marginal effect of a CLT model depends entirely on the level of subsidy passed to each successive buyer. The price of ownership may be lower due to the separation of land and structure, but the ground lease effectively reflects the value of the stream of services that the piece of land provides

57. See chapter 6 in this volume.
58. Federal Reserve Bank of Richmond (2012).
59. Temkin, Theodos, and Price (2010).
60. Munro (2007).
61. J. Davis(2006); Whitehead (2010).

to the homeowner. That is, the legal arrangement does not inherently lower the financial price of the home or enhance ownership opportunities. If the CLT is structured with subsidies that are sustainable and that lower the price of ownership relative to the housing attributes provided, then the CLT may in fact extend homeownership to households that otherwise would not have become owners.

The CLT model is easily targeted to low-income buyers based on means tests. In addition, the CLT can clearly recapture subsidies; in fact, this is a hallmark of the model. CLT models could recertify income and potentially renegotiate ground leases in cases where a homeowner's income increases dramatically; in practice, this is unlikely. The upfront and ongoing administrative costs of owning land, managing ground leases, and enforcing resale provisions are high. As such, this is among the more costly alternatives (as with down payment loans, the costs of recycling the subsidy offset the benefits of recapturing relative to a one-time subsidy). Yet this model has the potential to revitalize a neighborhood or community since it involves a number of homes within a local area. The CLT model also is likely to be associated with lower default risks.[62] Mobility is not restricted per se, but owners who sell shares in a CLT may be hard pressed to find another CLT for a subsequent purchase. Because the CLT is the buyer, a CLT model may actually offer greater liquidity to homeowners needing to sell. If the unit is truly discounted relative to the market, resale will be rapid as demand surely will be strong. Overall, the CLT model has several attractive aspects from a policy perspective, including the recapture of development and purchase price subsidies. The form of CLT, the design of the resale formula, and the administrative structure vary and largely determine the efficacy of this way of subsidizing low-income homeownership. Like other models, reaching more buyers will require changes in law and public administration.

There are several other approaches similar to the CLT model. One is a limited equity cooperative housing model. Like other housing cooperatives, residents own "shares" in a cooperative housing corporation. These shares provide the right to a housing unit (typically in a multifamily building) and joint management control. In a limited equity co-op, owners can resell their unit shares. The price is not determined by the market but instead by a formula similar to that of the CLT model, which returns paid-in equity and modest market appreciation. The subsidy typically applies when the co-op is initially developed, or when an existing property is recapitalized with public funds. The limited equity model is attractive from a policy perspective because a large one-time development subsidy can be retained in the unit for subsequent buyers. The administrative model is different from the CLT, but the issues of scale, administrative costs, and other factors shown in table 5-3 remain.

62. Jacobus and Abromowitz (2009); Temkin, Theodos, and Price (2010).

The deed-restricted home is another related approach. Typically designed for a high-demand housing market, this option does not function as a direct public subsidy but rather as a requirement that in order for a private developer to obtain a construction permit, he or she must include owner-occupied units that are affordable to lower-income families. The deed or covenant on the property restricts resale to another income-eligible homebuyer using a formula for the sale price. Such covenants typically provide that a unit must maintain its resale restriction for at least thirty years. While this approach has potential in some markets with active new construction, like other shared limited equity models, it is small in scale and requires ongoing administrative oversight.

There are several other variations on this theme. Shared ownership-equity models are not uncommon overseas and are used to support low-cost homeownership initiatives. In the United Kingdom, for example, shared ownership programs are structured so that the purchaser buys a proportion of the property (for example, 80 percent) with a traditional mortgage while the other portion (20 percent) is owned by a local public or nonprofit housing agency (called a "social landlord"). The homeowner pays rent to the landlord for the 20 percent share and pays a mortgage for the 80 percent share. Over time, as the owner's resources expand, the owner can buy out the 20 percent share and become the sole owner.[63] Somewhat similar approaches that use shared equity mortgages instead of ownership shares have been suggested in the United States.[64] While not aimed at using public subsidies to support low-income homeownership, these examples illustrate the innovative alternatives that partial ownership and shared equity models can present.

Conclusions

Homeownership entails risks and rewards for households. In some scenarios, extending the private benefits to lower-income families who could not otherwise afford to buy a home can enhance overall social welfare due to the potential positive externalities of homeownership. Even if the community benefits are not large, subsidies for low-income homeownership may be warranted out of a desire to promote socioeconomic equity or fairness, given the private benefits of owning a home. Access to these benefits underlies public policies that enhance ownership opportunities for low-income families who currently rent and for whom ownership is unlikely without public support. This chapter has focused on the role of public subsidies to promote ownership for low-income, first-time homebuyers. Once policymakers agree on the need for subsidies, the form of subsidy

63. Whitehead (2010); Whitehead and Yates (2010).
64. Caplin and others (2007).

and design of the specific program can have important effects on the sustainability of homeownership and the efficiency of the use of public funds.

There are three basic forms of subsidies for first-time buyers: payment subsidies to lower the monthly ongoing cost of owning a home, subsidies that lower the initial purchase price of the home, and subsidies that reduce the down payment required to qualify for a home mortgage. Recent federal regulations have added to the complexity of these alternatives by focusing on the ratio of maximum total debt to income. Although all three subsidies can lower debt burdens, lowering housing and other debt service costs may become more important as a means to expand homeownership in the future.

Currently federal subsidies for low-income homeownership focus on mortgage payments, purchase price, and down payments. Each kind of subsidy involves significant trade-offs and should be scrutinized for how well it serves the goal of promoting low-income ownership. The mortgage interest deduction, for example, offers little support for low-income buyers despite representing a large tax expenditure in the federal budget. Mortgage revenue bonds offer the potential to lower monthly payments for buying a home, but these bonds offer a very shallow subsidy in the current market. Down payment grants and loans can reduce the size of initial mortgages and reduce default risk but are more costly to administer. Purchase price–development subsidies can be large in magnitude and have positive effects on local housing markets but are not capable of serving a large number of first-time low-income homebuyers.

Alternative polices related to down payment savings initiatives and shared or limited equity models are worthy of consideration in light of the shortcomings of existing policies. Variations of these alternative models are used in limited instances in United States, and experiences from abroad can be useful for forming new approaches.

Policymakers considering subsidies for promoting low-income homeownership should more carefully evaluate the design and pilot of new programs according to specific criteria. No policy currently under consideration satisfies every criterion, however. There are further issues to consider, each of which triggers complicated trade-offs for policymakers. First, it is important to consider how the accumulation of home equity as wealth should be treated as a policy goal. Limiting equity erodes one of the benefits of owning a home but allows a subsidy to potentially support more households. A second issue is how structure type should be treated under any policy. Preferences for multifamily buildings have rarely been incorporated into policies but, at least in some markets, could be consistent with community planning goals. Finally, any subsidy for owning a home—regardless of whether it is designed as an income or wealth subsidy—alleviates the budget constraints on homeowners and leaves renters relatively worse off. The ratio of the costs of owning versus renting is shifted to favor owning. Although expanding homeownership is considered a worthy policy goal, incentives to buy a home may push some low-income households into owning a home when renting was actually their optimal choice. And if subsidies are large enough, housing markets may anticipate that certain classes of buyers will use public programs and respond by increasing the price of land and homes in equilibrium. Balancing these concerns is a challenge.

Despite the recent housing crisis, government policies continue to provide support and incentives for home-buying. These programs are not optimally designed for low-income renters who want to buy a home. Through a critical review of existing and innovative ways of delivering one-time and ongoing subsidies, policymakers can assess the efficacy of current programs and then focus subsidies on high-impact strategies.

References

Andrews, Dan, and Aida Caldera Sanchez. 2011. "Drivers of Homeownership Rates in Selected OECD Countries." Economics Department Working Paper 849. Paris: Organization for Economic Cooperation and Development.

Atterhog, Mikael, and Han-Suck Song. 2009. "A Survey of Policies That May Increase Access to Home Ownership for Low-Income Households." *Housing, Theory and Society* 26, no. 4: 248–70.

Basolo, Victoria. 2007. "Explaining the Support for Homeownership Policy in U.S. Cities: A Political Economy Perspective." *Housing Studies* 22, no. 1: 99–119.

Beracha, Eli, and Ken Johnson. 2012. "Lessons from over 30 Years of Buy versus Rent Decisions: Is the American Dream Always Wise?" *Real Estate Economics* 40, no. 2: 217–47.

Boehm, Thomas. P., and A. M. Schlottmann. 2009. "The Dynamics of Homeownership: Eliminating the Gap between African American and White Households." *Real Estate Economics* 37, no. 4: 599–634.

Bostic, Raphael W., and Kwan Ok Lee. 2009. "Homeownership: America's Dream?" In *Insufficient Funds: Savings, Assets, Credit, and Banking among Low-income Households,* edited by Rebecca M. Blank and Michael S. Barr, pp. 218–57. New York: Russell Sage Foundation.

Bourassa, Steven C., Alastair W. Greig, and Patrick N. Troy. 1995. "The Limits of Housing Policy: Home Ownership in Australia." *Housing Studies* 10, no. 1: 83–104.

Bourassa, Steven, and others. 2012. "Mortgage Interest Deductions and Homeownership: An International Survey." Research Paper 12-06. Zurich: Swiss Finance Institute.

Bratt, Rachel G. 2008. "Homeownership as Social Policy in the U.S.: Risk and Responsibility after the Subprime Crisis." Paper presented at the European Network for Housing Research Working Group, "Building on Home Ownership: Housing Policies and Social Strategies." Delft University of Technology, November 13–14.

Brogaard, Jonathan, and Kevin Roshak. 2011. "The Effectiveness of the 2008–2010 Housing Tax Credit." Working Paper (http://ssrn.com/abstract=1882599).

Caplin, Andrew, and others. 2007. "Shared-Equity Mortgages, Housing Affordability, and Homeownership." *Housing Policy Debate* 18, no. 1: 209–42.

Collins, J. Michael. 2007. "Federal Policies Promoting Affordable Homeownership: Separating the Accidental from the Strategic." In *Chasing the American Dream: New Perspectives on Affordable Homeownership,* edited by William M. Rohe and Harry L. Watson, pp. 69–95. Cornell University Press.

Cramer, Reid. 2009. "In Pursuit of a Responsible Homeownership Policy." *Shelterforce,* no. 158: 22–25.

Davis, John E. 2006. "Shared Equity Homeownership: The Changing Landscape of Resale-Redistricted, Owner-Occupied Housing." Montclair, N.J.: National Housing Institute.

Davis, Morris A. 2012. "Questioning Homeowership as a Public Policy Goal." *Policy Analysis,* no. 696: 1–16.

Drew, Rachel B., and Christopher Herbert. 2012. "Post-Recession Drivers of Preferences for Homeownership." Working Paper 12-4. Harvard University, Joint Center for Housing Studies.

Durning, Dan. 1987. "The Efficiency and Distribution of Mortgage Revenue Bond Subsidies: The Effects of Behavioral Responses." *Journal Policy Analysis and Management* 7, no. 1: 74–93.

Dynan, Karen. 2012. "Is a Household Debt Overhang Holding Back Consumption?" *BPEA* (Spring): 299–362.

Edmiston, Kelly D. 2012. "Nonprofit Housing Investment and Local Area Home Values." *Economic Review* (Federal Reserve Bank of Kansas City), Q1: 67–96.

Engelhardt, Gary V., and others. 2010. "What Are the Social Benefits of Homeownership? Experimental Evidence for Low-Income Households." *Journal of Urban Economics* 67, no. 3: 249–58.

Ergungor, O. Emre. 2010. "Homeownership for the Long Run: An Analysis of Homeowner Subsidies." Working Paper 10-21R. Federal Reserve Bank of Cleveland.

Federal Reserve Bank of Richmond. 2012. "Community Land Trusts: An Alternative Approach to Affordable Homeownership and Neighborhood Revitalization." *Marketwise Community* 3, no. 1:1–9.

Galster, George C., and Anna M. Santiago. 2008. "Low-Income Homeownership as an Asset-Building Tool: What Can We Tell Policymakers?" In *Urban and Regional Policy and Its Effects,* edited by Margery Austin Turner, Howard Wial, and Harold Wolman, pp. 60–108. Brookings.

Glaeser, Ed L. 2011. "Rethinking the Federal Bias toward Homeownership." 2011. *Cityscape* 13, no. 2: 5–37.

Goodwin, Kimberly R., and Leonard V. Zumpano. 2011. "The Home Buyer Tax Credit of 2009 and the Transition to Homeownership." *Journal of Housing Research* 20, no. 2: 211–24.

Government Accountability Office. 2010. "Usage and Selected Analyses of the First-Time Homebuyer Credit." GAO-10-1025R.

Haughwout, Andrew, Richard Peach, and Joseph Tracy. 2010. "The Homeownership Gap." *Current Issues in Economics and Finance* (Federal Reserve Bank of New York) 16, no. 5: 1–10.

Herbert, Christopher E., and Eric S. Belsky. 2008. "The Homeownership Experience of Low-Income and Minority Households: A Review and Synthesis of the Literature." *Cityscape* 10, no. 2: 5–60.

Herbert, Christopher, and Winnie Tsen. 2007. "The Potential of Downpayment Assistance for Increasing Homeownership among Minority and Low-Income Households." *Cityscape* 9, no. 2: 153–84.

Holupka, Scott, and Sandra J. Newman. 2012. "The Effects of Homeownership on Children's Outcomes: Real Effects or Self-Selection?" *Real Estate Economics* 40, no. 3: 566–602.

Hui, Eddie Chi Man, Ka Hung Yu, and David Kim Hin Ho. 2009. "Dynamics of Assisted Homeownership in Singapore." *Journal of Urban Affairs* 31, no. 2: 195–212.

Immergluck, Dan, and Phillip Schaeffing. 2010. "Responsible Lease-Purchase: A Review of the Practice and Research Literature on Nonprofit Programs." Working Paper (http://ssrn.com/abstract=1691194).

Internal Revenue Service. 2012. *Statistics of Income Bulletin* (Fall).

Jacobus, Rick, and David M. Abromowitz. 2009. "A Path to Homeownership: Building a More Sustainable Strategy for Expanding Homeownership." *Journal of Affordable Housing and Community Development Law* 19, no. 3-4: 313–44.

Jaffee, Dwight, and John Quigley. 2009. "The Government Sponsored Enterprises: Recovering from a Failed Experiment." Working Paper W09-001. University of California–Berkeley, Institute of Business and Economic Research.

Kennickell, Arthur B. 2012. "The Other, Other Half: Changes in the Finances of the Least Wealthy 50 Percent, 2007–2009." Working Paper 2012-40. Federal Reserve Board, Divisions of Research and Statistics and Monetary Affairs (http://ssrn.com/abstract=2191215).

Kocieniewski, David. 2010. "Home Tax Credit Called Successful, but Costly." *New York Times,* April 27, p. B1.

Lerman, Robert I., C. Eugene Steuerle, and Sisi Zhang. 2012. "Homeownership Policy at a Critical Juncture: Are Policymakers Overreacting to the Great Recession?" Policy brief. Washington: Urban Institute.

Listokin, David, and others. 2001. "The Potential and Limitations of Mortgage Innovation in Fostering Homeownership in the United States." *Housing Policy Debate* 12, no. 3: 465–513.

McKernan, Signe-Mary, and others. 2011. "Weathering the Storm: How Have IDA Homebuyers Fared in the Foreclosure Crisis?" *Housing Policy Debate* 21, no. 4: 605–25.

Mills, Gregory, and others. 2008. "Effects of Individual Development Accounts on Asset Purchases and Saving Behavior: Evidence from a Controlled Experiment." *Journal of Public Economics* 92, no. 5: 1509–30.

———. 2004. *Evaluation of the American Dream Demonstration. Final Evaluation Report.* Cambridge, Mass.: Abt Associates.

Moulton, Stephanie. 2010. "Originating Lender Localness and Mortgage Sustainability: An Evaluation of Delinquency and Foreclosure in Indiana's Mortgage Revenue Bond Program." *Housing Policy Debate* 20, no. 4: 547–83.

Munro, Moira. 2007. "Evaluating Policy towards Increasing Owner Occupation." *Housing Studies* 22, no. 2: 243–60.

Olsen, Edward O. 2007. *Promoting Homeownership among Low-Income Households.* Washington: Urban Institute.

Savage, Howard A. 2009. "Who Could Afford to Buy a Home in 2004?" *Current Housing Reports* (U.S. Census Bureau), May: 1–7.

Shlay, Anne B. 2006. "Low-Income Homeownership: American Dream or Delusion?" *Urban Studies* 43, no. 3: 511–31.

Temkin, Ken, Brett Theodos, and David Price. 2010. *Balancing Affordability and Opportunity: An Evaluation of Affordable Homeownership Programs with Long-Term Affordability Controls.* Report. Washington: Urban Institute.

U.S. Department of Housing and Urban Development. 2012. "Paths to Homeownership for Low-Income and Minority Households." *Evidence Matters* (Fall): 1–12.

Whitehead, Christine. 2010. "Shared Ownership and Shared Equity: Reducing the Risks of Home-Ownership?" Viewpoint. York, United Kingdom: Joseph Rowntree Foundation. September.

Whitehead, Christine, and Judith Yates. 2010. "Is There a Role for Shared Equity Products in Twenty-First Century Housing? Experience in Australia and the UK." In *The Blackwell Companion to the Economics of Housing: The Housing Wealth of Nations,* edited by Susan J. Smith and Beverley A. Searle, pp. 481–98. Malden, Mass.: Blackwell.

Wyly, Elvin K., and others. 2001. "Low-to-Moderate-Income Lending in Context: Progress Report on the Neighborhood Impacts of Homeownership Policy." *Housing Policy Debate* 12, no.1: 87–127.

6

Filling the Void between Homeownership and Rental Housing: A Case for Expanding the Use of Shared Equity Homeownership

JEFFREY LUBELL

Most discussions about expanding access to homeownership take as a given that we know exactly what homeownership is. The questions then usually fall into a predictable pattern: What are the risks and benefits of homeownership? How might it be expanded, and what are the costs and benefits of the different options for doing so? How can positive homeownership outcomes (for example, use of homeownership to access better neighborhoods) be maximized while minimizing negative ones (for example, foreclosure)?

But what if we were to take a step back and reexamine the definition and scope of the end goal itself? As others have observed, there is a lot of room in between the extremes of "rental housing" and "homeownership."[1] By considering alternative configurations of the bundle of attributes that make up the traditional definition of homeownership, we can open up new options for informing the policy debate and potentially develop new and more cost-effective approaches for advancing key societal goals.

Following some initial reflections on the definition of homeownership, this chapter focuses on a set of policy options that fall in between the traditional tenure options of rental housing and homeownership and are sometimes referred to

---

At the time of writing, the author was executive director of the Center for Housing Policy.

1. See, for example, Apgar (2004).

collectively as "shared equity homeownership."[2] As I use the term, shared equity homeownership (SEH) is a tenure choice that provides most of the benefits of homeownership at a lower price point, facilitating access to homeownership by low- and moderate-income households. Under SEH home price appreciation is shared between the homebuyer and the program sponsor to achieve a balance between the individual's interest in building wealth and the community's interest in ensuring long-term affordability.[3] Specific policy options for implementing SEH include community land trusts, limited equity cooperatives, deed restrictions, and shared appreciation loans.

The benefits of SEH go beyond initial affordability. When implemented effectively, SEH can reduce many of the risks of traditional homeownership, providing a safer and more sustainable housing option for low- and moderate-income households while still allowing sizable opportunities for households to build wealth. SEH also provides a mechanism for preserving the buying power of government and philanthropic investments in the face of rising home prices, allowing a single investment to help one generation of homebuyers after another. Because it can be used to assure long-term affordability of specific units, SEH also has an important role to play in helping to ensure that families of all incomes can afford to live in gentrifying areas near public transit stations, job centers, and effective schools.

I am acutely aware of the risks involved in asserting such sweeping benefits for a little-known and sparingly used tenure choice. It is justifiable to be skeptical of things that sound "too good to be true." But this is one time when I believe the case is so compelling that the field needs to be open to shifting its paradigms to accommodate it. There are certainly limitations to SEH—particularly challenges with scaling up and the potential for confusion among homebuyers. But I believe the policy case overwhelmingly favors greater use of these tools, particularly in cases where sizable public subsidies for homeownership are already being provided directly (for example, through grants or forgivable loans) or implicitly

2. It is important to note that "shared equity homeownership" is a term that has been superimposed upon a diverse landscape of alternative tenure options rather than one that grew organically from the field. Many practitioners of what I call SEH do not necessarily use or endorse this term, and as subsequently discussed, there are differences of opinion about which programs fall within SEH. Despite these issues, I find the term useful for categorizing a diverse set of programs that share related goals and can be used to produce similar outcomes. Most important, the programs that fit this definition provide a suite of benefits that, in my view, compare favorably with traditional homeownership and merit greater attention and investment.

3. Shared equity homeownership programs can help advance other individual and community goals, but their salient characteristic is a balance between individual wealth accumulation and long-term affordability. Other individual benefits of shared equity homeownership are discussed in the section "Rethinking the Traditional Homeownership Paradigm." Other community benefits include increased residential stability, improved diversity, and equitable access to neighborhoods of opportunity.

(such as through inclusionary zoning or density bonuses, as applied to home-ownership units).

Rethinking the Traditional Homeownership Paradigm

Current or prospective homeowners may view homeownership as a binary option—either you own a home or you do not. But I prefer to see it as part of a broader continuum of tenure choices, characterized by a particular set of attributes. These attributes generally cluster together closely so that they are regarded as a single package. But it is quite possible to reconfigure them so that a new tenure choice is created that contains some of these attributes and not others. For some people, or in some cases, this new tenure choice may be a better (or worse) option than traditional homeownership.

In defining these attributes, I prefer to use a policy lens—focusing on the benefits and risks—rather than a legal lens (that is, focusing on specific property rights). Box 6-1 lists selected benefits and risks of traditional homeownership that can help illustrate how it contrasts with shared equity homeownership. This comparison assumes a well-underwritten thirty-year fixed-rate mortgage.

As the nation has learned the hard way over the past half decade, homeownership can be a risky proposition.[4] Among other risks illustrated in box 6-1 are loss on resale, an inability to sell one's home and move to a new location when needed or desired, and assets that are overly concentrated in a single asset class. High transaction costs exacerbate many of these problems. In addition, homeownership remains out of reach for many households that might otherwise desire it because of high costs or credit requirements. While housing prices have come down significantly from their peak in 2006, credit requirements have gone up, so many would-be homebuyers are still unable to purchase.

Faced with these risks and drawbacks, one might be tempted to turn to rental housing as an alternative, and to a significant extent this is justified. But given the many benefits of homeownership noted in box 6-1—including security of tenure, greater freedom to shape one's physical environment, the freezing of most housing costs, and the ability to build assets through paydown of principal and home price appreciation—it is worth looking hard at whether homeownership can be modified in a way that substantially reduces the risks and drawbacks while preserving as many of the benefits as possible.

This is precisely what SEH seeks to accomplish by producing a new form of tenure that retains most of the benefits of traditional homeownership but with a much lower risk profile. While I do not believe that SEH is appropriate for everyone who wishes to purchase a home, I do think it is fair to say that for many

---

4. See generally, Apgar (2012) and Carr and Anacker (2012).

Box 6-1. *Benefits and Risks of Homeownership*

Benefits of Traditional Homeownership

—Generally provides security of tenure; if you pay your bills on time, you cannot be evicted.

—Homeowner has significant freedom to shape physical environment of the unit or property.

—Most housing costs are frozen at affordable levels, and as incomes rise, costs become even more affordable over time.

—Forced savings through paydown of principal.

—Opportunity to build sizable assets if home prices improve over time.

—It may be the only way to access certain neighborhoods with desirable features, such as high-performing schools.

Risks or Drawbacks of Traditional Homeownership

—Home prices may stagnate or decline, causing a loss upon resale.

—In certain markets or under certain conditions, it may be difficult to find a buyer at an acceptable price, inhibiting mobility.

—Many buyers end up with most if not all of their assets tied up in a single asset class (real property).

—Some homeowners may struggle with upkeep of their home.

—Many would-be buyers cannot afford to buy a decent quality home in a desirable neighborhood. As a result they either do not buy or buy a lower-quality home in a less desirable neighborhood.

low- and moderate-income households, SEH provides a superior risk-reward profile to traditional homeownership. I also believe that it is a more efficient and effective way to use scarce public funds as compared to large grants or forgivable loans (which convert to grants over time) for homeownership.

The rest of this chapter explores this argument in greater detail, focusing initially on describing how SEH works and the different forms it can assume, then discussing how it mitigates some of the risks of traditional homeownership while retaining most of the benefits. The final sections of the chapter describe the principal limitations of SEH and how those limitations might be addressed to help take it to scale.

How Does SEH Work and What Are Its Principal Benefits?

Under SEH as defined here, a program sponsor (such as a nonprofit organization, local government, community land trust, or philanthropy) provides a subsidy to reduce the costs of purchasing a home to a level affordable to a buyer at a target income level.[5] The buyer then purchases the home at the reduced level with standard financing—generally a thirty-year fixed-rate mortgage—and occupies the home as would a traditional homebuyer. On resale a formula is used to determine how any home price appreciation is shared between the homebuyer and the program sponsor. The sponsor's share is used to preserve affordability for the next buyer, which can be done in one of two main ways: keeping the subsidy in the property by capping the resale price (subsidy retention) or using the subsidy to augment the amount of assistance provided to the next buyer to keep pace with rising home prices (a shared appreciation loan or mortgage).[6]

To illustrate, assume a home sells for (and has a market value of) $250,000, but a household at the target income level can only afford a $200,000 mortgage plus a $10,000 down payment. In this case the program sponsor provides a $40,000 subsidy, allowing the buyer's $210,000 to be sufficient to purchase the home.

On resale a formula is used to determine how any home price appreciation is split. Say that this particular SEH program seeks to maintain the affordability of specific units by capping resale prices and requiring that the home be sold to a borrower at or below the target income level. Under this SEH program's formula, 75 percent of appreciation stays in the home and 25 percent goes to the buyer.

Assume the home is sold six years later, at which point it has a market value of $280,000 (after accounting for transaction costs)—$30,000 more than its original value of $250,000.[7] Based on the equity-sharing formula, the household receives 25 percent of this appreciation (or $7,500) and the rest stays in the home, lowering its cost to the next income-qualified buyer. This is implemented by restricting the resale price to the amount the buyer originally paid ($210,000) plus the buyer's share of home price appreciation ($7,500), for a total resale price of $217,500. The next buyer purchases the home with the same resale restrictions, as does the one after that, and so on, generally ensuring that the home stays affordable over time.

This process achieves several goals:

—It brings home purchase within reach of households that would not otherwise be able to afford it or that could not otherwise afford to purchase a decent quality home in a neighborhood with desired attributes (such as a good school district or within walking distance of public transit).

---

5. The target income level varies by program, but the basic idea is to help low- or moderate-income households that cannot afford market-rate homes in the neighborhood(s), city(ies), or market(s) served by the sponsor.

6. For more information on the latter option, see "Subsidy Retention versus Shared Appreciation Loans" later in this chapter.

7. This assumes a 3 percent annual appreciation rate and a 6 percent broker's commission—relatively conservative assumptions.

—It uses a single subsidy to provide long-term affordability to multiple purchasers of a home over time. The value of the subsidy actually grows over time, increasing from $40,000 initially to $62,500 for the second buyer, helping the second buyer afford the home.

—By preserving the affordability of specific homes, it can be used as a mechanism for ensuring that low- and moderate-income households have access to affordable homes in neighborhoods with good schools or that are likely to experience gentrification, such as high-demand neighborhoods near public transit stations or job centers.

The program also provides the buyer with an opportunity to build individual assets, composed of two parts: the buyer's share of home price appreciation and the forced savings achieved through the paydown of principal. If our hypothetical buyer took out a mortgage at 5 percent interest, he or she would have paid off $20,129 of the $200,000 mortgage after six years. Adding this to the $7,500 in home price appreciation, the buyer accumulates $27,629 in additional assets, more than two and a half times the buyer's original $10,000 investment. The buyer also gets its $10,000 down payment back through the sale process.

While this is certainly much less than the buyer would have garnered had that person purchased the home through traditional homeownership ($50,129), it greatly exceeds the return on investment one would expect from the stock market or just about any other form of investment other than traditional homeownership. And remember, the buyer could not have afforded to purchase the home at its full price in any event.

Now all this sounds good on paper, but how does SEH perform under real-world conditions? An evaluation by Kenneth Temkin, Brett Theodos, and David Price of the Urban Institute sought to answer this question by examining historical data on the performance of seven shared equity homeownership programs from around the country.[8] They found that the programs achieved their basic goals of providing homes that were affordable both to the initial buyers and to purchasers upon resale while generating returns on investment (overall and in six out of seven of the programs) that exceeded that of the stock market or a U.S. Treasury bond.

The seven programs examined in this study are not necessarily representative of all shared equity homeownership programs nationally, but because this study

8. Temkin, Theodos, and Price (2010). The evaluation is based primarily on administrative data held by each program, the time period of which varied from program to program. The seven programs covered were the "Champlain Housing Trust (CHT), located in Burlington, Vermont; Northern Communities Land Trust (NCLT) in Duluth, Minnesota; Thistle Community Housing in Boulder, Colorado; the Dos Pinos Housing Cooperative in Davis, California; Wildwood Park Towne Houses in Atlanta, Georgia; A Regional Coalition for Housing (ARCH) in eastern King County, Washington; and San Francisco Citywide Inclusionary Affordable Housing Program" (p. iii).

is the only available source of data on real-world performance of SEH programs collected in a consistent manner across multiple programs, it is worth pausing briefly to summarize the principal findings:

—The typical median income of purchasers ranged from a low of 35 percent of the HUD family area median income (AMI) in the Wildwood Park program in Atlanta to 73 percent of AMI in the Dos Pinos program in Davis, California, with typical participants' income in the five remaining programs ranging from 45 to 63 percent of AMI.

—On resale the homes generally remained affordable to low-income households, with the mean annual change in real income needed to afford the homes on resale falling in two sites, increasing by 0.5 percent or less in two other sites, and increasing by only 1–2 percent in two other sites. One site (A Regional Coalition for Housing, in King County, Washington [ARCH]), saw larger increases in required real income of 4 percent a year; yet even there homes remained affordable to buyers with incomes well below the median.

—The median amount spent by purchasers on down payment and closing costs was generally (but not always) very low, falling below $3,000 in three programs and equaling approximately $6,000, $18,000, and $40,000 in the remaining sites. (Data were not available for the seventh program, ARCH.)

—The median home price appreciation realized at time of resale ranged from a low of $2,015 in Atlanta to a high of $42,524 in King County, with four programs clustering between $4,171 and $8,107, and one program (in San Francisco) generating a median appreciation of $17,321. This was in addition to the principal paid down on mortgages, which generally fell between $2,400 and $4,000.

—As calculated by Temkin, Theodos, and Price, the internal rate of return on purchasers' investment of down payment and closing costs ranged broadly from 6.5 percent in Davis to 59.6 percent in King County, with San Francisco (11.3 percent), Atlanta (14.1 percent), Boulder (22.1 percent), Burlington (30.8 percent), and Duluth (39 percent) falling in between, beating the S&P 500 everywhere but in Davis—in most cases, by a long shot.

How Does SEH Mitigate the Risks and Drawbacks of Traditional Homeownership?

The discussion above focuses on what SEH provides: initial affordability, long-term subsidy preservation, long-lasting affordability, and substantial opportunities for owners to build assets (though the ability to accumulate assets through home price appreciation is admittedly reduced relative to traditional homeownership). But another beneficial feature of SEH is what it helps guard against: equity loss, immobility, and foreclosure.

A simple example illustrates how this works. Assume an individual buys a home with a market value of $300,000 through an SEH program for $240,000. Subsequently, market values go down by $10,000 so that at the time this home-owner wants to sell, the home is now worth only $290,000. Under traditional homeownership that person either would be stuck and unable to move or would have to sell at a loss. But the SEH owner may very well find a buyer willing to pay $240,000 (plus whatever transaction costs may be involved) to avoid a loss.[9] Indeed, if the resale formula were to permit a higher sales price because it was tied to something other than appraised values—for example, increases in incomes rather than home prices—it is even conceivable that the SEH purchaser would be able to find a buyer at the higher level (say $250,000 or $260,000), since these prices are still well below market value and thus likely a good deal for the buyer.[10] As this example illustrates, SEH can be used to guard against equity loss and immobility tied to home price declines, and when market prices go down, it may actually lead to greater asset accumulation for buyers than under traditional homeownership.

As one might expect, the ability of an SEH program to act as a cushion against home price declines depends to a large extent on the size of the subsidy: all things equal, the larger the subsidy is as a share of market value, the more likely it is to provide downside protection to an SEH owner. (If the subsidy is small to begin with and the market decline is large, an SEH buyer may still be forced to sell at a loss since SEH units will always sell at a discount relative to the market.) Since subsidies vary widely across SEH programs, some programs will provide better downside protection than others. But in a market in which home prices are generally rising faster than incomes over time—thus raising the possibility of a bubble that leads to a crash in home prices—the size of any subsidy is likely to grow over time (due to the retention of a share of home price appreciation) so that what starts out as a fairly modest subsidy could turn into a

9. Many SEH programs sell their homes directly and thus do not utilize brokers who charge commissions. They may nevertheless charge a fee to help cover the costs of monitoring affordability, qualifying the next buyer, and otherwise ensuring good stewardship of their homes. Other SEH programs do utilize real estate agents, though sometimes at reduced fees.

10. The owner's ability to sell the property for the higher price will depend both on whether a buyer can be found for that price and whether the higher price is allowed under the equity-sharing formula. As described under the summary of equity-sharing formulas below, different programs use different approaches for calculating the maximum resale price. A program that bases resale prices on changes in appraised values would not likely allow the higher price since appraised values have gone down, rather than up, but a program that bases resale prices on some other variable—for example, changes in the area median income—may well allow the higher price if that index has risen.

much larger subsidy twenty or thirty years down the road, increasing the down-side protection it provides.

Another benefit of SEH is the protection it offers against serious delinquency and foreclosure. An analysis of survey data provided in 2011 by a large sample of community land trusts—one approach to implementing SEH—found that just 0.46 percent of community land trust (CLT) homes were in foreclosure and just 1.3 percent of their loans were seriously delinquent.[11] These rates were much lower than comparable rates for the broader housing market, as measured by data from the Mortgage Bankers Association, which showed a foreclosure rate of 4.63 percent and severe delinquency rate of 8.57 percent.[12] This difference is all the more remarkable given that community land trusts tend to focus on assisting low-income buyers. The lower default and foreclosure rates are likely due to the greater affordability of the CLT homes at the outset—there was little chance for predatory lending—as well as the special efforts that CLTs made to manage their loans to help identify and assist owners in trouble before their problems escalated. Some SEH programs also impose limitations on the ability to refinance (generally a review and consent provision) to ensure that buyers do not end up refinancing into a predatory product.

It is difficult to isolate the impact on delinquency and foreclosure rates of effective stewardship of CLT homes—facilitated by very small portfolios and perhaps difficult to scale up—from the broader effect of the SEH structure used by CLTs, which helps to ensure both initial and ongoing affordability and generally provides some degree of cushion against market declines. It is also important to emphasize that SEH is no guarantee against foreclosure or equity loss. When faced with historic market declines in the late 2000s, even SEH homeowners were affected, with some unable to sell their homes for the prices they had expected or even at a level sufficient to repay their mortgages.

SEH provides a buffer, not foolproof insulation. But what it does do is essentially smooth out the rough edges of unpredictable homeownership markets. Under normal market conditions, SEH buyers have the opportunity to build predictable levels of assets but not the ability to make a killing if prices temporarily go through the roof. At the same time, they are provided with some downside protection that can help them weather modest market slowdowns without losing equity. SEH does all this while also expanding ownership opportunities to households that might not otherwise be able to purchase and preserving the buying power of public subsidies for the next group of households looking to get a start as homeowners.

11. Thaden (2011).
12. Thaden (2011).

What Are the Variations in Program Design among SEH Programs?

The above discussion generally treats SEH as a single construct. But as reflected in the evaluation by Temkin, Theodos, and Price and in Davis's encyclopedic examination of the subject, SEH programs are very diverse, spanning the spectrum from programs targeting very low-income households (incomes at or below 50 percent of the area median income) to programs targeting households right at or just above or below the median income.[13] Many programs operate in high-cost markets—particularly in California and the Pacific Northwest—where even moderate-income households struggle to purchase a home. Others operate in lower-cost markets, where SEH is used to push homeownership down to very low income households, build a sense of cohesion and community within specific developments, or simply keep pace with rising home prices.

SEH programs vary across many dimensions. The following is a brief overview of key programmatic differences.

Subsidy Retention versus Shared Appreciation Loans

Perhaps the most fundamental distinction among SEH models is between *subsidy retention* models that focus on maintaining the long-term affordability of specific housing units and *shared appreciation* loans or mortgages that preserve the capacity of program sponsors to assist future households in the face of rising home prices by requiring that a portion of home price appreciation be repaid along with the principal balance of a loan. These two program variations roughly mirror the split among rental assistance programs between project-based and tenant-based options: in the first instance, the subsidy stays with the unit; in the second, it is transportable to where beneficiaries choose to live.

The extended example discussed in the prior section falls into the first camp of subsidy retention, under which a subsidy is used to reduce the purchase price of a home, and then long-term affordability is ensured by specifying a maximum resale price of the home to the next buyer, who purchases the unit subject to the same basic resale restrictions. A similar outcome is achieved in a limited equity cooperative model (see next section) by regulating the resale price of cooperative shares. Subsidy retention models excel in maintaining the affordability of specific housing units, making them a good choice when the location of assisted units is particularly important. For example, a program seeking to maintain affordability in a neighborhood expected to experience gentrification may wish to lock up the affordability of specific homes within that neighborhood, as there is no assurance that similar units will be available when the next purchaser is looking to buy.

---

13. Temkin, Theodos, and Price (2010); Davis (2006).

Under a shared appreciation loan or mortgage, by contrast, the subsidy is provided in the form of a second or third mortgage that is repaid to the program sponsor at the time of resale along with a share of home price appreciation. (No payments are generally due while the buyer is living in the home, helping to ensure affordability.) This allows the program sponsor to provide a larger loan to the next purchaser, thus keeping pace with rising home prices and allowing subsequent buyers a similar range of choices as the prior buyers. Since the homes are sold at market prices to unrestricted buyers, these loans do not preserve the long-term affordability of specific units. However, they often provide greater choice to homebuyers, who can purchase any unit within a set price range rather than be limited to a narrower range of units subject to long-term resale restrictions. They are thus a good option for programs that are flexible about the location of assisted units, permitting purchasers a wide choice of units within the city or metro area or within a range of neighborhoods.

Practitioners generally agree that subsidy retention programs qualify as SEH. Opinions differ, however, on whether the second category of shared appreciation loans qualifies as SEH.[14] Excluding privately financed shared appreciation mortgages that provide short-term affordability to one buyer rather than long-term affordability for successive buyers, I consider most other shared appreciation loans to be a category of SEH.[15] This is because they can be used to achieve all of the basic goals of SEH, including initial affordability, long-term affordability, and individual asset building. Indeed, the exact same equity-sharing formulas can be used for both subsidy retention and shared appreciation models, with the same basic impact on long-term affordability and individual asset building.

By contrast, others see shared appreciation loans as a different concept altogether and choose not to categorize them together with subsidy retention models as SEH. One argument I have heard is that shared appreciation loans increase demand for market-rate homes, potentially leading to home price increases, whereas subsidy retention programs withdraw units from the private market and thus do not have this effect, at least for the reserved units.[16]

---

14. Compare Jacobus and Lubell (2007)—arguing that shared equity homeownership encompasses both subsidy retention models and shared appreciation loans—with Davis (2006), who only includes subsidy retention models within the definition of SEH.

15. See Lubell and Sherriff (2009).

16. Arguably there could be an inflationary effect on the broader market in either case—either by increasing demand for market-rate units or by decreasing the supply of market-rate units—but to the extent the shared equity activity helps support new construction or rehab activity, it could have an offsetting effect of boosting supply. Whether shared appreciation loans have an inflationary effect presumably has a lot to do with how the program is administered, the ratio of shared equity to market-rate buyers, the effective use of appraisals to keep prices reasonable, and broader market conditions. Note the interesting parallels to the debate on the relative merits of tenant-based versus project-based rental assistance.

Whether subsidy retention models and shared appreciation loans are classified together as SEH or not, it is clear that they use somewhat distinct mechanisms, so it may not ultimately matter too much how they are categorized. It is also important to note that in practice some programs combine the two approaches. This is accomplished by providing buyers with a shared appreciation loan but giving the program sponsor the right of first refusal to purchase the home on resale. This provides the program with an option on resale either to convert units to subsidy retention units or to recapture the subsidy and the sponsor's share of home price appreciation for relending to the next buyer, depending on the program's needs and market conditions.

Legal Structure

SEH can be implemented through a variety of legal structures. Shared appreciation loans are most commonly implemented through second mortgages (or, if the household already has a second mortgage, through a third mortgage). Subsidy retention, by contrast, can be implemented in multiple ways, including deed restrictions, limited-equity cooperatives, and community land trusts. The three approaches are described by Jacobus and Lubell:

> *Deed-Restricted Homeownership.* Under this common approach, the subsidy is applied to reduce the purchase price to a level affordable to homeowners at the target income level. Then, restrictions are put into place requiring that the units be sold to buyers meeting certain qualifications—for example, incomes below 80 percent of AMI [area median income]—at an affordable price as defined according to a formula set in the deed restriction or covenant. . . .

> *Limited Equity Cooperative.* Under this approach—typically, but not exclusively, applied in the context of an apartment or other multifamily development—families purchase a "share" in the cooperative, rather than a standard property interest in the home. Members of the cooperative receive a right to occupy one unit, as well as a vote on matters of common interest. Cooperative members share responsibility for maintaining common areas and other areas of joint responsibility (e.g., maintaining the roof), as well as the admittance of new members. Share prices are set by formula (contained in the co-op's bylaws, subscription agreement and stock certificates). . . .

> *Community Land Trust.* Under this approach, the land is owned by a community land trust (CLT) and then leased to families who purchase the

homes that sit on CLT land. Because the family needs to purchase only the building and not the land, a CLT home is more affordable than a conventional home. The ground lease establishes the conditions under which ongoing affordability is maintained, with the CLT always having the right to repurchase the property at an affordable price established by a resale formula built into the ground lease. . . .

One common approach to governing CLTs is to establish a board of directors consisting of an equal number of representatives of the following three groups: existing owners of homes on land leased from the CLT; residents from the surrounding community; and public officials or other supporters of the CLT.[17]

A full analysis of the benefits and limitations of these three approaches is beyond the scope of this article, but it is worth noting a few key issues:[18]

—*Limited equity versus no equity.* Some limited equity cooperatives provide little or no opportunity for individuals to build assets. Sometimes referred to as no-equity cooperatives, these developments focus primarily on maintaining ongoing affordability.[19] Because shareholders retain many of the other attributes of ownership (notably, security of tenure and as much ability as full-equity cooperatives to control their physical environment), they definitely fall between the tenure extremes of rental and ownership. But because this arrangement does not facilitate individual asset building, I would place no-equity cooperatives outside my definition of SEH.

—*Community-building features.* Cooperatives, by their very nature, have a communal aspect in that the shareholders own their development collectively and make decisions collectively about the future of the development. While community land trusts generally extend far beyond a single development, they also have a communal dimension, facilitated by their unique governance structure that involves resident representatives in the decisionmaking process. Deed restriction programs, by contrast, do not necessarily have a community-building component and may simply provide individual buyers with access to affordable homes.

—*Blurred lines.* As reflected in much of the discussion above, this is not a field that lends itself to sharp definitional boundaries. As might be expected, then, there is much blurring of the lines between these categories. For example, Davis describes the combined use of community land trusts and limited equity cooperatives, with the land trust existing primarily to prevent cooperative members

17. Jacobus and Lubell (2007, p. 23).
18. See Davis (2006) for a comprehensive discussion of these three approaches.
19. See Davis (2006).

from voting to turn themselves into an unrestricted market-rate cooperative.[20] Similarly, some community land trusts have started to use deed restrictions— rather than a ground lease—to maintain long-term affordability but still refer to themselves as community land trusts.

As of the time of his research, Davis estimated that, nationwide, there were 130,000 to 350,000 deed-restricted units, 425,000 limited or no-equity coopera- tive units (based on data provided by the National Association of Housing Coop- eratives), and 5,000 to 9,000 CLT units operated by about 200 land trusts.[21] A more recent analysis of survey data from a large sample of community land trusts notes a sharp rise in the establishment of CLTs between 2005 and 2010 but still estimates a total of only 7,139 CLT units nationwide.[22] Since there is no national source of data on deed-restricted units, the estimates on the scope of this inter- vention span a particularly wide range.

Equity-Sharing Formulas

Program sponsors have many options for sharing home price appreciation with the homeowner.[23] The following are some of the more common approaches.[24]

—*Appraisal-based formulas.* Under this approach the home is appraised at the time of sale and the time of resale, and the owner is allowed to retain a certain share of any home price appreciation. For example, the Champlain Housing Trust allows owners to sell their home for what they paid for it plus roughly 25 percent of home price appreciation. Many shared appreciation loan programs also use this approach but allow the owner to retain a much higher proportion of home price appreciation; for example, it is common for programs providing a shared appreciation loan equal to 20 percent of the home price to require repay- ment of only 20 percent of the home price appreciation, allowing the owner to keep 80 percent.

—*Index-based formulas.* With this approach an index—such as the consumer price index or the area median income—is used to determine how much appre- ciation is retained by the owner. For example, if the AMI has risen by 20 percent since the time of purchase, a program that bases equity sharing on the AMI

---

20. Davis (2006).

21. Davis (2006).

22. Thaden (2012).

23. Under any of these approaches, SEH programs have the option of increasing the resale price to account for investments by owners in home improvements, and many do so.

24. For a general overview of equity-sharing models, see Jacobus and Lubell (2007). Jacobus (2007a) provides a more detailed look at several of the models and how they work in different mar- ket conditions. An accompanying spreadsheet, accessible at www.nhc.org/shared_equity_suite.html, allows users to see the results of applying the different formulas to real-world situations.

would allow the owner to sell the property for 120 percent of the original purchase price. This has the advantage of ensuring that once a property is made
affordable to buyers at a target income level, it stays roughly affordable over time
to that same level (with affordability varying only based on changes in mortgage
interest rates).

—*Affordable housing cost.* This approach uses a formula to determine how
much a buyer at the target income level (for instance, 80 percent or 100 percent of AMI) can afford, in light of prevailing mortgage interest rates, without
reference to the original purchase price. This is the only approach that can truly
guarantee affordability to the next buyer at the target income level without a
new subsidy; however, it also places the risk from changing interest rates on the
owner. If interest rates rise significantly, the maximum resale price can decline
significantly—in some cases leading to losses on resale even when home prices
have otherwise increased.

As reflected in the description above of three very different approaches to
sharing home price appreciation, program sponsors have wide flexibility to tailor
resale formulas to meet the program's objectives. Aside from technical differences
among the various formulas, the principal decision point in setting a formula is
where to strike the balance between the goals of individual asset accumulation
and long-term affordability. The affordable housing cost model focuses primarily
on long-term affordability, even at the expense of individual asset building. The
common shared appreciation loan formula of requiring owners to repay only
20 percent of home price appreciation when the program invests 20 percent of
the purchase price in second mortgage assistance, on the other hand, places a
much greater emphasis on individual asset building, sometimes at the expense of
long-term affordability.[25]

I prefer the approach based on the AMI because it generally enables a predictable level of asset accumulation that helps ensure rough affordability over time to
the target income level. However, some practitioners argue that this may be more
difficult to explain to homebuyers than an appraisal-based formula.

Subsidy Sources

SEH is much more efficient than an outright grant in that it provides a mechanism for allowing a single investment to help one homebuyer after another.

---

25. Jacobus (2007a) provides a thorough analysis of this issue. Note that shared appreciation loan
programs do not have to follow this format and can in fact use any of the formulas that are used in
subsidy retention programs. The only difference is that instead of being used to determine the resale
price, the formula is inverted and used to determine the amount of appreciation that must be repaid
to the program sponsor at the time of resale, along with the original principal balance of the loan.

However, it is not free. Because the program's share of home price appreciation is used to retain affordability over time, it cannot be used to compensate the original lender for the cost of funds. A subsidy of some sort is thus needed to make the program work.

Precise data on the sources of subsidies for SEH programs are not available, but in general it appears that subsidy sources include federal HOME and CDBG funds as well as state and local funds from bond issues, housing trust funds, and other sources. Investments by philanthropies and large institutional employers (such as universities or hospitals) are also used to fund SEH units.

In considering the funds available to support SEH, it is important to note that the subsidy may be implicit as well as explicit. Inclusionary zoning programs that apply to homeownership developments, for example, result in units that sell for below-market rates without an explicit subsidy. If accompanied by long-term use restrictions (see below), the affordability of these units can be maintained over time.

Subsidy Duration

Ideally SEH programs would provide for permanent affordability, ensuring that an initial public or philanthropic investment is preserved and increased to keep pace with any growth in home prices and thus continue to help one generation of homebuyers after another. In practice some programs place limits on the duration of affordability covenants, such as thirty or forty years—a stipulation that gives owners the opportunity to outstay their covenant and receive ownership of their homes in fee simple, including the windfall of accumulated home price appreciation. These limits may be motivated by political concerns about what is feasible or by concerns that permanent affordability may run afoul of legal issues related to rules against perpetuities and unreasonable constraints.[26]

One approach taken in some communities is to combine a defined period of affordability with a requirement that the resale period restart whenever the property is transferred to a new party. This is the approach taken in the Fairfax County, Virginia, inclusionary housing program, which specifies a thirty-year affordability period that restarts with every ownership transfer. In Montgomery County, Maryland, owners must repay a portion of the proceeds of any inclusionary housing unit sold after expiration of the initial affordability period.

---

26. For a discussion of the legal issues, see Kelly (2009, 2010) and Davis (2006, pp. 78–80). The short version is that these legal barriers are more of a problem in some states than others and that state authorizing legislation can help clear up any ambiguity in the common law and assure everyone of the durability of permanent affordability covenants. See Sherriff (2010) for a review of state authorizing legislation.

What Are the Principal Limitations of SEH?

To sum up thus far: there is a broad and diverse spectrum of housing programs that fall between the extremes of rental housing and traditional homeownership. A large subset of this spectrum can be categorized as SEH programs that provide both initial and long-term affordability as well as substantial (though not unlimited) and generally fairly predictable (though not foolproof) opportunities to build assets, with varying degrees of downside protection against foreclosure and equity loss. For individuals who wish to access these monetary benefits, as well as the nonmonetary benefits of ownership (such as stability of tenure and ability to modify the home environment), SEH can be a good tenure choice.

So why aren't these kinds of options more widely available? Here are some of the principal obstacles to growth of SEH.

Limited Availability of Subsidy

In contrast to purely market-rate homeownership products, SEH requires a subsidy to work. This is a critical limitation that makes it difficult to scale up. At the same time, however, it is important to note that there is already substantial subsidy being spent on affordable homeownership.

Unfortunately, comprehensive data are not available on all sources of subsidy for homeownership and how much of this subsidy is going into SEH as opposed to grants or forgivable loans that essentially convert to grants over time.[27] But HUD data show that about one quarter of HUD's HOME Investment Partnerships Program funds is spent by local and state governments to assist homebuyers; this totaled roughly $7.5 billion in expenditures for homebuyer assistance through November 2013.[28] In addition, a 2004 HUD-sponsored study by Abt Associates indicated that about two-thirds of HOME-funded homeownership programs had not adopted long-term affordability rules beyond the minimum affordability periods required by the HOME program (five to fifteen years, depending on the amount of assistance) and that most HOME-funded homeownership programs provided assistance in the form of a grant or forgivable loan rather than through a mechanism that preserves long-term affordability.[29]

This suggests there may well be a potential to expand the available subsidy for SEH substantially by encouraging or requiring that a greater portion of the

27. Under a forgivable loan, a portion of the loan is forgiven each year. For example, in a fifteen-year forgivable loan, typically one-fifteenth of the principal balance is forgiven each year.

28. See the HOME Program National Production Report, showing cumulative production and expenditures through November 2013 (www.hud.gov/offices/cpd/affordablehousing/reports/production/103113.pdf).

29. See Turnham and others (2004); *Code of Federal Regulations,* Housing and Urban Development, title 24, sec. 92.254, "Qualification as Affordable Housing: Homeownership."

Box 6-2. *A Thought Experiment*

If we were to collectively develop 10,000 new SEH units per year, how many house-holds would we serve over a thirty- to fifty-year time horizon?

The answer depends largely on how often households move. Assuming that house-holds move once every twelve years, an estimated 662,500 households would be served over thirty years and 1.5 million households over fifty years. On the other hand, assuming that households move once every six years, an estimated 1 million households would be served after thirty years and 2.5 million households after fifty years.

These figures suggest that SEH could serve two to five times as many households for the same amount of money as a comparable grant program, which would serve 300,000 households over thirty years and 500,000 over fifty years.

See calculations available online at http://tinyurl.com/SEH123.

existing homeownership subsidy—both through the HOME program and other sources—be provided via an SEH format. Of course, as discussed in greater detail below, SEH may not be appropriate in all locations (for example, neighborhoods where little home price appreciation is expected or where there is a need to attract higher-income residents to achieve a mix of incomes) or for all programs (notably, down payment programs that provide a relatively small amount of assistance, where the incentive is not large enough to encourage buyers to agree to SEH restrictions). But for programs providing larger amounts of assistance in appropriate markets, the greater use of SEH in existing programs could well increase substantially the number of households served without increasing overall governmental expenditures. As outlined in box 6-2, over a thirty- to fifty-year period, a fixed amount of subsidy could serve roughly two to five times more households if structured as shared equity homeownership rather than outright grants for down payment.

The same point applies to inclusionary housing programs. Again, there are no good data on the extent to which inclusionary zoning programs attach resale restrictions to the below-market-rate ownership units they generate—and the duration of those restrictions. But the cautionary tale here is Montgomery County, Maryland—which has one of the oldest, largest, and most prominent inclusionary zoning programs—where the earliest produced units came with affordability covenants that lasted only five or ten years. Currently few of these units are still affordable, leading Montgomery County to revise its policy to require thirty years of affordability and the recapture of a portion of home price appreciation for units sold after the thirty-year period. By applying SEH principles to extend the affordability of all or nearly all units produced through inclusionary housing programs—whether mandatory or incentive based—the SEH inventory can be expanded with little or no additional subsidy.

Administrative Complexity and Expense

There is little question that SEH is more complex and expensive to adminis-ter than many other homeownership programs. This is one reason that some HOME-funded homeownership programs give for providing assistance in the form of a grant or forgivable loan rather than a binding covenant requiring resale to another qualified buyer.[30] In the latter case, as in SEH generally, the program sponsor must monitor the affordability of a growing portfolio (since units do not exit from the portfolio the way they do in non-SEH programs), find and determine the eligibility of qualified purchasers for resold units, review the quality of units turning over to determine if maintenance is needed before resale, and work with homeowners who fall behind on their mortgages. All of this takes time and money.

Rick Jacobus provides a comprehensive analysis of these tasks, which he calls "stewardship," as well as options for paying for them, which include govern-mental housing subsidy programs and operating subsidies from philanthropic sources, as well as (and perhaps more sustainably) fees charged to new SEH buy-ers or to sellers at the time of resale.[31] Typically, the fees charged at resale range from 1 to 4 percent of the sale price, well below the traditional real estate agent fee, which can often be avoided through the program's services, which include the marketing of resold homes to prospective purchasers.

One innovative approach is the New Jersey Housing Affordability Service, which performs stewardship services on a statewide basis to any jurisdiction that does not wish to provide these services on its own. This type of statewide entity enables assembly of the specialized expertise needed to ensure effective steward-ship of affordable units over time without each small jurisdiction needing to implement these services on its own.[32]

Variability in Local Conditions

SEH is best suited to areas where households at the target income level (for exam-ple, 60, 80, or 100 percent of the area median income) cannot afford to buy a home without assistance, and where home prices are expected to increase signifi-cantly over time—particularly when they are likely to increase faster than incomes, at least for certain stretches of time, such that families at the target income level will face increasing difficulties affording them. In some cases these criteria are sat-isfied for an entire city or metro area. In other cases the criteria are satisfied only

30. Turnham and others (2004).
31. Jacobus (2007b).
32. For more information, see Jacobus (2007b); see also New Jersey Housing and Mortgage Finance Agency, "New Jersey Housing Affordability Service (HAS)" (www.njhousing.gov/dca/hmfa/about/has/index.shtml).

for certain neighborhoods—such as a neighborhood that is in high demand or expected to be in high demand near a planned transit station or job center.

In practice this means that SEH is most important in strong housing markets or in gentrifying neighborhoods within otherwise weak markets. This said, there may be reasons to apply SEH to other markets—such as stable markets where home prices and incomes basically track, but the program sponsor wants to make homeownership possible at somewhat lower income levels than can be reached with FHA loans or by modest-sized down payment or interest subsidy programs. The question in these cases may be whether to use a shared appreciation loan or instead to provide a silent second mortgage. A silent second mortgage works much the same way as a shared appreciation loan—most important, no repayment is due until resale, ensuring affordability to lower-income households—but the program sponsor either forgoes interest entirely (in which case the loan's purchasing power will erode somewhat over time) or requires deferred interest to be paid at resale at fairly low levels (such as 2 percent).

Consumer Confusion

Needless to say, SEH homeownership is more complicated than traditional homeownership, and it may be difficult for prospective purchasers to fully understand how it works. This can be an obstacle in marketing SEH programs and may also create challenges for programs when purchasers of SEH homes come face-to-face with resale limitations or other features of SEH that they may have heard about but never fully internalized or understood. Some SEH programs have found it useful to recruit shared equity homeowners to help with the marketing efforts, as they may be more effective "messengers" to help prospective homebuyers overcome any initial skepticism and objectively consider the pros and cons. As with other aspects of SEH, market conditions are quite relevant since buyers may be more open to accepting limitations on asset growth when SEH purchase prices are far below prevailing market prices. Still, effective messaging is critical in all markets because consumer confusion can not only hinder recruitment efforts but potentially lead to political problems if SEH purchasers find themselves surprised by the resale limitations at the time of sale.[33]

Lack of Standardization

SEH can be complicated for political and financial institutions as well, especially given the broad diversity of programs. The lack of standardization can be particularly problematic for lenders financing the first mortgages on SEH homes. Naturally first mortgage lenders generally wish to understand and gain comfort with the resale restrictions and repayment requirements to ensure that the owner has

---

33. See Jacobus and Sherriff (2009).

strong incentives for keeping up the home and that the lender has full recourse to the property in the event of a foreclosure.

The process of educating lenders and obtaining their consent is complicated substantially by the wide variation in program models. During the strong market of the late 1990s and early 2000s, progress was made in working with Fannie Mae to develop a standardized rider for community land trusts and other SEH models. But with the tightening of Fannie Mae's credit requirements, many SEH purchasers and programs have turned to the FHA for financing, and some have run into difficulties gaining approval. Efforts are under way to work with the FHA to develop clearer guidelines regarding FHA financing for SEH.

Political Barriers

In many cases the political obstacles to SEH are among the biggest challenges to its adoption. Some policymakers and advocates view SEH a bit like "second-class" citizenship, arguing that low-income households should not be offered less opportunity to build wealth than higher-income households. Sometimes this argument is paired with very valid concerns about the prior history of redlining and other restrictions on the ability of minorities to purchase homes and benefit from home price appreciation.[34] Rather than seeing SEH as an opportunity to help a greater number of minority households build wealth, these critics argue that the limited equity buildup permitted under SEH further perpetuates the reduced access of minority households to the wealth-building benefits of traditional homeownership.

It is important to give these arguments fair hearing, and from the strict perspective of fairness, they seem well founded. From a practical perspective, however, they fail to account for limits on the amount of public subsidy available. Setting aside the important and related question of how to divide subsidy between rental and ownership, the question is really whether to spend limited homeownership subsidies on grants or forgivable loans that provide large asset-building opportunities to a relatively small number of households or to provide SEH to a much larger and growing number of households, creating a stock of permanently affordable homes that can eventually represent a significant (if still small) share of the overall housing stock.

As discussed in box 6-2 above, I estimate that over a thirty- to fifty-year period, one could serve roughly two to five times as many households with an SEH model as with comparable spending on grants. Is it worth sacrificing the opportunity to help so many additional households build predictable wealth through SEH just to give a smaller group the unrestricted ability to build assets (plus the windfall of the grant itself) by subsidizing traditional homeownership?

34. See Jacobus and Sherriff (2009).

Others may disagree, but for me the calculus is clear: if we are going to spend large sums of governmental or philanthropic funds to help bring the cost of homeownership down to more affordable levels, we ought to strongly consider using SEH instead. The larger the subsidy, the clearer it is that the policy calculus favors SEH.

The policy arguments in favor of SEH are enhanced by the experience of the homeownership boom and bust of the 2000s. During this period minorities and others gained expanded access to traditional homeownership, and many ended up worse off as a result once home prices plummeted and foreclosure rates rose. The great virtue of SEH is that it smooths out the rough edges of traditional homeownership, providing more predictable asset building tied to paydown of principal and modest home price appreciation, as well as some modest protection against home price declines.

Over the long run, the wealth-building potential of homeownership is tied mainly to the forced savings of principal reduction and modest home price appreciation. SEH expands opportunities for this type of wealth building while simultaneously enhancing the sustainability of ownership for low- and moderate-income families. Understood in this way, the risk-adjusted returns on SEH may actually be greater than those of traditional homeownership, which has a potential for faster rates of home price appreciation but also greater risk of loss.

How Could SEH Models Be Taken to Scale?

This topic has been anticipated by much of the discussion above, but by way of a conclusion, I would like to suggest some steps that could be taken to substantially expand the reach of SEH.

Revise HOME Program Rules and Guidance to Promote the Increased Use of SEH

HOME is a leading source of funding for homeownership assistance and also acts as a standard setter for other, locally funded programs. Right now, HOME regulations provide for a sliding scale of minimum affordability periods, ranging from five to fifteen years. While the HOME rules allow jurisdictions to set longer periods at their discretion, jurisdictions tend to adopt the default requirements, which are far too short to facilitate SEH. Therefore, one option is to change HOME regulations to make minimum affordability periods longer, so that the largest per-unit subsidy amounts lead essentially to required use of SEH.

An alternative approach would be to flip the current presumption so that long-term affordability (such as forty-five years of affordability that renews on resale) is the norm for large per-unit homeownership subsidies, with jurisdictions able to select shorter time periods at their discretion by documenting the reasons for their departure from the norm in their Consolidated Plan. While this would not force jurisdictions to adopt SEH, it would force them to think about the issue and provide a decision point that gives HUD an opportunity to educate jurisdictions about the pros and cons of SEH and the circumstances in which it is most important and effective. Because jurisdictions would have the option of selecting a shorter affordability period anywhere in the country, it would also avoid the problem of having to determine in advance, at the national level through a broadly applicable formula, the types of markets where SEH either is or is not most suitable.

Even without a change in the program regulations, HUD could provide more guidance to local jurisdictions about the benefits of SEH and encourage them to adopt it whenever they are considering large per-unit homeownership subsidies. HUD also could evaluate its policies to determine which ones are inadvertently acting as barriers to the use of SEH (for example, policies that create disincentives for jurisdictions to generate so-called program income or prevent jurisdictions from charging fees to cover stewardship costs) and adopt or propose changes to those policies to better support SEH.

Promote the Use of SEH in Inclusionary Housing Programs

As discussed earlier, a variety of inclusionary housing programs—such as inclusionary zoning and density bonuses—produce affordable homeownership units without the use of explicit public subsidy. I recognize that there are differences of opinion about the merits of these models, but at a minimum, whenever they are adopted, the affordability of the homeownership units ought to be sustained through the use of deed restrictions or other forms of SEH.

Ensure That SEH Purchasers Have Access to FHA Mortgages

As noted above, many SEH buyers seek to use FHA loans as the source of first mortgages, but some are running into a problem with approval of the resale restrictions. Adoption of clear guidelines from the FHA on the standards for approving these loans would help ensure that, at a minimum, those programs that can clear all the other hurdles for SEH have access to first mortgage financing from standard channels.

Move toward Greater Standardization of Program Documents

To a certain extent, the diversity of program models reflects differences in programmatic objectives and underlying philosophies. So some diversity is not only inevitable but probably desirable. At the same time, there are benefits to standardization, particularly in reducing obstacles to lender participation, developing standardized approval conditions by the FHA and any government-sponsored enterprises, and ultimately, reducing the costs to local programs of developing customized legal documents and program manuals.

The obvious compromise is to identify a limited number of models and encourage greater adoption of one of these standards. These models could still have some modest flexibility for local variation—for example, providing an option to select one of five standard resale formulas—without necessarily undermining the benefits of standardization.

Develop and Test Sustainable Stewardship Models

While the availability of subsidy will always be a limitation, we ought to be able to develop sustainable models for funding stewardship costs, especially through fees charged at resale or by ensuring the program's share of home price appreciation is sufficient to cover stewardship costs as well as maintaining affordability. To do this, we will need to better define stewardship, ensure that it is practiced effectively, document its benefits, and clarify available funding sources. It also may be worth following New Jersey's lead and establishing regional or state stewardship bodies to provide these services regionally. Among other benefits, this approach allows for the concentration of specialized expertise in a single organization, reducing the burden on many smaller governmental or nonprofit entities that may not have the capacity or the scale to provide it.

Ensure That Prospective Purchasers Can Find SEH Units and Information about SEH

As the number of SEH units increases, there may be opportunities to join forces and market SEH on a regional basis, providing a single source of information in a metro area where buyers can find out about available units and SEH programs and learn more about the basic principles underlying SEH. This may gradually help expand awareness of SEH as well as facilitate the linkage of interested buyers and available units.

References

Apgar, William. 2004. "Rethinking Rental Housing: Expanding the Ability of Rental Housing to Serve as a Pathway to Economic and Social Opportunity." Working Paper W04-11. Harvard University, Joint Center for Housing Studies. December.

————. 2012. "Getting on the Right Track: Improving Low-Income and Minority Access to Mortgage Credit after the Housing Bust." Harvard University, Joint Center for Housing Studies.

Carr, James H., and Katrin B. Anacker. 2012. "Long-Term Social Impacts and Financial Costs of Foreclosure on Families and Communities of Color: A Review of the Literature." Washington: National Community Reinvestment Coalition (October).

Davis, John Emmeus. 2006. "Shared Equity Homeownership: The Changing Landscape of Resale-Restricted, Owner-Occupied Housing." Montclair, N.J.: National Housing Institute.

Jacobus, Rick. 2007a. "Shared Equity, Transformative Wealth." Washington: Center for Housing Policy.

———. 2007b. "Stewardship for Lasting Affordability: Administration and Monitoring of Shared Equity Homeownership." Working Paper presented at NeighborWorks Training Institute Symposium, Portland, Ore., December 12.

Jacobus, Rick, and Jeffrey Lubell. 2007. "Preservation of Affordable Homeownership: A Continuum of Strategies." Washington: Center for Housing Policy.

Jacobus, Rick, and Ryan Sherriff. 2009. "Balancing Durable Affordability and Wealth Creation: Responding to Concerns about Shared Equity Homeownership." Washington: Center for Housing Policy.

Kelly, James J., Jr.. 2009. "Homes Affordable for Good: Covenants and Ground Leases as Long-Term Resale Restriction Devices." *St. Louis University Public Law Review* 29, no. 1: 9–39.

———. 2010. "Maryland's Affordable Housing Land Trust Act." *Journal of Affordable Housing and Community Development Law* 19, no. 3-4: 345–65.

Lubell, Jeffrey, and Ryan Sherriff. 2009. "What's in a Name? Clarifying the Different Forms and Policy Objectives of 'Shared Equity' and 'Shared Appreciation' Homeownership Programs." Washington: Center for Housing Policy.

Sherriff, Ryan. 2010. "Shared Equity Homeownership State Policy Review." Washington: Center for Housing Policy.

Temkin, Kenneth, Brett Theodos, and David Price. 2010. "Balancing Affordability and Opportunity: An Evaluation of Affordable Homeownership Programs with Long-Term Affordability Controls: Cross-Site Report." Washington: Urban Institute.

Thaden, Emily. 2011. "Stable Home Ownership in a Turbulent Economy: Delinquencies and Foreclosures Remain Low in Community Land Trusts." Working Paper. Cambridge, Mass.: Lincoln Institute of Land Policy.

———. 2012. "Results of the 2011 Comprehensive CLT Survey." Nashville, Tenn.: The Housing Fund.

Turnham, Jennifer, and others. 2004. *Study of Homebuyer Activity through the HOME Investment Partnerships Program.* Report prepared for the U.S. Department of Housing and Urban Development. Cambridge, Mass.: Abt Associates.

PART **III**

Assessing and
Mitigating Risk

7

Underwriting Standards, Loan Products, and Performance: What Have We Learned?

MARSHA J. COURCHANE, LEONARD C. KIEFER,
AND PETER M. ZORN

The mortgage market crisis of the past decade led to many changes in the structure of the industry and in the products being offered to borrowers. The beginning of the 2000s witnessed a surge in nonprime lending with an attendant proliferation of new products, including many that allowed borrowers who could not meet traditional underwriting standards to obtain home mortgages and achieve homeownership. By the end of the decade, however, delinquency and foreclosure rates had increased throughout the country, the nonprime sector had collapsed almost entirely, and these innovative products were largely gone from the offerings of mortgage lenders.

One immediate reaction to the crisis included a significant congressional response aimed at tighter regulation of the mortgage industry. Among other actions this entailed passage of the Dodd-Frank Wall Street Reform and Consumer Protection Act, with its introduction of the qualified mortgage (QM) and the qualified residential mortgage (QRM) requirements, as well as a variety of other restrictions on mortgage product offerings and extensions of consumer protections. Simultaneously lenders themselves tightened underwriting standards across the board and virtually eliminated product offerings requiring little or no documentation of income and assets, products with negative amortization options, and products specifically designed to meet the needs of nontraditional or nonprime borrowers.

Moreover, as the subprime sector collapsed, the government mortgage sector surged.[1] By 2009 lower-income home-purchase borrowers were disproportionately

---

1. See, for example, Courchane, Darolia, and Zorn (2013).

more likely to take out Federal Housing Administration (FHA) or Veterans Administration (VA) loans.[2] As a result by 2011 the market shares of the government-insured products, combined with those that met the credit standards of Freddie Mac and Fannie Mae (the government-sponsored enterprises, or GSEs), grew to account for over 90 percent of the market.[3]

Both the FHA and the GSEs have missions that support meeting the needs of underserved borrowers. The curtailment of nonprime mortgage offerings has nonetheless raised concerns that access to credit has been severely limited for borrowers with low down payments or poor credit histories or who are otherwise underserved by the prime market.[4] Moreover, underwriting and credit standards are currently as tight as they have been in decades. While likely providing assurance regarding the performance of current mortgage originations, this also restricts access to credit for targeted borrowers.

The history of mortgage performance over the last decade offers the opportunity to distinguish mortgage programs and combinations of borrower and loan characteristics that work (that is, perform well in stressful economic environments) from those that do not. Underwriting standards varied considerably in the earlier part of this decade, changing from restrictive to relaxed. This provides rich data on the performance of borrowers stretching for credit in a period of declining house prices and rising unemployment. Many of these loans performed poorly. However, throughout this critical period, state housing finance agencies and other homeownership programs offered loans to targeted populations that exhibited reasonable performance. These programs, however, were typically small in scale and have not been widely reproduced.

In this chapter we explore whether it is possible to achieve scale in providing underserved borrowers with access to mortgage credit at acceptable levels of risk. Specifically, we ask whether the data of the last decade offer the potential for creating a traditional automated underwriting scorecard that effectively and responsibly extends mortgage credit to borrowers who reside in low-income communities, make low down payments, and have poorer credit histories.

There are four steps necessary to complete this exercise:

—First, empirically estimate a mortgage delinquency model.

—Second, convert the estimated delinquency model to an underwriting scorecard for assessing risk.

—Third, determine a scorecard value ("cutpoint") that demarcates the marginal risk tolerance. Score values equal to or below the cutpoint are viewed as acceptable risk, while score values above the cutpoint are not.

---

2. See Avery and others (2010, p. A40).

3. See Inside Mortgage Finance (2012, p. 17).

4. See, for example, Courchane and Zorn (2012).

—Fourth, run targeted borrowers through this prototype of an automated underwriting system and determine the proportion of the population that is within acceptable risk tolerances.

The main data we use for this analysis are loan-level observations from Core-Logic on mortgages originated in the prime, subprime, and government sectors from 1999 through 2009. Using an enhanced version of these data, for each of the three market sectors, we separately estimate the probability that borrowers will become delinquent ninety days or more on their loans within the first three years after origination. Included in the model are controls for borrower and loan characteristics, as well as controls for key macroeconomic factors affecting mortgage performance post-origination (specifically, changes in house prices, interest rates, and unemployment rates).

Underwriting scorecards provide ex-ante assessments of risk (that is, they assess risk at origination), so creating scorecards requires appropriate treatment of the post-origination variables in our estimated models. We create two separate scorecards to bracket the possible approaches: on one side, making no forecast regarding the future values of post-origination variables; on the other side, perfectly accurately forecasting their future values. The first scorecard sets post-origination values of house prices, interest rates, and unemployment rates to their constant long-run levels (a "through-the-cycle" scorecard). The second scorecard sets post-origination values of house prices, interest rates, and unemployment rates to their varying ex-post realized values (a "perfect foresight" scorecard).

The next challenge is to determine appropriate scorecard cutpoints for delimiting loans within acceptable risk tolerances. The choice of cutpoint is a complicated policy-business decision, so we provide results for a variety of cutpoints, ranging from a low of a 5 percent delinquency rate to a high of a 20 percent delinquency rate. We also provide results for a representative set of cutpoints, set at 5 percent for prime loans, 15 percent for subprime loans, and 10 percent for government loans. We argue that these values represent reasonable risk tolerances and approximate the observed delinquency rates in 1999 through 2001 of the 90th percentile highest-risk loans originated in the prime market, the 50th percentile highest-risk loans in the subprime market, and the 60th percentile highest-risk loans in the government market.

The combination of scorecards and cutpoints creates working facsimiles of traditional automated underwriting systems, and we apply these systems to the target population.[5] For this exercise our target population is composed of borrowers with loan-to-value (LTV) ratios of 90 percent or above, with FICO scores

5. We weight the data based on the proportion of the target population in the Home Mortgage Disclosure Act (HMDA) data to ensure that the target population in our data is representative of the target population in HMDA data. This allows us to draw inferences to the full population.

of 720 or below or missing, and who are located in census tracts with median incomes below 80 percent of area median income.

Using our representative set of cutpoints, we find that 34 percent of the prime market targeted borrowers are viewed as acceptable risks by the through-the-cycle scorecard. The perfect foresight scorecard yields 42 percent. For the subprime market, these values are 26 and 39 percent, respectively, and for the government market, they are 39 and 44 percent, respectively. This suggests that automated underwriting systems offer some potential for responsibly extending credit to the target population. We also show that the through-the-cycle and perfect foresight scorecards offer competing policy trade-offs. The perfect foresight scorecard is more procyclical. However, it reduces credit losses and extends credit to a larger percentage of the target population, albeit by providing greater access during the up cycle.

Previous Literature

Many studies have looked at outcomes from the mortgage market crisis during the past decade. Of particular relevance for this research are studies that examine specific underwriting standards and products that may be intended for different segments of the population or that address outcomes for the target population.

Among many other studies produced over the last few years by the University of North Carolina Center for Community Capital is a recent paper by Quercia, Ding, and Reid that specifically addresses the balancing of risk and access for borrowers.[6] The paper narrowly focuses on the marginal impacts of setting QRM product standards more stringently than those for QM.[7] They find that such a setting of QRM standards would exclude many loans with low or no income documentation, hybrid adjustable rate mortgages, interest only, and negative amortization mortgages.

Quercia, Ding, and Reid also found that the benefits of reduced foreclosures resulting from the more stringent QRM product restrictions do not necessarily outweigh the costs of reducing borrowers' access to QRM mortgages. In particular, they conclude that LTV ratio requirements of 80 or 90 percent produce a smaller benefit when the resulting reductions in defaults are weighed against the number of borrowers excluded from the market. The results for debt-to-income (DTI) ratios and borrower credit scores similarly show that the most restrictive thresholds are less effective because they exclude a larger share of borrowers in relation to the percent of defaults they prevent. Of key importance is the finding that more stringent LTV and DTI ratios and credit score regulatory

---

6. Quercia, Ding, and Reid (2012).

7. For details of the QRM, see Federal Housing Finance Agency (2011).

requirements could disproportionately deny low-income and minority borrowers access to mortgage credit.

Pennington-Cross and Ho specifically examine the performance of hybrid and adjustable rate mortgages.[8] After controlling for borrower and location characteristics, they find that the type of loan product can have dramatic impacts on the performance of mortgages. Their specific focus is on hybrid adjustable rate loans. From 2001 through 2004, it was possible to refinance these products because house prices increased and interest rates decreased or stayed very low. However, interest rate increases over 2005–06 led to large payment shocks. Loans initially could still be refinanced due to rapid house price appreciation, but by 2007 house prices began to stabilize, and by 2008 house prices were declining so rapidly that only borrowers with excellent credit history and large amounts of equity and wealth could refinance. With large and unaffordable payment shocks, the only remaining option for many subprime borrowers was to default on their loans.

Amromin and Paulson also analyze the default experience of prime and subprime loans, although only over the period of 2004 through 2007.[9] They identify a decline in underwriting standards during this period for both prime and subprime loans. While they find that characteristics such as LTV ratio, FICO score, and interest rate at origination are important predictors of defaults for both prime and subprime loans, they do not believe that those changes were enough to have led to the observed increase in prime and subprime mortgage defaults over the past years. The authors firmly lay the cause of these defaults on house price declines but note that more pessimistic contemporaneous assumptions about house prices would not have significantly improved forecasts of defaults.

Courchane and Zorn look at changes to underwriting standards over time and their impact on access to credit for target populations of borrowers.[10] They use data from 2004 through 2009, specifically focusing on the access to and pricing of mortgages originated for African American and Hispanic borrowers, and for borrowers living in low-income and minority communities. The authors show that access to mortgage credit increased between 2004 and 2006 for targeted borrowers and declined dramatically thereafter. The decline in access to credit was driven primarily by the improving credit mix of mortgage applicants and secondarily by tighter underwriting standards associated with the replacement of subprime mortgages by FHA mortgages as the dominant mode of nonprime originations. Throughout the period of study, targeted borrowers also consistently paid higher prices for their mortgages; however, the extent of this

8. Pennington-Cross and Ho (2010).
9. Amromin and Paulson (2009).
10. Courchane and Zorn (2012). See also Courchane and Zorn (2011).

differential varied considerably over time and across groups. These pricing trends were driven primarily by the market's increasingly aggressive pricing of credit risk, mitigated somewhat by the FHA's increased share of mortgages and its more general reliance on average rather than marginal cost pricing.

These studies all suggest the critical importance of treating separately the three market segments—prime, subprime, and government—when assessing the changing access to credit over the past decade. They also provide some optimism that a careful examination of recent lending patterns will reveal opportunities for responsibly extending credit to targeted populations.

Data

Our analysis uses CoreLogic data on mortgages originated between 1999 and 2009.[11] The CoreLogic data identify prime (including Alt-A), subprime, and government loans serviced by many of the large national mortgage servicers. These loan-level data include information on borrower and loan product characteristics at the time of origination as well as monthly updates on loan performance through the third quarter of 2012. Merged to these data are annual house price appreciation rates at a zip code level from the Freddie Mac House Price Index and 2000 decennial census information on census tracts.[12] We also merge in unemployment rates from the Bureau of Labor Statistics as well as changes in the conventional market average thirty-year fixed-rate mortgage (FRM) reported in Freddie Mac's Primary Mortgage Market Survey®.[13]

The CoreLogic data are not necessarily representative of the overall population or of our target population. This is not necessarily a problem for estimating our delinquency model, but it does create concern for drawing inferences to our target population. To address this potential concern, we apply appropriate post-sample weights based on Home Mortgage Disclosure Act data to enhance the representativeness of our sample. We develop weights by dividing both the HMDA and the CoreLogic data into categories, and then creating weights for the CoreLogic

11. These data are made available to Freddie Mac by CoreLogic.

12. The house price index is the Freddie Mac House Price Index, Weighted Repeat Sales Index at the zip code level. While these data are not publicly available, the metro-state index can be found at www.freddiemac.com/finance/fmhpi/. The CoreLogic data do not provide census tract information, so we use a crosswalk from zip code tabulation areas to Census 2000 tracts. This crosswalk can be found at the Missouri Census Data Center (http://mcdc.missouri.edu/websas/geocorr12.html).

13. The unemployment rate is from the Bureau of Labor Statistics, "Local Area Unemployment Statistics" (www.bls.gov/lau/). We use county-level unemployment rates, which are seasonally adjusted by Moody's Analytics. These data are available publicly; see "30-Year Fixed-Rate Mortgages since 1971" (www.freddiemac.com/pmms/pmms30.htm).

Table 7-1. *Summary Statistics for Continuous Variables Used in the Estimations*

Units as indicated

Variable	Statistic	All Loans	Prime	Subprime	Government
LTV ratio	Mean	83	78	83	97
	SD	15	15	11	7
	Missing (percent)	1.8	10.1	2.8	1.9
FICO score	Mean	703	728	630	666
	SD	69	55	62	68
	Missing (percent)	15.5	16.8	8.1	15.2
Loan amount	Mean	190	207	173	143
(thousands of dollars)	SD	336	360	324	243
	Missing (percent)	. . . [a]	. . .	. . .	. . .
DTI ratio	Mean	36	36	n.a.	37
	SD	15	15	n.a.	15
	Missing (percent)	67.3	62.6	100	65.5
House price growth,	Mean	4.1	4.2	6.9	2.2
1 year post-origination	SD	10.3	10.6	10.1	8.9
(percent)	Missing (percent)	. . .	. . .	. . .	. . .
House price growth,	Mean	6.6	6.8	9.5	4.7
2 years post-origination	SD	19.8	20.3	20.7	16.9
(percent)	Missing (percent)	. . .	. . .	. . .	. . .
House price growth,	Mean	7.4	7.4	7.5	7.6
3 years post-origination	SD	27.5	28.3	29.1	23.8
(percent)	Missing (percent)	. . .	. . .	. . .	. . .
Change in mortgage rate,	Mean	−0.1	−0.1	0	−0.3
1 year post-origination	SD	0.6	0.6	0.6	0.6
(percentage point)	Missing (percent)	. . .	. . .	. . .	. . .
Change in mortgage rate,	Mean	−0.2	−0.2	−0.1	−0.3
2 years post-origination	SD	0.6	0.6	0.5	0.5
(percentage point)	Missing (percent)	. . .	. . .	. . .	. . .
Change in mortgage rate,	Mean	−0.2	−0.2	−0.3	−0.3
3 years post-origination	SD	0.6	0.6	0.5	0.6
(percentage point)	Missing (percent)	. . .	. . .	. . .	. . .
Unemployment rate,	Mean	5.6	5.4	5	6.5
1 year post-origination	SD	2.3	2.1	1.5	2.9
(percent)	Missing (percent)	. . .	. . .	. . .	. . .

(*continued*)

Table 7-1 (*continued*)

Variable	Statistic	All Loans	Prime	Subprime	Government
Unemployment rate,	Mean	6	5.9	5.4	6.7
2 years post-origination	SD	2.6	2.5	1.9	2.9
(percent)	Missing (percent)	...	...	...	...
Unemployment rate,	Mean	6.6	6.6	6.4	6.7
3 years post-origination	SD	2.8	2.8	2.7	2.7
(percent)	Missing (percent)	...	...	...	...

Source: Authors' calculations. See text for data sources.

a. We drop missing observations for continuous variables in the estimations except for FICO, where missing values are included through the use of a dummy variable. We include a missing observation category for discrete variables with missing observations.

data that ensure that the distribution of CoreLogic loans across the categories is the same as that for HMDA loans. The categories are a function of market segment (prime, subprime, and government), loan purpose (purchase or refinance), state, month of origination, and loan amount. Because we rely on a post-sample approach and cannot create categories that precisely define our target population, our weighting does not ensure representativeness of the CoreLogic data. However, it likely offers an improvement and is the best we can do under the circumstances.[14]

Consistent with our focus on identifying responsible credit opportunities for targeted populations, we restrict our analysis to first lien, purchase money loans. Summary statistics for the continuous variables used in our delinquency estimation are found in table 7-1; summary statistics for the categorical variables are shown in table 7-2.

As shown in table 7-1, the average LTV ratio for government loans is 97 percent. This is considerably higher than for the prime market, where first lien loans tend to have LTV ratios under 90 percent.[15] We also observe the expected differences in FICO scores, with an average FICO score in the prime sector of 728, a subprime average of just 630, and an average for government loans of 666. The prime market loan amount (that is, the unpaid principal balance at origination) averages $207,000, with the government loan amount the lowest at a mean of $143,000. While many claims about subprime loans focused on their fueling of

14. We do not use the weights for our delinquency estimations but do use them to draw any inferences about the population.

15. While table 7-1 lists the mean LTV ratio for subprime loans at 83 percent, this may reflect the absence of second lien loans, which led to the resultant higher combined LTV ratios for subprime borrowers.

Table 7-2. *Summary Statistics for Variables Used in Estimations (Class Variables)*

Percent

Variable	Class	All	Prime	Subprime	Government
Property type	Not condo	88.3	86.2	92.2	93.0
	Condo	11.7	13.8	7.8	7.0
Occupancy	Owner occupied	85.5	83.4	85.9	91.9
	Not owner occupied	14.5	16.6	14.1	8.1
Channel	Other	40.7	41.0	33.2	43.6
	Retail	29.9	33.7	21.2	22.1
	Wholesale	29.4	25.3	45.7	34.3
Product type	ARM	14.9	12.6	48.5	4.7
	Balloon	0.8	0.4	4.9	0
	FRM-15	5.6	7.7	1.6	1.2
	FRM-30	67.8	68.2	22.3	90.1
	FRM-other	3.8	4.5	1.7	2.7
	Hybrid	7.1	6.6	21	1.2
Documentation	Full documentation	34.5	29.9	49.4	41.8
	Missing	37.3	38.8	18.4	42.3
	Not full doc	28.1	31.3	32.2	15.9

Source: Authors' calculations.

the jumbo mortgage market, the mean value in this population is below that for prime at $173,000. DTI ratios do not differ much between prime and government loans, and the DTI for subprime is unavailable from the data.

The areas where the subprime loans were originated had the highest house price growth, at 6.9 percent one year after origination and 9.5 percent two years after origination. By the third year after origination, there was little appreciable difference in house price growth across market segments. The standard deviation of house price growth rates increased considerably over time, rising from about 10 percent the first year after origination to around 28 percent three years after origination. For all three time periods after origination, unemployment rates are highest, on average, in the areas with government loans.

Table 7-2 presents the summary statistics for the class variables in the Core-Logic population. Some expected results emerge. The subprime segment has the largest share of loans originated through the wholesale channel, at 45.7 percent. The wholesale share for the prime segment was only 25.3 percent. Nearly half (48.5 percent) of subprime loans were adjustable rate mortgage (ARM) loans while only 22.3 percent of subprime loans were the standard thirty-year FRM product. In contrast, 68.2 percent of prime loans were thirty-year FRMs while 7.7 percent were fifteen-year FRMs. Nearly all of the government loans were thirty-year FRMs. The documentation figures are somewhat surprising, with nearly half of subprime loans fully documented. The low share of fully documented loans in the prime sector likely reflects the inclusion of Alt-A loans, which are defined as prime loans in the CoreLogic data.

Many homeownership and affordable lending programs take a broad view of their constituent population. However, our interest is narrowly focused on assessing opportunities for responsibly extending mortgage credit to borrowers with low down payments and poor credit histories, or who are otherwise underserved by the prime market ("targeted population"). We define this specific population as borrowers taking out first lien, purchase money mortgages on owner-occupied properties located in census tracts with median incomes below 80 percent of the area median income, FICO scores less than or equal to 720, and LTV ratios greater than or equal to 90 percent.

Limiting our analysis to borrowers who live in lower-income census tracts is especially constraining, as many borrowers with high LTV ratios and lower FICO scores live elsewhere. However, our data lack accurate income measures, and policy considerations encourage us to include an income constraint in our definition of the targeted population. As a consequence, loans to targeted borrowers account for a small percentage of the total loans made during our period of study (roughly 4 percent). We can be assured, however, that our target population is composed of borrowers who are an explicit focus of public policy.

Figure 7-1 provides a graphic illustration of the distribution of target population loans across the three market segments. The dramatic shift over time in the share going to the government sector is obvious, as is the reduction in the number of loans originated to the target population after the crisis.

Analysis

The first step in our analysis is to estimate a model of loan performance over the crisis period. We use augmented CoreLogic loan-level data on originations from 1999 through 2009 to estimate a model of loans becoming ninety days or more delinquent in the first three years after origination. This model includes borrower and loan characteristics at origination as well as control variables measuring changes in house prices, unemployment rates, and interest rates post-origination. It also includes several interaction terms for the borrower, loan, and control variables.

We then use our estimated delinquency model to specify two representative underwriting scorecards—a through-the-cycle scorecard and a perfect foresight scorecard. Next we apply a variety of cutpoints to our scorecards. Loans with

Figure 7-1. *Loan Counts to Target Population by Market Segment and Origination Year, 1999–2009*

Thousands

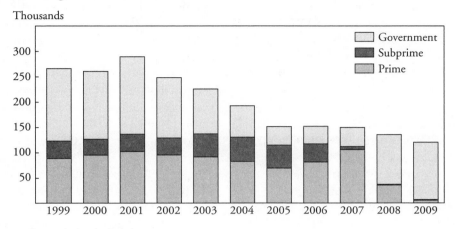

Source: Authors' calculations.

risk scores (delinquency probabilities) at or below the cutpoint are by definition assumed to be within appropriate risk tolerances.

The scorecard and cutpoint combinations provide working prototypes of an automated underwriting system. Our final step is to apply these prototypes to the target population and assess the results.

Estimating the Models

We estimate three separate delinquency models based on the CoreLogic population of first lien, purchase money loans. Separate models were estimated for prime loans (including Alt-A loans), subprime loans, and government loans, using an indicator provided in the CoreLogic data.[16] The estimation results for the prime market, subprime market, and government loans are presented in appendix A, tables 7A-1, 7A-2, and 7A-3, respectively.

Our process differs from the typical construction of underwriting systems in two important ways. First, while the CoreLogic data are reasonably rich in variables, they do not contain the detailed credit variables that are a key component of most underwriting models. As a result our model assesses risk less accurately than production versions. Second, typical models are estimated on historical data, but the resulting scorecards are applied to future applications (that is, out of sample). In our case, however, we apply our scorecard to the same historical

16. Because this field is determined by CoreLogic, we are unable to define the specific parameters of the subprime classification.

data we use for model estimation (that is, in sample). This, as a consequence, will tend to make our scorecard assess risk more accurately than production versions. These two factors counteract each other, and thus we believe they do not significantly bias our results.

The dependent variable in our estimation is a loan becoming ninety days or more delinquent in the first three years after origination. Continuous explanatory variables include borrower FICO scores, interest rates (Freddie Mac Primary Mortgage Market Survey® rates), house prices (based on the Freddie Mac House Price Index), and unemployment rates. The models also include categorical explanatory variables for loan amount ($50,000–$150,000, $150,000–$250,000, $250,000–$350,000, $350,000–$450,000, and greater than $450,000); documentation type (full documentation or missing documentation); LTV (less than 40 percent, 40 to 60 percent, 60 to 75 percent, 75 to 80 percent, 80 to 85 percent, 85 to 90 percent, 90 to 95 percent, 95 to 105 percent, 105 to 115 percent, and greater than 115 percent); product type (ARM, balloon, fifteen-year FRM [FRM-15], thirty-year FRM (FRM-30), and other FRM and hybrids (FRM-other); and condo and owner occupancy indicators. Finally, interactions were included between FICO score and loan amount, loan amount and LTV ratio, FICO score and LTV ratio, postorigination house price changes and LTV ratio, and FRM and LTV ratio.

Most of the variables in the prime delinquency model (table 7A-1) had the expected signs. Full documentation loans, retail channel loans, loans under the conforming limits, and FRM-30 loans are all less likely to become delinquent. As FICO score increases, the delinquency probability falls. Loans with higher LTV values have higher delinquency rates, with those characterized by LTV ratios greater than 100 most likely to go delinquent. Owner occupants are less likely to become delinquent.

Most of the subprime results (table 7A-2) are similar to those in the prime model. As in the prime segment, subprime borrowers with higher FICO scores are associated with lower delinquency rates, as are FRM-30 loans and those for owner occupants. The LTV ratio also exhibits a similar relationship with delinquency in both the prime and subprime models; however, the parameter estimates on the high-LTV ratio subprime loans are among the highest for both market segments. Still, there are some differences in the two models. For example, full documentation subprime loans are more likely to become delinquent, as are loans from the retail channel.

For the government segment (table 7A-3), the retail channel has the negative sign also observed in the prime segment. Full documentation loans are still marginally more likely to fall into delinquency, but given that nearly all government loans are full documentation, this result carries little weight. Finally, higher LTV ratio and lower FICO score government loans have an increased probability of delinquency.

In summary, the signs and magnitudes of our estimation parameters generally fit our expectations.

We next assess model fit by comparing model predictions to actual outcomes. The results of these comparisons are provided in appendix 7B as figures 7B-1, 7B-2, and 7B-3 for the prime, subprime, and government estimations, respectively.[17] In general we see that the models fit well. Specifically, the scatter plots remain relatively close to the 45-degree reference line. To the extent that there is any systematic error in the model, it occurs for lower-risk loans (toward the bottom left of the chart). This causes relatively little concern for our analysis because it is most important that the data points well fit the target population, which they do as shown in the higher-risk (upper right-hand) section of the charts.

Deriving the Scorecards

The second step of our analysis is to derive prime, subprime, and government scorecards from the estimated models. Scorecards are an ex-ante (that is, at origination) assessment of the credit risk associated with a particular borrower–loan combination. Our estimated delinquency models provide the basis for this assessment; however, these models include both ex-ante and ex-post (that is, post-origination) explanatory variables. The appropriate treatment of the post-origination explanatory variables is the key challenge for scorecard creation.

One approach, arguably the most typical, is to simply treat post-origination explanatory variables as controls in the scorecard—that is, to keep the value of these variables constant across borrowers and over time. We call this version a "through-the-cycle" scorecard. In our application we set post-origination variables to approximately their long-run means (house prices are set at a 2 percent annual increase, interest rates are assumed to remain unchanged after origination, and unemployment rates are set at 6 percent).

An alternative approach is to forecast at origination the future values of the ex-post explanatory variables. This is a challenging task in both theory and practice, and developing a representative prototype of this exercise is beyond the scope of our current analysis. Instead we pursue a simpler alternative that captures the concept of a scorecard incorporating forecasting.

The goal of forecasting is to accurately predict the future values of the ex-post explanatory variables. Our estimation data include the actual future values of these variables. Our approach, therefore, is to incorporate the actual future values

17. Loans in each segment are first grouped by model prediction and then divided into 200 equally sized buckets of loans with similar model predictions. The mean model prediction and actual delinquency rates are calculated for each bucket and then plotted in log-log scale. The model prediction is measured on the horizontal axis, and the actual delinquency rate is measured on the vertical axis. A 45-degree reference line is drawn in each chart, reflecting the combination of points where the models are perfectly predicting.

of the ex-post explanatory variables directly into our scorecard. We call this version our "perfect foresight" scorecard because it reflects the outcome of a scorecard with perfect forecasting. In this regard our scorecard represents an outer-bound possibility; scorecards that incorporate realistic forecasting will likely be less accurate.

Separate scorecards were created for each of the models-markets: prime, subprime, and government. We believe it is enlightening to compare and contrast the results of the through-the-cycle and perfect forecasting scorecards for each market. The through-the-cycle scorecard has the policy advantage of being relatively tight during the boom years and relatively loose during recessions (that is, it is countercyclical). As a result we expect it to be more "friendly" to the target population during recessionary periods such as those experienced recently. However, the through-the-cycle scorecard achieves this increased access to credit at the cost of potentially greater accuracy. For example, it systematically underassesses risk during down cycles.

In contrast, the perfect forecasting scorecard very accurately assesses the risk of loans. Realistic forecasting alternatives will not be as accurate, but nonetheless they can potentially do a better job than the through-the-cycle scorecard. The result is that scorecards incorporating forecasting can arguably better control risk but at the cost of a significant reduction in access to credit during recessionary periods. We expect the perfect foresight scorecard to be particularly "unfriendly" to the target population in recent years.

Choice of Cutpoints

The third step in our analysis is to choose scorecard cutpoints. The cutpoints set the marginal risk tolerance for the scorecards and so determine the levels at which loans switch from "acceptable" to "unacceptable" risks. All loans that the scorecards assess as less risky than the cutpoints are viewed as acceptable risks, all loans assessed as more risky than the cutpoints are viewed as unacceptable (too high) risks. The cutpoints, therefore, set the extreme bounds of within-tolerance risk for the scorecards.

Both policy and business considerations affect the judgmental determination of cutpoints. For example, a 10 percent delinquency rate might be viewed as an acceptable prime cutpoint during boom years when the market is optimistic and public policy is focused on expanding access to credit. However, the same 10 percent delinquency rate might be viewed as too high a prime cutpoint during a post-crisis recession, such as recently, when the market is trying to limit credit exposure and public policy has shifted to managing systemic risks and taxpayer losses.

It is not our intention to propose "correct" cutpoints for our scorecards. Rather, our goal is to illustrate how scorecards with reasonable cutpoints affect access to credit for the target population. Toward this end we provide a set of potentially reasonable cutpoints for each scorecard. Specifically, we provide results for cutpoints of 5 percent, 10 percent, 15 percent, and 20 percent delinquency rates for each of our scorecards. This provides a range of alternative impacts on the target population.

To simplify our presentation and focus our analysis, we also concentrate on a "representative" set of cutpoints that are determined by choosing among our four cutpoints for each market the one that most closely approximates the observed delinquency rate of marginal loans originated in the years 1999 through 2001. These years provide origination cohorts that experienced a relatively benign economic environment for the first three years after origination (neither expansive nor depressed), and so their realized performance is not unduly affected by factors outside the control of underwriting.

Underwriting in the prime market during the 1999 through 2001 period was relatively standardized (arguably, neither too loose nor too tight), so we set the representative cutpoint at the realized performance of borrowers around the 90th risk percentile of the perfect foresight scorecard. This performance is most closely approximated by a cutpoint of 5 percent delinquency rates, and by construction this results in about 90 percent of the prime loans originated in 1999, 2000, and 2001 being viewed as acceptable risk.[18]

The implication of this cutpoint for our two scorecards is illustrated in figures 7-2, 7-3, and 7-4, which show the results for the prime, subprime, and government markets, respectively. Each of these figures shows box-and-whisker plots of the scorecard score distributions by market and scorecard type for 1999 through 2009.[19] The box plots for the through-the-cycle scorecard are shown in panel A of figures 7-2 through 7-4; the box plots for the perfect foresight scorecard are shown in panel B of figures 7-2 through 7-4. We plot our representative cutpoints in each market as dashed lines.

The through-the-cycle scorecard makes specific, constant assumptions about the values of post-origination variables. As a consequence variation over time in the score distributions of the through-the-cycle scorecard is solely reflective of variation in observable-at-origination risk characteristics of the individual year cohorts. In contrast, variation over time in the score distributions of the perfect foresight scorecard also reflects variation in the economic environment

18. The 90th risk percentile is the scorecard prediction level that separates the 10 percent of borrowers with the highest predicted risks from the remaining 90 percent of borrowers with lower predicted risks.

19. The "box" in the box plot shows the interquartile range (IQR)—the scores between the 25th and the 75th percentiles. The "whiskers" go down to the 5th percentile, and up to the 95th percentile of scores. The 50th percentile (the median) is shown within the box as a short horizontal line. The average actual delinquency rate of loans originated in each year is shown with a diamond. The data are weighted via HMDA data to more accurately reflect the underlying population.

experienced post-origination. Moreover, because the perfect foresight scorecards are simply our model predictions from the first step, the models fit the data relatively well. That is, the box plots of the perfect foresight scorecard are closely reflective of the distributions of actual delinquency rates, as can be seen by the fact that the average actual delinquency rate (represented by a diamond) is generally toward the center of the interquartile range.

The resulting score distributions of the two scorecards are quite distinct. The box plots of the perfect foresight scorecard show relatively consistent risk distributions in years 1999 through 2004, a significant increasing of risk in the 2005 through 2007 period, and then declining risk with an ultimate return to the earlier levels by 2009. The impacts of the changing risk distributions are a function of a worsening credit mix of originations (due in part to loosening underwriting standards) and declining house prices after origination.

The through-the-cycle scorecard box plots show relatively consistent risk distributions in the origination cohorts throughout the entire period, albeit with a small change in the years 2005 through 2009. This suggests that a worsening post-origination macroeconomic environment was more likely to have been the cause of the poor credit performance of the 2005 through 2007 origination cohorts than a loosening in underwriting standards.

The horizontal dashed line in figure 7-2 plots the prime market representative cutpoint at 5 percent delinquency rates. This line in the through-the-cycle scorecard distributions (panel A) shows that the percentage of loans viewed as acceptable risk by this scorecard remains relatively constant throughout the period, albeit with a slight decline during the crisis years. That is, in most years the horizontal line runs between the 75th and 95th percentile risks (that is, between the top of the "box" and the highest "whisker"). In contrast, the perfect foresight scorecard (panel B) shows a significant reduction in the percent of originations viewed as acceptable risk in the 2005 through 2008 originations. In this regard the perfect foresight scorecard is clearly more procyclical during the recessionary period of 2007 and 2008.

Subprime market score distributions are shown in figure 7-3 and display a markedly different time trend than in the prime market. Both the box plots for the perfect foresight scorecard (panel B) and the average actual delinquency rates show that realized performance of origination cohorts in the years 1999 through 2001 was significantly worse than the performance of the 2002 through 2004 cohorts. This suggests that subprime underwriting in the 1999 through 2001 period was not as standardized in orientation as in the prime market. Moreover, the differential in risk between prime and subprime lending appears somewhat greater in 1999 through 2001 than in 2002 through 2004, suggesting that subprime lending was relatively less conservative than prime lending in the earlier period. Finally, the overall tolerance for accepting risk in mortgage lending has

Figure 7-2. *Prime Market Scorecard Distributions, 1999–2009*[a]

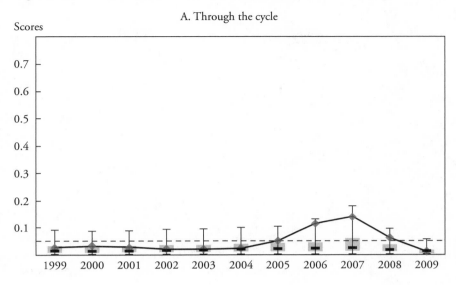

A. Through the cycle

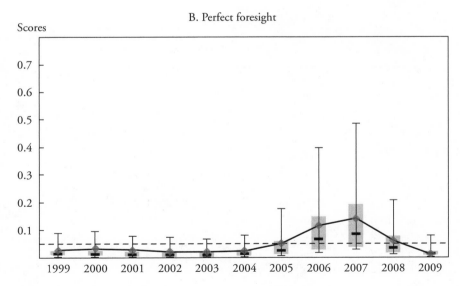

B. Perfect foresight

Source: Authors' calculations.

a. The "box" in the box plot shows the interquartile range (IQR; *shaded box*)—the scores between the 25th and the 75th percentiles. The "whiskers" go down to the 5th percentile, and up to the 95th percentile of scores. The 50th percentile (the median) is shown within the box as a *short horizontal line.* The average actual delinquency rate of loans originated in each year is shown with a *diamond.* The representative cutpoint is shown with a *dashed line;* the cutpoint for the prime market is a 5 percent delinquency rate.

The data are weighted via HMDA data to more accurately reflect the underlying population.

Figure 7-3. *Subprime Market Scorecard Distributions, 1999–2009*[a]

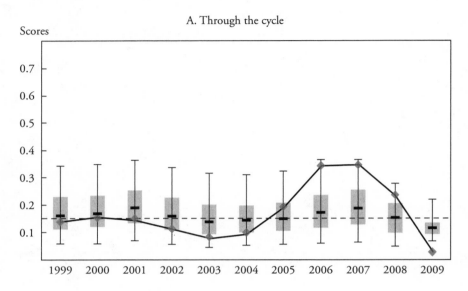

A. Through the cycle

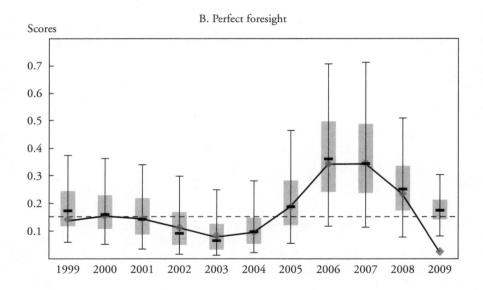

B. Perfect foresight

Source: Authors' calculations.

a. See note to figure 7-2 for explanation of abbreviations, symbols, and data weighting. The representative cutpoint for the subprime market is a 15 percent delinquency rate.

clearly declined in the recent environment. Reflecting these factors, we use a more restrictive standard for determining marginal borrowers in the subprime market than we do in the prime market. For the subprime market, we choose a representative cutpoint of 15 percent delinquency rates, which results in only about half of the subprime loans in the 1999 to 2001 cohort being viewed as acceptable risk.

Comparing the representative cutpoint lines and the subprime box plots in figure 7-3 also shows that the through-the-cycle scorecard (panel A) is the more countercyclical. Throughout the period the through-the-cycle scorecard consistently assesses about half of the subprime loans as being acceptable risk (that is, about 50 percent of subprime loans score below the cutpoint). The perfect foresight scorecard (panel B), however, shows significant variation in its assessment over the period—there is an increase in the percentage of acceptable risk loans from 1999 through 2003, at which point the percentage of acceptable loans declines rapidly to near zero levels, with only a slight rebound in 2009.

Government market scorecard distributions are shown in figure 7-4. As with the subprime market, the box plots for the perfect scorecard (panel B) suggest that underwriting was not as standardized or (relatively) conservative as in the prime market during 1999 through 2002. Particularly striking is the more limited relative increase in the risk distributions of the 2006–08 originations compared to the increase experienced by these cohorts in the subprime and prime markets. We therefore again impose a more restrictive standard for determining the marginal borrowers in the government market but mitigate this somewhat because of the government sector's explicit goal of providing credit to underserved borrowers. This yields a representative cutpoint for the government sector of a 10 percent delinquency rate, which results in about 60 percent of the 1999 through 2001 cohort being viewed as acceptable risk.

Applying Scorecards to the Target Population

Our last step applies our automated underwriting scorecards to the target population. The target population includes only borrowers residing in census tracts with median incomes below 80 percent of the area median who have low down payments (90 percent ≤ LTV ratio) and lower credit scores (FICO ≤ 720 or missing). As noted earlier, this represents only about 4 percent of overall originations during our period of study. In this regard it is a restrictive definition of the overall set of borrowers for whom there has been public policy concern (for example, first-time homeowners, low-income borrowers, minority borrowers, and borrowers underserved by the conventional mortgage market). We choose this more restrictive definition partially because we lack the data to accurately identify

Figure 7-4. *Government Market Scorecard Distributions, 1999–2009*[a]

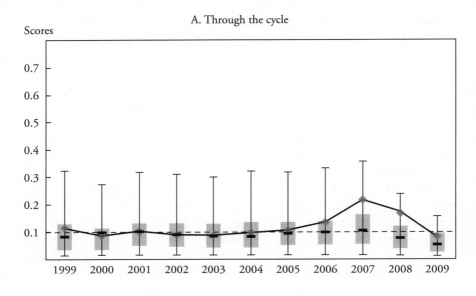

A. Through the cycle

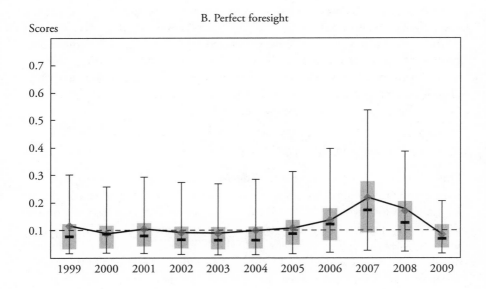

B. Perfect foresight

Source: Authors' calculations.

a. See note to figure 7-2 for explanation of abbreviations, symbols, and data weighting. The representative cutpoint for the government market is a 10 percent delinquency rate.

Table 7-3. *Percent of Acceptable Risk Borrowers within the Target Population, 1999–2009*

Scorecard	Market	Cutoff	1999	2001	2002	2003	2004	2005	2006	2007	2008	2009	All
Through the cycle	Prime	5	47	48	36	33	27	26	18	15	32	31	34
		10	83	86	80	78	75	73	63	53	77	74	75
		15	91	93	92	91	89	86	79	72	88	90	87
		20	95	96	96	96	94	92	87	82	93	95	93
	Subprime	5	0	0	0	0	0	0	0	0	0	0	0
		10	4	3	4	8	8	10	9	5	9	22	7
		15	16	17	23	33	35	32	26	17	38	78	26
		20	36	40	50	60	62	54	44	37	61	90	49
	Government	5	3	4	4	6	6	5	4	4	6	9	5
		10	34	33	37	42	43	38	35	36	49	60	39
		15	69	75	75	75	73	74	75	67	80	89	77
		20	79	84	85	85	83	84	84	79	91	96	86
Perfect foresight	Prime	5	55	65	64	67	55	26	2	1	4	15	41
		10	84	89	89	90	86	65	20	8	33	58	66
		15	92	95	95	95	93	81	42	23	60	81	77
		20	95	97	97	97	96	89	58	39	74	91	84
	Subprime	5	0	3	11	20	12	1	0	0	0	0	7
		10	5	19	38	51	41	10	0	0	0	0	23
		15	17	40	58	71	63	27	3	3	3	29	39
		20	36	58	75	84	78	44	9	7	21	63	54
	Government	5	8	13	23	25	23	9	2	0	1	3	11
		10	46	51	61	61	60	44	22	7	14	38	44
		15	73	80	83	82	80	74	54	24	37	72	72
		20	83	87	90	89	88	84	74	46	60	89	83

Source: Authors' calculations.

broader populations of policy focus, and partially to reflect postcrisis regulatory and market tightening (such as the QM and QRM criteria being promulgated by the Consumer Finance Protection Bureau) that has made it especially difficult for borrowers with poorer credit records or low down payments to obtain a mortgage. Moreover, although it is restrictive, we believe our target population highly reflects the population focused on by most affordable homeownership and underserved-groups policy initiatives.

We use our two scorecards to separately score target borrowers and then determine the percent of the population assessed as acceptable risks by the alternative cutpoints (5, 10, 15, and 20 percent delinquency rates). The results of this exercise for the through-the-cycle scorecard and the perfect foresight scorecard are provided in table 7-3, which clearly shows that the choice of cutpoint has a dramatic impact on the percent of the target population obtaining access to credit. For example, over the entire period, 34 percent of the target population is viewed as acceptable risk by the through-the-cycle scorecard when a cutpoint of 5 percent is used, whereas at a cutpoint of 10 percent, this figure jumps to 75 percent. The differential risk distributions of loans across the three markets are also clearly illustrated. Using the through-the-cycle scorecard, 75 percent of the target population in the prime market is viewed as acceptable risk at a cutpoint of 10 percent, but at the same cutpoint, this proportion declines to only 7 percent in the subprime market and to 39 percent in the government market. These three markets clearly, and deliberately, serve significantly different risk borrowers. This should be reflected in appropriately set cutpoints across the markets.

It is also interesting to compare results across the two scorecards. There is surprising similarity in the overall percentage of acceptable risk loans for the through-the-cycle and perfect foresight scorecards with the same cutpoints. For example, with a cutpoint of 5 percent, the through-the-cycle scorecard finds 34 percent of the prime market target population as acceptable risk, while the perfect foresight scorecard finds 41 percent meet that criterion. Similarly, at a cutpoint of 10 percent in the government market, the through-the-cycle scorecard finds 39 percent of the loans to the target population as acceptable risk versus 44 percent under the perfect foresight scorecard. The difference is somewhat larger in the subprime market, where a cutpoint of 15 percent results in 26 percent of loans being acceptable risk according to the through-the-cycle scorecard while the perfect foresight scorecard indicates that 39 percent meet that standard.

Moreover, there is a distinct pattern in these results. All things being equal, the perfect foresight scorecard yields a higher overall percentage of acceptable loans in the target population than the through-the-cycle scorecard. Looking at the yearly columns in the table 7-3 shows why. The perfect foresight scorecard views a substantially higher percentage of loans as acceptable risk in the years 1999 through 2004 than does the through-the-cycle scorecard. The pattern reverses in the 2006 through 2009 period, but the net impact is that over the entire period, more loans in total are viewed as acceptable risk by the perfect foresight scorecard.

These trends are more clearly illustrated graphically in figure 7-5, which plots the time trend of the percent of acceptable risk loans to the targeted population according to the through-the-cycle (panel A) and perfect foresight (panel B) scorecards. In comparing the two panels, it is clear that in the years leading up to the boom (2000 through 2005), the perfect foresight scorecard offers credit to a far greater percentage of the target population than does the through-the-cycle scorecard.

Figure 7-5. *Acceptable Risk Loans by Scorecard, 1999–2009*

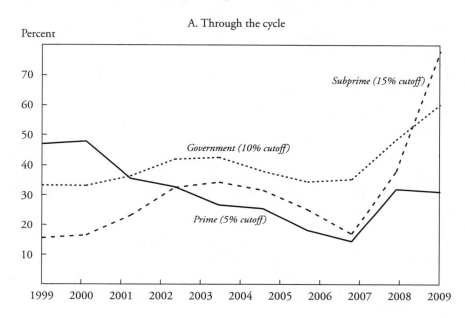

A. Through the cycle

Percent

Government (10% cutoff)

Subprime (15% cutoff)

Prime (5% cutoff)

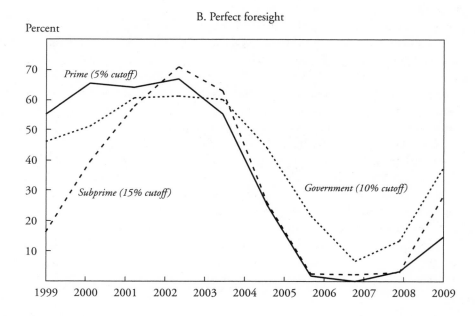

B. Perfect foresight

Percent

Prime (5% cutoff)

Subprime (15% cutoff)

Government (10% cutoff)

Source: Authors' calculations.

This increased access to credit is a two-edged sword. On one hand, the increased lending activity arguably contributed to the overstimulated housing market that was such a contributor to the recent recession—a public policy negative. On the other hand, however, the perfect foresight scorecard grants significantly more credit to the target population overall, albeit primarily in the early years of the decade—a public policy plus. Determining the preferred trade-off between these two outcomes is a public policy challenge.

Figure 7-5 also suggests that, at least using our representative cutpoints, it is possible to use automated underwriting systems such as our prototype scorecards to responsibly extend credit to targeted borrowers. Targeted borrowers have had difficulty obtaining credit in the recent market, arguably because of lower FICO scores and low down payments. Evidence that many of these loans may be acceptable risks offers a positive sign to people concerned with the access to credit of this population.

As a final part of our analysis, we illustrate the distributions of key risk characteristics of targeted borrowers with acceptable risk. Figure 7-6 shows the FICO score distribution for targeted acceptable risk borrowers, and figures 7-7 and 7-8 display the LTV and DTI ratio distributions, respectively.[20] Of most interest is examining the range of acceptable-risk values across these key characteristics in every market segment.

At the representative cutpoint for each market, figure 7-6 shows that acceptable risk prime target borrowers have a FICO score distribution with an interquartile range of 687 to 651, with an average of 666. For subprime the IQR falls between 651 and 589, with an average of 618. In the government segment, the IQR ranges from 677 to 639, with an average of 655. While these score ranges and averages vary by segment, all of them are considerably lower than the observed credit score averages of originations in the recent conventional or government markets. Rather, they represent scores that the current market considers very poor and would likely make it difficult to obtain credit.

A similar story holds for the LTV ratio (figure 7-7). Acceptable risk prime target borrowers have an LTV ratio distribution with an interquartile range of 90 to 95 percent. Acceptable risk subprime target borrowers also have an interquartile range of approximately 90 to 95 percent, while government borrowers' interquartile range falls at 98 to 99 percent. These are values well outside the cutoffs often discussed under QRM.

Finally, while we lack DTI data for the subprime market, acceptable risk prime targeted borrowers have a DTI ratio distribution with an interquartile range from around 47 to 56 percent. For the government market, the IQR goes

---

20. The box-and-whiskers plots are constructed the same way as in figures 7-2 through 7-4, but in this instance the diamond represents the average (mean) of the distribution.

Figure 7-6. *FICO Distribution for Targeted Accepts, by Mortgage Market*[a]

Score

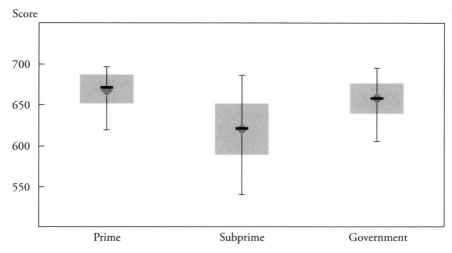

Source: Authors' calculations.

a. IQR (*shaded box*): scores between the 25th and the 75th percentiles. Whiskers go down to the 5th percentile, and up to the 95th percentile of scores. The 50th percentile (the median) is shown within the box as a *short horizontal line*. The average (mean) of distribution in each year is shown with a *diamond*.

The data are weighted via HMDA data to more accurately reflect the underlying population.

Figure 7-7. *LTV Ratio Distribution for Targeted Accepts, by Mortgage Market*[a]

Percent

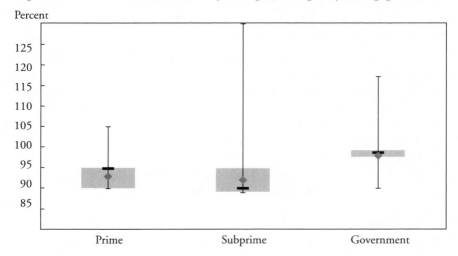

Source: Authors' calculations.

a. See note to figure 7-6 for explanation of abbreviations, symbols, and data weighting.

Figure 7-8. *DTI Ratio Distribution for Targeted Accepts, by Mortgage Market*[a]

Percent

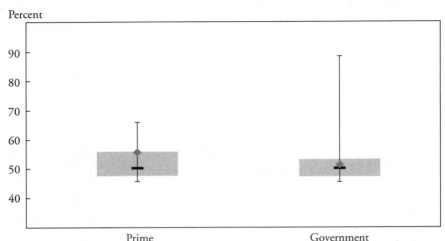

Source: Authors' calculations.
a. See note to figure 7-6 for explanation of abbreviations, symbols, and data weighting.

from 47 to 53 percent. In both instances these are values well above the proposed 43 percent threshold for QM. In fact, over 95 percent of the acceptable risk prime and government target borrowers have DTIs above the QM threshold.

Conclusions and Implications

Our delinquency estimations well fit our data, indicating the basic reasonability of the statistical models underlying automated underwriting systems. We use these estimations to construct two scorecards (through the cycle and perfect forecast) and then apply each scorecard to the historic population of targeted borrowers. Because these borrowers have lower FICO scores and make smaller down payments, they likely would face challenges obtaining mortgages in the current environment. It is instructive, therefore, to determine whether our scorecards suggest that it is possible to responsibly extend credit to a significant portion of this population.

The key to responsible lending is the appropriate setting of risk tolerances, and in automated underwriting systems this is operationalized by choosing the scorecard cutpoints that determine the maximum level of acceptable risk. This is not a science; rather, it is a judgment that balances policy, regulatory, and business considerations that all can change over time. The results of our analysis are very sensitive to the cutpoints we use. This simple observation highlights the temporal nature of responsible lending: risks that are viewed as acceptable in one period may be viewed as too high in another.

We focus our analysis on a representative set of cutpoints that we believe take a long-run view of risk. Using these cutpoints we find that it is possible to responsibly extend credit to a significant percentage of the targeted borrowers. Specifically, using the through-the-cycle scorecard, we assess 34 percent of the prime market targeted borrowers as acceptable risk, 26 percent of the subprime market targeted borrowers, and 39 percent of the government market targeted borrowers. Using the perfect foresight scorecard, we find it is possible to responsibly lend to 42 percent, 39 percent, and 44 percent of the prime, subprime, and government market targeted borrowers, respectively.

Our analysis is not definitive; it is sensitive to the choice of cutpoint (risk tolerance). It is, however, encouraging because it suggests that automated underwriting systems offer potential for responsibly extending credit to the target population. The size of this impact depends critically on the risk tolerances incorporated into the automated underwriting systems. But regardless of the chosen level of risk, our analysis identifies a portion of the target population to whom lenders can responsibly extend credit.

However, traditional automated underwriting systems are unlikely to be a panacea for providing credit access to the targeted population.[21] Successful homeownership outreach programs typically rely on prepurchase counseling and extensive (that is, high-touch) origination and servicing efforts. These programs also often consider nontraditional sources of data, such as rental payment history, when assessing borrower risk. None of these program aspects are recorded in the CoreLogic data, nor are they typically captured by automated underwriting models. Enhancing traditional automated underwriting along these dimensions is not a simple matter, but doing so offers the potential of further expanding access and increasing accuracy.[22] Even without this enhancement, however, automated underwriting is likely to remain only one of the effective tools used to responsibly extend credit to targeted populations.

Our analysis also highlights that choosing how a scorecard treats the postorigination environment has significant policy implications. From a macroeconomic perspective, the through-the-cycle scorecard has the desirable characteristic of being countercyclical—it tends to restrict credit during overheated markets and expand credit during recessions. The perfect foresight scorecard, in contrast, extends more overall credit (the expansion during the boom years is larger than the contraction during the recession). It also reduces total losses because

21. It is worth pointing out that most actual automated underwriting systems include many more detailed credit variables than are available in the CoreLogic data or included in our scorecard. The addition of these variables would certainly improve the accuracy of our delinquency model, but we expect they would have relatively little impact on extending credit to the target population.

22. See for example Avila, Nguyen, and Zorn (2013) on the value of counseling and chapter 8 in this volume on the use of alternative underwriting and servicing.

it "recognizes" when the post-origination environment will be more risky. This presents a challenging policy conundrum.

It is important to note that the benefits of a perfect foresight scorecard presume precisely that: perfect foresight. The overly optimistic view of most economic forecasters leading up to the last crisis suggests that this is an unrealistic expectation. It is beyond the scope of this chapter to create a scorecard that more reasonably mimics real-life forecasting. It seems reasonable to assume, however, that real-life forecasts will often be incorrect and that the promised loss reduction from incorporating forecasting into automated underwriting systems may be elusive.

Our analysis also has implications for QM and QRM regulations. QM standards focus on ability to repay while QRM addresses down payment considerations (that is, "skin in the game"). Very few if any of the target population borrowers would qualify for mortgages under strict QM and QRM constraints. For example, our analysis suggests that virtually all of the prime and government market targeted borrowers of acceptable risk have DTIs in excess of the 43 percent threshold proposed in QM regulations. Similarly, by construction our target borrowers make less than 10 percent down payments, well below the minimum 20 percent included in some initial proposals for a QRM. This illustrates both the disadvantage of regulation through single-metric thresholds and the advantage of taking into account compensating factors through statistical models. Model-based rather than simple threshold-based regulations offer the possibility of expanded access to credit at acceptable risk.

Finally, we note that mortgage products, especially the thirty-year FRM, and market segmentation likely play an important role in responsibly extending credit to the targeted population. There is no doubt that the thirty-year FRM has attractive characteristics from a risk perspective. And in our data, nearly 50 percent of the prime market targeted borrowers taking out thirty-year FRMs met our acceptable risk tolerances. However, this does not necessarily imply that all targeted prime borrowers could have, or should have, taken out a thirty-year FRM. Many non-FRM products offer significant reductions in monthly mortgage payments, at least initially, and have more relaxed underwriting standards.

Similarly, the prime market has historically provided a mortgage origination process that arguably would reduce the risk of lending relative to the subprime channel. It is tempting, therefore, to believe that moving borrowers from the subprime to the prime market could be a useful tool in responsibly extending credit. As with the thirty-year FRM, however, it is unclear whether this would ultimately benefit borrowers. The subprime market, for example, clearly has higher risk tolerances than the prime market, so all things being equal, it offers more access to credit. Fully exploring the value of the thirty-year FRM or prime lending for extending credit to targeted borrowers is an interesting but complex issue beyond the scope of this analysis.

Appendix 7A. Delinquency Models

Table 7A-1. *Delinquency Model, Prime Market Estimation Results*[a]
Units as indicated

Variable	Value	Estimate	SE	Prob χ²
Intercept	. . .	6.0511	0.0185	<.0001
LTV ratio	< 40	−2.0216	0.0383	<.0001
	40–60	−1.2569	0.0134	<.0001
	60–75	−0.4266	0.00841	<.0001
	75–80	−0.3532	0.00758	<.0001
	80–85	0.2441	0.0141	<.0001
	85–90	0.1925	0.00934	<.0001
	90–95	0.3963	0.00977	<.0001
	95–105	0.5549	0.00893	<.0001
	105–115	1.8594	0.0191	<.0001
	> 115	1.9365	0.0233	<.0001
DTI ratio	< 20	−0.2833	0.0062	<.0001
	20–30	−0.2094	0.00438	<.0001
	30–40	0.0668	0.003	<.0001
	40–45	0.2626	0.00348	<.0001
	45–50	0.2196	0.00413	<.0001
	> 50	0.2832	0.00389	<.0001
FICO score	. . .	−0.0123	0.000023	<.0001
Missing FICO	0	0.000145	0.000006301	<.0001
Loan amount (thousands of dollars)	50–150	−0.0346	0.00708	<.0001
	150–250	−0.1429	0.00817	<.0001
	250–350	−0.0867	0.0113	<.0001
	350–450	0.043	0.0143	0.0026
	> 450	0.0297	0.0164	0.0698
Documentation type	Full	−0.3883	0.00201	<.0001
	Missing	0.1165	0.00221	<.0001
Origination channel	Other	0.1946	0.0017	<.0001
	Retail	−0.1757	0.00185	<.0001
Owner occupied	Yes	−0.0675	0.00173	<.0001
Product	ARM	−0.0608	0.00644	<.0001
	Balloon	0.3316	0.0145	<.0001
	FRM-15	−1.021	0.01	<.0001
	FRM-30	−0.2932	0.00614	<.0001
	FRM-other	0.6934	0.00677	<.0001

(continued)

Table 7A-1. (*continued*)

Variable	Value	Estimate	SE	Prob χ^2
Condo	No	0.0191	0.00172	<.0001
Mortgage rate	1 year after	−0.0928	0.0028	<.0001
	2 years after	−0.0324	0.0031	<.0001
	3 years after	−0.0309	0.00283	<.0001
Unemployment rate	1 year after	−0.1203	0.00114	<.0001
	2 years after	0.0532	0.00131	<.0001
	3 years after	0.0661	0.000928	<.0001
House price appreciation	1 year after	−1.0398	0.0348	<.0001
	2 years after	−1.1007	0.0338	<.0001
	3 years after	−0.9109	0.0228	<.0001

Source: Author's calculations.

a. Also included in the estimation are interactions between: FICO score and loan amount, loan amount and LTV ratio, FICO score and LTV ratio, house price appreciation after 3 years and LTV ratio, and FRM and LTV ratio.

Table 7A-2. *Delinquency Model, Subprime Market Estimation Results*[a]

Units as indicated

Variable	Value	Estimate	SE	Prob χ^2
Intercept	. . .	2.5799	0.0265	<.0001
LTV ratio	< 40	−1.2988	0.1078	<.0001
	40–60	−0.8914	0.0347	<.0001
	60–75	−0.3043	0.0185	<.0001
	75–80	0.152	0.0151	<.0001
	80–85	0.339	0.019	<.0001
	85–90	0.2675	0.0168	<.0001
	90–95	0.3507	0.0182	<.0001
	95–105	0.3202	0.0173	<.0001
	105–115	1.1622	0.0396	<.0001
	> 115	0.9493	0.0568	<.0001
FICO score	. . .	−0.00681	0.000032	<.0001
Missing FICO	0	0.000375	0.000016	<.0001
Loan amount (thousands of dollars)	50–150	0.2089	0.0133	<.0001
	150–250	−0.0131	0.016	0.4133
	250–350	−0.1402	0.0273	<.0001
	350–450	−0.1274	0.038	0.0008
	> 450	−0.2051	0.0357	<.0001
Documentation type	Full	0.2048	0.00273	<.0001
	Missing	−0.4793	0.00387	<.0001
Origination channel	Other	0.2316	0.00265	<.0001
	Retail	0.0579	0.00322	<.0001
Owner occupied	Yes	−0.1238	0.0026	<.0001
Product	ARM	−0.1223	0.00595	<.0001
	Balloon	0.2676	0.00769	<.0001
	FRM-15	−0.5023	0.0154	<.0001
	FRM-30	−0.2281	0.00687	<.0001
	FRM-other	0.3455	0.0106	<.0001
Condo	No	0.0474	0.00325	<.0001
Mortgage rate	1 year after	0.0445	0.0036	<.0001
	2 years after	−0.0712	0.00429	<.0001
	3 years after	−0.1784	0.00439	<.0001
Unemployment rate	1 year after	−0.00534	0.00208	0.0103
	2 years after	−0.0566	0.00223	<.0001
	3 years after	0.0774	0.00146	<.0001
House prices	1 year after	−2.5146	0.0603	<.0001
	2 years after	−0.3572	0.0518	<.0001
	3 years after	−0.7534	0.0298	<.0001

Source: Author's calculations.

a. Also included in the estimation are interactions between: FICO score and loan amount, loan amount and LTV ratio, FICO score and LTV ratio, house price appreciation after 3 years and LTV ratio, and FRM and LTV ratio.

Table 7A-3. *Delinquency Model, Government Market Estimation Results*[a]
Units as indicated

Variable	Value	Estimate	SE	Prob χ^2
Intercept	. . .	6.0472	0.1869	<.0001
LTV ratio	< 40	−2.0861	1.834	0.2553
	40–60	−1.2143	0.2119	<.0001
	60–75	−0.252	0.1885	0.1813
	75–80	0.1252	0.1865	0.5021
	80–85	−0.0228	0.1884	0.9036
	85–90	−0.0116	0.1868	0.9506
	90–95	0.0871	0.1864	0.6403
	95–105	0.2927	0.1856	0.1148
	105–115	1.7592	0.1943	<.0001
	> 115	2.3596	0.2018	<.0001
DTI ratio	< 20	−0.5326	0.00905	<.0001
	20–30	−0.0622	0.00621	<.0001
	30–40	0.0422	0.00445	<.0001
	40–45	0.1667	0.00522	<.0001
	45–50	0.2094	0.00574	<.0001
	> 50	0.1949	0.00599	<.0001
Missing FICO	0	−0.00048	0.000019	<.0001
FICO score	. . .	−0.0127	0.000027	<.0001
Loan amount (thousands of dollars)	50–150	0.2099	0.1855	0.258
	150–250	0.0202	0.1871	0.9139
	250–350	0.1636	0.1925	0.3955
	350–450	−0.0661	0.2177	0.7616
	> 450	−0.4885	0.9169	0.5942
Documentation type	Full	0.0511	0.00241	<.0001
	Missing	−0.1051	0.00275	<.0001
Origination channel	Other	0.0923	0.00229	<.0001
	Retail	−0.1545	0.00264	<.0001
Owner occupied	Yes	−0.0981	0.00301	<.0001
Product	ARM	−0.3573	0.023	<.0001
	Balloon	−0.0615	0.0563	0.2748
	FRM-15	−0.5927	0.0264	<.0001
	FRM-30	−0.1334	0.0221	<.0001
	FRM-Other	1.1765	0.0226	<.0001
Condo	No	0.0853	0.00346	<.0001

Variable	Value	Estimate	SE	Prob χ²
Mortgage rate	1 year after	−0.0135	0.00279	<.0001
	2 years after	−0.047	0.00329	<.0001
	3 years after	0.0458	0.00329	<.0001
Unemployment rate	1 year after	−0.0392	0.00125	<.0001
	2 years after	0.0551	0.00187	<.0001
	3 years after	0.0247	0.00134	<.0001
House prices	1 year after	−2.3437	0.0486	<.0001
	2 years after	0.5796	0.0471	<.0001
	3 years after	−0.838	0.0403	<.0001

Source: Authors' calculations.

a. Also included in the estimation are interactions between: FICO score and loan amount, loan amount and LTV ratio, FICO score and LTV ratio, house price appreciation after 3 years and LTV ratio, and FRM and LTV ratio.

Appendix 7B. Comparison of Model Predictions to Actual Outcomes for Delinquency Rate

Figure 7B-1. *Goodness of Fit, Prime Estimation*[a]

Actual delinquency rate

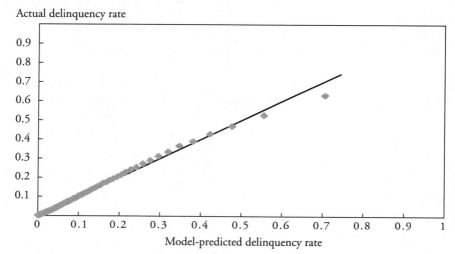

Model-predicted delinquency rate

Source: Authors' calculations.
a. See text for methodology.

Figure 7B-2. *Goodness of Fit, Subprime Estimation*

Actual delinquency rate

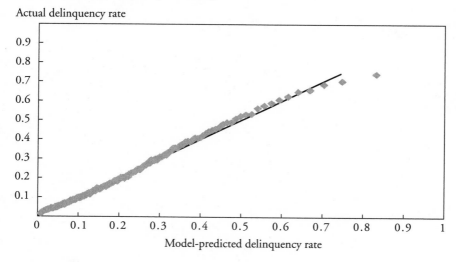

Model-predicted delinquency rate

Source: Authors' calculations.

Figure 7B-3. *Goodness of Fit, Government Estimation*

Actual delinquency rate

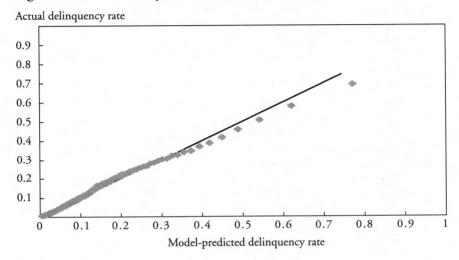

Model-predicted delinquency rate

Source: Authors' calculations.

References

Amromin, Gene, and Anna L. Paulson. 2009. "Comparing Patterns of Default among Prime and Subprime Mortgages." *Economic Perspectives* (Federal Reserve Bank of Chicago) 33, no. 2: 18–37 (www.chicagofed.org/digital_assets/publications/economic_perspectives/2009/ep_2qtr2009_part2_amromin_paulson.pdf).

Avery, Robert B., and others. 2010. "The 2009 HMDA Data: The Mortgage Market in a Time of Low Interest Rates and Economic Distress." *Federal Reserve Bulletin,* December: A39–A77 (www.federalreserve.gov/pubs/bulletin/2010/pdf/2009_HMDA_final.pdf).

Avila, Gabriela, Hoa Nguyen, and Peter Zorn. 2013. "The Benefits of Pre-Purchase Homeownership Counseling." Working Paper. Washington: Federal Home Loan Mortgage Corporation.

Courchane, Marsha J., Rajeev Darolia, and Peter M. Zorn. 2013. "The Downs and Ups of FHA Lending: The Government Mortgage Roller Coaster Ride." Working Paper (http://hofinet.org/documents/doc.aspx?id=2082).

Courchane, Marsha J., and Peter M. Zorn. 2011. "A Changing Credit Environment and Its Impact on Low-Income and Minority Borrowers and Communities." In *Moving Forward: The Future of Consumer Credit and Mortgage Finance,* edited by Nicolas Retsinas and Eric Belsky, pp. 86–117. Brookings.

———. 2012. "The Differential Access and Pricing of Home Mortgages: 2004–2009." *Real Estate Economics* 40 (December): S115–S158.

Federal Housing Finance Agency. 2011. "Qualified Residential Mortgages." *Mortgage Market Note* 11-02, April 11 (www.fhfa.gov/webfiles/20686/qrm_final_all_r41111.pdf).

Inside Mortgage Finance. 2012. *2012 Mortgage Market Statistical Annual,* vol. 1: *Primary Market.* Bethesda, Md.

Pennington-Cross, A., and G. Ho. 2010. "The Termination of Subprime Hybrid and Fixed Rate Mortgages." *Real Estate Economics* 38, no. 3: 399–426.

Quercia, Roberto G., Lei Ding, and Carolina Reid. 2012. "Balancing Risk and Access: Underwriting Standards for Qualified Residential Mortgages." Working Paper. Durham, N.C.: Center for Responsible Lending and Center for Community Capital, University of North Carolina (www.responsiblelending.org/mortgage-lending/research-analysis/Underwriting-Standards-for-Qualified-Residential-Mortgages.pdf).

8

Access and Sustainability for First-Time Homebuyers: The Evolving Role of State Housing Finance Agencies

STEPHANIE MOULTON AND ROBERTO G. QUERCIA

State Housing Finance Agencies (HFAs) entered the homeownership policy scene in the early 1970s through the sale of tax-exempt mortgage revenue bonds, which HFAs would then pass along as an interest rate savings on mortgages to qualified low- and moderate-income (LMI) first-time homebuyers. With mortgage interest rates rising as high as 18 percent in the early 1980s, many otherwise creditworthy homebuyers were cut off from the mortgage market simply because the monthly payments associated with the mortgage were too high. HFAs helped to reduce this barrier to entry by offering mortgages at below-market interest rates (often 2 to 4 percentage points below market), thereby reducing the monthly mortgage payment burden for the homebuyer. This mortgage payment "subsidy" was often viewed as the primary benefit of state HFAs for mortgage markets.

Since their creation four decades ago, HFAs have issued a cumulative total of nearly $260 billion in mortgage revenue bonds, funding mortgages for more than 2.9 million LMI households.[1] HFAs have further evolved to offer mortgage markets more than monthly payment subsidies. Many have helped develop statewide infrastructure that brings together lenders, real estate agents, nonprofit organizations, and local governments to address the needs of LMI first-time homebuyers. Through their structures and programs, HFAs not only offer subsidies to homebuyers, but they are positioned to address the kind of informational barriers that contributed to the recent financial crisis. Borrowers often lack information about

---

1. National Council of State Housing Agencies (NCSHA; 2012, p. 63, table 1).

loan products for which they can qualify, originators may lack information about borrowers' ability to repay their loan, and investors may lack information about the true default risk of a pool of mortgages. HFAs can address these challenges by increasing the flow of information about mortgage products, risks, and costs among borrowers, lenders, and investors, and by increasing the incentives for participants to use information in origination and servicing decisions. The Great Recession and its aftermath, along with recent regulatory reforms, have also created challenges and opportunities for HFAs to reassess their business models and strategies.

While state HFAs administer a variety of housing programs, including the Low-Income Housing Tax Credit program for rental housing development and the recent U.S. Treasury Hardest Hit Fund initiative for homeowners in financial distress, this chapter focuses on state HFA programs for single-family home purchase. More narrowly, using administrative and survey data, the chapter catalogs the different financing instruments, products, and activities employed by HFAs to promote and sustain first-time homeownership. It also discusses the central role that HFAs may be able to play in a national housing finance infrastructure after reform. As important as the latter point is, it has received little attention in the research literature. From this perspective alone, this chapter addresses an important void.

Overall, we find HFAs to be highly effective in addressing important market functions while at the same time fulfilling the public purpose of facilitating access to mortgages by creditworthy but otherwise underserved borrowers. The fact that the performance of HFA loans compares favorably with that of similar non-HFA loans reflects that effectiveness. While HFAs' traditional mortgage revenue bond business remains central, most HFAs are diversifying funding for single-family mortgage assets in significant ways, including direct participation in the mortgage-backed securities market. Not surprisingly, the capacity to undertake this and other new, flexible, and diversified activities varies by HFA. Efforts to increase HFA sophistication in these areas are likely to be critical to future success.

Pending regulatory changes may create opportunities for HFAs to develop new products to serve borrowers otherwise cut off from mortgage financing. HFAs have the potential to become a key mechanism to provide sustainable mortgage credit for low-income, minority, and other underserved borrowers in a future reformed national housing system. However, the discretion of HFAs to set innovative standards for their loan programs is often constrained by the private market participants on whom they rely for origination, servicing, and investments. Changes to servicing strategies and the secondary market environment, in addition to innovative product development, may be necessary to create additional demand for future HFA mortgage products.

State Housing Finance Agencies and Homebuyers

Two pieces of federal legislation in the 1960s led to the creation of state HFAs. The 1968 Housing Act provided federal funding to states to develop rental housing, and the 1968 Revenue and Expenditure Control Act permitted the use of tax-exempt industrial revenue bonds for "residential real property for family units." By 1987 forty-seven states had developed an HFA. By 2002 all states as well as Puerto Rico, the U.S. Virgin Islands, and the District of Columbia had functioning HFAs.[2] Not only did these agencies facilitate housing development, but their ability to issue tax-exempt bonds was viewed as a vehicle to attract new capital into the state, particularly institutional and individual investors in the long-term capital market who would typically purchase tax-exempt securities but not residential mortgage securities.[3] Furthermore state HFAs were largely self-sustaining, requiring no state budget allocations or subsidies beyond the federal tax expenditures to incentivize the bonds. Initially most state HFAs sold bonds to support rental housing development, but beginning with Virginia in 1974, HFAs began selling tax-exempt bonds to expand homeownership opportunities.

The entry of state HFAs into mortgage markets was initially justified by Congress as a way to benefit low- and moderate-income households unable to qualify for mortgage financing with conventional interest rates.[4] Extraordinarily high mortgage interest rates in the 1970s and early 1980s created substantial affordability barriers for households. State HFAs could use the proceeds from the tax-exempt mortgage revenue bonds (MRBs) to originate mortgages to borrowers at reduced interest rates. MRBs are tax exempt, private activity bonds purchased by investors at lower yields because of the tax-exempt status of interest income they receive; HFAs traditionally use the spread between the market rate and the issue rate to originate mortgages at below-market rates to homebuyers. HFAs are also permitted to use a spread between the interest rate on the MRBs and interest rate on mortgages originated (arbitrage), which they can apply to finance program administration and additional services, making the programs largely self-sustaining.[5] Changes in the prevailing interest rates and marginal tax rates over time have affected the magnitude of the interest rate subsidies, ranging from 360 basis points in 1981, to 200 basis points in 1985, down to 50–100 basis points in 1988, and on par with conventional mortgage rates today.[6]

2. NCSHA (2012, p. 3).
3. Stegman (1974).
4. U.S. Government Accountability Office (GAO) (1988).
5. The spread amount (arbitrage) is currently limited to 1.25 percent.
6. Because of lower marginal tax rates, the spread between the market rates and the MRB subsidized rate was permitted to decline, as investors needed more of a tax break to offset their lower total tax liability. See Durning (1992). See also Gross (1992, p. 126).

The early years of HFA homebuyer programs were marked by some controversy. Particularly some questioned the extent to which MRBs were effectively
targeted to underserved borrowers. Part of this controversy stemmed from the
entrance of local governments into the tax-exempt MRB market between 1978
and 1980, with much less regulation and oversight than state-administered
MRBs.[7] For example, one study found that two-thirds of the population would
have qualified for a local MRB subsidized mortgage based on income in 1978.[8]
Such coverage was beyond the intent of the enabling federal legislation. As a
result the 1980 Mortgage Subsidy Bond Tax Act limited the amount of MRBs
states could issue, thus granting states oversight of the amount of MRB volume
delegated to local authorities. Further restrictions required that borrowers be
first-time homebuyers (borrowers who have not owned a home in the previous
three years) buying homes below a specified price. Special treatment was permitted for targeted underserved areas. Restrictions were also placed on the amount
of fees that the implementers could earn from administering MRBs.

Despite the 1980 legislative changes, controversy over the targeting of the
MRB program continued, fueled by a 1983 report by the U.S. Government
Accountability Office (GAO) that found that 78 percent of 1982 recipients had
above median incomes, and the majority could have afforded homes without
additional subsidies.[9] Tax reforms in 1986 further reduced the amount of funds
that HFAs could leverage, making them competitive with other state private purpose bonds for total state bond limits.[10] Loan eligibility was limited to residents
earning less than 115 percent of the area (or state) median income, and eligible
homes were limited to less than 90 percent of area average home price, with some
exceptions for target areas (limits that are still in place today). Congress authorized an alternative Mortgage Credit Certificate (MCC) program in 1984, providing eligible homebuyers a tax credit for a set fraction of mortgage interest paid,
rather than a monthly payment subsidy.[11] Presumed to be more efficient and less
affected by interest rate fluctuations, MCCs could be used by states as a substitute
for MRB authority.[12] GAO studies also found that the cost to the federal govern-

7. Calkins and Aronson (1980); Cooperstein (1992); Durning (1992); GAO (1988).
8. Durning (1992).
9. GAO (1983).
10. From 1986 to 2000, the annual bond cap was set at $50 per capita, or $150 million if
greater, per state. Beginning in 2002 the bond cap was raised to $75 per capita ($225 million if
greater), and in 2003 it was indexed to increase annually for inflation. For 2013 the bond cap per
state was the greater of $95 per capita or $291.875 million. HFAs can carry forward unused bond
authority tied to a specific purpose or project for three years. See NCSHA (2012).
11. This fraction is typically 10–40 percent of total interest paid, or no more than $2,000. The
remaining amount can be taken as a typical mortgage interest deduction.
12. Greulich and Quigley (2009).

ment in terms of lost tax revenue from MRBs could be as high as four times the amount of the benefit provided as a monthly payment subsidy to homebuyers.[13] In addition, some research suggested that the monthly payment subsidies were being capitalized into higher asking home prices, particularly for new construction projects with seller financing.[14] The efficiency of the MCC could potentially address these concerns. However, because the MCC is a nonrefundable tax credit, demand has been limited to relatively higher-income borrowers.[15]

Aside from providing direct subsidies, HFAs have recently taken an important countercyclical role in stabilizing mortgage markets. For example, the 2008 Housing and Economic Recovery Act included a temporary increase of $11 billion in the annual private activity bond cap for housing activities (single- and multifamily).[16] In October of 2009, the Treasury Department launched the temporary HFA Initiative under the authority of the Housing and Economic Recovery Act in order to "maintain the viability of HFA lending programs and infrastructure."[17] The initiative increased the liquidity for HFA mortgages through the purchase of $13.9 billion in MRBs under the New Issue Bond Program.[18] This demonstrates the ongoing and important role of HFAs in mortgage markets.

The Role of HFAs in a Brave New World

HFAs combine both market- and mission-driven purposes, effectively balancing a sustainable business model while at the same time fulfilling their public purpose. A few important characteristics uniquely position state HFAs to fulfill these purposes. First, most HFAs are independent authorities (80 percent in 2010), benefiting from a quasi-governmental structure that provides them with more capacity for flexibility and innovation than mainline governmental entities.[19] Second, HFAs are largely self-sustaining, generating their own revenue (only 30 percent were even included in governors' budgets in 2010 for a direct appropriation).[20] Third, HFAs exist across all fifty states, as well as the District of Columbia, the U.S. Virgin Islands, and Puerto Rico, providing a common infrastructure while allowing for local variation in response to state-specific housing needs.

Rather than serving as an alternative to private market financing, HFAs leverage the private market to fund and guarantee mortgages. In fact, their historic

13. GAO (1983, 1988).
14. Durning and Quigley (1985); Cooperstein (1992); Durning (1992).
15. Greulich and Quigley (2009).
16. This increase was available through 2010.
17. U.S. Department of Treasury (2009).
18. NCHSA (2010).
19. NCSHA (2012).
20. NCSHA (2012).

reliance on mortgage revenue bonds to finance their operations tends to make HFAs more risk averse than other agencies, with some criticizing them for being too conservative.[21] Most state HFAs operate their homeownership initiatives within the origination channels and underwriting standards of conventional mortgages.[22] Most mortgages originated by HFAs are guaranteed by the federal government through Fannie Mae, Freddie Mac, or Ginnie Mae (for example, FHA insured mortgages) or limit investor risk through a moral obligation clause.[23]

What, then, is the benefit-added of HFA involvement in the mortgage market above and beyond what could be provided through the private market alone?

The role of state HFAs in mortgage markets is part of a broader discussion about government involvement in mortgage markets, which can be broken into two distinct justifications: government support for and promotion of *homeownership* to *increase access,* and government oversight of and intervention in consumer *mortgage transactions* to *reduce risk.* Traditionally the role of HFAs in mortgage markets has been defined as increasing access to homeownership for underserved populations, falling squarely under the first justification above. However, in this chapter we suggest that HFAs are increasingly evolving to play a second important role in reducing risk, as they are uniquely positioned to correct market failures related to the nature of exchange in the mortgage transaction. Both roles are described briefly below, followed by a presentation of survey data on current HFA strategies.

Access: Reducing Barriers to Entry

To the extent that owning one's home is associated with individual benefits for the owner as well as positive externalities for communities and markets, government intervention may be justified to remove barriers that prevent certain creditworthy individuals from entering the market. Such barriers could be financial (such as lack of sufficient funds to qualify) or structural (such as lack of access to affordable mortgage products). The exclusion of certain groups of individuals or neighborhoods from mortgage markets may not only be unfair but may also be economically inefficient, particularly to the extent to which otherwise creditworthy borrowers are denied access or are provided with unnecessarily high-cost products.[24]

State HFAs can help address these barriers by providing direct subsidies to homebuyers and by enhancing the lending infrastructure in local underserved communities. When HFAs entered the homeownership market in the 1970s,

21. Goetz (1993, p. 77).
22. Dylla and Caldwell-Tautges (2012).
23. A moral obligation clause is a nonbinding legislative commitment to ensure minimum levels of capital reserves for the HFA's origination activities. It provides a credit enhancement so that even if the borrower fails to make his or her mortgage payment, the MRB investor will be repaid.
24. Lax and others (2004); Belsky and Wachter (2010).

potential borrowers with otherwise good credit histories were excluded from the market because of high interest rates. Mortgage underwriting at the time relied heavily on "affordability ratios" to be approved for financing; generally mortgage payments (principal, interest, taxes, and insurance) had to be lower than 29 percent of a household's gross monthly income, and all financed debt including mortgage payments had to be below 36 percent. By lowering the interest rate on the mortgage, HFAs were effectively able to lower the monthly payment, thereby increasing the likelihood that a given homebuyer would qualify for a mortgage. Today lack of a down payment for home purchase presents a significant barrier for homebuyers.[25] Many HFAs thus offer up-front down payment subsidies to otherwise creditworthy borrowers by leveraging state and federal funds in conjunction with the affordable mortgage product.

Aside from direct subsidies, HFAs are also positioned to break down structural barriers that may reduce access to affordable mortgages for certain populations. Recent research suggests that LMI homebuyers do not necessarily self-sort into the lowest-priced product for which they may qualify. For example, a good portion of LMI homebuyers who received higher-cost subprime mortgages during the housing boom would have likely qualified for lower-cost sustainable conventional mortgages.[26] By building a network of community organizations, real estate agents, and lenders in underserved communities and strategically targeting affordable mortgage products to areas otherwise targeted for higher-cost lending, HFAs may help address issues of allocative inefficiency.[27]

Sustainability: Informational Barriers

While increasing access may help address market inefficiencies, market expansions created by increased access may not be sustainable if participants in the transaction lack full information and incentives for adequate screening and monitoring.[28] As was characteristic of subprime lending, incomplete information may lead borrowers, lenders, or investors to make decisions about mortgages that they would otherwise not make if they had full information. Insufficient incentives for careful screening and monitoring can lead lenders and investors to approve or finance loans in the short term with less than adequate scrutiny of the borrower's ability to repay the debt over the long term.[29] Both incomplete information and insufficient incentives have been cited as contributing factors to the recent mortgage crisis.[30]

25. Quercia, McCarthy, and Wachter (2003).
26. Carr and Schuetz (2001); Chomsisengphet and Pennington-Cross (2006).
27. Moulton and Bozeman (2011).
28. Glaeser and Kallal (1997); Belsky and Wachter (2010).
29. Agarwal, Chang, and Yavas (2012); Keys, Seru, and Vig (2012); Purnanandam (2011).
30. Jiang, Nelson, and Vytlacil (2009); Quercia, Freeman, and Ratcliffe (2011).

For individual borrowers mortgage decisions can be complex, requiring sufficient understanding of terms and conditions that many first-time homebuyers may not possess.[31] By incorporating education of and counseling to homebuyers as part of the mortgage product, HFAs can help improve the likelihood that borrowers make informed mortgage decisions, both before and after purchase. Furthermore the network of lenders, real estate agents, and nonprofits involved in HFA-funded mortgages increases the potential flow of information about borrowers and local markets, including "soft" information that may not be reflected in a borrower's credit report, such as commitment to repaying the mortgage as reflected in regular attendance at homebuyer education classes in the community.[32] There is some evidence suggesting that this type of "relationship lending" may reduce the probability of borrower default.[33]

Even if information is available, obtaining information can be costly, and thus market participants must have incentives to collect and use information in mortgage decisionmaking. HFAs face financial and reputational risk if loans within their portfolio default at rates higher than projected, including eventual downgrading of their bond issues (critical to their financial viability). Many HFAs monitor the performance of loans by participating lenders, with sanctions on or removal of lenders originating loans with high rates of default. On the servicing side, state HFAs often service the loans that they fund in house or contract with a master servicer or a limited set of servicers. Incentives to prevent default often lead to preventative servicing strategies, such as early interventions at the first sign of delinquency or immediate referral to a housing counselor. Research suggests that such preventative strategies may be associated with reduced default for otherwise similar borrowers.[34]

Current HFA Strategies

The following section describes the current scope and strategies of state HFAs, with information collected through two primary sources. First, we extracted data from the National Council of State Housing Agencies' (NCSHA) annual *Factbook*. NCSHA is a nonprofit membership organization representing the interests of state HFAs. Each year NCSHA conducts a survey to document the scope of HFA activities, with a 95–100 percent response rate. We primarily drew from data collected for the 2006 and 2010 *Factbooks* (2010 is the most recent available

31. Bucks and Pence (2008).
32. Ergungor (2010).
33. Ergungor and Moulton (2011); Moulton (2010).
34. Cutts and Green (2005); Stegman and others (2007).

Figure 8-1. *Number of MRB-Subsidized Home Purchases, 1993–2011*

Number of loans

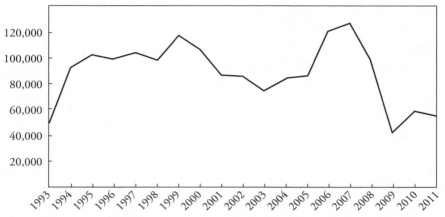

Source: Author's compilation of data provided by the National Council of State Housing Agencies.

at the time of this writing). Second, we administered our own web-based survey to state HFAs between December 2012 and January 2013, with a response rate of 71 percent, or thirty-seven out of fifty-two states and territories with active homebuyer programs. We supplemented these two surveys with data recently collected through a study on HFA homebuyer education and counseling programs, as well as statistics on loan performance from the National Delinquency Survey reported by the Mortgage Bankers Association.[35]

Size and Scope of Homebuyer Programs

From program inception through 2010, HFAs have funded nearly 3 million loans, 2.91 million through the sale of MRBs and 165,600 through MCCs.[36] The volume of loans closed by state HFAs (financed through MRBs) averaged about 100,000 a year from 1994 to 2008, with a peak of 126,611 loans in 2007. Loan volume dropped significantly two years later to a low of 41,857 loans in 2009, with a slight rebound to 59,127 loans funded in 2010 (figure 8-1). The decline in 2009 mirrors the overall decline in mortgage originations in the market. Despite fluctuations in loan volume, HFAs continue to extend credit to underserved

35. See, respectively, Dylla and Caldwell-Tautges (2012) and Mortgage Bankers Association (2012).
36. NCSHA (2012).

populations. In fact, in 2010 more than one-fourth of all loans originated were to minority households, one-third to female-headed households, and more than half to households with low incomes (less than 80 percent of area median).[37]

Loan Products, Securitization, and Financing

Most HFAs offset risk to investors by ensuring that loans are guaranteed in the case of default, either through conventional financing (for example, sold to Fannie Mae and Freddie Mac) or insured-guaranteed through the Federal Housing Administration, Veterans Administration, or the U.S. Department of Agriculture Rural Housing Service. The proportion of loans distributed by these three guarantors fluctuates over time, following general market trends. For example, FHA-insured mortgages as a share of total HFA portfolio increased from 38 percent in 2006 to 68 percent in 2012, due in part to the tightening of underwriting guidelines for conventional mortgages during the economic recession. Some states have offered other, uninsured loan products, although the proportion was higher during 2006 (16.4 percent of state HFAs) than in the more conservative lending environment of 2012 (only 5 percent of state HFAs offered these products) due to the need to offset investor risk and strengthen HFA credit ratings.

Indeed, many state HFAs have added their own underwriting criteria (credit enhancements, or overlays) on top of the secondary market criteria to preserve the quality of loans in their portfolios and to ensure standards in line with participating lender and servicer demands. Following general industry trends, this has increased substantially since 2006. For example, a recent survey of HFAs reveals that 75 percent of HFAs report having a minimum credit score requirement for at least some of their loan products in 2012, an increase from only 22 percent in 2006.[38] The credit score threshold fluctuates among agencies and over time; the majority (63 percent) of those with a requirement in 2012 set the minimum at 620, with 30 percent setting the floor at 640. In addition more than half (56 percent) report having a maximum debt service ratio in 2012, compared with only 36 percent in 2006. Some HFAs place additional requirements on all loan products; others only require additional underwriting criteria for particular loans (for example, those with HFA-funded down payment assistance).

Perhaps the most significant change is the gradual diversification of the financing mechanisms for HFA single-family mortgage assets. A significant number of HFAs have transformed their MRB financing structures from in-house ("whole loan") status to financing through mortgage-backed securities (MBS), potentially reducing credit risk (table 8-1). Under the whole loan structure, MRBs issued by state HFAs are backed by the full faith and credit of the state HFA,

37. NCSHA (2007, 2012).
38. 2012 authors' survey of state HFAs; $N = 37$.

Table 8-1. *Funding for Single-Family Mortgage Assets*[a]
Percent

	HFAs holding these assets		
	2006	*2012*	*Change*
MRB MBS	33.3	43.0	9.7
MRB whole loan	63.9	43.0	−20.9
Non-MRB MBS	0	37.0	37.0
Non-MRB whole loan	11.4	11.0	-0.4

Source: 2012 authors' survey of state HFAs.
a. $N = 37$.

collateralized by mortgage loans to borrowers. HFAs thus assume the risk for borrower repayment. When HFAs securitize mortgages financed by MRBs, the risk is passed on to the secondary market purchaser, guaranteeing that the MRB investors are repaid, regardless of borrower repayment (that is, the secondary market purchaser assumes the risk of borrower repayment). While MRBs are still the dominant source of financing, in light of forty-year record low interest rates and increasing regulations that limit the profitability of MRBs, HFAs are beginning to employ other mechanisms. For example, 37 percent of HFAs report selling non-MRB mortgage-backed securities to finance at least a portion of their single-family mortgage assets in 2012, compared with none in 2006. This strategy allows HFAs to bundle and sell a pool of loans directly into the MBS market—including the "to be announced" or TBA market—for an upfront financial return, rather than earning revenue over time from the mortgages backed by MRBs (which is less profitable when the spread between the MRB interest rate and conventional rates is very low to nonexistent). It is unclear the extent to which this shift will be temporary, reverting to MRB financing when interest rates rebound, or if this shift may bring with it a new era in single-family financing products and structures for state HFAs.[39]

Subsidies: Interest Rates and Down Payment Assistance

Historically, the benefit-added of state HFA mortgages has been defined as the interest rate subsidy provided to homebuyers. To the extent that interest rate subsidies reduced the monthly payment burden, which may have been a barrier for mortgage financing, HFAs were increasing access to credit for otherwise underserved populations. While the spread between conventional and MRB-subsidized interest rates has fluctuated over time, the recent economic

39. Moody's (2012).

downturn—with interest rates reaching forty-year lows—has resulted in the loss of the "interest rate advantage" for state HFA mortgage products. For example, the proportion of HFAs providing below-market interest rates decreased from 77 percent in 2006 to 19 percent in 2012. In fact 24 percent of HFAs reported financing mortgages with interest rates slightly above market rates in 2012. In the words of one state HFA executive, "The interest rate is no longer the driver of our perceived value." For better or worse, this shift has led HFAs to redefine their benefit-added to the market.

One advantage frequently cited by HFA executives is their provision of down payment assistance (DPA) subsidies. While some HFAs have historically offered DPA in conjunction with their affordable loan products, the recent tightening of underwriting standards, including lower loan-to-value thresholds, has increased demand for HFA-provided down payment assistance. For example, in 2011, 88 percent of HFAs offered some form of DPA.[40] Furthermore, HFA executives report that about 50 percent of HFA-financed loans included DPA in 2006, compared with about 70 percent of loans in 2012. This DPA is structured in a variety of ways, including grants, loans, and deferred or forgivable loans, or both.

Pre- and Postpurchase Support

Another benefit-added of HFA-funded mortgages is additional support provided to homebuyers before and after purchase. Prior to purchase many HFAs require or recommend that assisted borrowers participate in homebuyer education and counseling (HEC). According to a recent study, one-third of HFAs require HEC for all of their loan products, while an additional 49 percent require HEC for some of their loan products and 12 percent provide incentives to buyers to use HEC services.[41] In addition 59 percent of HFAs provide financial or technical support to other providers of HEC, while 14 percent provide HEC services directly. Aside from the instrumental benefits of HEC for borrowers, HFAs' involvement with HEC providers increases the capacity and diffusion of best practices statewide.

Almost all HFAs facilitating HEC services report that HEC "prepares borrowers for the complexities of the home-buying process" (97.5 percent) and "reduces loan delinquencies and foreclosures" (92.5 percent). The content of HEC may vary, covering topics such as assessing readiness for homeownership, general budgeting and credit, mortgage financing, and home maintenance. More than half of HFAs (55 percent) have adopted the guidelines from the National Industry Standards for Homebuyer Education and Counseling, which stipulate content and delivery standards for quality HEC programs, and 29 percent of HFAs have

40. Dylla and Caldwell-Tautges (2012).
41. Dylla and Caldwell-Tautges (2012).

established their own standards for HEC providers.[42] Simply by establishing a relationship between borrowers and HEC counselors prior to purchase (in house or within community organizations), HFAs help build bridges for vulnerable homeowners to seek help if they experience difficulties after purchase.

In addition to preparing borrowers prior to purchase, many state HFAs employ preventative servicing strategies to reduce mortgage defaults. These strategies can be structural, based on the servicing structure for HFA-funded mortgages and how servicers are held accountable, or programmatic, with specific interventions identified to respond to early delinquency. Structurally, many HFAs have reorganized servicing to allow for more direct agency oversight. This may be accomplished either by locating servicing in house rather than contracting out to single or multiple providers, or by contracting with one master servicer rather than several independent lenders, each with its own servicing procedures. In 2012, 67 percent of HFA executives reported using centralized servicing (in house or with a single master servicer), up from 62 percent in 2006. Shared servicing models are also developing, where one HFA will provide servicing for multiple HFA portfolios.

Forty-nine percent of HFA executives report programmatic strategies to help HFA-assisted homebuyers prevent default, above and beyond what the servicer would ordinarily provide for non-HFA mortgages. Of those with programmatic strategies, 82 percent intervene within thirty days of a missed payment, and 18 percent do so between thirty and sixty days of a missed payment. Some HFA executives report requiring borrowers to sign authorization for early default counseling at the time of closing, thereby giving permission for a housing counselor to make contact with delinquent borrowers as soon as they miss a payment.

Once a borrower enters default, HFAs employ a variety of different strategies to assist their borrowers. Figure 8-2 provides a breakdown of the strategies used by HFAs for loans funded in their single-family portfolios. For example, 71 percent report frequently offering counseling, and 63 percent report frequently offering temporary forbearance. Other strategies, such as permanent principal reduction and refinancing, are less common.

HFA Loan Performance

HFA single-family mortgages tend to be less likely to become delinquent or to default than non-HFA mortgages to otherwise similar borrowers. HFAs have not been immune to the effects of the housing market crash and related economic

---

42. See National Industry Standards for Homeownership Education and Counseling, "Guidelines and Code of Ethics Reference Guide" (www.homeownershipstandards.com/Uploads/National%20Industry%20Standards%20Code%20of%20Ethics%20Guidelines.pdf). Regarding HFA standards for HEC, see Dylla and Caldwell-Tautges (2012).

Figure 8-2. *Preventative Servicing Strategies for HFA Single-Family Mortgages*[a]

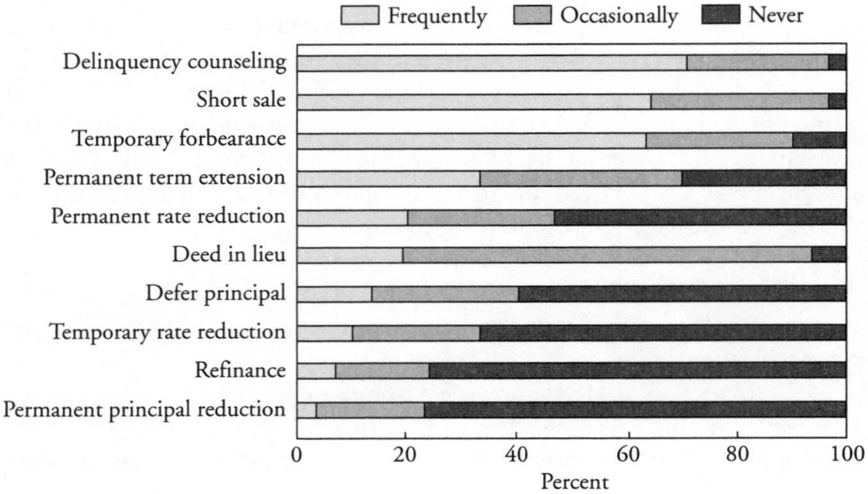

Source: 2012 authors' survey of state HFAs.
a. $N = 31$ (of those reporting any strategies).

shocks; the proportion of mortgages in HFA portfolios that are in distress has increased substantially since the economic crisis. Data on twenty HFAs with debt rated by Standard and Poor's indicate that delinquency rates for HFA-funded mortgages increased from 3.14 percent in 2006 to 7.1 percent during the third quarter of 2011.[43]

Despite increases in delinquencies due to the Great Recession, on average, HFA-funded mortgages perform relatively better than non-HFA mortgages, likely due to the proper underwriting of affordable loan terms, diligent screening and servicing, and the borrower support discussed above. Of the thirty HFAs reporting data on loan performance for our survey, the average proportion of loans ninety or more days delinquent as of June 30, 2012, was 3.10 percent, and the average proportion of loans in foreclosure was 1.89 percent. Comparatively, delinquency data from the Mortgage Bankers Association for the same period demonstrates that HFA mortgages outperform FHA delinquency rates (4.77 percent) and subprime mortgage delinquencies (9.16 percent) during the same period (see figure 8-3). While HFA delinquency rates are slightly higher than those for prime conventional mortgages, the risk characteristics of HFA first-time homebuyers are more similar to FHA and subprime borrowers, with higher loan-to-value ratios and lower incomes.

43. Standard and Poor's (2012).

Figure 8-3. *Loans 90+ Days Delinquent as of June 30, 2012*[a]

Percent delinquent

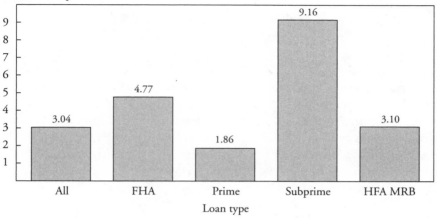

Source: Mortgage Bankers Association (2012); HFA self-reported loan performance data per 2012 authors' survey of state HFAs.

a. *N* = 30 HFAs with loan performance data.

Future Opportunities and Challenges for State HFAs

Several factors stemming from the Great Recession have challenged the traditional business models of HFAs: lower market interest rates that reduce the potential spread on MRB loans, fewer options for mortgage insurance or guarantees to reduce investor risk, and tightened regulations and underwriting standards for mortgages, specifically those with lower down payments and higher-risk borrowers. While interest rates will eventually rebound, changing market conditions and new legislation will likely continue to be part of the HFA reality.

On the survey we asked HFA respondents a series of questions about future opportunities and challenges. These responses sorted into four broad areas of action:

—increase flexibility and funding diversification,

—enhance agency capacity to implement change,

—maintain strong agency standards, and

—provide innovative products that meet local needs.

Each is described in more detail below.

Increase Flexibility and Funding Diversification

More than 70 percent of the HFA respondents mentioned "flexibility" or "funding diversification" as part of their response to the "single most important lesson their agency learned from the economic recession." The relatively nimble structure of HFAs as quasi-governmental entities allows them to adapt to changing economic circumstances. Several economic changes have led to new strategies, each with its own set of challenges.

Record low private market interest rates have reduced the potential spread between MRB-funded mortgages and conventional mortgages. This not only reduces the competitiveness of HFA mortgages for homebuyers, but it also reduces the revenue available to fund agency operations and additional services. HFAs generate revenue, in part, on the difference (spread) between the interest rate charged to the homebuyer and the interest rate on the MRB held by investors. Over time this spread has allowed HFAs not only to finance operations but also to develop substantial capital reserves (also important to preserving bond ratings). To the extent that the spread is no longer generating revenue, HFAs look to other strategies, such as short-term sale of bundled mortgages on the mortgage-backed securities market, with or without financing through mortgage revenue bonds.

This strategy can provide HFAs with immediate, short-term returns for their funded mortgages, rather than the longer-term revenues associated with traditional thirty-year MRB pools of mortgages. Furthermore, this strategy reduces the potential exposure (risk) of HFA-funded mortgages, particularly when compared with agencies that traditionally held all of their HFA mortgages in house (sometimes referred to as "whole loan states"). However, the challenge for HFAs will be balancing the potential short-term payoff with longer-term financial security. Balancing the risk and return associated with these different strategies requires a level of financial sophistication that many HFAs may not currently have. While new strategies are important for weathering economic cycles, MRBs have provided a historic benefit to HFAs that should remain part of their financing structures over the long term. In the words of one HFA executive, HFAs need to "adapt to the ever-changing market but be ready when the municipal bond market does return to be able to issue tax-exempt mortgage revenue bonds."

Enhance Agency Capacity to Implement Change

Many of the changes noted in the survey, including diversified funding for single-family assets, more complex loan products, increased servicing of HFA-funded "loans in house," and preventative servicing strategies, require concomitant adjustments in agency capacity. Indeed, many HFAs reported challenges related to developing a "new way to do business." These include investments in infrastructure and staff, designing new processes and procedures, and learning new technology and software. For many HFAs leveraging sufficient financial (and human) resources to make these sorts of capacity investments poses a significant challenge. According to our 2012 HFA survey, state HFAs employ on average 145 full-time staff persons, with 12 (8 percent) dedicated to single-family homeownership programs.

Figure 8-4. *HFA Self-Reported Capacity*[a]

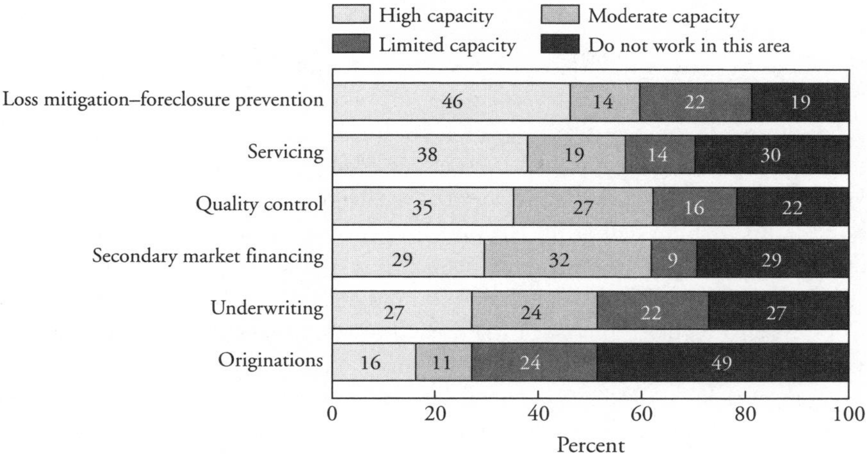

Source: 2012 authors' survey of state HFAs.
a. $N = 37$.

On the survey we asked HFA respondents to rate their capacity in a variety of areas related to single-family loan programs, if they engaged in that area at all (figure 8-4). Most HFAs expressed the strongest perceived capacity in areas such as foreclosure prevention and servicing, and less capacity in areas such as secondary market financing, underwriting, and quality control. For example, 40 percent of respondents reported moderate or limited capacity in secondary market financing, and more than 45 percent of respondents reported moderate or limited capacity in underwriting—both areas of significant (recent) change for HFAs that are critical to their long-term viability.

Maintain Strong Agency Standards

A key component of the relative success of HFA homeownership programs despite the economic downturn has been commitment to strong lending and financing standards. More than one-third of HFA respondents mentioned "financial strength," "moderation," or "strong lending standards" as being critical to their success through the Great Recession. Indeed, even the rating agencies that evaluate HFA bonds have indicated that HFAs have maintained a strong position and note that any downgrades in ratings to date have largely been due to downgrades in the federal government as a whole, which guarantees or insures many of the HFA-funded mortgages.[44]

44. Standard and Poor's (2012); Moody's (2012).

Maintaining strong financial performance is critical to HFAs. On the survey 92 percent of respondents identified bond ratings as being "very critical" to their agency, with the remaining 8 percent selecting "somewhat critical." A variety of factors affect the bond ratings of HFAs, including the proportion of delinquent HFA-funded loans, adequate mortgage insurance or credit enhancements for HFA-funded loans, securitization of HFA-funded loans, and agency financial position, including level of capital reserves relative to equity.[45] On the survey HFA respondents were asked to identify strategies they have used to preserve bond ratings. About half of the respondents noted decreased use of conventional mortgages with private mortgage insurance in favor of government-insured (FHA) loans, as well as the switch to MBS rather than whole loan assets.

HFAs also reported increased use of credit overlays, such as minimum credit score requirements or maximum debt-to-income ratios, in order to preserve the strength of their portfolios. Not unlike the rationales for the tightening of FHA underwriting criteria, the primary rationale for this change is to prevent HFA-funded mortgages from being adversely selected by higher-risk borrowers, concentrating those who would not otherwise qualify for mortgages in government-funded programs.[46] This presents a risk not only to the state HFAs but also to the market participants such as originators, lender servicers, and investors who are directly and indirectly invested in the performance of the program.

Future federal regulatory changes in the market that broadly limit the eligibility of certain types of loans or borrowers, such as those under the Dodd-Frank Act's qualified mortgage (QM) and qualified residential mortgage (QRM), will likely create opportunities and challenges for HFA-funded mortgages.[47] Because of the strong performance of HFA-funded mortgages, it is likely that they may be granted exemptions from some of the QM-QRM standards and requirements, similar to certain exemptions for GSE- and FHA-insured mortgages. This is important, as HFA-funded borrowers tend to have lower incomes with higher debt-to-income ratios and relatively high loan-to-value ratios (low down payments) that may be the target of regulatory changes. However, to the extent that a dual market develops, where HFAs only serve borrowers with higher risk profiles who would otherwise not qualify under new QM-QRM guidelines, the financial strength of HFA portfolios that has been critical to their viability may be threatened.

45. Standard and Poor's (2012); Moody's (2012).
46. Spader (2010).
47. For example, proposed QM rules require lenders to demonstrate a borrower's ability to repay the mortgage via set standards at the time of closing (including debt-to-income thresholds), or the originating lender could be held responsible for the loan if the borrower defaults. QRM rules require lenders to retain a set percentage (for example, 5 percent) of the loans that they originate and sell to the secondary market unless the loans meet certain eligibility criteria (for example, loans that fall under maximum loan-to-value thresholds).

Table 8-2. *Perceived Market Advantage of HFA Loans*[a]

Percent

Features	Top benefit	Top three benefits
Interest rate	14	81
Down payment assistance	72	94
Customer service	0	22
Flexible guidelines	6	17
Lender relationships	6	53
Other	3	19

Source: 2012 authors' survey of state HFAs.
a. $N = 37$.

Provide Innovative Products and Services That Meet Local Needs

The ultimate opportunity—and challenge—for state HFAs is to continue to provide homeownership products and services that fulfill their public purpose to meet housing needs not otherwise met by the private market, while at the same time balancing a successful business model. The supply- and demand-side factors that affect this delicate balance are dynamic. On the supply side, the types of products and services offered depend on financing structures available to HFAs, investor expectations, and financial return. On the demand side, the types of borrowers who are considered "underserved" also vary based on market dynamics, including interest rate structures, underwriting requirements, and mortgage availability. The key to HFA success is to provide access to *affordable mortgage financing* for *underserved but creditworthy LMI borrowers that will be sustainable over time.*

On the survey HFA respondents were asked to identify the top three advantages of HFA-funded mortgages in today's market environment (table 8-2). More than 70 percent of respondents listed down payment assistance as the number one benefit of HFA mortgages today. Affordable interest rates remain among the top three benefits for more than 80 percent of respondents, emphasizing the importance of affordability, despite the inability to offer below-market rates. Of note, lender relationships also were listed as an important benefit for more than half of HFA respondents. Lender relationships were identified as critical to reaching the first-time homebuyer market with affordable loan products. As noted previously, such relationships may also allow HFAs to overcome informational barriers in mortgage markets.

It is important to highlight that flexible underwriting guidelines are not mentioned frequently, as most HFA loans are securitized or government insured or both and currently abide by these preestablished underwriting standards. HFAs have historically stressed their role as increasing access to homeownership by providing affordable mortgages, not by lowering underwriting standards. In the future housing finance system, HFAs may have an opportunity to target borrowers who are cut off from private market financing because of new regulatory requirements (for example, QM-QRM) but are still considered to be creditworthy. For example, HFAs may allow relatively higher loan-to-value ratios or debt-to-income ratios than would be available through traditional channels, combining these relaxed standards with other tightened screening or servicing mechanisms. However, the discretion of HFAs to set their own underwriting standards for their loan programs may be constrained by the private market participants on whom they rely for origination, servicing, and investments. These entities may lack the capacity or willingness to adopt separate criteria for HFA-funded mortgages.

Conclusions

In this chapter we described the different financing instruments, single-family purchase products, and activities that characterize HFAs today. Since their creation HFAs have supported the extension of mortgage credit to more than 2.9 million low- and moderate-income households. HFAs have evolved into highly sophisticated financial entities that help creditworthy homebuyers access mortgage credit and promote postpurchase sustainability by addressing informational barriers. The added benefit of HFA participation in mortgage markets is not limited to below-market interest rates. While HFAs continue to offer this benefit, record low mortgage interest rates combined with tightening of underwriting standards has increased the salience of HFA-provided down payment assistance. In addition, many HFAs require homeownership education and counseling for borrowers, and some provide preventative servicing strategies to reduce mortgage default. Our analysis suggests that these various strategies seem to be working. From our survey data, we find that the ninety-day loan delinquency rate for HFA loans compares favorably with the performance of similar non-HFA loans.

The brave new world of housing finance, shaped by the Great Recession, creates both opportunities and challenges for state HFAs. While MRBs still remain a critical component of HFA financing strategies, many are diversifying funding for single-family mortgage assets, including through increased participation in the mortgage-backed securities market. Not surprisingly, we find that the capacity to undertake new, flexible, and diversified activities varies by HFA. For example, about four in ten HFAs report having limited capacity in areas such as secondary market financing, underwriting, and quality control. Ensuring HFAs' financial capacity and sophistication is critical to their future success.

It is likely that regulatory reforms, such as the Dodd-Frank Act's QM and QRM standards, will constrain the types of products and eligible borrowers receiving mortgages through private market channels. Otherwise creditworthy low- and moderate-income households may have difficulty obtaining mortgage credit through the mainstream private market, increasing the role for government involvement, such as through FHA-insured mortgages at the federal level and HFA-funded mortgages at the state level. As detailed in this chapter, HFAs offer strategic advantages for low- and moderate-income homebuyers, which include providing additional subsidies and addressing informational barriers that are likely to become increasingly more complex in a post–financial reform world.

However, originating mortgages that fall outside of conventional standards poses challenges for HFAs. Structurally, the discretion of HFAs to set their own underwriting standards may be constrained by the private market participants on whom they rely for origination, servicing, and investments. These entities may lack the capacity or willingness to adopt separate criteria for HFA-funded mortgages; thus product offerings by HFAs may become less flexible and more standardized. Changes to servicing strategies and the secondary market environment, in addition to innovative product development, may be necessary. Furthermore, to the extent that HFAs serve borrowers with higher risk, the strong financial performance of the HFAs could be put at risk. Thus new product development must be combined with an emphasis on creative strategies to mitigate risk, including education, counseling, and preventative servicing. Given their expertise and record, HFAs have the potential to become key lenders for low-income, minority, and other underserved borrowers.

References

Agarwal, Sumit, Yan Chang, and Abdullah Yavas. 2012. "Adverse Selection in Mortgage Securitization." *Journal of Financial Economics* 105, no. 3: 640–60.

Belsky, Eric, and Susan Wachter. 2010. "The Public Interest in Consumer and Mortgage Credit Markets." Research Paper 10-05. University of Pennsylvania Law School, Institute for Law and Economics (http://ssrn.com/abstract=1582947).

Bucks, Brian, and Karen Pence. 2008. "Do Borrowers Know Their Mortgage Terms?" *Journal of Urban Economics* 64, no.2: 218–33.

Calkins, Susannah E., and Leanne R. Aronson. 1980. "The Home Mortgage Revenue Bonds Controversy." *Publius* 10, no. 1: 111–18.

Carr, James H., and Jenny Schuetz. 2001. "Financial Services in Distressed Communities: Framing the Issue, Finding Solutions." Fannie Mae Foundation (August).

Chomsisengphet, Souphala, and Anthony Pennington-Cross. 2006. "The Evolution of the Subprime Mortgage Market." *Federal Reserve Bank of St. Louis Review* 88, no. 1: 31–56.

Cooperstein, R. L. 1992. "Economic Policy Analysis of Mortgage Revenue Bonds." In *Mortgage Revenue Bonds: Housing Markets, Home Buyers and Public Policy,* edited by Danny W. Durning, pp. 75–87. Boston: Kluwer Academic.

Cutts, Amy C., and Richard K. Green. 2005. "Innovative Servicing Technology: Smart Enough to Keep People in Their Houses?" In *Building Assets, Building Credit: Creating Wealth in Low-Income Communities,* edited by Nicolas P. Retsinas and Eric S. Belsky, pp. 348–77. Brookings.

———. 1992. "Policy Instruments and Policy Outcomes: Comparing the Arguments for Mortgage Revenue Bonds with Their Policy Results." In *Mortgage Revenue Bonds: Housing Markets, Home Buyers and Public Policy,* edited by Danny W. Durning, pp. 89–111. Boston: Kluwer Academic.

Durning, Danny W., and John M. Quiqley. 1985. "On the Distributional Implications of Mortgage Revenue Bonds and Creative Finance." *National Tax Journal* 38, no.4: 513–23.

Dylla, Doug, and Dean Caldwell-Tautges. 2012. *Winning Strategies: An Analysis of State Housing Finance Agency Support for Homeownership Education and Counseling Services.* Ithaca, N.Y.: Doug Dylla Consulting Services (February).

Ergungor, Ozgur Emre. 2010. "Bank Branch Presence and Access to Credit in Low- to Moderate-Income Neighborhoods." *Journal of Money, Credit and Banking* 42, no. 7: 1321–49.

Ergungor, Ozgur Emre, and Stephanie Moulton. 2011. "Beyond the Transaction: Depository Institutions and Reduced Mortgage Default for Low-Income Homebuyers." Working Paper 11-15. Federal Reserve Bank of Cleveland (http://ssrn.com/abstract=1903868).

Glaeser, Edward L., and Hedi D. Kallal. 1997. "Thin Markets, Asymmetric Information, and Mortgage-Backed Securities." *Journal of Financial Intermediation* 6, no. 1: 64–86.

Goetz, E. G. 1993. *Shelter Burden: Local Politics and Progressive Housing Policy.* Temple University Press.

Greulich, Erica, and John M. Quigley. 2009. "Housing Subsidies and Tax Expenditures: The Case of Mortgage Credit Certificates." *Regional Science and Urban Economics* 39, no. 6: 647–57.

Gross, David. 1992. "Program Effectiveness of Mortgage Revenue Bonds in a Changing Economic Environment." In *Mortgage Revenue Bonds: Housing Markets, Home Buyers and Public Policy,* edited by Danny W. Durning, pp. 125–33. Boston: Kluwer Academic.

Jiang, Wei, Ashlyn Aiko Nelson, and Edward J. Vytlacil. 2009. "Liar's Loan? Effects of Origination Channel and Information Falsification on Mortgage Delinquency." Research Paper 2009-06-02. Indiana University–Bloomington, School of Public & Environmental Affairs (http://ssrn.com/abstract=1421462).

Keys, Benjamin J., Amit Seru, and Vikrant Vig. 2012. "Lender Screening and the Role of Securitization: Evidence from Prime and Subprime Mortgage Markets." *Review of Financial Studies* 25, no. 7: 2071–108.

Lax, Howard, and others. 2004. "Subprime Lending: An Investigation of Economic Efficiency." *Housing Policy Debate* 15, no. 3: 533–71.

Moody's Investors Service. 2012. "Semiannual State HFA Delinquency Report: Seriously Delinquent Single Family Loans Continue to Rise." Special Comment, May 30.

Mortgage Bankers Association. 2012. "National Delinquency Survey Q3 2012." Washington.

Moulton, Stephanie, and Barry Bozeman. 2011. "The Publicness of Market Environments: An Evaluation of the Subprime Mortgage Lending Strategy." *Journal of Public Administration Research and Theory* 21, no. 1: 87–115.

National Council of State Housing Agencies (NCSHA). 2007. *State HFA Factbook: 2006 NCSHA Annual Survey Results*. Washington.

———. 2010. "State HFAs to Finance More Than 200,000 Affordable Homes under Administration's HFA Initiative." News release (January 13).

———. 2012. *State HFA Factbook: 2010 NCSHA Annual Survey Results*. Washington.

Purnanandam, Amiyatosh. 2011. "Originate-to-Distribute Model and the Subprime Mortgage Crisis." *Review of Financial Studies* 24, no. 6: 1881–915.

Quercia, Roberto G., Allison Freeman, and Janneke Ratcliffe. 2011. *Regaining the Dream: How to Renew the Promise of Homeownership for America's Working Families*. Brookings.

Quercia, Roberto G., George W. McCarthy, and Susan M. Wachter. 2003. "The Impacts of Affordable Lending on Homeownership Rates." *Journal of Housing Economics* 12, no. 1: 29–59.

Spader, Jonathan S. 2010. "Beyond Disparate Impact: Risk-Based Pricing and Disparity in Consumer Credit History Scores." *Review of Black Political Economy* 37, no. 2: 61–78.

Standard and Poor's Rating Services. 2012. "Housing Conference 2012: The Special eReport." *Credit Matters eReports,* March (www.standardandpoors.com/spf/swf/ereports/housing/Housing_revised/document/AveDoc.pdf.

Stegman, Michael. 1974. "Housing Finance Agencies: Are They Crucial Instruments of State Government?" *Journal of the American Institute of Planners* 40, no. 5: 307–20.

Stegman, Michael A., and others. 2007. "Preventive Servicing Is Good for Business and Affordable Homeownership Policy." *Housing Policy Debate* 18, no. 2: 243–78.

U.S. Department of Treasury. 2009. "Administration Announces Initiative for State and Local Housing Finance Agencies." Press release (October 19).

U.S. Government Accountability Office. 1983. "The Costs and Benefits of Single Family Mortgage Revenue Bonds: Preliminary Report." GAO-RCED-83-145 (April).

———. 1988. "Homeownership: Mortgage Bonds Are Costly and Provide Little Assistance to Those in Need." GAO/RCED-88-111 (March).

9

Mortgage Default Option Mispricing and Borrower Cost Procyclicality

ANDREW DAVIDSON, ALEX LEVIN, AND SUSAN WACHTER

This chapter examines the impact of mortgage supply characteristics on both housing affordability and financial risk outcomes in the wake of the mortgage crisis. A hallmark of the crisis was a shift toward nontraditional mortgage lending products. What impact did this have on consumers, investors, and the financial system? We address the performance of these products and their interaction with the financial sector in the production of systemic risk. While ex post the performance of these mortgages was disastrous and neither expected nor priced, we also show that ex ante the credit risk was also mispriced.

The links among mortgage lending instruments, such as Alt-A (income not documented), negative amortization or subprime mortgages, and underlying house price volatility and associated risks have been explored in recent empirical and theoretical research. While it may seem obvious that such instruments allow more borrowing than otherwise would occur in affordability- and credit score–constrained markets, and house prices rise as a result, the relationship may very well go both ways. That is, it is possible that markets with rising prices invite more supply of nontraditional mortgage products, and under certain conditions this could occur without an increase in credit risk—for example, if there is an innovation in lending technology that better discriminates good from bad risks and expands the credit box.

This paper reviews the literature on this question, summarizing models in which the expansion of nontraditional mortgages (NTMs) is associated with a decrease as well as an increase in overall financial risk. Increased risk may come from several sources. First, it is possible that the expansion of NTMs occurs along with the easing of credit constraints and underwriting standards associated with increased default risk, resulting in increased lending to riskier borrowers. Second, it is possible that the mortgage instruments themselves are riskier. Third, it is possible that the risk due to either of these factors is not priced. But, as noted, it is also possible that an increase in NTMs occurs without an increase in risk but rather with a decrease in risk. That is, NTMs expand when prices expand, and this is rational because prices increase due to a decline in risk, for example, as a result of an innovation in mortgage lending technology, as discussed further below.

The problem with this latter explanation as a model of the recent housing and mortgage market boom and bust is that there is evidence that during the expansion period, a key driver of default risk indisputably increased: the combined loan-to-value (CLTV) ratio. If technology also shifted so that risk could be calibrated or diversified better, then higher CLTVs could be sustainable. It may have been supposed that there was such a technology shift. But, as we discuss, in fact such a technology shift did not occur in the bubble years.

This chapter examines the impact of the provision of NTMs on credit risk, affordability, and systemic risk. The first section describes the expansion and performance of nontraditional mortgages. This is followed by a discussion of the cost of credit when combined loan-to-value ratios are accounted for and an analysis of the ex-ante pricing of risk for NTMs. The third section looks at the implications of the expansion in NTMs for affordability and homeownership. The chapter concludes with an examination of how and why credit risk in mortgage lending is related to systemic risk and procyclicality, particularly as demonstrated in the recent history of the mortgage crisis in the United States, and the consequent implications for policy.

The Expansion of Nontraditional Mortgage Instruments

The availability and use of NTMs expanded rapidly from 2000 through 2005.[1] In the first half of the 2000s, subprime mortgages, interest-only loans, negative amortizing loans, teaser rate ARMs, payment-option ARMs (option ARMs), and Alt-A mortgages as well as second liens dramatically increased their share of the overall mortgage origination market (figures 9-1 and 9-2).[2] As it expanded, the

1. See Levitin and Wachter (2012) for a description of the causes of the rise of NTM lending.

2. Interest-only loans allow borrowers to make no principal payments; negative amortizing loans have monthly payments that are less than the interest owed; payment-option adjustable rate mortgages (option ARMs) allow borrowers to choose the monthly payment level, including making interest only or negatively amortizing payments; and Alt-A loans, also called low-doc or no-doc loans, require little or no down payment, documentation, or proof of income.

Figure 9-1. *Market Share of Nontraditional Mortgage Products and Private-Label Securitization*[a]

Percent

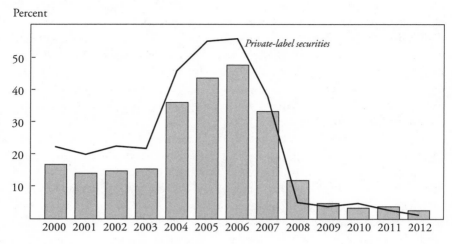

Source: Inside Mortgage Finance (2013).
a. Nontraditional mortgage products are subprime, Alt-A, and home equity loans.

Figure 9-2. *Origination Shares by Mortgage Type, 2000–12*

Percent of originations by dollar amount

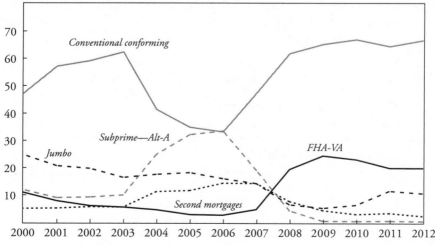

Source: Inside Mortgage Finance (2013).

subprime market developed new products whose features had never faced a market test. This included a particular class of initially discounted "hybrid ARMs" with short initial adjustment periods, also referred to as 2-28 and 3-27 loans (thirty-year loans with a fixed-rate teaser period of two or three years and annually adjusted rates thereafter). Buyers qualified based on the initial low "teaser" rate if they could not refinance to lower interest rate loans, even though they were not able to shoulder the higher payments that were scheduled. Over time, such products were increasingly overlaid with second liens and Alt-A mortgages such as low- and no-doc loans.

Subprime and low-doc loans had long existed as part of mortgage markets, but their share had remained limited from their origin in the 1970s through the early 2000s, with conforming, jumbo, and FHA loans representing a stable share of around 90 percent of all loans originated (as shown in figure 9-2). As of 2003 NTMs such as subprime and Alt-A loans only accounted for about 10 percent of mortgage origination. However, between 2003 and 2007, such NTMs acquired a significantly greater share of the mortgage finance market. A third of mortgages issued in 2006 were subprime or Alt-A mortgages. Including second liens, 47 percent of the market was made of NTMs in 2006 (figure 9-2). The growth in NTMs coincided with the growth in private label securities, which represented more than half of mortgage-backed securities issued in 2006, at their peak, and in which the vast majority of the NTMs were securitized (figure 9-1). After the housing bust, NTM products disappeared along with private-label securities.[3]

The development of NTM instruments after 2003 coincided with a rise in long-term interest rates that ended the market for prime refinancing and required the mortgage industry to develop new products to maintain its origination volumes and earnings level.[4] The growth in subprime and Alt-A mortgages, as well as in second mortgages (home equity loans and lines of credit) was accompanied by a loosening in underwriting standards with increased loan-to-value ratios and limited verification of borrowers' income. The relaxation of underwriting standards over the period was particularly concentrated in NTM products. In 2006 less than 20 percent of Alt-A mortgages had full documentation, and nearly 90 percent were interest only. Investors represented 16.5 percent of the Alt-A borrowers at the peak and were far greater users of both Alt-A and subprime than owner-occupants, adding to the default risk. For both subprime and Alt-A loans, there was a sharp increase in CLTV and in the proportion of borrowers who used a second lien after 2003.[5]

3. See Thomas and Van Order (2010) for a discussion of this relationship.
4. Levitin and Wachter (2012.)
5. See Levitin and Wachter (2012) for further discussion.

The development of NTM products contributed to an increase in the supply of credit. Current empirical evidence points to a relationship in which greater credit supply causes an increase in house prices, and reciprocally, the increase in house prices contributes to the relaxation of constraints and expansion in mortgage supply through new instruments.[6]

Housing prices and mortgage debt increased together from 1992 through 2005 with their ratio unchanged. What caused the expansion in both credit supply and housing prices? If the increased supply of NTMs is due to a risk-reducing innovation that allows the overcoming of former credit constraints, the result will be lower risk, lower required returns, and higher welfare. The argument is that innovations such as risk-based credit pricing and improved risk models could have allowed for the sustainable easing of constraints and an appropriate pricing of the risk associated with NTMs.[7] In a theoretical model, these innovations could lead to a permanent lowering of mortgage interest rate spreads over comparable Treasury rates and enable consumers to better smooth consumption over the life cycle.

In fact, the data show that NTMs had historically high rates of default and a far higher rate of foreclosure than other mortgage products. As shown in figure 9-3, which provides data on the quarterly rate of foreclosure by market segment, subprime ARMs had by far the highest foreclosure rate (almost 30 percent annually at the peak).

Option-pricing theory provides a structural framework for modeling ex-ante risk in mortgage instruments, including credit risk. At each period borrowers may continue to pay the mortgage, but they also have the choice to stop making payments and default, or to pay off the entire mortgage balance (by refinancing the loan or selling the property). These two choices may be considered as two embedded options: the option to "call" the mortgage by prepaying the loan, and the option to "put" the property to the lender in exchange for the loan. With nonrecourse loans, there is no other obligation to repay the loan.[8] The call option

---

6. Recent studies such as Anundsen and Jansen (2013) and Berlinghieri (2010) use structural vector error correction models to identify whether mortgage expansion Granger-causes price rises or whether rising prices Granger-cause an expansion in mortgage credit. Their findings generally support bidirectional causality. See Levitin and Wachter (2013) for a further discussion of the literature. Also see Coleman, LaCour-Little, and Vandell (2008) for a model of prices influencing supply, and see Pavlov and Wachter (2011) for a model of supply influencing prices.

7. See Favilukis, Ludvigson, and Van Nieuwerburgh (2012) for a description of a model in which financial innovations through financial market liberalization and technological gains allow households to smooth their consumption by reducing the risk in the economy and the risk of investments, enabling higher asset prices.

8. In many states mortgages are nonrecourse; in others they are effectively so, given costly and limited recovery.

Figure 9-3. *Foreclosure by Market Segment, 1998–2013*

Percent of loans going into foreclosure per quarter

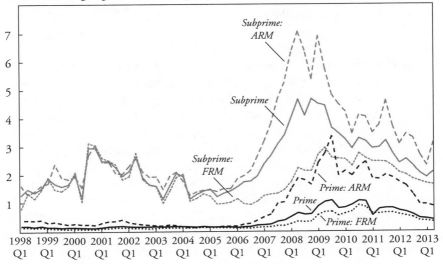

Source: Mortgage Bankers Association, *National Delinquency Survey*, various years.

allows refinancing when interest rates fall. In the subprime market, this option could also be used to refinance into the prime market if the borrower's credit condition improved.[9]

The literature establishes the likelihood of borrower distress and price declines as jointly contributing to default so that temporary price rises could conceal a heightened risk of default due to a shift in the composition of loans toward riskier products that are more likely to be associated with borrower distress. The higher default rates in the subprime segment are generally attributed to subprime borrowers' increased susceptibility to trigger events, a decline in their property's value (for example, due to neighborhood effects), or the risk of the instrument itself. More generally NTMs are likely to have higher credit risk ex ante; in fact, expected returns were somewhat higher. Next we turn to an empirical examination of these higher returns and the question of whether they reflected ex ante credit risk.

9. Cutts and Van Order (2005) posit that the dynamics of these options differ between prime and subprime borrowers. Within the prime market, when interest rates fall, rational borrowers exercise their call option to refinance into lower rates. On the other hand, subprime borrowers find it harder to qualify for a new loan and are therefore unable to optimally exercise their call option when rates decline.

A Hunt for Borrower Cost Reduction:
Evidence of Mispriced Mortgage Risk

This section first discusses the role of the decline in down payments in reducing all-in borrower costs and then quantifies how specific mortgage features contributed to that cost, combining evidence from origination data with models of borrower behavior. To do so for prime and nonprime home purchase loans, we decompose total borrower cost into the two terms: the loan payment rate at origination and the down payment. Then the loss-adjusted lending rate is calculated based on projected credit losses and the origination rate. The results show the ex ante (based on information available at the time) uneconomically low loan origination rates for Alt-A and subprime loans, given the credit risk.

This analysis follows the work of Davidson and Levin, which analyzes the history of the mid-2000s housing bubble and the subsequent decline in home prices to reveal the contribution of each of the constituent components.[10] The conclusions here generally agree with those of other studies that place the root of the crisis in the availability of credit stemming primarily from unregulated nonagency securitization and loans with nonstandard features.[11]

The Role of the Down Payment (Equity)

When entering into a loan, borrowers need to come up with equity or "borrow" a down payment at an equity rate. Blending the loan rate (payable on debt) with equity rates (applied to down payments) may provide a better gauge of what the loan really costs. For example, combining a traditional 20 percent down payment at a 20 percent return-on-equity rate (20.08 percent payment rate assuming a thirty-year amortization) with an 80 percent debt at a 6 percent rate (7.3 percent payment rate) produces a 9.9 percent annual total cost measured off the full price of a home. If the loan rate drops to 4 percent (5.8 percent payment rate), the total cost will go down to 8.7 percent. In this example loan payments fall by 20 percent, but the total cost moved down only 12 percent.

Naturally, a reduced requirement for a down payment will be shown as a lower equity cost on a borrower's balance sheet—even with an unchanged loan rate. If, in the above example, the 20 percent down payment were replaced with a 10 percent down payment, the total cost would drop from 9.9 percent to 8.7 percent, or by 13 percent.

---

10. Davidson and Levin (2012).

11. On unregulated nonagency securitization, see Levitin and Wachter (2009). On loans with nonstandard features, see Berkovec, Chang, and McManus (2012).

Figure 9-4. *Historical CLTV Ratio and Loan Cost at Origination (U.S. Average, Purchase Loans)*[a]

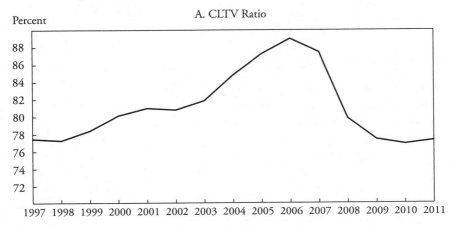

A. CLTV Ratio

Percent

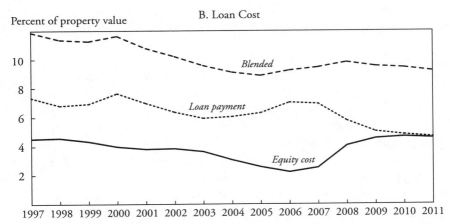

B. Loan Cost

Percent of property value

Source: Authors' calculations based on data from Intex and Freddie Mac.
a. Pre-2008: nonagency loans; 2008–11: agency loans.

These examples give a hint of what happened in the 2000s. Panel A in figure 9-4, shows that during the housing bubble, the CLTV ratio on nonagency *purchase* loans rose significantly. That trend was reversed in 2008–11; for that period the data in panel A reflect agency loans rather than nonagency loans, given the lack of new nonagency origination.

Using the concept of the equity cost, we can state with certainty that the shift in down payment alone moved the combined borrower cost down from 2000 to 2006 and up since 2006. The drop in interest rates in recent years was largely offset by the increase in down payment cost. Therefore, even in a falling interest rate environment, housing could become less affordable. As is shown in panel B of figure 9-4, by the end of 2011, the loan cost constituted only about 50 percent of the blended cost of debt and equity.

Credit Risk Underpricing

A historical chart of blended financing rates would not yield sufficient information without also considering loan quality. A pool of subprime loans that is projected to lose 20 percent of its principal over a five-year average life can be viewed as losing 4 percent a year. If that pool has a 7 percent weighted average coupon, it will effectively be paying only 3 percent—if one attempts to monetize borrowers' economics (regardless of whether the investor is protected by loan insurance or not). Such a loan instinctively catches the attention of borrowers (especially those who are purchasing for investment), even if they cannot assess their own credit risk objectively. This example shows that an undervalued risk may lead to a strong demand to buy homes. It is the loss-adjusted rate that matters for modeling the borrower incentive. Creating financing privileges and loopholes for weak borrowers stimulates them and inflates demand for housing.

How can one determine whether the credit risk was or was not correctly priced in newly originated loans? We conducted the following quantitative study. For each nonagency origination quarterly cohort, starting from 2000, we ran a credit- and option-adjusted spread (credit OAS) model to assess expected loan losses and—after dividing by the projected weighted average life—annualized them.[12] This approach utilized an empirical model of borrower behavior (Andrew Davidson and Company [AD&Co.] LoanDynamics Model) and a risk-adjusted home price index (HPI) stochastic simulation model (see table 9-1). For each of these analyses, we employed economic data (interest rates, home prices) that were available only at the time of analysis (for example, we did not use future actual economic trajectories).

There are four components to this valuation approach. The first component is simulation of interest rates and home prices. The analysis relies on hundreds of random paths that depend on past home prices as well as projected interest rates. Rising home prices in the recent past contribute to rising home prices in the future. Rising interest rates produce falling home prices over the first few years of the forecast and then produce higher home prices over longer time horizons as home prices adjust to inflation imbedded in higher interest rates.

The second component is a forecast of month-by-month prepayments, defaults, and loss severity for the mortgages. The forecast takes into account the economic

---

12. For the credit OAS model, see Levin and Davidson (2008).

Table 9-1. *Forward, Risk-Adjusted HPA*[a]

Percent

	2000	2001	2002	2003	2004	2005	2006	2007
HPA outlook								
2-year cumulative	11.5	12.8	12.8	8.0	9.3	4.1	−11.8	−10.7
5-year cumulative	28.4	26.0	22.0	11.5	14.3	9.3	−11.8	−10.5
Prior-year HPA								
1-year cumulative	10.4	10.7	10.5	11.0	14.0	14.0	7.0	−0.3

a. Produced by the AD&Co. HPI2 model for the 25-MSA Composite index using forward interest rates at each analysis date and a constant risk adjustment for HPA. These are median scenarios shown for illustration purposes; the actual credit OAS model works with random interest rates and HPA paths.

variables (interest rates and home prices) from the simulation. The forecast also considers the nature of the collateral, the terms of the mortgage, the creditworthiness of the borrower, and the delinquency status of the loans at the start of the analysis. For this analysis we used the AD&Co. LoanDynamics Model.

The form of the modeling is a dynamic transition matrix or Markov model. The model assumes that the state of the loan is determined by its delinquency status. A loan can be current, delinquent (two to five months), seriously delinquent (more than six months), or terminated. The transitions between these states are dynamic models based on borrower, collateral, loan, and economic variables.

The third component is the cash flow generator. For loans this is a relatively simple process of transforming the prepayment, default, and severity forecasts into monthly forecasts of principal and interest payments, based upon the characteristics of the loans.

The final component is the computation of the credit OAS, which represents the spread that when added to the discount rates for each path results in an average price across all paths that equals the market price, or in this case, the proceeds from the borrower (par less points). In this phase of the analysis, other analytical metrics such as the average lifetime loss can also be computed. The average loss we use in the analysis is not the loss from a single path but reflects the average of paths—some with greater losses, some with little or no loss—reflecting the option-like feature of mortgage default. This approach differs from standard rating agency models in that it dynamically assesses the value of the embedded options, whereas rating agency methods generally are not designed to vary as market conditions change. Results for U.S. averages are shown in figure 9-5.

Panel B of figure 9-5 shows that before 2004 loss-adjusted rates had been strikingly similar among prime, Alt-A, and subprime loans, suggesting that the

Figure 9-5. *Projected Credit Losses and Rates*

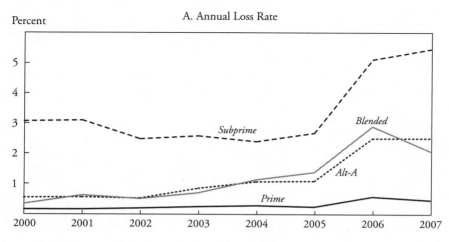

A. Annual Loss Rate

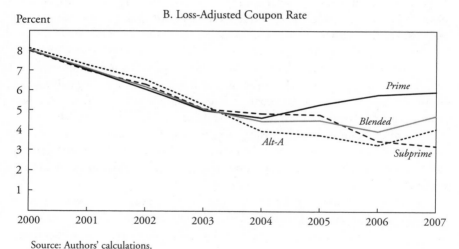

B. Loss-Adjusted Coupon Rate

Source: Authors' calculations.

risk had been priced fairly. Since 2004 the low-quality loans were underpriced, with the loss-adjusted rate falling below that of top-quality loans.[13]

We have further analyzed the cause of this phenomenon in detail and found that the credit risk mispricing could be attributed to

13. This is consistent with findings by Levitin and Wachter (2012) and Courchane and Zorn (2012) showing that after 2004 the spread between prime and subprime mortgages narrowed even as risk mounted.

—uneconomically low loan origination rates for Alt-A and subprime loans,

—the growing percentage of ARMs and option ARMs, and

—the increase of CLTV ratios,

with the worsened ex-ante HPI outlook not appropriately priced into nonconventional products. In particular, the reduced down payment standards affected both the equity cost and the expected credit losses, effectively reducing the borrower cost in each case.

The critical economic driver, the home price appreciation (HPA) outlook, is shown in table 9-1. In forming this assumption, our model reacts to the observed HPA trend and statistically separates systematic (diffusive) term from nonsystematic (jumpy) term. It also gauges the total cost of financing that affects changes in HPI equilibrium. In particular, the worsening in the HPI outlook from 2004 to 2005 and again from 2005 to 2006 was mostly due to the change of trend in HPA. The fact that HPA stopped growing suggests a reversion in the second-order differential equations that describe the HPA diffusion term in the model. In contrast, the persistent pessimism through 2007 was fueled by the quick increase in financing cost that occurred when poorly underwritten loan products ceased to exist and the low down payment regime ended (figure 9-4).

Appendix 9A lists results of the analysis by market segment and loan type. It shows some of the key variables that affect credit cost. In general, there was an increase in the CLTV ratio in many of the segments and a move toward riskier products and lower loss-adjusted rates.

In the beginning of the 2000s, the blended rate's spread of nonprime loans above the prime-borrower rate was in the 50–100 basis point range for Alt-A borrowers and about 300 basis points for subprime borrowers. These spreads did not widen and in some cases tightened by 2006—contrary to the worsening dynamics of the HPA outlook. A rising share of nonprime and option ARMs that offered below-market introductory rates was another problem. Even with comparable FICO and LTV levels, adjustable rate mortgages are proven to be riskier products relative to fixed-rate mortgages due to both the reset-related payment shocks and the way borrowers are self-selected and qualified for the product. In addition, the quality of so-called Alt-A loans deteriorated, as evidenced by the falling percent of fully documented loans. Interestingly, FICO scores did not deteriorate and mostly improved in each loan category, which, rather than being an objective trend, may have been a scoring system's compromise.

All-in Cost

With the loss component detected, we now can compute the all-in cost rate (figure 9-6), combining the loan origination rate with the impact of down payment and mispriced credit risk.

Figure 9-6. *All-In Cost of Borrowing (Nonagency Loans)*[a]

Percent of property value

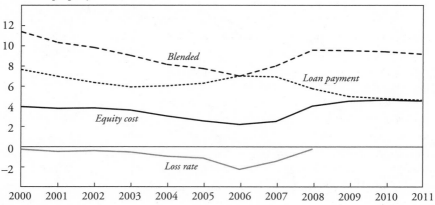

Source: Authors' calculations.
a. All-in borrower cost = loan payment + loss rate (negative) + equity cost.

The blended lines in figure 9-6 clearly depict the mid-2000s "dent" in effective cost despite an increase in loan rates. It was caused by the plummeting equity cost and the increased credit risk underpricing. The existence of the dent in financing cost history matched the actual HPI dynamics fairly well. The effect was even stronger in those regions, such as California, that originated more ARMs, option ARMs, and nonstandard loans in general (see next section).

Geographic Market Composition

Studies by Levin and by Pavlov and Wachter show that the peak-to-first-trough of HPI measured across U.S. states closely followed the proliferation of non-standard loans.[14] Understanding mortgage market composition is critical in explaining the geographic dynamics of housing markets. Compositional factors contributing to the mid-2000s run-up of home price indexes were concentrated geographically in states with large shares of non-conforming loans, nonprime loans, and ARMs in general and option ARMs in particular. Naturally, the difference in the presence of these three could be used to explain the differences in borrower cost across geographic regions. Table 9-2 summarizes the dynamics of mortgage market origination for the United States (bubble), California (stronger bubble), and Texas (no bubble). Due to the lack of GSE and Ginnie Mae (GNMA) data, we do not separate loans by purpose.

14. Levin (2010); Pavlov and Wachter (2011).

Table 9-2. *Comparison of Origination Shares in 2000, 2006, and 2011 (All Loans)*

Percent

Origination	United States			California			Texas		
	2000	2006	2011	2000	2006	2011	2000	2006	2011
GSE	47.2	33.2	66.4	29.9	15.4	70.2	74.5	53.8	59.1
GNMA	11.0	2.7	21.6	2.0	0.1	14.3	4.7	9.2	29.9
Nonagency	41.8	64.1	11.9	68.1	84.5	15.5	20.8	37.0	11.0
Nonprime	21.3	53.1	6.7	26.3	67.3	3.6	11.1	31.9	8.0
Nonagency ARMs[a]	10.1	33.0	1.1	21.6	43.6	0.8	3.7	15.3	0.0
Non-Agency Option ARMs	0.2	9.7	0.1	0.5	20.4	0.0	0.0	0.9	0.0

Source: Inside Mortgage Finance, *Mortgage Market Statistical Annual,* various years.
a. Excluding option ARMs.

Shares of loan types associated with underpriced credit risk rose prominently by 2006 and declined or disappeared as the crisis began. While these loan types dominated the California market in 2006, they were not prominent in Texas, which mostly borrowed conventionally. It is not that subprime loans in Texas were much better than those in California; rather, there were many fewer of them.

In California the history of the negative-amortization poison repeated itself. Origination of cost of funds indexed ARMs (coincidentally, up to 20 percent of market share) in the second half of the 1980s caused some decline in home prices in the upcoming years. Back then, negative amortization was an innocent by-product feature arising from the mismatch between frequent rate resets and less frequent payment resets. In contrast, the second wave of "neg-am" innovation in option ARMs was flawed by design: homeowners-to-be were provided a mechanism to increase their debt in hopes of selling homes later at a higher price and paying off the loan.

In each case the "neg-am" volume had a remarkable coincidence with HPI booms and busts, although it remains a chicken-and-egg dilemma. Option ARMs could only be offered with confidence that home prices would grow. The low-cost financing they offer propels the HPI further. Once it reaches its peak, option ARMs stop being offered. Their death caused the HPI to decline more deeply as new homebuyers could not afford prices paid by previous owners who used option ARMs. Nevertheless it is unlikely that home prices could be sustained without the presence of option ARMs and other low down payment loans.

The share of nonstandard loans fell sharply in recent years, which the increase in the conforming loan limit helped. However, loan origination also notably shifted from GSEs to GNMA, the Federal Housing Administration, in particular.

Figure 9-7. *Total Home Financing Cost as Percent of Property Value*

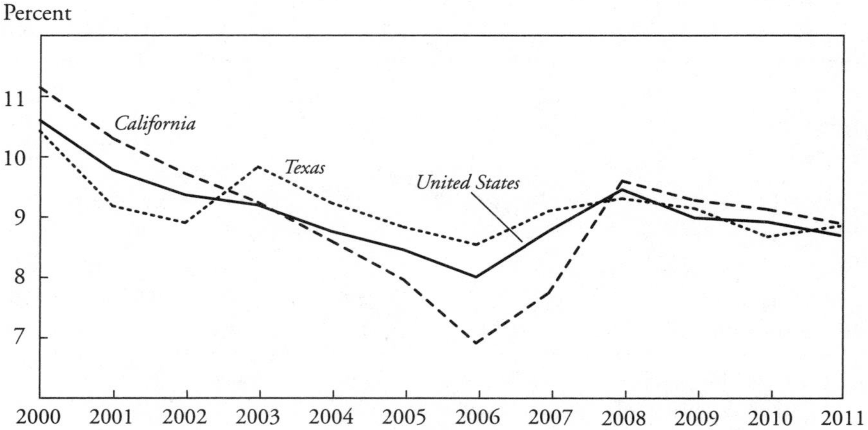

Percent

Source: Authors' calculations.

This GNMA-sponsored, high-LTV origination has grown. It is evident that the low down payment requirement made those loans popular.

Using the origination market's composition, we computed and compared the total cost of borrowing that blends loan rates, the cost of down payment, and credit risk underpricing. Computations are carried first for each loan type and then weighted by market shares. Results are shown in figure 9-7, which demonstrates a remarkable mirror-reflection of the respective home price dynamics. It is worth mentioning that regional elasticity of supply was also a factor in dampening spikes of demand.

Relaxation of Standards in the Bubble Years: Lack of Impact on Access to Homeownership

In this section, we provide evidence of the impact of the expansion of NTMs on the credit constraints to homeownership and consider the potential role of credit risk underpricing on actual homeownership outcomes. The research literature has established that credit standards can result in lower homeownership rates for those who are subject to borrowing constraints, especially among low-income and minority households.[15] Three types of constraints have been identified that affect the probability of homeownership: credit, income, and wealth. Of these,

15. Linneman and Wachter (1989); Haurin, Hendershott, and Wachter (1996, 1997); Rosenthal (2002); Barakova and others (2003).

the wealth constraint is the most likely to prevent a household from obtaining a mortgage to finance a home purchase.

Given the relaxation of credit standards between 2003 and 2007, along with the expansion in mortgage products (subprime, Alt-A, and other nonstandard mortgages), the expectation is that borrowing constraints became less of a barrier to homeownership, increasing the affordability of homeownership for households previously unable to obtain financing. Despite the increase in the supply of mortgage lending and the shift in the supply toward products that were initially more affordable, from 2004 through 2007, the homeownership rate did not increase. In fact, the homeownership rate decreased after 2004.[16]

To address the question of why this was so, Barakova and colleagues measure the impact of constraints on homeownership using data from the National Longitudinal Survey of Youth.[17] The study finds that between 2003 and 2007, income and credit barriers were largely eliminated, which means that through the changes in credit supply, households were not constrained by their income or credit history in the purchase of a target valued home. But one constraint did remain binding: as prices dramatically increased over the period, the wealth constraint continued to affect homeownership.[18] It may have been that the high CLTV lending went to people for whom wealth was not a binding constraint but for whom low down payments enabled a cheaper put option. This is very different from the interpretation that these new borrowers were credit constrained, which is consistent with new borrowers being disproportionately investors.

The easing of mortgage lending underwriting by relying on the collateral's value and its expected appreciation did, however, enable single-family residential real estate investors to take advantage of a less expensive put option to increase leverage. This agrees with findings by Haughwout and his colleagues on the role played by real estate investors in the boom.[19] They show that in states that experienced the largest volatility in house prices over the boom and bust, almost

---

16. The rate of homeownership reached a high of 69 percent in 2004. See U.S. Census Bureau, "Current Population Survey/Housing Vacancy Survey," Series H-111, table 14: "Homeownership Rates for the U.S. and Regions: 1965 to Present" (www.census.gov/housing/hvs/data/histtabs.html).

17. See Barakova and others (2003, 2013).

18. The finding of the persistence of the negative effect of the lack of wealth on homeownership may seem surprising given that during this period 100 percent combined LTV (CLTV) loans were available. Several factors may have contributed to the persistence of the wealth constraint. First, in order to obtain a 100 percent CLTV loan, a borrower needs to combine a first and second lien, generally through an 80-20 piggyback loan, which would come with a relatively high blended rate due to risk-based pricing, acting as a disincentive. Second, borrowers would still need to have disposable savings to cover closing, moving, and fix-up costs, even if they are able to finance 100 percent of the purchase price. Third, wealth might remain binding in situations where the asking price for the home is higher than the appraised value used to underwrite the loan.

19. Haughwout and others (2011).

half of the purchases at the peak of the market were associated with investors. These investors used higher leverage and, in the bust period, exhibited higher delinquency rates, which is consistent with their exercise of the put option. In addition, Chinco and Mayer examine the role played by second homebuyers in particular markets.[20] They hypothesize that these buyers are more likely to rely on capital gains than on returns from rent income and to be less knowledgeable about local market conditions. They find that the share of the purchase made by these "distant speculators" is correlated with higher house price increases and higher implied-to-actual price-to-rent ratios that can be used as a proxy for mispricing. They also find that these distant speculators had a particularly large impact in "sand state" markets like Las Vegas, significantly contributing to the increase in prices in these areas during the boom, concluding that second home-buyers in these markets behaved like overconfident or uninformed speculators. It appears from these findings that if the lending environment allows uncon-strained investors to enter markets and to increase their leverage, thereby lower-ing the cost of the put option, these actors may buy into and support the forma-tion of asset bubbles. But in efficient markets such price rises would ordinarily be countered by short selling to bring prices back in line with fundamentals.

Price Expectations, Nontraditional Mortgage Supply, and Procyclicality

Due to limits to arbitrage in real estate markets, property markets are prone to booms and busts. The creation of cycles in real estate is worsened by the fact that supply is inelastic in the short run. The fundamental cause of bubbles, however, is the inability to sell real estate short, thereby limiting downward pressure on prices.[21] As a result, prices can be bid up by "optimists" and become disconnected from fundamentals through an absence of downward pressure either in the form of increased supply or short selling.[22] When the behavior of optimists is not coun-terbalanced by short selling from "pessimists," the price of real estate is pushed beyond its fundamental value. The potential for overvaluation derives from the heterogeneity of expectations. The key role of expectations in the determination of real estate prices is made clear from the user cost equation, which links asset prices to rents. A common approach is to compute the user cost, defined as

20. Chinco and Mayer (2012).

21. While vehicles exist for short selling, such as real estate investment trusts and futures mar-kets, they are limited in their impact. See Levitin, Pavlov, and Wachter (2009).

22. Herring and Wachter (1998) develop a model of land prices that serves as a straightforward framework for evaluating price cycles in the presence of fixed supply. This model helps demonstrate the role of optimists in determining real estate prices. Pavlov and Wachter (2006) show the source of the incentives to supply mortgage finance to overpriced homes.

$$P \times u = P(rf + \rho + tx + d - g),$$

where P represents price in dollars; $P \times rf$, forgone interest (at the risk-free rate); $P \times \rho$, the risk premium for housing; $P \times tx$, annual property taxes; $P \times d$, annual depreciation; and $P \times g$, the expected appreciation in house prices.

With frictionless arbitrage,

$$R = P \times u,$$

where R represents the rent in dollars for an asset priced at P, which implies that

$$P/R = 1/u = 1/[rf + \rho + tx + d - g].$$

The equation above can then be compared with the observed price-to-rent ratio to determine whether observed house prices are out of line with fundamentals. There are two core issues in the above methodology that make real estate prone to credit-induced bubbles. First, the expected appreciation term, g, must be based upon the modeled change in prices as opposed to the actual change in prices, since we are talking about future values. If the model is based on historical price appreciation, this will lead to incorrect forecasts. Moreover, after a price rise when expectations on future prices correct, the result will be a decline in prices rather than a leveling off of prices. This is because price expectations are capitalized into current house prices.

The second core issue is with the ρ term, which represents the risk premium (or cost of capital) for housing lending. A decline in this risk premium is commonly observed in credit-induced asset bubbles. In credit-induced bubbles, the risk premium falls as price appreciation rises, as shown in a study by Pavlov and Wachter.[23] As demonstrated in country data analysis by Pavlov and Wachter, the symptom of a bubble is the negative correlation between lending spreads (that is, the risk premium ρ) and real estate price appreciation, g, all else being equal.[24] The empirical evidence shows that when compressed lending spreads are associated with rising prices, all else being equal, subsequent price collapses are greater.

The common factor that characterizes markets where, ex ante, housing prices are more likely to fall, is a relatively high correlation of expected price appreciation g (not based on fundamentals) and a decreased risk premium ρ. This is due to the inconsistency of high expected price appreciation g (not based on fundamentals) along with a lower risk ρ.

Underpriced financing induces borrowers not only to overpay for assets, because they obtain cheap financing, but also to borrow more. The interplay of these two effects magnifies price increases, especially in markets that are

23. Pavlov and Wachter (2009a). See also Pavlov and Wachter (2009b) and Levitin, Pavlov, and Wachter (2012).

24. Pavlov and Wachter (2009b).

more supply constrained. If this occurs, housing prices will be inflated through increased demand (dampening default risk during the period of rising prices), and these price rises may result in higher price growth expectations that in turn are capitalized into higher prices. When the NTM expansion comes to an end, in the absence of a fundamental cause for an increase in prices, prices will decline, as the expectation of future price increases is not ratified, with a turn to higher lending standards and a higher cost of lending in response to defaults.

While it is clear that systemic risk can derive from the procyclical erosion of lending standards, there is no consensus on how to avoid this. While no system is perfect, fixed-rate long-term mortgages with robust, standardized securitization historically have been consistent with financial stability. Standardization promotes liquidity, ensures suitability, and enhances transparency so that increased risk can be monitored. A market and a formal trading exchange for buying and short selling real estate securities could be helpful in bringing about increased transparency and price discovery. Securitization has become an essential component of consumer finance and of real estate finance in particular. But to make securitization work, clear rules of the game that help achieve transparency and ensure against counterparty risk are needed as well as data provision to inform trading. Markets can price and expose risk, but the tools and information must be there to do so. Historically, lenders in the U.S. mortgage market who made noninvestment grade loans were forced to keep the mortgages—and the credit risk—on their books. However, mortgage markets in the United States began to change in the mid-1990s, and a rapid transformation occurred after 2000 when lenders discovered that they could securitize mortgages through private conduits managed by investment banks.

Investors assumed the credit risk on these MBS, which meant on the underlying mortgages. Because private label MBS did not have the GSE payment guarantee (with implicit or explicit government backing), they were designed with other forms of credit enhancement, most notably the division of the securities backed by a pool of mortgages into a cash flow waterfall that allocated default risk on the mortgages by a hierarchy of "tranches." The result was the creation of AAA securities from risky underlying mortgages. The riskiest tranches received the lowest ratings from the credit rating agencies and therefore paid the highest yields, and they were the first to lose value if borrowers fell behind on their payments. On top of this, financial firms leveraged private label MBS by using them as collateral for additional debt, in the form of collateralized debt obligations (CDOs). CDOs were constructed by pooling and tranching CDOs themselves. Leverage on top of leverage left the system vulnerable to even the slightest decline in prices or increase in loan defaults.

But the extent of this systemic increase in leverage was not known. Looser standards and the lowered price of the embedded put option buoyed housing prices in the short term. In particular, CDOs retained strong buyers of private-label credit risk throughout this period as CDO managers relied on ratings rather than the underlying credit characteristics of the loans. In addition, this reliance led to deterioration in the underwriting process and a substantial increase in fraud and misrepresentations, the magnitude of which was not fully understood at the time.[25] The race for market share fueled the extension of these increasingly risky loans to borrowers without the capacity to repay—a process likely exacerbated by short-term fee seeking. While long-term performance would be an important metric for those whose profits were tied to long-term results, in a market where the put option is in the money, participants are increasingly likely to be short-termers.

Aggressive lenders gained market share and fees by offering loans with low upfront costs, attracting repeat buyers purchasing pricier homes and second homes as well as speculators. The result was a rise in housing prices that could not be sustained, and with an end to the price rise, one that would be followed by a price decline. This would call into question the solvency of the lending institutions that relied on the collateral behind these loans. But the very complexity of the loans and the securities through which they were funded made it difficult to determine solvency implications. The result was a liquidity crisis for many lending institutions and the historic fiscal and monetary bailouts. Another result was the seizing up of NTM lending through the implosion of institutions that had been providing these nonstandard products. In response, credit constraints have since been set at historically high levels which, despite the Federal Reserve's persistent support of low interest rates, results in a high cost of homeownership, as shown above.[26] The after-the-fact identification of risk caused lenders to restrict access to lending across the board, resulting in procyclical lending terms. Despite the unprecedented Fed support for low interest rates, the all-in costs of homeownership have increased. The right level of credit constraints is currently the subject of rule making to implement the Dodd-Frank measures regarding provision of credit. At the same time, the form of the GSEs as they emerge from conservatorship is also under discussion. What should be clear is that a new housing finance structure, whatever form it takes, will itself affect the volatility of housing prices and thus the lending standards necessary for systemic stability.

25.While some investors may have recognized the declining credit quality, as in physical real estate, it was difficult to take short positions in these securities because there was no effective mechanism to short private label MBS, until the development of the pay-as-you-go credit default swap (CDS) mid-2005. The introduction of the asset-backed securities index (ABX) index in early 2006 provided an additional mechanism to short private label MBS. The CDO bid was stronger than the CDS-ABX short through 2006. See Levitin and Wachter (2012) for discussion.

26. See Bernanke's comments in Appelbaum (2013).

Appendix 9A. *Credit-Risk Mispricing in Detail (Historical Averages for U.S. Purchase Loans), 2000–07*

Percent except for FICO

Loan type	2000	2001	2002	2003	2004	2005	2006	2007
Prime FRM								
Share	66.0	51.3	45.6	35.0	10.8	10.6	11.6	29.8
Input data								
FICO score	695	709	714	737	744	745	744	748
CLTV ratio	74.5	76.7	77.4	78.1	77.3	80.9	83.5	84.9
Full doc	65.2	71.8	62.3	57.1	46.2	41.5	40.4	40.9
Rate	8.23	7.37	6.79	5.88	5.90	5.90	6.50	6.41
Results								
Annual loss	0.07	0.07	0.09	0.07	0.07	0.10	0.30	0.25
Loss-adjusted rate	8.16	7.29	6.69	5.81	5.83	5.80	6.19	6.16
Prime ARM[a]								
Share	17.3	12.2	23.4	30.4	26.6	16.2	13.0	13.3
Input data								
FICO score	711	724	730	737	737	744	742	750
CLTV ratio	81.1	71.9	77.7	81.6	82.8	81.1	81.3	81.6
Full doc	22.6	52.7	42.6	46.3	48.1	43.7	42.2	38.6
Rate	7.86	6.45	5.10	4.35	4.44	5.25	6.20	6.30
Results								
Annual loss	0.41	0.43	0.38	0.37	0.35	0.26	0.63	0.55
Loss-adjusted rate	7.45	6.02	4.73	3.98	4.09	5.00	5.57	5.75
Alt-A FRM								
Share	8.9	21.6	15.5	12.9	9.1	10.3	13.3	16.1
Input data								
FICO score	675	697	707	710	715	723	716	722
CLTV ratio	77.9	77.4	79.6	81.5	83.7	87.9	90.1	89.6
Full doc	38.2	28.6	33.5	30.1	29.4	25.2	16.6	20.2
Rate	9.11	7.96	7.32	6.47	6.47	6.43	7.16	7.12
Results								
Annual loss	0.60	0.54	0.39	0.45	0.37	0.38	1.12	1.26
Loss-adjusted rate	8.50	7.42	6.93	6.01	6.10	6.05	6.04	5.86
Alt-A ARM[b]								
Share	1.4	1.4	3.6	6.1	19.5	19.1	17.0	16.1
Input data								
FICO score	676	708	713	703	710	714	712	718
CLTV ratio	78.4	79.5	75.5	81.5	87.0	89.1	91.8	91.6
Full doc	9.8	70.2	45.4	35.1	29.8	23.9	14.1	14.0
Rate	7.30	6.63	6.32	5.76	5.56	6.13	7.14	7.44

Loan type	2000	2001	2002	2003	2004	2005	2006	2007
Alt-A ARM (continued)								
Results								
Annual loss	0.21	1.20	1.26	1.70	1.51	1.16	2.69	2.95
Loss-adjusted rate	7.09	5.44	5.06	4.07	4.04	4.97	4.45	4.50
Alt-A Option ARM								
Share	0.4	0.0	0.2	0.5	5.8	10.8	11.4	9.3
Input data								
FICO score	711		696	710	727	723	723	727
CLTV ratio	77.5		76.3	76.0	78.4	82.6	85.2	85.3
Full doc	18.4		17.9	19.5	23.3	16.6	10.4	10.6
Rate	4.27		4.55	2.52	1.72	1.72	2.70	4.82
Results								
Annual loss	0.88		1.07	1.30	1.06	1.45	3.04	2.59
Loss-adjusted rate	3.39		3.49	1.22	0.67	0.28	-0.34	2.24
Subprime FRM								
Share	1.8	3.9	2.8	4.1	4.7	4.9	6.5	2.9
Input data								
FICO score	590	613	636	656	659	658	650	640
CLTV ratio	89.1	94.5	93.8	87.3	84.7	91.9	94.1	92.7
Full doc	30.0	29.4	44.5	42.1	42.0	38.9	40.3	54.8
Rate	11.14	10.26	9.32	8.16	8.04	8.55	9.44	9.61
Results								
Annual loss	2.17	1.61	0.74	0.78	0.72	0.67	1.68	2.39
Loss-adjusted rate	8.97	8.65	8.59	7.38	7.32	7.88	7.75	7.22
Subprime ARM[c]								
Share	4.1	9.6	8.9	11.0	23.6	28.1	27.3	12.4
Input data								
FICO score	593	598	619	631	648	646	642	638
CLTV ratio	92.0	92.7	91.7	89.3	88.5	91.5	92.2	91.0
Full doc	37.5	25.8	47.4	46.0	43.5	37.8	33.6	40.9
Rate	11.10	10.22	8.79	7.70	7.28	7.45	8.58	8.68
Results								
Annual loss	3.66	3.87	3.32	3.50	3.04	3.20	6.04	6.01
Loss-adjusted rate	7.43	6.35	5.47	4.21	4.23	4.25	2.53	2.67

Sources: Intex and AD&Co.
a. Including a small share of option ARMs.
b. Excluding option ARMs.
c. Including a small share of option ARMs.

References

Anundsen, A. K., and Eilev S. Jansen. 2013. "Self-Reinforcing Effects between Housing Prices and Credit." *Journal of Housing Economics* 22, no. 3: 192–212.

Appelbaum, Binyamin. 2013. "Fed to Maintain Stimulus Efforts despite Jobs Growth." *New York Times,* March 20 (www.nytimes.com/2013/03/21/business/economy/fed-maintains-rates-and-strategy.html).

Barakova, Irina, and others. 2003. "Does Credit Quality Matter for Homeownership?" *Journal of Housing Economics* 12, no. 4: 318–36 (http://dx.doi.org/10.1016/j.jhe.2003.09.002).

———. 2013. "Borrowing Constraints during the Housing Bubble." Working Paper 741. Wharton Real Estate Center (http://ssrn.com/abstract=2229571).

Berkovec, Jim, Yan Chang, and Douglas A. McManus. 2012. "Alternative Lending Channels and the Crisis in U.S. Housing Markets." *Real Estate Economics* 40, no. s1: S8–S31.

Berlinghieri, L. 2010. *Essays on House Price Fluctuations in the U.S.* Ph.D. thesis, University of Washington.

Chinco, A., and C. Mayer. 2012. "Distant Speculators and Asset Bubbles in the Housing Market." Working Paper. Columbia Business School (www.econ.yale.edu/~shiller/behfin/2012-04-11/Chinco_Mayer.pdf).

Coleman, M., IV, M. LaCour-Little, and K. D. Vandell. 2008. "Subprime Lending and the Housing Bubble: Tail Wags Dog?" Working Paper (http://ssrn.com/abstract=1262365).

Courchane, Marsha J., and Peter M. Zorn. 2012. "Differential Access to and Pricing of Home Mortgages: 2004 through 2009." *Real Estate Economics* 40, no. s1: S115–S158.

Cutts, Amy Crews, and Robert A. Van Order. 2005. "On the Economics of Subprime Lending." *Journal of Real Estate Finance and Economics* 30, no. 2: 167–96.

Davidson, A., and A. Levin. 2012. "Measuring Housing Affordability and Home Price Equilibrium: Revisiting the Housing Bubble and Bust and HPI Modeling." AD&CO *Quantitative Perspectives* (June).

Favilukis, J., S. Ludvigson, and S. Van Nieuwerburgh. 2012. "The Macroeconomic Effects of Housing Wealth, Housing Finance, and Limited Risk-Sharing in General Equilibrium." Working Paper 15988. Cambridge, Mass.: National Bureau of Economic Research (www.nber.org/papers/w15988.pdf).

Haughwout, Andrew, and others. 2011. *Real Estate Investors, the Leverage Cycle, and the Housing Market Crisis.* Staff report 514. Federal Reserve Bank of New York (www.newyorkfed.org/research/staff_reports/sr514.pdf).

Haurin, D. R., P. H. Hendershott, and S. M. Wachter. 1996. "Wealth Accumulation and Housing Choices of Young Households: An Exploratory Investigation." *Journal of Housing Research* 7, no. 1: 33–58 (http://papers.ssrn.com/sol3/papers.cfm?abstract_id=9143).

———. 1997. "Borrowing Constraints and the Tenure Choice of Young Households." *Journal of Housing Research* 8, no. 2: 137–54 (http://papers.ssrn.com/sol3/papers.cfm?abstract_id=9139).

Herring, R. J., and S. M. Wachter. 1998. "Real Estate Cycles and Banking Crises: An International Perspective." Working Paper 298. Wharton Real Estate Center (http://knowledge.wharton.upenn.edu/papers/510.pdf).

Inside Mortgage Finance. 2013. *Mortgage Market Statistical Annual.* Bethesda, Md.: Inside Mortgage Finance Publications.

Levin, Alex. 2010. "HPI Modeling: Forecasts, Geography, Risk and Value." Presentation given at the Eighteenth Andrew Davidson and Company Conference, New York, June.

Levin, Alexander, and Andrew Davidson. 2008. "The Concept of Credit OAS in Valuation of MBS." *Journal of Portfolio Management* 34, no. 3: 41–55.

Levitin, Adam, Andrey Pavlov, and Susan Wachter. 2009. "Securitization: Cause or Remedy of the Financial Crisis?" Georgetown Law and Economics Research Paper 146285 (http://ssrn.com/abstract=1462895).

———. 2012. "Will Private Risk-Capital Return? The Dodd-Frank Act and the Housing Market." *Yale Journal on Regulation* 29, no. 1: 155–80.

Levitin, Adam, and Susan M. Wachter. 2012. "Explaining the Housing Bubble." *Georgetown Law Journal* 100, no. 4: 1177–258.

Linneman, Peter, and Susan Wachter. 1989. "The Impacts of Borrowing Constraints on Homeownership." *Real Estate Economics* 17, no. 4: 389–402.

Pavlov, Andrey, and Susan M. Wachter. 2006. "The Inevitability of Marketwide Underpricing of Mortgage Default Risk." *Real Estate Economics* 34, no. 4: 479–96 (http://papers.ssrn.com/sol3/papers.cfm?abstract_id=944969).

———. 2009a. "Mortgage Put Options and Real Estate Markets." *Journal of Real Estate Finance and Economics* 38, no. 1: 89–103 (http://papers.ssrn.com/sol3/papers.cfm?abstract_id=1285517).

———. 2009b. "Systemic Risk and Market Institutions." *Yale Journal on Regulation* 26, no. 2: 9–26 (http://papers.ssrn.com/sol3/papers.cfm?abstract_id=1462360).

———. 2011. "Subprime Lending and Real Estate Prices." *Real Estate Economics* 38, no. 1: 1–17 (http://papers.ssrn.com/sol3/papers.cfm?abstract_id=1489435).

Rosenthal, Stuart S. 2002. "Eliminating Credit Barriers: How Far Can We Go?" In *Low-Income Homeownership: Examining the Unexamined Goal,* edited by Nicolas P. Retsinas and Eric S. Belsky, pp. 111–45. Brookings.

Thomas, Jason, and Robert Van Order. 2010. "Housing Policy, Subprime Markets and Fannie Mae and Freddie Mac: What We Know, What We Think We Know and What We Don't Know." Paper presented at the conference Past, Present, and Future of the Government Sponsored Enterprises, Federal Reserve Bank of St. Louis (http://research.stlouisfed.org/conferences/gse/Van_Order.pdf).

IV

The Government's Role in
the Evolving Mortgage Market

10

Rethinking Duties to Serve in Housing Finance

ADAM J. LEVITIN AND JANNEKE H. RATCLIFFE

If the housing crisis has had a silver lining, it is the opportunity to rethink our housing finance policy. The U.S. housing finance system and its regulation evolved to address particular crises and problems—the Great Depression, the postwar housing crunch, the 1960s budget crises, redlining, the savings and loan crisis—rather than as a planned, comprehensive system.[1] Taking into account how the mortgage finance market has been restructured in the wake of the 2008–09 financial crisis, it is essential to ensure that it better serves the housing needs of all Americans. Thus, an important question going forward concerns the role of duties to serve (DTS)—obligations on lending institutions to reach out to traditionally underserved communities and borrowers. Should there be DTS, and if so, who should have the responsibility to serve whom, with what, and how?

As an initial matter, it is important to distinguish fair lending from DTS. Fair lending concerns the obligation not to discriminate on unlawful grounds in the actual granting of credit and its terms. The duties to serve concept is broader, recognizing that merely prohibiting discriminatory lending is insufficient to address the disparity of financial opportunity. DTS involve taking affirmative steps to reach out to communities traditionally underserved by the housing finance market to ensure not just that credit is granted on nondiscriminatory terms, but that there is also equal access to credit-granting institutions. DTS imply that a financial institution ensures its services are available to *all*

1. Levitin and Wachter (2013).

eligible consumers. Currently the U.S. housing finance system features DTS in two major ways: depository institutions are subject to the Community Reinvestment Act of 1977, and Fannie Mae and Freddie Mac—two government-sponsored enterprises (GSEs)—are subject to specific housing goals. In addition, on a smaller scale, each of the Federal Home Loan Banks (FHLBs) is required to target a share of profits to affordable housing. The financial system has changed since these regulations were first conceived, with the rise of interstate branch banking, secondary markets, nondepository lenders, and new technologies. Yet despite these changes, some of the fundamental issues regarding access to credit for people of color, or those of low-to-moderate income (LTMI) or living in LTMI communities or communities of color, are still operative, whether in the form of redlining or predatory lending.[2] Today's low regulatory and investor tolerance for risk may usher in a new phase of limited access to credit. DTS need to be revised and updated so that it aligns with the constantly evolving nature of the financial market.

This paper argues that DTS must be conceived of as a question of public benefit and purpose, not strictly as a question of social justice, redress, or mandated subsidy. Financial services are not just another type of business: the U.S. financial system functions because of the legal and financial infrastructure provided by the federal government, and government is constitutive of the market.[3] To the extent that private firms are suffered to operate in the system, it is conditioned on provision of equal access, much like a public utility or common carrier.[4]

Put differently, like transport and telecom providers, financial services providers have a social responsibility as well as a shareholder responsibility. Their right to do business is a limited one. First, unlike general corporate charters, neither bank charters nor the GSEs' charters are freely granted. Bank and GSE charters are also limited, special-purpose charters that restrict the business these entities

---

2. Quercia, Freeman, and Ratcliffe (2011).

3. As the 1912 Democratic Party platform put it, "Banks exist for the accommodation of the public." American Presidency Project, Democratic Party Platform of 1912 (www.presidency.ucsb. edu/ws/index.php?pid=29590#axzz2isKCn5Lr).

4. A "common carrier" is defined in Merriam-Webster's dictionary as "a business or agency that is available to the public for transportation of persons, goods or messages." Common carriers, such as airlines and shippers, offer these services to the general public in a nondiscriminatory manner under a licensing and regulatory framework that serves the public interest. Specifically, they may not unreasonably refuse service to anyone willing to pay the fare. Another example is the universal service aspect of the Telecommunications Act of 1996, the goal of which is to ensure broad, nondiscriminatory access to advanced telecom services "to all consumers, including those in low-income, rural, insular and highest-cost areas at rates that are reasonably comparable to those charged in urban areas." To spread the costs, all telecom providers pay an assessment on their revenues that goes to the Universal Service Fund, which also specifically funds the provision of services to schools, libraries, and rural health care providers (www.transition.fcc.gov/wcb/tapd/universal_service/).

can undertake to a specific type of economic activity thought to be in the public interest. Doing business under these special-purpose charters confers certain benefits and comes with a set of social responsibilities, namely ensuring that financial services are available and accessible to all communities within the constraints of financial institution safety-and-soundness.

DTS are part and parcel of the purpose for granting special-purpose charters for financial intermediation and for government support of the market, which comes in a variety of forms—economic, regulatory, and infrastructure—that benefit stakeholders directly and indirectly. For example, federal deposit insurance enables the scope and scale of depositories' business. Likewise, mortgage banks, though not directly backed by the government, can operate only because of the secondary mortgage market, much of which is government backed. Even the purely private segments of the secondary market rely on the framework provided by government-supported segments of the market. Similarly, private mortgage insurance (PMI) companies do the lion's share of their business on GSE-backed loans, because PMI is specifically required by the GSEs' charters. In the recent crisis, the expansion of the Federal Housing Administration (FHA) program played a countercyclical role in stabilizing the housing market, indirectly reducing potential losses for a range of stakeholders.[5] As these examples show, the government provides a supportive framework to the benefit of a range of market participants, who interdependently benefit from, and should contribute to, a vibrant and accessible market.

Further, we argue that DTS go beyond simply doing business with LTMI and minority communities as has been traditionally mandated. DTS must include offering the *same types of products* to all communities, adjusted for the needs of communities (for example, seasonal income in rural agricultural communities). DTS should not sanction a type of separate but equal approach to housing finance; rather, DTS must involve ensuring access to substantively similar credit as is available to well-served communities.

We are *not* suggesting that lenders could or should offer identical loans to all borrowers. DTS must exist within the bounds of safe-and-sound lending practices. There cannot, however, exist a two-tracked, separate, and unequal housing (and consumer) credit system in the United States, with wealthier (and whiter) communities offered traditional, nonpredatory products from depositories and prime lenders, such as long-term, fully amortized, fixed-rate mortgages, while LTMI and minority communities go unserved or served only by non-banks offering higher cost and nontraditional products that expose borrowers to greater risks than traditional products. Because of the constitutive role of government in the financial marketplace, and its direct and indirect support of the entire

5. Quercia and Park (2012).

housing finance system, all entities in the system must have DTS that is consistent with safety and soundness. DTS might reduce (but not eliminate) profitability in some cases, but that is the cost of doing business in a government-constituted market. Simply put, consumers' access to a government-constituted market must be offered in a nondiscriminatory and accessible manner to all.

This paper proceeds as follows: First, it discusses the importance of homeownership and housing finance for economic opportunity. It then reviews the regulatory framework and history underlying the present set of DTS, addressing the policy concerns underlying DTS and how they have changed. The paper identifies several problems in the existing DTS framework that will continue to limit the impact of DTS unless remedied. A discussion of the public purposes of financial services follows. The paper concludes with recommendations for operationalizing DTS conceived of as public accommodations within the bounds of prudential regulation, laying out a quartet of reforms that will make DTS more effective. In particular, it proposes the creation of an independent DTS commission that would serve as an advocate for DTS and a check on financial institutions' compliance *outside* the prudential bank regulators.

The Importance of Homeownership for Economic Opportunity

Homeownership has long been a keystone for the economic vitality of America's broad middle class, conferring financial and social benefits on families and communities.[6] Homes provide more than just shelter; they are also a long-term savings vehicle and nurture stable communities. Homeownership also generates various macroeconomic benefits through new construction, real estate transactions, and financial services employment. The individual and social benefits from homeownership, however, come largely from the way it is financed: since the 1930s, the housing finance system has been designed to provide affordability, stability, and societal benefits through consumer-friendly mortgages.

This has not always been the case. Before the 1930s, housing finance was a private business; mortgages were usually short-term balloon loans so that the rates could be readjusted regularly. Large down payments were required, and the homeownership rate was below 50 percent.[7] Recurrent boom-bust cycles made homeownership a risky investment. These cycles culminated in the Great Depression, and when lending collapsed, 1,000 families were foreclosed on per day.[8]

---

6. We emphasize that while there are particular benefits from homeownership, there is a role for stable rental housing as well.

7. Levitin and Wachter (2013).

8. Immergluck (2009).

In response, President Herbert Hoover in 1932 initiated a new housing finance process with the establishment of the Federal Home Loan Bank (FHLB) system.[9] Following this action, a series of federal initiatives over the years served to improve and strengthen homeownership financing, including:

—The New Deal, under the Roosevelt administration, launched the Home Owners' Loan Corporation in 1933 to purchase and restructure distressed mortgages with consumer-friendly terms.

—Federal deposit insurance was also introduced in 1933 to encourage people to put their money into banking institutions so depositories could resume lending.

—The Federal Housing Administration (FHA) was established in 1934 to provide a full government guaranty so lenders would extend fixed-rate, fully amortizing long-term loans adhering to a set of standards.

—The Federal National Mortgage Association (FNMA, or Fannie Mae) was created in 1938 as a government-owned corporation to provide low-cost liquidity for FHA-insured loans so as to enable further FHA-insured lending in the primary market.

—The Veterans Administration (now the U.S. Department of Veterans Affairs) began to guarantee mortgages in 1944 as part of the GI Bill.

Even with the privatization of Fannie Mae in 1968 and the creation of the Federal Home Loan Mortgage Corporation (FHLMC, or Freddie Mac) in 1971 (originally owned by the Federal Home Loan Banks), the federal government continued to play a critical role in housing finance, both explicitly, through the Government National Mortgage Association's (GNMA, or Ginnie Mae) guarantee of mortgage-backed securities built on FHA-insured/VA-guaranteed loans, FDIC deposit insurance, and through the implicit guarantee of the GSEs.

Whether through guaranteeing lending institutions, mortgages, or secondary market entities, the government has taken the ultimate credit risk on most mortgages made in the United States since the 1930s. The major exception occurred during the mid-2000s when private-label securitization briefly and disastrously became a dominant source of mortgage capital, forcing the government to step in to bail out institutions for which it did not have an explicit guaranty. Postcrisis, government-supported financing of mortgages through FHA and the GSEs (by then in conservatorship and fully taxpayer supported) sustained the lifeblood of capital to the housing market. The importance of the housing finance system to the U.S. economy is such that the system will always be implicitly or explicitly guaranteed against catastrophic losses.

Today, housing equity is by far the largest source of net wealth for U.S. households.[10] The median wealth of a home-owning household in the country

9. Levitin and Wachter (2013).
10. Taylor and others (2011).

is $174,500, compared to $5,100 for the median renter.[11] In survey after survey, Americans—whether renters or owners, whether stable or recently foreclosed on—overwhelmingly aspire to own homes. Macroeconomically, economic recovery depends heavily on the housing market.[12]

The same government policy that over the decades facilitated these housing-related opportunities also set up barriers to participation by minority families, many of these explicit. Federal policies once disfavored racially mixed neighborhoods, promoting the institutionalizing of redlining. For many of their initial years, FHA and VA programs favored white borrowers; indeed, from 1934 to 1959, when FHA guaranteed more than half the home purchase mortgages in the United States, only 2 percent of the loans went to African Americans.[13]

Though antidiscrimination and fair lending laws eventually outlawed racially discriminatory housing and lending practices (which is not to say that they do not persist),[14] the long-term effects still influence lending disparities. Today, while 74 percent of white households own their own homes, less than half of black and Hispanic households do.[15] Prevented from full participation in homeownership over the second half of the twentieth century, minorities have not been able to accumulate the same wealth as whites.

The collapse of the housing bubble has exacerbated racial wealth gaps. Today the median white household holds $20 of wealth for every $1 held by the median Latino or black family.[16] In a study following the same households over the quarter century from 1984 to 2009, the wealth gap between white and black households in the study tripled (in 2009 dollars), from a starting point of $85,000 to $236,500. While the median wealth of the African American household grew from just under $6,000 to $28,500, the median white household saw wealth increase from $90,851 to $265,000.[17]

The primary driver of this gap is homeownership, accounting for 27 percent of the difference. A higher share of whites attain homeownership, and they do so at an earlier age, which is in part attributable to greater access to resources for

11. Bricker and others (2012).

12. Bernanke (2012).

13. Immergluck (2009, ch. 2).

14. In 1948 a Supreme Court decision banned judicial enforcement of racially restrictive covenants in real estate. *Shelly* v. *Kraemer,* 334 U.S. 1 (1948). In 1950 FHA ended its practice of favoring racial covenants; a 1962 Executive Order by Kennedy banned discrimination in federal housing programs; Title VIII of the Civil Rights Act of 1968—the Fair Housing Act—prohibited discrimination in housing markets. In 1976 the Supreme Court found this prohibition included denying loan applications in specific neighborhoods. The Equal Credit Opportunity Act of 1974, amended in 1976, prohibited lending discrimination, including disparate impact.

15. U.S. Census Bureau (data as of fourth quarter 2012).

16. Taylor and others (2011).

17. Shapiro, Meschede, and Osoro (2013).

down payments from inheritances or family assistance. Thus, wealth advantages compound intergenerationally.[18]

Moreover, at least partly as a result of inequities in the terms of mortgage financing, minority borrowers and high minority neighborhoods experienced greater wealth stripping, less appreciation, and higher foreclosure-related wealth loss than white households and neighborhoods in the mortgage boom and bust. Hispanic and African American households hold a greater share of their net worth in home equity.[19] They were also more likely to receive high-cost, risky loans, even when controlling for credit risk, and while white borrowers have experienced the most foreclosures, minority borrowers have been more than twice as likely to lose their homes to foreclosure.[20] As a result, from 2005 to 2009, the median wealth for white households fell 16 percent, for African American households 53 percent, and for Hispanic households 66 percent. By 2009, with black and Hispanic household median wealth at its lowest level in twenty-five years by some measures, the wealth gap between white households and black and Hispanic households stood at its highest level in twenty-five years.[21]

Thus, access to nonpredatory finance is central to addressing self-compounding inequalities in financial opportunities that have far-reaching externalities, particularly for communities of color. Systems of economic opportunity, such as homeownership, can actually contribute to inequality if equal access to those systems is hindered at any point.

Fair Lending and Duties to Serve: The Existing Regulatory Framework

DTS are the result of a variety of laws. While DTS are distinct from fair lending, their role needs to be understood in the context of supplementing and expanding fair lending laws.

Fair Housing Act of 1968

The Fair Housing Act (Title VIII of the Civil Rights Act of 1968) was a central piece of civil rights legislation from the 1960s. It originally prohibited discrimination in the sale, purchase, rental, or financing of residential real estate on the basis of race, color, religion, or national origin.[22] The act has subsequently been expanded to prohibit discrimination on the basis of gender, familial status, and

18. Shapiro, Meschede, and Osoro (2013).
19. Taylor and others (2011).
20. Bocian and others (2011).
21. Taylor and others (2011).
22. 42 U.S.C. § 3601 et seq. The Civil Rights Act of 1968 also prohibited discrimination in housing, but required a showing of intentional discrimination.

disabilities. The act does not create an affirmative DTS. Instead, as applied to housing finance, it mandates nondiscriminatory extensions of credit. The act is enforced by the Department of Housing and Urban Development (HUD) secretary, the attorney general, and by private rights of action.

Equal Credit Opportunity Act of 1974

The Equal Credit Opportunity Act (ECOA) of 1974 originally prohibited discrimination against applicants for any sort of credit on the basis of gender or marital status. It was subsequently amended to prohibit discrimination based on race, color, religion, national origin, age, or because the applicant receives public income assistance.[23] ECOA is enforced by the Consumer Financial Protection Bureau (CFPB) for large banks and non-banks and by the Office of the Comptroller of the Currency, Federal Reserve Board, FDIC, and National Credit Union Administration (NCUA) for small banks and credit unions. The CFPB interprets ECOA as prohibiting both disparate treatment and disparate impact based on neutral policies.[24] There is also a private right of action. Like the Fair Housing Act, ECOA does not mandate that access to credit be provided in any particular community, and ECOA's protected classes do not include LTMI (except to the extent individuals receive public assistance).

The Home Mortgage Disclosure Act of 1975

The Home Mortgage Disclosure Act (HMDA) of 1975 was an important step in identifying patterns of redlining.[25] Originally, the law required lenders to report lending volumes by census tract but was amended in 1989 by the Financial Institutions Reform, Recovery, and Enforcement Act (FIRREA) to require loan-level reporting of mortgage applications and originations. HMDA does not direct particular practices, but it is a key tool in policing discriminatory mortgage lending.

The Community Reinvestment Act of 1977

In 1977 Congress enacted the Community Reinvestment Act (CRA), which created a continuing and affirmative obligation for depository institutions (other than credit unions) with federal deposit insurance to "help meet the credit needs of the local communities in which they are chartered consistent with the safe and sound operation of such institutions."[26] The CRA only applies to a depository's

---

23. 15 U.S.C. § 1691.

24. CFPB (2012).

25. For more information on the history of HMDA, see FFIEC (2012).

26. 12 U.S.C. § 2901. For a comprehensive history of the CRA, see Art (1987), MacDonald (1995), Joint Center for Housing Studies (2002), Barr (2005), and Bernanke (2007).

activities, not the activities of its nondepository affiliates or holding company (except at the depository's election to include affiliate activity).

Enactment of the CRA was motivated, at least in part, by frustration that fair lending laws alone were not eliminating redlining. The intent behind the CRA was a fundamental change in lenders' attitudes and responsibilities toward serving traditionally underserved communities.

The CRA settled the core philosophical dispute over whether depository institutions enjoying the benefits of federal charters and federal deposit insurance owe any duty to consider the impact on neighborhoods when determining their lending policies. The CRA was a legislative mandate for a change in policy and a rebuke to financial institutions and the federal supervisory agencies that had previously sanctioned and even encouraged redlining.[27]

While this obligation applies to financial services, investments, and mortgages, we focus mainly on the mortgage aspect here.[28] In addition to the safety and soundness provision, the hallmark principles of this law include flexibility and adaptability by giving regulators the authority to set and revise performance criteria; a public role in "regulating from below" through public disclosure and input; a balance of quantitative and qualitative measures that considers efforts and activities in tandem with lending volumes; and a context-based approach for evaluating an institution's performance, in which each institution is examined against the backdrop of a particular market.[29]

The financial world has changed significantly since the CRA became law. In 1977 depository institutions—particularly savings and loans—funded and held most mortgages. By the early 1990s, however, through the increased use of mortgage securitization, the GSEs were funding more than half of all new loans, and depositories' share of originations was declining, thereby lessening the share of the mortgage origination market covered by the CRA.[30]

The Housing Goals

As the secondary market replaced deposits as the primary source of funding for mortgages, it came to play a critical role in determining who gets access to credit and under what terms. The CRA does not apply to the GSEs, which are privately owned firms operating under special-purpose federal charters. These charters specify the public purposes of the GSEs, which include "provid[ing] ongoing

---

27. Art (1987).

28. Details on the mechanics of CRA are available at www.ffiec.gov/cra/default.htm.

29. Quercia, Ratcliffe, and Stegman (2009).

30. Immergluck (2009, p. 45). For a good history of adjustments to CRA over the following three decades, see Ludwig, Kamihachi, and Toh (2009).

assistance to the secondary market for residential mortgages (including activities relating to mortgages on housing for low- and moderate-income families involving a reasonable economic return that may be less than the return earned on other activities)" and "promot[ing] access to mortgage credit throughout the Nation (including central cities, rural areas, and underserved areas)."[31]

In the 1970s HUD set goals that 30 percent of GSE funding go to central cities and 30 percent go to households earning below area median income (AMI). This goal was nonbinding, and HUD did not monitor performance.[32]

In 1992, as the influence of GSEs in the housing market increased and concerns mounted that they were contributing to redlining, their public purposes were operationalized with the establishment of housing goals (HGs), part of the Federal Housing Enterprises Financial Safety and Soundness Act (FHEFSSA).[33] These are purely quantitative targets measured as the annual percentage of loans funded by the GSEs that fall in one of several target categories, defined by borrower income or census tract median income or minority population share. The performance of the GSEs on these measures is benchmarked against the overall conventional conforming market ("benchmark market").[34]

Several adjustments were made to the GSEs' DTS regime through the Housing and Economic Recovery Act of 2008 (HERA). Those implemented, beginning in 2010, include separate goals for refinance and purchase mortgages; a lowering of income thresholds, generally to 80 percent of area median income (and thus better aligned with the CRA); other adjustments to the underserved areas goals; and exclusion of loans determined by the regulator to be inconsistent with safety and soundness. Loans in private label securities purchased by the GSEs are also no longer counted.[35]

Several other important changes have not yet been implemented. First, HERA adds a "duty-to-serve" underserved markets (manufactured housing, affordable housing preservation, rural housing, and other segments that may later be deemed to qualify) through a more CRA-like approach that incorporates context and level-of-effort measures. Second, it calls for the GSEs to allocate 0.042 percent of the value of new loan purchases to a dedicated fund to support housing for the lowest income families and certain related economic development

---

31. Fannie Mae and Freddie Mac Charter Acts (www.fhfa.gov/GetFile.aspx?FileID=29).

32. Immergluck (2009).

33. A history of events leading to the establishment of the goals can be found in Fishbein (2003).

34. Weicher (2010). The benchmark market excludes loans above the GSEs' loan limits or otherwise ineligible for purchase by the enterprises, government insured loans, second liens, high-cost loans, and loans from "segments of the market determined to be unacceptable or contrary to good lending practices, [or] inconsistent with safety and soundness." Housing and Economic Recovery Act of 2008.

35. Federal Housing Finance Agency (2010).

activities in underserved communities. With these changes, the secondary market DTS would become more multifaceted, using a combination of broad goals, targeted qualitative measures, and subsidies.[36]

Comparing CRA and the HGs

The HGs were a step toward aligning secondary market affirmative obligations with those of CRA-covered lenders in the primary market.[37] Similar to the CRA, the HGs allow for public comment, and results are reported annually. The GSEs provide a limited public data set on their HG eligible loans. There is also a contextual element implied in the process for establishing the HGs, as they are to be based on housing needs, macroeconomic and demographic conditions, and other factors.

This alignment has not been perfect, however. The CRA gives credit for income categories different from those of the HGs. Also, the HGs are entirely quantitative, whereas the act's measures have a strong subjective element. The CRA is based largely on local market activities, whereas the HGs are purely national in scope.

In terms of incentive for good performance, under the CRA, there is both a public perception risk and a material business concern for failure to earn a passing grade. Regulators are required to consider an institution's CRA performance when reviewing applications for mergers, and for such activities as opening and closing branch banks. How heavily to weigh CRA performance is largely left to the regulator's discretion, although the public nature of the process gives advocates some leverage over the determination. However, in practice, sanctions have been little used. Since 1990 only 0.35 percent of exams have resulted in a failing grade, while 96 percent earned satisfactory or higher.[38] From 1985 to 1999 only eight applications for actions subject to the CRA had been denied out of 92,177 applications submitted.[39]

The GSEs met or exceeded their HGs in nearly all years,[40] although the penalty for failing to meet them—a requirement to create a strategic plan for

36. The Housing and Economic Recovery Act of 2008; Public Law 110-289 (July 30, 2008). Title I Subtitle B—Improvement of Mission Supervision (www.gpo.gov/fdsys/pkg/PLAW-110 publ289/html/PLAW-110publ289.htm).

37. 12 U.S.C. § 4565.

38. The CRA ratings database can be downloaded at www.ffiec.gov/craratings/Rtg_spec.aspx. From 1990 to December 2012, out of 69,792 ratings, there were 246 of "substantial noncompliance," many related to the same institution for different exam periods. There were 2,517 "needs to improve" ratings. Since the beginning of 2008, of 8,822 exams, 0.2 percent were rated "substantial noncompliance," while 97.5 percent earned "satisfactory" or higher.

39. Barr (2005).

40. Financial Crisis Inquiry Commission (2010); Weicher (2010).

improving performance—is not particularly burdensome. However, reputational concerns likely exerted strong influence in this case as well.

Perhaps most important, both of these affirmative obligation regimes incorporate a safety and soundness requirement. The GSE charter specifies that activities be undertaken "at reasonable economic return," and the 1992 act establishing the goals required them to be based on "the need to maintain the sound financial condition of the enterprises."[41]

FIRREA Requirements for Federal Home Loan Banks

A final and distinct DTS rests with the FHLB system, a system of twelve federally chartered member-owned banks that provide liquidity to the housing finance market by issuing tax-exempt bonds to finance the rediscounting of mortgages held by member banks.[42] The FHLB charter conveys privileges on the FHLB system (passed on to its members, which are commercial banks and S&Ls) in the form of access to low-cost liquidity and dividends.

Prior to 1989 the FHLB's mission was to provide liquidity to the S&L sector. In the aftermath of the S&L crisis, FIRREA created a specific DTS for the FHLB system in two forms. First, all FHLBs must offer Community Investment Programs (CIPs) to provide lower-cost advances for loans that provide housing and certain commercial activities for LTMI households and neighborhoods, though the size and scope of these activities are not mandated.[43] More explicit is the requirement that 10 percent of each FHLB's profits (or at least $100 million per year in aggregate) must go to affordable housing programs (AHPs) "to subsidize the interest rate on advances to members engaged in lending for long term, low and moderate-income, owner-occupied and affordable rental housing at subsidized interest rates."[44]

Like Fannie Mae and Freddie Mac's goals, this duty to serve applies to the secondary market entities only (the FHLBs themselves); most members of the FHLBs are subject to the CRA. The FHLB profit diversion is a distinct form of DTS. Though easier to measure and implement, it may not reach as far and leans toward providing special programs rather than expanding access to mainstream offerings. In contrast to the CRA and HGs, the AHP requirement is

---

41. Housing and Community Development Act of 1992, Public Law 102-550, 102nd Congress (October 28, 1992), §1331-8.

42. See Levitin and Wachter (2013) regarding the history of the FHLBs.

43. Federal Home Loan Bank Act § 10 (12 U.S.C. §§ 1430) requires, "Each bank shall establish a program to provide funding for members to undertake community-oriented mortgage lending. . . . Advances under this program shall be priced at the cost of consolidated Federal Home Loan Bank obligations of comparable maturities, taking into account reasonable administrative costs." See www.fhfa.gov/Default.aspx?Page=113.

44. Federal Home Loan Bank Act (12 U.S.C. §§ 1421.

more redistributive. Some within the FHLB system view it as a reasonable and effective tax; others consider it core to the system's mission.[45] HERA has called for the establishment of HGs similar to those of Fannie Mae and Freddie Mac on FHLBs' mortgage purchase programs.

Effectiveness of Existing Duties to Serve— A Review of the Evidence

There is little consensus about the impact of existing DTS. One school of thought holds that affirmative obligation requirements have improved access to credit, though more can be done. A second posits that affirmative obligation requirements led lenders to make riskier loans, eventually leading to the financial crisis of 2008. A third view holds that the affirmative obligations have not accomplished much for good or bad. The accumulated evidence indicates that DTS have changed institutional behavior and had a modest impact on increasing underserved communities' access to housing finance without compromising safety and soundness.

Change in Institutional Behavior?

The evidence is consistent in identifying changes in institutional behavior. Harvard's Joint Center for Housing Studies found that the CRA "influences the plans of most lenders at the margin."[46] A Federal Reserve survey found that 73 percent of institutions had implemented at least one special CRA program. While more than 40 percent reported they were motivated by the opportunity to earn additional profits, the most common reasons for these programs were "responding to the credit needs of the community" and "promoting community growth and stability," suggesting that lenders' view of the CRA had aligned with the spirit of the act.[47]

Other documented changes made by CRA-covered lenders include setting up dedicated CRA units; working with community partners and local governments; investing in community development corporations, loan consortia, and community development financial institutions; and funding borrower counseling.[48] Many lenders also entered into "CRA Agreements," which are "a pledge signed by a community organization(s) and a bank outlining a multi-year program of lending, investments, and/or services."[49] A 2007 study by the National Community Reinvestment Coalition reported 446 of these agreements.[50]

45. Hoffman and Cassell (2002).
46. Joint Center for Housing Studies (2002, p. vi).
47. Avery, Bostic, and Canner (2000).
48. Barr (2005).
49. National Community Reinvestment Coalition (2007, p. 4).
50. National Community Reinvestment Coalition (2007, p. 4).

Likewise, research shows that the GSEs responded to the HG challenge by offering more flexible lending programs.[51] Fannie Mae's Office of Low- and Moderate-Income Housing opened in 1987, some five years before the goals were established; by 1990 this office had committed $5 billion, and in March of 1991 Fannie Mae launched "Opening Doors," a $10 billion initiative expanding its LTMI housing programs.[52] Fannie Mae's "trillion dollar commitment" to affordable housing was announced in 1994 and achieved by 2000. Similarly, Freddie Mac made a $3 billion commitment in 1991 and 1992 for affordable homeownership and rental.[53]

In pursuit of these commitments, the GSEs developed new programs in partnership with other agencies and mortgage insurers such as the "3/2" program launched in 1991.[54] The GSEs also incrementally introduced flexibilities in reviewing credit history and debt-to-income ratios, funded employer-assisted housing, engaged in special efforts in rural areas and for elderly borrowers, made investments in low-income rental housing and state housing finance agency bonds, and made targeted purchases of "goals-rich" loans.

Change in Lending Practices?

Did these organizational changes translate into lending activities? Case study evidence confirms they did. For example, Self-Help, a nonprofit financial institution in North Carolina, found in the early 1980s that many banks had special CRA programs but did not have a secondary market outlet for these loans, which constrained the amount of lending they could do. Self-Help started buying these portfolios, and demonstrated that they performed well, despite having characteristics that disqualified them from purchase by the GSEs. In 1998 Fannie Mae entered into an agreement where Self-Help, with $50 million in capital backing from the Ford Foundation, would serve as a conduit and guarantor of such loans originated to satisfy the CRA and HGs and subsequently sold to Fannie Mae. Self-Help's national affordable mortgage secondary market program, the Community Advantage Program (or CAP), funded 46,500 mortgages originated by thirty-six lenders.[55] These loans did not comply with standard, conforming underwriting requirements, yet they proved profitable. This is just one of many cases of the lending motivated by DTS programs.

---

51. Listokin and others (2000); Temkin, Quercia, and Galster (2000).

52. Levine (1993).

53. Brendsel (1991).

54. The 3/2 Option program permits the homeowner to make a down payment of 3 percent of the property value, with another 2 percent being contributed by a family member, grant, or loan from a government or nonprofit agency. Fannie Mae boasts no fewer than ten "Community Lending" products for LTMI borrowers.

55. Quercia, Freeman, and Ratcliffe (2011).

A few studies have examined the relationship between CRA agreements and lending activity. Schwartz found that banks with CRA agreements had higher shares of mortgages approved to targeted borrowers and lower denial disparity rates than other banks, though these differences could not be conclusively tied to the agreements.[56] In case studies, Shlay found that CRA-eligible lending increased in all the markets examined, irrespective of agreement activity, and among all the lenders, though the lenders with CRA agreements increased their CRA lending activity more than others.[57] Bostic and Robinson found a statistically significant and sustained increase in CRA-qualified volumes by lenders entering an agreement, although this finding is not benchmarked against change in the institutions' overall lending activity or other lenders' CRA activity.[58]

Interestingly, banks receiving downgrades were not found to subsequently improve their performance.[59] More recently, Agarwal and others compared the rate at which applications were converted to mortgages by CRA-covered institutions undergoing CRA examinations to those not undergoing examinations. They observed a relative increase in conversions among the banks undergoing CRA examinations only among the forty-nine large banks out of the more than 5,000 studied.[60] The study's findings have been questioned, however, because the periods studied do not correspond with the period considered in CRA examinations.[61]

In terms of the GSEs, the HGs corresponded with a substantial increase in funding to LTMI homeowners and multifamily properties. For example, in 1993, 32 percent of the GSEs' activities met the low-and-moderate income goal,[62] but by 2001 this share regularly represented at least half of their activity. This represents a sizable increase in LTMI financing in the market as a whole, given the GSEs' expanding market share. Moreover, by 2002 the GSEs steadily closed the gap by which they lagged the benchmark market. From 1995 through 2008, the level of such lending activities by the benchmark market remained essentially flat.[63]

There is a paucity of research on the impact of FHLB advances and the AHP and CIP programs in particular on the provision of housing finance to underserved segments.[64] Higher FHLB advances are associated with higher levels of

56. Schwartz (1998).
57. Shlay (1999, pp. 35, 247).
58. Bostic and Robinson (2004).
59. Dahl, Evanoff, and Spivey (2010).
60. Agarwal and others (2012).
61. Reid and others (2013).
62. HUD (1998).
63. Weicher (2010).
64. McCool (2005).

mortgage lending, generally,[65] and FHLB members originate a higher proportion of loans to targeted areas and minority borrowers than non-members,[66] but there has been no link established between FHLB advances, let alone AHP program usage, and increased lending to underserved markets. Simply in terms of activity, the FHLB system reports that "more than 776,000 housing units have been built using AHP funds" totaling more than $4.6 billion since 1990.[67]

Impact on Profitability?

What about costs to the institutions? Gunther proposed that profitability concerns conflict with CRA objectives.[68] As noted, however, both the CRA and the HGs stress that DTS exist within the boundaries of safety-and-soundness. CRA-covered institutions surveyed reported that 78 percent of CRA lending was at least break-even. At the same time, respondents reported that their special CRA lending programs had comparable or better delinquency and charge-off rates than all mortgage lending.[69] Addressing the notion that noncredit costs can be a factor, Willis lays out a number of categories of costs arising from the CRA, from administrative and production costs to perceived pressures to reduce pricing to uneconomic levels.[70] To this latter point, however, Federal Reserve economists compared interest rates charged by institution type and borrower CRA eligibility and found no evidence of a bank subsidy to attract CRA loans.[71]

The evidence regarding the impact on credit losses is fairly consistent and does not support the contention that these laws have materially harmed institutions. Evidence from Self-Help's CAP confirms that CRA lending can be undertaken profitably, even in tumultuous times. CAP loans have gone to borrowers with a median income of $30,792. Half the borrowers had credit scores below 680, and most made down payments of under 5 percent. Despite the recent economic and housing market challenges, the portfolio has continued to perform relatively well and within the risk tolerance supported by the program's pricing.[72]

Agarwal and coauthors find no material difference in the risk factors for loans made by institutions undergoing exams versus those not being examined, and finds no increase in defaults associated with CRA exams, except for in 2004–06

---

65. Tuccillo, Flick, and Ranville (2005).
66. Courchane and Steeg (2005).
67. See www.fhlbanks.com/programs_affordhousing.htm.
68. Gunther (2000).
69. Avery, Bostic, and Canner (2000).
70. Willis (2009).
71. Canner and others (2002).
72. Quercia, Freeman, and Ratcliffe (2011).

originations, where defaults among examined banks were slightly higher than for banks not undergoing exams. Since most of the elevated defaults were due to loans made *after* the CRA exam or in tracts not eligible for CRA credit, this suggests that factors other than the CRA drove performance. In fact, the authors attribute this effect to the then vibrant private-label securities market.[73]

A review of goal-qualifying loans made by the GSEs from 2005 to 2008 found that loans that could be "clearly attributed to the increase in goals" constituted only 8 percent of their ninety-or-more-day delinquencies.[74] Weicher provides compelling evidence that factors other than HGs led the GSEs to pursue the risky subprime and Alt-A lending that ultimately accounted for a disproportionately higher share of their delinquencies.[75]

The FHLB economic model is quite different. Only 10 percent of an FHLB's net income is directed to funding the AHP programs, so the allocation varies with the FHLB's ability to pay it.

Risk to the Financial System?

Federal Reserve Board governors, the Comptroller of the Currency, and the Financial Crisis Inquiry Commission have all concluded that the CRA was not responsible for the risky lending that led to the foreclosure crisis.[76] Indeed, the evidence suggests that the CRA was a deterrent to risky lending.[77] Returning to the CAP study, a comparison of CAP borrowers with similar borrowers who received subprime and private-label mortgages shows that the private-label borrowers defaulted at three to five times the rate of comparable CAP-borrowers. CAP loans, motivated by both the CRA and HGs, were prime-priced, fully underwritten, long-term fixed-rate mortgages. In contrast, loans made through the private-label sector, which were generally not subject to CRA or GSE housing goals, carried more of the high-risk features that have been associated with increased likelihood of default.[78] Other studies have shown that loans made by CRA lenders within their assessment areas to LTMI borrowers were less likely to have risky product features than loans made by independent mortgage companies.[79] Federal Reserve economists found that CRA loans made in 2006 performed better than all loans combined and have had defaults a quarter of the

73. Agarwal and others (2012).
74. Seiler (2010).
75. Weicher (2010).
76. Kroszner (2009); OCC (2008); Financial Crisis Inquiry Commission (2010).
77. Reid and Laderman (2011); Traiger and Hinckley (2008).
78. Ding and others (2011).
79. Laderman and Reid (2009).

level of 2006 higher-priced loans.[80] In an empirical study of the impact of both the CRA and HGs on lending patterns, Avery and Brevoort summarize: "Our lender tests indicate that areas disproportionately served by lenders covered by the CRA experienced lower delinquency rates and less risky lending."[81]

Research has absolved the HGs of causing the financial crisis as well. Ghent, Hernández-Murillo, and Owyang do not find any increase in subprime lending or differential pricing that would be expected if lenders were seeking riskier loans to meet the HGs.[82] Thomas and Van Order conclude that the evidence proves that "Fannie and Freddie did not cause the subprime boom and bust."[83] Their evidence suggests that the goals explain only a small element of risk taking. Notably, less than 10 percent of the credit books of the GSEs were for loans with high loan-to-values (LTVs)—a proxy for lending to lower wealth households—as of June 2008, just prior to conservatorship and less than 1 percent were for borrowers with higher LTVs and a low credit score.[84] Instead, disproportionate credit losses arose from their Alt-A loans, which, with generally lower LTVs and higher loan amounts, did not, on net, help satisfy the chief LTMI lending goals.[85]

The influence of both the CRA and the GSEs waned during 2004–06 as the share of all mortgages made by CRA lenders declined,[86] and Fannie and Freddie's share of mortgage securitizations fell below that of the private-label sector. In fact, only 6 percent of the high-cost high-risk mortgages made during this period were eligible for CRA credit, accounting for only 1.3 percent of all originations.[87] As one scholar concludes, "Put simply, when so much subprime lending was performed by financial institutions acting beyond the scope of the CRA, it is hard to argue that the CRA was responsible for the type of risky lending that led to the financial crisis."[88]

Greater Access to Credit?

The ultimate question is whether these provisions produced systemic improvements in access to credit. On the one hand, there was a clear increase in lending to LTMI and minority borrowers and communities over the last three decades.

---

80. Bhutta and Canner (2013).

81. Avery and Brevoort (2011).

82. Ghent, Hernández-Murillo, and Owyang (2013).

83. Thomas and Van Order (2011, p. 25).

84. LTV more than 90 percent and Credit Score less than 620.

85. According to Seiler (2010, p. 11), "Alt-A and IO made it harder to achieve the goals but easier to achieve the purchase subgoals."

86. Essene and Apgar (2009).

87. Park (2010).

88. Brescia (2013)

On the other hand, since the mid-1990s, the CRA's influence has declined. And, despite the increase in HGs from 1995 to 2007, the share of overall benchmark market lending that went to target borrowers and neighborhoods remained largely static or even declined.

The empirical evidence generally suggests these rules have had, on the whole, modest but positive effects on overall credit flows. Earlier studies find increased volumes of lending, though broad-based growth in lending to LTMI borrowers and neighborhoods makes it hard to discern how much to attribute to the CRA.[89] A detailed analysis of 30 million loans made from 1993 to 2000 found that CRA-covered lenders originated a greater share and rejected a smaller share of CRA-eligible home purchase loans "than they would have if CRA were not in place."[90] Barr's review of the collective evidence finds "a statistically significant and economically important role for CRA."[91]

CRA-motivated lending also appears to have had positive effects on target neighborhoods. Avery, Calem, and Canner found mixed results in terms of the neighborhood outcomes associated with the CRA.[92] Reviewing the literature on neighborhood outcomes, An and Bostic noted that increased GSE housing goal lending was offset by a reduction in FHA lending.[93] This is still a positive outcome, as FHA loans are generally considered more expensive than conventional conforming loans, and it indicates increased options and competition for borrowers in those neighborhoods.

Indeed, Spader and Quercia found that CAP lending at the neighborhood level in 2000–02 offset only a small number of FHA loans, and that most of the CAP loans represented loans that would not otherwise have been made. But in 2004–06, CAP loans were much more likely to supplant subprime lending, which carried higher default risk, suggesting that such loans can have beneficial neighborhood impacts in a variety of market environments.[94]

Using discontinuity analysis of neighborhood lending patterns, Bhutta found a statistically significant if modest increase in bank lending attributable to the CRA—sixty-five loans per census tract over a nine-year period.[95] Using the same approach, Bhutta found a similarly modest effect associated with the geographically based HG of twenty-three originations per tract over a seven-year period, concluding that "these results do not provide much support of the notion that the

89. Avery and others (1996); Belsky, Schill, and Yezer (2001); Evanoff and Siegal (1996); Litan and others (2001); Gunther (2000); Barr (2005).

90. Joint Center for Housing Studies (2002, p. 76).

91. Barr (2005, p.164).

92. Avery, Calem, and Canner (2003).

93. An and Bostic (2007).

94. Spader and Quercia (2012).

95. Bhutta (2011).

GSE act had a major impact on homeownership and household debt by expanding credit supply to marginal groups from the mid-1990s to the mid-2000s."[96]

Summary of the Evidence

Were the CRA and the HGs effective, ineffective, or disastrous? The evidence confirms that these DTS provisions changed lenders' basic approach to serving LTMI and minority borrowers. It also confirms that institutions have not compromised safety and soundness in efforts to satisfy these provisions. Finally, while there is strong empirical evidence that credit flows to these segments have improved, they have not been substantial enough to address the market failures that DTS seek to correct.

Critically, however, DTS may have affected the credit availability in LTMI and minority communities in a qualitative manner. If DTS did not exist, there would likely be housing finance available, but less of it, and it would be qualitatively different. Even with DTS, a two-tracked credit system emerged, but it would likely have been worse without DTS.

Barriers to Effective DTS

Several factors appear to have limited the effectiveness of DTS, and going forward, DTS need to be crafted to address these factors. The effectiveness of DTS has been undermined by three factors: changes in the institutional composition of the mortgage market, regulatory failures, and the advent of risk-based pricing and "reverse redlining."

Change in the Mortgage Market

Since the CRA and HGs were instituted, the financial landscape has undergone a series of tectonic shifts in the sources of credit, underwriting, and terms of credit. These changes have significant impact on the flows of mortgage credit to minority and LTMI households and communities. The CRA and HGs have not kept pace with these changes. For example, the CRA, despite some modernization attempts, is still largely predicated on the structure of the financial services market in 1977, when direct mortgage lending was done overwhelmingly by local depositories.[97] CRA assessment areas are generally the counties in which a depository institution has offices or deposit-taking ATMs. By 2006, however, only about 25 percent of mortgages were made by depository institutions in

---

96. Bhutta (2010).

97. In 2000, citing increased regulatory flexibility, better information technology, and increased flow of mortgages to minority and LTMI communities particularly from institutions not covered by the CRA, Gunther claimed that the CRA was no longer relevant. Gunther (2000).

markets where they had a physical presence.[98] Meanwhile, non-bank lenders had come to originate a large share of mortgages.

The optional inclusion of non-bank affiliates in CRA exams allowed depository institutions to provide limited service to underserved markets, while serving that same segment with a non-bank arm that specialized in higher-cost products.[99] From 1994 to 2007, banks grew the LTMI share of their lending faster among subsidiaries/affiliates than through their depositories.[100] Depositories also began making more of their loans outside of their assessment areas. In 1990 banks of all sizes originated about 70 percent of their mortgages within their assessment areas, but by 2006 the large banks originated more mortgages outside their assessment areas than within them.[101]

A similar story occurred with the HGs. The GSEs lost market share rapidly to the private-label securitization market from 2004 to 2006.[102] This meant that the HGs, like the CRA, simply applied to a smaller part of the market. In fact, the majority of toxic loans that triggered the recent financial crisis were financed by the market sectors that were subject to neither the CRA nor the HGs: nondepository lenders and private-label securitization.

Regulatory Failure

The effectiveness of DTS is necessarily dependent on their enforcement. DTS are only enforced publicly; no private right of action exists. History suggests that regulators have been lenient in their application of the duties. The CRA was designed to discipline regulators who disregarded the new fair lending regulations,[103] yet over the course of the CRA's history, few sanctions have been levied for failure to engage in sufficient community reinvestment.[104] It is hard, however, to attribute this to industry success in community reinvestment. Rather, it seems to reflect regulatory enforcement attitudes.

Even so, regulators have staked out different positions in enforcing the CRA. In the first decade after passage, while the FHLB board labored to implement the law, the Federal Reserve was blatant in "resistance to CRA," never declining a merger application and unconditionally approving many that were strongly protested.[105] In 1990 the Office of Thrift Supervision (OTS) (successor to the

98. Essene and Apgar (2009).

99. The CRA itself only covers depositories. The optional inclusion of affiliates is part of the regulatory implementation.

100. Avery, Courchane, and Zorn (2009).

101. Avery, Courchane, and Zorn (2009).

102. Levitin and Wachter (2012).

103. Immergluck (2009).

104. Barr (2005).

105. Art (1987, p. 1122).

FHLB board) gave out more than twice as many unsatisfactory ratings as the other regulators, but as regulatory competition for chartering increased, CRA laxity became a method for federal bank regulators to distinguish themselves and thereby attract chartering business (which provides the bulk of some regulators' operating budgets).[106] Thus, by 2007 OTS was awarding about twice as many "outstanding" evaluations as the other federal regulators. Moreover, in a 2005 joint rulemaking, the OTS took a separate path from other regulators and exempted 88 percent of its supervised institutions from significant CRA obligations, and, perhaps more important, set a precedent for regulator defection.[107]

The GSEs, in contrast, have met their goals almost consistently, but there are no material repercussions for failing. In the most recent HGs proposal, the regulator set the goals to levels well below those set previously, and below current performance of the GSEs.[108]

DTS measures were motivated in large part by public engagement. The CRA provided explicit ways for the public to regulate the regulators. The HG process also allows for public comment. Over time, however, the public voice has been muffled. For example, since 1990 there has been tremendous volume in bank merger activity, but the Federal Reserve has only held thirteen public meetings on community reinvestment in relation to mergers. Regulators have pointedly refused to consider CRA agreements in the merger approval process, yet merger approval is one of the primary CRA enforcement levers.[109]

Reverse Redlining and Risk-Based Pricing

Another factor that undermined the effectiveness of DTS was the rise of risk-based pricing in mortgage underwriting. New, data-driven technologies for assessing and sorting borrower risk enabled lenders to charge based on a borrower's characteristics and thus eschewed the rate-based credit rationing of earlier underwriting methods. The prospect of high returns also enabled lenders to lend in communities they previously saw as too risky. In 2005 Federal Reserve Board Chairman Alan Greenspan applauded these innovations, noting that "lenders have taken advantage of credit-scoring models and other techniques for efficiently extending credit to a broader spectrum of consumers. . . . These improvements have led to rapid growth in subprime mortgage lending. . . . Unquestionably, innovation and deregulation have vastly expanded credit availability to virtually all income classes."[110]

---

106. On chartering competition, see generally Levitin (2009, 2013).
107. See Marsico (2006).
108. See Federal Housing Finance Agency (2012).
109. Taylor and Silver (2009).
110. Greenspan (2005).

Risk-based pricing, however, did not simply result in the extension of credit where it had not been granted before. Instead, credit was granted on substantively different terms than the standard, prime-priced, long-term, fixed-rate, fully amortized mortgage. As a result, the subprime and alternative lending that emerged with risk-based pricing was not evenly distributed. Although most subprime borrowers were white, and most subprime loans were made in higher-income neighborhoods, a disproportionate share of this lending was concentrated in LTMI and minority communities[111] and among LTMI and minority buyers even after controlling for risk factors.[112]

DTS efforts were supposed to encourage well-regulated depository institutions to lend. Despite the progress made in the 1990s, these markets still suffered from lack of equal access to credit. Essene and Apgar report that borrowers in high minority, lower-income neighborhoods were less likely to receive a loan from a CRA-regulated lender lending in their assessment area than borrowers in higher-income and whiter neighborhoods.[113] Areas that exhibited "high latent demand" in 1996, by virtue of high mortgage denial rates, experienced the most growth in loans originated for sale to private-label securitization conduits in 2002–05, and subsequently experienced the elevated defaults associated with such loans. These areas were characterized by lower socioeconomic conditions and a higher share of minority residents.[114] Thus, once redlined communities became targets of "reverse redlining." In this sense, the concentration of high-cost, high-default lending in LTMI and minority markets was a result of inadequate access to standard prime credit.

The Home Mortgage Disclosure Act, the CRA, and the HGs were inadequate to address the change in credit terms. The act did not contain information about pricing until 2004, and even then did not contain adequate borrower and product information. The CRA did not consider loans made outside of assessment areas or loans made by depositories' affiliates except by a depository's request. The GSEs were allowed to count qualified high-cost loans, as well as nonprime loans packaged into private-label mortgage-backed securities that they purchased, toward their HGs.

A major lesson from the housing bubble should be that loan characteristics are important. To the extent that the policy goal of the CRA and HGs is to ensure equal access to mortgage credit, it must also be equal access to similar products, structured to be sustainable and affordable.

---

111. See Ding and others (2008).
112. Jackson and Burlingame (2007).
113. Essene and Apgar (2009).
114. Mian and Sufi (2009).

Since the financial crisis, some of these shortcomings have been addressed by the Housing and Economic Recovery Act (HERA) of 2008. But these adjustments are still inadequate and nothing has been done to bring DTS in line with the realities of the current mortgage finance market. Overall, so much has worked against effective implementation of DTS—lack of market coverage, weak regulatory engagement, and the development of risk-based pricing—that we cannot really know how effective they could be if properly designed and implemented.

Rethinking Duties to Serve

The aftermath of the housing bubble presents an opportunity to rebuild DTS. The subsequent regulatory focus has been on rules emphasizing safety and soundness in mortgage lending. A spate of new and pending regulations aimed at ensuring safety and soundness portend an institutionalization of postcrisis credit constriction. These new policies include Title XIV of the Dodd-Frank Wall Street Reform and Consumer Protection Act and its regulatory implementation by the CFPB, particularly the ability-to-repay requirement, new mortgage servicing regulations, and ongoing changes in FHA's single-family mortgage insurance. These changes could greatly and permanently limit the availability of credit, especially from prime, well-regulated sources, and particularly to borrowers with less wealth and income. If safety-and-soundness regulations are not adequately balanced with efforts to ensure access to credit broadly and equitably, they could exacerbate disparities in access to the mortgage finance system and in so doing, undermine the market in many communities.

Now as much as ever, DTS need to be understood as a fundamental part of the financial system. The federal government is constitutive of the financial market from the most basic levels, such as enforcement of contracts, up to direct assumption of credit risk on mortgages, deposits, and secondary market entities. The financial system only operates because of the legal and financial infrastructure provided by the government. This infrastructure is costly to provide. Moreover, private market participants benefit from government support of the market. This is perhaps most obvious in the case of depositories with FDIC insurance; absent FDIC insurance, depositories' cost of funds would presumably be higher and their deposit funding base smaller.

The benefits of federal support for financial markets extend past depositories, however. Absent the federal government's support, it is difficult to imagine a secondary mortgage market of any size, thereby forcing more balance-sheet lending by financial institutions, which would in turn limit the volume of business they could do. Similarly, non-banks benefit indirectly from federal deposit insurance as they rely on insured depositories for their warehouse lines of credit. Absent federal deposit insurance and the liquidity from the secondary mortgage market, warehouse line availability might be more limited or more expensive, or both.

Because of the public cost and private benefits from constituting financial markets, it is quite reasonable to require that financial services firms operate in the public interest, as well as in their own private financial interests. Fulfilling certain public mandates is a precondition of market participation and enjoyment of the federal government's support for the financial marketplace. As the federal government has a deep policy interest and, arguably, duty to ensure the availability of economic opportunities to all Americans, DTS should be seen as a basic obligation of all financial institutions.

Accordingly, we suggest a quartet of reforms to make future DTS more effective and appropriate to the modern mortgage marketplace. Implementing these reforms calls for more complexity than it is possible to present in this paper, but future success will rest on these fundamental principles.

DTS Should Apply Universally to the Entire Primary Market

DTS should cover the entire marketplace, depositories and nondepositories alike, so we do not repeat the situation where nonregulated entities have a competitive advantage and can crowd out regulated purveyors. Nondepository lenders are virtually all dependent on depositories for warehouse lines of credit and other funding; accordingly, as they benefit indirectly from federal support of depositories, they should be held to similar standards. DTS should depend on activities, not on the identity of the financial institution. Applying DTS to all mortgage lending institutions would help reduce regulatory arbitrage incentives.

DTS Should Apply Equally for All Secondary Market Entities

DTS must apply not only at the primary market level, but also at the secondary market level, and the primary and secondary market DTS must be aligned. Application of DTS to the secondary market should not be restricted to the GSEs or whatever federally backed entity or entities eventually fill their role; it should also apply to depositories that are active in funding the primary mortgage market. The very largest banks have outgrown the role that the CRA originally envisioned for them. These institutions have national service areas and undertake significant lending through affiliates and subsidiaries that do not fall under the CRA. They also serve secondary market functions through warehouse and wholesale lending, and securitization. As such they should be subject to additional and exceptional DTS, akin to those applied to the mortgage GSEs.

DTS Must Be Good Business but Must Also Be Supported by Evaluative Tools, Metrics, and Incentives

While we believe that DTS should be understood as a cost of doing business in exchange for privileges previously described, we acknowledge that specific DTS provisions must make business sense. The evidence indicates that DTS activities can be undertaken profitably, sometimes even more so than nontargeted business lines as in the subprime lending spree.

There are proven ways to extend mortgages to target segments in ways that mitigate risk—through products, underwriting, servicing, and partnerships. However, the experience to date with DTS shows us that just because a DTS activity is profitable does not necessarily mean that lenders will pursue it. After the financial crisis, regulatory policy, investors, and lenders have become risk-averse as new rules and practices are put in place, making it harder for all but the strongest borrowers to get credit.[115] It is therefore essential that DTS mechanisms act as a thumb on the scale to lead institutions to invest in and sustain meaningful DTS activities over the long term.

DTS experience to date shows us that profitability alone is not enough to change resource allocation. The incentives for compliance must encourage long-term investment in targeted activities, linked to measurable outcomes, without encouraging excessive risk taking. This includes appropriate sanctions and rewards, as well as tools and benefits for compliance that have a tangible economic benefit or a risk-mitigating effect. Material incentives could include a menu of sanctions and benefits, such as various levels of fines, adjustments to the cost of FHLB advances or dividends, guaranty fees, or deposit insurance. These activities could be staged so that regulators have alternatives to "nuclear options" like cease-and-desist orders and denial of bank mergers. Importantly, the soundness imperative should include consequences for serving underserved segments with inferior alternatives. DTS must mean serving all communities with appropriate products.

The metrics employed should be both quantitative and qualitative, neither relying on good faith efforts alone, nor solely on hard quotas. Rather, they should be framed around identified financing gaps and policy goals and represent actionable objectives that relate to an institution's function within the system.

In terms of tools, requirements should be accompanied by mechanisms that can facilitate expanding access safely. One example is a research and development fund to be built into the secondary market to support efforts to safely serve more borrowers.[116] In a similar vein, the Affordable Housing Trust Fund and the

---

115. Parrott and Zandi (2013).
116. Mortgage Finance Working Group (2011, 2014).

Capital Magnet Fund, envisioned in HERA but not yet funded, are important complementary tools. Such tools, of course, should be deployed alongside, not instead of, DTS obligations. On a smaller scale, the AHP program, taken as part of a CRA effort, is a model to build on; doubtless many depositories have earned CRA credit in connection with projects that benefited from the AHP program. Similarly, regulatory waivers from some consumer protection laws (namely disclosure requirements of dubious effectiveness) could be granted to approved test programs, much as the CFPB's Project Catalyst is considering enabling innovations in consumer disclosures.

DTS Must Have a Credible Enforcement Mechanism

DTS are unlikely to be effective absent true commitment from federal regulators to their application. To ensure that DTS are in fact observed, regulators must be held accountable, which requires greater transparency in the regulatory review process. Public participation is a hallmark of the creation of these rules, as well as their continued improvement and effectiveness.[117] Yet while the CRA has the public role conceptually right, in practice the public role has become muted. Transparency of data, public input into the planning process, and public review of performance of both institutions and regulators should be reinvigorated and central to all DTS provisions. Moreover, the public should be given greater leverage so that regulators cannot simply ignore DTS. One possibility is to create an independent DTS commission, ombudsman, or inspector general (perhaps based in the CFPB, which has an explicit access to credit mission) charged with reviewing regulatory enforcement of DTS and formally commenting on regulatory decisions (such as merger applications under the current CRA).[118] The idea is to provide sufficient resources for an institutional actor whose single duty is to advocate for DTS for all regulators (thereby reducing regulatory arbitrage incentives).

Conclusion

The original motivations for DTS were about disparate access to credit, as measured by gaps in lending and denial rates between borrowers and communities that are white or higher income and minority or LTMI borrowers and communities, respectively. But by the mid-2000s, these disparities manifested in differences in terms of credit, with minority and LTMI borrowers and neighborhood residents much more likely to receive loans with disadvantageous terms.

117. See, for example, MacDonald (1995).

118. 12 U.S.C. § 5511(a): "The Bureau shall seek to implement and, where applicable, enforce Federal consumer financial law consistently for the purpose of ensuring that all consumers have access to markets for consumer financial products and services."

Today we are facing a potential "back to the future" where tight credit is disparately constraining access to credit for minority and LTMI households and communities. At the same time, we are facing a massive demographic shift in household formation and housing demand. Future housing demand will be driven by a greater share of LTMI, minority, and younger households.[119] These demographics mean that market stability converges with the access-related issues of equity. To the extent that LTMI and minority borrowers have difficulty accessing the housing finance markets, the effects will be felt in those communities and more broadly because of the suppressed demand for home purchases. Persistent lending disparities that prevent these potential homebuyers from obtaining mortgages could have broad and far-reaching effects by depressing the real estate economy and curbing household wealth formation.

Certainly, caution is warranted in the wake of the devastating crisis that grew out of the lending excesses of the mid-2000s, when unregulated lenders disproportionately targeted traditionally underserved segments with products that were less safe. These lenders were less likely to be subject to the CRA,[120] and the private-label securitization channel that financed the majority of loans during the bubble years of 2004–06 was not subject to any HGs. It would be a regrettable mistake to conflate reckless (and frequently fraudulent) lending based on inadequate underwriting and risky repayment terms with prudent lending that enables lower wealth and lower income borrowers to safely become homeowners.

Each of the competing tensions—safety and soundness on the one hand and access on the other—carries its own systemic risks. Leaving a large part of the market underserved produces a negative externality on the entire economy, while miss-serving market segments with unproven products contributes to a global economic crisis. Neither approach serves to foster equity and economic opportunity. Effectively resolving these tensions presents another strong rationale for mechanisms that explicitly motivate lenders to balance access to credit with safety and soundness to all potential homebuyers.

References

Agarwal, Sumit, and others. 2012. "Did the Community Reinvestment Act (CRA) Lead to Risky Lending?" Working Paper 18609. Cambridge, Mass.: National Bureau of Economic Research (www.nber.org/papers/w18609).

An, Xudong, and Raphael W. Bostic. 2007. "GSE Activity, FHA Feedback, and Implications for the Efficacy of the Affordable Housing Goals." *Journal of Real Estate Finance and Economics* 36, no. 2: 207–31.

---

119. Masnick, McCue, and Belsky (2010).
120. Gunther (2000).

Art, Robert C. 1987. "Social Responsibility in Bank Credit Decisions: The Community Reinvestment Act One Decade Later." *Pacific Law Journal* 18: 1071–40 (http://hein online.org).

Avery, Robert B., Raphael W. Bostic, and Glenn B. Canner. 2000. "CRA Special Lending Programs." *Federal Reserve Bulletin* 86: 711–31 (www.federalreserve.gov/pubs/bulletin/2000/1100lead.pdf).

Avery, Robert B., and Kenneth P. Brevoort. 2011. "The Subprime Crisis: Is Government Housing Policy to Blame?" Finance and Economics Discussion Paper 2011-36. Washington: Federal Reserve Board (www.federalreserve.gov/pubs/feds/2011/201136/index.html).

Avery, Robert B., Paul S. Calem, and Glenn B. Canner. 2003. "The Effects of the Community Reinvestment Act on Local Communities." In *Proceedings of Seeds of Growth: Sustainable Community Development: What Works, What Doesn't, and Why.* Conference sponsored by the Federal Reserve System (www.federalreserve.gov/communityaffairs/national/ca_conf_suscommdev/pdf/cannerglen.pdf).

Avery, Robert B., Marsha J. Courchane, and Peter M. Zorn. 2009. "The CRA within a Changing Financial Landscape." In *Revisiting the CRA: Perspectives on the Future of the Community Reinvestment Act.* Federal Reserve Banks of Boston and San Francisco.

Avery, Robert B., and others. 1996. "Credit Risk, Credit Scoring, and the Performance of Home Mortgages." *Federal Reserve Bulletin* 82 (July): 621–48.

Barr, Michael S. 2005. "Credit Where It Counts: The Community Reinvestment Act and Its Critics." *New York University Law Review* 80, no. 2: 513–652.

Belsky, Eric, Michael Schill, and Anthony Yezer. 2001. *The Effect of the Community Reinvestment Act on Bank and Thrift Home Purchase Mortgage Lending.* Research note. Harvard University, Joint Center for Housing Studies.

Bernanke, Ben S. 2007. "The Community Reinvestment Act: Its Evolution and New Challenges." Speech at the Community Affairs Research Conference, Washington. March 30 (www.federalreserve.gov/newsevents/speech/bernanke20070330a.htm).

———. 2012. "The Economic Recovery and Economic Policy." Speech at the New York Economic Club. November 20 (www.federalreserve.gov/newsevents/speech/bernanke20121120a.htm).

Bhutta, Neil. 2010. "GSE Activity and Mortgage Supply in Lower-Income and Minority Neighborhoods: The Effect of the Affordable Housing Goals." *Journal of Real Estate Finance and Economics* 45, no. 1: 238–61.

———. 2011. "The Community Reinvestment Act and Mortgage Lending to Lower-Income Borrowers and Neighborhoods." *Journal of Law and Economics* 54, no. 4: 953–83.

Bhutta, Neil, and Glenn Canner. 2013. "Mortgage Market Conditions and Borrower Outcomes: Evidence from the 2012 HMDA Data and Matched HMDA-Credit Record Data." *Federal Reserve Bulletin* 99, no. 4: 1–58 (www.federalreserve.gov/pubs/bulletin/2013/pdf/2012_HMDA.pdf).

Bocian, Debbie Gruenstein, Wei Li, Carolina Reid, and Roberto G. Quercia. 2011. *Lost Ground: Disparities in Mortgage Lending and Foreclosures.* Durham, N.C.: Center for Responsible Lending.

Bostic, Raphael W., and Breck L. Robinson. 2004. "Community Banking and Mortgage Credit Availability: The Impact of CRA Agreements." *Journal of Banking and Finance* 28, no. 12: 3069–95.

Brendsel, Leland. 1991. "Secondary Mortgage Markets and Redlining." Testimony before the U.S. Senate Subcommittee on Consumer and Regulatory Affairs of the Senate Committee on Banking, Housing, and Urban Affairs. February 28 (http://babel. hathitrust.org/cgi/pt?id=pst.000018076325;seq=1;view=1up).

Brescia, Raymond H. 2013. "The Community Reinvestment Act: Guilty, but Not as Charged." Working Paper (draft). Albany Law School. March 2 (http://ssrn.com/ abstract=2227520).

Bricker, Jesse, and others. 2012. "Changes in U.S. Family Finances from 2007 to 2010: Evidence from the Survey of Consumer Finances." *Federal Reserve Bulletin* 98, no. 2 (www. federalreserve.gov/pubs/ bulletin/2012/pdf/scf12.pdf).

Canner, Glenn B., and others. 2002. "Does the Community Reinvestment Act (CRA) Cause Banks to Provide a Subsidy to Some Mortgage Borrowers?" Finance and Economics Discussion Paper 2012-19. Washington: Federal Reserve Board (www.federal reserve.gov/pubs/feds/2002/200219/200219abs.html).

CFPB (Consumer Financial Protection Bureau). 2012. *Bulletin 2012–04 (Fair Lending)* (http://files.consumerfinance.gov/f/201404_cfpb_bulletin_lending_discrimination. pdf).

Courchane, Marsha J., and Darcy Steeg. 2005. "A Comparative Analysis of FHL Bank Member Mortgage Lending." Washington: ERS Group and Welch Consulting. April 27.

Dahl, Drew, Douglas D. Evanoff, and Michael F. Spivey. 2010. "The Community Reinvestment Act and Targeted Mortgage Lending." *Journal of Money, Credit and Banking* 42, no. 7: 1351–72.

Ding, Lei, and others. 2008. "Neighborhood Patterns of High-Cost Lending: The Case of Atlanta." *Journal of Affordable Housing and Community Development Law* 17, no. 3: 193–217.

———. 2011. "Risky Borrowers or Risky Mortgages: Disaggregating Effects Using Propensity Score Models." *Journal of Real Estate Research* 33, no. 2: 245–78.

Essene, Ren S., and William C. Apgar. 2009. "The 30th Anniversary of the CRA: Restructuring the CRA to Address the Mortgage Finance Revolution." In *Revisiting the CRA: Perspectives on the Future of the Community Reinvestment Act,* edited by Prabal Chakrabarti and others, pp. 12–19. Federal Reserve Banks of Boston and San Francisco.

Evanoff, Douglas D., and Lewis M. Siegal. 1996. "CRA and Fair Lending Regulations: Resulting Trends in Mortgage Lending." *Economic Perspectives* 20, no. 6: 19–46.

Federal Housing Finance Agency. 2010. "2010–2011 Enterprise Housing Goals; Enterprise Book-Entry Procedures." *Code of Federal Regulations,* title 12, parts 1249, 1282. RIN 2590-AA26. Final Rule (www.fhfa.gov/webfiles/16603/finalruleaffhsggoals 9210.pdf).

———. 2012. "2012–2014 Enterprise Housing Goals. Final Rule." *Federal Register* 77, no. 219 (www.gpo.gov/fdsys/pkg/FR-2012-11-13/pdf/2012-27121.pdf).

FFIEC (Federal Financial Institutions Examination Council). 2012. "History of HMDA" (www.ffiec.gov/hmda/history2.htm).

Financial Crisis Inquiry Commission. 2010. "Government Sponsored Enterprises and the Financial Crisis." Preliminary staff report. April 7 (http://fcic-static.law.stanford.edu/cdn_media/fcic-reports/2010-0409-GSEs.pdf).

———. 2011. *The Financial Crisis Inquiry Report.* U.S. Government Printing Office. January.

Fishbein, Allen J. 2003. "Filling the Half-Empty Glass: The Role of Community Advocacy in Redefining the Public Responsibilities of Government-Sponsored Housing Enterprises." In *Organizing Access to Capital—Advocacy and the Democratization of Financial Institutions,* edited by Gregory D. Squires, pp. 102–18. Temple University Press.

Ghent, Andra C., Rubén Hernández-Murillo, and Michael T. Owyang. 2013. "Did Affordable Housing Legislation Contribute to the Subprime Securities Boom?" Working Paper (www.public.asu.edu/~aghent/research/AHG_Oct29_2013.pdf).

Greenspan, Alan. 2005. "Consumer Finance." Remarks at the Federal Reserve System's Fourth Annual Community Affairs Research Conference. Washington, April 8 (www.federalreserve.gov/boarddocs/speeches/2005/20050408/default.htm).

Gunther, Jeffrey W. 2000. "Should CRA Stand for Community Redundancy Act?" *Regulation* 23, no. 3: 56–60.

Hoffman, Susan, and Mark Cassell. 2002. "What Are the Federal Home Loan Banks Up To? Emerging Views of the Purpose among Institutional Leadership." *Public Administration Review* 62, no. 4: 461–70.

HUD (Department of Housing and Urban Development). 1998. "HUD Prepares to Set New Housing Goals." U.S. Housing Market Conditions Summary. HUD, Office of Policy Development and Research (www.huduser.org/Periodicals/ushmc/summer98/summary-2.html).

Immergluck, Dan. 2009. *Foreclosed: High-Risk Lending, Deregulation, and the Undermining of America's Mortgage Market.* Cornell University Press.

Jackson, Howell E., and Laurie Burlingame. 2007. "Kickbacks or Compensation: The Case of Yield Spread Premiums." *Stanford Journal of Law, Business and Finance* 12 (Spring): 289–361.

Joint Center for Housing Studies. 2002. *The 25th Anniversary of the Community Reinvestment Act: Access to Capital in an Evolving Financial Services System.* Harvard University.

Kroszner, Randall. 2009. "The Community Reinvestment Act and the Recent Mortgage Crisis." In *Revisiting the CRA: Perspectives on the Future of the Community Reinvestment Act,* edited by Prabal Chakrabarti and others, pp. 8–11. Federal Reserve Banks of Boston and San Francisco.

Laderman, Elizabeth, and Carolina Reid. 2009. "CRA Lending during the Suprime Meltdown." In *Revisiting the CRA: Perspectives on the Future of the Community Reinvestment Act,* edited by Prabal Chakrabarti and others, pp. 115–33. Federal Reserve Banks of Boston and San Francisco.

Levine, Martin. 1993. "Fannie Mae's Affordable Housing Initiatives: Historical Perspective and Future Prospects." In *Housing America: Mobilizing Bankers, Builders and*

Communities to Solve the Nation's Affordable Housing Crisis, edited by Jess Lederman, pp. 63–72. Chicago: Probus Publishing.

Levitin, Adam J. 2009. "Hydraulic Regulation: Regulating Consumer Credit Markets Upstream." *Yale Journal on Regulation* 26, no. 2: 143–227.

———. 2013. "The Consumer Financial Protection Bureau: An Introduction." *Review of Banking and Financial Law* 31, no. 2: 321–70.

Levitin, Adam J., and Susan M. Wachter. 2012. "Explaining the Housing Bubble." *Georgetown Law Journal* 100, no. 4: 1177–258.

———. 2013. "The Public Option in Housing Finance." *U.C. Davis Law Review* 46, no. 4: 1111–39.

Listokin, David, Elvin K. Wyly, Larry Keating, Kristopher M. Rengert, and Barbara Listokin. 2000. "Making New Mortgage Markets, Case Studies of Institutions, Home Buyers and Communities." *Housing Facts and Findings* 2, no. 3. Fannie Mae Foundation.

Litan, Robert E., Nicolas P. Retsinas, Eric S. Belsky, Gary Fauth, Maureen Kennedy, and Paul Leonard. 2001. *The Community Reinvestment Act after Financial Modernization: A Final Report.* U.S. Treasury Department.

Ludwig, Eugene, James Kamihachi, and Laura Toh. 2009. "The Community Reinvestment Act: Past Successes and Future Opportunities." In *Revisiting the CRA: Perspectives on the Future of the Community Reinvestment Act,* edited by Prabal Chakrabarti and others, pp. 84–104. Federal Reserve Banks of Boston and San Francisco.

MacDonald, Heather. 1995. "The Politics of Mortgage Finance: Implementing FIRREA's Reforms." *Journal of Planning, Education, and Research* 15, no. 1: 3–15.

Marsico, Richard D. 2006. "The 2004–2005 Amendments to the Community Reinvestment Act Regulations: For Communities, One Step Forward and Three Steps Back." *Clearinghouse Review* 39 (January-February): 534–45.

Masnick, George S., Daniel McCue, and Eric S. Belsky. 2010. "Updated 2010–2020 Household and New Home Demand Projections." Working Paper W10-9. Harvard University, Joint Center for Housing Studies.

McCool, Thomas J. 2005. "Federal Home Loan Bank System: An Overview of Changes Affecting the System." Testimony before the Committee on Banking, Housing and Urban Affairs, U.S. Senate. U.S. Government Accountability Office.

Mian, Atif, and Amir Sufi. 2009. "The Consequences of Mortgage Credit Expansion: Evidence from the U.S. Mortgage Default Crisis." *Quarterly Journal of Economics* 124, no. 4: 1449–96.

Mortgage Finance Working Group. 2011. *A Responsible Market for Housing Finance.* Washington: Center for American Progress. January.

———. 2014. *Expanding Access through Responsible Innovation: The Market Access Fund.* Washington: Center for American Progress. January.

National Community Reinvestment Coalition. 2007. *CRA Commitments.* Washington.

OCC (Office of the Comptroller of the Currency). 2008. "Comptroller Dugan Says CRA Not Responsible for Subprime Lending Abuses." Press release. November 19 (www.occ.gov/news-issuances/news-releases/2008/nr-occ-2008-136.html).

Park, Kevin. 2010. "CRA Did Not Cause the Foreclosure Crisis." Policy brief. University of North Carolina, Center for Community Capital (www.ccc.unc.edu/cra.php).

Parrott, Jim, and Mark Zandi. 2013. *Opening the Credit Box*. Washington: Urban Institute (www.urban.org/UploadedPDF/412910-Opening-the-Credit-Box.pdf).

Quercia, Roberto, Allison Freeman, and Janneke Ratcliffe. 2011. *Regaining the Dream: How to Renew the Promise of Homeownership for America's Working Families*. Brookings.

Quercia, Roberto G., and Kevin A. Park. 2012. *Sustaining and Expanding the Market: The Public Purpose of the Federal Housing Administration*. University of North Carolina, Center for Community Capital (http://ccc.unc.edu/contentitems/sustaining-and-expanding-the-market-the-public-purpose-of-the-federal-housing-administration/).

Quercia, Roberto, Janneke Ratcliffe, and Michael A. Stegman. 2009. "The Community Reinvestment Act: Outstanding and Needs to Improve." In *Revisiting the CRA: Perspectives on the Future of the Community Reinvestment Act*, edited by Prabal Chakrabarti and others, pp. 47–58. Federal Reserve Banks of Boston and San Francisco.

Reid, Carolina, and Elizabeth Laderman. 2011. "Constructive Credit: Revisiting the Performance of the Community Reinvestment Act during the Subprime Crisis." In *The American Mortgage System: Crisis and Reform*, edited by Susan M. Wachter and Marvin M. Smith, pp. 159–86. University of Pennsylvania Press.

Reid, Carolina, and others. 2013. *Debunking the CRA Myth—Again*. Research report. University of North Carolina, Center for Community Capital (http://ccc.sites.unc.edu/files/2013/02/DebunkingCRAMyth.pdf).

Schwartz, Alex. 1998. "Bank Lending to Minority and Low-Income Households and Neighborhoods: Do Community Reinvestment Agreements Make a Difference?" *Journal of Urban Affairs* 20, no. 3: 269.

Seiler, Robert S., Jr. 2010. "Affordable Housing Goals and the Performance of Single-Family Mortgages Acquired by Fannie Mae and Freddie Mac, 2004–2008." Presentation at the FDIC–Federal Reserve System Symposium on Mortgages and the Future of Housing Finance. Arlington, Va., October 26.

Shapiro, Thomas, Tatjana Meschede, and Sam Osoro. 2013. "The Roots of the Widening Racial Wealth Gap: Explaining the Black-White Economic Divide." Research and policy brief. Brandeis University, Heller School for Social Policy and Management, Institute on Assets and Social Policy.

Shlay, Anne B. 1999. "Influencing the Agents of Urban Structure: Evaluating the Effects of Community Reinvestment Organizing on Bank Residential Lending Practices." *Urban Affairs Review* 35, no. 2: 247–78 (http://uar.sagepub.com/cgi/content/abstract/35/2/247).

Spader, Jonathan S., and Roberto G. Quercia. 2012. "CRA Lending in a Changing Context: Evidence of Interaction with FHA and Subprime Originations." *Journal of Real Estate Finance and Economics* 44, no. 4: 505–25.

Taylor, John, and Josh Silver. 2009. "The Community Reinvestment Act: 30 Years of Wealth Building and What We Must Do to Finish the Job." In *Revisiting the CRA: Perspectives on the Future of the Community Reinvestment Act*, edited by Prabal Chakrabarti and others, pp. 148–59. Federal Reserve Banks of Boston and San Francisco.

Taylor, Paul, Rakesh Kochhar, Richard Fry, Gabriel Valesco, and Seth Motel. 2011. *Twenty-to-One: Wealth Gaps Rise to Record Highs between Whites, Blacks, Hispanics*. Washington: Pew Research Center (www.pewsocialtrends.org/files/2011/07/SDT-Wealth-Report_7-26-11_FINAL.pdf).

Temkin, Kenneth, Roberto G. Quercia, and George C. Galster. 2000. "The Impact of Secondary Mortgage Market Guidelines on Affordable and Fair Lending." *Review of Black Political Economy* 28, no. 2: 29–52.

Thomas, Jason, and Robert Van Order. 2011. "Housing Policy, Subprime Markets and Fannie Mae and Freddie Mac: What We Know, What We Think We Know, and What We Don't Know." Working Paper. George Washington University (http://business.gwu.edu/creua/research-papers/files/fannie-freddie.pdf).

Traiger and Hinckley. 2008. *The Community Reinvestment Act: A Welcome Anomaly in the Foreclosure Crisis: Indications That the CRA Deterred Irresponsible Lending in the 15 Most Populous U.S. Metropolitan Areas*. January 7. New York.

Tuccillo, John A., Frederick E. Flick, and Michelle R. Ranville. 2005. *The Impact of Advances on Federal Home Loan Bank Portfolio Lending: A Statistical Analysis*. Arlington, Va. (www.fhlbanks.com/assets/pdfs/section-newsevents/related_research/Tuccillo Report.pdf).

Weicher, John C. 2010. *The Affordable Housing Goals, Homeownership and Risk: Some Lessons from Past Efforts to Regulate the GSEs*. Paper presented at the conference Past, Present, and Future of the Government-Sponsored Enterprises, Federal Reserve Bank of St. Louis (http://research.stlouisfed.org/conferences/gse/Weicher.pdf).

Willis, Mark. 2009. "It's the Rating, Stupid: A Banker's Perspective on the CRA." In *Revisiting the CRA: Perspectives on the Future of the Community Reinvestment Act*, edited by Prabal Chakrabarti and others, pp. 59–70. Federal Reserve Banks of Boston and San Francisco.

11

Dual Mortgage Markets: What Role Has the Government Played and How Likely Will One Emerge in the Future?

RAPHAEL W. BOSTIC

Dual mortgage markets are a direct descendant of key policy responses to the Great Depression. Before the Depression, nearly all mortgages were five-year balloons, so that homeowners needed to refinance their mortgage every five years. The capital crisis of the Depression limited the ability of households to find new credit when their mortgages reached maturity, which resulted in massive foreclosures. The policy response was to bolster the housing finance system by creating institutions, including Fannie Mae and the Federal Housing Administration (FHA), to provide access to credit for these populations who would otherwise be forced into foreclosure and be shut out of the market for the foreseeable future. In so doing, Fannie Mae and FHA helped provide access to mortgage credit and homeownership for millions of families, but at a higher cost. In later years, both institutions, but particularly the FHA, would evolve to play a leading role in providing access to borrowers who would be unable to get a mortgage under prevailing underwriting standards but who could afford and reliably repay a mortgage if they were able to get one. In essence, the creation of Fannie Mae and FHA created a dual mortgage market, and in so doing expanded access to mortgage credit.

The author thanks Eric Belsky, Bill Apgar, Barry Zigas, and conference participants for helpful comments and suggestions. I thank Glenn Canner, Madura Watanagase, Ed Szymanoski, and Arthur Acoca-Pidolle for their assistance with data analysis.

Today, however, a Google search on the phrase "dual mortgage market" yields over 1.5 million hits. A casual review of the listing makes clear one thing: a dual mortgage market is considered a problem. To the extent that a dual market exists, the view is that it needs to be eliminated. For example, in response to a report showing black and Hispanic borrowers being more likely to receive government-backed loans, Deyanira Del Rio writes: "Moreover, the existence of a dual mortgage market is, in itself, problematic and warrants ramped-up enforcement of fair lending laws."[1]

This view, widely held in the advocacy community, arises from the notion that market forces, market discipline, and regulation are less effective in markets serving minority and lower-income communities. As a result, borrowers that rely on these markets are inherently disadvantaged and subject to abuse, and these abuses can impose costs that exceed any potential benefits of homeownership. This view has been an important voice in discussions on the desired structure of the next generation housing finance system.[2]

How should one reconcile these two pictures of dual markets? What should we think about dual markets in the context of housing finance reform efforts as they continue during Obama's second term? This chapter explores these questions. It first explains the dual market and what it has meant for borrowers and neighborhoods, for both good and bad. A particular focus is placed on the role that government played in its creation and persistence. The discussion reveals that there are several dualities in the market, and that these interact in ways that can yield net benefits but can also expose borrowers to abuse and significant risks. The analysis concludes that a dual mortgage market is unavoidable, if one believes that broad access to mortgage credit and homeownership is an important policy objective, and argues that policymakers must position the government to limit the risks and abuses that such a market structure can produce.

Mortgage Underwriting and Finance: The Foundation for a Dual Market

Though this chapter focuses on government involvement in the persistence of dual mortgage markets, it is important to recognize that this market has been a large driver in its existence. The issues associated with dual mortgage markets emerge from the basics of banking finance and underwriting, coupled with the dynamics pertaining to how equilibria are achieved. Lenders make decisions on whether to extend credit to borrowers based on a set of factors, including interest rate risk, liquidity risk, and credit risk, among others.

1. Del Rio (2011).
2. Mortgage Finance Working Group (2011).

Interest rate risk exists because market interest rates could increase or decrease in the future. Lenders that have extended loans at prior lower rates are unable to take advantage of a more favorable environment until those loans become due. In U.S. mortgage markets, interest rate risk for lenders is compounded because borrowers generally have the ability to prepay their mortgages without cost when rates fall. The presence of interest rate risk is reflected in the differential pricing for fixed- and adjustable-rate mortgages, with fixed-rate products having a higher price commensurate with the higher exposure to this risk the product represents.

Liquidity risk arises because once a loan is extended, a lender is less liquid and thus less able to provide credit in the event that an attractive loan option presents itself in the future. Liquidity risk pricing is observed in the market as differential pricing across loans of different terms, with longer-term loans featuring higher interest rates.

Credit risk represents the likelihood that a borrower will repay a loan. Repayment is a function of two options that borrowers face. One option—the "call" option—presents the borrower with decision criteria on whether to prepay the mortgage. This option depends largely on prevailing interest rates and the transaction costs of prepayment. The "put" option presents the borrower with decision criteria on whether to stop paying the mortgage and give it back to the lender, otherwise known as default. Pure finance theory suggests the default decision is made exclusively by comparing the value of the home and the value of the mortgage. If the mortgage is worth more (that is, the put option is "in the money"), then the borrower should default. The purest form of this suggests that a borrower will default if the mortgage is a penny more valuable than the home, though this ruthless exercise of the option is not expected due to transaction costs associated with default. A second theory of mortgage performance holds that performance can be influenced by the occurrence of so-called trigger events. These events are personal crises that either disrupt income or demand significant financial resources that limit the ability to repay debt. Losing a job, divorce, and sudden illness are typical trigger events. Empirical evidence supports the view that both option theory factors and trigger event factors are associated with loan performance.[3]

Recognizing that the value of a property is typically a function of macroeconomic factors that are beyond the control of individual borrowers, most key variables involved in credit risk underwriting are those that indicate a borrower's historical propensity to repay loans and likelihood of succumbing to a trigger event. These include, among other factors, a potential borrower's employment and income history, available financial reserves, and credit score, which is a summary

---

3. Quercia and Stegman (1992); Berkovec and others (1994); Deng, Quigley, and Van Order (2000); Van Order, Firestone, and Zorn (2007).

Table 11-1. *Median Value of Family Wealth, Income, and Savings, by Ethnicity*
Thousands of dollars

	Net worth		Financial holdings		Income	
Year	White	Non-white, Hispanic	White	Non-white, Hispanic	White	Non-white, Hispanic
1989	121.7	10.6	27.3	3.4	51.0	24.6
1992	105.7	18.2	23.8	4.5	46.6	28.0
1995	108.8	22.0	26.8	7.9	46.4	29.0
1998	128.0	22.1	40.5	8.7	51.4	31.1
2001	150.6	22.4	48.6	8.9	55.4	31.5
2004	162.2	28.6	42.1	5.8	56.7	34.3
2007	179.7	29.5	47.4	9.4	54.5	38.8
2010	129.8	20.5	37.1	6.0	52.9	34.6

Source: *Survey of Consumer Finances*, Board of Governors of the Federal Reserve System, multiple years.

measure of an individual's past performance in repaying debts and other obligations. The major factor used to assess the likelihood that a loan will have negative equity is the down payment, which establishes a loan-to-value ratio. The interest rate charged for a mortgage loan varies with the estimated probability of repayment: borrowers with lower estimated probabilities of repayment have to accept loans with higher interest rates and more restrictive terms, often referred to as subprime loans.

This underwriting approach establishes a framework through which a dual market can arise, because the characteristics used in credit underwriting decisions are not randomly distributed across the population, with ethnic minorities and lower-income people generally holding a weaker position along nearly all the key dimensions. Many studies have documented wealth differences among people with different ethnic backgrounds.[4] Table 11-1 shows the extent of these differences and demonstrates that income and wealth-based differences have been long-standing and continuous. The table shows that median income for non-white and Hispanic families has remained at about 60 percent of the median income for white families for the past twenty years. Regarding liquid assets, the median value of financial holdings for white families has, with one exception, stood at five to eight times that for minority and Hispanic families over the same period. The multiples for net worth over this period are typically between five and seven.

4. Gittleman and Wolff (2004); Avery and Rendall (2002).

Table 11-2. *Median Value of Family Wealth, Income, and Financial Assets, by Income*
Thousands of dollars

Year	Net worth		Financial assets		Income	
	Second quintile	Fourth quintile	Second quintile	Fourth quintile	Second quintile	Fourth quintile
1989	41.8	113.9	7.4	25.5	24.6	68.6
1992	42.1	114.3	5.9	26.4	23.3	63.7
1995	49.1	106.8	8.7	30.5	24.7	63.8
1998	46.2	149.0	8.9	48.4	27.1	71.7
2001	47.2	173.5	10.0	68.6	30.2	79.4
2004	39.6	184.1	5.7	55.8	29.5	78.0
2007	39.6	214.5	7.4	62.3	30.2	78.7
2010	27.7	127.1	5.3	39.2	28.5	71.2

Source: *Survey of Consumer Finances,* Board of Governors of the Federal Reserve System, multiple years.

There are also major differences by income and ethnicity in individual credit scores, and evidence is clear that minorities are disadvantaged where credit scores are concerned.[5] Moreover, the differences are large. For example, Courchane, Gailey, and Zorn show that African American and Hispanic borrowers have credit scores that are on average about 100 points and 50 points lower than the average score for white borrowers (a FICO score of 700).[6] Similar disparities are observed among families grouped by income. Not surprisingly, as seen in table 11-2, lower-income families are at distinct disadvantages regarding income (by definition), financial asset wealth, and net worth.

The presence of these differences has significant implications for the allocation of mortgage credit, and lenders can pursue two distinct approaches in response. In one approach, all lenders might implement a unified underwriting scheme—one set of rules for all borrowers—and there will necessarily be differential access to mortgage credit and ultimately homeownership. Figure 11-1 represents this graphically. The two subgroups in the population shown in the figure both have uniform credit quality distributions; one group has a lower credit quality distribution than the other. The top panel shows the effect of using a single threshold for making allocation decisions. In this scenario, a greater proportion of members from Group A will receive a mortgage, and much of Group B will be shut out of the market completely.

5. Board of Governors (2007).
6. Courchane, Gailey, and Zorn (2007).

Figure 11-1. *Lender Underwriting Policies and Access to Credit*

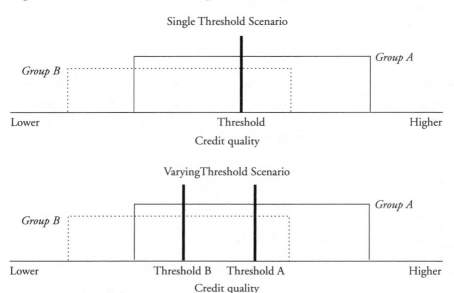

Alternatively, the market could evolve and provide different products tailored to serve borrowers with varying credit profiles. This would widen the availability of mortgage credit and leave only the most risky borrowers fully excluded from the market, as shown in the bottom panel of figure 11-1. Here, more members of both groups receive mortgages, but nearly half of the members of group B—rather than only 20 percent as in Panel A—now have access to the credit market. While those receiving the second tier loans may pay a higher rate, they are able to receive a mortgage if they can pay the higher price as opposed to being shut out completely. Thus, we observe an expansion of access to credit with a dual market.

This dual market approach has been operationalized in the mortgage market through differentiation in product diffusion across population subgroups and neighborhoods segmented by race and income. Two key product categories emerged to serve those with weaker average credit profiles: loans guaranteed by the Federal Housing Administration (FHA) and subprime loans.

The FHA provides a 100 percent guarantee for loans that fit a specific profile that other sources generally bypass—low risk on the income dimension but higher risk along the down payment and credit repayment dimensions. Thus, the FHA product is attractive for families with a steady (and strong) income stream but little wealth, which limits how much can be offered as a down payment, and for those with damaged credit history, which will translate into a low credit score.

Table 11-3. *FHA Purchase Loan Share for All Borrowers, Minority Borrowers, and Borrowers in Lower-Income Neighborhoods, 2001–11*
Percent

Year	All loans	African American borrowers	Hispanic borrowers	Lower-income neighborhoods
2004	9	17	12	14
2005	6	10	6	8
2006	6	10	6	8
2007	8	15	10	11
2008	29	50	44	39
2009	42	62	63	54
2010	41	62	64	54
2011	35	56	59	48
2012	31	54	55	44

Source: Home Mortgage Disclosure Act data; count includes all owner-occupied first-lien loans; calculations by Madura Watanagase.

FHA loans are priced to account for these borrower characteristics: they have higher interest rates than those of loans serving borrowers with stronger credit profiles and also require borrowers to pay a mortgage insurance premium (that can be rolled into the mortgage payment).

Table 11-3 provides a snapshot demonstrating the FHA's importance for minority and lower-income communities. It shows that penetration of FHA loans has been and generally continues to be far greater among minority and lower-income communities. The table reports trends several years into the house price run-up, and we observe market shares in decline from the FHA's historical 10 to 15 percent home purchase market share.[7] The erosion in market share was driven by aggressive expansion by lenders offering subprime and alternative mortgage products, which began to outcompete those from the FHA. Even through this period of shrinking FHA market share, though, FHA had larger shares in minority and lower-income communities, with their share almost double the overall share among African American borrowers. The pattern of low overall FHA market shares changed only at the depth of the crisis, when the supply of loans lacking government support dried up.[8] Since then, FHA presence has been strong

7. For consistency, data are reported only from 2004. Home Mortgage Disclosure Act (HMDA) data reporting requirement changes in 2004 allow for the identification of loans by lien status. Comparable figures for earlier years cannot be obtained.

8. The FHA itself notes that it has become the primary source of mortgage credit for minorities and lower-income families. The FHA is also critical for first-time homebuyers.

Table 11-4. *FHA Refinance Loan Share for All Borrowers, Minority Borrowers, and Borrowers in Lower-Income Neighborhoods, 2001–11*
Percent

Year	All Loans	African American borrowers	Hispanic borrowers	Lower-income neighborhoods
2004	3	8	1	5
2005	2	1	3	3
2006	2	4	2	3
2007	5	9	4	6
2008	17	35	20	24
2009	16	42	29	28
2010	12	29	21	20
2011	8	20	15	14
2012	10	20	18	15

Source: Home Mortgage Disclosure Act data; count includes all owner-occupied first-lien loans; calculations by Madura Watanagase.

across the entire home purchase mortgage market, and its total market share has consistently exceeded 30 percent. Despite this rise, FHA home purchase market shares still remain higher for minority and lower-income communities.

Table 11-4 reports shares for refinance loans only. FHA shares in this segment of the market were uniformly lower than those in the home purchase market and were low in absolute terms for many years. This makes clear that the FHA presence was strongest for home purchase lending and that refinances, which often led to subsequent problems, were less of an FHA issue.

Subprime loans are the other major product that caters to those with weaker credit profiles. Like FHA loans, subprime loans have features that better accommodate the lower-wealth, lower-credit-quality profiles of many minority and lower-income borrowers. First, subprime loans are typically more lenient regarding credit quality requirements. Second, these loans often have repayment structures that vary monthly payments and interest rates in ways that reduce payments significantly in early years. These features also hold appeal for prospective borrowers with limited or little wealth and perhaps weaker credit histories. That noted, subprime loans have other features that could significantly damage borrowers. Monthly payments can jump significantly and leave borrowers with a heavy mortgage burden relative to income. Moreover, these loans often feature prepayment penalties that could prevent already vulnerable borrowers from transitioning to more attractive, lower cost products if they became available.

The evidence is clear that subprime loans are also more prevalent in minority and lower-income communities. A series of HUD reports in 2000 showed the penetration of loans with subprime characteristics into lower-income and minority neighborhoods in six metropolitan areas.[9] They found that high-cost subprime loans were three times more likely in lower-income neighborhoods than in high-income neighborhoods. The pattern was more extreme across neighborhoods grouped by racial composition, with African American neighborhoods showing subprime prevalence five times higher than predominantly white neighborhoods. In addition, research has found these neighborhood-level relationships for individuals grouped by race or income, and some of it has demonstrated the persistence of these neighborhood and individual relationships even after controlling for other relevant characteristics. For example, Mayer and Pence find that "even controlling for credit scores and other zip code characteristics, race and ethnicity appear to be strongly and statistically significantly related to the proportion of subprime loans."[10] The effects are large: moving from the median zip code to the 90th percentile in terms of black or Hispanic population share increases the estimated prevalence of subprime loans by between 30 and 45 percent.

As an interesting sidebar, evidence on the performance of these loans through the housing crisis suggests that all loans in the higher risk portion of the dual market are not created equal. While default and foreclosure rates rose among both FHA and subprime loans, the performance of subprime loans was much worse. According to data from the Mortgage Bankers Association, subprime mortgage delinquencies and foreclosures from the middle of 2008 through 2012 exceeded 30 percent and were over 40 percent for much of 2009 and 2010, whereas the FHA loans show combined delinquency and foreclosure rates of between 15 and 18 percent during the same period.[11] Thus, there may be a compelling interest in regulating this segment of the market or, at a minimum, ensuring that information is available on the varying qualities of the products that serve it.

Other Dualities: Institutions and Compensation Practices

In addition to product differences across the segments of the dual market, we also observed differences in the players. These differences became acute in the 1990s as the market evolved. As noted by Apgar and Calder, the United States housing market underwent a major transformation starting in the 1990s.[12] The market originally was dominated by large financial institutions that provided retail delivery of services through loan officers resident in bank branches. The repeal of the Depression-era Glass-Steagall Act, which established firewalls limiting

9. HUD (2000).
10. Mayer and Pence (2008, p. 14).
11. Mortgage Bankers Association (2012).
12. Apgar and Calder (2005).

the potential scope of banking institutions, reintroduced interstate banking and opportunities for financial institutions to achieve scale economies. The market responded strongly, and in just over ten years the mortgage origination market share of the largest banks grew from about 28 percent in 1990 to more than 75 percent in 2003. This concentration has increased even more since 2003; indeed, in the first quarter of 2012, one bank was responsible for more than one-third of all mortgage originations.[13] These large banks have increasingly relied on secondary markets to provide the long-term funding and carry the long-term risk associated with markets.

These two trends—consolidation of lenders and the rise of the secondary market—helped spark the rise of the correspondent sector of the market. Banks became willing to accept loans that could be funded through the secondary market from (virtually) any source that could reliably generate volume, allowing brokers to establish more extensive networks of banks to serve and giving their business model increased viability. The business model for independent mortgage companies also relied on securitization, and the increased prevalence of secondary mortgage markets allowed these institutions to expand their scale and scope as well.

In the evolution of the dual market, these correspondent players performed a more significant role as mortgage-related intermediaries in minority and lower-income communities. Some have argued that this is partly because lenders do not adequately provide banking services to residents in these neighborhoods thus allowing them to establish familiarity and relationships with bankers who could extend mortgage credit. This scenario may be due to discrimination or because bankers in concentrated markets are not ruthlessly maximizing profits.[14] Some have pointed to regulatory disincentives for serving customers with somewhat higher risk profiles on safety and soundness grounds. Others argue that banks do not engage with residents of underserved neighborhoods because bank staff do not match the demographics of those communities.[15] Finally, some argue that banks have been less creative in developing attractive products and reaching out to potential borrowers in these neighborhoods and point to the prevalence of check cashing institutions in minority and lower-income neighborhoods as evidence of this.[16] Their presence, the argument goes, arises because banks do not offer products that appeal to people living in such communities.

In the 1970s these concerns, among others, led to a set of legislative responses to promote increased bank engagement in minority and lower-income

---

13. Campbell and Son (2012).
14. Munnell and others (1996); Berger and Hannan (1998).
15. Kim and Squires (1995).
16. Rhine, Greene, and Toussaint-Comeau (2006); Caskey (1994).

neighborhoods. The Home Mortgage Disclosure Act of 1975 (HMDA) mandated the public reporting of data on mortgage lending activity, so that the extent to which banks were serving communities could be verified independently. The data that resulted from this act have become a powerful tool for regulators and activists alike in monitoring and providing discipline to banks.[17] The Community Reinvestment Act of 1977 (CRA) was motivated by a desire for banks to invest local deposits more intensively in the neighborhoods from which the deposits originated. It resulted in the creation of a periodic bank examination scheme that assesses how banks are responding to local community needs. The Federal Housing Enterprises Financial Safety and Soundness Act of 1992 (also known as the 1992 GSE Act) engaged the secondary market in this area by mandating that secondary market institutions provide liquidity to historically underserved minority and lower-income mortgage markets. This was put into practice through the establishment of annual affordable housing goals, such that the main government-sponsored mortgage enterprises (GSEs), Fannie Mae and Freddie Mac, had to meet purchase volume and transaction targets in specified minority and lower-income communities. Research has shown that these pieces of legislation have been associated with increased lending and the origination of loans with positive profits.[18]

Research has also shown that these acts have reshaped the distribution of loans and the character of the two parts of the dual mortgage market. An and Bostic, for example, examine the impact on market structure brought about by the GSE affordable goals. Their research finds that the goals have been effective in increasing the competition among lenders for borrowers at the margin between the two parts of the dual market.[19] The evidence shows that the GSEs promote prime market competition against the FHA and subprime lenders in places where goal activity is higher, resulting in an increased relative presence of less expensive prime loans and a reduction in the relative prevalence of pricier FHA and subprime loans. The research shows that these relationships are strongest in high-minority neighborhoods. Simulations suggest the substitutions resulted in aggregate savings in excess of $2 billion.

One can thus think of the activity spurred by these legislative responses as a mechanism for establishing the boundaries of the dual market. Loans associated with compliance with the CRA, the GSE affordable goals, and other similar requirements lie in the margin between the underwriting standards of the two markets. Experiences with these loan products can in principle cause lenders to assess their underwriting guidelines and, to the extent that these loans exceed

17. Bostic and Robinson (2005).
18. See, for example, Bostic and Robinson (2003, 2005), and Avery, Bostic, and Canner (2000).
19. An and Bostic (2008, 2009).

profitability thresholds, adjust them to incorporate more loan products to serve borrowers with stronger credit profiles. In the framework of figure 11-1, this is the equivalent of shifting the higher threshold slightly to the left—an initial rationale for these acts. The open question is whether experience has shown these loans to be sufficiently profitable and, if so, whether underwriting guidelines have been adjusted to reflect this market reality. Considerable debate exists on both issues.[20]

Another important mortgage market duality arose because of differences in pricing and compensation practices across origination channels (that is, between banks and non-bank correspondent institutions). It had been common practice for agents working on behalf of lenders to receive higher compensation if they were able to get a borrower to agree to a mortgage with an interest rate higher than the benchmark rate for that mortgage product. For brokers and correspondent agents, the difference between the loan interest rate and the benchmark rate is called a yield spread premium; for bank loan officers, the spread is known as an overage.

Rose summarizes the logic and evidence in support of the view that yield spread premiums are more significant in broker compensation than overages are for bank loan officers.[21] Briefly, because banks more often incur costs if a loan defaults, they have an incentive to limit overage size to constrain default risk. Because correspondents typically lack this concern, fewer constraints are applied. Moreover, bank loan officers often have additional volume-based compensation incentives, further reducing the overage incentive effect. In addition, evidence shows that the amount of profit from yield spread premiums and overages varies by origination channel, with potential profitability being higher for a given-sized spread at non-bank lenders compared to bank lenders.[22]

Taken together, these suggest that the non-bank correspondent channel has greater incentive to put borrowers in more expensive mortgage products. The many subsequent lawsuits and settlements associated with non-bank institutions' steering of borrowers to less advantageous (read: more expensive) products, which some call "push marketing," bear this out.[23]

---

20. Research on CRA-related lending conducted by the Federal Reserve showed these loans to be profitable, though less profitable than other loans in lender portfolios. See Board of Governors (2000). Others have noted that CRA-related and affordable housing goal loans have performed better than projected in general. This suggests that underwriting should be adjusted to accommodate this. However, others have argued that the incentives established by the CRA and other acts have been, on balance, detrimental to housing markets, families, and communities.

21. Rose (2012).

22. Woodward (2008).

23. See, for example, Savage (2011).

Problems with the Dual Mortgage Market

While a dual mortgage market offers clear benefits by expanding access to mortgage credit and homeownership, it can have inherent problems that could induce inequities in access to mortgage credit and could even leave those most disadvantaged worse off than if they had not pursued homeownership at all. Imperfect information in the higher-risk portion of the market may create information asymmetries that leave prospective borrowers at risk of exploitation. Such asymmetries may arise for several reasons. Primary among these is the fact that lower-income and lower-wealth borrowers often have less direct experience with mortgage markets, and their unfamiliarity with how their application is likely to be perceived and with the process generally can leave them vulnerable. Borrowers could accept terms and conditions that are worse than they otherwise might have been able to obtain. Furthermore, to the extent riskier borrowers are more likely to be served in the risk-based price proportion of the market, the interest rate offer they receive comes only after application is made or at least after information like the credit score is retrieved. Thus, the costs of comparison shopping are higher than in the prime market and the risk of price discrimination higher.

Research strongly suggests that conditions are ripe for these negative outcomes. Evidence shows that higher-risk borrowers often have an inaccurate perception of their credit quality, and that minority borrowers often believe their credit quality is worse than it actually is.[24] Evidence also clearly demonstrates the efficacy of housing counseling that increases familiarity with the mortgage process and basic underwriting and finance rules of thumb. Borrowers who receive counseling before entering the home-buying process have better outcomes in terms of obtaining a lower cost and more sustainable mortgage product, performing better once they have their mortgage, and curing when they face mortgage difficulties.[25]

There is ample evidence these negative outcomes do occur and that they are more prevalent in minority and lower-income communities. The HUD report, cited above, offers clear evidence of this.[26] Additional evidence shows that loan officers who are given discretion often seek additional rents from minority, lower-income, and other "disadvantaged" borrowers and are rewarded with risk-spread premiums.[27] Moreover, there is reason to believe that these abuses increase in frequency as the marketplace becomes more complex and a broader set of products is available in these neighborhoods.

24. Courchane, Gailey, and Zorn (2007).
25. Hirad and Zorn (2002); Collins (2007); Abt Associates (2012a, 2012b).
26. HUD (2000).
27. Ayers and Siegelman (1995).

This information problem, and the fact that it was concentrated geographically and in some segments of the population, meant that the issues associated with the three dualities identified in the previous section—products, institutions, and practices—were exacerbated in lower-income and minority communities. Borrowers in these areas were left especially vulnerable because the agents they were most likely to interact with were precisely those for whom the incentive to push market and engage in other abuses was highest. Few effective protections existed for these borrowers.

This problem was further amplified by the prevailing market dynamics. The rise of the housing market in the early and mid-2000s featured opposing trends for the two main product types of the higher-risk portion of the dual market: subprime share grew dramatically during the period, while FHA shares fell sharply. This highlights institutional differences in the response to changing market conditions. Subprime lenders aggressively innovated, finding new outlets for their products and new customers to engage. By contrast, the FHA did not significantly change its product mix or business strategy during this time. Indeed, even in the face of mounting evidence that some product offerings, such as loans featuring seller-financed down payments, were producing large losses, congressional action, via the FHA Seller-Financed Downpayment Reform Act of 2009, was required to eliminate the product. Nimble responses were not possible.

One might draw a conclusion that this higher-risk portion of the dual market might simultaneously, and perhaps paradoxically, have had too much and not enough innovation. Rapid innovation can create conditions that increase the likelihood that the individual treatment and problematic outcomes described above will occur. As new products and pitches flood the market, a premium will be placed on knowledge and understanding of the mortgage process. This is a clear stress point.

At the same time, our understanding of the nature of credit risk and loan performance evolves over time. As this knowledge base changes, one would like to see corresponding changes in products and practices. It is therefore desirable to have institutions and a legislative environment that are able to incorporate such changes seamlessly and without long time lags. Otherwise, those who rely on the higher-risk portion of the dual market for access to mortgage credit could be stuck in products that cause them to fall further and further behind the mainstream. Ultimately, they might find themselves unable to leverage their initial access into a more favorable financial position.

Next Steps: Government's Role in Shaping the Dual Market

This discussion makes clear that the government played an explicit role in the creation and perpetuation of a dual market. Legislative and regulatory actions as well as policy decisions that shaped the mix of available products and their character all contributed to the creation of this market structure. The result was an expansion of access to mortgage credit and the benefits such an expansion generated. However, this expansion did not come without a corresponding set of problems, as discussed in the preceding section.

The basics of underwriting and finance suggest that if maintaining broad access to mortgage credit is to remain a key objective of policy, a dual mortgage market of some form, embodied in the presence of a range of product options, will be necessary. Assuming this goal is preserved during deliberations on the next generation of housing policy, a position I believe is desirable, the issue therefore is not if there should be a dual market, but rather how to have a dual market that features adequate protections to prevent or at least limit abuse.

In this regard, government will clearly play a central role. There are at least three areas in which the government must take major steps in order to achieve a successful dual market that reaps its potential benefits while minimizing its costs and risks. These areas can be broadly thought of as products, players, and preparation. Significant steps have been taken already.

Perhaps the most important innovation has been the Dodd-Frank Wall Street Reform and Consumer Protection Act of 2010. Among other things, Dodd-Frank created the Consumer Financial Protection Bureau (CFPB), an agency with responsibility for pursuing an explicitly consumer-oriented regulatory agenda. A major problem with the regulatory regime that prevailed before the act's passage was that conflicts between industry and consumer interests played out behind closed doors, in the halls of regulatory agencies whose primary charge was preserving the safety and soundness of financial institutions and minimizing systemic risk. This limited the extent of vigorous public debate and prevented consumer safety and soundness from having as strong an influence on policy as it might otherwise have. The creation of the CFPB changes this, which is a very welcome change.

Beyond internal institutional dynamics, the creation of the CFPB established important market-level reform. Importantly, it unifies a previously distributed regulatory structure, removing many aspects of the institution-based duality that allowed excesses and abuses to proliferate. CFPB's authority to write and enforce regulations that apply to both banks and non-banks offering financial products represents an opportunity to remove differences in regulatory rules that made conditions ripe for confusion and abuse. Moreover, this structure places clear regulatory responsibility in a single agency, which clarifies accountability. Taken together, these are important steps to promote the expansion of access to credit in ways that are not associated with significant increases in risk or the potential for abuse.

Regarding products, consistent with the approach taken in Dodd-Frank, the government's primary role will be regulatory, with an approach of using pricing to signal relative safety rather than banning products outright. Such an approach recognizes that every product can be appropriate in the right circumstance; indeed, no-documentation loans existed or were used long before the troubles experienced in the 2000s. However, every product is not necessarily the best for every borrower. Dodd-Frank takes key steps in this direction through its call for the creation of a regulatory scheme that signals to consumers a set of products that are relatively safe and more sustainable than many of the products that were promulgated during the housing run-up in the early 2000s. In addition, the act moves regulators to provide incentives for borrowers to use such products.

The housing crisis revealed a fundamental flaw in the prevailing system of housing finance—the dominance of a transaction-based compensation scheme that had at best weak connections to subsequent loan performance coupled with a reliance on a secondary market that limited the risk exposure of most parties. This structure left no interest in the origination of a loan (save the consumer, sometimes) with an incentive to stop a deal if its details suggested excessive risk or imprudence. This "no skin in the game" feature helped accelerate some of the worst trends during the early 2000s and resulted in a deeper crisis. Dodd-Frank addressed this to some extent with its realignment of incentives to give financial institutions more accountability for loan performance by requiring that they hold a loss position in the event of poor future performance and by changing regulations concerning loan officer compensation. Furthermore, mortgage brokers and correspondents had an incentive to sell borrowers on an interest rate higher than demanded by the lender because they could earn the difference back in the form of a yield spread premium.

However, in the context of dual markets, there are players other than large lenders who are particularly significant and warrant direct attention. For example, independent mortgage companies and similar institutions lacking bank charters historically have received less regulatory scrutiny than other financial institutions that are important for mortgage markets. The development of a robust examination framework that permits the identification of problems and potential abuses in a timely manner must be a high priority for policymakers and regulators.

Credit rating agencies were another key player in the crisis. These agencies failed to accurately assess the risks represented by pools of subprime and other dual market loan products, which resulted in outsized unexpected losses to investors, banking institutions, and ultimately the entire financial system. Moving forward, one must consider whether the structure that prevailed at the time of the crisis, with ratings agencies acting on behalf of the issuers of securities, is prudent. One might expect agency problems, such that risks are underemphasized, to emerge through such an arrangement, and it could be that this structure exacerbated underlying market problems. Perhaps one should explore a return to the historic role of rating agencies being agents for buyers, either through individual investors establishing policies whereby they will only rely on ratings generated via a buyer-based set of rules or by regulatory fiat.

Finally, as noted earlier, mortgage brokers emerged as an important conduit for families seeking mortgage finance during the 1990s and 2000s. If they remain so, then the regulation of brokers will help determine access to mortgage credit and homeownership for minority and lower-income families. As was the case for lenders, broker compensation was tied to the completion of a transaction and not linked to the performance of the loan that emerged from that transaction. This incentive structure allowed brokers to have little concern about the viability of a mortgage arrangement and undoubtedly contributed to the widespread prevalence of the unsustainable loans that were at the heart of the mortgage crisis in many markets.

There are at least two possible approaches to changing broker incentives. One would be to create a structure that parallels that for lenders and require them to have "skin in the game," perhaps through a bonding requirement tied to loan volume, an origination fee schedule where the fee is paid over time based on continued loan performance, or by establishing some broker liability in the event that a loan's performance fell outside some predetermined range and was identified to be a clear outlier. Alternatively, one might use information as a market discipline. In this approach, the performance of all loans in a broker's portfolio would be tracked and assessed relative to a performance benchmark, and this assessment could be made public, perhaps in the form of a letter grade. This information-based system would be similar to the reporting system used for restaurant inspections in California, which has been shown to positively impact restaurant adherence to inspection guidelines.[28]

Considering the part of brokers points to an important reality: the government role in managing the dual mortgage market must extend beyond the federal government. Brokers are regulated at the state level. Effective closure of broker "holes" that allow for possible abuse will require fifty distinct regulatory actions. Coordination of this effort will be a significant challenge. Policymakers must find methods for overcoming it.

Ultimately, though, one should have serious doubts about the ability of a rule- and regulation-based system to consistently prevent abuses from arising in markets, especially as time passes. There is a long history of market players finding the weak spot or spots in a regulatory system and devising schemes to exploit them. Moreover, there are few examples of "foolproof" regulatory regimes if market forces are allowed to freely operate in some fashion. This truth is reflected in

28. Simon and others (2005).

the fact that laws require virtually every regulation to be evaluated and assessed over time for efficacy and effectiveness (and all are ultimately reviewed at some point); experience always uncovers problems and loopholes.

This agility of markets suggests that an important, and perhaps more enduring, approach is to work to reduce the asymmetries creating the conditions that allow abuses to occur. Much of the abuse we observed during the housing crisis resulted from minority and lower-income borrowers' unfamiliarity with the mortgage process or with their own credit quality coupled with misaligned incentives that generated significant financial gains for those who put borrowers in expensive higher-risk mortgages. Evidence on mortgage counseling has shown that strategies can be effective in increasing familiarity and thereby reducing the potential for abuse. Clearly, the recent past has shown that a system in which mortgage counseling is optional or passively made available to borrowers will not be adequate to counter rapidly evolving markets where product offerings can change significantly. New strategies are needed to prepare people for homeownership.

One possible approach here is to diffuse knowledge on the home-buying process, mortgage underwriting, and credit quality more thoroughly through society. An obvious vehicle for this is the education system, particularly at the secondary school level. Since nearly all Americans pass through some sort of secondary school education, introducing a curriculum requirement on home-buying financial literacy would ensure a minimum level of knowledge and awareness for all. With an increased knowledge base among borrowers, we should observe a squeezing out of the least sophisticated exploitation techniques. In an optimal world, we will create a wary population of homebuyers that understands the basics of underwriting and has an intuitive feel for when abusive behavior might be in the air.

Another Government Role: Creating a Bridge between Markets

One further role that government should play in the context of dual markets is the promotion of responsible and sustainable innovation. As noted, the higher risk portion of the dual market can have both too much and too little innovation as market conditions change. This can leave borrowers either vulnerable to serious abuses or stuck in products far less beneficial than others that could be accessible in an appropriately evolved market. The government will be needed to mediate this dynamic.

The government historically has played this role through its support of community-based institutions via the Community Development Financial Institution fund as well as through enforcement of the Community Reinvestment Act and the affordable housing goals for Fannie Mae and Freddie Mac. The government should continue to play this role in a future housing finance system. One interesting proposal is to establish a mortgage transaction fee and use the proceeds to create a fund, called a Market Access Fund, providing competitive grants to test innovative products that lie in the space between the two portions of the dual market.[29] This type of proposal merits serious consideration. Perhaps the FHA could be a "locus of innovation" regarding products to serve these margins.

Concluding Thoughts

The 2006 housing crisis and subsequent collapse of the institutional foundations of the housing finance system have sparked a vigorous debate about the shape and nature of the next generation system of housing finance. In August 2010, then Treasury Secretary Timothy Geithner, in his remarks opening a major conference focused on the subject, clearly laid out the objectives of this pursuit: "a carefully designed guarantee in a reformed system, with the objective of providing a measure of stability in access to mortgages."[30] In considering these remarks, one should view stability as referring not only to the broad financial system—undoubtedly a key concern for Geithner—but also to the finances of households considering how to be housed. These households face risk to be managed as well. Achieving this goal will require a multifaceted approach. The Dodd-Frank financial reform act was a first salvo in the reframing of housing finance. It established some high-level policy objectives, but left many details to regulatory bodies to hash out.

Discussions at that conference and in many other forums on that topic invariably migrated to the issue of a "dual mortgage market" and its desirability. While it is clear that this type of market structure carries risks, the fundamentals of underwriting and the realities of the distribution of wealth and income across the population make clear that dual markets will be necessary if the charge to keep access to credit broad and affordable is taken seriously. The challenge for policymakers remains how to accomplish this in a safe and sound fashion.

References

Abt Associates. 2012a. *Housing Counseling Outcome Evaluation—Foreclosure Counseling Outcome Study: Final Report.* Prepared for the U.S. Department of Housing and Urban Development, Washington.

———. 2012b. *Housing Counseling Outcome Evaluation—Pre-Purchase Counseling Outcome Study: Research Brief.* Prepared for the U.S. Department of Housing and Urban Development, Washington.

29. Mortgage Finance Working Group (2011).
30. Geithner (2010).

An, X., and R. W. Bostic. 2008. "GSE Activity, FHA Feedback, and Implications for the Efficacy of the Affordable Housing Goals." *Journal of Real Estate Finance and Economics* 36, no. 2: 207–31.

———. 2009. "Policy Incentives and the Extension of Mortgage Credit: Increasing Market Discipline for Subprime Lending." *Journal of Policy Analysis and Management* 28, no. 3: 340–65.

Apgar, W. C., and A. Calder. 2005. "The Dual Mortgage Market: The Persistence of Discrimination in Mortgage Lending." In *The Geography of Opportunity: Race and Housing Choice in Metropolitan America,* edited by X. de Souza Briggs, pp. 101–26. Brookings.

Avery, R. B., R. W. Bostic, and G. B. Canner. 2000. "CRA Special Lending Programs." *Federal Reserve Bulletin* 86 (November 11): 711–31.

Avery, R. B., and M. S. Rendall. 2002. "Lifetime Inheritances of Three Generations of Whites and Blacks." *American Journal of Sociology* 107, no. 5: 1300–46.

Ayers, I., and P. Siegelman. 1995. "Race and Gender Discrimination in Bargaining for a New Car." *American Economic Review* 85, no. 3: 304–21.

Berger, A. N., and T. H. Hannan. 1998. "The Efficiency Cost of Market Power in the Banking Industry: A Test of the 'Quiet Life' and Related Hypotheses." *Review of Economics and Statistics* 80, no. 3: 454–65.

Berkovec, J. A., G. B. Canner, S. A. Gabriel, and T. H. Hannan. 1994. "Race, Redlining, and Residential Mortgage Loan Performance." *Journal of Real Estate Finance and Economics* 9, no. 3: 263–94.

Board of Governors of the Federal Reserve System. 2000. *Report to Congress on the Performance and Profitability of CRA-Related Lending.* Washington.

———. 2007. *Report to Congress on Credit Scoring and Its Effects on the Availability and Affordability of Credit.* Washington.

Bostic, R. W., and B. Robinson. 2003. "Do CRA Agreements Increase Lending?" *Real Estate Economics* 31, no. 1: 23–51.

———. 2005. "What Makes CRA Agreements Work? A Study of Lender Responses to CRA Agreements." *Housing Policy Debate* 16, nos. 3-4: 513–45.

Campbell, D., and H. Son. 2012. "Wells Fargo Dominates Home Lending as BofA Retreats: Mortgages." *Bloomberg News Online,* May 3 (www.bloomberg.com/news/2012-05-03/wells-fargo-dominates-home-lending-as-bofa-retreats-mortgages.html).

Caskey, John P. 1994. *Fringe Banking: Check-Cashing Outlets, Pawnshops, and the Poor.* New York: Russell Sage Foundation.

Collins, J. M. 2007. "Exploring the Design in Financial Counseling for Mortgage Borrowers in Default." *Journal of Family Economic Issues* 28, no. 2: 207–26.

Courchane, M., A. Gailey, and P. Zorn. 2007. "Consumer Credit Literacy: What Price Perception?" Working Paper, Federal Reserve Bank of Chicago (April 16).

Del Rio, D. 2012. "Homeowners Face Segregated Mortgage Market." *Huffington Post* blog, August 1 (www.huffingtonpost.com/deyanira-del-rio/homeowners-face-deeply-se_b_1706275.html).

Deng, Y., J. M. Quigley, and R. Van Order. 2000. "Mortgage Terminations, Heterogeneity and the Exercise of Mortgage Options." *Econometrica* 68, no. 2: 275–307.

Geithner, T. 2010. "Opening Remarks at the Conference on the Future of Housing Finance." *Real Clear Politics*, August 17 (www.realclearpolitics.com/articles/2010/08/17/geithners_opening_remarks_at_the_conference_on_the_future_of_housing_finance_106788.html).

Gittleman, M., and E. N. Wolff. 2004. "Racial Differences in Patterns of Wealth Accumulation." *Journal of Human Resources* 39, no. 1: 193–227.

Hirad, A., and P. Zorn. 2002. "Prepurchase Homeownership Counseling: A Little Knowledge Is a Good Thing." In *Low-Income Homeownership: Examining the Unexamined Goal*, edited by N. P. Retsinas and E. S. Belsky, pp. 146–74. Brookings.

HUD (U.S. Department of Housing and Urban Development). 2000. *Unequal Burden: Income and Racial Disparities in Subprime Lending in America*. Washington.

Kim, S., and G. D. Squires. 1995. "Lender Characteristics and Racial Disparities in Mortgage Lending." *Journal of Housing Research* 6, no. 1: 99–113.

Mayer, C., and K. Pence. 2008. "Subprime Mortgages: What, Where and to Whom?" Finance and Economics Discussion Series Working Paper 2008-29. Washington: Board of Governors of the Federal Reserve System.

Mortgage Bankers Association. 2012. *MBA National Delinquency Survey, Third Quarter*. Washington.

Mortgage Finance Working Group. 2011. *A Responsible Market for Housing Finance: A Progressive Plan to Reform the U.S. Secondary Market for Residential Mortgages*. Washington: Center for American Progress (January).

Munnell, A. H., G. M. B. Tootell, L. E. Browne, and J. McEneaney. 1996. "Mortgage Lending in Boston: Interpreting HMDA Data." *American Economic Review* 86, no. 1: 25–53.

Quercia, R. G., and M. A. Stegman. 1992. "Residential Mortgage Default: A Review of the Literature." *Journal of Housing Research* 3, no. 2: 341–79.

Rhine, S. L. W., W. H. Greene, and M. Toussaint-Comeau. 2006. "The Importance of Check-Cashing Businesses to the Unbanked: Racial/Ethnic Differences." *Review of Economics and Statistics* 88, no. 1: 146–57.

Rose, M. J. 2012. "Origination Channel, Prepayment Penalties, and Default." *Real Estate Economics* 40, no. 4: 663–709.

Savage, C. 2011. "Countrywide Will Settle a Bias Suit." *New York Times*, December 21 (www.nytimes.com/2011/12/22/business/us-settlement-reported-on-countrywide-lending.html).

Simon, P. A., P. Leslie, G. Run, G. Z. Jin, R. Reporter, A. Aguirre, and J. E. Fielding. 2005. "The Impact of Restaurant Hygiene Grade Cards on Foodborne-Disease Hospitalizations in Los Angeles County." *Journal of Environmental Health* 67: 32–36.

Van Order, R., S. Firestone, and P. M. Zorn. 2007. "The Performance of Low Income and Minority Mortgages." University of Michigan, Ross School of Business Paper 1083 (April).

Woodward, S. E. 2008. *A Study of Closing Costs for FHA Mortgages*. Washington: Department of Housing and Urban Development, Office of Policy Development and Research.

12

The Role of Mortgage Finance in Financial (In)Stability

MARK CALABRIA

Empirical research on the causes of financial crises has grown in recent decades.[1] Early work, such as that by Kaminsky and Reinhart, helped establish the link between asset prices and banking crises.[2] While this initial research focused on equity prices, subsequent research expanded the analysis to include residential property prices. This subsequent research is briefly reviewed here. After establishing the link between residential property prices and banking crises, I discuss the role of various credit policies, both for their impact on property prices and for the stability of the financial system in the face of declining property prices. The role of specific loan characteristics, such as loan-to-value (LTV) ratios, is discussed first, followed by the role of institutional leverage. Policy recommendations conclude.

Costs of Financial Crises

Policy choices are ultimately about deciding which costs are worth bearing to achieve a particular set of benefits. Debates regarding homeownership—and by extension, mortgage finance—have a tendency to tout the benefits with little, if any, discussion of the costs. Numerous studies document a variety of benefits,

1. Demirguc-Kunt and Detragiache (1998).
2. Kaminsky and Reinhart (1999).

both public and private, that are correlated with homeownership.[3] Other studies find correlations that are not so beneficial, such as increased structural unemployment.[4] While correlation is obviously not causality, the positive benefits of homeownership appear to be robust, at least for the average homeowner—even if not for the marginal one. Those benefits, however, must be weighed against the costs that are associated with banking crises, to the extent that banking crises are either driven by or exacerbated by mortgage policies.[5] This chapter argues that U.S. mortgage finance policies were direct contributors to the recent financial crisis.

Housing busts are costly. Examining housing booms and busts across industrial economies between 1971 and 2001, Helbling finds that GDP levels are, on average, around 8 percent below trend three years after the beginning of a housing bust.[6] Of the twenty housing busts defined by Helbling, only one was not associated with a recession. More recent estimates from Reinhart and Rogoff support these findings, wherein financial crises are associated with an average decline of GDP of 9 percent and an average increase in unemployment of 7 percentage points (for the recent U.S. episode, unemployment increased from 4.5 percent to 10 percent).[7] Financial crises, associated with housing busts, also result in substantial increases in government debt.

A harder to quantify but no less real consequence of financial crises is the increased state ownership of financial institutions that often follows. At the time of this writing, the United States government, via the Troubled Asset Relief Program, maintained an interest in 270 financial institutions, most of which are small institutions.[8] Of more consequence is the federal rescue of Fannie Mae and Freddie Mac. For some, such as General Motors' former financing arm Ally Bank, government ownership represents a majority (74 percent for Ally Bank). The United States is not alone in this regard: for instance, the Royal Bank of Scotland is still majority owned by the U.K. government.

Beginning with the seminal contribution of La Porta, Lopez-de-Silanes, and Shleifer, researchers have identified several negative aspects of increased state ownership of banks.[9] Greater government ownership of financial institutions is correlated with lower economic growth and, in particular, lower growth in labor

---

3. For a brief review of the literature on the benefits of homeownership, see Coulson (2002).

4. Blancher and Oswald (2013).

5. Mian and Sufi (2011); Taylor (2012); Fostel and Geanakoplos (2008).

6. Helbling (2005).

7. Reinhart and Rogoff (2009).

8. See Office of the Special Inspector General for the Troubled Asset Relief Program, Quarterly Report to Congress, July 2013 (www.sigtarp.gov/Quarterly%20Reports/July_24_2013_Report_to_Congress.pdf).

9. La Porta, Lopez-de-Silanes, and Shleifer (2002).

productivity (the ultimate driver of wages). More recent research by Shen and Lin suggests that these negative effects arise from increased political interference with bank lending and investment decisions.[10] To the extent that financial crises result from housing and mortgage finance policies, such policies appear to have long-run negative impacts on the economy due to expanded state control of the financial system.[11]

House Prices and Financial Crises

Scholarship on financial crises had long been dominated by either verbal story-telling or stylized mathematical models.[12] Friedman and Schwartz's groundbreaking contribution introduced a more empirical analysis of both financial crises and business cycles.[13] Their work, however, focuses exclusively on the United States and almost exclusively on monetary factors. Despite its empirical nature, much of the interpretation of Freidman and Schwartz remains verbal. Extensive panel studies of financial crises would not appear until the 1990s.

On the one hand, American researchers are fortunate that financial crises are relatively uncommon in the United States. On the other hand, infrequent occurrences leave us with too few observations to ascertain significant statistical patterns. Even for the sake of science, few of us would wish for another Great Depression. Keeping in mind the institutional differences, however, country panel studies have greatly increased our degrees of freedom and knowledge. Beginning with Kaminsky and Reinhart, researchers utilized panel data spanning a number of decades in several countries.[14]

Using a database spanning seventy-six currency crises and twenty-six banking crises between 1970 and 1995, Kaminsky and Reinhart identify booms in equity prices as significant predictors of banking crises. Reinhart and Rogoff extend this analysis to include residential property prices; with similar findings, they show that substantial real increases in housing prices characterize banking crises in advanced economies.[15]

Earlier theoretical work by Gorton and by Calomiris and Gorton place the bursting of asset bubbles at the center of their analysis of banking crises.[16] Asset busts can lead to crises because depositors lack the ability to fully evaluate the

10. Shen and Lin (2012).

11. On the relation between federal housing policy and the recent financial crisis, see Wallison (2010).

12. Kindleberger (2005); MacKay (1841).

13. Friedman and Schwartz (1963).

14. Kaminsky and Reinhart (1999).

15. Reinhart and Rogoff (2008).

16. Gorton (1988); Calomiris and Gorton (1991).

net worth of banks and, accordingly, take observable declines in asset prices as a proxy for bank health. If the funding of said assets is highly leveraged, as is generally the case with real estate, then significant declines in asset values are likely to lead to some financial insolvency.

The association of housing price declines and financial fragility is not an artifact of only modern economies. Calomiris and Gorton attribute 40 percent of national bank failures during the Panic of 1890 to real estate depreciation and about a third of such failures during the Panic of 1884 to similar causes.[17]

Empirical and theoretical research indicates an important role for asset price booms and busts in the frequency of financial crises. But is there anything special about housing? Or is residential real estate simply another asset class for regulators and bankers to monitor? The empirical evidence suggests that, yes, there is something special about housing. Bordo and Jeanne, when examining asset booms and busts in OECD countries between 1970 and 2001, find the probability of a property boom ending in a bust is 52.5 percent.[18] The corresponding probability of a stock market boom ending in a bust is only 12.5 percent in their sample. Put simply, stock market booms generally do not end in busts, whereas property booms do, suggesting that housing markets demand particular attention in terms of financial stability.

More recent research attempts to quantify the marginal impact of housing price appreciation on the probability of a financial crisis. Barrell and others estimate that a 1-percentage-point increase in real house prices raises the probability of a financial crisis by 0.07 percent in the United States.[19] To offset the impact of house price increases, Barrell and others estimate that, for every 3 percent rise in real house prices, a bank's unweighted capital adequacy ratio would have to rise by 1 point.

The unique role of housing prices in financial crises is the result of the high level of dual leverage in the U.S. mortgage finance system. The dual nature of this leverage arises from the elevated debt-to-equity ratios of both mortgagees and mortgagors. In the face of declining asset prices, equity held by borrowers and financial institutions can cushion this decline, avoiding widespread household and financial insolvencies. One can envision the property owner as the first equity cushion. With sufficient declines in asset prices, property owners may default, often in the presence of an adverse income shock. The smaller the cushion of equity, the more likely defaults occur. In the event of a default, the holder of the mortgage becomes the owner of the underlying asset. At this point, the holder's equity cushion becomes the primary determinant of whether it is pushed into insolvency due to a decline in property values.

---

17. Calomiris and Gorton (1991).
18. Bordo and Jeanne (2002).
19. Barrell and others (2010).

Housing is, of course, not the only asset acquired with debt. Financial institutions are required to hold capital against both housing and nonhousing loans. The extremely high level of dual leverage in the U.S. residential mortgage market is, however, unmatched in other sectors of the U.S. economy. Examine, for instance, the U.S. rental market. Moody's apartment price index displays a boom and bust history more extreme than even that of the market for single-family homes. Yet there is little evidence that the U.S. apartment market contributed to the recent crisis, other than its impact on employment and residential investment. Defaults in the apartment sector contributed to the failure of small and regional banks, but the role of these institutions in contributing to any financial "panic" appears trivial.[20] As it relates to taxpayer-provided assistance, direct taxpayer costs have largely been to cover losses in the single-family-home sector. Despite the very large losses associated with the failures of Fannie Mae and Freddie Mac, those are almost exclusively a result of their activities in single-family housing.Comparing differences between the apartment market and the single-family housing market, let us start with the borrower. During the recent housing boom, purchases of single-family homes averaged an LTV ratio of close to 80 percent, as reported by the Federal Housing Finance Agency's "Monthly Interest Rate Survey." The typical purchaser of an apartment complex, in contrast, purchased the property with an LTV ratio of around 60 percent.[21] This difference alone explains a considerable amount of the variation in default rates between owners of single-family homes and owners of apartments.

Let us now take a look at the lender's cushion. The most straightforward cushion is the risk weighting of the apartment loan. Under Basel capital requirements, a bank would hold all of the risk. An adequately capitalized bank keeps 8 percent as a cushion.[22] If the lender holds the single-family house mortgage, the risk weighting equals 50 percent, or 4 percent capital. If, as was typical during the boom, the lender sold the mortgage along with other loans, and reacquired a mortgage-backed security (MBS) containing the loan, the risk weighting was 20 percent, or 1.6 percent capital.

To make the comparison more concrete, assume that there are two properties, both worth $1 million. One is a single-family residence, the other a small apartment complex. For the single-family home, the borrower takes a mortgage for $800,000. If the lender holds this loan on its balance sheet, it reserves 4 percent, or $32,000, against the loan. The apartment complex purchaser takes a mortgage for $500,000, which the lender holds, and sets aside $40,000. Under

---

20. See Felton and Nichols (2012); Bhaskar, Gopalan, and Kliesen (2010).

21. See American Council of Life Insurers (2007).

22. For regulatory definitions of bank capitalization, see *Code of Federal Regulations*, Capital Measures and Capital Category Definitions, title 12, sec. 325.103.

this example, there is a combined $232,000 cushion to absorb loss for the single-family home loan and $560,000 to absorb loss for the apartment loan. Although it is a highly stylized example, this comparison illustrates why a boom and bust in the apartment market does not result in a systemic crisis, whereas similar losses in the single-family housing market can.

In the following sections, I examine the drivers of this dual leverage and offer policy proposals to minimize the risk arising from housing booms and busts.

Demographics and Loan-Level Characteristics

This section argues that reduced down payments for borrowers have been a significant driver of mortgage defaults, particularly when the borrowers have low credit ratings. The connection between low down payment lending and population demographics, particularly the age profile, is then examined. I argue that low down payment lending dramatically increased homeownership among households under the age of thirty, arguably allowing such households to skip the process of saving for a down payment. Low down payment lending also played a critical role among older borrowers and among investors, which, while contributing to increased defaults, added little to short-term gains in homeownership.

Given that economists still debate the causes of the Great Depression, it should be of little surprise that scholars are divided over the causes of the recent Great Recession. Among the topics debated are the drivers of mortgage default. The arguments in this chapter are built upon the relationship between borrower equity and mortgage default.[23] The theory is that, in the face of an adverse income shock such as job loss, households with less equity will be less likely to be able to maintain their mortgage payments and will have fewer incentives to do so.

One element of public debate regarding mortgage default is the contribution of loan features deemed unfair or even predatory. The theory, to the extent there is one, behind Dodd-Frank's Mortgage Reform and Anti-Predatory Lending Act is that abusive loan features pushed borrowers into default, triggering the crisis. To abstract away from these loan features, table 12-1 presents normalized claim rates for the Federal Housing Administration's single-family housing loans. Each cell is a multiple of the normalized 1.0 in the upper right cell; for instance, a rate of 5.6 would represent a claim rate 5.6 times that observed for the cell 1.0. FHA loans are almost always fixed-rate, thirty-year mortgages with no prepayment penalty, no teaser rate, and various fees capped either by regulation or statute. FHA is essentially the benchmark for a "safe loan" under most definitions of

---

23. For a review of this literature, see Ayres and Mitts (2012); Foote, Gerardi, and Willen (2008); Vandell (1995).

Table 12-1. *Claim Rates, FHA Single-Family Insured Loans*[a]

Loan-to-value ratios (percent)	Credit scores			
	500—79	*580–619*	*620–79*	*680–850*
Up to 90	2.6	2.5	1.9	1.0
90.1–95	5.9	4.7	3.8	1.7
Above 95	8.2	5.6	3.5	1.5

Source: Galante (2011).
a. Claim rates relative to that of the lowest-risk cell.

abusive lending, such as that used under the risk-retention requirements of section 941 of the Dodd-Frank Act.

As one reads right to left across the table, borrower credit quality declines, and as one descends down the rows, borrower down payment declines. What is immediately obvious is the exponential nature of increasing loan loss, as the LTV ratio increases and credit quality declines. Similar results have been documented outside of the FHA as well as being established within the FHA, controlling for a variety of other variables and for earlier time periods.[24]

Research since the crisis has questioned whether cheap credit, particularly as measured by the LTV ratio, can explain the crisis. Glaeser, Gottlieb, and Gyourko suggest that trends in the average LTV ratio cannot explain the housing bubble.[25] Subsequent analysis by Duca, Muellbauer, and Murphy, however, expands the analysis to examine trends in LTV ratios for first-time homebuyers.[26] Estimates by Duca, Muellbauer, and Murphy suggest that about half of the real appreciation in home prices between the fourth quarters of 2001 and 2005 can be attributed to an increase in LTV ratios among first-time homebuyers.

While LTV ratios among first-time buyers have been trending upward since the early 1990s, the early 2000s witnessed a significant acceleration of that trend. The increase in first-time-buyer LTV ratios also closely tracks the private label, MBS share of the mortgage market, although one must bear in mind the large private-label MBS purchases by the government-sponsored enterprises, particularly from 2002 to 2005.[27] Even had there been no expansion of mortgages to borrowers with a weak credit history, the increase in LTV ratios among first-time buyers would have significantly increased delinquencies in the face of a housing bust.

24. See Anderson, Capozza, and Van Order (2008); Hendershott and Schultz (1993); Von Furstenberg (1969).
25. Glaeser, Gottlieb, and Gyourko (2010).
26. Duca, Muellbauer, and Murphy (2011).
27. Calabria (2011).

Given the usual necessity of saving for a down payment, and the normal amortization of most mortgages, LTV ratios differ dramatically across homeowners. The highest ratios are among the youngest households. Among all homeowners (not just recent buyers) LTV ratios averaged just below 40 percent in 2010, up from around 30 percent during the boom. Households with heads under age forty, on average, display LTV ratios just over 70 percent, up from around 60 percent during the boom. Younger households are also more likely to have a mortgage. Despite a dramatic increase in mortgage use by elderly households, partly driven by the expansion of FHA's Home Equity Conversion Mortgage program, over half of elderly households still own their homes free and clear. Among families under age forty, less than 10 percent own their homes free and clear.[28]

The decade from 1994 to 2004, essentially moving from the trough to near the peaks of both the housing boom and trends in age-specific ownership rates, witnessed a 5-percentage-point increase in homeownership, from 64 percent to 69 percent. This increase was not spread evenly across age groups. Amazingly, households under age twenty-five saw an almost doubling in their homeownership rate, an 11-percentage-point increase (from 15 percent to almost 26 percent). The increase among households twenty-five to twenty-nine years of age was almost as impressive, with an 8-percentage-point increase (from 34 percent to 42 percent). Figure 12-1 illustrates this increase, by five-year age increments, for families under forty years of age.

As the cliché goes, What goes up must come down. The dramatic increase in homeownership rates among younger households has been somewhat matched by an equally dramatic reversal. The largest declines in homeownership, since the ending of the boom, occurred among households under age forty. By contrast, homeownership rates for households over age seventy-five have actually increased since the onset of the bust. To the extent that the increase in homeownership among younger households was driven by increases in LTV ratios, the decline in homeownership among this group is also a result of the interaction of high LTV ratios with a downturn in home prices.

One measure of distress is the degree to which households are underwater on their mortgage (that is, the value of their mortgage exceeds the value of their home). Carter calculates the percentage of households underwater, by age, between 1997 and 2009.[29] A number of trends emerge.

The age trend displays a larger frequency of young households being underwater: the frequency in 2009 for households under thirty-five was almost three times that for households over sixty-five. Even after the onset of the bust, the

---

28. For age-related homeownership rates, see Emmons and Noeth (2013).

29. Carter (2012). Separately calculated figures from the Survey of Consumer Finance yield slightly smaller frequencies but qualitatively similar results. See Wolff (2012).

Figure 12-1. *Homeownership Rates, by Age Group, 1994–2012*[a]

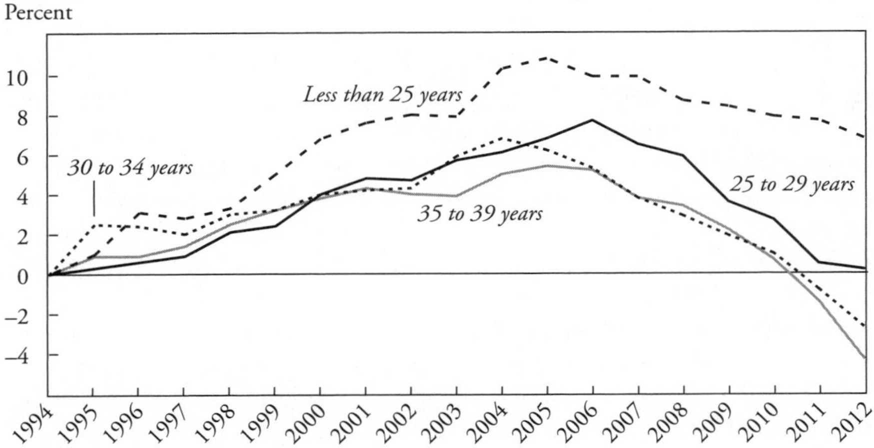

Percent

Source: Emmons and Noeth (2013); U.S. Census Bureau (2013).
a. Five-year age groups are younger than forty years.

frequency of underwater households over age sixty-five was less than that of households under age thirty-five at the peak of the boom in 2005.

To the extent that negative equity is a driver behind mortgage default, and negative equity is also the result of younger households entering homeownership earlier due to a relaxation in down payment requirements, we can connect the age of borrowers with mortgage defaults.[30] This is not to imply that age itself is an independent driver of mortgage default but rather that low or negative equity has been the result of expanding homeownership to younger households and that the resulting reduction in equity among those borrowers has driven mortgage delinquencies.

Because younger households started out with less equity, their percentage reductions in equity during the bust were greater as well, magnifying the impact of the recession on the balance sheet of younger households. Homeowners under age thirty-five have witnessed an average decline in home equity of around 60 percent, whereas owners over age seventy-five experienced a decline of less than 10 percent.[31] Between these extremes, increasing age is associated with smaller reductions in home equity. Wolff also finds mortgage delinquency rates to loosely decline with age. This section suggests that a significant contributor to the rise in mortgage delinquencies is the reduction in down payments, particularly

30. Bhutta, Dokko, and Shan (2010).
31. Wolff (2012).

among first-time, generally younger, homebuyers. Such an outcome was not only foreseeable but, in at least one instance, predicted. Deng, Quigley, and Van Order simulate the outcome of a policy of offering low down payment mortgages.[32] Their results indicate that if a zero down payment option were offered priced as a conventional mortgage, the expected losses could exceed 10 percent of the funds loaned. The sensitivity of their results is highly dependent upon the rate of house price appreciation, unemployment, and household income relative to area median household income. Their "extreme" case of zero price appreciation, zero down payment, 8 percent unemployment, and an income 60 percent of the median yields a cumulative fifteen-year default rate of 35 percent.

Obviously, events of the last several years make this "extreme" case look relatively mild. Even under the sunny situation of 10 percent price appreciation, 4 percent unemployment, and 150 percent of area median income, Deng, Quigley, and Van Order still find zero down payment loans to have a fifteen-year cumulative default rate of 4.4 percent.[33] If anything, history shows the cost estimates of Deng, Quigley, and Van Order to be on the conservative side. Gerardi, Shapiro, and Willen also provide evidence that the primary driver of default is a combination of the LTV ratio and continued borrower equity.[34]

The arguments presented here are consistent with the theory of low-equity clustering proposed by Ayres and Mitts, who argue that it is not simply the average level of negative equity that matters but also—and more important—the distribution of negative equity.[35] Consider two populations, both with average LTV ratios of 90 percent and both suffering a fall in house prices of 15 percent. In population A, where all households have an LTV ratio of 90, the entire population is underwater. In population B, where 50 percent have an LTV ratio of 100 and 50 percent have an LTV ratio of 80, only half the population is underwater. Ayres and Mitts suggest that geographic clusters of low-equity borrowers explain the mortgage defaults.

I suggest that low-equity clustering also occurred by age, more specifically among younger households. Given the lower attachment of younger households to the labor market, low-equity clustering among the young also makes such households more vulnerable to the double-trigger models of default that incorporate both job loss and negative equity. Johnson and Mommaerts estimate that younger households, particularly those under age twenty-five, are significantly more likely than older households to lose their jobs.[36] Among those whose jobs

32. Deng, Quigley, and Van Order (1996).
33. Deng, Quigley, and Van Order (1996).
34. Gerardi, Shapiro, and Willen (2009).
35. Ayres and Mitts (2012).
36. Johnson and Mommaerts (2011).

ended during the study period were 29.1 percent of workers aged eighteen to twenty-four. Other age groups' job losses were smaller: 17.3 percent for ages twenty-five to thirty-four, 13.0 percent for ages thirty-five to forty-nine, 12.5 percent for ages fifty to sixty-one, and 17.9 percent for ages sixty-two and older.

The focus on younger households also derives from the policy objective of increasing homeownership via the reduction of down payments. For many younger households, the need to save for a down payment can delay the transition to homeownership. Older homeowners are also likely to take advantage of reduced equity requirements but without a corresponding gain in homeownership rates. The discussion here does not intend to imply that the recent boom was driven solely, or even mainly, by young households but that the policy relevance of reduced down payment requirements is largely an issue for younger households. Although the prevalence of negative equity is greater for younger households, the depth for those households underwater is often greater for older households, due largely to borrower extraction of equity via refinance. This suggests different policy responses. For younger households, down payment requirements are likely more binding, whereas for older households restrictions on federal support of equity extraction is more important. To the extent that federal backing is provided, such backing can be limited to purchase loans and not to cash-out refinancing.

The preceding focuses upon the increase in leverage during the recent boom by homeowners. Investors, those not intending to live in the home, also played an important role in driving both increased leverage and home prices. Researchers at the Federal Reserve Bank of New York have documented both the increasing percent of purchases made by investors and increasing leverage among these investors.[37] Calabria also documents the increasing investor share of Fannie Mae and Freddie Mac purchases.[38] Given the greater propensity for investors to default, federally backed loans to investors should be subjected to a higher level of underwriting than comparable purchase loans. Haughwout and others focus on "self-reported" investor loans, whereas many investor loans were initially reported as owner occupied.[39] Piskorski, Seru, and Witkin note that "more than 6% of mortgage loans reported for owner-occupied properties were given to borrowers with a different primary residence."[40] Their research suggests that increased fraud by both borrowers and originators was in part due to the increased use of securitization.

37. Haughwout and others (2011). See also Robinson (2012).
38. Calabria (2011).
39. Haughwout and others (2011).
40. Piskorski, Seru, and Witkin (2013, p. 3).

Figure 12-2. *Home Mortgages Securitized, 1962–2010*

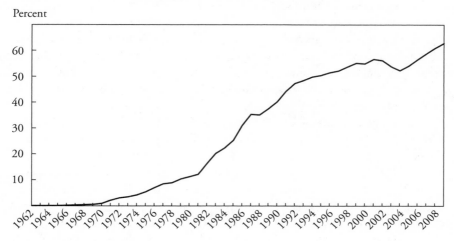

Source: Federal Reserve (2011).

Mortgage defaults, of any level, need not result in insolvencies among financial institutions. Nor does any level of mortgage delinquency guarantee a financial crisis. The level of mortgage default, along with the severity of loss, determines the losses that holders of mortgages incur. Whether holders become insolvent is also a function of the equity capital held to absorb losses. Losses can be offset by equity. Such was not to be, however: as leverage increased on the part of borrowers, so did leverage increase on the part of mortgage investors and lenders. The following section examines this trend.

Securitization and Financial Stability

With the exception of information technology, there are probably few sectors of the economy that have changed as dramatically in the last few decades as the financial sector. Among the most significant changes is how the mortgage market is funded (figure 12-2). It is hard to grasp the fact that, as President Reagan took office in 1981, government-sponsored enterprises owned or guaranteed only about 17 percent of the mortgage market. Around a third of that share was held directly on portfolio, with the remainder representing virtually all the securitized mortgage activity. The private issuance of MBSs was trivial. Over two-thirds of residential mortgages were held directly on the balance sheet of depositories. By the end of 2006, at the height of the housing boom, 56 percent of residential mortgages were held either in agency pools or as private label securities. Thirty-one percent were held as whole loans on the balance sheets of banks, thrifts, and credit unions.

Securitization had its benefits, though some were more perceived than real.[41] Certainly MBSs were, in general, more liquid than the underlying mortgages. They were also priced more regularly in the market, offering institutions a more accurate measure of the value of the assets on their balance sheets. Those values, of course, might be more representative of market opinion, but they were also likely to be more volatile.

One of the benefits of securitization for financial institutions was that it allowed for significant reductions in required capital, the flip side of which is increased leverage. Under both Basel I, published in 1988, and Basel II, published in 2004, securitized mortgages required far less capital than whole mortgages. The risk weight for whole mortgages, under Basel, is 50 percent, whereas the risk weight for MBSs is 20 percent. Many of the recent banking problems in Europe are a direct result of capital standards placing a zero risk weighting on OECD government debt. Any system of banking regulation that calls Greek sovereign debt risk free is a system likely to fail.

Much of this impact was recognized before the crisis. Ambrose, Lacour-Little, and Sanders find evidence consistent with the notion that securitization is driven by an arbitrage of capital standards.[42] They focus on the arbitrage within a bank's own portfolio. The International Monetary Fund also notes that, during the expansion of the housing boom, the largest banks significantly expanded their total assets with only a relatively modest increase in total risk-weighted assets, allowing for a significant increase in leverage.[43] This was accomplished not by increasing the loans-to-assets ratio but by increasing the holdings of securities.

Capital arbitrage also works across institutions. To some degree, the growth of Fannie Mae and Freddie Mac was likely the result of mortgage credit risk flowing to the most highly leveraged segments of the financial system.

Perhaps the most egregious element of the Basel capital standards was the allowance of a zero risk weighting on off-balance-sheet, short-term "liquidity" guarantees. Banks could originate (or purchase) mortgages and mortgage-backed securities and place them in off-balance-sheet, special-purpose entities (also known as special investment vehicles). Such entities were then funded in the short-term commercial paper market, with the investor usually being a money market mutual fund. Banks could choose to incorporate these entities as separate corporations, in which case the banks would retain no risk. Most banks, in order to increase the attractiveness (and credit rating) of these vehicles, offered liquidity

41. Shin (2009).
42. Ambrose, Lacour-Little, and Sanders (2005).
43. IMF (2008).

Table 12-2. *Alternative Capital Holdings for Financial System Mortgage Holdings, 2006*

Millions of dollars unless otherwise noted

	Mortgage holdings	Minimum capital ratio (percent)	Minimum capital	Minimum 10% capital ratio	Minimum capital	No-risk weights (percent)	Minimum capital
Depositories	2,932,733	4.00	117,309	5.00	146,637	8.00	234,619
Agency, whole loans	457,587	2.50	11,440	2.50	11,440	2.50	11,440
Agency, MBS guarantees	3,749,120	0.45	16,871	0.45	16,871	0.45	16,871
ABS private issuers	2,167,117	0.00	. . .	0.00	. . .	0.00	. . .
Bank GSE debt holdings	786,654	1.60	12,586	2.00	15,733	8.00	62,932
Total capital	. . .	. . .	158,207	. . .	190,680	. . .	325,862
Alternate scenario (all bank, whole loan)	9,306,557	4.00	372,262	5.00	465,328	8.00	744,525
Additional capital	. . .	. . .	214,056	. . .	274,647	. . .	418,663

Source: Author's calculations; Federal Reserve (2007).

guarantees behind these entities. As long as these guarantees were under a year in duration, the Basel rules provided a zero risk weight for capital purposes.

The zero risk weight on short-term bank guarantees interacted in a perverse manner with the regulation of money market mutual funds (MMMFs). By regulation, MMMFs are limited to holding only short-term, highly rated securities. Such a system provided a ready source of demand for short-term, asset-backed commercial paper issued by banks, especially in a low interest rate environment where funds were pushed to reach for yield. Since neither the MMMFs nor the short-term bank guarantees required capital, the interaction of these two separate regulations resulted in a financing of mortgages that could be leveraged on a massive scale. Acharya, Schnabl, and Suarez estimate that this combination of regulatory incentives reduced banking system capital by almost $70 billion, had such loans been held on the balance sheet of depositories.[44]

To give an indication of the impact of capital arbitrage, table 12-2 represents alternative scenarios. Total U.S. home mortgages held in 2006 equaled

44. Acharya, Schnabl, and Suarez (2012).

$10.48 trillion. Depository institutions, government-sponsored enterprises, and private asset-backed security pools held $9.3 trillion, which forms the basis of the figures below.

The table also shows present capital requirements and additional system capital if all $9.3 trillion mortgages in 2006 were held as whole loans on the balance sheet of depositories. As the FDIC requires a 10 percent risk-weighted capital ratio for banks to be considered "well capitalized," the table shows this comparison with a 10 percent ratio. Finally, the table presents estimates for a flat 8 percent unweighted capital ratio. All of the alternatives make the assumption that neither the demand nor the supply of mortgage credit is affected by changes in capital requirements. I revisit that assumption later.

A mortgage finance system characterized by the holding of whole mortgages on bank balance sheets would also be a system with over $200 billion more in equity, a cushion of equity that could have strengthened confidence as the crisis hit—and a cushion that could have stood before any taxpayer losses. At a 10 percent risk-weighted capital ratio, that cushion increases to almost $300 billion. An elimination of risk weighting would, all else equal, raise that cushion to over $400 billion.

Reducing the leverage of the U.S. mortgage finance system obviously raises the issue of whether there would be sufficient capital to support the mortgage market. I discuss the role of household mortgage leverage earlier: reducing the level of individual household mortgage leverage would allow for some reduction in overall system leverage. For instance, in 2007 households held real estate valued at $20.8 trillion, backed by mortgage debt totaling $10.5 trillion, yielding a ratio of equity to value of 49.4 percent. Increasing that value to 57.5 percent would reduce total mortgage debt outstanding by $1 trillion, allowing for a reduction in financial system leverage as well.

The preceding discussion assumes that the levels of leverage observed in the mortgage market accurately mirror the true levels of leverage. During the peak of the boom, valuations in both single-family and multifamily markets were driven by comparables that reflect the boom. The possibility of using a more comparable trend for appraisals, rather than a snapshot, could potentially reduce the procyclical nature of the appraisal process. Booms can also lead to aggressive assumptions regarding income growth for income-producing properties. Again, using assumptions that dampen cyclical factors would provide more stable measures of leverage. To some extent the growth of government-backed securitization has reduced the incentives for originators to gather more accurate and stable measures. Compared to the current mortgage finance system, moving toward a greater reliance on bank balance-sheet funding would not only increase the capital in the system but also better align the incentives for tracking and measuring leverage at the loan level.

Another benefit of increased equity on the part of both borrowers and lenders is that it provides a greater cushion in the event that property valuations contain large errors. To some extent, neither regulators nor market participants can ever truly know the actual amount of leverage in the system. Valuations can change quickly, even when they are measured accurately. Such errors become more important as leverage increases. For simplicity, posit that the true price of a home observed by lenders or investors is plus or minus 10 percent of the observed price, with a 0.5 probability of either. With a 10 percent down payment, half the time the actual borrower equity is zero. A similar analysis holds for the examination of bank solvency. Again, a higher equity cushion on the part of borrowers and lenders will reduce the likelihood that measurement errors result in insolvencies.

Policy Recommendations

Incentives facing both the borrower and the lender greatly contributed to increased leverage in the mortgage finance system. Given the social harm from housing busts and any accompanying financial crisis, policies to reduce these costs appear badly needed.

On the part of borrowers, federally backed mortgages should require modest down payments.[45] Hatchondo, Martinez, and Sánchez estimate that a minimum down payment of 15 percent would reduce mortgage defaults by 30 percent.[46] If house prices did not adjust (fall), homeownership rates would fall by an estimated 0.2 percent. A full downward adjustment in house prices of 0.7 percent would result in no decline in homeownership rates. In any event, it appears that large reductions in mortgage defaults can be achieved with a relatively low impact on both homeownership and house prices.

Alternatively Hatchondo, Martinez, and Sánchez estimate that garnishing the income of defaulters, in excess of 43 percent of median consumption, would achieve similar declines in defaults but with lower required down payments. It would result in an increase in both homeownership and housing prices. Despite the vast welfare improvements of such a proposal, I believe the time-inconsistency problem facing policymakers would render it ineffective.[47] Policies facing borrowers need to endure housing busts. While Athreya, Tam, and Young find that "harsh" penalties for defaulting borrowers would improve social (and borrower) welfare, these policies again strike me as politically unsustainable, accepting that

45. Hong Kong Monetary Authority (2011).
46. Hatchondo, Martinez, and Sánchez (2011).
47. Kydland and Prescott (1977).

Figure 12-3. *Homeownership Rate and Loan-to-Value Ratios, by Decade, 1950–2010*

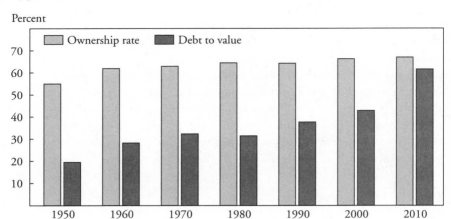

Source: Federal Reserve (2011).

the development of a model of political behavior regarding borrowers is beyond the scope of this chapter.[48]

In assessing the impact of down payment requirements on homeownership, history suggests that the bulk of the impact will be manifested more in home prices than in homeownership rates. Figure 12-3 displays the national home-ownership rate and the average owner's loan-to-value ratio. What is immediately obvious is that long-run homeownership gains since 1960 have been relatively modest, while average leverage has more than doubled.

From 1960 to 1980, the average LTV ratio remained relatively stable. Beginning in the 1990s, after the Tax Reform Act of 1986 eliminated the deductibility of all but mortgage debt, the LTV ratios dramatically increased to the point that in 2010 they were double what they had been in 1980. When comparing this trend to Shiller's time series on real house prices, prices follow a similar trend: relatively stable until the 1990s and then a massive boom that corresponds to the increase in leverage.[49] Again, the time series suggests that the most significant impact of the increased leverage was increasing prices, not homeownership. Setting aside the most recent boom, the Shiller series also raises a basic question about the value of homeownership as an investment, as between 1950 and 1997 the series fluctuated around an index value of 107. It is simply hard to conclude from the last 120 years of data that housing in the United States has been a

48. Athreya, Tam, and Young (2009).
49. See www.econ.yale.edu/~shiller/data.htm. Also see Shiller (2005).

good investment. If one plots five-year rolling changes in real house prices (not shown), it also becomes readily apparent that housing is a risky investment.

A contributing factor to the increased leverage on the part of homeowners is the confusion between ownership and debt. At the extreme, if one has zero (or negative) equity in a property, it is hard in any real sense to label one an owner. A contributor to the increase in household leverage has been the mortgage-interest deduction. While others offer more complex proposals to reform the deduction, a gradual elimination would likely be both the easiest to implement and the most effective at reducing household leverage.[50]

As the chapter emphasizes, it was the unique combination of high leverage on the part of both borrowers and lenders that contributed to the crisis. Financial reform efforts to reduce this leverage should include an elimination of Basel's risk-weighting system to be replaced with a simple, flat leverage ratio of around 10 percent, with an equal treatment of on- and off-balance-sheet funding. As important, any federally chartered institution, whether a depository or a government-sponsored enterprise, must be subject to equal capital treatment for the holding of mortgages. Raising bank capital requirements while leaving those of even more highly leveraged institutions unchanged would be to double down on the mistakes of the past. Equal capital treatment should also apply to both whole loans and mortgage-backed securities. Regulators in the United Kingdom have proposed increasing capital standards required for mortgages in line with increases in housing prices. While such an idea has considerable merit and attractiveness, the political pressure during a housing boom would be to continue the boom and not "lean against the wind." Accordingly, the policy proposals suggested here have intentionally not relied on the discretion of bank regulators or politicians but do have the advantage of being hardwired into statute.

A potential counter to the proposals raised here, especially those regarding increased down payments, is that a modest increase in down payments of, say, 5 or even 10 percent would have made little difference in a market where prices were falling 20 or 30 percent. First, the depth of negative equity is directly related to default.[51] Even if households were still underwater, being *less* underwater would likely reduce mortgage delinquencies. Second, increased down payment requirements on federally backed loans would also reduce the demand for housing, with the result that housing prices in the boom period would increase by less, suggesting that housing price declines that followed the boom would be more modest. At a very basic level, the policies here are aimed less at cushioning the bust than at restraining the boom. Gerardi, Shapiro, and Willen also provide evidence that, even in the face of large price declines, mortgages with initial

---

50. Ayres and Mitts (2012).
51. Bhutta, Dokko, and Shan (2010).

combined LTV ratios of under 90 percent performed reasonably well during the recent crisis.[52]

Conclusions

The housing bubble and financial crisis were the result of a multitude of policy choices.[53] This chapter does not attempt a comprehensive analysis of the crisis, nor are its proposals comprehensive. The focus is instead on forces unique to the U.S. system of mortgage finance. Reform in other areas, including monetary policy, is also badly needed.

Banking crises, particularly those associated with housing busts, are quite costly. While a variety of policies, such as monetary policy, were likely contributors to the financial crisis of 2008, this chapter argues that the uniquely high levels of "dual" leverage in the mortgage finance system were the primary drivers of the losses to both households and financial institutions. Policies that directly reduce household and financial system leverage should, however, be at the heart of mortgage finance reform.

Homeownership policies that leave households deeply underwater or in foreclosure are not sustainable policies. On the tax side, the mortgage interest deduction provides an incentive for households to become more leveraged, just as the expensing of interest encourages higher corporate leverage. An elimination of the mortgage interest deduction should be part of any reform debate. Subsidies for low down payment lending, such as those provided by FHA and the government-sponsored enterprises, should also be scaled back if not eliminated. To the extent that government chooses to subsidize homeownership, those subsidies should be targeted at home equity rather than home debt.

On the bank regulatory side, a substitute of the Basel risk weights for a flat leverage ratio could reduce both the herding of banks into mortgage assets as well as decreasing overall bank leverage, if done correctly. Additionally, policies that continue to tap households, in their role of taxpayers, to recapitalize financial institutions are also not sustainable.

References

Acharya, Viral, and Matthew Richardson. 2009. "Causes of the Financial Crisis." *Critical Review: A Journal of Politics and Society* 21, no. 2–3: 195–210.

Acharya, Viral, Philipp Schnabl, and Gustavo Suarez. 2010. Working Paper 15730. Cambridge, Mass.: National Bureau of Economic Research.

---

52. Gerardi, Shapiro, and Willen (2009).
53. Acharya and Richardson (2009).

————. 2012. "Securitization without Risk Transfer." *Journal of Financial Economics* 107, no. 3: 515–36

Ambrose, Brent, Michael Lacour-Little, and Anthony Sanders. 2005. "Does Regulatory Capital Arbitrage or Asymmetric Information Drive Securitization?" *Journal of Financial Services Research* 28, no. 1–3: 113–33.

American Council of Life Insurers. 2007. "Commercial Mortgage Commitments." Washington.

Anderson, Charles, Dennis Capozza, and Robert Van Order. 2008. "Deconstructing the Subprime Debacle Using New Indices of Underwriting Quality and Economic Conditions: A First Look." North Palm Beach, Fla.: Homer Hoyt Advanced Studies Institute.

Athreya, Kartik, Xuan Tam, and Eric Young. 2009. "Are Harsh Penalties for Default Really Better?" Working Paper 09-11. Federal Reserve Bank of Richmond.

Ayres, Ian, and Joshua Mitts. 2012. "Three Proposals for Regulating the Distribution of Home Equity." Working Paper. Yale Law School.

Barrell, Ray, E. Philip Davis, Dilruba Karim, and Iana Liadze. 2010. "Bank Regulation, Property Prices and Early Warning Systems for Banking Crises in OECD Countries." *Journal of Banking and Finance* 34, no. 9: 2255–64.

Bhaskar, Rajeev, Yadav Gopalan, and Kevin Kliesen. 2010. "Commercial Real Estate: A Drag for Some Banks but Maybe Not for U.S. Economy." *Regional Economist* (Federal Reserve Bank of St. Louis), January.

Bhutta, Neil, Jane Dokko, and Hui Shan. 2010. "The Depth of Negative Equity and Mortgage Default Decisions." Finance and Economic Discussion Series Paper 2010-35. Washington: Federal Reserve Board.

Blancher and Oswald. 2013. "Does High Home-Ownership Impair the Labor Market?" Working Paper 19079. Cambridge, Mass.: National Bureau of Economic Research.

Bordo, Michael, and Olivier Jeanne. 2002. "Boom-Busts in Asset Prices, Economic Instability, and Monetary Policy." Working Paper 8966. Cambridge, Mass.: National Bureau of Economic Research.

Calabria, Mark. 2011. "Fannie, Freddie, and the Subprime Mortgage Market." Briefing Paper 120. Washington: CATO Institute.

Calomiris, Charles, and Gary Gorton. 1991. "The Origins of Banking Panics: Models, Facts, and Bank Regulation." In *Financial Markets and Financial Crises*, edited by R. Glenn Hubbard. University of Chicago Press.

Carter, George R., III. 2012. "Housing Units with Negative Equity, 1997–2009." *Cityscape: A Journal of Policy Development and Research* 14, no. 1: 149–65.

Coulson, Edward. 2002. "Housing Policy and the Social Benefits of Homeownership." *Business Review* (Federal Reserve Bank of Philadelphia) 2Q: 7–16.

Demirguc-Kunt, Asli, and Enrica Detragiache. 1998. "The Determinants of Banking Crises in Developing and Developed Countries." *IMF Staff Papers* 45: 81–109.

Deng, Yongheng, John Quigley, and Robert Van Order. 1996. "Mortgage Default and Low Down Payment Loans: The Costs of Public Subsidy." *Regional Science and Urban Economics* 26, no. 3–4: 263–85.

Duca, John, John Muellbauer, and Anthony Murphy. 2010. "Housing Markets and the Financial Crisis of 2007–2009: Lessons for the Future." *Journal of Financial Stability* 6: 203–17.

———. 2011. "Credit Standards and the Bubble in US House Prices: New Econometric Evidence." *BIS Papers* 64: 83–89.

Emmons, William, and Bryan Noeth. 2013. "Why Did Young Families Lose So Much Wealth during the Crisis? The Role of Homeownership." Federal Reserve Bank of St. Louis *Review* 95, no. 1: 1–26.

Federal Reserve. 2007. "Flow of Funds Accounts of the United States Statistical Release Z.1."

———. 2011. "Flow of Funds Accounts of the United States Statistical Release Z.1. "

Felton, Andrew, and Joseph B. Nichols. 2012. "Commercial Real Estate Loan Performance at Failed US Banks." *BIS Papers* 64: 19–24.

Foote, Christopher, Kristopher Gerardi, and Paul Willen. 2008. "Negative Equity and Foreclosure: Theory and Evidence." *Journal of Urban Economics* 64, no. 2: 234–45.

Fostel, Ana, and John Geanakoplos. 2008. "Leverage Cycles and the Anxious Economy." *American Economic Review* 98, no. 4: 1211–44.

Friedman, Milton, and Anna Schwartz. 1963. *A Monetary History of the United States, 1867–1960*. Princeton University Press.

Galante, Carol. 2011. "Testimony before the Subcommittee on Insurance, Housing, and Community Development, Committee on Financial Services, United States House of Representatives." September 8.

Gerardi, Kristopher, Adam Hale Shapiro, and Paul Willen. 2009. "Decomposing the Foreclosure Crisis: House Price Depreciation versus Bad Underwriting." Working Paper 2009-25. Federal Reserve Bank of Atlanta.

Glaeser, Edward, Joshua Gottlieb, and Joseph Gyourko. 2010. "Can Cheap Credit Explain the Housing Boom?" Working Paper 16230. Cambridge, Mass.: National Bureau of Economic Research.

Gorton, Gary. 1988. "Banking Panics and Business Cycles." *Oxford Economic Papers* 40: 751–81.

Haughwout, Andrew, Donghoon Lee, Joseph Tracy, and Wilbert van der Klaauw. 2011. "Real Estate Investors, the Leverage Cycle, and the Housing Market Crisis." Staff Report 514. Federal Reserve Bank of New York.

Hatchondo, Juan Carlos, Leonardo Martinez, and Juan M. Sánchez. 2011. "Mortgage Defaults." Working Paper 2011-019A. Federal Reserve Bank of St. Louis.

Helbling, Thomas. 2005. "Housing Price Bubbles—A Tale Based on Housing Price Booms and Busts." *BIS Papers* 21: 30–41.

Hendershott, Patric, and William Schultz. 1993. "Equity and Nonequity Determinants of FHA Single-Family Mortgage Foreclosures in the 1980s." *Journal of the American Real Estate and Urban Economics Association* 21, no. 4: 405–30.

Hong Kong Monetary Authority. 2011. "Loan-to-Value Ratio as a Macroprudential Tool—Hong Kong SAR's Experience and Cross-Country Evidence." *BIS Papers* 57: 163–78.

IMF (International Monetary Fund). 2008. *Global Financial Stability Report*. April.

Johnson, Richard, and Corina Mommaerts. 2011. "Age Differences in Job Loss, Job Search and Reemployment." Discussion Paper 11-01. Washington: Urban Institute.

Kaminsky, Graciela, and Carmen Reinhart. 1999. "The Twin Crises: The Causes of Banking and Balance-of-Payments Problems." *American Economic Review* 89, no. 3: 473–500.

Kindleberger, Charles. 2005. *Manias, Panics and Crashes: A History of Financial Crises.* 5th ed. Hoboken, N.J.: Wiley.

Kydland, Finn, and Edward Prescott. 1977. "Rules Rather than Discretion: The Inconsistency of Optimal Plans." *Journal of Political Economy* 85, no. 3: 473–92.

La Porta, Rafael, Florencio Lopez-de-Silanes, and Andrei Shleifer. 2002. "Government Ownership of Banks." *Journal of Finance* 57, no. 1: 265–301.

MacKay, Charles. 1841. *Memoirs of Extraordinary Popular Delusions.* London: R. Bentley.

Mian, Atif, and Amir Sufi. 2011. "House Prices, Home Equity-Based Borrowing, and the US Household Leverage Crisis." *American Economic Review* 101, no. 5: 2132–56.

Piskorski, Tomasz, Amit Seru, and James Witkin. 2013. "Asset Quality Misrepresentation by Financial Intermediaries: Evidence from RMBS Market." Research Paper 13-7. Columbia Business School.

Reinhart, Carmen, and Kenneth Rogoff. 2008. "Is the 2007 U.S. Subprime Crisis So Different? An International Historical Comparison." *American Economic Review* 98, no. 2: 339–44.

———. 2009. *This Time Is Different: Eight Centuries of Financial Folly.* Princeton University Press.

Robinson, Breck. 2012. "The Performance of Non-Owner-Occupied Mortgages during the Housing Crisis." *Economic Quarterly* (Federal Reserve Bank of Richmond) 98, no. 2: 111–38.

Shen, Chung-Hua, and Chih-Yung Lin. 2012. "Why Government Banks Underperform: A Political Interference View." *Journal of Financial Intermediation* 21, no. 2: 181–202 (www.sciencedirect.com/science/article/pii/S1042957311000271).

Shiller, Robert. 2005. *Irrational Exuberance.* 2nd ed., revised and updated. New York: Currency/Doubleday.

Shin, Hyun Song. 2009. "Securitisation and Financial Stability." *Economic Journal* 119 (March): 309–32.

Taylor, Alan. 2012. "The Great Leveraging." Working Paper 18290. Cambridge, Mass.: National Bureau of Economic Research.

U.S. Census Bureau. 2013. *Housing Vacancies and Homeownership.*

Vandell, Kerry. 1995. "How Ruthless Is Mortgage Default? A Review and Synthesis of the Evidence." *Journal of Housing Research* 6, no. 2: 245–64.

Von Furstenberg, George. 1969. "Default Risk on FHA-Insured Home Mortgages as a Function of the Terms of Financing: A Quantitative Analysis." *Journal of Finance* 24, no. 3: 459–77.

Wallison, Peter. 2010. "Government Housing Policy and the Financial Crisis." *Cato Journal* 30, no. 2: 397–406.

Wolff, Edward. 2012. "The Asset Price Meltdown and the Wealth of the Middle Class." Working Paper 18559. Cambridge, Mass.: National Bureau of Economic Research.

PART V

Sustaining Homeownership

13

Engaging Distressed Homeowners

MARK COLE

For most families, a central part of the American Dream has been the goal of homeownership. In 2004 consumer attitudes, public policy, and the private sector were all integrally involved in driving the rate of homeownership to a record high of 69 percent.[1] The prevailing opinion was that homeownership was a sound economic investment and that it built stronger families and enriched community life. However, the Great Recession and the lingering economic hardship afterward had a devastating effect on individuals, families, neighborhoods, and communities across the United States. The record numbers of unemployed and underemployed, foreclosures, significant drops in home values, and loss of retirement savings and investments caused many to question this conventional wisdom as they grappled to understand and solve these problems.

Many factors can threaten the sustainability of homeownership, including income and budget shocks, life events, unexpected repair costs, falling home prices, and interest rate risk. These and other challenges encountered in the past few years have caused many to reassess the value of homeownership and forced everyone to reconsider the way they think about the loss of their home. This chapter offers insights on these factors through data on the individuals and families who sought help from a housing counseling organization during this tumultuous period. By assessing the data and performance from a variety of the agency's programs and services, we can gain insights into how to help

---

1. Joint Center for Housing Studies (2012).

homeowners resolve mortgage delinquencies and help others ultimately achieve sustainable homeownership.

CredAbility is a full-service, nonprofit, financial counseling agency headquartered in Atlanta, formerly known as CCCS of Greater Atlanta. Founded in 1964, CredAbility provides bilingual, personal, round-the-clock counseling in five states in the Southeast and, via telephone and the Internet, to people in all fifty states. CredAbility is a HUD-certified national intermediary and a member of both the National Foundation for Credit Counseling and the Homeownership Preservation Foundation. Its mission is to help people resolve financial challenges and build economic security for themselves and their families. It uses comprehensive, holistic counseling to help clients assess their situation, set priorities and clear goals, and establish a realistic, written action plan to achieve them. It has helped more than 3 million households nationally since 2007 through its preventive and remedial services.

Although CredAbility offers a broad range of education and counseling services, I focus here on the challenges distressed homeowners face and how new methods of outreach and approaches to providing support are improving their likelihood of sustaining homeownership. Specifically, I review counseling data on foreclosure prevention, early intervention, and the support program after loan modification. The counseling data offer a view of who is seeking help and the challenges they face in sustaining homeownership. For delinquent homeowners discouraged from trying to resolve their delinquency, early intervention by nonprofit counseling agencies can encourage them to act. Many attempts at loan modification failed because they did not address the family's entire financial obligations. Ongoing engagement after a loan modification makes a significant difference for financially fragile families as they recover and rebuild their financial lives.

The data offered here represent the personal stories of millions of people who have faced a potential or an actual loss of their home. The chapter tries to answer two questions: What should we—as counselors, policymakers, lenders, government, friends, and community leaders—do to help these people? And, What should they do to address their situation? The answers are vital to both the national economic recovery and to the prevention of another such crisis in the future.

The Historic Scope of the Problem

Before I review the data or explore the effectiveness of the programs, I want to fully consider the challenges average families (low-to-moderate income and struggling middle class) faced during the Great Recession. There is a variety of tools and indexes to assess individual components at a macroeconomic level, but none of these measures tells the story from the individual family's perspective and none looks holistically at the key elements of what average families face. Cred-Ability, with its nearly fifty years of experience in helping consumers in financial distress, built the CredAbility Consumer Distress Index to measure the financial condition of the average American household.

The index is a quarterly, comprehensive picture of the average American household's financial condition. Using the key elements of financial health and distress, it converts a complex set of factors into a single, easy-to-understand number. The index measures the country as a whole, each of the fifty states, and seventy-seven metropolitan areas (national and state reports date back to 1980; metropolitan reports date back to 1990). Five categories of personal finance that reflect or lead to a secure, stable financial life are measured: employment, housing, credit, household budget, and net worth. All are equally important, so each category is equally weighted. More than sixty-five data points are used.[2] Key data include unemployment and underemployment, mortgage and rental delinquencies, housing cost as percentage of budget, credit scores, use of lines of credit, credit delinquencies, per capita bankruptcies, disposable income, savings, consumer confidence, and household net worth.

Financial distress is measured on a 100-point scale; a score below 70 indicates financial distress. In general, lower scores equate to a weaker financial position, a greater urgency to act, resolutions that will take longer and be harder to achieve, and the increased probability of needing third-party help. The index score is tied to one of five general rating categories (secure, stable, weak, distressed, and crisis), which reflect the strength and stability of the consumer's position. During the period from 1980 to the end of 2012, no quarters were rated as secure, sixty-eight were rated as stable (51.5 percent), fifty were rated as weak (37.8 percent), fourteen were rated as distressed (10.6 percent), and no quarters were rated as in crisis. Figure 13-1 offers a broad historical perspective of the scores for the period. The average quarterly score during this period was 79.3, with a high of 87.2 in 1995 and a low of 64.3 in 2009.

Figure 13-2 displays the index scores from the Great Recession, 2007 through the end of 2012. The overall score and the scores for each of the five elements are charted here to show the drivers of the overall score and trends across time. Nationally, the country was in a state of distress from the third quarter of 2008 to the second quarter of 2012, or fourteen consecutive quarters. Employment and housing were the primary drivers of distress, but it also interesting to note how consistently strong and poor credit and net worth were and how household budgets fluctuated as families adjusted to their evolving situations The key takeaway here is that, by historical standards, this has easily been the most stressed

2. CredAbility client data are not a data source for the index. More information and historical data for the index are available at www.credability.org/consumerdistressindex.

Figure 13-1. *Historical National Scores, CredAbility Consumer Distress Index, 1980–2012*

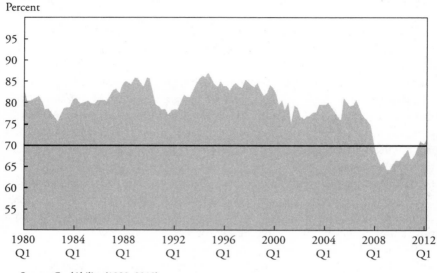

Figure 13-2. *CredAbility Consumer Distress Index, Five Variables, 2007–12*

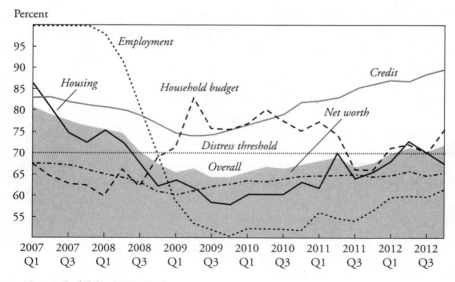

period in recent history and these nineteen quarters were the worst nineteen quarters in the past thirty-one years. So it is no surprise that the families seeking help face very difficult circumstances.

Faces of the Crisis: Overview of CredAbility's Counseling Client Profile

Before CredAbility can create a solution and action plan, it works with clients, one on one, to understand the individual's or the family's entire story. This allows for the gathering of unique data and insights. Such comprehensive data are necessary to properly assess clients' situations and to craft professional advice to help them implement plans to achieve their goals. The counseling sessions yield data in the following categories:

—Demographic: age, gender, marital status, ethnicity, and household size

—Financial: income and expenses, assets and liabilities, and debt obligations

—Credit: reports, credit and bankruptcy risk scores at counseling and one year later

—Cause of problem: primary and secondary reasons that they are seeking assistance.

CredAbility aims for a unique, holistic view of clients' situations, as clients are willing to tell a neutral, nonjudgmental third party much more about their true situation than they would anyone else. CredAbility now holds more than 3 million records of first counseling sessions in its data warehouse and, because of its national work, affiliations, and partnerships, these data generally reflect the national geographic distribution of problems. Overall, the data reveal very financially fragile households. Since CredAbility serves people of all socioeconomic levels and demographic groups—literally, people from food stamp users to those earning six-figure salaries—there is no typical client. However, the average (mean) of all 1.6 million first counseling sessions completed across all lines of service from 2007 to 2012 looks like this:

—Forty-six-year-old, married Caucasian female

—2.8 persons in household

—68 percent are homeowners

—548 credit score, 137 Bankruptcy Navigator Index score

—$44,418 gross annual income

—$1,441 monthly budget deficit (the amount left over after paying all scheduled bills)

—$30,134 unsecured debt

—32.5 percent monthly housing costs to income ratio (front-end ratio); 54.1 percent total monthly recurring debt payments to income ratio (back-end ratio)

—$49,090 net worth.

Understanding these characteristics allows others to realize their circumstances, how they arrived there, and how to prevent a recurrence. This group would historically be in an asset accumulation phase of their lives to prepare for retirement in twenty or so years. Instead, they find themselves in a deep financial hole, saddled with a substantial negative net worth, unsecured debt, ruined credit, difficult employment and income prospects, and serious questions about the value of homeownership. Historians will debate whether the Great Recession was the product of a housing bubble, subprime lending, government inaction, consumer greed, market failures, or some combination of these and other factors. What is beyond dispute, though, is that the event was much, much more than a housing crisis and that the impacts on spending and borrowing, perspectives on household income and employment, and the shattered dreams of this generation's retirement plans will reverberate for years in our national economy and psyche. Any serious discussion about long-term solutions must take these factors into consideration.

To help understand the specific challenges of homeowners who identified their mortgage delinquency as their primary financial problem, I next look in depth at a subset of these 1.6 million first counseling sessions. Data gathered from more than 422,000 foreclosure prevention clients through counseling sessions offer a unique perspective and better understanding of many of their specific issues.

Changing Demographics

As outlined in table 13-1, the demographic characteristics of those seeking foreclosure prevention help changed dramatically between 2007 and 2012.

—Age. One of the most discouraging trends has been the steadily increasing age of CredAbility clients, moving from forty-four in 2007 to fifty-one in 2012. Historically, clients have been in their late thirties or early forties. *Implication: People in their forties and fifties traditionally have been stable financially, but this generation is dealing with employment issues and aging with unprecedented levels of debt. Most important, this age group has less time to recover from the financial crisis. The cumulative impact of these challenges means that this generation will face the most uncertain retirement in generations, one in which it will be more responsible for and less prepared to handle its financial responsibilities.*

—Gender. Women have always been the majority of clients seeking counseling, but during this recession the percentage seeking help moved downward from 61.3 percent in 2007 to 52.3 percent in 2009, as more married couples and single men sought help.

—Ethnicity. In the early years of the housing crisis, a disproportionate number of people of color sought help. In the 2006–08 time frame, the majority of people seeking assistance (57–61 percent) was from minority groups and most had nontraditional or subprime mortgage products. However, as the housing

Table 13-1. *Client Demographics, CredAbility Foreclosure Prevention, 2007–12*

Percent except as indicated

Demographic information	2007	2008	2009	2010	2011	2012
Age in years	44	44	46	48	49	51
Gender						
Female	61.3	56.8	52.3	52.9	53.5	55.5
Male	38.7	43.2	47.7	47.1	46.5	44.5
Marital status						
Married	53.2	57.7	60.4	56.9	55.9	53.9
Divorced	14.7	13.8	13.3	15.2	15.7	15.8
Single	32.1	28.6	26.3	27.9	28.4	30.3
Female-headed household	33.9	27.8	24.0	25.9	27.5	30.1
Ethnicity						
Caucasian	38.6	42.2	44.2	49.1	51.5	50.9
African American	39.8	29.1	19.9	21.1	20.6	23.4
Hispanic	15.8	22.1	29.4	22.6	20.5	18.6
Asian	1.3	2.4	3.0	3.0	2.7	0.5
Native American	0.4	0.4	0.4	0.4	0.3	4.1
Other	4.1	3.8	3.1	3.8	4.3	2.6
Household size (number)	3.2	3.3	3.2	3.0	3.0	2.9

Source: CredAbility (2007–12).

crisis has evolved and become an employment-driven problem versus a product-driven issue, the distribution of clients changed to mirror the nation's broader demographics, reaching a majority Caucasian (51.5 percent) client base by 2011.

Changing Reasons for Distress

While there may be significant volatility in the reasons cited for financial distress from year to year, people generally face financial distress for one of two basic reasons: the consequence of behavior or unpreparedness for unplanned circumstances. Traditionally, the causes of financial problems fall into four groups:

—Reduced income from job loss, temporary underemployment, or cutbacks in hours worked

—Changes in marital status, such as separation, divorce, or becoming widowed

—Medical issues, ranging from one-time events to chronic conditions or disability

—Overspending or accumulating too much debt.

Table 13-2. *Causes of Client Financial Problem, CredAbility Foreclosure Prevention, 2007–12*

Percent

Cause	2007	2008	2009	2010	2011	2012
Reduced income/unemployment	48.8	47.7	55.8	52.9	58.4	43.8
Overobligation/overspending	29.9	13.2	7.0	6.8	8.5	25.7
Divorce/separation/death	8.7	6.7	9.3	5.1	7.5	3.8
Medical/accident/disability	2.0	11.1	6.9	6.9	10.1	8.5
Other/not provided	10.6	21.4	21.0	28.2	15.5	18.2

Source: CredAbility (2007–12).

Historically, when the economy is good, people who get into trouble tend do so as a result of overspending or overobligation. During recessions, it is job loss, temporary underemployment, and other reductions in hours or income that drive financial distress. Table 13-2 shows the clear shift away from behavior-based problems to income-related problems in 2007 and 2008 and the reverse trend in 2011 and 2012. This last shift was the result of a drop in the unemployment rate, as people secured permanent work at lower rates of pay. This new reality—of a permanently reduced income with significant financial obligations—is part of the face of the current economic recovery. Interestingly, there is also a rise in combination (versus single) problems as well as the emergence of student loans as an issue. These appear in both the Other and Overobligation categories in the table and are cited as a cause of distress by 8–13 percent of homeowners.

A Daunting Financial Picture

Average families use a limited number of relatively simple financial products in their financial lives, but these clients face a complicated situation. At the heart of every counseling session is a detailed review and frank conversation about their goals, habits, and overall financial picture. Table 13-3 shows the financial information gathered from foreclosure prevention sessions.

Key observations from these data include:

—Household income. While CredAbility serves clients from all socioeconomic groups, its work has historically been with low-to-moderate-income families. However, this recession definitely impacted the middle class and above. Gross income jumped from $40,534 in 2006 to $45,423 in 2007 to $51,341 in 2008, primarily as a result of higher-income families dealing with job loss or underemployment issues. The average client's income now mirrors that of the U.S. median household income. It has become very common to see people who

Table 13-3. *Client Financial Information, CredAbility Foreclosure Prevention, 2007–12*

U.S. dollars except as indicated

Financial information	2007	2008	2009	2010	2011	2012
Gross annual income	45,423	51,341	50,520	50,889	51,081	51,948
Monthly net income	3,097	3,463	3,464	3,410	3,376	3,352
Monthly living expenses	1,963	2,154	2,110	2,108	2,150	2,178
Monthly debt payments	2,289	2,655	2,601	2,498	2,420	2,261
(Monthly surplus/deficit)	(1,125)	(1,346)	(1,247)	(1,196)	(1,194)	(1,087)
Surplus/deficit as percent of gross income	−29.7	−31.5	−29.6	−28.2	−28.0	−25.1
Secured debt payments						
Housing expense (Mortgage/rent)	1,441	1,671	1,652	1,568	1,529	1,444
Nonmortgage debt (auto)	483	507	496	475	465	457
Unsecured debt						
Total debt	14,627	19,091	18,137	18,321	17,063	14,412
Minimum payment	365	477	453	455	426	360
Number of creditors	5.0	5.3	4.6	4.6	4.4	3.9

Source: CredAbility (2007–12).

have previously supported the work of nonprofit and social service agencies and food banks to now be their clients. *Implication: Many people who traditionally had discretionary income or access to home equity are now struggling to keep their mortgage current. This change in income has also affected their ability to refinance their mortgage and have funds available for maintenance or repairs.*

—Household expenses. The average starting budget during 2007–12 for foreclosure prevention clients was based on $3,400 a month in take-home pay and a monthly deficit of $1,209. Clearly, many of these family budgets were built on a different income level or were enabled by access to credit cards or home equity to deal with any budget shortfall. Instead, they found themselves forced to juggle their finances, deciding which bill to pay or whether to borrow and slip into deeper debt over time. *Implication: Credit cards have become critical to households' financial survival, as they provide needed cash flow for basic living expenses, like gas and groceries, and are the only shock absorbers for unexpected expenses, since most of these families have little to no savings. As a result, many families have reprioritized payment of credit cards ahead of their mortgage. This picture may also explain why gasoline and food price swings are much more impactful on psychology and consumer spending than stock market volatility.*

Table 13-4. *Client Debt-to-Income Ratios, CredAbility Foreclosure Prevention, 2007–12*

Percent

Debt-to-income ratios	2007	2008	2009	2010	2011	2012
Housing as percent of gross income	38.1	39.1	39.2	37.0	35.9	33.4
Housing as percent of net income	46.5	48.3	47.7	46.0	45.3	43.1
Nonmortgage debt as percent of gross income	22.4	23.0	22.6	21.9	20.9	18.9
Nonmortgage debt as percent of net income	27.4	28.4	27.4	27.3	26.4	24.4
Combined debt as percent of gross income	60.5	62.1	61.8	58.9	56.9	52.2
Combined debt as percent of net income	73.9	76.7	75.1	73.3	71.7	67.5

Source: CredAbility (2007–12).

—Unsecured debt. One of the positive trends emerging over the past few years is that Americans have finally become serious about dealing with their unsecured debt. At the peak of the crisis in 2009, the average CredAbility client was carrying between 3.5 times to 7.7 times more credit card debt than the average American, depending on what type of counseling assistance they were seeking. For foreclosure prevention clients, credit card debt peaked in 2008 at $19,091 and dropped steadily to $14,412 by 2012. *Implication: This deleveraging, first due to charge-offs and more recently by people paying down debt, is being driven by three factors. People who doubt the stability of their jobs or who have seen no real growth in wages are loath to risk carrying unnecessary debt. People who have damaged credit or poor credit scores cannot get new credit and must manage their existing credit better in order to keep it. People who have paid off debt and are now enjoying the flexibility of being debt free do not want to go back to the bondage of carrying too much debt.*

Poor Debt-to-Income Ratios

CredAbility clients also have difficult debt-to-income ratios. For decades, mortgages were underwritten with a 28/36 rule, in which borrowers were limited to a 28 percent front-end debt-to-income ratio, calculated as the mortgage payment divided by monthly gross income, and a 36 percent back-end debt-to-income ratio (calculated by dividing all secured and unsecured debt payments by gross income). Table 13-4 shows these ratios.

Table 13-5. *Client Net Worth, CredAbility Foreclosure Prevention, 2007–12*

U.S. dollars

Financial information	2007	2008	2009	2010	2011	2012
Net worth	8,168	72,630	88,936	64,923	44,388	20,029
Assets	188,390	173,460	178,636	202,080	211,502	210,561
Liabilities	196,558	246,090	267,572	267,003	255,890	230,590

Source: CredAbility (2007–12).

During this time period, the front-end ratios for clients in all other lines of service were not terrible, ranging from 23.8 to 32.8 percent. However, foreclosure prevention clients had front-end debt-to-income ratios ranging from 33.4 to 39.2 percent and back-end ratios (which are more attuned to their obligations) ranging from 52.2 to 76.7 percent. It is very difficult to make housing sustainable with these kinds of ratios. *Implication: It is not surprising that many early loan modification attempts failed, because these early efforts did not look at the clients' entire financial picture, and the problem was not solvable by adjusting a single payment or recapitalizing the arrearages. A second implication is that these back-end ratios make coordination between secured and unsecured creditors difficult—that is, deciding which creditor should take write-offs or make other concessions.*

Negative Net Worth

Calculating net worth for the average American family is a simple exercise. Average family assets are composed primarily of a home, autos, a checking account, a savings account, and a very modest 401k. Liabilities include mortgages, auto loans, credit card debt, and student loans. And while CredAbility stresses to clients that their net worth does not define self-worth, it is still not a cheery exercise for most people to see where they stand. Table 13-5 shows the net worth of the average client during this time period.

The debt from of underwater homes weighed heavily on families' balance sheets. The shift in net worth from about $8,000 in 2007 to $89,000 in 2009 to $44,000 in 2011 was driven primarily by the declines in home values relative to the balances owed on mortgages. With these deficits, it would take many years of monthly payments for many homeowners to get back to just owing what the house is worth. *Implication: It is important to understand homeowners' mindsets; specifically, do they see their property as a house or as a home? A house is a place to live and a financial investment, with limited emotional attachment. A home is a place with deep emotional meaning that offers social status and a connection to*

Table 13-6. *Client Credit Profile, CredAbility Foreclosure Prevention, 2007–12*

Units as indicated

Credit scores	2007	2008	2009	2010	2011	2012
Credit risk score	511	519	546	561	564	576
Bankruptcy risk score	114	113	133	145	154	180
Probability of bankruptcy (%)	77.9	78.3	70.0	64.8	61.1	54.0

Source: CredAbility (2007–12).

neighborhood, community, and schools. As a result, the attitude and range of acceptance options for each group are quite different based on their mind-set. Also, CredAbility's analyses show that net worth is one of the best predictors of client success, as it impacts the willingness and capacity to implement and fight for the success of an action plan. This makes for interesting policy discussions around a variety of options and tools, from accelerated foreclosures to shared equity arrangements to principal write-downs.

Distressed Credit Profile

One surprising, and little known, fact is that the credit scores of CredAbility clients actually improved during the recession. This was not a result of recovery but rather a reflection of the breadth of the crisis, as more people with traditionally higher scores fell into distress. Table 13-6 shows the beginning credit profile of counseled clients.

—Credit risk score. For ten years the average credit score for clients across all other lines of services was in the high 520s to low 530s. Foreclosure prevention clients were below that average during the 2007–08 time frame, but their scores increased dramatically, by 57 points, between 2008 and 2012. This increase was primarily the result of people with traditionally higher credit scores seeking counseling after they encountered employment and income problems.

—Bankruptcy risk score: Another helpful tool in assessing the strength and future performance of clients is bankruptcy risk scores. While credit risk scores typically predict the chance that borrowers will miss a payment in the next two years, bankruptcy risk scores predict the likelihood that they will default entirely and file for a chapter 7 liquidation or a chapter 13 repayment plan. While dropping from a peak of 78.3 percent in 2008 to 54.0 percent in 2012, CredAbility clients had a very high statistical risk of failure.

Implication: With these credit profiles, it is almost impossible for clients to take advantage of refinancing at today's record low rates. And given the time it will take their credit to recover and in an era of significantly tougher underwriting, it will be a long time before they are likely to become homeowners again. Ironically, given the increased costs of filing after bankruptcy reform in 2005, some clients can't afford the filing fees and are too broke to file for bankruptcy.

Encouraging Results from Counseling

Despite all these dramatic shifts and significant challenges, foreclosure prevention counseling is a very effective tool. Once a person seeks help, a significant mind-set shift occurs. With the full picture laid out, they can then decide on their goals and priorities and make the necessary choices in the proper context of priorities, trade-offs, and time frames. Between 2007 and 2012, there was an average 40-point increase in the confidence to successfully reach their financial goals after counseling (from 37 to 77 percent), and more than 85 percent of clients would recommend this service to someone they knew facing a similar problem.

In addition to confidence gains, recent studies point to counseling's effectiveness. Ding, Quercia, and Ratcliffe's study of outbound calls to mortgage borrowers forty-five days delinquent finds that the odds of curing the default are 50 percent higher for borrowers who accepted and received counseling than for noncounseled borrowers; Collins and Schmeiser's work finds that counseling increases by 58 percent the probability of receiving a loan modification; and the Urban Institute's study on national foreclosure mitigation counseling clients finds that counseled borrowers are more likely than noncounseled borrowers to cure (89–97 percent), to receive higher reductions in monthly payments ($176), and to have lower redefault rates nine months after serious delinquency (67–70 percent).[3] CredAbility's internal analysis of its foreclosure prevention counseling clients shows that 81 percent were still in their home one year after counseling and that 72 percent had no foreclosure activity on their credit report.

Outreach: Early Intervention

Given the financial distress experienced by many homeowners during the recession, it is easy to understand why one of the biggest challenges in dealing with individuals and families during this period was simply making contact with them. Whether as a result of feelings of shame or embarrassment or being paralyzed by misconceptions about the intentions of their servicer or investor, people often stop answering the telephone or opening the mail in a financial crisis. Given the traditionally low rate of mortgage delinquencies and defaults, the servicing world was equally unprepared from both a systems perspective and a staffing perspective to tackle this new world of double-digit delinquencies. Freddie Mac estimated at one point that it had no contact with approximately 50 percent of the homeowners it had foreclosed on.

3. Ding, Quercia, and Ratcliffe (2008); Collins and Schmeiser (2013); Mayer and others (2011).

In late 2005 Freddie Mac engaged CredAbility and several other counseling agencies to determine if there was a way to reach and engage hiding or discouraged homeowners. This pilot kicked off in 2006 with three goals:
—Increase the contact rate with delinquent homeowners
—Assess the efficacy of counseling at forty-five days of delinquency
—Decrease the number of delinquent loans that result in foreclosure and prevent future delinquencies.

The Pilot and Its Results

The pilot was designed to reach homeowners who were in the early stage of delinquency, primarily forty-five to sixty days delinquent.
—Identifying delinquent borrowers. Individual companies servicing for Freddie Mac identified borrowers who were forty-five days delinquent and who had no contact with the servicer since the delinquency began. Lists of these borrowers were sent to Freddie Mac, excluding certain types of loans such as FHA, VA, and those known to be in bankruptcy.
—Mailing the offer. Upon receipt of the list, Freddie Mac mailed a solicitation letter to homeowners, on joint Freddie Mac/counseling agency letterhead, encouraging them to make contact with the servicer, offered free counseling, and informed them to expect a call from the counseling agency.
—Reaching out. Within seven days from the date of the solicitation mailing, if homeowners had not contacted the counseling agency or brought their account current, the counseling agency placed the first call in an attempt to reach the homeowner. The counseling agency made at least three attempts to reach the homeowner by calling at different hours and different days of the week.
—Encouraging action. The content of the contact was simple and straightforward. Homeowners were encouraged to act—either by contacting the servicer directly or scheduling a counseling session—versus continuing to ignore the problem.
The pilot concluded at the end of 2007, having engaged almost 17,000 homeowners, and exceeded the targeted results for contact rates, counseling outcomes, and decreases in delinquencies.

Broader Goals, Continuing Success

With these promising initial results, the pilot was moved into full program status in 2008. Program goals for each contact expanded to five:
—Reach the homeowner by phone
—Establish the homeowner's intention
—Provide counseling (priority budget, importance of mortgage, options)
—Initiate a conversation between the homeowner and the servicer
—When appropriate, complete a workout package and forward to the servicer.

Table 13-7. *CredAbility–Freddie Mac Early Intervention Program Data*
Unit as indicated

Step	Number or percent	Activity explanation
Letters mailed	955,768	Homeowner receives letter with offer of assistance
Contacts by agency	239,454	Right party contacts made by agency
Foreclosures avoided	64,922	Homeowner contact that avoided foreclosure
Contact rate	25.1%	Agency makes right party contact with homeowner receiving letter
Counsel rate	36.2%	Agency counsels homeowner after contact
Delinquency cure rate	24.8%	Homeowners contacted by agency that cures their delinquency
Foreclosure avoided rate	27.1%	Homeowners contacted by agency that avoids foreclosure

Source: CredAbility (2006–12).

To date, the program has yielded some impressive results, as outlined in table 13-7.

Lessons Learned

In addition to these results, the company learned some important lessons about how to make outreach contacts and engage homeowners through this process.

—Value of an endorsed, neutral third party. Homeowners who hide from their servicer are skeptical of third parties. They are often bombarded with calls and solicitations from organizations that purport to want to help, but it is difficult to tell legitimate organizations from potential scams. Homeowners liked receiving a letter to introduce the counseling agency and to see the endorsement of the financial institution, even though they were afraid to speak directly to the financial institution themselves. By endorsing free access to a trustworthy nonprofit agency, the servicer showed that its true intent was to work with the homeowner to find a solution, not just to foreclose on the property.

—Less demand for counseling than expected. While CredAbility was successful in contacting 25 percent of these delinquent borrowers, the rate of those agreeing to counseling was just 36 percent of the contacted group. Perhaps this low demand for counseling is the result of not wanting to interject a third party into the process or otherwise complicate working with the servicer. But it is unfortunate that these families missed out on an opportunity to address their entire financial picture and challenges and to take advantage of a wide variety of tools and programs versus just changing their monthly mortgage payment amount.

—Cures from a single phone contact. It was a surprise that many homeowners required just the nudge of a call from a counseling agency to get them to act, resulting in a cured delinquency. This represents a remarkable return on investment and mission for counseling agencies, servicers, and homeowners alike.

—Packages remain problematic. The rate of document collection and submission is 20 percent for counseled clients, a rate for delinquent loans that is just too low to affect the overall problem. Financially distressed people are notoriously poor record keepers, and changing requirements during the early years of the crisis made it tough to pull together a package and get a decision within the allotted time frames. Progress continues, and third parties like CredAbility are critical to this effort, but better systems (like Hope LoanPort) and streamlining the movement of homeowners through a full range of retention and exit options need more attention.

Support after Loan Modification

Since the early days of the housing crisis, when counseling was almost exclusively offered in person by most housing counseling agencies, engagement models with homeowners have been forced to evolve. From offering counseling via a national hotline to connecting homeowners with servicers to gathering documentation for decisions on workouts, counseling agencies have continued to adapt to the changing needs of the families they serve. A program to support homeowners after their loans are modified is just one example of this continuing innovation.

Loan modifications quickly became the preferred tool in the attempt to keep homeowners in their homes, with more than 6 million government and private modifications completed since 2007. However, in the first wave of loan modifications, redefault rates of 50–60 percent were common. This high percentage was due to several factors: the single focus on lowering mortgage payments or recapitalizing arrearages, the lack of focus on the client's whole range of financial problems, and the lack of ongoing support for financially fragile homeowners. Many homeowners who have experienced delinquency on their mortgage need ongoing education, counseling, and coaching to successfully maintain homeownership. In the experience of CredAbility, it takes a family between nine and eighteen months to get into financial trouble before they reach out for help, and it takes two or three times that long to work out of the problem. In light of the client profile outlined earlier, it is clear that these families' financial challenges will not go away overnight.

The Process

CredAbility's support program for clients following their loan modification is designed to engage and coach homeowners about how to manage their priorities and finances in order to maintain homeownership. After a loan modification is established, whether a trial modification or a permanent modification, CredAbility provides outreach, counseling, education, and follow-up coaching to homeowners identified by an investor or servicer, following the process outlined below.

—Identifying homeowners. The servicer sends to CredAbility a list of homeowners who have entered into a loan modification agreement and who have been targeted to receive the offer of ongoing support. This homeowner contact information includes homeowner's name, phone numbers, street address, city of residence, zip code, investor and servicer loan number, payment amount, and payment due date.

—Extending the offer. The homeowner receives a letter from Fannie Mae or the servicer, introducing CredAbility, describing the services available, and alerting the homeowner of CredAbility's intent to telephone the homeowner. The letter also includes a dedicated toll-free number and dedicated web address that homeowners can use to contact CredAbility directly to get more information or to opt out of the program.

—Making initial contact. CredAbility makes at least three attempts to telephone each homeowner and places these calls at three different times of day and on different days within a thirty-day period. The conversation with the homeowner includes a live exchange of information (not just a series of messages or voicemails) and information about the availability of free education and counseling resources. Having the homeowner agree to participate in ongoing outreach or a counseling session is the goal.

—Counseling the homeowner. For borrowers who accept the offer of free service, CredAbility schedules a telephone counseling session to be held as soon as possible and no more than thirty days following the date of the initial conversation with the homeowner.

The first counseling session consists of a comprehensive review of the homeowner's current financial situation including the following:

—A review and discussion of current debt payment obligations, including mortgage payments, with attention to trial modifications that could help the homeowner achieve a permanent modification

—A review and discussion of the homeowner's credit report and credit score

—The creation of a budget designed to enable the homeowner to manage regular monthly obligations and household expenses and to establish long-term financial stability

—Identification of unsecured debt that may be compromising the homeowner's financial situation and develop strategies to address it, including the creation of a debt management plan or other debt reduction strategy

—Development of a personalized action plan for the individual or family to follow

—Sending the homeowner a written summary of the session, including the action plan, educational materials, and additional resources

—Offering a second counseling session.

The second counseling session consists of education on how to maintain stable finances for the longer term, using a broad range of financial concepts and remedial and preventive strategies and goals; a review of the credit report to ensure accurate reporting and to address any issues; and modifications to the budget to achieve longer term goals such as planning for home maintenance expenses, establishing adequate emergency savings, saving for retirement, education and other needs, and repayment of unsecured debts.

At the heart of the support program is a regular series of contacts and conversations designed to build a relationship with the homeowner. CredAbility makes up to ten monthly education and coaching check-in contacts with homeowners to offer additional assistance, including online educational resources and coaching on the action plan and budget during the twelve-month period following initial acceptance of assistance. Contacts are broken up into three four-month segments, with specific content designed for each period. The goal of these scheduled contacts is to build a relationship with the homeowner by imparting relevant information to the homeowner in small doses at teachable moments. These periodic contacts are designed to not be intense or intrusive. They employ a variety of methods, including telephone calls, e-mails, and texts. Counseling is always available, and these regular contacts offer a nonthreatening way for homeowners to discuss emerging problems or recent events that might otherwise jeopardize the stability of their situation. This is important, because it is typically four to six months after the loan modification that the first serious problem arises.

Promising Results, Lessons Learned

Early results are promising. Contact was made with about 50 percent of the homeowners targeted; about 86 percent of these accepted the offer of ongoing support. Additional results are shown in table 13-8.[4] The following lessons have been learned:

---

4. Note that, although loan performance for this group appears to be strong, results versus a randomized control group have not been released, and I am not at liberty to discuss these results.

Table 13-8. *CredAbility Support Program Following Loan Modification*
Unit as indicated

Step	*Activity*	*Percent*	
Referrals received	26,152		
Made right party contact	13,005	49.7	of referrals
Opted out	1,833	14.1	of those contacted
Entered ongoing support	11,172	85.9	of those contacted
Remained in ongoing support after 4 months	6,012	62.7	continued to next 4-month cycle
Chose a counseling session	2,435	21.8	of participants
Chose a second session	1,170	48.0	of counseled

Source: CredAbility (2010–12).

—Homeowners like regular contacts. While CredAbility has a specific topic or agenda item to cover in each contact, these cumulative engagements build a relationship. Recorded interactions between counselors and the homeowner show how quickly this rapport can be built and how appreciative clients are of the continued support.

—Changing habits takes time. Setting new goals and starting a plan is exciting, but sticking with it as life happens is hard. A trusted third party can offer suggestions and have tough conversations about the consequences of bad choices.

—Problems will happen. The fragile nature of homeowners' finances almost makes it inevitable that they will experience financial challenges in the first year of a modification. Problems typically arise four to six months into the plan, which is why it is critical to have an established line of communication so that a homeowner can address a problem before it spirals out of control.

—It works. CredAbility's internal models show a sustained and positive benefit to homeowners.

Conclusions

At the beginning of this chapter I posed two questions: What should we do to help these people? And, What should they do to address their situation? Unfortunately, even at this point, the answers are not clear. So instead of policy recommendations, I offer six practical parting thoughts and observations:

—Reexamine conventional wisdom periodically. Homeownership is not for everyone, and historical views of the value and benefits of homeownership proved to be false and damaging to many families. We must regularly and publicly examine and debate conventional views to ensure their validity in a rapidly changing world.

—Encourage people to build margin into their lives. People should not make lending or borrowing decisions based on the assumption that things will always go well. Breathing room must be maintained in their financial lives if they are to succeed in the uncertain world that they will navigate in the years ahead.

—Understand that bad things happen to good people. We must discern between sweeping events beyond anyone's control and poor personal choices. It seems obvious that there are clear differences between being an irresponsible real estate speculator and being a person who has always paid the bills until a disaster strikes. However, designing a system to objectively recognize this difference is very difficult.

—Engage overwhelmed and paralyzed people. We must find new ways to communicate and engage with people struggling through a financial crisis. Crises take time to develop and even longer to resolve. Throughout that time, families remain financially fragile and are almost guaranteed to face setbacks along the way. We must find simple ways for these people to have endorsed access to a neutral, trusted adviser and easy access to the tools and services that will enable them to resolve their situation.

—Require a comprehensive view. We must view family finances through a holistic lens and fashion goals and solutions accordingly. In the recent crisis, housing debt often surfaced as the problem both because it is the single largest bill people face and because failing to pay has such dire consequences. However, at the heart of the problem was the layering of multiple risks and the mass of other debts that made the family's position untenable. Every lender needs to worry about these other debts, because it affects his or her returns and losses.

—Acknowledge that there are no quick or easy solutions. Like losing weight or staying healthy, it is not knowledge but rather the willingness and discipline to apply that knowledge that ultimately yield results. It requires time, support, and the proper motivation to tackle and resolve the complicated financial problems that people in a crisis face. Unfortunately, the money and resources for third-party counselors and advisers to assist in these situations often arrive too late or leave too early. We need sustainable fee-for-service funding models and infrastructure for those critical financial first responders.

References

Collins, J. Michael, and Maximilian D. Schmeiser. 2013. "The Effects of Foreclosure Counseling for Distressed Homeowners." *Journal of Policy Analysis and Management* 32, no. 1: 83–106.

CredAbility. 1980–2012. "Consumer Distress Index" (www.credability.org).

————. 2006–12. "Freddie Mac EI Program Activity Report" (www.credability.org).

————. 2007–12. "Foreclosure Prevention Client Profile" (www.credability.org).

————. 2010–12. "Post Modification Support Program Activity Report" (www.cred ability.org).

Ding, Lei, Roberto G. Quercia, and Janneke Ratcliffe. 2008. "Post-Purchase Counseling and Default Resolutions among Low- and Moderate-Income Borrowers." *Journal of Real Estate Research* 30, no. 3: 315–44.

Joint Center for Housing Studies. 2012. *State of the Nation's Housing 2012.* Cambridge, Mass.

Mayer, Neil, Peter A. Tatian, Kenneth Temkin, and Charles A. Calhoun. 2011. "National Foreclosure Mitigation Counseling Program Evaluation Final Report Rounds 1 and 2." Washington: NeighborWorks America (www.nw.org/network/foreclosure/nfmcp/documents/NFMCEval_Rounds1-2_Final.pdf).

14

The Home Mortgage Foreclosure Crisis: Lessons Learned

PATRICIA A. McCOY

From 2007 through 2011, the United States housing market suffered from a severe imbalance in supply and demand.[1] On the supply side, there were too many homes for sale, and too many of those listings were for foreclosed homes. In addition, there were several million homes awaiting sale in the foreclosure pipeline.[2] Many of these homes in the so-called "shadow housing inventory" eventually came on the market and pushed down house prices.

The demand for homes was also depressed. In the aftermath of the financial crisis, banks tightened their lending standards. Meanwhile, millions of households suffered a decline in creditworthiness, making it difficult or impossible for them to get loans.

Reducing the shadow housing inventory is one method to help correct the imbalance in housing supply. There are two ways to reduce that inventory. One is through foreclosure prevention, to keep homes with distressed loans from entering the shadow inventory to begin with. The other is to speed up sale of real estate owned on the back end.

The author thanks Eric Belsky, Chris Herbert, the Joint Center on Housing Studies at Harvard University, and the University of Connecticut School of Law for their generous support of this research and the anonymous reviewers who read this work. She also gives special thanks to Jennifer Molinsky for her meticulous editorial work on this chapter.

1. For example, Goodman and others (2012a, p. 2).
2. CoreLogic (2013) estimated this inventory at 2.3 million houses as of October 2012.

In this chapter I focus on foreclosure prevention. Foreclosure prevention addresses the front end of the problem by keeping distressed borrowers in their homes. Where that is not possible, foreclosure prevention partly addresses the back end of the problem by seeking a "graceful exit" for the borrower while expediting sale of the home to a new owner.

Investors take heavy losses on foreclosures: on average, 50 percent or more.[3] This suggests that a significant portion of distressed mortgages could and should be resolved short of foreclosure. In theory servicers and investors should be willing to do a loan workout whenever the net present value (NPV) of loss mitigation exceeds the net present value of foreclosure. This NPV test defines the outer parameters of the loan workouts most servicers will perform.

From society's viewpoint foreclosure prevention should have two major objectives. The first is designing loss mitigation plans to minimize the chance of redefault. The second is to keep homes occupied whenever possible. Avoiding vacant homes is crucial to remedying the shadow inventory. Not only do these homes deteriorate in value, they attract crime and push down the value of neighboring homes.

Consequently, foreclosure prevention should strive for a solution that keeps the homeowner in the home. That means negotiating a loan modification whenever possible that satisfies the NPV test and is designed for success. But when that is not possible, the goal should be a short sale to a buyer who will keep the home occupied. Doing so will help reduce the negative externalities from abandoned homes.

Most first-time loan modifications are behind us now, and we have substantial empirical evidence about what worked and what did not.[4] In this chapter, I discuss the four main lessons from the last several years' experience with loss mitigation, including structural challenges to reaching the right level of loan modifications.

Loss Mitigation: Its Rationale and Techniques

The high loss severity for foreclosures creates space for loss mitigation strategies that resolve distressed mortgages at lower cost to both investors and borrowers. The most common test for making that determination is the net present value or NPV test. Under the NPV test, a loan modification or other workout technique is deemed cost-effective when the net present value of the workout exceeds that of going to foreclosure. Pooling and servicing agreements (PSAs) normally impose the NPV test on workouts of private-label loans and also require servicers

3. Bernanke (2008); Capozza and Thomson (2006); Cordell and others (2008, pp. 3, 11–12).
4. For example, Moody's Investors Service (2012d, p. 4).

to maximize recovery for the benefit of the investors in the trust as a whole. Servicers are supposed to implement this requirement by choosing the higher NPV, as between a loan workout and foreclosure. Federal loss mitigation programs impose their own NPV tests, and many servicers also apply proprietary NPV tests to distressed loans held in portfolio.

NPV tests have their limitations. For one thing, NPV tests can be manipulated because PSAs give servicers of private-label loans wide discretion in how to calculate the values. Servicers can choose whatever values they want for variables, such as the expected sales price from foreclosure, the discount rate applied to projected revenues from loan modification, and the chance of redefault. Investors have little ability to monitor or change the values that servicers use for these inputs.[5] As a result servicers can manipulate the NPV calculation for many distressed private-label loans to achieve the outcomes they want. The same problem affects the NPV test for federal loan modifications and for loans held in portfolio, although to a lesser extent.[6]

In addition, it can be hard for distressed borrowers to meet the NPV test when their incomes have plummeted. During the financial crisis, the collapse in home values caused more than one quarter of all borrowers to go underwater on their mortgages. Normally, negative equity is a necessary condition for default but not sufficient. Most underwater borrowers who default also suffer an income shock.[7] If that income shock is too severe—as is often the case with unemployment—the borrower may not qualify for a loan modification under the NPV test.

When loans go delinquent or are in danger of default, servicers have a variety of workout techniques at their disposal to resolve those loans short of foreclosure. (I use "loan workout" broadly in this chapter to refer to the full spectrum of techniques used to resolve distressed loans short of refinancing or foreclosure.) This large menu of options gives servicers discretion about which technique to use.

Like refinancing, some workout techniques allow the homeowner to retain ownership of the home. Of those, some lower monthly payments while others do not. *Capitalization* takes the borrower's arrears and tacks them onto the principal, thereby increasing the monthly payments, either immediately or later on. When capitalization includes *forbearance,* the servicer temporarily lowers the borrower's monthly payments but adds the forborne sums to the loan balance, meaning

---

5. Cordell and others (2008, p. 18); Thompson (2009, pp. 6-9, 18); Kiff and Klyuev (2009). For Fannie Mae and Freddie Mac loans and loans evaluated for the Home Affordable Modification Program (HAMP) modifications, this discretion is more limited. The HAMP program, Fannie Mae, and Freddie Mac require servicers to use standardized software to calculate NPV. Cordell and others (2008, p. 18); Credit Suisse (2007).

6. Office of the Special Inspector General for the Troubled Asset Relief Program (2012c).

7. See Foote and others (2009a), who note that the exception is for deeply underwater homeowners, who may decide their homes are worthless investments and walk away from their mortgages.

that the loan payments will eventually go even higher than the original payment amount. When capitalization does not involve forbearance, the monthly payments immediately go up. One way or the other, capitalization alone does not involve modification of any loan terms.

Loan modifications, in contrast, alter the loan terms, either by extending the term of the loan, reducing the interest rate, lowering the principal, or some combination of the three. Many loan modifications have the effect of lowering monthly payments.

Capitalization and modifications share the ostensible objective of keeping homeowners in their homes. Other workout techniques result in liquidation and normally require homeowners to vacate their homes. In a *short sale,* for example, the servicer allows a borrower to sell the home for less than the outstanding loan balance and often forgives the remaining amount due. In a *deed-in-lieu of foreclosure,* the borrower deeds the house to the servicer and moves out, in exchange for full forgiveness of the debt. In some cases, however, the servicer may lease the home back to the borrower, relieving any need to vacate the home.

The Federal Government's Evolving Approach to Loss Mitigation during the Crisis

In 2007 and 2008, the first two years of the financial crisis, private loss mitigation efforts by servicers were haphazard, with low success rates. In mid-2007, at the urging of the George W. Bush administration, the mortgage industry launched the HOPE NOW Alliance to promote greater foreclosure prevention. The objective of HOPE NOW was to get distressed borrowers into loan counseling and to convince servicers to grant them proprietary loan modifications whenever possible.

HOPE NOW's initial performance was disappointing. During 2007 and 2008, only 8.5 percent of mortgages that were at least sixty days past due received loss mitigation of any kind (whether a loan modification, a short sale, or a deed-in-lieu of foreclosure).[8] Furthermore, the majority of loan modifications in 2007 and 2008 actually *raised* borrowers' monthly payments instead of lowering them.[9] For homeowners who were already struggling to meet their payments, these loan modifications were often destined to fail.

Some of the reasons for this disappointing performance were the voluntary nature of HOPE NOW, its lack of financial incentives for loss mitigation, and the absence of a standardized template for loan modifications or a numerical target for lower loan payments. Servicers varied widely in their approach to and

---

8. Adelino, Gerardi, and Willen (2009, pp. 13–18 and table 5).
9. Adelino, Gerardi, and Willen (2009, pp. 11–12 and table 3).

handling of loan workout requests: of 15 million workouts between July 2007 and October 2012, only 32 percent (4.81 million) were proprietary loan modifications, while the remaining 68 percent (10.34 million) resulted in liquidation or deferred or rescheduled borrowers' payments temporarily without permanently lowering those payments.[10]

The Federal Deposit Insurance Corporation's (FDIC) "Mod in a Box" program attempted to correct some of these deficiencies. When FDIC took over as conservator of the mortgage lender IndyMac in 2008 and assumed servicing for its more than 60,000 seriously delinquent loans, Chairman Sheila Bair implemented a uniform template for loan modifications designed to handle the growing volume of IndyMac's distressed loans.[11] Under the Mod in a Box program, the FDIC's goal was to lower monthly payments, not raise them, by reducing the borrower's front-end debt-to-income (DTI) ratio to 38 percent, subject to maximizing NPV. To get the DTI down to 38 percent, Mod in a Box instituted a standardized "waterfall" of workout techniques that included capitalizing arrears and, if necessary, lowering the interest rate. After that, the term could be extended, and if more was needed to hit the 38 percent target, the FDIC could grant the borrower principal forbearance.[12] The FDIC paid servicers $1,000 for every IndyMac loan modified through Mod in a Box. By February 1, 2009, 9,901 or about 26 percent of IndyMac's seriously delinquent loans had been modified.[13] Over time the FDIC succeeded in lowering the redefault rates on later IndyMac loan modifications compared with those performed before April 2009.[14]

In late 2008 the new Federal Housing Finance Agency (FHFA) unveiled a parallel streamlined loan modification program for delinquent loans guaranteed by Fannie Mae and Freddie Mac.[15] The program replaced proprietary loss mitigation programs begun in the 1980s that had not used a standardized waterfall designed to lower mortgage payments.[16] These older programs had had disappointing results, partly attributable to lack of affordability (in 2008 over half

---

10. HOPE NOW (2012, pp. 4, 7).

11. Brown (2010).

12. Brown (2010).

13. Kiff and Klyuev (2009, pp. 16–18).

14. Brown (2010, pp. 5, 11).

15. Cordell and others (2009, p. 19); Federal Housing Finance Agency (2010, p. 18); Kiff and Klyuev (2009, pp. 16–18).

16. See Federal Housing Finance Agency (2009, p. 8), comparing the GSEs' prior proprietary loan modification programs with HAMP. For example, Crews Cutts and Green (2004) described GSE repayment plans at the time, which typically resulted in higher rather than lower monthly payments because the plans required people to resume their regular monthly payments plus pay off the arrears (pp. 6, 21).

of GSE loan modifications increased monthly loan payments).[17] As a result redefault rates for GSE loan modifications made in 2008 and 2009 were substantially worse than in later years, after both GSEs overhauled their proprietary loan modification protocols to lower monthly payments.[18]

Frustrated with approaches to foreclosure prevention that did not result in lower payments for distressed borrowers, the Obama administration announced its own loss mitigation program, called Making Home Affordable (MHA), in February 2009. MHA was funded with $36.9 billion in Troubled Asset Relief Program (TARP) funds. Mod in a Box and FHFA's own streamlined program formed the model for the Obama administration's approach to loan modifications.

MHA's main feature was a loan modification program called the Home Affordable Modification Program, or HAMP, which revamped the protocol for loan modifications in three important ways. First, HAMP sought to alter the NPV calculus and servicer compensation incentives by paying subsidies for modifications of owner-occupied loans that were NPV-positive. Second, HAMP instituted a standardized loan modification waterfall for participating servicers to make modifications more successful and to bring them to scale. Finally, as part of that waterfall, HAMP required servicers to lower borrowers' monthly payments to 31 percent of gross monthly income for five years, first by lowering interest rates as far down as 2 percent, then by extending the loan term to up to forty years, and then, if necessary, by forbearing (or, at the servicer's option, forgiving) part of the principal.

When HAMP was unveiled, the administration predicted that it would help 3 to 4 million homeowners restructure their mortgages by its original end date of December 31, 2012.[19] HAMP fell short of that goal, completing only 1.136 million permanent loan modifications as of December 2012.[20] Meanwhile, newly initiated foreclosures consistently outstripped permanent modifications (taking proprietary and HAMP modifications together) from third quarter 2011 through third quarter 2012, sometimes by as much as two to one (figure 14-1). The trend for earlier quarters was similar.[21]

Despite this track record, HAMP had certain successes. The program's emphasis on lower monthly payments and lower interest rates cut redefault rates substantially. Furthermore, HAMP improved over time in response to feedback. Some of the later changes to HAMP—especially the decision to triple

17. See Federal Housing Finance Agency (2011, p. 4).
18. Compare Federal Housing Finance Agency (2011, pp. 4–8) with Federal Housing Finance Agency (2009, p. 12).
19. U.S. Department of the Treasury (2009a). The Treasury Department later extended the HAMP program through December 31, 2015.
20. Making Home Affordable (MHA; 2013, p. 3).
21. Office of the Comptroller of the Currency (OCC; 2012a, pp. 22, 24; 2012c, pp. 5, 24).

Figure 14-1. *Total Foreclosure Starts to Total Modifications,*
Third Quarter 2011 to Third Quarter 2012

Number

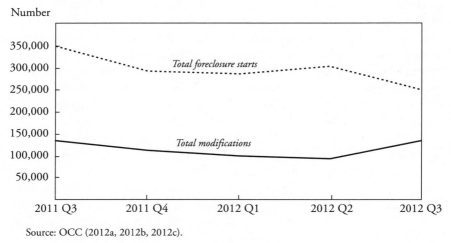

Source: OCC (2012a, 2012b, 2012c).

the subsidies for principal reductions—further raised the success rate of HAMP
modifications.

A Taxonomy of Distressed Mortgages

In thinking about the best way to resolve distressed mortgages, it is worthwhile
to evaluate loans along three different dimensions: the home's *occupancy prospects*
(whether the house is occupied and, if so, whether there is a cost-effective loss
mitigation technique that will keep the house occupied, either by the borrower or
someone else); the *ownership status of the loan* (that is, whether the loan is held in
portfolio or sold and, if so, to whom), and the *presence or absence of junior liens.*

Occupancy Prospects

Occupancy prospects can be broken down into three basic categories: currently
occupied homes involving delinquent borrowers with sufficient cash flow to pass
an NPV test; currently occupied homes that involve delinquent borrowers without sufficient cash flow; and vacant homes.

Most servicers, before they agree to modify a loan, will first determine
whether a modification will increase the net present value of the loan relative to
foreclosure. When an owner-occupant borrower has enough cash flow to make
a loan modification NPV-positive, normally a loan modification can and should
be designed to keep the homeowner in the home.

Owner-occupant borrowers who lack sufficient income to qualify for a traditional loan modification under an NPV test present a different and more complicated situation. There are various reasons why a borrower might experience such a large cash shortfall: an income shock that is long-term or permanent in nature, for instance due to disability, retirement, a spouse's death, or divorce; or job loss resulting in a steep income loss that may nevertheless be temporary. Another situation involves borrowers who could meet their loan payments when they lived in their homes but had to move—often for new job postings—and could not sell their old homes for enough to pay off their mortgages due to negative equity. Some borrowers in this situation cannot afford dual housing payments and end up defaulting. In the most extreme version of this scenario, the borrowers are members of the U.S. armed forces who have received orders to move.

Finally, some distressed borrowers move out of their homes. Sometimes the departing borrowers rent their houses out; more often, their houses become vacant when they leave. Some vacant houses are awaiting foreclosure and will eventually go to sheriff's sale. Other vacant houses have gone through foreclosure and sale and are now sitting in inventory as bank real estate owned. In the most difficult cases, sometimes referred to as "zombie loans," servicers refuse to even initiate foreclosure, sometimes because the owner of the loan does not want to assume title or the legal obligations that go with it, putting the house in legal limbo.[22] In other cases second lien holders create holdup problems that discourage the first lienholder from proceeding to foreclosure.[23]

Ownership Status of the Loan

The ownership status of a distressed loan can also affect the servicer's flexibility to grant loss mitigation and the type of mitigation that can be offered.[24] Distressed mortgages held in portfolio are the easiest to resolve short of foreclosure because the servicer has the full panoply of loss mitigation tools at its disposal.

The remaining mortgage loans are owned by investors. In the main these investors are divided into two groups: investors in mortgage-backed securities issued by Ginnie Mae or the GSEs (Fannie Mae and Freddie Mac) and investors in private-label securities. Both the GSEs and private-label securitizations place limitations on the types of loss mitigation techniques that may be used. As of this writing, for example, the GSEs do not permit principal forgiveness in loan modifications.

Similarly, in private-label securitizations, the pooling and servicing agreement for the loan pool usually places constraints on the servicer's ability to negotiate a workout. Nevertheless, the majority of PSAs permit some degree

22. See U.S. Government Accountability Office (GAO; 2011).
23. Agarwal and others (2011, pp. 16–17, 19).
24. See, for example, Gelpern and Levitin (2009).

of loan modifications in the event of default, imminent default, or reasonably foreseeable default.[25]

Most PSAs give servicers broad discretion to negotiate forbearance that temporarily extends delinquent payments but does not require a change of loan terms, so long as the servicer forwards the missed payments to investors in a timely fashion.[26] While PSAs are usually stricter about permanent loan modifications, they vary widely from deal to deal.[27] A small percentage of PSAs—roughly 10 percent—prohibit any material loan modifications.[28] The remaining PSAs permit material loan modifications only when they are in the best interest of investors.[29] In such cases the servicer's precise latitude to negotiate a loan modification will depend on the PSA. Many PSAs permit modification of all loans. Another group, consisting of about 35 percent of PSAs, limits modifications to 5 percent of the loan pool (measured by the loan amount or number of loans). PSAs may contain other restrictions on loan modifications such as mandatory trial modification periods, use of specific resolution procedures, caps on interest rate reductions, restrictions on the types of eligible loans, and limits on the number of modifications in any one year.[30]

For the 90 percent or so of private-label securitizations that allow loan modifications to some degree, it is not clear whether PSA limits on those modifications ever became binding. A Berkeley, California, survey of PSAs concluded that "large-scale modification programs [could] be undertaken without violating the plain terms of PSAs in most cases."[31] Even for securitizations that prohibit loan modifications outright or cap them at 5 percent, some of those PSAs were amended to allow more modifications.[32] In addition, credit rating agencies no longer count modified loans that are current twelve months after modification against the 5 percent cap where one exists.[33] Thus, while servicers faced challenges in complying with multiple PSAs containing a hodgepodge of provisions, for the most part, those agreements did not constrain their ability to modify distressed loans.

25. Credit Suisse (2007, p. 6); Hunt (2009, p. 7). Among other things this has the salutary benefit of allowing servicers to contact borrowers before any payments are missed to determine the borrower's ability to handle the new payments and, if not, to explore other options.

26. Credit Suisse (2007, p. 6); Hunt (2009, p. 7).

27. See generally Eggert (2007).

28. Credit Suisse (2007); Hunt (2009, p. 6).

29. Hunt (2009, pp. 7–9). In general, any change in the principal balance, the interest rate, or the final maturity will constitute a "material" modification (p. 7).

30. Credit Suisse (2007, pp. 6–7); Kiff and Klyuev (2009, p. 11).

31. Hunt (2009, p. 10). See also Adelino, Gerardi, and Willen (2009, pp. 13–18 and table 5); Thompson (2011, p. 755).

32. Most PSAs allow caps on loan modifications to be waived upon consent by a rating agency or a bond insurer; only a few require investor approval. Kiff and Klyuev (2009, p. 11).

33. Thompson (2011, p. 755).

Lien Status

The lien status of a distressed mortgage can also affect the prospects for loss mitigation because the presence of a junior lien can complicate a loan workout. About 25 percent of mortgages originated between 2004 and 2009 had one or more junior liens.[34] Junior liens were even more prevalent among borrowers with first mortgages held in private-label securitized trusts: by year-end 2009, over half of private-label mortgages had second liens compared to 18 percent of GSE loans.[35]

Borrowers with negative equity are also more likely to have junior liens. That comes as no surprise because junior liens boost combined loan-to-value ratios. As of second quarter 2012, 4.2 million underwater borrowers had second liens, with an average combined loan-to-value ratio of 128 percent.[36]

It is also instructive to look at who owns junior liens. In the first quarter of 2011, only 2 percent of the outstanding $929 billion in closed-end junior mortgages and home equity lines of credit were held by securitized trusts; the vast majority of the rest was held by depository institutions and credit unions. Together that quarter, four of the nation's largest banks—Bank of America, Wells Fargo, JPMorgan Chase, and Citigroup—held 43 percent of all outstanding closed-end junior mortgages and home equity lines of credit in portfolio.[37]

This imbalance between bank ownership of junior liens and investor ownership of private-label securitized first lien loans creates principal-agent conflicts for banks that service private-label first liens and their own junior liens. From the viewpoint of investors, servicers should write down their seconds before modifying distressed private-label firsts. However, servicers may be reluctant to do so because write-downs will reduce earnings as well as bank capital.[38] The capital implications alone are staggering given that total outstanding second mortgages on banks' books equaled over half of all bank capital in 2011.[39]

Evidence suggests that junior liens impede loan modifications. In general, it is difficult to study the effect of the presence of junior liens on a distressed homeowner's prospects for loan modification because most data sets do not allow researchers to identify which second liens are linked to particular first-lien loans. Two innovative studies overcame that hurdle, however, and found that first-lien mortgages with junior liens were less likely to be modified than first liens with none.[40] A

34. Been, Jackson, and Willis (2012, p. 4).

35. Goodman and others (2010); Prior (2012).

36. CoreLogic (2012, p. 2).

37. Goodman and others (2011a, pp. 38–40); see also Been, Jackson, and Willis (2012, p. 4); Goodman and others (2010, pp. 25–27).

38. See, for example, Agarwal and others (2010, p. 16).

39. Lee, Mayer, and Tracy (2013).

40. Agarwal and others (2011, pp. 5, 18); Chan and others (2011).

third study reported that junior liens were 11.3 percent less likely to be modified than first liens, which suggests that distressed borrowers who have those liens have greater difficulty in negotiating a comprehensive loan modification package.[41]

There are several reasons why first-lien loan modifications are harder to negotiate when junior liens are present. For one thing a surprising proportion of junior liens continue to perform after borrowers default on the firsts.[42] Other junior liens are both underwater and delinquent and thus often lack real worth apart from possible recourse or demanding a holdup payment from the first lienholder in order to approve a workout.[43] Junior lien holders may perceive holdup power in that regard because first lien holders usually require them to sign an agreement to continue to subordinate their claims before modifying a first mortgage.[44] Junior lien holders are often reluctant to agree or demand several thousand dollars in order to resubordinate.[45] In other circumstances the junior lien holder may not even be found because there is no central registry of junior liens.

Lessons Learned

The experience of the past few years provides three important lessons about the right way to do loss mitigation. First, when loan modifications are NPV-positive, they should incorporate lower monthly payments and principal reduction to minimize the risk of redefault. Second, loan modifications should be granted as early as possible in the delinquency process, once again to lower the risk of default. Finally, top priority should be given to solutions that keep homes occupied, even if the homeowners can no longer afford to remain in their homes.

Lesson One: Give Modifications with Lower Monthly Payments and Principal Reduction to Distressed Borrowers Who Have Sufficient Cash Flow.

Where a distressed homeowner wants to stay in his or her home and has sufficient cash flow to make a loan modification NPV-positive, the outcome should

---

41. Agarwal and others (2010).

42. See Goodman and others (2010, p. 28); Jagtiani and Lang (2011, p. 7); Lee, Mayer, and Tracy (2013).

43. See Cordell and others (2008, p. 27); see also Agarwal and others (2011, pp. 2–3, 5).

44. Randolph (2010). First lien holders require these agreements even though the second lienholder would not gain priority over the first lienholder where the loan modification would not prejudice its rights. Loan modifications that drop the interest rate, extend the loan term, or reduce principal do not prejudice junior lien holders because they improve the lien holders' ability to collect on their loans. In contrast, refinancings, short sales, and deeds-in-lieu of foreclosure would require a resubordination agreement because they have a prejudicial effect on junior lienholder interests. See also Been, Jackson, and Willis (2012, pp. 6–8).

45. Cordell and others (2008, pp. 26–27).

be clear. Under these circumstances there is no good reason for a servicer to deny a loan modification (unless a pooling and servicing agreement precludes one). That is because a loan modification will keep the house occupied and increase net recovery for both the homeowner and the owner of the loan.

The more compelling question is how to best structure loan modifications to minimize the chance of redefault. This is not a hypothetical concern. Consider the experience in 2008, when loans serviced by the largest banks and thrifts had a discouraging total twelve-month sixty-day-plus redefault rate of 58 percent. After that, servicers and policymakers learned a lot about how to cut the risk of redefault. Subsequently, with every passing year, the twelve-month sixty-day-plus redefault rate dropped steadily, down to 23 percent for modifications made in 2011. That was a 60 percent decline from 2008. Loan modification data for 2012 indicate that the redefault rate is generally holding steady or continuing to fall.[46]

What led to that improvement? Overwhelming evidence shows that the right kind of loan modification significantly lowers redefault risk. The lesson is this: lower monthly payments reduce the risk of redefault, and principal reduction lowers it even more.

Through 2008 the vast majority of loan workouts capitalized arrears without other measures designed to reduce payments.[47] Perversely, this *increased* the borrowers' monthly mortgage payments. For borrowers with cash-flow problems—especially problems that were indefinite or permanent in nature—many of these workouts failed and later had to be redone.[48]

In contrast, there is abundant evidence that loan modifications that lower monthly payments, either through reduced interest, principal reductions, or extensions of the maturity date, result in substantially lower redefault rates.[49] Workouts that cut interest rates perform better than workouts that only capitalize

46. OCC (2012a, pp. 37–38; 2012c, pp. 34–36).

47. In two path-breaking studies that brought this problem to light, Alan White reported that over two-thirds of loan workouts studied increased both the borrowers' loan payments and principal by adding in overdue interest and fees without taking other steps to reduce monthly payments. The average principal increase was a whopping $10,800. White (2009a, p. 1114; 2009b, p. 509). A study by the Boston Fed confirmed White's findings: see Adelino, Gerardi, and Willen (2009, pp. 11–12 and table 3). By the end of 2008, plans increasing principal remained the most common type of workout by far. See Adelino, Gerardi, and Willen (2009); Agarwal, Amromin, and Ben-David (2011); Collins and Reid (2011); Goodman and others (2011a, p. 34); Mason (2009, p. 32); Quercia and Ding (2009, p. 171).

48. Goodman and others (2012b, p. 55); see also Agarwal and others (2010, p. 20)

49. See Adelino, Gerardi, and Willen (2009) (lowering payments cuts redefault rates by 20 percent to 40 percent); Agarwal, Amromin, and Ben-David (2011, p. 5); Agarwal and others (2010, p. 22); Brown (2010, p. 10); Goodman and others (2011a, p. 29); Haughwout, Okah, and Tracy (2010); MHA (2012b, p. 7); OCC (2012a, pp. 41–43); Quercia and Ding (2009); Voicu and others (2011).

arrears. The bigger the interest rate cut, the lower the rate of redefault.[50] Cutting principal has the lowest redefault rate of all, probably because doing so lowers monthly payments while reducing the effect of negative equity as an independent driver of default.[51]

In response to this experience, interest rate reductions and principal reductions and deferrals became more common in recent years. According to the Office of the Comptroller of the Currency (OCC), the proportion of loan modifications reducing the interest rate grew markedly following the introduction of HAMP, hitting a high of 84 percent before falling to slightly lower levels in 2011 and 2012.[52] Over that same period, principal reductions and principal deferrals also grew quickly, albeit from very low levels. By third quarter 2012, 17.1 percent of loan modifications reduced principal and 19.1 percent deferred it.[53] That trend was especially pronounced in the private-label space, where principal reductions and principal deferrals made up 38.0 percent and 28.2 percent, respectively, or two-thirds of all private-label loan modifications in third quarter 2012.[54] In contrast, principal write-downs accounted for 37.8 percent of modifications to loans held in portfolio, while principal deferrals accounted for 8.4 percent (totaling 46.2 percent) in third quarter 2012. Fannie Mae and Freddie Mac granted principal write-downs on no loans.[55]

The growing trend toward principal relief was partly spurred by increased incentives under HAMP. In March 2010 the HAMP program started offering carrots to servicers to write down principal and extinguish junior liens.[56] Under the Principal Reduction Alternative, or PRA, offered to any underwater borrower owing more than 115 percent of the current value of his or her home (except for

50. Agarwal, Amromin, and Ben-David (2011); Fuster and Willen (2012); Goodman and others (2012a, p. 5); OCC (2012b, pp. 43-44); Voicu and others (2011).

51. Bajari, Chu, and Park (2008, pp. 32–33); Das and Meadows (2011); Goodman and others (2011a, p. 29; 2012a, pp. 4, 9; 2012b, p. 55); Haughwout, Okah, and Tracy (2010); Moody's Investors Service (2012a, pp. 5–6); Quercia and Ding (2009); Voicu and others (2011). See also Board of Governors of the Federal Reserve (2012, p. 4).

52. OCC (2012a, p. 26; 2012c, p. 25).

53. OCC (2012c, p. 25).

54. OCC (2012c, p. 28). That represented a significant increase from earlier years. Agarwal, Amromin, and Ben-David reported that from January 2008 to May 2009, no private-label loan modifications in the OCC Mortgage Metrics data set featured principal deferral or write-downs; meanwhile, over that same time period, only 3 percent of portfolio loan modifications involved principal deferral and only 1 percent involved principal write-downs. Agarwal, Amromin, and Ben-David (2011).

55. See OCC (2012c, p. 28), which shows that Fannie and Freddie did grant principal deferrals in 31 percent and 44.5 percent, respectively, of their loan modifications in third quarter 2012. Those borrowers will eventually have to repay the deferred principal, however.

56. U.S. Department of the Treasury (2013b).

borrowers with GSE loans), HAMP servicers had to calculate the borrower's net present value using both the standard approach and an alternative approach that moved principal reduction to the top of the HAMP waterfall (with the objective of lowering principal to a loan-to-value ratio of 115 percent). If a principal write-down was needed to reduce the borrower's monthly payment to 31 percent of income, the servicer could—but was not obliged to—reduce principal. To encourage principal write-downs, the federal government offered to pay 10 to 21 cents for each dollar of unpaid principal written down (depending on the loan-to-value ratio).[57] In January 2012 the administration tripled that subsidy to as much as 63 cents for every dollar written off.[58] Gradually, the increased subsidy worked, and this voluntary program took hold. For instance, in November 2012, 77 percent of all new trial modifications for non-GSE loans that were eligible for a principal reduction received one.[59]

The $25 billion state and federal mortgage servicing settlement in March 2012 boosted the incentives for principal write-downs even more. Under that settlement the five largest servicers—Bank of America, JPMorgan Chase, Wells Fargo, Citicorp, and Ally Financial—agreed to a total of at least $10 billion in principal reductions to underwater borrowers who were past due or at risk of default.[60] In 2012 there was a big upswing in non-PRA principal reductions that did not qualify for a subsidy under HAMP, in all likelihood due to the settlement.[61] As of December 31, 2012, the five servicers reported granting $6.04 billion in first-lien principal forgiveness and $11.6 billion in second-lien modifications and extinguishments. Over 25,000 other borrowers were in active first-lien trial modifications that, if successful, could result in $3.49 billion in additional write-downs.[62] This trend was poised to accelerate as the result of a later $8.5 billion settlement between federal banking regulators and ten large

57. If the servicer opted to reduce principal, it would initially treat the reduction as forbearance. To encourage borrowers to remain current on their new, lower loan payments, servicers would then forgive the forborne amount in three equal steps over three years, as long as the homeowner remained current on the payments. U.S. Department of the Treasury (2013b).

58. Massad (2012). The January 2012 directive also offered the first principal reduction incentives for GSE loans. As of this writing, the GSEs were still not availing themselves of those incentives.

59. MHA (2012c, p. 4).

60. U.S. Department of Justice (2012). Eventually, the total principal write-downs under the agreement were expected to exceed $10 billion because of the way those write-downs are credited toward the settlement. See *United States of America, et al.* v. *Bank of America Corp. et al.,* Consent Judgment. Civil Action 12-00361, Document 11 (D.D.C. April 4, 2012), exhibit D-1, table 1. See also Office of Mortgage Settlement Oversight, "About the Mortgage Settlement" (www.mortgage oversight.com/about-the-mortgage-settlement/).

61. MHA (2012c, p. 4).

62. Office of Mortgage Settlement Oversight (2013, p. 3).

servicers in January 2013 for foreclosure abuses.[63] Under that settlement the banks agreed to devote up to $5.2 billion in loan modifications and forgiveness of deficiency judgments.

While the spurt in principal relief was notable, interest rate reductions still outstripped principal reductions by more than two to one in 2012, despite their higher redefault rates. Fannie Mae and Freddie Mac continue to refuse to grant principal write-downs at all at the insistence of their conservator, the Federal Housing Finance Agency, which maintains that principal forgiveness will increase the GSEs' accounting losses to the detriment of taxpayers.[64] Meanwhile, over 83 percent of all loan modifications made in the second quarter of 2012— and over 96 percent of those involving Fannie Mae, Freddie Mac, and federally insured mortgages—capitalized arrears.[65] Those capitalization plans undercut other loan modification terms such as rate reductions and term extensions by increasing the outstanding principal of the capitalized loans and thereby boosting the default risk of underwater borrowers.[66] As a result we still have not achieved the optimal mix of loan modification techniques.

What explains the continued resistance to principal reductions? While there are several reasons, typically servicers and FHFA cite moral hazard as the main concern.[67] They argue that principal modifications will induce other borrowers who are able to pay their mortgages to strategically default (or threaten to default) in order to reduce their loan payments.[68]

The severity of negative equity in this country following the financial crisis intensified this debate. As of June 30, 2012, 10.8 million borrowers (more than one out of every five homeowners) had underwater mortgages. Even that was an improvement over previous quarters.[69] The concern is that homeowners have

63. Board of Governors of the Federal Reserve System and the OCC (2013). The ten servicers were Aurora, Bank of America, Citibank, JPMorgan Chase, MetLife Bank, PNC, Sovereign, SunTrust, U.S. Bank, and Wells Fargo.

64. See DeMarco (2012b); OCC (2012c, p. 28). FHFA maintains that position even though it has conceded that when the higher HAMP subsidies were taken into account, principal reduction by the GSEs compared to principal forbearance would reduce taxpayer losses by $1.7 billion. DeMarco (2012a, pp. 17–19). Fannie Mae and Freddie Mac's resistance to principal write-downs also explains the extremely low take-up rate on the principal reduction program paid for by the Hardest Hit Fund under the Troubled Asset Relief Program. See GAO (2012b, pp. 24–25 and figure 4); Office of the Special Inspector General for the Troubled Asset Relief Program (2012a).

65. OCC (2012b, p. 30).

66. See Collins and Reid (2011).

67. See, for example, DeMarco (2012b). For discussion of other explanations for this pattern, see McCoy (2013).

68. See, for example, Ambrose and Capone (1996, p. 105); Posner and Zingales (2009, p. 577); Quercia and Ding (2009, p. 171).

69. See CoreLogic (2012); see also Board of Governors of the Federal Reserve (2012, p. 4).

growing incentives to walk away from their mortgages as their loans go more and more deeply underwater.

Moral hazard concerns are real.[70] Guiso, Sapienza, and Zingales estimate, for instance, that 26 percent of mortgage defaults were strategic, based on surveys conducted in late 2008 and early 2009.[71] Still, it is important not to overstate the extent of moral hazard. The vast majority of underwater borrowers do not default. In second quarter 2012, for instance, almost 85 percent of underwater borrowers were current on their payments.[72] Furthermore, a large proportion of underwater borrowers who default do so due to cash flow difficulties, not strategic behavior.[73] Studies have concluded that underwater borrowers remain deeply averse to walking away from their mortgages until they reach high levels of negative equity, in part due to morality.[74] Underwater borrowers who default on their mortgages also suffer major damage to their credit records for several years at a minimum.[75]

Moral hazard objections to principal reduction ignore the fact that all forms of loan modification trigger moral hazard to some degree.[76] If moral hazard were of overriding concern, one would expect servicers to resist interest rate reductions too. Moreover, the strategic default objection does not take into account the benefits of a smaller shadow inventory to society or the fact that principal reductions, used wisely, *reduce* overall incentives toward strategic default by alleviating the negative equity that fuels that behavior.[77]

Furthermore, there are techniques to discourage moral hazard when granting principal reductions.[78] One way is to restrict principal reductions to financially struggling homeowners and deny them to homeowners who default for purely strategic reasons. For this reason the HAMP program limits principal forgiveness and other types of modifications to borrowers who can show financial hardship, thereby allowing servicers to distinguish borrowers with proven

70. Several studies have found evidence of strategic default by deeply underwater borrowers. See Bajari, Chu, and Park (2008); Bhutta, Dokko, and Shan (2011); Elul and others (2010, pp. 10–13); Goodman and others (2011a, p. 29); Haughwout, Okah, and Tracy (2010); Jagtiani and Lang (2011, p. 7); Mayer and others (2011). But see Foote, Gerardi, and Willen (2008, p. 234), who found little evidence of strategic default during the Massachusetts housing downturn in the early 1990s.

71. Guiso, Sapienza, and Zingales (2011).

72. CoreLogic (2012); see also Foote and others (2009a, pp. 2–3 and n. 8); DeMarco (2012b).

73. For example, Bhutta, Dokko, and Shan (2011); Foote and others (2009a, p. 1, note 1).

74. Bhutta, Dokko, and Shan (2011); Guiso, Sapienza, and Zingales (2009, 2011).

75. For example, Brevoort and Cooper (2010, p. 2).

76. For example, Goodman and others (2012a, p. 13).

77. For example, Moody's Investors Service (2012a, pp. 5–6; 2012b, pp. 6–8; 2012c, pp. 5–6; 2012d, p. 5).

78. See generally Goodman and others (2012a, pp. 15–16).

cash flow problems from those who are still able to pay their mortgages in full.[79] Another approach is to limit principal modifications to borrowers who became delinquent before the principal reduction program was announced.[80] Similarly, restricting principal reductions to borrowers with lower FICO scores and fully amortizing mortgages can constrain moral hazard because borrowers with higher FICO scores and less than fully amortizing mortgages are more apt to strategically default.[81]

There are also ways to design principal reductions to discourage strategic default. For instance, the special servicer Ocwen uses several design features in the principal modifications it grants to underwater borrowers to reduce moral hazard. First, Ocwen writes down eligible loans to 95 percent of the current appraised value, in order to restore the borrower to positive equity. This draws on the insight that borrowers are unlikely to strategically default if their mortgages are "in the money."[82] Second, to discourage redefault Ocwen forgives one-third of the write-down each year for three years, as long as the borrower continues to perform. Finally, the borrower must agree to share 25 percent of any future home price appreciation with the investor, to limit any upside from strategic default.[83] At other times servicers who write down principal may insist on a short sale that requires the borrower to move out instead of a partial charge-off that keeps the borrower in the home. This too is intended to discourage strategic default.[84]

Lesson Two: Do Not Put Off Granting Loan Modifications.

Speed is of the essence when it comes to granting loan modifications to eligible borrowers. The evidence on this point is clear. Distressed borrowers redefault

79. MHA (2011a, p. 51). The mortgage servicing settlement is somewhat more ambiguous about a financial hardship test. While the settlement appears to limit principal write-downs to underwater owner-occupant borrowers "with economic hardship" who were at least sixty days delinquent as of January 31, 2012 (before the settlement was signed), it does not define "economic hardship." Elsewhere in the settlement, the consent decree also seems to contemplate possible principal relief to current borrowers who are "at imminent risk of default due to [their] financial situation." See, for example, *United States of America* v. *Bank of America Corp.,* Consent Judgment (2012, pp. D-2, I-1, I-7 through I-8). The settlement gives servicers broad discretion to define their own financial hardship test.

80. The mortgage servicing settlement takes this approach. See, for example, *United States of America* v. *Bank of America Corp.,* Consent Judgment (2012, p. I-7).

81. Amromin and others (2012).

82. Compare with Moody's Investors Service (2012d, pp. 1–2, 5). Even reducing negative equity to combined loan-to-value ratios of around 120 percent or less can sharply reduce incentives to engage in strategic default. See Bhutta, Dokko, and Shan (2011); Guiso, Sapienza, and Zingales (2009, 2011). See also Agarwal and others (2010, pp. 21–23).

83. Prior (2011); see generally Goodman and others (2012a, p. 14). For similar equity sharing proposals, see Posner and Zingales (2009, p. 577); Das and Meadows (2011).

84. Thompson (2011, p. 755).

at significantly lower rates when they receive loan modifications earlier in the delinquency process.[85] This effect is particularly pronounced for borrowers with lower FICO scores.[86]

Disturbingly, recent trends have being going the wrong way. In the private-label market in 2008, only 5 percent of loan modifications were made after twelve months' delinquency; in 2012 that number jumped to over 40 percent.[87] What makes this even more surprising is that in July 2011 the HAMP program started making higher payments for modifications issued sooner rather than later following default.[88] Despite this subsidy the proportion of private-label modifications made more than a year after default continued to rise.[89]

Lesson Three: For Distressed Borrowers Lacking the Cash Flow to Make a Loan Modification NPV-Positive, Find a Solution That Will Keep the Home Occupied.

Some distressed homeowners do not have sufficient cash flow to satisfy the NPV test for a loan modification. Nor do they often qualify for a refinance.[90] These homeowners fall into a variety of groups, with different solutions. In some cases it may be possible to keep people with inadequate cash flow in their homes. When that is not possible, top priority should be given to solutions that keep the home otherwise occupied.

UNEMPLOYED AND UNDEREMPLOYED BORROWERS

The single biggest group of distressed borrowers who may lack sufficient cash flow to meet the NPV test consists of people who are unemployed or underemployed. As of year-end 2012, 12.2 million individuals were unemployed in the United States.[91] Up to two-thirds of these were homeowners.[92] In 2010 jobless and underemployed homeowners constituted up to 23 percent of distressed

---

85. Brown (2010, p. 6); Goodman and others (2011b, p. 57); Quercia and Ding (2009, p. 171).

86. Goodman and others (2012a, pp. 5, 8).

87. Goodman and others (2012a, pp. 5–6).

88. MHA (2011b). HAMP now pays servicers $1,600 for modifications completed within 120 days of delinquency, $1,200 for those completed within 121 days to 210 days of delinquency, and only $400 for modifications completed more than 210 days following delinquency. Previously, HAMP paid a flat $1,000 for all modifications completed, regardless of when they were done. See also MHA (2011a, p. 106).

89. Goodman and others (2012a, pp. 5–6).

90. The early refinance programs of the Bush and Obama administrations did not have promising records. More recently, the GSEs and the FHA agreed to refinance borrowers with Fannie, Freddie, and FHA loans into lower interest rate loans regardless of whether they were underwater on their mortgages.

91. Bureau of Labor Statistics (2013b).

92. See Foote and others (2009a, p. 10).

borrowers.[93] Almost 68 percent of the people who applied to HAMP through November 2012 gave lost income from reduced pay or job termination as their reason for applying.[94]

Many jobless homeowners do not qualify for a traditional HAMP loan modification because their drop in income is so severe that they would need a 50 percent payment reduction or more in order to afford their mortgage. A loan modification that large will usually not pass the NPV test, eliminating any private incentive for servicers and investors to grant a workout.[95]

Nevertheless, there are good public policy reasons for the government to intervene in conditions of mass unemployment. While the income disruption from joblessness is large, it also is temporary for most unemployed homeowners who plan to return to work. In December 2012, for example, it took eighteen weeks on average—three and a half months—for the median jobless person to find new work.[96] Government relief makes sense under these circumstances by giving jobless borrowers breathing room to locate new work without losing their homes and thereby generating the negative spillover effects that come with ouster.

When HAMP was first announced in early 2009, it did not contemplate special relief for unemployed borrowers. But by year-end 2009, the Obama administration became concerned that HAMP was ignoring the millions of borrowers suffering catastrophic income drops due to job loss or reduced hours. By that point the national unemployment rate was hovering around 9 percent and 25 percent of homes had underwater mortgages.[97] Many underwater borrowers who lost their jobs were trapped because they could not make the payments and could not sell their homes for enough to pay off their mortgages. In response, by mid-2010 the administration rolled out three programs to address the situation of these borrowers.

The Hardest Hit Fund. The administration's first step in February 2010 was to create the Hardest Hit Fund (HHF) to funnel money to unemployed homeowners in the worst-off states to help them pay their mortgages. The Hardest Hit Fund is financed through TARP and is meant to pay for "innovative measures"

93. As of 2009, for instance, Herkenhoff and Ohanian (2012, pp. 2–3) estimated that unemployed borrowers held around 6 percent of mortgages, more than double the rate in 2005.

94. MHA (2012c, p. 6).

95. See Foote and others (2009a, pp. 3–4).

96. Bureau of Labor Statistics (2013b). The average spell of joblessness was longer, however, clocking in at 38.1 weeks as of December 2012.

97. Office of the Special Inspector General for the Troubled Asset Relief Program (2012a, summary on p. 1).

by state housing finance agencies (HFAs) to assist borrowers in states hit hardest by the financial crisis.[98]

The Hardest Hit Fund originally was envisioned as a $1.5 billion program making grants to the five states with home price declines of 20 percent or more. Eventually, after four rounds of funding, the HHF expanded into a $7.6 billion TARP program extending assistance to eighteen states and the District of Columbia.[99] The Department of the Treasury approved state plans to use the HHF to address a variety of local housing challenges, including jobless and underemployed borrowers, underwater borrowers, and second liens.[100] While state HFAs can use their HHF grants for any or all of these reasons with Treasury's approval, all of them targeted unemployed homeowners.[101] This is reflected in the demographic makeup of the borrowers who received assistance through the HHF. As of September 30, 2012, 92 percent of the borrowers assisted by the HHF gave unemployment or underemployment as their reason for applying. About half had underwater mortgages, and about 64 percent were delinquent on their mortgages when they applied for help.[102]

The Hardest Hit Fund got off to a disappointingly slow start. Collectively, the nineteen HFAs estimated that the HHF would assist up to 486,000 borrowers by the program's end in 2017. But two and half years after it started, the Hardest Hit Fund had only helped 77,164 borrowers and had only spent $742 million— less than one-tenth of its TARP allotment—as of September 30, 2012. About 27 percent—$199 million—of that money went to administrative costs.[103]

According to the U.S. Government Accountability Office and the Special Inspector General for TARP (SIGTARP), there were several reasons for the slow rollout. For one thing, the Treasury Department "rushed out the program without appropriate collaboration of key stakeholders."[104] For another, administration of the program was entrusted to state HFAs, which often lacked experience

98. Office of the Special Inspector General for the Troubled Asset Relief Program (2012a, summary on p. 1). Formally, funding for the Hardest Hit Program was authorized in the Emergency Economic Stability Act of 2008.

99. U.S. Department of the Treasury (2013a, 2010b); Office of the Special Inspector General for the Troubled Asset Relief Program (2012a, summary on p. 1).

100. Office of the Special Inspector General for the Troubled Asset Relief Program (2012a, summary on p. 1); White House (2010).

101. See Congressional Oversight Panel (2010, p. 40); GAO (2012b, p. 24).

102. U.S. Department of the Treasury (2012).

103. U.S. Department of the Treasury (2012); Office of the Special Inspector General for the Troubled Asset Relief Program (2012a, summary on pp. 1–2).

104. Office of the Special Inspector General for the Troubled Asset Relief Program (2012a, summary on pp. 2–3).

in running programs of this type.[105] On top of that, large national mortgage servicers refused to participate in the program for nine months, until Fannie Mae and Freddie Mac issued guidance for HHF servicing in October 2010.[106]

Based on this lackluster performance, SIGTARP warned: "If Treasury cannot achieve the desired level of homeowners assisted . . . Treasury should put the funds to better use toward [other] programs that are reaching homeowners."[107] SIGTARP and the GAO were also concerned about the Hardest Hit Fund's lack of transparency.[108] Treasury delayed reporting aggregate results for the HHF until mid-2012. Even today those results do not appear in the Treasury Department's monthly HAMP report or the administration's housing scorecard. Instead, they are buried on the Treasury Department's website.[109] Four years into the program, there are still no publicly available data on the success rate of HHF borrowers.

Despite these obstacles, the HHF's payment assistance provisions for unemployed and underemployed borrowers proved substantially easier to implement than its provisions for principal forgiveness, reducing second liens, or transition aid. As of first quarter 2012, less than 5 percent of HHF funds for borrowers had been spent on the latter three activities, while 96 percent was spent on assisting jobless borrowers make mortgage payments or pay off past due amounts.[110] According to the GAO, it was easier for HFAs to top off loan payments or pay off arrearages because those two types of relief required minimal servicer involvement. In contrast, principal reduction, second-lien relief, and transition assistance required active decisionmaking involvement by servicers. That, plus the GSEs' refusal to adopt the principal reduction program, impeded the success of those aspects of the Hardest Hit Fund.[111]

The HAMP Unemployment Program. One of the Hardest Hit Fund's biggest drawbacks was in limiting relief to homeowners in the targeted states. By mid-2010 federal data suggested that income loss had become the most common reason for mortgage defaults.[112] The high correlation between job loss and default

105. See GAO (2012b, pp. 27–28).

106. See GAO (2012b, p. 28); Office of the Special Inspector General for the Troubled Asset Relief Program (2012a, summary on pp. 2–3).

107. Office of the Special Inspector General for the Troubled Asset Relief Program (2012a, summary on p. 3).

108. See GAO (2012b, highlights and pp. 22, 35, 37); Office of the Special Inspector General for the Troubled Asset Relief Program (2012a, summary on pp. 2–3). See also Congressional Oversight Panel (2010, p. 107).

109. See U.S. Department of the Treasury (2012). The Treasury Department's monthly TARP reports to Congress contain only a cursory update on the Hardest Hit Fund program.

110. See GAO (2012b, pp. 24-25 and figure 4).

111. See GAO (2012b, p. 25).

112. See for example Foote and others (2009b).

drove home the importance of addressing the plight of unemployed homeowners nationwide, not just in the worst-off states.

Consequently, in March 2010 the federal government broadened HAMP to help any out-of-work homeowners, regardless of their state. Under the Home Affordable Unemployment Program (UP), the government encouraged servicers to cut the mortgage payments of unemployed borrowers eligible for HAMP to 31 percent of gross income or forbear payments altogether for three to six months (later expanded to twelve months or more) while the homeowners looked for work.[113] If a borrower assisted through UP later regained employment, he or she had to be considered for a traditional HAMP modification. Any payments forborne under the UP plan would be capitalized if the borrower qualified for a HAMP modification. Otherwise, if the UP forbearance period ended, and the borrower did not qualify for traditional HAMP relief, he or she would be considered for a short sale or a deed-in-lieu of foreclosure under the Home Affordable Foreclosure Alternatives program.[114]

For a variety of reasons, the Unemployment Program barely got off the ground. Two and a half years after its inception, as of October 31, 2012, only 29,050 UP forbearance plans had been started.[115] In all likelihood this disappointing take-up rate is partly due to the fact that the government gave servicers no added financial incentives for participating in UP.[116] Furthermore, Fannie Mae and Freddie Mac refused to participate in the program, probably because servicers were encouraged (but not required) to grant principal modifications under the UP program.[117]

The Emergency Homeowners Loan Program. Whatever its merits, one reason the UP program fell short was that it did not provide servicers with financial incentives for assisting unemployed borrowers. Consequently, in the Dodd-Frank Wall Street Reform and Consumer Protection Act (Dodd-Frank) in July 2010, Congress authorized the U.S. Department of Housing and Urban Development

---

113. To qualify, the loan in question had to be for an owner-occupied principal residence, have a mortgage balance of less than $729,750, and be originated before 2009. The borrower also had to prove financial hardship and receipt of unemployment benefits. After six months borrowers who found work with lower pay or who did not find work at all would be considered, respectively, for a permanent HAMP modification or for a short sale combined with relocation assistance. U.S. Department of the Treasury (2013b).

114. Office of the Special Inspector General for the Troubled Asset Relief Program (2012b, pp. 77–78).

115. MHA (2012c, p. 4). Of those forbearance plans, 25,045 required a reduced mortgage payment and 4,005 required no payment at all.

116. MHA (2010).

117. See U.S. Department of the Treasury (2013b).

(HUD) to create a third program—the Emergency Homeowners Loan Program, or EHLP—providing $1 billion in aid to unemployed homeowners in the remaining thirty-two states and Puerto Rico that did not receive Hardest Hit funds.[118] That aid consisted of zero-interest, nonrecourse, subordinate loans for up to $50,000 to help unemployed or underemployed borrowers stay current on their mortgage payments for up to twenty-four months.[119] No payments were due during the five-year term of the loan as long as the recipient used the home as his or her principal residence and remained current on the first mortgage. With each passing year of satisfactory performance, 20 percent of the balance would be retired and the EHLP note would be extinguished after five successful years.[120] On the other hand, if the homeowner did not meet the repayment obligations, the loan would be paid out of any home equity that remained after the other loans were retired, without recourse against the borrower.[121]

To qualify for EHLP assistance, borrowers had to meet a complicated set of strict criteria, including receipt of a notice of intention to foreclose and loss of at least 15 percent of gross income due to unemployment, underemployment, or a medical emergency. In addition, applicants needed to show that they had a reasonable likelihood of being able to resume repayment on their first mortgage loans within two years.[122]

Congress imposed a tight application deadline of September 30, 2011, on all EHLP loans.[123] Unfortunately, HUD did not start taking applications until June 20, 2011, eleven months after Dodd-Frank's passage.[124] HUD allowed five states to disburse their EHLP funds directly; NeighborWorks America distributed the funds in Puerto Rico and the other twenty-seven states.[125] In the end less than 12,000 of the approximately 100,000 people who applied for EHLP loans qualified for them, and HUD left nearly half of the funds unspent.[126] That was less than half of the 30,000 families HUD originally projected the program

---

118. *Dodd-Frank Wall Street Reform and Consumer Protection Act,* Public Law 111-203, *U.S. Statutes at Large* 124 (2010): 2208–09, § 1496 (amending *U.S. Code* 12, §§ 2702–2708).

119. U.S. Department of the Treasury (2010b).

120. U.S. Department of Housing and Urban Development (2010).

121. U.S. Department of Housing and Urban Development (2010).

122. U.S. Department of Housing and Urban Development (2010).

123. Dodd-Frank, § 1496.

124. U.S. Department of Housing and Urban Development, Office of Inspector General (2011, p. 69).

125. Connecticut, Delaware, Idaho, Maryland, and Pennsylvania were the states that served as direct providers. GAO (2012a, pp. 30–31).

126. See Buckley (2011); Dennis (2011); U.S. Department of Housing and Urban Development, Office of Inspector General (2011, pp. 69–70); GAO (2012a, pp. 30–31); Schmit (2011). Author's calculations from USASpending.gov.

would assist.[127] In addition, of the money that was disbursed, almost half went to borrowers in three states: Connecticut, Maryland, and Pennsylvania, states which directly disbursed EHLP funds.[128]

The department's inspector general blamed EHLP's disappointing performance on HUD's "delays in establishing EHLP." According to the inspector general's report, those delays were due to "the uniqueness of the program, outsourced application intake and evaluation, lack of a permanent management structure, and the aggressive timeframe for obligating the funds."[129]

Program Performance. When the history of the federal government's recent loss mitigation programs for unemployed borrowers is considered to date, it is apparent that the three programs fell short of their goals. Through the third quarter of 2012, those programs only helped a total of 117,235 unemployed or underemployed borrowers. This number pales compared to the estimated 902,000 to 1.297 million delinquent borrowers who were unemployed as of September 2012.[130] Furthermore, billions of dollars in federal aid to unemployed borrowers remain unspent.

There are several reasons for this poor performance. First, the federal approach to unemployed homeowners was piecemeal in multiple respects. The only ongoing program with funding—the Hardest Hit Fund—applied to less than 40 percent of the states. EHLP covered the entire country and was funded but was only a one-time Band-Aid with a tight statutory deadline, expiring before more than a few thousand households could be helped, most in just three states. Meanwhile, HAMP's Unemployment Program is still in operation (and applies to every state), but servicers have largely ignored it, probably because it does not pay servicer or borrower subsidies.

Lack of GSE cooperation further hindered the take-up rate of two of the programs. Fannie Mae and Freddie Mac were slow to issue guidance for the payment assistance provisions of the Hardest Hit Fund and refused to participate in its principal reduction provisions. Similarly, the GSEs boycotted HAMP's Unemployment Program, probably because servicers are encouraged (but not required) to consider principal forgiveness.

Little is known about the performance of these programs. The Hardest Hit Fund makes its aggregate statistics difficult for the public to locate and does not

127. See Dennis (2011).

128. Schmit (2011).

129. U.S. Department of Housing and Urban Development, Office of Inspector General (2011, p. 69).

130. According to Lender Processing Services (2012, p. 18), as of September 30, 2012, approximately 5.64 million borrowers were delinquent on their mortgages or in foreclosure. Extrapolating from Herkenhoff and Ohanian (2012, pp. 2–3), this estimate assumes that somewhere between 16 percent and 23 percent of those borrowers were unemployed.

publicly report the success rate of its borrowers. The EHLP program has not issued statistical reports at all (leaving it to HUD's inspector general and the GAO to ferret out basic data on that program). HAMP's Unemployment Program does report the number of borrowers assisted in the Treasury Department's monthly HAMP report, but the success rate of those borrowers is unknown.

Without results on borrower performance, it is difficult to draw firm conclusions about features of these programs that are likely to have greater success. But some tentative conclusions can be drawn. First, the Hardest Hit Fund's program to pay mortgage arrears and upcoming mortgage payments for borrowers who have suffered job loss or reductions in pay for up to twenty-four months has had the biggest take-up rate of any of the administration's three foreclosure prevention programs for unemployed borrowers. In all likelihood direct payments were successful because they did not require servicers or investors to write down the interest rate or principal.[131]

Second, and related to the first point, foreclosure prevention efforts for unemployed borrowers are likely to fail if servicer participation is voluntary and unfunded. The HAMP UP offers no financial incentives to servicers to forbear on mortgage payments. In contrast, HHF directly subsidizes mortgage payments for unemployed borrowers, which helps explain why it has had almost three times the take-up rate of the UP in a smaller number of states.

Third, the federal government should have provided targeted relief to jobless borrowers on a nationwide basis from the outset. Instead, the government delayed providing nationwide assistance, and when it finally did provide that assistance, it did so on a short-fuse deadline (the EHLP program) or without funding and on terms that the GSEs opposed (HAMP UP).

Fourth, any program of broad geographic scope for individual relief to borrowers will necessarily have implementation delays on the ground. Dividing that relief among three different programs run by two different federal departments using different local delivery mechanisms compounded those implementation delays and spawned borrower confusion and resistance by servicers.

Fifth, the one-shot fix in EHLP was a serious mistake, particularly with that program's unrealistic application deadline. Unemployment is an ongoing problem, and consequently relief needs to be ongoing too.

Finally, the problems in rolling out the Hardest Hit Fund and HAMP UP point out the need for cooperation and closer involvement by the Federal Housing Finance Agency, Fannie Mae, and Freddie Mac. The GSEs dragged their feet in issuing servicing guidelines for the Hardest Hit Fund, which seriously delayed its implementation. Meanwhile, the GSEs' opposition to voluntary principal

---

131. See Foote and others (2009a).

reduction features helped neuter HAMP UP and limit the success of the Hardest Hit Fund program.

RATE RESETS AND OPTION ARM RECASTS

Performing borrowers facing unaffordable rate resets on adjustable rate mortgages (ARMs) formed another group who could have stayed in their homes with the right type of loan modification. When the foreclosure crisis unfolded in 2007 and early 2008, policymakers' main concern was about the payment shock from pending rate resets on hybrid ARMs, interest-only ARMs, and option ARMs.[132] The Bush administration's first response was an FHA refinance program called FHASecure, rolled out in August 2007, which gave borrowers facing unmanageable increases in their mortgage payments due to upcoming rate resets on their adjustable rate loans the chance to refinance into FHA-insured fixed-rate loans. Most servicers refused to participate in the program, however, because they would have to take a write-down of up to 10 percent on the borrower's existing mortgage in order for the debtor to qualify for an FHASecure loan. At the end of the day, the program only assisted 4,200 total borrowers, and the federal government wound it down in late 2008.[133]

In late 2007 policymakers and industry also began to consider tackling the rate reset problem through loan modifications. In December 2007 the American Securitization Forum unveiled a plan for voluntarily freezing interest rates on securitized subprime ARMs.[134] Meanwhile, FDIC Chairman Sheila Bair started giving speeches arguing that ARMs should be frozen at their initial rates to avoid defaults from sudden payment shock. She urged servicers to adopt her plan, saying that if the industry did not adopt voluntary modification programs, Congress would "do it for them."[135]

After LIBOR and other ARM indexes plunged in the fall of 2008, concerns over payment shock eased and attention turned to other causes of mounting delinquencies.[136] As the crisis unfolded, early payment defaults shot up,

---

132. For a description of the payment shock problem, see McCoy (2007, p. 123). A related problem involved recasts on option ARMs, which had a negative amortization feature that allowed borrowers to defer principal and even part of their principal payments during the initial period of their loans. Under the terms of those loans, eventually the loan "recast," and the borrowers had to start amortizing the skipped principal and interest, which had been added to the principal. Together, a rate reset combined with a recast could significantly boost the monthly payments on an option ARM loan. See McCoy (2007).

133. Cordell and others (2009); Corkery (2008, p. C1).

134. See American Securitization Forum (2007).

135. Terris (2007).

136. For example, see LIBOR (2013).

indicating that large numbers of homeowners could not afford their monthly mortgage payments even at the initial interest rates. Some early payment defaults were attributable to reckless underwriting or fraud, particularly in cases of low- or no-documentation (the so-called liars') loans. In the meantime rising unemployment emerged as the new, main driver of mortgage delinquencies. Between May 2007 and October 2009, unemployment soared from 4.4 percent to 10 percent.[137] Others who kept their jobs experienced cuts in hours or in pay.

While concerns over rate resets and option ARM recasts abated over time, a not insignificant fraction of mortgage delinquencies were associated with these features, particularly during the early phase of the crisis. One group of researchers placed an upper bound on delinquencies from rate resets at around 12 percent.[138]

Although this group of borrowers was smaller than those hit by unemployment and reductions in pay, loan modifications offering payment reductions could have helped borrowers facing prohibitively expensive rate resets to stay in their homes. That is particularly true for borrowers in unaffordable ARMs who were able to make their mortgage payments before their rates reset.

People with Dual Housing Payments

Job relocation is another reason why some underwater homeowners ran out of money to pay their mortgages. One group of researchers recently estimated a nationwide baseline two-year mobility rate of 10 to 11 percent from 1985 through 2009. Relatively few of those individuals had negative equity during that period, even though home prices had started to fall in 2007.[139] However, home prices continued to decline after 2009 and did not stabilize until 2012. In the process a growing number of homeowners became underwater on their mortgages, including some who needed or wished to relocate.

Civilian Homeowners. Some underwater borrowers who had been current on their mortgages had to move away for new job assignments but could not sell their homes for enough to retire their mortgages. Their challenge was to juggle their old mortgage payments plus their new rent or mortgage in the new location. Some of these homeowners made enough to manage both payments, while others made do by renting out the old home or negotiating lower payments on their mortgages.[140] Other homeowners who relocated fell behind on their old mortgages.

---

137. See Bureau of Labor Statistics (2013a).

138. See Foote, Gerardi, and Willen (2012, pp. 5–7). This estimate is not far from the 10.9 percent of borrowers in active permanent HAMP modifications who reported an "excessive obligation" as their primary hardship reason. MHA (2012c, p. 6).

139. See Ferreira, Gyourko, and Tracy (2011, pp. 9–10, 16, and tables 1, 3).

140. Generally, however, civilians who relocate are not eligible for HAMP modifications on the mortgages on their old homes because they are no longer owner occupants.

For homeowners who cannot generate enough cash to manage dual housing payments, a short sale would often be beneficial. Before 2011 servicers were highly resistant to short sales, even when those sales were NPV-positive, for the same reason they were resistant to other types of principal reduction. Thus the eight largest servicers reported that only 6.2 percent of their borrowers who applied for but were rejected for HAMP trial modifications were in the process of short sales or deed-in-lieu of foreclosure transactions as of July 2010.[141]

This resistance to short sales ebbed over time, partly due to increased federal subsidies. The Obama administration started down this path in March 2009, when the Treasury Department announced it was offering financial incentives to servicers for alternatives to foreclosure. These incentives included payments to servicers for approving short sales and payments to investors to extinguish second liens that could impede those sales.[142]

After those measures failed to gained traction, the Treasury Department revamped the program, renaming it the "Home Affordable Foreclosure Alternatives" program (HAFA) in March 2010. HAFA increased the incentive payments to servicers to approve short sales from $1,000 to $1,500, on the condition that they excuse any deficiency and not require a financial contribution or promissory note from the borrower. As another incentive, the government increased subsidies to junior lien holders to 6 percent of the outstanding loan balance, up to $6,000, to induce them to release their liens. The government also doubled its relocation payments to borrowers who completed short sales or deed-in-lieu transactions, up to $3,000.[143]

In 2010 Fannie Mae and Freddie Mac allowed short sales but only under relatively stingy circumstances. In April 2012, under pressure from the administration, the Federal Housing Finance Agency liberalized the GSEs' short sale guidelines to increase the number of short sales for distressed GSE loans. Those measures included a sixty-day deadline for responding to short sale offers and enhancements addressing borrower eligibility, documentation, appraisals, antifraud safeguards, payments to junior lien holders, and mortgage insurance.[144] A few months later, in a highly significant move, FHFA announced that Fannie Mae and Freddie Mac would henceforth allow underwater homeowners to complete short sales even if they were current on their mortgages so long as they had an eligible hardship. The GSEs defined "eligible hardship" to include job relocation, the death of a borrower or coborrowers, divorce, or disability. In addition, the GSEs agreed to waive deficiencies from short sales under certain

141. U.S. Department of the Treasury (2010a).
142. U.S. Department of the Treasury (2009b).
143. U.S. Department of the Treasury (2013b). See also MHA (undated, 2012a).
144. Federal Housing Finance Agency (2012a).

circumstances and started offering second lien holders up to $6,000 to agree to a short sale.[145]

The March 2012 state-federal mortgage servicing settlement added to the impetus toward short sales. Under that settlement the nation's five largest mortgage servicers agreed to grant at least $10 billion in principal reductions, partly in the form of short sales.[146] In addition to procedural protections meant to spur short sales, the agreement gave the five servicers different amounts of credit, depending on lien status, for short sales that forgave the deficiency balances of the borrowers.[147]

These developments contributed to a surge in short sales by the fall of 2012. HAFA completed a total of 78,260 short sales by September 30, 2012.[148] Meanwhile, the Office of Mortgage Settlement Oversight reported that 113,534 short sales and deeds-in-lieu of foreclosure had been granted under the mortgage servicing settlement for the six-month period ending September 30, 2012, totaling about $13.13 billion in total relief, or an average of $115,672 per borrower. No other category of consumer relief under the settlement agreement during that period was remotely as large.[149]

RealtyTrac reported that short sales outside of foreclosure accounted for 22 percent, or slightly over 220,000 of all residential sales during third quarter 2012, up from 17 percent during third quarter 2011.[150] The GSEs took credit for 33,972 of those third quarter short sales, up from 8,054 short sales by the GSEs in first quarter 2009.[151] Meanwhile, in the so-called fiscal cliff legislation in early January 2013, Congress laid the groundwork for a continuation of this trend by extending the Mortgage Forgiveness Debt Relief Act, excusing homeowners doing short sales from federal income tax on any deficiency balances forgiven through December 31, 2013.[152]

This new, greater ease in arranging short sales was not a panacea. Short sales present major coordination problems. For one, they depend on borrowers taking

145. Federal Housing Finance Agency (2012b).

146. U.S. Department of Justice (2012); *United States of America* v. *Bank of America Corp.,* Consent Judgment (2012).

147. See *United States of America* v. *Bank of America Corp.,* Consent Judgment (2012, exhibit D-1, table 1).

148. MHA (2012d, p. 4). The following month, that total rose to 83,741 short sales over the life of the HAFA program. MHA (2012c, p. 4).

149. Office of Mortgage Settlement Oversight (2012, p. 3).

150. RealtyTrac (2012); computations by author. According to RealtyTrac, the average short sale price in third quarter 2012 was $82,312 lower than the combined outstanding loans on the properties being sold.

151. Federal Housing Finance Agency (2012d, p. 32).

152. The American Taxpayer Relief Act of 2012, 112 Cong. 2 sess., § 204(a), amending *U.S. Code* 26, § 163(h)(3)(E)(iv).

the initiative to list the short sale, but too many distressed homeowners facing eviction become discouraged and abandon the property. Short sales also depend on servicers and investors being willing to give approval (which the subsidies have had partial success in addressing). Even when approval is forthcoming, it may take too long, causing the sale to fall through.

Nevertheless, barriers to short sales are falling at the margin, which should encourage more underwater borrowers to attempt them. This will benefit both civilians relocating elsewhere and members of the armed services who were ordered to transfer.

Military Homeowners with Permanent Change of Station Orders. An especially compelling case of the relocation issue involves members of the armed forces who receive Permanent Change of Station (PCS) orders—commands to move to a new military installation for reassignment, often under short deadlines. Servicemembers who received PCS orders but were underwater on their mortgages faced often difficult options. Generally, they did not earn sufficient salary to make double housing payments on their new homes and their old. While they had a right to be evaluated for foreclosure prevention under the Servicemembers Civil Relief Act (SCRA), servicers did not always cooperate with that request.[153] Some servicers pressured servicemembers to waive their statutory rights; others stalled processing requests for relief. In the worst cases, servicers illegally foreclosed on soldiers' homes or told servicemembers that they must be delinquent before they could qualify for assistance. Such a delinquency, however, would likely jeopardize the servicemember's security clearance and, with it, his or her job.[154] This sequence of events was not only of grave concern to the individuals involved but also had broader implications for military readiness and national security.

Even if the SCRA were consistently observed, the act would not fully alleviate this situation. The SCRA only applies to mortgage loans originated before the homeowner's military service began.[155] And even when the SCRA applies, if the servicer is seeking foreclosure, the homeowner has already gone delinquent in all likelihood and put his or her security clearance and job at risk.

In response, federal officials announced several new initiatives to improve the loss mitigation options for military homeowners facing PCS orders. In the March 2012 state-federal mortgage servicing settlement, for instance, the five large servicers that were party to that agreement agreed to measures to protect SCRA rights, including mandatory look-backs and compensation where they

153. *U.S. Code* 50 (1942), appendix, §§ 501–597b.

154. For example, Henriques (2011a, 2011b); Petraeus (2012).

155. *U.S. Code* 50 (1942), appendix, § 533(a). In those instances, if the servicemember defaults on the mortgage during the period of military service or within ninety days thereafter, no foreclosure, sale, or seizure of the property is valid unless there is a court order or the servicemember waived his or her rights under the act. 5 *U.S. Code* 50 (1942), appendix, § 533(c) and § 517.

had improperly denied benefits under the act. As part of the settlement, the servicers agreed to provide short sale opportunities and to waive deficiencies for underwater military homeowners in PCS order cases.[156]

Three months later the Federal Housing Finance Agency announced that under new agency guidelines, Fannie Mae and Freddie Mac would approve short sales by military homeowners who received PCS orders without first requiring those borrowers to go delinquent. In addition, FHFA confirmed that servicemembers with Fannie or Freddie loans would not be required to contribute financially to obtain approval for a short sale. Nor would they be liable for any deficiency.[157]

In some cases servicemembers with PCS orders planned to return to their homes and wished to renegotiate their mortgages. To assist those borrowers, the HAMP program modified its guidelines effective June 1, 2012, to allow certain military homeowners with PCS orders to qualify for traditional HAMP loan modifications.[158]

Taken together, these provisions represent a sea change in the treatment of distressed military homeowners with PCS orders. The short sale provisions, however, do not cover all mortgages. Furthermore, in order for those provisions to be successful, servicers have to observe them. Mindful of that challenge, in June 2012 federal banking regulators issued an interagency guidance advising compliance. The guidance was relatively weak, however, and simply flagged concerns about certain servicer practices regarding military homeowners with PCS orders without requiring those practices to be reformed.[159]

OTHER CASH-STRAPPED DELINQUENT HOMEOWNERS

The last group of cash-strapped, distressed homeowners consists of those whose incomes have become permanently or indefinitely impaired. If they cannot meet the NPV test for a loan modification and cannot refinance their mortgages, it will be difficult for them to stay in their homes.

---

156. See *United States of America, et al.* v. *Bank of America Corp. et al.,* Consent Judgment (2012, A-32 through A-35, E-5, exhibits H through H-2). Importantly, the five servicers agreed not to require a servicemember to be delinquent to qualify for a short sale, loan modification, or other loss mitigation relief if the servicemember was suffering financial hardship and was otherwise eligible for such loss mitigation. *United States of America, et al.* v. *Bank of America Corp. et al.,* Consent Judgment (2012, A-34).

157. Federal Housing Finance Agency (2012c). Previously, in 2011 the two GSEs had published guidance confirming that PCS orders constituted a hardship for purposes of forbearance and loan modifications.

158. Under the revised guidelines, servicemembers who had to move due to PCS orders but who planned to return to their houses and did not buy a house somewhere else could now qualify as "owner occupants," qualifying them for HAMP loan modifications. Petraeus (2012).

159. Board of Governors of the Federal Reserve System and others (2012).

In some circumstances it may be possible for an investor to take a deed-in-lieu of foreclosure and rent back the home to the borrower at a market rate. This is easier said than done, however. First, the homeowner must be able to afford the rental price. In many areas, however, increasing demand since 2008 for rental housing caused rental prices to rise. Second, whoever assumes the deed must be willing to own and maintain the property and to act as a landlord. Servicers and private-label investors are unlikely to volunteer for this role. As a result transfer-leaseback programs have not come to scale, and an organized response will be needed if that option is to become viable.

Barring a rental solution, other distressed borrowers who have suffered such large shocks to income that they do not qualify for a loan modification will probably have to move out. If matters come to that, the priority should be on helping the affected borrower transition to more affordable lodgings while finding a new owner to occupy the home. If the mortgage is underwater, this will usually require a short sale combined with relocation assistance for the borrower.

In March 2009 the administration announced subsidies to encourage these types of alternatives to foreclosure. In addition to subsidies for short sales and releases of second liens that could impede those sales, the Treasury Department offered borrowers $1,500 to cover their expenses of relocation.[160] A year later, in its new HAFA program, Treasury announced that it was doubling relocation assistance and boosting payments to servicers and second lien holders to agree to short sales.[161]

To date, despite the rise in short sales, HAFA's progress has been discouraging. As of November 2012, only 85,881 HAFA plans had been completed, with 83,741 involving a short sale.[162] That number paled compared to the approximately 3 million foreclosures that were completed between April 2009 and November 2012.[163]

Final Lesson: Current Subsidies Are Not Enough to Overcome the Existing Barriers to Cost-Effective Loss Mitigation.

So far this analysis has proceeded on the assumption that investors will approve loan modifications and short sales that have a higher net recovery than going to foreclosure. The reality has been otherwise. Most observers agree that there have been too few cost-effective loan modifications and short sales. And even if loss mitigation were granted whenever it was NPV-positive, the NPV test would still

160. U.S. Department of the Treasury (2009b).
161. U.S. Department of the Treasury (2013b).
162. MHA (2012c, p. 2).
163. U.S. Department of Housing and Urban Development and U.S. Department of the Treasury (2012, p. 3).

not take into account society's interest in preventing abandoned homes and the negative spillover effects that result from them.

In too many cases, the slow pace of workouts is the result of incentive structures that cause servicers to prefer foreclosure to NPV-positive loan modifications or short sales.[164] The leading source of those incentives is today's system of servicer compensation.[165] Loss mitigation is costly to staff, and servicers receive too little for that labor-intensive task under today's flat-fee compensation system. In addition, servicers are positively rewarded for rejecting NPV-positive loss mitigation solutions because their only real assurance of collecting advances and penalties such as late fees, default management fees, and the like is by going to foreclosure.[166] The same incentives encouraged the nation's largest servicers to cut costs through robo-signing and other abuses of the foreclosure process, which eventually resulted in enforcement decrees and the multi-billion-dollar mortgage servicing settlement.

The Obama administration tackled the issue of servicer compensation with subsidies that were meant to reverse the incentives created by the current system of servicer compensation. The subsidy experience had mixed effectiveness. HAMP's biggest success was in reversing the trend from loan modifications that *increased* monthly payments—with high redefault rates—to loan modifications that *lowered* monthly payments, often substantially. The federal government accomplished this objective in two ways: first, by paying servicers to cut loan payments and interest rates and second, by publicizing the effect of those lower payments in reducing redefault rates. This aspect of HAMP was so successful that proprietary loan modification programs migrated toward the HAMP approach over time as the redefault rates of HAMP modifications steadily dropped.

One can see a similar though less pronounced effect in HAMP's principal reduction program. HAMP never made principal reductions a mandatory part of the HAMP waterfall for participating servicers; instead, HAMP encouraged servicers to consider principal forgiveness and paid them for granting it. Principal reduction modifications became much more common after the administration tripled its payments for those features and after the superior performance of principal write-down modifications became known. Similarly, short sales—which also involve principal write-downs—surged after the HAMP program upped its subsidies for those workouts.

164. See McCoy (2013).

165. For a full analysis of that compensation system and the incentives it creates, see McCoy (2013, pp. 755–58).

166. McCoy (2013, pp. 757–58); McBride (2007); Thompson (2009, p. 17). Servicers have additional incentives to artificially generate late fees by not posting on-time payments promptly or postponing collection until late fees can be assessed. Thompson (2009, p. 17).

There are three takeaways from the principal write-down experience. The first involves transparency. From 2008 onward, a growing body of publicly available studies by securities analysts and university and government researchers found that principal write-downs had better redefault rates than interest rate reductions or capitalization of arrears.[167] In all likelihood this evidence encouraged servicers and investors to approve more of them (in the HAMP and proprietary spheres alike). Second, tripling the HAMP subsidies noticeably boosted the number of principal forgiveness workouts. Finally, despite that surge, interest rate reductions still outpaced principal reductions as of late 2012, even though principal reductions do better in lowering redefault rates. And the heightened subsidies did nothing to bring Fannie Mae, Freddie Mac, or the FHFA on board with the principal reduction strategy. As this suggests, federal subsidies for voluntary principal write-downs—at least at the subsidies' current levels—go only so far in overcoming resistance to modifications using principal forgiveness.

Other aspects of HAMP demonstrate the limited power of subsidies. This can be seen in the disappointingly low number of total loss mitigation plans approved, the high number of loan modifications that still capitalize arrears, and the failure to process workout requests more quickly over time on average.

The administration's foreclosure prevention programs for jobless and under-employed homeowners epitomize these problems. One conclusion from that experience is that subsidies worked better than having none. The program with the best take-up rate—the Hardest Hit Fund—eclipsed servicer resistance to some extent by directly subsidizing loan payments for unemployed borrowers. In contrast, the HAMP Unemployment Program provided no subsidies whatsoever, which doomed that program from the start.

Even with subsidies, however, the Hardest Hit Fund to date has only made a dent in the problem of unemployed borrowers. Despite HHF's generous funding, the take-up rate has been too low. So while HHF subsidies made some difference at their current level, they were not enough to tackle the unemployment problem wholesale.

Finally, the checkered experience with the three foreclosure prevention programs for the unemployed underscores the need for transparency. Given their limited success, one must ask whether easy-to-find online monthly reports about total take-up rates and results would have spurred those programs to improve. If the federal government is going to spend billions of dollars on foreclosure prevention, then it has a responsibility to the public to release data on the outcomes of all of those programs voluntarily, regardless of their funding source.

167. See note 51.

Going Forward

In retrospect, the foreclosure prevention experience of the past six years was a mixed success. The number of loan modifications and other workouts was lower than expected. Meanwhile, too many unnecessary foreclosures occurred, inflicting needless, widespread losses not only on homeowners and investors but also on surrounding communities in the form of depressed housing values, shrinking tax bases, crime, and neighborhood decay.

At the same time, loss mitigation initiatives in recent years provide a rich lode of data and experiences that can inform policymaking. These initiatives offer two sets of overarching insights. One set concerns the question of which workout techniques work best. The other set addresses the question of how to overcome the barriers to adoption of the most effective workout techniques.

Best Practices in Workouts

With respect to the first set of insights on the most effective workout methods, it is important to keep the objectives of foreclosure prevention in mind. From the viewpoint of investors, loss mitigation should be granted where it will increase net recovery relative to foreclosure. Subject to that condition, from the viewpoint of society, loss mitigation should strive to keep the affected home occupied in order to avoid the fallout that comes from a vacant home. Preferably this should be accomplished by keeping the homeowner in the home or, where that is not possible, through a short sale to a new homeowner. Finally, design matters: loan workouts should be designed to minimize the risk of redefault.

To achieve those objectives, HAMP and its predecessor, Mod in a Box, drove home the importance of using a standardized loss mitigation template. The emergence of these templates had several salutary effects. They helped focus workout evaluations on home retention at the individual borrower level. As a result loan modifications rose noticeably after HAMP was implemented. In addition, the templates helped servicers process high volumes of distressed mortgages more efficiently and improved redefault rates substantially by requiring the use of algorithms designed to produce lower monthly payments.

The emphasis on lower monthly payments turned out to be crucial to success. Furthermore, the *way* in which monthly payments were lowered also had an effect on redefault rates. In particular, dollar for dollar, reducing principal is a more powerful way of avoiding redefault than lowering interest rates, at least for deeply underwater borrowers.

The recent history of loss mitigation also demonstrates the importance of early intervention. Redefault rates improved noticeably on average for loan modifications granted in the first few months of delinquency.

Finally, the disorganized and disappointing approach to the plight of unemployed homeowners makes clear that more could have and should have been done. From the outset the government should have offered foreclosure prevention to jobless homeowners on an ongoing basis without artificial deadlines and regardless of their state of residence. Moreover, policymakers needed to recognize that loan modifications for the unemployed will often fail the NPV test because their income loss is so severe. For this reason direct assistance with mortgage payments until the homeowners find new jobs will be more effective than expecting servicers to undertake the likely futile exercise of evaluating those individuals for loan modifications under the NPV test.

Reducing Barriers to Optimal Loss Mitigation

During the financial crisis and its aftermath, policymakers struggled to improve the disappointing take-up rate on foreclosure prevention. The George W. Bush administration used a voluntary approach to loss mitigation, which did not work. Things improved once the Obama administration adopted the HAMP waterfall template and handed out subsidies for HAMP participation. Still, loss mitigation rates were below what the administration originally had projected. This suggests that going forward, subsidies alone will not be enough to produce the right level of loss mitigation. Instead, the lessons from the foreclosure crisis will need to explicitly be made part of the servicing industry's institutional design.

The first task will be to reform servicing guidelines to institutionalize the parts of HAMP that worked, especially the standardized waterfall, the emphasis on early intervention, and the attention to lower monthly payments, including through principal reduction.[168] Right now, the federal government has a historic window in which to accomplish that task. That window has opened because the nation's system of housing finance is currently in flux. One thing is certain: that system will change. The eventual reform of the housing finance system will give the government a rare opportunity to standardize loss mitigation protocols for future generations. It is imperative, moreover, that the government take action because the spillover effects of the foreclosure crisis were too costly to relegate foreclosure prevention to private contracting alone.[169]

In standardizing loss mitigation protocols, one task will be to amend federal servicing guidelines. Today, virtually all home mortgages are federally guaranteed

168. The Consumer Financial Protection Bureau has taken major strides toward early intervention by requiring servicers to notify delinquent borrowers in writing of their loss mitigation options within fifteen days of the second missed payment. Consumer Financial Protection Bureau (2013b).

169. The Government Accountability Office recently estimated, for instance, that cumulative output losses from the recent financial crisis could exceed $13 trillion. See GAO (2013, pp. 17, 23–24).

or insured, either by the GSEs, FHA, the VA, or the Rural Housing Service. Because these instrumentalities are all within the executive branch's control, the administration should take measures to incorporate HAMP's features into the servicing guidelines for all four of their mortgage programs going forward.

In addition, the administration needs to find a way to make FHFA and the GSEs include principal reduction in their loss mitigation arsenal. Some of the strongest resistance to key provisions of HAMP came from FHFA, Fannie Mae, and Freddie Mac. The GSEs and FHFA refused to participate in principal reductions and undermined HAMP's Unemployment Program because HAMP UP merely required GSE servicers to consider principal forgiveness. Convincing FHFA and the GSEs to drop their resistance and come on board will be essential to any meaningful plan to boost the number of cost-effective loan modifications.

Another task will be to revamp private-label pooling and servicing agreements for future securitizations. In 2007 and 2008, the private-label mortgage-backed securities market collapsed and that market remains moribund today. Investors are not likely to return to the private-label market without major reforms, including enhanced disclosures, more robust data, improved due diligence, stronger representations and warranties, credible credit ratings, stronger structures, and revamped PSA provisions. The need to change pooling and servicing agreements provides a ripe opportunity to institutionalize the HAMP protocols in the private-label market of the future.

Strong consideration should also be given to requiring servicers to adopt HAMP protocols for loans held in portfolio, given the heavy negative externalities from needless foreclosures. If federal banking regulators early on had insisted on deeper write-downs to distressed mortgage loans—especially distressed junior liens—that would have removed a powerful obstacle to loan modification relief. Requiring banks to mark down their distressed loans more promptly would increase their incentives to engage in the right level of loss mitigation.

While reforming servicing guidelines is necessary, it is not enough. The experience of the past few years made clear that the current servicing system presents other institutional barriers to the right level of loss mitigation. Chief among those barriers is our broken system of servicer compensation. Today, servicers are overpaid for servicing current loans and underpaid for processing delinquent loans.

Servicer compensation reform is not an immediate fix because the current compensation arrangements apply to the delinquent loans now in the pipeline. However, revamping servicer compensation to properly pay servicers for processing and approving NPV-positive loan modifications would help avoid servicing breakdowns in the future. In particular, servicing compensation needs to be redesigned to reduce the amount paid for performing loans and to properly reward servicers for processing loss mitigation for distressed loans.

Of course, one cannot discuss servicer compensation without discussing subsidies. The whole point of HAMP subsidies was to reverse the incentives toward excessive foreclosures that the current system of servicer compensation creates. While those subsidies had some success, that success was only partial. In light of this experience, some argue that HAMP subsidies should have been higher. But if servicer compensation is meaningfully reformed and servicing guidelines are appropriately amended, possibly future subsidies could actually be reduced. The Consumer Financial Protection Bureau's new ability-to-repay and qualified mortgage rule will also likely help by limiting at origination the number of poorly underwritten mortgages that likely would require loss mitigation.[170]

Finally, there is serious reason to be concerned about the wide variation in servicers' propensity to grant workouts.[171] Relatively little is known about the reasons for this disparity, and more research is needed into the possible causes, including whether they stem from differences in business models, investor types, or other factors.

In the meantime, the Consumer Financial Protection Bureau has come out with new rules that will help hold all servicers to the same high standard. Under those rules servicers *must* evaluate borrowers who apply in a timely manner for all loss mitigation options permitted by the investor for which the borrower may be eligible. Similarly, servicers may not initiate foreclosure if a timely application is pending for a loan modification or other alternative to foreclosure.[172] Importantly, the bureau can examine mortgage servicers for compliance with these rules and initiate enforcement in the event of violations.

Differences in servicers' batting averages also underscore the importance of transparency in holding servicers accountable. The HAMP program publishes loss mitigation statistics for the largest individual servicers every month. In addition, HAMP audits servicers for compliance with its protocols and has called out servicers by name in public for subpar performance. These "naming-and-shaming" tactics have pressured servicers to clean up compliance.[173]

Transparency also has another valuable effect in disseminating knowledge and best practices. After the recent spate of studies on the effect of different workout techniques on redefault rates, servicers increasingly gravitated toward techniques

---

170. Consumer Financial Protection Bureau (2013a).

171. See, for example, Agarwal, Amromin, and Ben-David (2011); Been and others (2011); Collins and Herbert (2009); Goodman and others (2012b, p. 55). See MHA (2013) for statistics on the modification activities of individual large servicers.

172. Consumer Financial Protection Bureau (2013b).

173. Eventually, the state-federal mortgage servicing settlement and the later federal settlement of the robo-signing enforcement actions addressed some of the same problems. However, those settlements were limited to the largest servicers.

that were more successful. This suggests that the studies may have served an educational role in bringing about that change. If the future mortgage default database mandated by the Dodd-Frank Wall Street Reform and Consumer Protection Act contains robust data fields on loss mitigation methods, that database could help government and independent researchers alike to extend that research in the future.

The federal government should also work with the servicing industry to make sure that servicers take advantage of the best technologies available. It is unimaginable, for instance, that servicers still expect borrowers to fax in their loan modification requests and supporting documentation when secure digital transmission would avoid lost paperwork and be centrally accessible for all of a servicer's employees to read. Eliminating outdated technologies such as fax submissions should substantially reduce some of the most maddening and protracted breakdowns in the loss mitigation process.

In conclusion, this country's recent experience with foreclosure prevention has yielded a number of concrete lessons. While those lessons are clear and progress has been made, successfully implementing those lessons in the current servicing environment is not an easy matter. It is crucial not to let the memory of loss mitigation's challenges fade as the inventory of distressed mortgages declines. Instead, regulators, the servicing and securitization industries, and the public at large should make good use of the coming years to adopt the structural changes that are needed to improve loss mitigation once and for good.

References

Adelino, Manuel, Kristopher Gerardi, and Paul S. Willen. 2009. "Why Don't Lenders Renegotiate More Home Mortgages? Redefaults, Self-Cures, and Securitization." Public Policy Discussion Paper 09-4. Federal Reserve Bank of Boston (www.bos.frb.org/economic/ppdp/2009/ppdp0904.pdf).

Agarwal, Sumit, Gene Amromin, and Itzhak Ben-David. 2011. "The Role of Securitization in Mortgage Renegotiation." Working Paper 2011-2. Columbus, Ohio: Charles A. Dice Center for Research in Financial Economics.

Agarwal, Sumit, and others. 2010. "Market-Based Loss Mitigation Practices for Troubled Mortgages Following the Financial Crisis." Working Paper 2010-19. Columbus, Ohio: Charles A. Dice Center for Research in Financial Economics.

———. 2011. "Second Liens and the Holdup Problem in First Mortgage Renegotiation." Working Paper. Ohio State University.

Ambrose, Brent W., and Charles A. Capone Jr. 1996. "Cost-Benefit Analysis of Single-Family Foreclosure Alternatives." *Journal of Real Estate Finance and Economics* 13: 105–20.

American Securitization Forum. 2007. "Streamlined Foreclosure and Loss Avoidance Framework for Securitized Subprime Adjustable Rate Mortgage Loans: Questions and

Answers." New York and Washington (www.americansecuritization.com/uploaded Files/ASFStreamlinedFrameworkQA121707.pdf).

Amromin, Gene, and others. 2012. "Complex Mortgages." Working Paper. Chicago: American Finance Association.

Bajari, Patrick, Chenghuan Sean Chu, and Minjung Park. 2008. "An Empirical Model of Subprime Mortgage Default from 2000 to 2007." Working Paper 14625. Cambridge, Mass.: National Bureau of Economic Research.

Been, Vicki, Howell Jackson, and Mark Willis. 2012. "Sticky Seconds—The Problems Second Liens Pose to the Resolution of Distressed Mortgages." New York University, Furman Center for Real Estate and Urban Policy (http://furmancenter.org/files/publications/Essay_Sticky_Seconds_-_The_Problems_Second_Liens_Pose_to_the_Resolution_of_Distressed_Mortgages.pdf).

Been, Vicki, and others. 2011. "Determinants of the Incidence of Loan Modifications." Law and Economics Research Paper 11-37. New York University.

Bernanke, Ben S. 2008. "Housing, Mortgage Markets, and Foreclosures." Speech at the Federal Reserve System Conference on Housing and Mortgage Markets. Washington, December 4 (www.federalreserve.gov/newsevents/speech/bernanke20081204a.htm).

Bhutta, Neil, Jane Dokko, and Hui Shan. 2011. "Consumer Ruthlessness and Mortgage Default during the 2007–2009 Housing Bust." Working Paper (http://papers.ssrn.com/sol3/papers.cfm?abstract_id=1626969).

Board of Governors of the Federal Reserve. 2012. "The U.S. Housing Market: Current Conditions and Policy Considerations." White Paper.

Board of Governors of the Federal Reserve System and Office of the Comptroller of the Currency. 2013. "Independent Foreclosure Review to Provide $3.3 Billion in Payments, $5.2 Billion in Mortgage Assistance." Press release (http://occ.treas.gov/news-issuances/news-releases/2013/nr-ia-2013-3.html).

Board of Governors of the Federal Reserve System and others. 2012. "Interagency Guidance on Mortgage Servicing Practices Concerning Military Homeowners with Permanent Change of Station Orders." Press release, June 21 (www.federalreserve.gov/newsevents/press/bcreg/bcreg20120621a1.pdf).

Brevoort, Kenneth P., and Cheryl R. Cooper. 2010. "Foreclosure's Wake: The Credit Experiences of Individuals Following Foreclosure." Working Paper 2010-59. Federal Reserve Board of Governors.

Brown, Richard A. 2010. "The FDIC Loan Modification Program at IndyMac Federal Savings Bank" (www.fdic.gov/bank/analytical/cfr/mortgage_future_house_finance/ppt/Brown.PDF).

Buckley, Cara. 2011. "U.S. Mortgage-Aid Program Is Shutting Down, with up to $500 Million Unspent." *New York Times,* September 28.

Bureau of Labor Statistics. 2013a. "Labor Force Statistics from the Current Population Survey." February 5 (www.bls.gov/cps/cpsaat24.htm).

———. 2013b. "The Employment Situation—December 2012." January 4 (www.bls.gov/news.release/archives/empsit_01042013.pdf).

Capozza, Dennis R., and Thomas A. Thomson. 2006. "Subprime Transitions: Lingering or Malingering in Default?" *Journal of Real Estate Finance and Economics* 33, no. 3: 241–58.

Chan, Sewin, and others. 2011. "Pathways after Default: What Happens to Distressed Mortgage Borrowers and Their Homes?" Law and Economics Research Paper 11-33. New York University.

Collins, J. Michael, and Christopher E. Herbert. 2009. "Loan Modifications as a Response to the Foreclosure Crisis: An Examination of Subprime Loan Outcomes in Maryland and Surrounding States." Working Paper. Cambridge, Mass.: Abt Associates.

Collins, J. Michael, and C. K. Reid. 2011. "Who Receives a Mortgage Modification? Race and Income Differentials in Loan Workouts." Working Paper 2010-07. Federal Reserve Bank of San Francisco.

Congressional Oversight Panel. 2010. *December Oversight Report: A Review of Treasury's Foreclosure Prevention Programs.* 111 Cong. 2 sess. (www.gpo.gov/fdsys/pkg/CPRT-111JPRT62622/html/CPRT-111JPRT62622.htm).

Consumer Financial Protection Bureau. 2013a. "Ability-to-Repay and Qualified Mortgage Standards under the Truth in Lending Act (Regulation Z)." Final rule; official interpretations. *Federal Register* 78, no. 20 (January 30): 6408.

———. 2013b. "Mortgage Servicing Rules under the Real Estate Settlement Procedures Act (Regulation X)." Final rule; official interpretation. *Federal Register* 78, no. 31 (February 14): 10696.

Cordell, Larry, and others. 2008. "The Incentives of Mortgage Servicers: Myths and Realities." Finance and Economics Discussion Paper 2008-46. Federal Reserve Board.

———. 2009. "Designing Loan Modifications to Address the Mortgage Crisis and the Making Home Affordable Program." Finance and Economics Discussion Paper 2009-43. Federal Reserve Board.

CoreLogic. 2012. "CoreLogic® Reports Number of Residential Properties in Negative Equity Decreases Again in Second Quarter of 2012" (www.corelogic.com/about-us/news/corelogic-reports-number-of-residential-properties-in-negative-equity-decreases-again-in-second-quarter-of-2012.aspx).

———. 2013. "CoreLogic® Reports Shadow Inventory Continues Decline in October 2012" (www.corelogic.com/about-us/news/corelogic-reports-shadow-inventory-continues-decline-in-october-2012.aspx).

Corkery, Michael. 2008. "Mortgage 'Cram-Downs' Loom as Foreclosures Mount." *Wall Street Journal,* December 31.

Credit Suisse. 2007. "The Day after Tomorrow: Payment Shock and Loan Modifications" (www.credit-suisse.com/researchandanalytics).

Crews Cutts, Amy, and Richard K. Green. 2004. "Innovative Servicing Technology: Smart Enough to Keep People in Their Houses?" Working Paper 04-03. McLean, Va.: Freddie Mac.

Das, Sanjiv R., and Ray Meadows. 2011. "Strategic Loan Modification: An Options-Based Response to Strategic Default." Working Paper (www.fdic.gov/bank/analytical/cfr/mortgage_future_house_finance/papers/Das.PDF).

DeMarco, Edward. 2012a. "Addressing the Weak Housing Market: Is Principal Reduction the Answer?" Remarks prepared for delivery before the Brookings Institution. April 10 (www.fhfa.gov/webfiles/23876/Brookings_Institution_-_Principal_Forgiveness_v11R-_final.pdf).

————. 2012b. Letter to the Honorable Elijah B. Cummings, Ranking Member, and the Honorable John Tierney, Member, Committee on Oversight and Government Reform, U.S. House of Representatives. May 1 (www.fhfa.gov/webfiles/23919/Cummings TierneyResponse5112F.pdf).

Dennis, Brady. 2011. "HUD Program to Help Struggling Homeowners Falling Short." *Washington Post,* September 21.

Eggert, Kurt. 2007. "Comment on Michael A. Stegman et al.'s 'Preventive Servicing Is Good for Business and Affordable Homeownership Policy': What Prevents Loan Modifications?" *Housing Policy Debate* 18, no. 2: 279–97.

Elul, Ronel, and others. 2010. "What 'Triggers' Mortgage Default?" Working Paper 10-13. Federal Reserve Bank of Philadelphia, Research Department.

Federal Housing Finance Agency. 2009. *Foreclosure Prevention Report: Second Quarter 2009* (www.fhfa.gov/webfiles/23152/2Q09ForeclosurePrevention100209F.pdf).

————. 2010. *Foreclosure Prevention & Refinance Report: Third Quarter 2009* (www.fhfa. gov/webfiles/15345/3Q2009ForeclosurePreventionRefinanceRpt10810.pdf).

————. 2011. *Report to Congress: 2010* (www.fhfa.gov/webfiles/21570/FHFA2010Rep ToCongress61311.pdf).

————. 2012a. "Fannie Mae and Freddie Mac to Streamline Short Sales to Help Borrowers and Communities." News release, April 17 (www.fhfa.gov/webfiles/23887/ Short_Sales_release_041712.pdf).

————. 2012b. "FHFA Announces New Standard Short Sale Guidelines for Fannie Mae and Freddie Mac; Programs Aligned to Expedite Assistance to Borrowers." News release, August 21 (www.fhfa.gov/webfiles/24211/shortsalesprfactfinal.pdf).

————. 2012c. "FHFA Announces Short Sale Assistance for Military Homeowners with Fannie Mae or Freddie Mac Loans." News release, June 21 (www.fhfa.gov/webfiles/ 24026/CFPBFinalwFS.pdf).

————. 2012d. *Foreclosure Prevention Report: Third Quarter 2012* (www.fhfa.gov/ webfiles/24858/3q12FPR_final.pdf).

Ferreira, Fernando, Joseph Gyourko, and Joseph Tracy. 2011. "Housing Busts and Household Mobility: An Update." Staff Report 526. Federal Reserve Bank of New York (www.newyorkfed.org/research/staff_reports/sr526.pdf).

Foote, Christopher L., Kristopher Gerardi, and Paul S. Willen. 2008. "Negative Equity and Foreclosure: Theory and Evidence." *Journal of Urban Economics* 64, no. 2: 234–45.

————. 2012. "Why Did So Many People Make So Many Ex Post Bad Decisions? The Causes of the Foreclosure Crisis." Public Policy Discussion Paper 12-2. Federal Reserve Bank of Boston (http://economics.mit.edu/files/8621).

Foote, Christopher L., and others. 2009a. "A Proposal to Help Distressed Homeowners: A Government Payment-Sharing Plan." Public Policy Brief 09-1. Federal Reserve Bank of Boston.

————. 2009b. "Reducing Foreclosures." Public Policy Discussion Paper 09-2. Federal Reserve Bank of Boston (www.bostonfed.org/economic/ppdp/2009/ppdp0902.pdf).

Fuster, Andreas, and Paul S. Willen. 2012. "Payment Size, Negative Equity, and Mortgage Default." Staff Report 582. Federal Reserve Bank of New York (www.newyork fed.org/research/staff_reports/sr582.pdf).

GAO (U.S. Government Accountability Office). 2011. *Vacant Properties: Growing Number Increases Communities' Costs and Challenges.* GAO-12-34. November 4.

————. 2012a. *Foreclosure Mitigation: Agencies Could Improve Effectiveness of Federal Efforts with Additional Data Collection and Analysis.* GAO-12-296. June (www.gao.gov/assets/600/592028.pdf).

————. 2012b. *Troubled Asset Relief Program: Further Actions Needed to Enhance Assessments and Transparency of Housing Programs.* GAO-12-783. July (www.gao.gov/assets/600/592707.pdf).

————. 2013. *Financial Regulatory Reform: Financial Crisis Losses and Potential Impacts of the Dodd-Frank Act.* GAO-13-180. January (www.gao.gov/assets/660/651322.pdf).

Gelpern, Anna, and Adam J. Levitin. 2009. "Rewriting Frankenstein Contracts: Workout Prohibitions in Residential Mortgage-Backed Securities." *Southern California Law Review* 82, no. 6: 1075–1152.

Goodman, Laurie S., and others. 2010. "Second Liens: How Important?" *Journal of Fixed Income* 20, no. 2: 19–30.

————. 2011a. "The Case for Principal Reductions." *Journal of Structured Finance* 17, no. 3: 29–41.

————. 2011b. "Modification Success—What Have We Learned?" *Journal of Fixed Income* 21, no. 2: 57–67.

————. 2012a. "Modification Effectiveness: The Private Label Experience and Their Public Policy Implications." Working Paper. Austin, Tex.: Amherst Securities Group.

————. 2012b. "Mortgage Modification Activity—Recent Developments." *Journal of Fixed Income* 55, no. 4: 55–68.

Guiso, Luigi, Paola Sapienza, and Luigi Zingales. 2009. "Moral and Social Constraints to Strategic Default on Mortgages." Working Paper 15145. Cambridge, Mass.: National Bureau of Economic Research.

————. 2011. "The Determinants of Attitudes towards Strategic Default on Mortgages." Working Paper 11-14. University of Chicago, Booth School of Business.

Haughwout, Andrew, Ebiere Okah, and Joseph Tracy. 2010. "Second Chances: Subprime Mortgage Modification and Redefault." Staff Report 417. Federal Reserve Bank of New York (www.newyorkfed.org/research/staff_reports/sr417.pdf).

Henriques, Diana B. 2011a. "A Reservist in a New War, against Foreclosure." *New York Times,* January 26.

————. 2011b. "Mortgage Companies Settle Suits on Military Foreclosures." *New York Times,* May 26.

Herkenhoff, Kyle F., and Lee E. Ohanian. 2012. "Foreclosure Delay and U.S. Unemployment." Working Paper 2012-017A. Federal Reserve Bank of St. Louis.

HOPE NOW. 2012. "Industry Extrapolations and Metrics." October (www.hopenow.com/industry-data/2012-12-11-HOPENOW-Full-Report-(October).FINAL.pdf).

Hunt, John P. 2009. "What Do Subprime Securitization Contracts Actually Say about Loan Modification? Preliminary Results and Implications." Berkeley Center for Law, Business, and the Economy (www.law.berkeley.edu/files/Subprime_Securitization_Contracts_3.25.09.pdf).

Jagtiani, Julapa, and William W. Lang. 2011. "Strategic Default on First and Second Lien Mortgages during the Financial Crisis." *Journal of Fixed Income* 20, no. 4: 7–23.

Kiff, John, and Vladimir Klyuev. 2009. "Foreclosure Mitigation Efforts in the United States: Approaches and Challenges." Staff Position Note SPN-09-02. International Monetary Fund (www.imf.org/external/pubs/ft/spn/2009/spn0902.pdf).

Lee, Donghoon, Christopher Mayer, and Joseph Tracy. 2013. "A New Look at Second Liens." In *Housing and the Financial Crisis,* edited by Edward Glaeser and Todd Sinai, pp. 205–34. University of Chicago Press.

Lender Processing Services. 2012. "LPS Mortgage Monitor: October 2012 Mortgage Performance Observations" (www.lpsvcs.com/LPSCorporateInformation/Communication Center/DataReports/MortgageMonitor/201209MortgageMonitor/Oct2012.pdf).

LIBOR. 2013. "History of the LIBOR Rates (2013)" (www.wsjprimerate.us/libor/libor_rates_history-chart-graph.htm).

Massad, Tim. 2012. "Expanding Our Efforts to Help More Homeowners and Strengthen Hard-Hit Communities." *Treasury Notes* blog, January 27 (www.treasury.gov/connect/blog/Pages/Expanding-our-efforts-to-help-more-homeowners-and-strengthen-hard-hit-communities.aspx).

MHA (Making Home Affordable). 2010. "Home Affordable Unemployment Program: An Overview for Servicers of Non-GSE Loans" (www.hmpadmin.com//portal/programs/docs/hamp_servicer/upoverviewfornongseservicers.pdf).

———. 2011a. *Handbook for Servicers of Non-GSE Mortgages: Version 3.4* (www.hmpadmin.com/portal/programs/docs/hamp_servicer/mhahandbook_34.pdf).

———. 2011b. "Supplemental Directive 11-06: Making Home Affordable Program—Updates to Servicer Incentives" (www.hmpadmin.com/portal/programs/docs/hamp_servicer/sd1106.pdf).

———. 2012a. "Home Affordable Foreclosure Alternatives (HAFA) Program" (www.makinghomeaffordable.gov/programs/exit-gracefully/Pages/hafa.aspx).

———. 2012b. "Program Performance Report through March 2012." (www.treasury.gov/initiatives/financial-stability/reports/Documents/Mar%202012%20MHA%20Report%20Final.pdf).

———. 2012c. "Program Performance Report through November 2012" (www.treasury.gov/initiatives/financial-stability/reports/Documents/November%202012%20MHA%20Report%20Final.pdf).

———. 2012d. "Program Performance Report through October 2012" (www.treasury.gov/initiatives/financial-stability/reports/Documents/October%202012%20MHA%20Report%20Final.pdf).

———. 2013. "Program Performance Report through December 2012" (www.treasury.gov/initiatives/financial-stability/reports/Documents/December%202012%20MHA%20Report%20Final.pdf).

———. Undated. "Home Affordable Foreclosure Alternatives Program: Overview" (www.hmpadmin.com//portal/programs/foreclosure_alternatives.jsp).

Mason, Joseph R. 2009. "Subprime Servicer Reporting Can Do More for Modification than Government Subsidies." Working Paper (http://papers.ssrn.com/sol3/papers.cfm?abstract_id=1361331).

Mayer, Christopher, and others. 2011. "Mortgage Modification and Strategic Behavior: Evidence from a Legal Settlement with Countrywide." Working Paper 17065. Cambridge, Mass.: National Bureau of Economic Research.

McBride, Bill. 2007. "Tanta: Mortgage Servicing for UberNerds." *Calculated Risk*, February 20 (www.calculatedriskblog.com/2007/02/tanta-mortgage-servicing-for-uber nerds.html).

McCoy, Patricia A. 2007. "Rethinking Disclosure in a World of Risk-Based Pricing." *Harvard Journal on Legislation* 44, no. 1: 123–54.

———. 2013. "Barriers to Home Mortgage Modifications during the Financial Crisis." *Arizona Law Review* 55, no. 3: 723–73.

Moody's Investors Service. 2012a. "Principal Reduction Helps to Reduce Re-default Rates in the Long Run." *ResiLandscape*, January 20.

———. 2012b. "Rising Home Prices Reduce Default Risk in Private-Label RMBS." *ResiLandscape*, November 20.

———. 2012c. "The Impact of the Mortgage Settlement on RMBS Investors." *ResiLandscape*, February 22.

———. 2012d. "U.S. Private-Label RMBS and Servicer Quality: 2013 Outlook." December 13.

OCC (Office of the Comptroller of the Currency). 2012a. *OCC Mortgage Metrics Report: Fourth Quarter 2011*. March (www.occ.treas.gov/publications/publications-by-type/ other-publications-reports/mortgage-metrics-2011/mortgage-metrics-q4-2011.pdf).

———. 2012b. *OCC Mortgage Metrics Report: Second Quarter 2012*. September (www. occ.treas.gov/publications/publications-by-type/other-publications-reports/mortgage-metrics-2012/mortgage-metrics-q2-2012.pdf).

———. 2012c. *OCC Mortgage Metrics Report: Third Quarter 2012*. December (www. occ.treas.gov/publications/publications-by-type/other-publications-reports/mortgage-metrics-2012/mortgage-metrics-q3-2012.pdf).

Office of Mortgage Settlement Oversight. 2012. *Continued Progress: A Report from the Monitor of the National Mortgage Settlement* (www.mortgageoversight.com/reports/ monitors-second-report/).

———. 2013. *Ongoing Implementation: A Report from the Monitor of the National Mortgage Settlement* (www.mortgageoversight.com/wp-content/uploads/2013/02/Ongoing-Implementation.pdf).

Office of the Special Inspector General for the Troubled Asset Relief Program. 2012a. *Factors Affecting Implementation of the Hardest Hit Fund Program*. SIGTARP 12-002. April 12 (www.sigtarp.gov/Audit%20Reports/SIGTARP_HHF_Audit.pdf).

———. 2012b. *Quarterly Report to Congress*. October 25 (www.sigtarp.gov/Quarterly %20Reports/October_25_2012_Report_to_Congress.pdf).

———. 2012c. *The Net Present Value Test's Impact on the Home Affordable Modification Program*. SIGTARP 12-003. June 18 (www.sigtarp.gov/audit%20reports/npv_report.pdf).

Petraeus, Hollister K. 2012. "Written Testimony before the Senate Committee on Banking, Housing and Urban Affairs." June 26 (www.consumerfinance.gov/speeches/writ-ten-testimony-of-holly-petraeus-before-the-senate-committee-on-banking-housing-and-urban-affairs/).

Posner, Eric A., and Luigi Zingales. 2009. "A Loan Modification Approach to the Housing Crisis." *American Law and Economic Review* 11, no. 2: 575–607.

Prior, Jon. 2011. "Ocwen Unveils New Principal Reduction Program." *Housing Wire,* July 26 (www.housingwire.com/news/2011/07/26/ocwen-unveils-new-principal-reduction-program-0).

———. 2012. "Less than One-in-Five GSE Loans Hold a Second Lien." *Housing Wire,* April 5 (www.housingwire.com/news/2012/04/05/less-one-five-gse-loans-hold-second-lien).

Quercia, Roberto G., and Lei Ding. 2009. "Loan Modifications and Redefault Risk: An Examination of Short-Term Impacts." *Cityscape* 11, no. 3: 171–94.

Randolph, Patrick A., Jr. 2010. "Mortgage Modification and Alteration of Priorities between Junior and Senior Lienholders" (http://dirt.umkc.edu/alterationofpriorities.htm).

RealtyTrac. 2012. "Foreclosure Sales Increase 21 Percent in Third Quarter, Short Sales Biggest Share of Distressed Sales" (www.realtytrac.com/content/foreclosure-market-report/q3-2012-foreclosure-sales-and-short-sales-market-report-7499).

Schmit, Julie. 2011. "$1B Homeowner Program Mainly Benefited 3 States." *USA Today,* November 21.

Terris, Harry. 2007. "ARM Workout Calls Trigger Fierce Debate." *American Banker,* October 9.

Thompson, Diane E. 2009. *Why Servicers Foreclose When They Should Modify and Other Puzzles of Servicer Behavior: Servicer Compensation and Its Consequences.* Boston: National Consumer Law Center (www.nclc.org/images/pdf/pr-reports/report-servicers-modify.pdf).

———. 2011. "Foreclosing Modifications: How Servicer Incentives Discourage Loan Modifications." *Washington Law Review* 86, no. 4: 755–840.

U.S. Department of Housing and Urban Development. 2010. "Emergency Homeowner Loan Program—Summary" (www.hud.gov/offices/hsg/sfh/hcc/msgs/EHLP100810.pdf).

U.S. Department of Housing and Urban Development, Office of Inspector General. 2011. *Audit Report.* 2012-FO-0003 (www.hudoig.gov/pdf/Internal/2012/ig12f0003.pdf).

U.S. Department of Housing and Urban Development and Department of the Treasury. 2012. "The Obama Administration's Efforts to Stabilize the Housing Market and Help American Homeowners." National Scorecard, December (http://portal.hud.gov/hudportal/documents/huddoc?id=HUDDecNat2012_SC.pdf).

U.S. Department of Justice. 2012. "$25 Billion Mortgage Servicing Agreement Filed in Federal Court." Press release, March 12 (www.justice.gov/opa/pr/2012/March/12-asg-306.html).

U.S. Department of the Treasury. 2009a. "Homeowner Affordability and Stability Plan Executive Summary." Press release, February 18 (www.treasury.gov/press-center/press-releases/Pages/tg33.aspx).

———. 2009b. "Making Home Affordable: Updated Detailed Program Description." Press release, March 4 (www.treasury.gov/press-center/press-releases/Documents/housing_fact_sheet.pdf).

————. 2010a. "Making Home Affordable Program: Servicer Performance Report through August 2010" (www.treasury.gov/initiatives/financial-stability/reports/Documents/AugustMHAPublic2010.pdf).

————. 2010b. "Obama Administration Announces Additional Support for Targeted Foreclosure-Prevention Programs to Help Homeowners Struggling with Unemployment." Press release TG-823, August 11 (http://portal.hud.gov/hudportal/HUD?src=/press/press_releases_media_advisories/2010/HUDNo.10-176).

————. 2012. "Q3 2012, Consolidated Performance Report" (www.treasury.gov/initiatives/financial-stability/TARP-Programs/housing/Documents/HFA%20Quarterly%20Report.Q32012.pdf).

————. 2013a. "Hardest Hit Fund: Program Purpose and Overview" (www.treasury.gov/initiatives/financial-stability/TARP-Programs/housing/hhf/Pages/default.aspx).

————. 2013b. "Making Home Affordable Program Enhancements to Offer More Help for Homeowners" (www.makinghomeaffordable.gov/programs/Documents/HAMP%20Improvements_Fact_%20Sheet_032510%20FINAL2.pdf).

Voicu, Ioan, and others. 2011. "Performance of HAMP versus Non-HAMP Modifications—Evidence from New York City." Law and Economics Research Working Paper 11-41. New York University.

White, Alan M. 2009a. "Deleveraging the American Homeowner: The Failure of 2008 Voluntary Mortgage Contract Modifications." *Connecticut Law Review* 41, no. 4: 1107–31.

————. 2009b. "Rewriting Contracts, Wholesale: Data on Voluntary Mortgage Modifications from 2007 and 2008 Remittance Reports." *Fordham Urban Law Journal* 36, no. 3: 509–35.

White House. 2010. "President Obama Announces Help for Hardest Hit Housing Markets." Press release, February 19 (www.whitehouse.gov/the-press-office/president-obama-announces-help-hardest-hit-housing-markets).

Contributors

Eric S. Belsky is managing director of the Joint Center for Housing Studies of Harvard University, a lecturer at the Harvard Graduate School of Design, and coeditor of several Brookings/JCHS collaborations.

Raphael W. Bostic is the Bedrosian Chair on Governance and the Public Enterprise at the Sol Price School of Public Policy, University of Southern California, Los Angeles.

Mark Calabria serves as the director of Financial Regulation Studies at the Cato Institute in Washington.

Kaloma Cardwell studies law at the University of California, Berkeley School of Law.

Mark Cole is executive vice president and chief strategy officer at Hope Loan-Port. At the time of writing, he served as executive vice president–chief operations officer at CredAbility in Atlanta.

J. Michael Collins is faculty director at the University of Wisconsin–Madison Center for Financial Security.

MARSHA J. COURCHANE is vice president and practice leader at Charles River Associates in Washington.

ANDREW DAVIDSON is president of Andrew Davidson and Company in New York.

CHRISTOPHER E. HERBERT serves as research director for the Joint Center for Housing Studies of Harvard University.

LEONARD C. KIEFER serves as deputy chief economist at Freddie Mac in McLean, Virginia.

ALEX LEVIN is director of financial engineering at Andrew Davidson and Company, New York.

ADAM J. LEVITIN is professor of law at Georgetown University Law Center. At the time this book was written, he was visiting professor of law at Harvard Law School.

MARK R. LINDBLAD serves as research director for the Center for Community Capital, University of North Carolina at Chapel Hill.

JEFFREY LUBELL is director of housing initiatives for Abt Associates in Bethesda, Maryland. At the time this book was written, he served as executive director of the Center for Housing Policy in Washington.

PATRICIA A. McCOY is Connecticut Mutual Professor of Law at the University of Connecticut School of Law.

DANIEL T. McCUE is a research manager at the Joint Center for Housing Studies of Harvard University.

JENNIFER MOLINSKY is a research associate at the Joint Center for House Studies of Harvard University.

STEPHANIE MOULTON is assistant professor at the John Glenn School of Public Affairs, Ohio State University.

john a. powell is the executive director of the Haas Institute for a Fair and Inclusive Society, University of California, Berkeley.

ROBERTO G. QUERCIA serves as chair of the Department of City and Regional Planning and director of the Center for Community Capital, University of North Carolina at Chapel Hill.

JANNEKE H. RATCLIFFE is executive director of the Center for Community Capital, University of North Carolina at Chapel Hill.

CAROLINA REID is assistant professor of city and regional planning, Department of City and Regional Planning, University of California, Berkeley.

WILLIAM M. ROHE is the Cary C. Boshamer Distinguished Professor and director of the Center for Urban and Regional Studies, University of North Carolina, Chapel Hill.

ROCIO SANCHEZ-MOYANO is a research assistant at the Joint Center for Housing Studies of Harvard University.

SUSAN WACHTER is the Richard B. Worley Professor of Financial Management at the Wharton School, University of Pennsylvania.

PETER M. ZORN serves as vice president, Housing Analysis and Research, at Freddie Mac in McLean, Virginia.

Index